Principles of Management

Principles of Management

Text and Cases

Dipak Kumar Bhattacharyya

Professor

Xavier Institute of Management

Bhubaneswar

Pearson

Original edition, entitled *Principles of Management*, 1 by Dipak Bhattacharya, published by Pearson Education Ltd., Copyright © <Copyright Year of the Original Book>.

Indian Subcontinent Reprint

ISBN 9788131754214

First Impression, *2012*
Eighth Impression, 2023
Ninth Impression, 2024

Published by Pearson India Education Services Pvt. Ltd, CIN: U72200TN2005PTC057128.

Head Office: 1st Floor, Berger Tower, Plot No. C-001A/2, Sector 16B, Noida - 201 301, Uttar Pradesh, India.
Registered Office: Featherlite, 'The Address' 5th Floor, Survey No 203/10B, 200 Ft MMRD Road, Zamin Pallavaram, Chennai – 600 044.
Website: in.pearson.com; Email: companysecretary.india@pearson.com

Printed in India at Repro India Limited

To Tapodeep, Sudip, and Sutapa, who encourage me to write.

About the Author

Dipak Kumar Bhattacharyya, currently a professor of organizational behaviour and human resource management at the Xavier Institute of Management, Bhubaneswar, completed his master's in economics from Jadavpur University and his doctoral work in management from the University of Calcutta. He worked in industry for several years before turning to academia in 1988 as a professor of human resource management in the ICFAI Business School, Kolkata. Since then he has worked with several prominent institutes including the Kolkata branch of the Institute of Management Technology; the Indian Institute of Social Welfare and Business Management (IISWBM); and the Institute of Engineering and Management as both an academic and an administrator. Prior to joining XIMB, Professor Bhattacharyya was the corporate director of the Kolkata-based Camellia Group. In addition, he has been involved in preparing the Entrepreneurship Development Programme at IISWBM conducted in association with Entrepreneurship Development Institute of India, Ahmedabad. He has been a visiting faculty at XLRI School of Business and Human Resources, Jamshedpur and the Indian Institute of Foreign Trade (IIFT), Kolkata. He was also attached to several universities including the external programmes of foreign universities such as the University of London and the DeSales University.

Professor Bhattacharyya has over 35 years of experience in academia and industry across various aspects of management including total quality management, quality circles, statistical quality control and human resource management. He has published two edited volumes—*Organizational Development* (1994) and *Training and Development* (1995)—and several textbooks such as *Labour Economics and Productivity* (1995), *Production and Operations Management* (1999), *Management Principles and Practices* (2005), *Industrial Management* (2010) and *Cross-Cultural Management* (2010). He has to his credit more than 100 research papers in prominent academic journals including *Management Research* and *Indian Journal of Labour Economics*. He continues to pursue research in the area of human resource development, cross-cultural management, six-sigma practices, human resource control systems, and organizational systems.

Professor Bhattacharyya provides consultancy services to organizations such as the IndianOil Corporation Ltd, and the Mitsubishi Chemical Corporation. He is also a member of different committees and institutes such as the Industrial Relations Committee of the Bharat Chamber of Commerce, and the State Labour Institute under the Department of Labour, West Bengal.

Contents

Preface

During the years since Independence, Indian organizations have evolved to adopt and implement management practices adhering to global standards. Today, many Indian organizations have a dynamic presence in industrially advanced countries, competing with the best-in-class organizations globally. For Indian companies to sustain their competitive advantage and gain a stronger foothold in the international business scenario, it is imperative for students (and future managers) to understand the fundamentals of management clearly and imbibe the essence of Indian business practices. They need a textbook that will help them achieve this goal.

Principles of Management: Text and Cases addresses these needs of students. It is designed to cater to the requirements of undergraduate and postgraduate students of management. Written in accordance with the curriculum requirements of management courses, this book integrates theory with practice. The 26 case studies in the book along with the opening vignettes introduce students to real-world situations and problems that managers face. These cases also highlight the management practices of successful Indian and foreign companies. Samples of a leave policy, a code of ethics, etc., have been appended as annexures to some chapters to further illustrate the way these organizations function.

In creating this textbook I have drawn on my experience as an academic and industry professional. Written in a crisp, lucid, and business-like style, it covers all facets of the principles of management. Each chapter is structured as a self-sufficient unit addressing each concept in its totality. The end-of-chapter questions have been framed to review the comprehension of concepts and foster the development of students' managerial skills. Additional material on skill development has been provided on the companion site of the book to enhance the managerial skills of students.

THE ORGANIZATION OF THE BOOK

The book is divided into 21 chapters covering all aspects of the principles of management.

Chapter 1, 'Introduction to Management', discusses the concepts and process of management, its various functions, important characteristics, and different dimensions, structures and systems. It also explains the evolution of various management thoughts and the differences between them.

Chapter 2, 'Organizational Planning', elaborates on the concepts of planning in organizations, encompassing policy formulation, framing of strategies, budgeting and forecasting, and various forms of decision making.

Chapter 3, 'Organizing', presents the various methods of organizing, types and forms of organization structures, line and staff management issues, processes of delegation, centralization and decentralization of authority, span of management, systems view of organization, the relationship of organizational systems with structure, and the open systems approach in an organization.

Chapter 4, 'Staffing in Organizations', explains the functions of recruitment, the methods of recruitment, the process of induction and orientation after recruitment, and the process of the placement of the employee.

Chapter 5, 'Directing Through Motivation', begins with a discussion of the meaning and characteristics of directing. It then delves into the concepts and process of motivation, relating motivation to employees' morale and productivity. It concludes with a discussion on the different theories of motivation.

Chapter 6, 'Directing Through Leadership', elaborates on the theories of leadership, outlines the differences between a leader and a manager, discusses the different styles of leadership, highlights the importance of leadership in managing an organization, and finally, suggests how leadership can be developed in an organization.

Chapter 7, 'Introduction to Control', describes the essentials of good control, interdependence of control on other functions of management, steps, methods and importance of control, and the various tools and techniques used in enforcing control.

Chapter 8, 'Coordination in Organizations', elaborates on the needs, the significance, principles, objectives and purposes of coordination, the various types of coordination, and the concepts of internal and external coordination.

Chapter 9, 'Organizational Forms', explains various organizational forms and their relative advantages and disadvantages, with a specific focus on multinational, transnational, and globally integrated enterprises.

Chapter 10, 'Business Environment and Social Responsibility', presents the reasons for organizational responsibility to the society, the advantages and disadvantages of social responsibility, and internal task environmental issues.

Chapter 11, 'Ethics and Values in Organizations', discusses the concepts of ethics and values, and the benefits of ethical practices in organizations. It also elaborates on the various components of a code of ethics, the process of building an ethical culture in organizations, different views on managerial ethics, and ethical decision making.

Chapter 12, 'Communication and Negotiation in Organizations', explains the concepts of communication and negotiation, the various types and nature of communication, effective techniques of communication, psychological and behavioural influences on communication, group communication, and barriers to communication. It also examines the use of transaction analysis.

Chapter 13, 'Organizational Systems, Structure, and Design', discusses the systems view of organization, the principles of systems theory, and organizational structure and its relationships with the systems. It also talks about the open systems approach in an organization, the viable systems approach, the business process approach, socio-technical systems, and the relationship of organizational culture with organizational design.

Chapter 14, 'Technology Management in Organizations', defines the concept of technology management, sociological issues related to it, and its link with innovation. It covers issues pertaining to strategic technology management, technology planning, and technology transfer.

Chapter 15, 'Globalization and Business Organizations', begins by explaining the context of globalization. It then elaborates upon the benefits of globalization to organizations, various factors involved in promoting globalization, process of development of globalization, important players of globalization, and the relation of globalization to international marketing, culture and talent management.

Chapter 16, 'Organizational Culture', examines organizational culture and its influences, mergers and their implications on organizational culture, Hofstede's cultural orientation model, relationship of organizational culture, climate and structure, cultural issues across nations, managing corporate cultural change, organizational diagnostics, and various organizational development issues.

Chapter 17, 'Managing Conflict and Stress in Organizations', highlights the causes of conflict and stress in organizations, and explains the process of conflict management and stress management.

Chapter 18, 'Individual Behaviour and its Characteristics', discusses the process of perception, relationship between perception and individual decision-making styles, personality and its constructs, and the influence of personality, attitude and emotional intelligence on individual behaviour.

Chapter 19, 'Managing People in Groups', discusses the concept of groups, types of groups, theories of group formation, and the effectiveness of groups. It also explains the group-decision making process, the influence of groups on organizational culture, the process of team development through group formation, group roles and norms, and group dynamics and group conflict.

Chapter 20, 'Capability Development, Innovation, and Creativity', focuses on the concept of capability development, the use of the people capability management model, organizational life cycle analysis, and talent management. It then goes on to elaborate on the concepts of innovation, creativity, and critical success factors which help in building organizational capability.

Chapter 21, 'Quality Management Practices in Organizations', elaborates on the basics of quality management practices, and their impact on the people management function in organizations and on customer satisfaction. It touches upon the concepts of six sigma, lean management, employee empowerment, quality of work life, quality circles, Toyota production systems, and quick response manufacturing.

FEATURES

Each chapter contains useful pedagogical features to facilitate the understanding of students.

- **Learning objectives:** Well-defined learning objectives specify the learning outcome of each chapter.
- **Opening vignettes:** A short opening vignette introduces students to real-world situations which lay the foundation for the concepts discussed in the chapter.
- **Closing cases with case questions:** Chapter-end case(s) depict real-life situations and problems which help students correlate theory with practice. The case questions specify the line of inquiry students need to take while analysing the case.
- **Summary:** A chapter-end summary recapitulates important concepts and definitions.
- **Key terms:** A list of key terms captures the important terminology for a quick review.
- **Review questions:** Review questions help students assess their understanding of concepts.
- **Critical thinking questions:** Critical thinking questions encourage students to apply the concepts to real-world situations.
- **Further reading:** A list of articles and books is provided for the benefit of those students who want to delve deeper into the concepts discussed in the chapter.

THE TEACHING AND LEARNING PACKAGE

A number of resources have been provided on the companion site (www.pearsoned.co.in/dipakkumarbhattacharyya) to facilitate the teaching and learning process.

For Students

- **Question bank:** A chapter-wise question bank has been provided for practice.
- **Additional online material:** The additional online material for skill development includes Management Exercises and Doing Management Research focusing on tools and techniques that managers use and the methodologies of management research, respectively. Aimed at helping students hone their managerial skills, this material discusses important skill-development techniques such as role plays, brainstorming sessions, and business simulations.

For Teachers

- **PowerPoint presentations:** PowerPoint slides capturing the major points from each chapter have been provided for instructors.
- **Instructor's manual:** An instructor's manual, which is mapped to the PPTs, explains the approach to be used in each chapter. The manual also includes solutions to end-of-chapter questions and detailed case teaching notes.

ACKNOWLEDGEMENTS

I would like, first and foremost, to thank Sudipti Banerjea, my mentor in the University of Calcutta. I would also like to acknowledge Fr P. T. Joseph, S. J., Director, Xavier Institute of Management, Bhubaneswar (XIMB); N. R. Datta, Chairperson and Managing Director, Camellia Group; Partha Pal, Deputy Director (Academics), Camellia Group; Aveek Bhattacharyya, Business Development Head, Camellia Group; and Sumit Shome, Deputy Manager (Operations), Camellia Group as well as my friends and colleagues in XIMB and the Camellia School of Business Management (CSBM). Their support has been invaluable to me while writing this book.

A word of thanks is due to all my students in XIMB, CSBM and the Indian Institute of Social Welfare and Business Management. Without their inputs, this book would not have materialized. Writing this book would also not have been possible without the support of my wife and children. Finally, I would like to acknowledge the contribution of the Pearson editorial team in bringing out this book in the best possible form.

I welcome comments and suggestions from my readers.

Dipak Kumar Bhattacharyya

1

Introduction to Management

After going through this chapter, you will be able to understand:

- the concept and process of management
- the various functions of management
- the characteristic features of management and its different dimensions
- the importance of management in studying organizational structures and systems
- modern management thoughts

Monkey Management

'Carrying other peoples' monkeys' is a typical syndrome of managers globally. Despite clear job descriptions and adequate briefing about their job roles, managers often find themselves doing the jobs of their subordinates to meet deadlines. Often, it may not be because the subordinates are incapable of doing their jobs. Rather, it is that the managers cannot repose their trust in people down the line. As time-bound achievement is necessary in the competitive corporate world, managers always chase deadlines to achieve results. The subordinates' propensity to 'pass the buck', on one pretext or the other, increases when they find their managers' shoulders always ready to take on their jobs. The resultant effect is that managers need to overstretch and skip their weekends while their subordinates enjoy the idle time. Management practices, therefore, call for a more inclusive approach of partnering with people, irrespective of their hierarchical level. Subordinates need to be made to feel responsible for their jobs. Managers need to help them understand how important their contributions are to the success of the organization. Finally, managers need to explain the subordinates' jobs to them, train them, and allow them to do their jobs.

Note: Monkey management ('carrying one's own monkeys' is the metaphor used here to denote responsibilities) implies delegation of responsibilities to subordinates and ensuring that such responsibilities (monkeys) do not return to the managers. This seminal idea was pioneered by William Oncken, Jr, and Donald L. Wass in their classic article 'Management Time: Who's Got the Monkey?' in *Harvard Business Review* in 1974.

INTRODUCTION

'Principles of management' is a baseline management course for students of management at both postgraduate and undergraduate levels. A basic knowledge of management principles is very crucial as subsequent management courses rest on an understanding of the core concepts. Students of management, therefore, need to learn the basic concepts of management for developing application-based knowledge of the subject.

Modern organizations apply management practices to achieve their goals and objectives. The complexity of businesses has further made it imperative to apply management practices, without which organizations cannot survive their competition. Application of management theories and concepts is now required in every activity of an organization. This means that management theories and practices are applied by not only a manager but also an engineer, an accountant, or a security-in-charge of a company. It is due to this reason that the managerial role needs to be tested in the light of Henry Mintzberg's theory (1979).

Mintzberg classified managerial roles into interpersonal, informational, and decisional roles. In their *interpersonal role*, managers need to interact and communicate with the people (working both under and above them) and manage their behaviour to get the desired results. The *informational role* requires managers to collect, monitor, and disseminate information to keep their workplace updated with global changes. Managers play their *decisional role* every now and then while they manage their jobs. To perform all these roles, the study of principles of management is important for students of management as they are the future managers of organizations. It is often argued that management knowledge is inbuilt and, hence, it requires no formal study of theories and concepts. However, this statement can be refuted. It is important to understand that application-based management knowledge has its basis in the theoretical understanding of the principles of management.

A BACKDROP TO MANAGEMENT

To understand the principles of management, it is important to understand the concept of an organization and its various subsystems. An *organization* is made of a group of people with some specific goals, objectives, and activities. *Organization* is also defined as the relations among the components of a system. *Organization structure* denotes the components and relations that bind the people working within the organization.

The three major kinds of issues in an organization relate to the people, the organization itself, and the technology it uses. *People issues* encompass education, training, and attitudes. *Organization issues* cover strategy, policy, culture, and bureaucracy. *Technology issues* encompass hardware, software, telecommunications, and information systems.

The three different levels of organization structure are strategic, tactical, and operational. The *strategic level* represents decision making, that is, the corporate or the top level of an organization. The *tactical* or *business level* is the level of middle management where strategic decisions are transformed into tactics to achieve the strategic intents of the organization. The *operational level* represents actual implementation where first-level employees and workers execute the tactics, adopting the action plan of the organization.

The success of an organization largely depends on the management practices prevalent in the organization. This chapter, therefore, introduces the basics of management to lay the foundation for subsequent chapters.

History of Management

The history of management can be traced back to the mid-1700s, that is, the period when the Industrial Revolution took place in Europe. Before the Industrial Revolution, economic activities used to be managed through home-centre production systems. During this period, since the owner of the means of capital and the owner of the labour services was the same, participation in work was more spontaneous and limited to family members. Self-motivated family members used to do their best to achieve excellence in their work and optimize their gains.

With the Industrial Revolution and its cascading effect, significant advancements took place in technology, communication, transportation, and market expansion. Traditional market areas were confined to areas near family-managed production centres. Subsequent to the Industrial Revolution, though, the market domain expanded, resulting in an increased demand for produced goods in family-run production systems. It was not possible to cater to the increased demands through the family-run production systems. Improved technology and other infrastructural support systems resulted in a major transition from family-centred to home-centred production systems. Such organized production activities needed engagement of people who were not family members, and who would render their services against some economic consideration.

The evolving complexity of technology-supported production systems resulted in the need for people to work in groups to accomplish the jobs and the goals of an organization. A separation of the two entities, one the owner of the means of capital and the other the owner of labour services, made it difficult and impractical to manage on the basis of spontaneous participation in work. It was then important to use management principles and practices to coordinate individual efforts and translate these to a group effort.

Gradually, the need was felt for a separate group of professional managers in organizations to achieve results. With the spread of globalization and advancements in technology, the task of the manager not only became important but also started to require institutionalized knowledge. The principles of management provide such basic and institutionalized knowledge to prepare individuals to take responsibility as future managers of organizations.

In this chapter, the definitions and concepts of management have been discussed and the key management thoughts have been elaborated upon with emphasis on the pioneering contributions of Frederick Winslow Taylor, Henri Fayol, Elton Mayo, Mary Parker Follet, and Max Weber.

Nature and Process of Management

The needs of people are to some extent satisfied through the economic activities of organized groups and associations. It is mainly to cater to one's own interests that people come together and accomplish goals through cooperation. However, to be more effective in this pursuit, it is essential that group efforts be properly organized, directed, and coordinated, that is, there is a need for result-oriented management. Therefore, management can be said to be as old as civilization or organized life. The systematic study of management, however, started only six to seven decades ago.

After World War II, the literature on management has grown at an unprecedented rate. This trend has been reinforced by improved research, teaching, and practices. At the same time, there are huge differences of opinion and controversies around the concepts of management. Although one can find some commonality in the way various schools of thought define 'management', these schools consider management from different perspectives. These schools range from the operational school to the mathematical school, the human behaviour school, the systems school, and the decision theory school. The many divergent views have made the task of defining management extremely difficult. Operationally, *management* can be defined as a dynamic process that helps to get things done, through and with the efforts of people. However, this definition is rather inadequate. In this competitive world, management as a process helps in optimizing scarce resources (all the inputs to achieve the intended goals and objectives of the organization).

Today, one organization is differentiated from another based on the degree of efficient management practices. Efficient management practices add to the competitive strength of organizations. The term *management* may be defined differently by different scholars, but its approaches, environment, and processes are essentially the same for organized activities. It encompasses all hierarchical levels in the organization.

Dimensions of Management

In the preceding section, there has already been an attempt to provide a holistic definition of management. However, to authenticate such a definition, one has to first validate it through a review of the standard definitions of management provided by scholars in the field. From this point, the definitions of management can be categorized into different approaches according to their different dimensions:

- **Productivity orientation**: Taylor and John F. Mee have pioneered this concept. Their definitions are primarily concerned with increased productivity as the basic goal of management.
- **Human-relations orientation**: This concept was pioneered by Lawrence A. Appley and Harold Koontz. Their definitions of management primarily emphasize people and the relationships among people as the focus of management.
- **Decision-making orientation**: Definitions under this category focus on decision making as the primary function of management. Ross Moore and Stanley Vance pioneered this concept.
- **Leadership orientation**: This concept views leadership as the essence of management. The proponents of this concept are Donald J. Clough and Ralph C. Davis.
- **Process orientation**: This concept views management as a process. Numerous authors including James L. Lundy, Dalton E. McFarland, Howard M. Carlisle, F. E. L. Brech, Robert L. Trewatha, M. Gene Newport, and George R. Terry are proponents of this concept.

Understanding the dimensions of management in the different definitional contexts helps to develop a holistic, all-inclusive, and all-purposive definition. Thus, *management* can now be defined as the optimization of constraining resources to achieve intended goals.

Resource is a broad term and it encompasses everything that one requires as inputs (including knowledge and information inputs). Resources are not available in abundance. There are always resource constraints. Every organization tries to achieve their charted goals and objectives through efficient management, by proper allocation of constraining resources. Goals and objectives emanate from strategic plans of organizations, which have been explained in detail in Chapter 2.

FUNCTIONS OF MANAGEMENT

The functions of management relate to those activities that help in value addition and also in achieving the goals and objectives of organizations. Production, purchasing, selling, advertising, finance, and accounting are examples of such functions. The nature of such functions varies from organization to organization, but there are certain commonalities. Fayol (1949), the founder of modern management theory, divided all the activities of an organization into six groups: (1) technical, (2) commercial, (3) financial, (4) security, (5) accounting, and (6) managerial.

Fayol distinguishes between the principles and the elements of management. *Principles* are rules and guidelines, while *elements* are functions of management. Fayol has grouped the elements into five managerial functions: (1) planning, (2) organizing, (3) commanding, (4) coordinating, and (5) controlling.

Fayol's classification is widely accepted. Luther Gullick (1937) used the term POSDCROB for Fayol's classification. The initial letters of the term indicate management functions, viz. planning (P), organizing (O), staffing (S), directing (D), coordinating (CO), reporting (R), and budgeting (B). Reporting is a part of the control function while budgeting is a part of both planning and controlling. William H. Newman and Charles E. Summer, Jr, (1961) classified the management process into the functions of organizing, planning, leading, and controlling. The most useful method of classifying managerial functions is to group them around the components of planning, organizing, staffing, directing, and controlling.

The given functions of management are common to all business enterprises and organizations in other fields as well, but the manner in which these are carried out will not be the same across organizations. All these functions constitute the job of a manager though the relative importance of each of them will vary from time to time. Thus, tight economic conditions might force a firm to lay more emphasis on control for the time being, while a growing concern may have to devote more time to organizational problems.

Another way of describing the functions of management is to consider them as a series of interrelated functions—planning, organizing, staffing, leading, coordinating, and controlling—constituting a process.

Planning

Planning is deciding in advance what is to be done, how it is to be done, and when it is to be done. It involves projecting the future course of action for the business as a whole and also for different sections within it. Planning is, thus, the preparatory step for taking action and helps in bridging the gap between the present and the future. Since planning is essentially choosing, it is dependent upon the availability of alternatives. It is through this process of choosing that decision making can be seen as an obvious and important aspect of planning. Thus, planning is an intellectual process and signifies the use of a rational approach to the solution of a problem. In a more concrete sense, the planning process comprises determination and laying down of objectives, policies, procedures, rules, programmes, budgets, and strategies. Management might plan for a short period and also for the long run. For improved efficiency and better results, short-range plans need to be properly coordinated with long-range plans.

Planning is a fundamental function of management and all other functions of management are greatly influenced by the planning process. The importance of planning is amply manifested by the increasing interest evinced in planning in business, government, and other organizations. Very often, the planning process is erroneously described to be the prerogative of the top management. The fact, though, is that planning permeates all levels in the organization and every manager, irrespective of their position in the management hierarchy, must plan within the limits of their authority and the decisions of their seniors.

Organizing

Organizing is the next function of management. It may be conceived of as the structuring of functions and duties to be performed by a group of people for the purpose of attaining enterprise objectives. The functions and activities of the enterprise depend upon the objectives to be accomplished and are also directed towards fulfilment of such objectives. This necessitates establishment of activity–authority relations throughout the enterprise.

More specifically, organization as a function of management involves the following steps:

1. Determination of the activities of the enterprise keeping in view its objectives
2. Classification of such activities into convenient groups for the purpose of division

3. Assignment of these groups of activities to individuals
4. Delegation of authority and fixing of responsibility for carrying out such assigned duties
5. Coordination of these activities and authority relations throughout the organization

Thus, division of work among people and coordination of their efforts to achieve specific objectives are the fundamental aspects of organizations. Problems of organizing arise only when group efforts are involved. Activities by one person cannot possibly be organized in the sense in which the term is used. Similarly, an organization always intends to achieve objectives and, thus, it is a means to an end and never an end in itself. For better results, it is, therefore, implied that organizations be based upon practical prudence and sound application of organizational principles.

Staffing

Organization as a function of management helps the executive to establish positions and lay down their functional relations to each other. It is through the function of *staffing* that different positions in the organization structure are filled. The staffing process, therefore, provides an organization with an adequate number of competent and qualified personnel at all levels in the enterprise. Since successful performance by individuals largely determines the success of the structure, the staffing function deserves sufficient care and attention of the management. This requires managers to properly estimate the workforce requirements of the organization, consistent with the qualifications expected for proper and efficient discharge of duties of existing and possible jobs in the organization. Managers should also be able to lay down suitable selection and placement procedures, develop employee skills through training and appraisal schemes, and devise suitable schemes of compensation.

Staffing is a continuous function. A new enterprise has to employ people to fill in positions in the organization. In an established concern, factors such as death or retirement of employees and frequent changes in the organization's objectives as well as changes within the organization itself make staffing a continuous function of management.

Directing

Mere planning, organizing, and staffing are not sufficient to set tasks in motion. The management may have well-coordinated plans, properly established duties and authority relations, and able personnel, but it is through the function of *directing* that the manager is able to get the employees to accomplish their tasks. This function involves making the employees integrate their individual efforts with the interests and objectives of the enterprise. It calls for properly motivating, communicating with, and leading the subordinates. Motivation induces and inspires employees to perform better, while through competent leadership the manager is able to make the employees work with zeal and confidence. Directing the subordinates embraces three essential activities:

1. Issuing of orders and instructions
2. Guiding and counselling the subordinates in their work with a view to improving their performance
3. Supervising the work of subordinates to ensure that it conforms to plans

Control

While directing, the manager explains to subordinates the work expected of each of them and also helps them to do their respective jobs so that enterprise objectives can be achieved. Yet, even then there is no guarantee that work will always proceed according to one's plans. It is this possibility of actions deviating from the plan that necessitates constant observation of actual performance so that appropriate steps may be taken to ensure conformance. Thus, *control* involves compelling events to conform to plans. The important steps to be initiated in this direction are:

1. Measurement of accomplishment against the standard and recording of deviations
2. Analysing and probing the reasons for such deviations
3. Fixing of responsibility in terms of persons responsible for negative deviations
4. Correction of employee performance so that group goals are accomplished

From this discussion, it is evident that control is closely related to the planning job of the manager. However, it should not be viewed merely as a post-mortem of past achievements and performance. In fact, a good control system should suggest corrective measures so that negative deviations may not recur. The principle of feedback, when incorporated in the control system, can be of great use. To enforce control on the activities of the organizations, the *project evaluation and review technique* (PERT) is extensively used. PERT requires plotting the activities and then allocating time for each such activity. Using the *critical path method* (CPM), PERT helps in optimizing the time required to accomplish the tasks.

Coordination

Coordination has been advocated as a separate function of management by many authorities including Fayol. However, since coordination is all-pervasive and encompasses every function of management, it may be better understood as the essence of management than a separate management function. Poor coordination is attributed to failure to perform all of the listed management functions.

Coordination deals with harmonizing work relations and efforts at all levels for some common purpose. It may be described as the process of unifying individual efforts for the purpose of accomplishing group goals. The whole idea of coordination is to adjust, reconcile, and synchronize individual efforts, so that group efforts become more effective and common objectives are met.

Sometimes, *coordination* is confused with *cooperation* and it is thought, though erroneously, that if there is cooperation, coordination will automatically follow. While cooperation helps achieve coordination, it is by no means the sole condition for the latter to follow. One can take the example of a cricket match. Without coordinated efforts on the part of the players, it is difficult for the team to win a match. Coordination is not spontaneous. Differences in understanding, approach, timing, interest, or efforts have to be reconciled while synchronizing individual efforts.

A manager coordinates the work of their subordinates. For better results, the following guidelines are suggested:

- Coordination should be viewed as the responsibility of every manager right from the bottom to the top, and every individual should know how their job contributes towards accomplishing the objectives of their department and also the dominant goals of the enterprise. Even when a supervisor is able to accomplish the objectives of their department, they should be made to realize that their achievement is useless unless it is combined with the achievements of the other units and is contributing to the attainment of the larger objectives of the organization. Thus, every manager should understand and appreciate the hierarchy of objectives.
- Individual efforts are more easily synchronized if coordination is achieved in the early stages of planning and policymaking. Thus, where production and marketing policies are at cross-purposes, coordination between the two groups of activities will be a serious problem.

- Coordination is better achieved through understanding of interpersonal and horizontal relationships of people rather than through vertical relationships in the organization and by issuing of orders for coordination.
- Another essential requirement is good communication. As a result of constant change in the business environment, plans and policies are frequently revised and compromises and adjustments are reached. If the required information is not communicated well in time, then unifying individual efforts for accomplishment of enterprise goals becomes difficult.

CHARACTERISTICS OF MANAGEMENT

In the context of the various definitions of management and subsequent discussions, one can enumerate certain important features of the discipline of management:

- **Management is organized activities**: Management is essentially a group effort. Unless groups are properly organized through coordination and control, management loses its essence. Proper organizing of activities with a clear structure showing authority relationships is important for managing an organization.
- **Management is aligned with organizational objectives**: Every organization develops clearly stated objectives. Peter F. Drucker (1954) had emphasized *management by objectives* (MBO) for achieving results in an organization. For deciding the objectives of an organization, a participative approach is followed to elicit commitment from the cross-sections of employees working in an organization. Even though MBO traditionally puts stress on deciding the objectives at the corporate or the highest level in the organization, in order to make it participative, *key result areas* (KRAs) or *key performance areas* (KPAs) are framed for individual employees of the organization. KRAs/KPAs are individual, qualitative, and quantitative targets and are mutually decided by the manager and the subordinates. KRAs/KPAs are framed within the ambit of MBO. Aggregation of KRAs/KPAs leads to the achievement of MBO.
- **Management optimizes constraining resources**: Appropriate resource allocation and optimization of the resources is an important feature of management. Objectives are set keeping in view the resource constraint. A manager has to rationalize the utilization of constraining resources to achieve the best results. Let us understand this with an example. A manager has two options before him: one is to buy new technology with a huge capital investment and the other is to sub-contract or outsource the job. Capital investment will require the organization to borrow the fund required, the payback period of which is more than 10 years. On the other hand, sub-contracting will enable the organization to manage the activity once a proper vendor is identified. If the manager faces this situation, what will he do? He will obviously go for the second option. It has been seen that there are many companies who are doing very well with the second option and are even outsourcing their manufacturing activities.
- **Management works with and through people**: An organization is not just brick and mortar, nor is it just system and structure. It consists of its people, or employees. The competitive advantage of any organization is its people. Hence, managing people successfully is the most important priority for an organization. Encyclopaedia Britannica, Inc. which was more than two centuries old, collapsed because it could not manage its people to respond to change. When Microsoft's sister concern Encarta introduced a CD version of the encyclopaedia in the market, Britannica could not respond with a competing product as the CD version would reduce the commission income of its sales force.

Ultimately, the company had to sell its stake to another new investor at less than half of its price. This shows that management cannot succeed without taking people into confidence.

- **Management is decision making**: One of the most important tasks of a manager is decision making. A manager has to evaluate various decisional alternatives and select the best one. Proper decision making minimizes the risk involved in decisions.
- **Management is a science as well as an art**: Learning management is possible through a scientific process. Therefore, as a discipline, management is a science. However, effective application of management is an art. That is why managerial styles differ. A manager may be too formal with subordinates and maintain a task-oriented relationship, while another may be informal and people-oriented. Both may lead to results but long-term effectiveness is achieved only through people orientation.
- **Management is universal**: Management encompasses everything, not merely a business organization. Even for managing a temple, a church, or a mosque, one has to apply management principles. Approaches may differ, though. Universality also implies transferability of management knowledge and skills across countries. It may be noted that there are arguments that are for and against universality. Proponents of cross-cultural management are against universality of management as they consider management to be situational. Those who subscribe to the concept of universality of management suggest that management is universal and can be found in all types of organizations.
- **Management is intangible**: Management is not something that is tangible or visible. It is an intellectual process that facilitates the management of an organization. Information and knowledge are the key elements of management and these become the most important inputs. The entire process of management, including planning and organizing, comprises intangible inputs that add value to the organization.
- **Management is an interdisciplinary approach**: Management is a structured approach encompassing different fields like political science, economics, sociology, psychology, mathematics, statistics, anthropology, and even engineering. Inputs from all these disciplines have strengthened management and managerial functions.
- **Management is a social process**: As a social process, management has to be responsive to social needs. The social responsibility of an organization is now a well-developed concept that requires management to take inputs from society and give output to society. Efficient management through proper utilization of resources of society can improve the quality of life. A. Dasgupta (2009) pointed out that the activity of every enterprise must be conducted in such a manner that it can serve its own objectives as well as its social purpose. Social responsibilities of management are not always fixed. These keep on changing. To focus on the importance of social responsiveness of an enterprise, William C. Frederick, James E. Post, and Keith Davis (1992) said social responsiveness is 'the ability of a corporation to relate its operations and policies to the social environment in ways that are mutually beneficial to the company and to the society'. It is measured in terms of organizational contributions to charitable and civic projects, assisting voluntary social organizations (NGOs) in fundraising, employee involvement in civic activities, emphasis on equal-employment opportunity, extent of fair treatment of employees, fair pay and safe working conditions, safe and quality products to consumers, and pollution avoidance and control. Howard R. Bowen (1953) advocated the concept of *social audit*, defining it as 'a commitment to systematic assessment of and reporting on some meaningful, definable domain of the company's activities that have social impact'. It is categorized into two types: (1) those required by the government and (2) those that are voluntary in nature. Since organizational social responsibility and responsiveness ultimately depend on the

ethical standards of managers, many organizations also try to impart training on managerial ethics and values to make managers more socially responsive.

- **Management is a system of authority**: Management involves decision making. In any organization, the onus of decision making is ultimately on the management. Organizational structure, therefore, traditionally puts management at the top, from where authority and reporting relationships flow. Even though there are attempts to make the organization more participative through horizontal, matrix, and to some extent hybrid organizational structures, ultimately the planning and controlling functions still rest with the management.
- **Management is dynamic**: Since an organization has to keep environmental forces in context and adapt to changes, it has to be dynamic. Without a dynamic approach, an organization may lose its competitive advantage. Using the *strength–weakness–opportunities–threat* (SWOT) model, the Boston Consulting Group (BCG) matrix, or Porter's model, an organization decides its course of action to respond to the changing requirements and frames its plans and strategies accordingly.
- **Management principles are relative and not absolute**: The application of management principles depend on the situation. Each organization may have a situation different from that of others. Such difference may be in terms of time, place, or sociocultural factors. Therefore, principles of management should be understood in the light of the prevailing culture or situations. This can be illustrated through an example. A multinational organization wanted to apply the same principles that were applicable in their branch in the United States, in the branches in Peru and Mexico. The result was disastrous since, in comparison to the United States, the working hours and business etiquette are completely different in these countries. One of the many differences is that workers in Peru and Mexico usually get a long lunch break between their working hours, which can extend up to three hours, allowing them time to even enjoy a nap. However, they start very early in the morning to maintain the schedule of their working hours. Hence, the principles of management that were applicable in the United States could never have been successfully applied in this context.
- **Management is a profession**: The word *profession* has a variety of meanings. It is characterized as an occupation based on specialized knowledge and skill, a theoretical structure, and a learning of science. Management as an occupation has these characteristics. On the other hand, management lacks the characteristic of a profession because it does not fulfil certain other requirements. In order to be a profession in the true sense, the field of management has to satisfy certain other characteristics, namely, the existence of an organized and systematized body of knowledge, a formal method of acquisition of knowledge, the existence of an association with professionalization, the formulation of ethical codes, and the existence of service motives. Many theorists argue that management does not satisfy all these characteristics and, hence, it is wrong to designate management as a profession. They believe that it is better to call it an emerging profession. Whatever the contention, management is increasingly gaining recognition as a profession and has, in fact, become one of the most well-recognized professions in India. To substantiate this claim, there are a number of professional management bodies like All India Management Association, National Institute of Personnel Management, and Indian Society for Training and Development, which are furthering the cause of management through regular membership services. They have come up with the idea of professional ethics, which largely focuses on service motives, taking the profession beyond the ambit of one's individual livelihood.
- **Management is a strategic function**: Every organization has to move strategically to chart their action plan in order to sustain their competitive edge in a changing environment. It is the strategic choice of the organization to decide whether to emphasize *new-market development* or to enhance the scope for repeat buying with better *customer relationship management* (CRM). This aspect has been discussed in detail in Chapter 2.

Management: Is it a Science or an Art?

Science can be defined as a body of knowledge encompassing the systematic study of the structure and behaviour of the physical and natural world through observation and experiment. Observation and experiment, therefore, comprise the scientific method. Thus, chemistry as a science refers to a systematic body of knowledge accumulated through the application of the scientific method in a particular area. Science is systematic in the sense that certain relationships, principles, and their limitations have been discovered, tested, and established. However, it does not mean that the principles and laws so established are immutable. Discovery of new knowledge and phenomena can always change any principle, irrespective of its standing and respect. Management can be described as a science but it is an inexact science when compared to the physical sciences. Management is a theory possessing a number of principles relating to coordination, organization, decision making, and so on. It is true that one cannot have the same kind of experimentation in management as is possible in the natural sciences. It is the same case with economics, political science, military science, and a number of other sciences dealing with the complex structure of group norms and behaviour. It is, however, appropriate to emphasize that management is as yet a growing science.

The *art* of doing something implies a skill acquired through repeated efforts. In this context, management is also an art as it can only be perfected through practice. Management principles are necessary not only for the sake of knowledge alone but also for their application to real-life situations. In fact, skill in application of principles to work situations is so important to the job of an executive that some authorities regard it as the art of management. However, this does not mean that the science and the art of management are mutually exclusive; they are, instead, complementary to each other. Hence, the theory and the practice of management are mutually helpful.

Management: A Profession

The corporate form of organization that separates ownership from management, the growing complexities in managing the activities of an organization, and the development of an organized body of systematic knowledge of management are essential factors responsible for raising management to the status of a distinct profession. A *field* is normally characterized as a profession when the following features are present:

- A systematic body of knowledge
- Need for learning and proper organization
- Entry restricted on the basis of examination or education
- Dominance of the service motive over the profit motive

Except for the requirement of restricted entry, management qualifies for all other tests of a profession. It is now backed by a systematic body of knowledge. A number of management principles have been developed which need to be imbibed through proper learning and education. Besides, in a number of countries, institutes, associations, and universities are now imparting knowledge relating to management. Moreover, the social and moral climate has created new challenges for this field. The management of today must be creative rather than adaptive and be conscious of its ethical and social responsibilities towards the society. Another important development in the field of management has been that professional management consultants are growing both in terms of numbers and quality. However, as mentioned, management fails to qualify for the test of professionalism on the point of restricted entry. Although there is growing preference for properly educated and trained people for managing business enterprises, self-made managers cannot altogether be eliminated. Thus, the field of management may not strictly be a profession like the legal or the medical professions, though professional attributes are very much present in it.

Significance of Management

Management is important due to the following reasons:

- It optimizes use of scarce resources.
- It ensures effective leadership and motivation.
- It promotes harmony among industrial relations.
- It facilitates the achievement of goals.
- It facilitates change and growth.
- It enhances the quality of life.
- It improves productivity.
- It contributes to organizational competitiveness.
- It develops professionalism.
- It contributes to organizational growth.

DIFFERENT APPROACHES TO MANAGEMENT

As mentioned in the earlier sections, management was influenced by various disciplines like sociology, economics, political science, anthropology, psychology, and even literature. Due to such multidisciplinary influences, even authors like Harold Koontz (1961) referred to management as a 'jungle'. Even then, differences exist in the classification of approaches. Although one of the ways to classify management approaches is from the analysis of John G. Hutchinson (1971), which considers the development of management from five different perspectives, the history of management can be broadly classified into three groups: (1) the classical approach, (2) the neo-classical approach, and (3) the modern approach.

The *classical approach* has conventionally implied traditionally accepted views. This approach emphasizes organizational efficiency to increase organizational success. It believes in functional interrelationships, following of certain principles based on experience, a bureaucratic structure, and a reward–punishment nexus. The classical school of thought developed in three different directions: the scientific management approach, the administrative approach, and the bureaucratic approach, which also falls under the administrative school of thought. The *bureaucratic approach* was pioneered by Weber (1920), the *scientific management approach* by Taylor (1903), and the concept of *administrative theory* by Fayol (1949).

The *neo-classical approach* emphasized human relations, the importance of the person behind the machine, individual as well as group relationships, and social aspects. This approach was pioneered by Mayo and his associates (1933). It was further extended to the *behavioural sciences approach*, pioneered by Abraham Maslow (1968, 1971), Chris Argyris (1957), Douglas McGregor (1960), and Rensis Likert (1961). The *quantitative approach* (which developed during World War II and believes in economic effectiveness to solve business problems) and the *contingency approach* (which discards the concept of universality and determines managerial decisions by considering situational factors) also form a part of the *neo-classical approach*.

Modern management thought combines concepts of the classical school with social and natural sciences. It basically emerged from systems analysis.

Even though most discussions on the evolution of management thought start with the classical approach, a brief acknowledgement of the contributions of the pre-classical theorists is useful to appreciate the process of development in management thought. A list of the contributions by pre-classical theorists has been provided in Table 1.1.

Table 1.1 Contributions of Pre-classical Theorists

Contributor	Pioneering ideas
Robert Owen (1771–1858)	He is considered to be a pioneer of the human resource management process. He advocated the necessity of concern for the welfare of workers.
Charles Babbage (1792–1871)	As an inventor and a management scientist, he built the practical mechanical calculator, which is considered to be the basis of the modern computer. He also advocated the idea of specialization of mental work and suggested the necessity of profit sharing.
Andrew Ure and Charles Duplin (1778–1857)	They emphasized the necessity of management education, which further paved the way to professionalize management functions.
Henry Robinson Towne (1844–1924)	He emphasized the significance of skills in running a business.

Reviewing the contributions of the pre-classical theorists, it is clear that their focus was more on developing some specific techniques to solve some identified problems. Due to their obvious technical background, they could not think of management as a separate field. By and large, they integrated management with their respective areas of specialization. Andrew Ure, Charles Duplin, and Henry Robinson Towne largely laid the foundation of management theory, which has ultimately shaped modern management thought.

Classical School of Thought

This school of thought is divided into two approaches—the scientific school and the administrative school. The theorists of this school laid down the foundation of managing an organization in accordance with certain principles. In Table 1.2, the contributions of each theorist have been highlighted.

Scientific management

Scientific management is a classical approach that emphasizes the scientific study of work methods to improve efficiency of workers. Among all the contributors to this school of thought, the contribution

Table 1.2 Contributions of Classical Theorists

Scientific management	
Frederick W. Taylor (1856–1915)	Development of scientific management
Frank B. and Lillian M. Gilbreth (1868–1972)	Time and motion studies
Henry L. Gantt (1861–1919)	The Gantt chart
Administrative theory	
Henri Fayol (1841–1925)	General theory of management
Max Weber (1864–1920)	Rules of management

of Taylor is thought to be the most important. Regarded as the father of scientific management, Taylor developed specific principles for this field in 1911. He started his experiments with the concept of scientific management in 1878 at Midvale Steel Co. During his days at Midvale, he saw that employees were 'soldiering', that is, deliberately working at a pace slower than one's capabilities. He concluded that workers indulged in 'soldiering' primarily for three reasons: (1) fear of losing their jobs if they increase their output, (2) faulty wage systems, and (3) outdated methods of working.

For eliminating this problem, Taylor developed the principles of scientific management, emphasizing five important issues:

1. Emphasize organized knowledge rather than rely on rule of thumb
2. Obtain harmony in group action
3. Achieve cooperation
4. Work for maximum output rather than restricted output
5. Develop the potential of the workers both for their self-development and organizational prosperity

In essence, Taylor emphasized the following points to achieve organizational efficiency:

- Develop a scientific way of performing jobs
- Train and develop the potential of the workers to perform the job
- Establish harmonious relations between management and workers

In order to ensure that such objectives are achieved, Taylor suggested two important managerial practices: the piece-rate incentive system and time and motion study. The *piece-rate incentive system* rewards the worker who produces maximum output. Such an incentive system will motivate workers to work more to maximize their earnings. This system requires workers to perform at some pre-decided standard rate to earn their base wages. Standards are decided using time and motion study. If workers are able to produce more, then in addition to their base rate they get incentives on the number of excess units produced over and above the standard units. This serves the interest of workers as well as management—workers feel motivated to maximize their earnings, while management gets the benefit of increased productivity.

Time and motion study, as already pointed out, facilitates the determination of the standard time required for performing a job. Time study helps in the determination of time required, duly defining the art of recording, analysing, and synthesizing the time elements of each operation. *Motion study*, on the other hand, involves study of movements in doing a job in parts. It eliminates wasteful movements and retains only the necessary ones. Thus, it makes a job simple, easier, and better.

Taylor developed the time and motion study concepts in association with Frank and Lillian Gilbreth. Like Taylor, Frank Gilbreth is also known as the father of motion study. Lillian Gilbreth conducted research on motion studies. Both of them explored ways of reducing fatigue. They had classified seventeen basic hand motions including search, select, position, and hold, which they called 'therbligs' (*Gilbreth* spelled backward with 'th' treated as one letter). Their approach helps us to analyse the exact elements of a worker's hand movements. A simple modification of a brick-laying approach, following the Gilbreths' studies, helped to increase hourly output from 120 bricks to 350.

Henry Laurence Gantt also worked as a close associate of Taylor at Midvale and subsequently at Bethlehem Steel. His contributions to the scientific management school of thought are the *task and bonus system* and a chart commonly known as the Gantt chart, developed in the years 1910–1915. As per his incentive plan, workers receive their day wages even when they do not perform their complete job. On the other hand, they get a bonus when they take less than the normal standard time to complete the work. It was further recommended that there be payment of bonus to foremen as well, based on the incremental performance of workers.

The *Gantt chart* is used for production planning to compare actual and planned performances. It is a visual device for production control, indicating progress of production in terms of time rather than quantity. In fact, the programme evaluation and review technique (PERT) concept was subsequently developed based on the Gantt chart. In Chapter 7, the Gantt chart has been illustrated in detail.

Some of the drawbacks of scientific management are:

- The basic principles of scientific management revolve around operations problems and do not focus on managerial issues, essential for managing an organization. That is why it is often said that it is more focused on engineering than on management.
- The assumptions of this theory about people in general are that they are rational and primarily driven by their desire to fulfil material gains. Only the economic and physical needs of people are emphasized, to the exclusion of their social needs.
- This theory also ignores the human desire for job satisfaction.

Administrative theory

Administrative theory, another part of the classical school of thought, focuses on principles to coordinate the internal activities in an organization.

General theory of management The French industrialist Fayol, through his pioneering work *General and Industrial Management* published in English in 1949, explained that satisfactory results can be achieved with scientific forecasting and proper methods of management. At the outset, Fayol classified the business operations of an organization into six activities and then outlined 14 principles of management. The six activities are:

1. **Technical**: It is concerned with production and manufacturing.
2. **Commercial**: It includes all activities related to buying, selling, and exchange.
3. **Financial**: It ensures optimal use of capital.
4. **Security**: It ensures the protection of employees and property.
5. **Accounting**: It is concerned with costs, profits and liabilities, maintaining balance sheets, and compiling statistics.
6. **Managerial**: It is a functional approach to management and is concerned with planning, organizing, commanding, coordinating, and controlling.

After detailing all these activities, Fayol primarily focused on the managerial activities and outlined 14 principles to achieve efficiency. These 14 principles are as follows:

1. **Division of labour**: If people are specialized at their work, they can perform their task better. This principle recommends grouping of people as per their area of specialization. The modern assembly-line concept is an outcome of division of labour.
2. **Authority**: Managers must have authority to get things done. Yet, formal authority alone may not help to compel obedience from subordinates; managers must have the expertise to exert personal authority.
3. **Discipline**: People working in an organization need to comply with rules and agreements that govern the organization. Without discipline, results cannot be achieved. Strong discipline and leadership are inter-connected and these can together create an environment of positive work culture.

4. **Unity of command**: Members in an organization must receive instructions from only one person. Conflict will arise when one receives orders and instructions from multiple managers. Therefore, the reporting relationship of one subordinate should be with one superior.
5. **Unity of direction**: All operations in an organization need to be directed towards one objective. Without this, achievement of goals cannot be ensured.
6. **Subordination of individual interest to the common good**: The interests of an individual employee should not take precedence over the interests of the organization as a whole.
7. **Remuneration**: It should be fair to both employees and employers.
8. **Centralization**: Centralization reduces the role of the subordinates in decision making, while decentralization enhances it. Managers should retain responsibility through centralization but at the same time give their subordinates enough authority to do their jobs properly.
9. **Hierarchy**: There should be a line of authority, illustrated in the form of an organization chart clearly showing the structure of authority from the top management to employees down the line.
10. **Order**: People and materials should be in the right place at the right time. Job allocation to people should be made in a way that suits them.
11. **Equity**: Managers should be fair to their subordinates.
12. **Stability of staff**: Employee turnover should be less to ensure efficiency of an organization.
13. **Initiative**: Subordinates should have the freedom to conceive new ideas and do their task, even though they may commit mistakes.
14. **Esprit de corps**: Team spirit should be promoted to develop a culture of unity in the organization. Use of verbal communication instead of formal written communication, wherever possible, may help in developing the team spirit in an organization.

Bureaucratic theory The *bureaucratic theory* pioneered by Weber (1920), which falls under the administrative school of thought, emphasizes authority structures and description of an organization based on the authority relations. According to Weber, 'a bureaucracy is highly structured, formalized, and impersonal organisation'. In fact, he has advocated the necessity of a formal organization structure with set rules and regulations. The characteristics of a bureaucratic organization as described by Weber are shown in Table 1.3.

Bureaucracy is often misunderstood as being a web of red tape and too many rules. However, Weber's concept is intended to remove ambiguity, inefficiencies, and patronage.

Criticism of the classical school of thought

Behavioural theorists criticized the classical theorists on a number of grounds. First of all, management principles are not universally applicable in today's complex business situation. Some principles of Fayol are also contradictory, for example, the principle of specialization contradicts the principle of unity of command. Similarly, Weber's bureaucracy also takes away the individual's creativity and flexibility, and dissuades them from responding to a complex situation in a global environment. Further, classical theorists also ignored the important aspects of organizational behaviour. These theories do not deal with the problems of leadership, motivation, power, or informal relations. They also fail to consider the internal and external environmental forces affecting an organization. These stress the necessity of achieving productivity, more than anything else.

Neo-classical School of Thought

This school of thought, which was a transitional phase, basically emphasized human relations.

- Workers assign meaning to their status in the organization and give value to events, objects, and specific features of their environment (hours of work, wages, etc.).
- Workers derive satisfaction or dissatisfaction from the social status of an organization. This means that they also look for social rewards, associating them with an organization.
- Workers' social demands are influenced by social experiences in groups, both inside and outside the workplace.

Bank wiring observation room experiment This part of the Hawthorne experiments was conducted to test some of the ideas that the researchers formed during the interview phase. It was conducted between 1931 and 1932. In this experiment, there were fourteen participants (samples) including wiremen, solder men, and inspectors. There was no change in the physical working conditions. Sample workers were paid based on an incentive pay plan, relating their pay to output. They had the opportunity to earn more by increasing the output. However, as the researchers observed, the output was constant at a certain level. Analysis of the results showed that the group encourages neither too much nor too little work. They enforce 'a fair day's work' on their own. Group norms, therefore, are more important to the worker than money. The study, thus, provided some insights into informal social relations within groups.

The Hawthorne experiments, by focusing on the importance of human relations, contributed immensely to management theory.

In the behavioural school of thought, other contributors like Abraham Maslow, Douglas McGregor, and Chris Argyris also left a significant impact. While Maslow focused on the importance of human needs, which are major driving forces for human motivation, McGregor made certain assumptions about people, categorizing them under theory X and theory Y. Theory X essentially represents a negative view about people, that is, people are lazy by nature, have little ambition, dislike work, avoid responsibility, and require direction to work. Theory Y, on the contrary, assumes that people are more positive, capable of self-control, innovative and creative, and they do not inherently dislike work. These theories have been further discussed in detail in Chapter 5.

Chris Argyris's contributions to the behavioural school of thought are extremely important. His contributions comprise the maturity–immaturity theory, the integration of individual and organizational goals, and the patterns of model I and model II. According to the maturity–immaturity theory, people progress from a stage of immaturity and dependence to a state of maturity and independence. If organizations keep their employees in a dependent state, they allow them to remain immature and thereby prevent them from achieving their potential. Argyris further contended that a formal organization develops a rigid structure, compelling people to behave in an immature way. This leads to incongruence between the individual and organizational goals, hinders organizational development, leads to failure, and fosters frustration and conflict. People end up showing their aggression, regression, and suppression in various ways. Model I and model II patterns are two different assumptions. Workers in the model I type of organization are motivated by the desire to manipulate others and protect themselves from others. Workers in the model II type of organization are less manipulative and more willing to learn and take risks. Argyris, therefore, suggested that managers try to create a model II type of organization.

Likert and Drucker have also contributed significantly to this school of thought. Likert attributes low productivity and poor morale of employees to a typical job-centred supervision technique. He has suggested some typical leadership styles to ensure better productivity and improved morale of workers. These have been discussed in detail in Chapter 6. Drucker, on the other hand, pioneered several modern management concepts in the fields of innovation, creativity, problem solving, organization design, and management by objectives (MBO). All his principles have been acknowledged and are referred to throughout this book.

Criticism of the neo-classical school of thought

Despite the brilliant contributions by the behavioural school of thought to the theories of management, it was criticized on the following grounds:

- It is believed that the procedures and analysis of the findings and the conclusions drawn thereon have little relevance. In fact, the conclusions are not supported by adequate evidence.
- The relationship between satisfaction of workers and productivity was established with simplistic assumptions, while in reality the situation is more complex due to behavioural phenomena.
- Further, all these studies failed to focus on the attitudes of workers, although attitudes play a crucial role in influencing workers' performance and productivity.

Modern Approaches

Some modern approaches have played a significant role in the evolution of management theories, such as the quantitative school, the systems theory, and the contingency theory.

- The *quantitative school of thought* emerged during World War II. During the war, managers, government officials, and scientists were brought together to help the army to effectively utilize resources. These experts, using some earlier mathematical approaches to the concepts advocated by Taylor and Gantt, solved many logistic problems in the war. Subsequent to the war, such techniques were applied by many organizations to solve their business problems. This school of thought extensively utilizes statistics, optimization models, information models, and computer simulations for decision making and economic effectiveness to solve business problems. It has various branches, such as management science, operations management, and management information systems.
    - The *management science approach* visualizes management as a logical entity, expressing management in terms of mathematical symbols, relationships, and measurement data. Also known as the *operations research approach*, it is applied in areas like capital budgeting and cash-flow management, production scheduling, product strategy development, human resource planning, and inventory management. Various mathematical tools like queuing theory, linear programming, PERT, CPM, decision theory, simulation, replacement, probability theory and sampling, time-series analysis, and index numbers are used to minimize the error in management decisions.
    - The *operations management approach* is primarily concerned with production management and its related areas. In fact, it is difficult to draw a line between management science and operations management. Most of the mathematical tools mentioned earlier are used in operations management. Moreover, this approach also helps in decision making in other functional areas like finance, marketing, and human resource management.
    - The *management information systems approach* focuses on designing and implementing computer-based information systems for use by management. It converts raw data into information inputs, which are subsequently used by management for decision making. Modern management information systems help in enterprise-wide decision making, integrating all functions of management. Enterprise-wide decision support systems (such as human resource information systems) are used for critical or strategically important decisions, as these provide valuable information inputs.
- An extension of the quantitative school of thought is the *systems theory approach*. This approach considers the organization as a whole because of the interdependent nature of activities, requiring the organization to interact with external environmental factors. In this competitive scenario,

organizations cannot function in isolation. It has to operate in open systems, interacting with the environment. Whether it is new-product development or employee selection, the organization has to consider them as open systems, as its decisions are interrelated and interdependent with the environmental situation. *Synergy* is the phenomenon of open systems of management by which the total system is more than a simple sum of its parts. It means that if a manager effectively coordinates the efforts of related sub-systems, the result will be greater than the sum total of such independent efforts, that is, 2 + 2 will be greater than 4. The systems approach to management is also important because it helps in avoiding entropy. *Entropy* is a syndrome wherein systems and processes eventually decay. By relating the organization to the environment, following a systems approach, such a situation can be averted.

- The *contingency theory approach* discards the concept of universality in management principles and determines managerial decisions considering situational factors. The task of a manager, as per this theory, is to identify which techniques will—in a particular situation, under particular circumstances, at a particular point of time—best contribute to achieving organizational goals. The theory contends that organizational phenomena exist in a logical pattern, which managers can understand gradually by interpreting various situations. They can thereby frame their managerial styles, which vary from situation to situation.

The contingency theory and the systems theory are together classified as the *integrative school of management thought* because these two theories integrate the classical, behavioural, and quantitative theories into a framework that uses only the best of each approach in a given situation.

CONTEMPORARY SCHOOL OF MANAGEMENT THOUGHT

The *contemporary school of management thought* provides a framework of management practices based on more recent trends like globalization, theory Z concepts, McKinsey's 7-S approach, excellence models, and productivity and quality issues.

With the pervasiveness of the World Trade Organization (WTO) and the European Economic Community (EEC), everyone is now operating in a global economy. Managers are now required to think globally even to operate in domestic markets. Market shares are lost in domestic markets because of competing foreign companies. Hence, understanding management from a global perspective has now become important.

Theory Z concepts, pioneered by W. G. Ouchi and A. M. Jaeger (1978), incorporate elements of Japanese and American management culture and emphasize the need to study and adopt appropriate management practices from other countries. The underlying concept can be better understood through a reading of the information provided in Table 1.5.

McKinsey's 7-S framework developed by T. J. Peters and R. H. Waterman (1982) identified seven independent organizational factors that need to be managed by today's managers.

1. **Strategy**: To determine allocation of scarce resources and commit the organization to a specific course of action
2. **Structure**: To determine number of levels (in hierarchy) and authority centres
3. **Systems**: To determine organizational process, procedures, reports, and routines
4. **Staff**: To determine key human resource groups in the organization and describe them demographically
5. **Style**: To determine the manner in which managers should behave in achieving organizational goals

Table 1.5 Different Types of Management Practices

Type A (American)	Type J (Japanese)	Type Z (Modified American)
Short-term employment	Lifetime employment	Long-term employment
Individual decision making	Consensual decision making	Consensual decision making
Individual responsibility	Collective responsibility	Individual responsibility
Rapid evaluation and promotion	Slow evaluation and promotion	Slow evaluation and promotion
Explicit, formalized control	Implicit, informal control	Implicit, informal control with explicit, formalized measures
Specialized career path	Non-specialized career path	Moderately specialized career path
Segmented concern	Holistic concern	Holistic concern, including family

6. **Superordinate goals (shared vision)**: To determine the guiding concepts that an organization has to instil in its members
7. **Skill**: To determine the abilities of people in the organization

The 7-S framework suggests that any change in any S factor may lead to adjustment of other S factors. Meanwhile, the concept of 8S has been introduced with the addition of one more S, namely, streaming. Streaming includes those areas that either indirectly or directly influence or shape the other S factors. A graphical representation of the model is given in Figure 1.1.

Peters and Waterman (1982) in their pioneering work, *In Search of Excellence,* identified some common characteristics of excellent organizations. Such characteristics have now become important management principles. They have been listed in Table 1.6.

Global competition has further accentuated the need for enhancing quality and productivity. These two attributes are the basic requirements for any organization to retain competitive advantage. Hence, management practices should focus on these by developing human resources to sustain their competitive advantage.

MANAGEMENT BY OBJECTIVES

Drucker (1954) emphasized for the first time the organizational need for setting objectives to make performance more measurable. When objectives are set in a systematic manner, consciously directed towards effective and efficient achievement of organizational and individual targets, it is known as *management by objectives* (MBO). General Electric Company used the elements of MBO while reorganizing itself, introducing decentralized decision making. For most organizations, MBO is required for performance appraisal as it calls for active involvement of subordinates in setting objective standards. Moreover, MBO also acts as a motivating factor for employees because they can understand their specific objectives and assess the degree of their achievement themselves. Thus, MBO helps in managing an organization with clarity, encourages personal commitment, and creates effective controls. In a way, MBO has paved the way for participative management, involving people in framing objectives and aligning their individual goals with the organizational goals or vice versa.

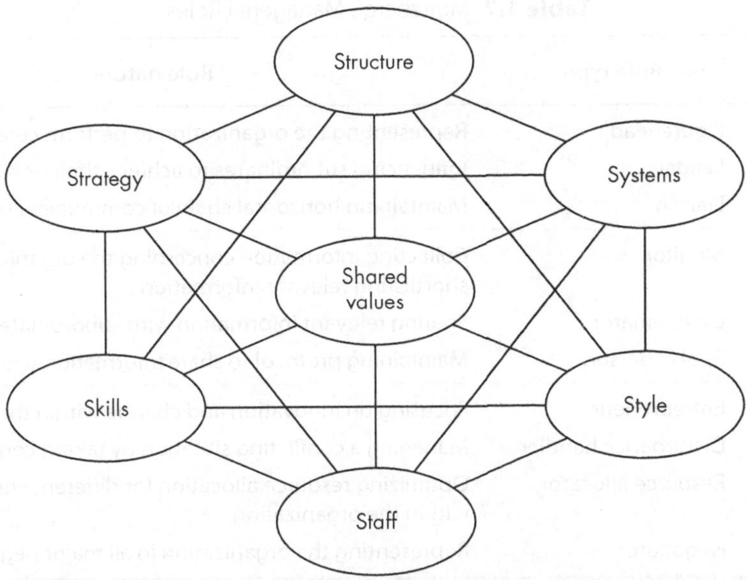

Figure 1.1 McKinsey's 7-S Model (*Source:* Mckinsey & Company)

Table 1.6 Characteristics of Excellent Organizations

Management principles	Characteristics of excellent firms
A bias for action	Excellent firms make things happen.
Closeness to the customer	These firms know their customers and their needs.
Autonomy and entrepreneurship	They value these qualities in each employee.
Productivity	They achieve productivity through relationships with people based on trust.
Hands-on, value-driven management	These firms make such management mandatory.
'Sticking to the knitting,' that is, staying with the business one knows best	They always work according to their strengths.
Simple form, lean staff	These firms develop cost-effective work teams.
Simultaneous loose–tight properties	They decentralize many decisions, while at the same time retaining tight overall control.

MANAGERIAL ROLES

Managerial roles denote position-specific behavioural patterns of managers. Mintzberg (1979), based on his study of five organizations, identified ten roles of managers, classifying these into three broad roles, namely, interpersonal, informational, and decisional. *Interpersonal roles* are classified into figurehead,

Table 1.7 Mintzberg's Managerial Roles

Role category	Role type	Role nature
Interpersonal	Figurehead	Representing the organization to perform ceremonial duties
	Leader	Influencing subordinates to achieve their goals and objectives
	Liaison	Maintaining horizontal chain of communication
Informational	Monitor	Collecting information concerning the organization and shortlisting relevant information
	Disseminator	Sharing relevant information with subordinates
	Spokesperson	Maintaining protocol to share information with outsiders
Decisional	Entrepreneur	Focusing on innovation and change within the organization
	Disturbance handler	Managing a conflicting situation by taking corrective action
	Resource allocator	Optimizing resource allocation for different competing needs within the organization
	Negotiator	Representing the organization in all major negotiations

leader, and liaison roles; *informational roles* are classified into monitor, disseminator, and spokesperson roles; and *decisional roles* are classified into entrepreneur, disturbance handler, resource allocator, and negotiator roles. In Table 1.7, the nature of these managerial roles has been explained in detail.

MANAGERIAL SKILLS AND COMPETENCIES

The skills of managers have now become an important factor to address global competitiveness at the organizational level and also at the national level. However, imparting skills through training and development is not yet recognized as an important initiative to be taken at the organizational level due to the problem of quantification of benefits. *Skills* developed through training are a coordinated series of actions that serve to attain some goal or accomplish a particular task. Operationally, *skills* are defined widely as overt responses and controlled stimulation. Overt responses may be verbal, motor, or perceptual. Verbal responses typically stress on speaking (which requires memorization of words), motor responses stress on movements of limbs and body, and perceptual responses stress on understanding of sensory responses.

It takes months to acquire motor skills which further require sustained practice. Through controlled stimulations, these acquired skills can be retained, as workers are exposed to the application of skill. When a machine operator is taken through the training and learning process involving new technology, they cannot make use of their knowledge unless they put the learned skills into operation. The process of controlled stimulation, that is, the irritation of the muscles, nerves, or sensory organs is used to evoke a response to particular activities, which gradually develops the skill of the workers in the post-learning phase. Therefore, controlled stimulations are energy inputs to workers, which are expressed in units of frequency, length, time, and weight.

Technological change and skill requirements have been made a subject of investigation in enormous studies across the world. There is a general consensus that technological change alters the job but the observations differ on the aspects of nature and form. The *neo-classical economic theory* stated that technological changes require a broader variety of skills and higher average skills from workers. New forms of skill and responsibility along with technological change have been studied in continuous process industry and chemical manufacturing units, petroleum refining, metal working industries, banking operations, and many other industries that use advanced mechanization. Another school of thought advocates that technology is instrumental in fractionating and de-skilling of jobs. Redesigning of jobs subsequent to technological change separates the planning and the concept of the job in its totality from the execution aspect of work. De-skilling and skill downgrading also occur due to differential growth of high- versus low-skill occupations and industries. The focal point of this hypothesis is that technology induces differential points of growth for sectors of the economy and produces skill polarization through eventual occupational shift to skilled jobs in some industries and unskilled jobs in many others. These phenomena are especially evident in India. From the 1981 Census onwards, one finds a major occupational shift of workers from the primary sector to the secondary sector and from the secondary sector to the tertiary sector. Simultaneous structural change in occupational patterns is also evident, as the number of blue-collar workers has been drastically reduced while the number of white-collar workers has significantly increased. In contrast, another school of thought argues that de-skilling is a secondary consequence of de-industrialization, which again is prompted by technological change. One other approach, which is the mixed change or conditional position, is more a characterization of the empirical evidence than a well-developed theory.

Transformations in skill due to technological change occur along two tracks:

1. Compositional shift, that is, structural change in occupational pattern due to the creation or elimination of jobs of a given level of skill, and the sudden distribution of jobs in the sectoral economy to people
2. Changes in work content (the technical nature of work and the role relations surrounding work performance)

Internationally, the future careers will require greater education (more in the form of institutionalized knowledge) at the job-entry level and will also demand continuing education to keep pace with technological dynamism. Greater levels of technological literacy, even for lower-skill and low-paying occupations, will be in demand in the future.

Going back in history, one finds that the Indian social system had a definite inclination towards developing and maintaining different social groups in terms of certain crafts. The quality elements in a particular craft and the attendant necessary skills were the deciding factors for the purpose of ranking that craft along with others in order of importance.

Skill can be categorized as either generic or technical, or entry-level or advanced. Conventionally, *skill* can be defined as the amount of knowledge or attributes deemed vital to organizational success. There are four general types of skills:

1. **Technical**: It relates to concepts, methods, and tools specific to an organization.
2. **Supervisory**: It enables one to effectively supervise others.
3. **Interpersonal**: It enables people to communicate and interact effectively.
4. **General business**: It helps in business and support infrastructure.

Technical skills are observable, demonstrable, and testable. The other skill types are more subjective, and difficult to quantify.

Any organization going for skill renewal or a skill-change exercise needs to undertake the following tasks:

- Profile the skills required by jobs
- Assess the skill levels acquired by individuals
- Conduct a gap analysis between required and acquired skill

Training should ideally occur before the skill is needed so that daily work can be reinforced with training.

Skills Inventories

A *skills inventory* is a device for pinpointing information about individuals and their suitability for different jobs. Skills inventories include the name of the employee and a listing (or inventory) of job-related skills, training, and/or experience that could prove useful in a future assignment. The purpose of skills inventories is to provide the organization with quick, accurate information on all employees in order that the management can choose the best and the most qualified person for promotion or transfer. For example, a skills inventory may consist of the following information: age, address, health, education, willingness to travel, experience in past and present jobs, and foreign languages spoken. If an overseas assignment requiring the speaking of German should suddenly become vacant, the skills inventory could quickly identify those candidates who possess the needed qualifications.

Multi-skilling

Multi-skilling is the process of training employees in specific skills that cross the traditional trade-specific or craft-specific skill sets. Thus, to develop multi-skills, employees require additional training to enable them to perform more jobs within the same job family or to do the entire job from a holistic point of view. Multi-skilling is often misconstrued to imply that it is consequent upon downsizing. However, downsizing occurs due to skill obsolescence, while multi-skilling is due to a holistic development of human potentialities. This holistic development takes place to effectively address the requirements of a changing production process (more flexible and customized), organizational systems (decentralized control), and state-of-the-art technology (numeric control, computer numeric control, direct numeric control, etc.). Multi-skilling facilitates intra-occupational and inter-occupational job mobility and thereby reinforces human resource planning (HRP).

Competencies

Competencies are sets of behaviours that encompass skills, knowledge, abilities, and attributes. Competencies need to be assessed at the organizational level as well as the individual level. Individual competencies together reinforce organizational competencies. However, there always exists the possibility of a major incongruence between individual competencies and organizational competencies. Exercises in workforce planning help to analyse such gaps and develop a competency model. A competency model is a map to display a set of competencies. It is future-oriented and helps to describe an ideal workforce. A documented competency model helps in managerial decision making since it is aligned with the vision, mission, objectives, goals, and strategies of an organization. It also helps the employees of an organization to understand the organization's functional requirements and work towards the enrichment of their skills, knowledge, abilities, and attributes. This can be independent of an organization-wide competency-enrichment exercise.

Case National Bank's Change in Crisis Management

National Bank is an excellent example of a highly successful organization that has been able to maintain its success in a rapidly changing environment through an incremental adjustment process. During the 1990s, changes occurred in the environment of Indian financial institutions.

These included rapid deregulation of the financial services sector by the Indian government. The critical moves involved were the partial convertibility of the rupee, foreign institutional investors' (FII) participation in the financial market in India, foreign equity participation, and foreign direct investments (FDIs) in the Indian industry (including banking). As a result, a number of foreign-owned banks started operating in India.

From its inception, the bank's strategic focus has been merchant banking (investment banking). In the 1980s, the bank commenced a process of diversification. However, with deregulation in the 1990s, it diversified further, building up strength in specialist markets, particularly in high-value-added niches (market segments) like corporate services, mutual funds, insurance-product selling, and project financing. The pace of diversification in subsequent years required the bank to manage the organizational change with multi-pronged strategies. Apart from growing with diversification, the bank also acquired some regional banks to consolidate its market position.

Change in National Bank has been a process of constant adjustment. Continuous change is embedded in its corporate philosophy. In all change processes, the bank adopts the partnership concept. The idea behind this is to let the process of change evolve, rather than to impose it. With the rapid growth in its product mix, the bank had to increase its workforce, creating the increasing problem of coordination in a collegial/partnership system. In a collegial/partnership system, product heads are hardly required to report to the CEO, as every unit runs like an independent business unit. To deal with the increase in size and the complexity of operations, the bank had to create additional structures, systems, and controls, much against the collegial/partnership system. However, fresh recruitment of professionals was not adaptable to the collegial culture. Although an attempt was made to frame strategies for well-articulated goals and objectives, an internalized collegial culture of collaboration was in direct conflict with the same. The management at National Bank then focused on creating autonomous profit centres, achieving cross-functional synergies. More emphasis was laid on systematic communication across the profit centres to supplement the effort of coordination. Unfortunately, various strategies like adopting a consultative style of management, forming more executive committees to take participative decisions, and an open-plan office could not yield any result.

CASE QUESTION

National Bank has approached you at this point of crisis. Suggest an action plan to ease the situation.

Case Mind Your Attitude

Vinod is the works manager at Lakshmi Engineering. Rahul has been with the company for some time as finance manager and head of the accounts and finance division, but he reports to the works manager.

Rahul's general attitude is to be tight-fisted about financial matters. He has always been conscious of the need to conform to company policies and procedures, and he firmly opposes any deviation from these, but is often willing to explain the reasons for his view. He prides himself as a man of principles. Vinod, in contrast, wants to take action regardless of past practice or policy. He considers himself to be a 'result-oriented' manager.

The differing attitudes of the works manager and the finance manager had led to conflict on past occasions, and Vinod had warned Rahul on two occasions that if Rahul could not carry out his instructions, he was free to search for a job elsewhere. Rahul argued his case with a measure of success, stating that his approach was proper and that in financial matters the policy guidelines had to be observed.

One afternoon, Vinod approached Rahul and said, 'Here is an incentive plan for the maintenance group. I am notifying it today and introducing it from tomorrow. Have a look at it.' Rahul appeared to be surprised. He had not known that an incentive plan was being contemplated for maintenance workers, as the company's policy till then was to pay incentives only to direct production workers. Nevertheless, he took the plan with him and returned to Vinod a couple of hours later. He said to Vinod, 'You can't introduce this plan straightaway. We have to give this some more thought. Our maintenance costs are too high, mainly due to the lack of adherence to norms on consumption of spare parts. This incentive plan gives no weight to the consumption of spare parts. Further, it will only add to maintenance costs without any real benefits to the company.'

Vinod's reaction was one of anger. 'You understand nothing of incentive plans,' he retorted. He further added, 'Spare-parts consumption is high because of the poor quality of spares bought by the materials department. Anyway, I don't intend to waste time on this with you. I am notifying this incentive plan today.'

An altercation followed, and Rahul and Vinod's argument got so loud that it attracted the attention of others in the hall, outside Vinod's office. 'I am the boss here,' screamed Vinod, and added, 'If you can't work with me and obey my instructions, you are free to leave your job and go elsewhere.'

A few moments later, Rahul was back in his office, tired and sullen. He called in the secretary and said, 'No, I have no option. Please write this down.' He dictated his letter of resignation.

CASE QUESTIONS

1. Discuss the leadership style used by Vinod. How effective is his style? What changes will you advise?
2. To what extent were Rahul's needs being considered? What kind of organizational climate was created?

SUMMARY

- Every organization applies management practices that rest on a theoretical understanding of management principles. To understand the principles of management, it is important to understand the concept of an organization and its various sub-systems.
- The history of management can be traced back to the mid-1700s, that is, the period when the Industrial Revolution took place in Europe. With the gradual expansion of industrial activities and cross-border business, management principles and practices have become more important to coordinate individual efforts and translate the same to group efforts.
- *Management* is a dynamic process to get things done through and with the efforts of people. In this competitive world, management as a process helps in optimizing scarce resources (all the inputs required to achieve the intended goals and objectives of the organization).
- The four dimensions of management are productivity, human relations, decision making, and leadership.
- The functions of management relate to those activities that help in value addition and also in achieving the goals and objectives of the organization. Production, purchasing, selling, advertising, finance, and accounting are examples of such functions. The nature of such functions varies from organization to organization but still has certain commonalities.

- Management functions can also be described as a process, that is, related activities like planning, organizing, staffing, leading, coordinating, and controlling.
- Management theories can be discussed from three perspectives: classical, neo-classical, and modern.
- Some important management practices that are a part of the contemporary school of management thought are McKinsey's 7-S framework and theory Z concepts.
- There are three main roles of managers, namely, the *interpersonal*, *informational*, and *decisional* role. Different managerial skills and competencies are required to perform such roles.

KEY TERMS

Classical approach: The classical approach to management has conventionally implied traditionally accepted views. This approach emphasizes organizational efficiency to increase organizational success. It believes in functional interrelationships, following of certain principles based on experience, bureaucratic structure, and a reward–punishment nexus.

Control: The possibility of actions deviating from the plan necessitates constant observation of actual performance so that appropriate steps may be taken to ensure conformance. Thus, control involves compelling events to conform to plans.

Coordination: Coordination deals with harmonizing work relations and efforts at all levels for some common purpose. It may be described as the process of unifying individual efforts for the purpose of accomplishing group goals. The whole idea of coordination is to adjust, reconcile, and synchronize individual efforts, so that group efforts become more effective and common objectives are met.

Decision-making orientation: This concept focuses on decision making as the primary function of management. Moore and Vance pioneered this concept.

Directing: Directing is a function that enables the manager to get the employees to accomplish their tasks. This function involves making the employees integrate their individual efforts with the interests and objectives of the enterprise. It calls for properly motivating, communicating with, and leading the subordinates.

Human-relations orientation: This concept was pioneered by Lawrence A. Appley and Harold Koontz. Their definitions of management primarily emphasize people and the relationships among people as the focus of management.

Leadership orientation: This concept views leadership as the essence of management. The proponents of this concept are Donald J. Clough and Ralph C. Davis.

Management: Management is the optimization of constraining resources to achieve intended goals.

Management by objectives: Management by objectives emphasizes management of an organization focusing primarily on objectives and then managing the whole organization with the directions set by the objectives.

Managerial competencies: Competencies are a set of behaviours that encompass skills, knowledge, abilities, and attributes. Competencies need to be assessed at the organizational level as well as the individual level. Individual competencies together reinforce organizational competencies.

Managerial role: Managerial roles denote position-specific behavioural patterns of managers. Mintzberg identified ten roles of managers, classifying them into three broad roles: interpersonal, informational, and decisional.

Modern management approach: The modern management approach combines concepts of the classical approach with the modern management social and natural sciences. It emerged from systems analysis.

Neo-classical approach: The neo-classical approach emphasizes human relations, that is, the importance of the person behind the machine, individual as well as group relationships, social aspects, etc.

Organizing: Organizing is the second function of management. It is the structuring of functions and duties to be performed by a group of people for the purpose of attaining enterprise objectives. The functions and activities of the enterprise depend upon the objectives to be accomplished and are also directed towards fulfilment of such objectives. This necessitates establishment of activity–authority relations throughout the enterprise.

Planning: Planning is the first function of management. It is deciding in advance what is to be done, how it is to be done, and when it is to be done. It involves projecting the future course of action for the business as a whole and also for different sections within it.

Process orientation: This concept views management as a process. Lundy, McFarland, Carlisle, Brech, Trewatha, Newport, and Terry are proponents of this concept.

Productivity orientation: Taylor and Mee have pioneered this concept. This concept believes in increased productivity as the basic goal of management.

Staffing: Staffing is the function through which different positions in the organization structure are filled. The staffing process, therefore, provides an organization with an adequate number of competent and qualified personnel at all levels in the enterprise.

Theory Z: Theory Z concepts, pioneered by Ouchi and Jaeger, incorporate elements of Japanese and American management culture, and emphasize the need to study and adopt appropriate management practices from other countries.

REVIEW QUESTIONS

1. Define the term *management*. Which approach or approaches to management is/are more relevant in modern organizations?
2. Using a diagram, describe the management process. Explain each process keeping in view its importance in modern organizations.
3. Examine the following statements critically:
   i. Management is both a science and an art.
   ii. Management principles are not universal.
   iii. Management lacks in social responsiveness.
   iv. Management optimizes the utilization of constraining resources.
4. 'Planning, organizing, coordination, and control are the basic functions of management'. Comment on this statement.
5. Examine the following statements:
   i. 'Management is a profession'. Do you agree with this statement? Give reasons. Also, explain the social responsibility of management.
   ii. 'Management principles are universally applicable'. Critically comment on this statement. Briefly explain the various principles of management.
6. Briefly discuss various schools of management thought.

7. What are the important features of a bureaucratic organization? Point out the merits and demerits of a bureaucratic organization.
8. Explain briefly the contributions of F. W. Taylor to the evolution of management thought.
9. What are the principles of management as per Henri Fayol? Do you think all these principles are relevant to the modern organization?
10. Discuss the major findings of the human relations theory and examine how this theory contributes to organizational effectiveness.
11. Distinguish between the *neo-classical* and *classical* approaches to management. What are their advantages and disadvantages?
12. What are the important characteristics of modern management thought? How are they different from earlier approaches?
13. Examine the importance of the contingency approach and the systems approach to management.
14. Discuss the contributions of McKinsey, Peters, and Waterman in the development of modern management thought.
15. Write short notes on the following:
    i. Social audit
    ii. Managerial activities
    iii. Management by objectives
    iv. Decision making
    v. Staffing
    vi. Hawthorne experiments
    vii. Situational approach
    viii. Esprit de corps
    ix. Contemporary school of management thought
    x. McKinsey's 7-S framework
    xi. Theory Z
    xii. Characteristics of excellent organizations

CRITICAL THINKING QUESTIONS

1. Visit an organization of your choice and identify the nature of management practices. Classify their managerial practices into a specific school of thought (there may be some variations) and explain it in detail.
2. In many manufacturing organizations, the classical approach to management exists even today. Take the examples of cement-, steel-, and jute-manufacturing units and identify the way they function.

REFERENCES

Argyris, C. (1957). *Personality and Organization*. New York: Harper Collins.

Bowen, Howard R. (1953). *Social Responsibilities of the Businessman*. New York: Harper & Brothers.

Dasgupta, A. K. (2009). *The Collected Works of A. K. Dasgupta, Volume I: Two Treatises on Classical Political Economy*. Edited by Alaknanda Patel. New Delhi: Oxford University Press.

Drucker, Peter (1954). *The Principles of Management*. New York: HarperCollins Publishers.

Fayol, Henri (1949). *General and Industrial Management*. Translated from the French edition by Constance Storrs. London: Pitman.

Frederick, William C., James E. Post, and Keith Davis (1992). *Business and Society: Corporate Strategy, Public Policy, and Ethics*, 7th ed. New York: McGraw-Hill.

Gullick, Luther (1937). 'Notes on the Theory of Organization', in Luther Gulick and Lyndall Urwick (eds), *Papers on the Science of Administration*. New York: Institute of Public Administration.

Hutchinson, John G. (1971). *Management Strategy and Tactics*. New York: Holt, Rinehart and Winston.

Koontz, H. (1961). 'The Management Theory Jungle', *Academy of Management Journal*, 4(3): pp. 174–188.

Likert, R. (1961). *New Patterns of Management*. New York: McGraw-Hill.

Maslow, Abraham H. (1971). *The Farther Reaches of Human Nature*. New York: Esalen Books, Viking Press.

——— (1968). *Toward a Psychology of Being*. New York: D. Van Nostrand Company.

Mayo, Elton (1933). *The Human Problems of an Industrial Civilization*. New York: Macmillan.

McGregor, Douglas (1960). *The Human Side of Enterprise*, annotated ed. New York: McGraw-Hill.

Mintzberg, H. (1979). *The Structure of Organizations*. Englewood Cliffs, NJ: Prentice Hall.

Newman, William H., J. R. Summer, and E. Charles (1961). *The Process of Management: Concepts, Behavior and Practice*. Englewood Cliffs, NJ: Prentice Hall.

Ouchi, W. G. and A. M. Jaeger (1978). 'Type Z Organization: Stability in the Midst of Mobility', *Academy of Management Review*, April, pp. 305–314.

Peters, T. J. and R. H. Waterman (1982). *In Search of Excellence: Lessons from America's Best Run Companies*. New York: Harper & Row.

Taylor, Frederick Winslow (1903). *Shop Management*. New York: American Society of Mechanical Engineers.

——— (1911). *The Principles of Scientific Management*. New York: Harper & Brothers.

Weber, Max (1920). *Collected Essays in the Sociology of Religion*, vol. 1. Tübingen: J. C. B. Mohr (Paul Siebeck).

FURTHER READING

Bhattacharyya, Dipak Kumar (2009). *Organizational Behaviour: Text and Cases*. New Delhi: Oxford University Press.

——— (2010). *Industrial Management*. New Delhi: Vikas Publishing.

Dale, Ernest (1965). *Management: Theory and Practice*. New York: McGraw-Hill.

George, C. S., Jr (1968). *The History of Management Thought*. Englewood Cliffs, NJ: Prentice Hall.

Massie, Joseph L. (1986). *Essentials of Management, 4th ed.* New Delhi: Prentice Hall.

2

Organizational Planning

After going through this chapter, you will be able to understand:

- the concept and definitions of planning
- the importance of planning in an organization
- policy formulation for plans in an organization
- the concept of a strategy and its various levels
- strategy formulation
- the ways in which budgets facilitate plans
- forecasting
- various forms of decision making

Planning: An All-encompassing Managerial Function

Planning is of prime importance at the operations level. The marketing department puts up requisitions to the operations department after booking orders to ensure the supply of produced goods according to the requirements of customers. The operations department then needs to schedule activities, balancing cost optimization and on-time delivery. Customers' orders and specifications may vary, which is why the operations department needs to schedule production ensuring that the least amount of time is spent on interchanging machines (shifting from production of one type of item to another), without, however, prejudicing the interest of customers in general. Any mistake may ultimately result in inappropriate resource allocation, customer dissatisfaction, and poor return on investment.

One of the important areas of operations planning is supply chain management, which balances the organizational capacity to produce and manage supply. It requires, among other things, cross-functional (across various functions like marketing, human resources, finance, and operations) coordination. There are many debates surrounding forecasting, another important component of planning. Operationally, organizations use forecasting as an input for holistic planning processes. For example, for effective inventory planning, one needs to forecast the inventory requirements. Here, therefore, forecasting of inventory requirements becomes the input for comprehensive inventory planning. However, some organizations still continue to use forecasting independent of planning. Such organizations translate their mission into specific objectives and accordingly drive the organizational activities. In an economic downturn, however, sustaining a mission may become difficult.

Organizations are then required to scale down their activities after reviewing their planning premise (the assumptions based on which they draw their plan). In such cases, they make use of business forecasting, extrapolating the present market realities.

INTRODUCTION

Planning is the most basic managerial function and is all-encompassing in nature. All other functions of management are largely dependent on the effectiveness of planning. For example, the control function of management becomes meaningless without planning. Through planning, organizations decide what is to be done to achieve some decided goals and by enforcing control one can ascertain whether everything is being done properly to meet the goals. Being the primary and basic managerial function, planning also guides and motivates people to achieve results. People get a sense of direction and are able to achieve their goals along with the organization's goals.

In Chapter 1, it was explained that management is a dynamic process. Since planning constitutes the core of management, it is also dynamic, that is, the plans need to be changed from time to time, keeping pace with the changing planning premises. With changes in the business environment, organizations need to change or alter the plan, to ensure that the desired results are achieved.

CONCEPT OF PLANNING

Planning involves deciding the future course of action in advance. A manager has to plan what is to be done, where, how, and by whom. Planning helps the manager to understand in advance the future activities that need to be performed to achieve the desired results for the organization as a whole and also for each department. Effective planning requires not only assessing the future, but also making adequate provision to face the future. From this perspective, planning is a rational approach to the future. Managers are, therefore, required to plan and initiate necessary actions for successful implementation of their plans.

At the organizational level, planning is done by choosing from different alternatives. Proper study of alternatives facilitates correct courses of action that are less prone to risk, based on which organizations take decisions. In fact, both planning and decision making can be considered to be an intellectual process. Through planning, managers can minimize the risk of decisional errors. Since planning is an intellectual process, managers need to be mentally prepared and consciously determine future courses of action. It requires consideration of objectives, facts, and forecasts.

It is also important to remember that planning is useful to every hierarchical level of an organization. For example, a marketing manager makes use of planning to decide the courses of action for new-market development. Similarly, a salesperson reporting to the same marketing manager needs to plan to meet the sales target. Therefore, one must not erroneously construe that planning is the prerogative of only the top management. The planning process involves choosing the best course of action from different alternatives, and it has to be implemented by all people, irrespective of their hierarchical level.

Importance of Planning

Since planning is one of the primary functions of management, it provides the framework within which organizing, staffing, directing, and controlling are undertaken. The enormous importance of planning is understood in the context of its dynamic equation with other management functions and also with the organization's objectives.

- **Planning clarifies the objectives of the organization**: In planning, the first stage is the deliberate statement of organizational and departmental objectives. The statement of objectives helps employees to visualize the organization in its entirety and see how their actions contribute to its ultimate goals. Since objectives represent end points of planning, management should be prepared to face the future and revise its plans in the light of possible changes so that goals can be accomplished more effectively.
- **Planning economizes operations**: Planning is done considering the factors of economy and efficiency in operations. As an all-pervasive function, planning improves the effectiveness of all other functions of management and also helps to secure coordinated efforts throughout the organization. Since it involves choosing, planning facilitates choice of the best method and also helps to identify alternatives expected to produce the desired results with minimum cost and risk.
- **Planning precedes control**: Control ensures that everything conforms to one's plans. Planning is, therefore, an important prerequisite for control. The management function of control seeks to check performance against a predetermined standard of projected courses of action established through the planning process, and in this process control ensures conformance to plans.
- **Planning provides for the future**: Planning, by definition, means providing for the future and deciding the course of action. Every plan, therefore, requires adequate provisioning for future contingencies. During the planning process itself, organizations need to look to the future and discover suitable alternative courses of action. Depending on the quality of prediction (making use of scientific forecasting tools), managers can have a relatively realistic idea of the future and chalk out suitable programmes of action. As a rational approach, planning provides for unexpected events and can, accordingly, enable the management to prepare against any eventual and undesirable change.
- **Planning increases the efficiency of all managerial functions**: Planning, organizing, staffing, directing, and controlling together contribute to the accomplishment of organizational, departmental, and group goals. Each function of management has its respective importance. However, since planning is the primary function and precedes all other managerial functions, effective plans can increase the efficiency of all other managerial functions.

Limitations of Planning

Even though planning is all-pervasive and a primary function of management, it is subject to certain limitations. Without proper understanding of such limitations, planning may result in futile exercises. Some limitations of planning have been listed here and awareness of these may improve the efficiency of planning.

- **Planning premises may be wrong**: The premises of planning are the basis and framework for any decision. Understanding the planning premises with absolute accuracy is not possible. There always exists some margin of error that may vitiate the plans.
- **Rapidity of change**: Every organization operates in the context of a certain internal and external environment. The environment cannot always be stable. Thus, the extent of change in the internal and external environment creates various situations of instability, making the planning job extremely difficult.
- **Time and cost constraints**: Every organization has to plan within given time and cost constraints. Such constraints stand against the efficiency of planning. In a situation of crisis, organizations may even have to take decisions on war footing, in which case planning itself becomes redundant. Non-availability of time and resources may compel the organization to settle for the most convenient business plan.

- **Planning may limit new ideas**: New ideas or innovativeness in planning may not be encouraged because of the traditional mindsets of people. If the vision and the philosophy of the organization are not progressive, it may limit the planning initiative of the management. Similarly, procedural and policy rigidities also come in the way of planning. Procedures, rules, and policies once documented are difficult to change. Such inflexibility obviously affects planning.
- **Capital investment constraint**: Capital invested in a business, in the form of both equipment and employees (investment in training), often limits the planning initiative. Managers are quite often compelled to set their planning premises keeping in mind the capital investment, which cannot be foregone.
- **Lack of control over external factors**: Some external factors may seriously impede the process of planning, for example, a sudden change in government policies, union pressure for a wage hike, war, and international policies (like WTO, EEC, or ASEAN resolutions).

Yet, despite such limitations, organizations cannot do away with planning. Every manager has to systematically plan to achieve the desired results.

COMPONENTS OF PLANNING

Having understood the meaning and context of planning, it is now important to elaborate upon the various components of planning. Planning components are usually classified as objectives, policies, procedures, programmes, budgets, and strategies.

Policy

A *policy* is a predetermined and established guideline aimed towards the attainment of accepted goals and objectives. Such guidelines help to accomplish the strategic intent through properly designed efforts. Policies should not be interpreted as strategies or tactics. A *strategy* is a proposed course of action to exert a far-reaching impact on the ability of the enterprise to attain its goals. Therefore, a strategy relates to the means.

Policies can be differentiated from objectives, programmes, and procedures. Policies relate to the fundamental framework of principles and rules that are used as reference information for decision making and provide a constant pattern of decisions and structured thought processes. *Objectives*, on the other hand, are specific goals or aims, preferably in quantitative terms, and can be considered as something that an individual or a group seeks to accomplish. Hence, an objective is something to accomplish, while a policy is a guide to accomplish it.

Again, a policy is different from a procedure, as a *procedure* defines the manner of accomplishing something. A procedure comprises the process and the method. While policies form part of a framework of general principles, a procedure necessarily indicates how to do something and directs employees towards the accomplishment of the goal. Policies are also differentiated from programmes. *Programmes* are developed on the basis of policies with a view to implementing them and, accordingly, programmes involve an additional step beyond the policies to simplify decisions. The execution of programmes leads to specific actions including practices and procedures.

Policies cover a wide variety of subjects. A comprehensive coverage of policies embraces any action or decision taken by either employees or management in relation to the working environment, the rights and responsibilities of employees and management, and the actions of both parties. Thus, one policy may be a statement of standards for employee attendance and another may be a statement of management obligations in grievance administration. One policy may explain conditions under which loans will be granted, whereas another may indicate conditions under which an employee is subjected to discharge.

Inputs for policies may be from both internal and external sources. Internally, policies are developed based on employees' suggestions or complaints, terms of reference in collective bargaining, quality circles, total quality management teams, value engineering teams, self-managed teams, etc. External sources could be compliance with legislative norms, norms of the society and community, national and global economic changes, political changes, etc. Once the organization finalizes the policy documents, subsequent changes, if any, can only be carried out with vetting from the top management. Each documented policy needs to be communicated to everyone, especially when such policies concern them either directly or indirectly. Communication of policies can be made in the form of standing orders, house journals, circulars, or documented policy manuals.

Procedures prescribe the details for carrying out policies. They spell out the specific rules and regulations, and the steps, time, place, and personnel responsible for implementing policies. Procedures also clarify what is to be done in particular circumstances. For example, to manage the grievances of employees, organizations may have a grievance-handling procedure.

Purposes of policies

Through policy statements, one basically provides guidelines for decision making. A policy-bound decision-making process can be delegated, and decision making by default becomes easier, consuming less time as it does not require a detailed analysis of any decisional problem or issue. Policy-bound decisions are routine and repetitive by nature. On the other hand, since strategic decisions are highly situation-specific, they cannot be taken based on policy guidelines.

Based on the inputs given earlier, one can say that policies provide a clear idea of what management and employees can expect. Policies promote consistency and fairness of action under conditions that are similar in character and eliminate any bias in employee-related decisions. In this way, policies help to avoid confusion and misunderstandings. For example, a disciplinary policy spells out minor and major violation of disciplinary norms and, accordingly, lists the disciplinary actions. To ensure the implementation of disciplinary action, one needs to follow specific steps, which are usually documented in organizations as part of the disciplinary procedure.

Framing or developing policies

In framing policies, at the outset, it is important to consider objectives or purposes. Operationally, in policy framing, it is also important to consider the cost–benefit aspects, keeping in context the size and complexity of the organization. A policy on medical reimbursements to retired employees cannot be sustained by the organization in the long run, when the number of retired employees is more. For example, the Andrew Yule Group, an erstwhile multinational operating in India, still continues with its age-old policy of reimbursement of medical expenses for its retired employees. The company cannot sustain such a burden in its present state of financial health and is, therefore, running on loss.

While determining the policies, it is also important to ensure their acceptability to management as well as to employees. Such acceptance largely depends on the degree of administrative feasibility and fairness to employees.

Framing of policies requires a high degree of imagination. Policy-bound decisions are taken subsequent to policy framing. Hence, imaginative managers can visualize the nature and context of future decisions, and accordingly, can draw the current policy. Along with imagination, policy framing also requires knowledge, understanding of the operating problems, etc.

Guidelines for policy formulation

A number of guidelines for policy writing have been well established and are worth enumerating.

- **Purpose**: It is a statement of purpose or rationale that clarifies the need for a policy and also ensures its acceptance.
- **Semantics**: The wording should be as simple as possible, so that the intent of the policy is understood clearly. For example, a standing order cannot be written in a way that employees at the lower rungs find it difficult to understand. Also, a normative approach to policy framing requires avoidance of any expression that may malign or antagonize people.
- **Tone**: The tone of a policy document needs to exude warmth and understanding. A positive tone can also evoke quick responses from the people who are influenced by a policy.
- **Form**: Many organizations provide policy statements in the form of an outline. This approach is good for managerial reference and applications, but difficult for the employees to follow. Often, an employee's interpretation of policy documents may be wrong. Moreover, policy statements in the form of an outline are cold and distant. Policy statements articulated in the form of short paragraphs always encourage reading.
- **Clarity**: Clarity in policy statements is ensured through short sentences. It is always preferable to use a single short sentence to carry one statement. Putting multiple statements in one sentence confuses the employees, and they fail to comprehend the meaning.

Communicating policies

After finalizing the policy documents, it is desirable for the management to communicate the same to the employees. Successful communication of a policy means that employees have understood it clearly. For communication of policies, organizations make use of written media such as employee handbooks, bulletin boards, and company periodicals. In some cases, organizations may also conduct policy-familiarization workshops to make employees understand the policies and their compliance in day-to-day work. In such workshops, employees can interact and understand the policy documents, and have their doubts clarified. For better clarity in employees' understanding, various visual aids like film strips, placards, and funnel boards may be used. Any subsequent policy change also needs to be communicated appropriately.

Administration of policies

Uniformity in policy administration is very important. Under similar circumstances, individuals and group members need to be treated similarly according to policy. At the outset, it has already been stated that policies are the guidelines for routine or repetitive decision making. Hence, it is important that every policy-bound decision is fair and uniform, irrespective of the rank and the file of the employee. However, operationally, policy administration may adopt an approach of differentiation between the office and the shop floor. In office, a minor policy violation may require rigid imposition of penalty, if any. In the case of shop-floor workers, who are unionized, flexibility in policy administration may be required or it may be just the reverse. While adopting a flexible approach in policy administration, an organization may consider issues like work record, demonstrated capability, knowledge level of the employee, and the circumstances under which the policy violation occurred. If the case of policy violation is rare and accidental for the person concerned, who otherwise has a good track record of performance, often the organization becomes flexible in policy administration. However, in all such cases where the organization adopts a flexible approach in policy administration, there must be adequate justification. A sample of a policy document has been appended at the end of this chapter as Annexure 2.1 for better understanding.

Programme

A *programme* consists of the entire broad course of action governing employees at all levels (including management) in an organization. It can be thought of as a stable plan of action that continues over an extensive period of time. It is the end product of the organization's philosophy, values, concepts, principles, policies, and procedures. For example, for human resource (HR) functions of any organization, there may be programmes on recruitment and selection, grievances and discipline, benefits and compensation, etc.

Strategy

Strategy is the long-term direction and scope of an organization, matching its resources to its changing environment and in particular its markets, customers, or clients, to meet stakeholders' expectations. To achieve results and excellence in business performance, most organizations around the world take the initiative to align their strategies with their business goals and objectives. A well-developed strategy map for any organization gives a sense of direction to all cross-sections of organizational members. Linking such strategies with individual performance goals in the form of *key performance areas* (KPAs) and *key result areas* (KRAs) benefits the organization as they reap the advantage of competitiveness through the high performance level of organizational members. Strategies are put into practice through plans. Tactics are the action plans through which strategies are executed. Hence, action plans help in the various managerial functions of an organization including human resource management (HRM).

A strategy is primarily concerned with:

- The scope of an organization's activities
- Matching the activities of an organization to the environment in which it operates
- Resource implication
- Effects on operational decisions
- The values and expectations of stakeholders
- The long-term direction of the organization

Levels of strategy

There are three levels of strategies:

1. **Corporate-level strategy**: Corporate-level strategies are influenced by the mission of the organization. They address the following issues:
   - Overall scope of an organization
   - How an organization is managed in structural and financial terms
   - How resources are allocated to different operations
2. **Competitive or business strategy**: These strategies are adopted in order to strengthen the position of the organization in the market. They explain:
   - How to compete in a market
   - Which products or services should be developed and offered to which markets
   - The extent to which customers' needs are met
   - If it is possible to achieve the objectives of the organization, viz. long-term profitability, market growth, and efficiency
3. **Operational strategies**: These are adopted at the functional level and the success at the functional or operational level ultimately enables an organization to achieve corporate-level and competitive strategies.

Strategy, therefore, is either the plans made or the actions taken to help an organization fulfil its intended purposes. Strategic plans for the future are called *intended strategy* and strategic actions are known as *realized strategy*. *Strategic means* are plans and policies, while *strategic ends* may be either a broad vision and mission or focused goals and objectives.

Framing a strategy

Strategic plans are a process of thinking through the current mission of the organization with due cognizance of current environmental conditions—both external and internal. Such plans, therefore, set the guidelines for future decisions and results. A strategy map elaborating the details of vision, mission, goals, objectives, strategies, and action plans is appended as Annexure 2.2.

Vision

A *vision* consists of the organization's intentions that are all-inclusive and forward-thinking. It is the driving force of the organization. A *vision* has certain characteristics, such as:

- It describes aspirations for the future.
- It does not specify the means that are used to achieve the desired ends.
- It must be inspirational.
- It is often unwritten.
- It must be communicated.

Communication of a vision can be done in two ways: in the form of a mission statement and through personal selling (personal interactions with customers to build relationships and communicate one's vision). The attitude towards the quality of products and customers' complaints are examples of the vision or intentions of an organization.

Mission

A vision in tangible form is a *mission statement*. Therefore, a mission statement verbalizes the vision.

A mission statement attempts to answer the following issues:

- Basic purpose of an organization
- Uniqueness or distinctiveness of the organization
- Likely difference in business three to five years in the future
- Principal customers, clients, or key market segments
- Principal goods and services in the present and the future
- Principal economic concerns
- Basic beliefs, values, aspirations, and philosophical priorities of the firm

Some of the key elements of a mission statement are:

- **View of the future**: The anticipated regulatory, competitive, and economic environment
- **Competitive arenas**: The business and geographic business arenas where the company will compete
- **Sources of competitive advantage**: The skills that the company will develop and a description of how the company intends to succeed

Some of the benefits of a mission statement are:

- It establishes boundaries to guide strategy formulation.
- It acknowledges responsibilities to various stakeholders and establishes standards of organizational performance.
- It suggests standards of individual behaviour.

Goals

A mission statement tries to make a vision more specific, while *goals* are attempts to make a mission statement more concrete. Goals have several defining features, such as:

- They address both financial and non-financial issues.
- They facilitate reasoned trade-off (the range of goals should be perfectly consistent with one another).
- They can be reached with a stretch.
- They cut across functional areas.

Objectives

Objectives are the operational definitions of goals. They describe what organizations hope to accomplish in specific measurable terms within a given time frame. The top management of an organization decides the overall objectives, which then cascades to divisional, departmental, and individual employee-level objectives. Individual employee-level objectives are variously known as *key result areas* (KRAs), *key performance areas* (KPAs), *key performance indicators* (KPIs), or *key sales objectives* (KSOs). Such individual-level objectives then become the basis for performance evaluation. Thus, characteristically, objectives can be measured; they have a time dimension; and they reduce conflicts (misunderstandings) by setting a common direction for all those who work for the organization.

Two important components of planning, namely, strategy and policy, are put into practice by means of plans. A comparison has been provided in Table 2.1.

STRATEGIC CONTROL

Organizational strategy is selected and implemented over time. Since strategies are designed to accomplish future objectives, it is necessary to enforce control over strategy. This is known as *strategic control*.

Table 2.1 Comparative Study of Policy and Strategy

Policy	Strategy
Policies are general statements or understandings.	Strategy is the direction and scope of an organization.
Policies guide managers' thinking in decision making.	Strategies are concerned with deployment of human and material resources.
Policies ensure that decisions fall within certain boundaries.	Strategies increase the chance of achieving selected objectives.

Strategic controls, which can be enforced through certain operational controls, are designed to answer the following questions:

- Are we moving in the right direction?
- Are key things falling into place?
- Are our assumptions about major trends and changes correct?
- Are the critical things we need to do being done?
- Do we need to adjust or abort this strategy?
- How are we performing?
- Are we meeting objectives and schedules?
- How are costs, revenues, and cash flows matching projections?
- Do we need to make operational changes?

Establishing Strategic Control

Strategic control can be established in the following ways:

- Allow time between initial implementation and achievement of intended results
- Steer the organization through different actions (like undertaking of projects and investments) and also through the environmental situation as well as the firm's internal situation
- Correct the actions and directions of the firm as required by certain developments and changes in the external environment and the internal situation

Types of Strategic Control

There are four basic types of strategic control:

1. **Premise control**: *Premise control* is designed to check systematically and continuously whether or not the premises set during the planning and implementation process are still valid. For example, a bank may adopt an aggressive marketing strategy to achieve 15 per cent annual growth, establishing a planning premise that not more than 10 per cent would be their non-performing assets. Premise control in this case should be ensured by monitoring the non-performing assets at the branch level on a regular basis.
2. **Implementation control**: *Implementation control* is designed to assess the overall strategy results associated with incremental steps and the actions that implement the overall strategy. For example, an internationally known fast-food centre decided to maintain a 3:1 company–franchise ratio of ownership as part of their expansion strategy, to ensure control over quality of foods, rates, etc. However, the growing competition in this business later forced them to reverse the ratio to accelerate their ability to open outlets at new locations.
3. **Strategic surveillance**: *Strategic surveillance* is designed to monitor a broad range of events inside and outside the company that are likely to threaten the course of the organizational strategy. For example, right from its inception, IBM focused on computer hardware and became one of the best in the world even in the desktop business. However, with the emergence of Dell and HP's Compaq series, IBM was unable to sustain itself in the market of price-sensitive desktops and, as a result, gradually had to change its business focus. Today, IBM has withdrawn from the desktop business and made a foray in the IT-enabled services (ITeS) market. Also, strategic surveillance helped IBM

to understand that a new market for their mainframe computers could be the libraries around the world, apart from the corporate houses.

4. **Special alert control**: *Special alert control* is the need to thoroughly and, often, rapidly reconsider the firm's basic strategy, based on a sudden, unexpected event. For example, a political coup or a home war in Afghanistan will put pressure on exporters to Afghanistan, who may have to thoroughly reconsider their export market strategy. Another instance is the Lehman Brothers' collapse (the firm borrowed significant funds from the market to fund their mortgage business, making itself highly vulnerable to a downturn in the market), which resulted in a sub-prime mortgage crisis cascading into a global economic meltdown and adversely affected the business plans of several organizations across the globe.

OPERATIONAL CONTROL

Strategic controls are useful to top management in monitoring and steering the basic strategic direction of the company. Apart from this, operating managers also need to enforce strategic control befitting the nature of the strategy. The primary concern at the operating level is allocation and use of the company resources. *Operational control systems* guide, monitor, and evaluate progress in meeting annual objectives. Usually, the following steps are taken for operational control:

1. Set standards of performance
2. Measure actual performance
3. Identify deviations from standards
4. Initiate corrective action or adjustment

There are three types of *operational control systems*: budgets, schedules, and key success factors.

Functional and Grand Strategies

Functional strategies guide functional actions towards implementation of the grand strategy. The *grand strategy* provides general direction while functional strategies give specific guidance to managers for accomplishing annual objectives. Functional strategies, therefore, translate grand strategy at the business level into action plans for the organization. Operating or functional managers develop such strategies taking into cognizance the policy guidelines. Therefore, the time horizon for such strategies may be a year or less. Grand strategies, on the other hand, are framed with a long-term perspective at the corporate level.

Formulating functional strategies at each operational level, at the outset, requires identification of critical success factors. For example, marketing strategies need to focus on product, price, marketplace, and market promotion. Finance strategies may focus on capital acquisition, allocation, dividend, and working-capital management. Research and development (R&D) strategies focus on basic research, commercial development, time horizon, organizational fit, and basic R&D posture (defensive, offensive, innovation, development, etc.).

For evaluating strategy, one needs to consider its internal and external consistency, its appropriateness in terms of available resources, its degree of risk (which should be reasonable), its time horizon (not too long to face the risk of becoming obsolete), and its workability.

Operational Strategy Factors

From an operations manager's point of view, it is important to study the following factors while adopting an operations strategy:

- The number, type, size, and location of operations facilities
- The type of equipment that will be utilized (focused and specific, general-purpose and flexible, automated or principally manual)
- Make (producing an item internally) or buy (buying an item externally) decision
- Organization structure (whether it is suitable to accomplish and coordinate all the necessary efforts)
- The workforce selection, employment security, compensation methods, and management style
- The information systems that will be used to collect, analyse, and distribute information on production, purchasing, inventory, quality, personnel, etc.
- Production planning, scheduling and control, system and inventory policy
- The quality control and improvement methods that will be used
- The productivity improvement methods—machine/human resources

Budgeting

Budgeting is the formulation of plans for a given future period in numerical terms. It is a statement of anticipated results in financial terms (as in revenue and expense, and capital budgets) or in non-financial terms (as in budgets of direct labour hours, materials, physical sales volume, or units of production). The Chartered Institute of Management Accountants (CIMA, 2005), defines a budget as the 'quantitative expression of a plan for a defined period of time. It may include planned sales volumes and revenues; resource quantities, costs and expenses; assets, liabilities and cash flows.' As budgets provide standards of performance, they usually become the basis for control. All results and performances are measured and appraised against *budget standards*, which are developed through a comprehensive budgetary programme. Control exercised for the execution of budgets is known as *budgetary control*.

Budget making is concerned with the planning function of management, while budgetary control is associated with controlling in organization. CIMA defines budgetary control as the establishment of a 'master budget, devolved to responsibility centres, (which) allows continuous monitoring of actual results versus budget, either to secure by individual action the budget objectives or to provide a basis for budget revision'.

Characteristics of budgets

From the given concept and definitions of budgets, the following characteristics can be listed:

- A budget is essentially for a given period.
- It differs from objectives and policies because it is set down in specific numerical terms.
- A good budget is flexible.
- It secures maximum participation of the entire organization both in preparation and follow-up.
- A budget is fundamental to the organization. It generally receives attention and support of the top management.

Purposes of budgeting

Budgeting is used for a variety of purposes. Some of the purposes are:

- **To use it as an organized procedure for planning**: Budgeting is used as an aid to planning and a budget is sometimes known as the *profit plan*. A budget requires planning and is also in itself an instrument of planning. Budgeting involves anticipation of results and expressing these in numerical terms. Forecasting or projecting a future course of action, as implied in budgeting, is essentially a planning process. Comprehensive budgeting forces the management to develop a network of objectives, policies, and plans for all phases of operations of the enterprise.

- **To use it as a means of coordination**: Budgeting is also used for coordinating the activities of the various divisions of a business. While preparing budgets, information is required relating to divisions and activities in the enterprise. A sales budget, for instance, cannot be prepared without knowing about the production programme of the enterprise. The very act of preparing budgets, therefore, forces coordination. The process of integrating various budgets into a master budget also highlights the importance of coordination implied in budgeting.
- **To use it as a basis for control**: Control represents the most widely known use of budgeting. Events can be compelled to conform to plans only when there are predetermined objectives and standards. Budgeting forces the management to lay down objectives, goals, and plans in numerical terms. It, thus, provides the yardstick for measurement of performance which is so essential for effective control. Budget reports analyse the deviations and, also, suggest corrective actions. Thus, budgeting is also used as an aid to managerial control.
- **To enforce control of cost**: An individual budget for each operation or department helps the management to know the cost for each of them separately and, thus, exercise effective control over cost. The departmental manager who notices substantial deviations from budgeted costs for operations under their control feels compelled to curtail extra expenditure and think very seriously about controlling the cost.
- **To increase efficiency in the field of production**: More often than not, budgetary control necessitates preparation of a separate production budget and, thus, helps determine progress and efficiency of the production.
- **To determine capital requirements**: Budgeting is also employed to determine capital requirements of the enterprise. This is possible through computing financial flows at different phases of all the operations of the enterprise as reflected in various budgets.
- **To encourage research and development**: Budgeting aims at encouraging research and development. Comparison of actual performance with the budgeted goals and plans and thorough analysis of deviations, particularly of key factors, provide a sound basis for research and development.
- **To increase utility of cost records**: Budgeting entails considerable use of cost information and records. Thus, budgetary control adds meaning to cost records and increases their utility.

Reporting

The essence of budgeting lies in taking proper corrective actions to rectify the negative deviations. This can be achieved if the management has full information about deviations. This is called *reporting*. Management can have access to the requisite information if an effective system of reporting is in operation. Reporting is, therefore, extremely important in a system of budgetary control.

Reports should be drawn up in such a manner that they enable the management to realize at a glance where its attention is needed. Hence, the application of the principle of *management by exception* (wherein the management pays special attention to material deviations requiring investigation) is inevitable here.

The whole system should work like the nervous system in a human body where all information about whatever is happening is noted, but the mind is burdened only with that information which requires some action.

The following factors merit consideration with respect to reports:

- The report should be factual and objective.
- The report should relate to a definite period of activity, and should be prepared in such a way that the responsibilities of various persons and departments are clearly demarcated.
- The report should be brief, concise, and clear.
- The report should be specific with respect to exceptional aspects so that immediate action can be taken by the management.
- Reports that no one uses should be immediately stopped.
- A copy of the report should be sent to the person responsible for the activity covered, so that they are kept informed about the progress of their work.
- Above all, the report should be prompt even if it contains a permissible degree of inaccuracy.

FORECASTING

Forecasting is defined as either an estimate or an inference of a future event. It may not always be an accurate estimate or inference as it is based on past trends. However, forecasting provides an effective basis for planning different activities of an organization. From a managerial point of view, forecasting is important for planning, scheduling, and controlling the system to achieve efficient results.

Steps in Forecasting

The following steps are required for effective forecasting:

1. Identify the objectives for which forecasting is done. From a manager's point of view, forecasting objectives may be reducing queuing problems of customers by enhancing the number of service counters, initiating changes in the design of a product, measuring customers' response patterns, etc.
2. Determine the time period of forecast, which may be a long-term or a short-term period. Depending on the time period, managerial decisions and actions may vary. For example, if an organization requires extra workforce for a period less than one year, instead of direct recruiting they may avail the services of an outsourcing agency (who make people available on hire).
3. Select the right forecasting method in line with the objective and the time frame. For example, annual sales forecast (for an existing organization) is better done using time-series analysis, while Delphi technique or market research methods are best applied where collective opinions are required to be assessed.
4. Collect required data and information matching the selected forecasting method. For time-series analysis past data is collected, while for market research primary data is gathered by conducting surveys.
5. Implement results for managerial decisions (planning and control).
6. Periodically evaluate forecasting by assessing degree of error and reliability, and revise accordingly.

Types of Forecasting

Forecasting techniques can be broadly categorized under three types: qualitative or judgemental, time-series analysis, and cause-effect models (see Table 2.2). Depending on the type chosen, different techniques are adopted. *Qualitative forecasts* involve collection of opinions and preferences, which are

Table 2.2 Forecasting Models and Techniques

Forecast type	Techniques used
Qualitative methods	Delphi technique Nominal group method Market research method
Time-series analysis	Last period method Simple average method Moving average method Exponential smoothing Trend projections Tracking signal
Cause-effect models	Correlation regression method Econometric method Input-output analysis End-user analysis

then, quantified using different statistical tools. Delphi method, nominal group technique, and market research are the commonly used qualitative techniques.

Quantitative forecasts are divided into time-series analysis and cause-effect models. *Time-series analysis* uses historical data to calculate the average of past demand and the results thus obtained (average) are used as forecasts. Last period demand, simple average, moving average, exponential smoothing, and trend projections are among the most frequently used techniques under time-series analysis.

Forecasting using *cause-effect models* is done using correlation regression or econometric techniques. *Correlation regression technique* shows the cause-effect relationship between an organizational past sales data and market or economic forces that caused changes (either negative or positive) in the demand pattern. *Econometric models* are used to forecast economic conditions. For example, when principles of consumption theory are used to forecast demand pattern, this technique is used. Similarly, *input-output analysis* is another quantitative model that looks at an economy as a system of interrelated economic sectors where changes in one can be used to predict changes in the other. *End-user analysis* is used to predict sales prospects through an appraisal of the level of customer satisfaction.

We now discuss in detail the forecasting techniques that fall under qualitative methods and time-series analysis.

QUALITATIVE METHODS

Qualitative methods use collections of opinions and preferences for forecasting.

Delphi Technique

The word *Delphi* has come from Greek. In Athens (the capital of Greece), it was a convention to consult an oracle representative of the Greek god Apollo during ancient times. The advice of the oracle could, however, be interpreted only by the priest.

In modern times, this method is essentially a group process to achieve a consensus forecast. This method calls for selection of a panel of experts from within or outside the organization, whose comments are crystallized from a series of questionnaire responses and then used as the basis to forecast. The series of questionnaire is prepared from the responses received from a prior set of questions in a sequencing manner. At every stage, information obtained from the previous questionnaire is shared among the participating members, without, however, disclosing the majority opinion, which otherwise may have peer-group influence on minority opinion.

The procedure of the Delphi technique may be enumerated as follows:

1. To start with, it requires selection of a coordinator and a panel of experts both inside and outside the organization.
2. The coordinator circulates questions in writing to each such expert.
3. The experts then write their observations.
4. The coordinator edits those observations and summarizes, without, however, disclosing the majority opinion in the summary.
5. On the basis of the summary, the coordinator develops a new questionnaire and circulates it among the experts.
6. The experts answer the new set of questions.
7. The coordinator repeats the process until such time as he/she is able to synthesize a forecast from the opinion of the experts.

The success of the process depends on the following factors:

- Experts should be so chosen that they have the requisite knowledge and skills to give pertinent answers.
- Questions should be relevant to the objective.
- Criteria for evaluating responses should be consistent, unbiased, and befitting the objectives. Although there is no universal set of criteria for evaluating responses, it is often considered necessary to follow certain guidelines:
    - ❑ Consider the assessment made by the experts in terms of their knowledge in the area
    - ❑ Consider the assessment in terms of feasibility, objectives, time, and resource requirement
    - ❑ Consider the assessment in terms of desirability
    - ❑ Consider the assessment in terms of extraneous factors

Nominal Group Method

Like the Delphi method, the *nominal group method* also involves a panel of experts. The major difference is that while under the Delphi technique experts are not allowed to discuss among themselves for assessing the questions, under the nominal group method experts are given the opportunity to discuss among themselves. In this method, the coordinator assumes the role of a facilitator, allowing the experts to sit together to discuss their ideas, and records of such discussions are made on a flip chart. After this round-table discussion of ideas, the experts are asked to rank their ideas according to their perceived priority. The group consensus is then derived mathematically in terms of individual rankings. The process, therefore, affords creativity and facilitates scientific group consensus, unlike the consensus by qualification (as the coordinator ultimately decides the best course of action) arrived at under the Delphi technique.

Market Research

This qualitative method of forecasting is used to develop a model for consumer buying behaviour. From the published secondary-source data, parameters such as market size, population size and its biographical characteristics, income distribution pattern, past sales data, product groups, and competitive advantages are synthesized to develop the desired consumer behaviour model. To supplement this, surveys may be conducted interviewing the target population (samples) by administering a structured questionnaire. Such supplementary efforts concretize the preceding observation and make the forecast more effective. The market research technique is usually employed by organizations to forecast new product sales or sales of established products in new markets, or for long-range market forecasts.

TIME-SERIES ANALYSIS

Data over a time period (time-series data) are used under this method as the basis of forecast. However, mere projecting the past into the future, without considering endogenous and exogenous changes, will increase the forecasting errors, which may result in either over- or under-forecasting, and both may have an adverse effect on managerial decisions. There are five distinct elements in time-series analysis to be taken into account:

1. **Trend**: It is the fluctuation in forecast over a time period.
2. **Cyclical effects**: It is the change in forecast in relation to some particular event, which could be economic liberalization, global meltdown, WTO resolutions, etc.
3. **Seasonality**: It is a seasonal fluctuation if it occurs more than once in a given time period, for example, the requirement of more maintenance staff members in power utility services during the summer and rainy seasons, compared to the winter season.
4. **Step**: This is caused by sudden change due to the economic environment or increased market share, or procurement of some new machines, etc.
5. **Random fluctuations**: These fluctuations do not follow any obvious pattern. While forecasting, such random fluctuations can be taken into consideration following the moving average method.

Last period method, simple average method, and trend projections are some of the forecasting techniques used during time-series analysis. When the forecast for the next period is the last observed value in the time-series data, it is known as the *last period method*. In the *simple average method*, the average of the time-series data (according to months or years) is calculated along with the average for the period. The percentage constituted by the average of the data to the average for the period is the seasonal index, which is used for forecasting. *Trend projection* requires extensive and reliable time-series data that studies the movement of the variable (for example, sales) over time and, thus, predicts the future on the basis of past trends. Moving average method, exponential smoothing, and tracking signal are the other techniques that will be discussed in detail in the following sections.

Moving Average Method

Let us illustrate the moving average method in the context of workforce forecasting. In workforce forecasting, the average of the combined employment-level data for the recent past is considered as the forecasted employment level for the next period. This technique is useful to guard against random fluctuations. However, it requires careful selection of time periods, which may be a six-period, ten-period, or twelve-period moving average. If the time periods chosen are too few, we may get a wide variability in our forecast. Considering more time periods will always give better results. Whatever time period we select for forecast, it is necessary to continue with the same number of periods for our computations. After each period elapses, the figure for the oldest period is dropped and the figure for the newest period is added for our subsequent computation of workforce requirements. Example 2.1 gives an illustration of the moving average method.

Example 2.1 Illustration of the Moving Average Method

The workforce data of X & Co. for their healthcare division for the past six years is shown in Table 2.3. (a) Forecast their workforce requirement in 2011 using a six-period moving average and a four-period moving average. (b) After assigning weights to different time periods, forecast the workforce requirement for 2011 again.

Table 2.3 Workforce in the Healthcare Division of X & Co.

Year	Workforce
2005	500
2006	600
2007	800
2008	1,000
2009	1,100
2010	1,300

Solution: (a) The forecasted workforce in 2011 using a six-period moving average is

$$F_m = \frac{500+600+800+1000+1100+1300}{6}$$

$$= \frac{5300}{6} = 883$$

If we were asked to use a four-period moving average to forecast workforce requirement for 2011, we would need to drop the data of 2005 and 2006 and compute the workforce as follows:

$$F_m = \frac{800+1000+1100+1300}{4} = \frac{4200}{4} = 1{,}050$$

From the above variation in results, we can well understand the danger of considering lesser time periods in workforce forecasting.

(b) For achieving better results, weights may be assigned for different time periods at the discretion of the analyst. For example, workforce levels of 2005, 2006, and 2007 may be less relevant and, hence, for these years weights may be assigned as 1 in each case. For 2008 the weight may be 2, for 2009 it may be 3, and for 2010 it may be 4. Now, the forecasted workforce for the year 2011 will be as follows:

$$F_m = \frac{1(500)+1(600)+1(800)+2(1000)+3(1100)+4(1300)}{\sum w}$$

$$= \frac{500+600+800+2000+3300+5200}{12}$$

$$= \frac{12400}{12} = 1{,}033$$

Exponential Smoothing

In the moving average method, we need to carry forward a large volume of historical data. The need for such past records can be eliminated by adopting the exponential smoothing method. This method smoothes out random errors by giving exponentially decreasing weights to historical data.

The weight factor is indicated by alpha (α), which is a smoothing constant, a non-linear decimal value that lies between zero and one. The formula for the exponential smoothing model is:

$$F_m = F_t + \alpha - (A_{t-1} - F_{t-1})$$

Where, F_m = Forecasted workforce
F_{t-1} = Forecasted demand for the previous period
α = Smoothing constant
A_{t-1} = Actual workforce required for the previous period

Example 2.2 depicts the way in which this method works by using this formula.

Double exponential smoothing can also be done to ensure further cushion in workforce forecasting.

Tracking Signal

An automatic monitoring mechanism to keep track of accuracy of forecasting models is known as *tracking signal*. It is the ratio of cumulative forecasting error to the *mean absolute deviation* (MAD). *Cumulative forecasting error* or *running sum of forecasting error* (RSFE) is indicated by:

$$\sum_{t=1}^{n} (A_t - F_t)$$

Where,
A_t = Actual demand for period t
F_t = Forecasted demand for period t

Therefore, $$\text{Tracking signal} = \frac{RSFE}{MAD} = \frac{\sum_{t=1}^{n} (A_t - F_t)}{MAD}$$

The *tracking signal* (TS) is recalculated every time there is availability of actual demand data and in sync with any update of the forecast. The TS should be fairly small and then only can it be said that the forecasting is accurate or near accuracy. If a TS moves outside some pre-established range, it is known as *tripping of signal*. Every time a signal trips, one adjusts one's forecasting method. Usually, the limit

Example 2.2 Illustration of Exponential Smoothing

Assume that the forecasted workforce requirement for an organization was 500, while its actual requirement was 480. Considering the alpha value of 0.4 (which the company feels will produce the best results), compute the workforce requirement for the current period.

Solution: $F_m = F_t + \alpha - (A_{t-1} - F_{t-1}) = 500 + 0.4\ (480 - 500) = 492$

of the TS is taken to vary between three and eight. Example 2.3 illustrates TS with an example of actual demand data and forecasted demand data.

In Example 2.3, the TS is less than the limit of 3 to 8 up to period 9. In periods 10 and 11, it undershoots the limit. As of now, the forecasting model is considered to be functioning well. However, if the trend persists even in subsequent periods, one may have to reassess the forecasting model.

Example 2.3 Illustration of Tracking Signal

In Table 2.4, actual demand data and forecasted demand data for periods 1 to 11 have been provided. Calculate the TS to formulate a forecasting model.

Table 2.4 Actual and Forecasted Demand Data

Period	Actual demand (A_t)	Forecasted demand (F_t)
1.	125	132
2.	144	139
3.	133	136
4.	130	134
5.	137	136
6.	143	141
7.	137	140
8.	138	141
9.	133	139
10.	131	136
11.	130	134

Solution: An assumption up to period 5 has been made to make an initial estimate of the MAD to test the accuracy of the forecasting model. For each subsequent period, the TS value has been computed to understand whether it is within the accepted range of 3 to 8. This data has been provided in Table 2.5.

Table 2.5 Forecasting Model

Period	Actual demand (A_t)	Forecasted demand (F_t)	Errors ($A_t - F_t$)	Sum of ($A_t - F_t$) errors (*RSFE*)	*MAD*	*TS* = *RSFE*/*MAD*
1.	125	132	−7	–	–	–
2.	144	139	+5	–	–	–
3.	133	136	−3	–	–	–
4.	130	134	−4	–	–	–
5.	137	136	+1	–	4.00	–
6.	143	141	+2	+2	3.67	+0.54
7.	137	140	−3	−1	3.57	−0.28
8.	138	141	−3	−4	3.50	−1.14
9.	133	139	−6	−10	3.78	−2.65
10.	131	136	−5	−15	4.30	−3.49
11.	130	134	−4	−19	3.91	−4.86

DECISION MAKING

Decision making is the process to select a course of action from a number of alternatives. Like planning, decision making is all-pervasive. Also, much like forecasting, decision making is an important part of planning. It has been explained earlier how policy documents help in taking managerial decisions. However, these are decisions of routine nature and are also called operational decisions. Strategic or important decisions are taken considering different alternatives. In order to be a successful manager, one has to necessarily develop decision-making skills. The decision-making process is similar to strategic planning, which has been explained earlier. Decision making involves:

- Diagnosing, defining, and identifying the source of the problem
- Information gathering and analysis of the facts required to solve the problem
- Developing and evaluating alternative solutions to the problem
- Choosing the best decision alternatives
- Communicating the decisions
- Implementing the decisions

Various forecasting tools help in decision making. These have been explained earlier. Another important tool, that is, decision tree, for evaluating decision making is explained here.

Decision Trees

A decision tree is a graphic representation of the sequence of decisions required in determining the expected values of alternative courses of action. Each decision alternative is weighed by developing a pay-off matrix, which depicts the probable value of each of the decision alternatives by quantifying the various outcomes and probabilities of their occurrence. Probability is the degree of likelihood that a particular event will occur. It varies from zero (no chance of occurring) to one (certain chance of occurring). Outcomes are quantified in terms of expected value (EV). It is the sum of values of the expected outcomes multiplied by their respective probabilities. For example, a manager expects 0.20 probability of earning INR 60,000 from a business, 0.40 probability of earning INR 30,000 from the business again, and 0.30 probability of losing INR 20,000 from the business. Such assumptions are based on past experience or from the general trend analysis in the industry. Their EV can be computed in the following manner:

$$\begin{aligned}\text{Expected value} &= 0.20(60{,}000) + 0.40(30{,}000) + 0.30\ (-20{,}000)\\ &= (12{,}000 + 12{,}000) - 6{,}000\\ &= 24{,}000 - 6{,}000\\ &= 18{,}000\end{aligned}$$

Likewise, the manager can now compare the expected value of INR 18,000 with other alternatives and decide on the best alternative based on the higher expected value. Thus, the pay-off matrix as given in Table 2.6 is now analysed.

From the pay-off matrix one has to first compute the expected value company-wise for each decision alternative, and the values can then be represented in the form of a decision tree.

The EVs for companies are as follows:

Company A, investment alternative 1: 0.60(30,000) + 0.40(–15,000) = 12,000

Company B, investment alternative 2: 0.60(70,000) + 0.40(–30,000) = 30,000

Company C, investment alternative 3: 0.60(40,000) + 0.40(–10,000) = 20,000

Table 2.6 Pay-off Matrix

Investment alternatives	High sales (probability = 0.60)	Low sales (probability = 0.40)
Investment alternative 1, Company A	30,000	−15,000
Investment alternative 2, Company B	70,000	−30,000
Investment alternative 3, Company C	40,000	−10,000

It is evident that investment in Company B, that is, investment alternative 2, is the best option. Hence, the observations can now be represented in the form of a decision tree. A template of a decision tree has been provided in Figure 2.1.

Apart from the pay-off matrix and decision tree, queuing models, distribution models, inventory models, and game theory are also used as decision tools. A queuing model helps to reduce waiting time to ensure better service to customers, while a distribution model helps to determine the most cost-effective way of distribution of products and services. Inventory models help to determine the optimum inventory level for both inputs (raw materials and spares/components) and output (finished goods). Game theory helps to measure the decision outcomes under different situations of uncertainty.

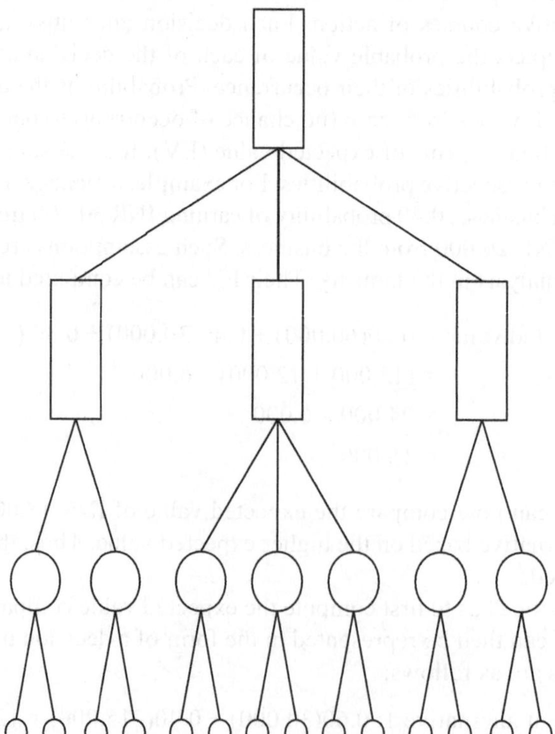

Figure 2.1 A Decision Tree

Apart from these models, all the forecasting techniques discussed earlier in the chapter serve as important tools in managerial decision making. The Delphi technique and the nominal group technique are examples of group decision making. Group decisions are also taken by forming various committees.

Management Information Systems and Decision Support Systems

Management information system (MIS) gathers comprehensive data and organizes and summarizes the same in a form that adds value to managerial decision making. It is a computer-based information system that aims to enable more effective planning, decision making, and control. A typical MIS has four major components: data gathering, data entry, data transformation, and information utilization. Most organizations keep a centralized database that can be used for a wide variety of applications.

Decision support system (DSS) is an interactive computer system that is easily accessible to and operated by people who are not computer-friendly. DSS helps them to plan and make decisions. A typical DSS consists of the following elements:

- An MIS to support several ways for accessing and summarizing data
- A sophisticated database that allows information to be accessed in various ways
- A user-friendly interface that allows the user to use simple commands (rather than complicated computer terms) while communicating with the DSS
- A database containing both internal and external information, which helps managers to relate and benchmark (compare) their decisions
- Rapid response time, which makes the system more effective than a conventional MIS

SCENARIO PLANNING

Scenarios are the alternative views of the future primarily based on some events or changes that have occurred or are likely to occur. From the organization point of view these help in identifying the strategic fit, pending some future developments. Essentially, scenarios are reflections on future situations with some frame of reference. We can also define scenarios as a tool to prioritize our perceptions about future alternatives. Using a set of stories, scenarios are plotted and used as the basis for framing plans and strategies. Using scenarios, mangers forecast their proposed change initiatives reflecting future situations—a process that is known as *scenario planning*. For scenario planning, managers or decision makers are required to question the broadest assumptions about the way the world in general, and the organization in particular, work, so that decisions can be taken beforehand to meet the gap, if any. Thus, to explore the scenarios, managers essentially think about uncertain aspects that may have a bearing on any eventuality of relevance to the organization.

With the increasing impact of economic globalization, understanding the global business environment has now become an important imperative for the organization. The global business environment gets affected by political changes and new emerging technologies, among other factors. Such changes create discontinuity in the business and to sustain itself, the organization needs to prepare itself in advance, chasing events. Scenario planning helps in exploring the eventualities and developing a shared understanding of, or commitment to, strategic interventions to help the organization adapt, before unforeseen changes gag the organization.

In a turbulent market environment, organizations need to quickly adapt themselves to change. Quick response to change is possible only when organizations are capable of preconceiving different scenarios of the environment with prior plans and programmes, and accordingly are capable of responding to the changes with adequate contingency plans and prestructured strategies. Gil Ringland (1998) and Peter

Schwartz (1991) have identified that organizations worldwide are developing scenario plans to respond to unforeseen-change situations. According to Schwartz, *scenarios* are future contingencies considering which organizations are able to determine their future directions with contingency plans.

Literally, a scenario is a script for a play. It is a tool to consolidate one's perception about alternative future environments, to take decisions at the right time. According to Pierre Wack (1985), *scenario planning* involves development of three or four different plots along with the associated narratives to illustrate the major driving forces for change and the critical uncertainties in the environment.

Thus, scenario planning denotes the creative foresight of managers and decision makers to keep pace with the changing environmental uncertainty. It is also considered to be a strategic planning method. The key driving forces for scenario plans are the changing social, technical, economic, environmental, educational, political, and aesthetic (STEEEPA) trends. Globally, organizations such as Shell and Siemens AG have made extensive use of scenario plans.

Shell as an organization has made the most extensive use of scenario planning since 1973, primarily to cope with the oil crisis sparked off by the Organization of Petroleum Exporting Countries (OPEC). Shell's strategy was to cope with the environmental turbulence often sparked by the non-compromising OPEC members, who rarely reached an agreement on collective price rising or production strategy. This non-compromising attitude often caused operational discontinuities in petroleum, oil, and lubricants (POL) companies worldwide. Peter Drucker (1954) more appropriately said that 'the greatest danger in times of turbulence is not the turbulence; it is to act with yesterday's logic'. Drucker's argument also emphasized the need for strategic forecasting making use of scenario plans to cope with organizational changes.

Forces of Scenario Planning

The major driving forces of scenario planning can be placed into four categories:

1. **Social dynamics**: Social dynamics in the broadest sense incorporate major demographic trends in age mix, income, education, and lifestyles, and even change in the value systems. For example, a prominent lifestyle change is represented by the shift in customers' perceptions about value-added products and services. Customers are now more informed and they can question the company's products and services when they fail to meet their expectations. Changes in the income level (particularly when it is on the higher side and frees more disposable income) lead customers to solicit premium products and services.
2. **Economic issues**: Both macro and microeconomic trends influence the scenario plans. Macroeconomic trends shape the economy as a whole. With more global interrelatedness, failure of one major multinational or transnational organization (for example, Lehman Brothers) can have a cascading effect, causing failures in many other organizations and also in the larger economy. The recent global meltdown and its ripple effect is a case in point. Similarly, microeconomic issues like the modus operandi of competing organizations can also spark off the need for change and become a basis for scenario planning.
3. **Political issues**: Political beliefs and ideologies of ruling parties and oppositions, legislative and regulatory changes, etc., can also be the basis for scenario plans for an organization. The US policy on outsourcing can be a major issue for the Indian outsourcing business and also for the IT-enabled services (ITeS).
4. **Technological issues**: New emerging technologies influence the business per se. With the development of plasma and LCD technology, conventional CTVs have now become almost obsolete. Similar

changes in code-division multiple access (CDMA) and global system for mobile communications (GSM) technologies have revolutionized the mobile phone industry. Similarly, in many other areas, changes in technology have influenced the product or service mix. Organizations that could understand and gauge such changes beforehand developed appropriate action plans to respond and strategize accordingly.

Steps for Scenario Planning

After understanding the key drivers for scenario plans, it is necessary to follow certain steps in a sequential order. Each step necessitates certain actions and after completion of one step, another needs to be started. In line with the practices at Shell, the steps can be enumerated as follows:

1. Identify the drivers for change/assumptions
2. Draw a framework of drivers
3. Develop some mini-scenarios, preferably seven to nine
4. Reduce these scenarios to a manageable number, preferably two or three
5. Prepare the draft of the scenarios
6. List the issues arising in each scenario

The various types of drivers for scenarios have been explained already. To understand which driver or drivers is/are important at a particular point of time, managers need to first delineate the circumstances under which the organization operates. Therefore, managers need to make an informed assumption. Brainstorming, application of the Delphi technique, and focus-group interviews are some of the common techniques for informed assumptions. To draw a framework of informed assumptions, managers can make extensive use of their intuition or can follow a structured pattern, more in the form of a flow chart. Finally, there is the need to act upon each step to finally draw the scenario and make use of the scenario for framing the future strategies of the organization. These steps are also known as *Shell's model of scenario planning.*

Case Kumar.com: Problems Suffered due to Poor Planning

Problems started for Kumar.com when it tried to leverage its experience in the textile business in a totally different domain, that is, internet services. Throughout the country, they opened thousands of outlets through the franchise route, against hefty association-fee deposits for admission. At the time the company started its venture, the global IT industry was booming and India had just started experiencing its effects, with many new entrepreneurs eyeing investments in the industry for making a quick buck. For Kumar.com, this was an immense business expansion move. With the scrapping of the multi-fibre agreement (MFA) by the World Trade Organization (WTO), the textile export business of the company (which had until then prospered due to preferential export quota against MFA) had suffered a serious jolt. Perhaps this had prompted the company to change their business focus to a new challenging area, that is, to become an internet service provider (ISP). The company, however, failed to take off mainly due to lack of infrastructure. Government regulations also stood in the way of using the government-controlled gateway, as the market then was more controlled and regulated.

In early 1995, the company observed a steep fall in their share prices in the market, which almost went to the level of 50 per cent less than the price of their face value. Mounting pressure from the franchisees to get back their deposits and a series of litigations on the same issue pushed the company to a serious liquidity crunch. The company had to then draw an immediate restructuring plan, which caused huge redundancies in the workforce, including their top-brass executive team members; drastic curtailment of benefits of those employees who still continued in their jobs; and a refocusing on their erstwhile flagship textile business. That was the time when the company introduced new lifestyle fabrics at a very competitive rate. Kumar Fabrics were earlier not in the affordable price range for the common people in India, but when the prices came down, the domestic market responded positively.

In their new strategic restructuring programme, the company adopted multi-pronged strategies in terms of systems thinking and teamwork, holistic strategic planning with transformed leadership, focus on new product development, and customer relationship management. With extensive employee participation in framing and implementing such strategies, the company ultimately earned back its fortune and returned to its original business track, that is, textile manufacturing. The new strategy document of the company focused on plan objectives, inbound forces, insights, product direction, implementation, actions, and commitment. As a system, the company revisits this document and makes necessary adjustments, keeping pace with the changing planning premises. Direct participation of employees and regular communication to them about plans and strategies made the transition of the company a mega success. Thus, the company rose from the brink of bankruptcy to the highest level, and today, Kumar Fabrics is a household name in India. Effective planning and framing of strategy can, therefore, benefit any company in any situation.

CASE QUESTION

List the possible reasons for the failure of Kumar.com. Also, identify the lessons learnt from the case.

SUMMARY

- *Planning* is an all-pervasive and fundamental function of management. It involves deciding in advance what is to be done, where, how, and by whom. Through planning, the manager projects a course of action for the future aimed at achieving desired results for the enterprise as a whole and each department within it.
- Planning provides the framework within which organizing, staffing, direction, and controlling are undertaken. Planning components are usually classified as objectives, policies, procedures, programmes, budgets, and strategies.
- A *policy* is a predetermined and established guideline aimed towards the attainment of accepted goals and objectives. Such guidelines facilitate properly designed efforts to accomplish the strategic intent.
- *Programme* consists of the entire broad course of action governing employees at all levels (including management) in an organization.
- *Strategy* is the direction and scope of an organization over the long term, matching its resources to its changing environment and in particular its markets, customers, or clients, so as to meet stakeholders' expectations.

- *Objectives* are the operational definitions of goals. It describes what the organization hopes to accomplish.
- *Budgeting* is the formulation of plans for a given future period in numerical terms. It is a statement of anticipated results in financial terms (as in revenue and expense, and capital budgets) or in non-financial terms (as in budgets of direct labour hours, materials, physical sales volume, or units of production). The essence of budgeting lies in taking proper corrective actions to rectify the negative deviations.
- *Forecasting* is defined as either an estimate or an inference of a future event. Forecast may not always be an accurate estimate or inference as it is based on past trends. However, it provides an effective basis for planning different activities of an organization. At the organization level, various tools are used to ensure minimum forecasting errors.
- Modern organizations also make use of scenario planning to preset their strategies in order to be prepared for future ambiguities. *Scenarios* are alternative views of the future primarily based on some events or changes that have occurred or are likely to occur. Essentially, *scenario planning* is the reflection on future situations with some frame of reference.

KEY TERMS

Budgeting: Budgeting is the formulation of plans for a given future period in numerical terms. It is the statement of anticipated results in financial terms (as in revenue and expense, and capital budgets) or in non-financial terms (as in budgets of direct labour hours, materials, physical sales volume, or units of production).

Decision support system: Decision support system (DSS) is an interactive computer system that is easily accessible to and operated by people who are not computer-friendly. DSS helps them to plan and make decisions.

Decision tree: A decision tree is a graphic representation of the sequence of decisions required in determining the expected values of an alternative course of action. Each decision alternative is weighed by developing a pay-off matrix, which depicts the probable value of each decision alternative by quantifying the various outcomes and probabilities of their occurrence.

Forecasting: Forecasting is defined as either an estimate or an inference of a future event. It may not always be an accurate estimate or inference as it is based on past trends. However, forecasting provides an effective basis for planning different activities of an organization.

Management information system: A management information system (MIS) gathers comprehensive data and organizes and summarizes the same in a form that adds value to managerial decision making. It is a computer-based information system that aims to enable more effective planning, decision making, and control.

Mission: A vision in tangible form is a mission statement. Hence, a mission statement verbalizes the vision and attempts to answer the basic purpose of an organization.

Objectives: Objectives describe what organizations hope to accomplish in specific measurable terms within a given time frame. The top management of an organization decides the overall objectives, which then cascades to divisional, departmental, and individual employee-level objectives.

Planning: Planning involves deciding the future course of action in advance to achieve the desired results for the organization as a whole and also for each department. Effective planning requires not only assessing the future, but also making adequate provision to face the future.

Policy: A policy is a predetermined and established guideline aimed towards the attainment of accepted goals and objectives. Such guidelines help to accomplish the strategic intent through properly designed efforts. Policies are not the same as strategies or tactics.

Programme: A programme consists of the entire broad course of action governing employees at all levels (including management) in an organization. It is the end product of the organization's philosophy, values, concepts, principles, policies, and procedures.

Scenario planning: Using a set of stories, scenarios are plotted and used as the basis for framing plans and strategies. Managers forecast their proposed change initiatives reflecting future situations using scenarios. This process is known as scenario planning.

Strategic control: Since strategies are designed to accomplish future objectives, it is necessary to enforce control over strategy. This is known as strategic control.

Strategy: Strategy is the long-term direction and scope of an organization, matching its resources to its changing environment and in particular its markets, customers, or clients, to meet stakeholders' expectations. To achieve results and excellence in business performance, most organizations around the world take the initiative to align their strategies with their business goals and objectives.

Vision: A vision consists of the organization's intentions that are all-inclusive and forward-thinking. It is the driving force of the organization. However, while it describes aspirations for the future, it does not specify the means that should be used to achieve the desired ends.

REVIEW QUESTIONS

1. Explain the nature of planning. Is *planning* different from *decision making*?
2. Discuss how policies and procedures of an organization influence planning.
3. How are the planning premises set? How does forecasting help in setting the planning premises?
4. 'Planning is an important strategic function.' Discuss.
5. Explain important qualitative and quantitative decision-making tools.
6. Explain the importance of the Delphi technique. Do you think this method ensures a consensus forecast? If yes, why? If no, what alternative method would you suggest?
7. Explain the importance of cause-effect models in forecasting the sales of a fast-food centre.
8. In what way is *exponential smoothing* a better alternative than the *moving average method* in long-range forecasting?
9. Differentiate between the following:
   i. Planning and decision making
   ii. Planning and forecasting
   iii. Planning and strategy formulation
   iv. MIS and DSS
   v. Planning and budgeting
10. What are the limitations of planning? Do you think planning is necessary despite its serious limitations?
11. What are the implications of policies and procedures on strategies?

12. Write short notes on the following:
    i. Vision and mission
    ii. Strategic control
    iii. Grand strategies
    iv. Strategy and action plan
    v. Operational strategy factors

CRITICAL THINKING QUESTIONS

1. ABC Corporation has experienced steady growth in annual sales in its seven-year history. The firm has traditionally used a three-year moving average to predict sales for the coming year. The newly appointed CEO of the company feels that a simple three-year moving average is too unrealistic and results in extremely poor sales forecasts. As inaccuracies in forecast may affect many important managerial decisions, the CEO of the organization has asked you to determine the best time-series technique for estimating sales by comparing a weighted seven-year moving average using the following weights: 0.1, 0.1, 0.2, 0.2, 2, 3, and 3, respectively, from the oldest to the most recent year, with a simple exponential smoothing model using an α of 0.35.

   Assume a 1997 sales forecast of INR 305,000. The forecasts for subsequent years are the annual sales of previous years as given in Table 2.7.

   Table 2.7 Annual Sales and Forecast Data

Year	1997	1998	1999	2000	2001	2002	2003
Sales (INR)	305,000	328,000	345,000	370,000	387,000	404,000	405,000

   Which forecasting method (three-year moving average, seven-year moving average, or exponential) would you recommend for this historical data and why?

2. The mission statement of Simon India is as follows:
    i. To achieve excellence in manufacturing world-class medical equipment
    ii. To achieve customer satisfaction
    iii. To get recognized as the best company in after-sales service
    iv. To ensure talent retention

   The company envisages an annual growth rate of 20 per cent in their business. Based on the given information, frame a strategy map.

REFERENCES

Chartered Institute of Management Accountants (2005). *CIMA Official Terminology*. Oxford: CIMA Publishing, An imprint of Elsevier.

Drucker, Peter (1954). *The Principles of Management*. New York: HarperCollins Publishers.

Ringland, G. (1998). *Scenario Planning—Managing for the Future*. New York: John Wiley & Sons.

Schwartz, P. (1991). *The Art of the Long View*. New York: Doubleday.

Wack, P. (1985). 'Scenarios: Shooting the Rapids'. *Harvard Business Review*, 63 (6): pp. 139–150.

FURTHER READING

Barney, J. (1977). 'Firm Resources and Sustained Competitive Advantage', *Journal of Management*, 17, pp. 99–120.

Becker, B. E. and M. A. Huselid (1998). 'High Performance Work Systems and Firm Performance: As Synthesis of Research and Managerial Implications', *Research in Personnel and Human Resources Journal*, 16 (1): pp. 53–101.

Becker, Gary S. (1964). *Human Capital: A Theoretical and Empirical Analysis, with Special Reference to Education*. New York: Columbia University Press.

Bhattacharyya, D. K. (2007). *Human Resource Research Methods*. New Delhi: Oxford University Press.

——— (2009). *Organizational Behaviour: Text and Cases*. New Delhi: Oxford University Press.

——— (2010). *Industrial Management*. New Delhi: Vikas Publishing.

——— (2010). *Organizational Change and Development*. New Delhi: Oxford University Press.

Dale, Ernest (1965). *Management Theory and Practice*. New York: McGraw-Hill.

Eisenhardt, K. M. (1989). 'Agency Theory: An Assessment and Review', *Academy of Management Review*, 14 (4): pp. 57–74.

Eric, Flamholtz (1981). *Personnel Management, Human Capital Theory and Human Resource Accounting*. University of California: Institute of Industrial Relations.

Hamel, G. and C. K. Prahalad (1994). *Competing for the Future*. Boston: Harvard Business School Press.

Jackson, S. E. and R. S. Schular (1995). 'Understanding Human Resource Management in the Context of Organizations and Their Environments', *Annual Review of Psychology*, 46, pp. 237–264.

Katz, R. and D. Khan (1978). *The Social Psychology of Organizations*. New York: John Wiley & Sons.

Koontz, H. (1961). 'The Management Theory Jungle', *Academy of Management Journal*, 4 (3): pp. 174–188.

Meyer, John W. and Brian Rowen (1977). 'Institutionalized Organizations: Formal Structure as Myth and Ceremony', *American Journal of Sociology*, 83, pp. 34–363.

Miles, R. H. and C. C. Snow (1984). 'Designing Strategic Human Resource Systems', *Organizational Dynamics*, 13 (1): pp. 36–52.

Mintzberg, H., B. Ahlstrand and J. Lampel (1998). *Strategy Safari: A Guided Tour through the Wilds of Strategic Management*. New York: The Free Press.

Pfeffer, J. and G. R. Salanick (1978). *The External Control of Organizations: A Resource Dependence Perspective*. New York: Harper & Row.

Porter, M. (1985). *Competitive Advantage: Creating and Sustaining Superior Performance*. New York: Free Press.

Powel, Walter W. and Paul J. DiMaggio (1991). *The New Institutionalism in Organizational Analysis*. Chicago: University of Chicago Press.

Prahalad, C. K. and G. Hamel (1990). 'The Core Competence of the Corporation', *Harvard Business Review*, 68 (3): pp.79–91.

Sanz-valle, R., R. Sabater-Sanchez and A. Aragon-Sanchex (1999). 'Human Resource Management and Business Strategy Links: An Empirical Study', *International Journal of Human Resource Management*, 10 (4): pp. 655–671.

Williamson, Oliver E. (1981). 'The Economics of Organization: The Transaction Cost Approach', *The American Journal of Sociology*, November 1981, 87, pp. 548–577.

Wright, P. and G. McMahan (1992). 'Theoretical Perspectives for Strategic Human Resource Management', *Journal of Management*, 18, pp. 295–320.

Annexure 2.1
Leave Policy of a Hypothetical Organization

Policy Number: ____________
Coverage: All employees of Future India including the managerial level and executive directors
Board's Approval: ________________ Effective Date: ________________

EMPLOYEE LEAVE POLICY

Policy

Future India always aspires to establish and maintain an orderly system of administration and towards that end, the company's policy with regard to the various forms of leave available to employees of the company is laid down as follows.

1.0 Specific Objectives

1.1 The objectives of this policy are to:

i. Ensure uniform standards and procedures for administration of leave within the company.

ii. Provide an employee leave programme that will facilitate monitoring the various forms of leave, ensure accurate application, detect potential abuses, and keep a full record of the leave system.

iii. Ensure that employees, supervisors, and departmental heads are familiar with the company's leave programme.

2.0 Responsibilities

2.1 The Board (or its designated committee) will:

i. Review, amend, and adopt changes in the Employee Leave Policy

ii. Approve changes in the actual leave benefits, as considered appropriate

2.2 The Chief Executive Officer (or designate) will:

i. Provide for administration of the procedures outlined in the Employee Leave Policy

ii. Assist department heads, supervisors, and employees in the implementation and administration of the Employee Leave Policy

iii. Recommend to the Board changes in the Employee Leave Policy or changes in the actual benefits and leave granted to employees, where considered appropriate

2.3 Department heads and supervisors will:

i. Ensure the completion of all required forms and records regarding the Employee Leave Policy

ii. Ensure that employees are aware of the Employee Leave Policy

iii. Ensure that employees provide complete information and all necessary documentation for required forms, in accordance with the Employee Leave Policy

iv. Assist employees by clarifying their eligibility for leave programmes and helping them complete the necessary documentation

v. Recommend changes to the Employee Leave Policy where considered appropriate

2.4 All employees will:

i. Make themselves familiar with the Employee Leave Policy

ii. Comply with all regulations and procedures as outlined in the Employee Leave Policy

3.0 General Provisions

3.1 Leave rules of the company:

i. Employees eligible for leave will complete the Leave Application in accordance with the policy outlined herein. This application will be forwarded to the supervisor and/or department head for consideration and, where necessary, forwarded to the Chief Executive Officer for consideration.

ii. The leave will be approved or denied as appropriate and the employee will be notified of the decision in writing.

iii. The individual(s) responsible for payroll will be notified as necessary.

iv. The employee's personal file will be updated.

3.2 Specific procedures

i. The following are the various types of leave included in the leave programme of the company:

- Leave without pay
- Annual leave
- Medical or sick leave
- Statutory holidays
- Casual leave

Each type of leave is explained here.

3.3 Leave without pay

i. **Eligibility:** Leave without pay is not normally granted unless all leave to which the employee is entitled has been completely availed of prior to the application.

Upon application by an employee, leave without pay may be granted to an employee according to the following stipulations:

- Employee having completed less than one year of service: to be granted up to 10 working days
- Employee having completed one to five years of service: up to 20 working days in a year
- Employee having completed more than five years of service: up to 45 working days in a year

ii. **Up to one week of leave (five working days):** Applications are to be submitted in writing, to the appropriate superior, who may grant up to five working days' leave without pay when grant of this leave will not involve extra expenses for the company in the form of overtime payments or hiring of additional staff.

iii. **Longer than one week of leave:** Applications are to be referred by the department head through the Human Resource Department to the Chief Executive Officer.

Payroll staff is to be advised of all leaves as and when granted, and also immediately when the employee returns to work. A copy, each of the application and authorization, are to be added to the employee's personal file.

3.4 Effect of leave without pay on employee benefits: The following clause would be applicable to all leave without pay exceeding 15 days.

During the period of leave without pay, no employee will be eligible for any benefits. The company can recover the actual cost of any such benefits, payable to the employee as terminal benefit like insurance contribution, gratuity, etc. For leave of absence less than 15 days, however, the company will accommodate such cost, provided the leave of absence granted to the employee did not cause any pecuniary loss to the company by way of the need for engaging extra hand to complete the assigned tasks of the employee. No pay will be granted for any statutory holidays, if such holidays fall within the period of leave.

4.0 Annual Leave

4.1 General provisions

i. All employees on satisfactory completion of their period of probation will be entitled for annual leave.

ii. The period of the annual leave calendar year is January 1 to December 31.

iii. After satisfactory completion of the period of probation, all employees will receive a maximum of 30 days' annual leave in a calendar year and such leave would be credited at the rate of two and a half days for each completed month. For availing annual leave during the year, the period of annual leave would be restricted to the number of days credited in the account of the employee taking into account the number of months served. However, the company can grant annual leave in advance, considering the merits of the individual case.

iv. A maximum of 180 days can be accumulated as annual leave.

v. Unavailed portion of annual leave (subject to the limit of 180 days) can be encashed by an employee during normal retirement. In cases of resignation, encashment of annual leave will be subject to the acceptance of resignation of an employee by the company.

vi. Under no circumstances can an employee be granted annual leave exceeding 15 days consecutively.

All annual leave applications are to be routed through Departmental Heads to the Chief Executive Officer for prior sanction under intimation to the HR Department.

5.0 Medical or Sick Leave

5.1 General provisions

i. The company will provide medical or sick leave to all employees on their satisfactory completion of the probation period. The period of medical leave shall be restricted to 15 days (half pay) in a calendar year. Hence, an employee can commute such medical leave with full pay for a maximum period of seven and a half days in a calendar year.

ii. Medical leave is given to an employee as protection of loss of wages due to illness. Hence, employees intending to avail medical leave should intimate their respective Head of the Department during the period of absence on grounds of illness, enclosing a certificate from a registered medical practitioner. After joining back, the employee should also produce a certificate of fitness to their Head of the Department to regularize their period of absence. The Head of the Department will accordingly forward the documents with due recommendation to the HR Department.

6.0 Statutory Holidays

6.1 General provisions

A list of statutory holidays is prepared and circulated during every calendar year and such lists vary according to the declaration of the statutory bodies.

7.0 Casual Leave

7.1 General provisions

i. All employees, including those who are on probation, shall be entitled to get a maximum of six days' casual leave in a calendar year. For availing casual leave, it is mandatory to obtain prior approval from the Head of the Department. However, if an employee suddenly requires casual leave to meet any exigency, and if the period exceeds one working day, the employee must ensure that their Head of the Department has been informed, or else, their period of absence shall be treated as unauthorized absence and will render them liable to face disciplinary action.

ii. Unavailed casual leave expires on completion of the calendar year. Hence, it cannot be accumulated and encashed.

Annexure 2.2

A Strategy and Action Plan for the HRM Function of a Hypothetical Organization

VISION

1. We are committed to provide an enjoyable work environment to our employees to promote teamwork, improvement in quality, and excellence.
2. Our employees are our valued customers and the most important stakeholders.
3. We are committed to achieve financial growth of our organization by fostering growth and creativity among our valued employees.

MISSION

To achieve excellence in human resource management, and foster growth and creativity

GOALS

1. To promote teamwork
2. To ensure improvement in quality
3. To foster growth and creativity

OBJECTIVES

Goal 1

- Achieve group cohesiveness by inculcating participative management
- Reduce dissonance in managerial decisions
- Reduce conflict and grievances to achieve zero loss of man- days and increase productivity

Goal 2

- Achieve higher levels of quality consciousness in the organization
- Reduce costs of quality to zero within the next five years
- Provide error-free products and services to customers to increase customer-retention levels and to further increase market share

Goal 3

- Promote creativity in the organization
- Provide opportunities for growth of the employees
- Increase the retention levels of employees so as to reduce current employee turnover by 80 per cent in next five years

STRATEGIES

Goal 1: Improve participative management

Goal 2: Initiate organization-wide quality improvement

Goal 3: Develop a culture that promotes growth and creativity

ACTION PLANS

Strategy 1

- Establish small group forums like quality circles (QCs), self-managed teams (SMTs), value-engineering teams (VETs), and total quality management (TQM) clubs in the organization
- Shift focus from statutory participation to total participation
- Empower employees by involving them in the decision-making process
- Implement an organization-wide transparent communication network

Strategy 2

- Implement quality-awareness programmes through regular training and development
- Develop TQM culture by increasing formal and informal interaction among all the cross-sections of employees
- Practice TQM philosophy through personal selling (reflected in the behaviour of all)

Strategy 3

- Encourage directed-creativity culture and practices with a clear documented policy
- Emphasis on in-house talent rather than on outsourcing
- Implement a reward system for focused and need-based creative ideas
- Implement documented promotion policy to provide growth opportunities for employees

Figure 1 gives a pictorial representation of the strategy and action plan of an organization.

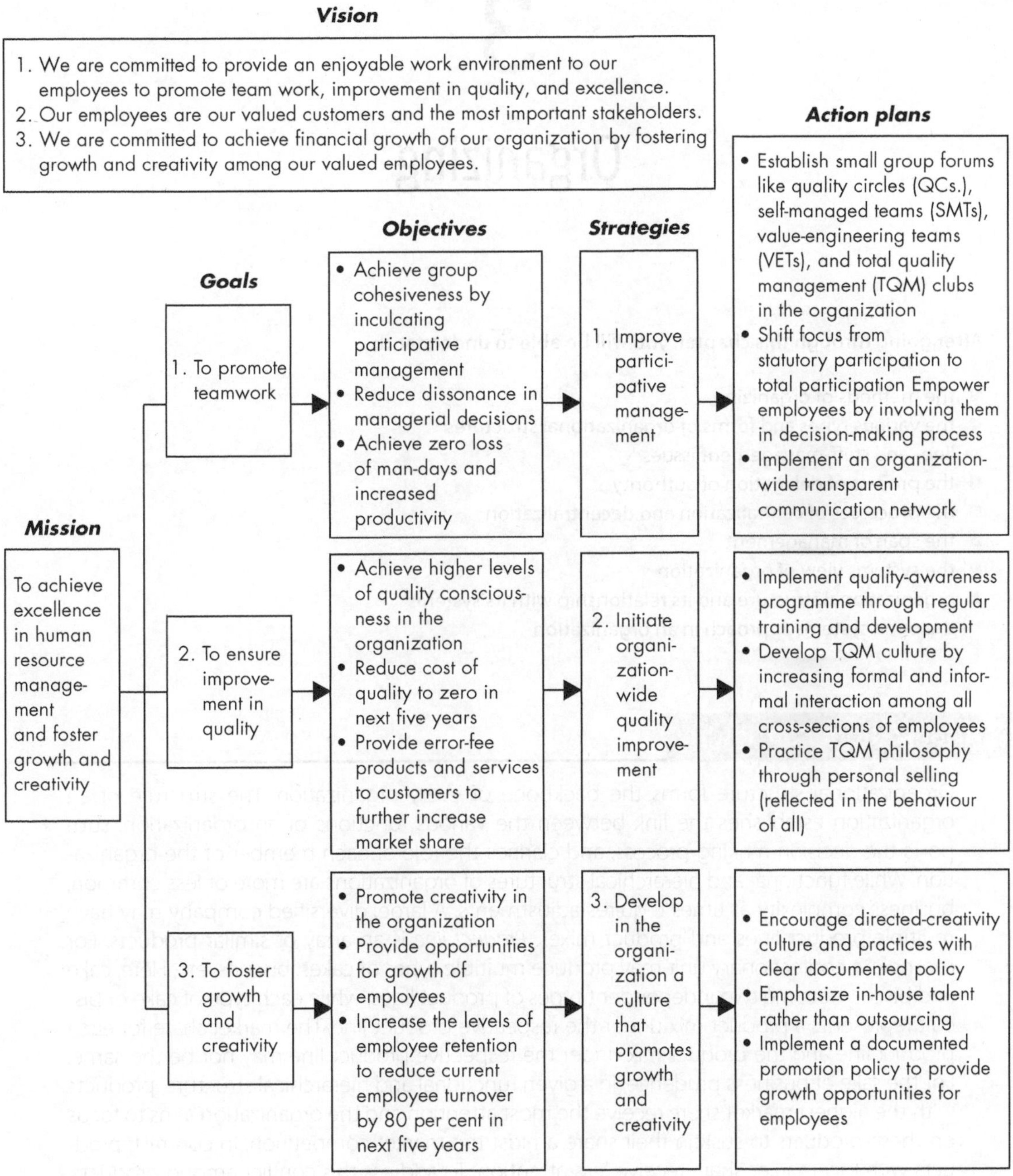

Figure 1 Strategy Action Map

3

Organizing

After going through this chapter, you will be able to understand:

- the methods of organizing
- the various types and forms of organizational structures
- line- and staff-management issues
- the process of delegation of authority
- the processes of centralization and decentralization
- the span of management
- the systems view of organization
- organizational structure and its relationship with its systems
- the open systems approach in an organization

Organizational Structure

Organizational structure forms the backbone of every organization. The structure of an organization establishes the link between the various functions of an organization, supports the decision-making process, and clarifies the role of each member of the organization. While functional and hierarchical structures of organizations are more or less common, business complexity at times requires adjustments. A large, diversified company may have multiple product lines and product mixes. *Product line* is an array of similar products. For example, a confectionary unit may produce multiple types of cakes, biscuits, etc. Here, cake and biscuit become two independent types of product lines, while each type of cake or biscuit represents a product mix under the respective product line. The market share for each product line and the product mix under the respective product line may not be the same. For the sake of business prudence, in a given functional and hierarchical structure, products with the highest market share receive the most attention and the organization aims to focus on these products to sustain their share amidst the market competition. In contrast, products with low market share receive less attention. To address this conflict among products, organizations around the world are now focusing on developing each product line or product mix as their strategic or independent business unit. In a *strategic business unit* (SBU) or an *independent business unit* (IBU), heads run their activities independently and, in the process, benefit the company, helping it to grow in all spheres of business.

INTRODUCTION

As explained in Chapter 2, planning is one of the most important steps in management. After finalizing the plan, managers need to allocate and use the resources available in the organization in the right way. Managers create appropriate conditions for the employees of the organization to work in a concerted manner to achieve the desired goals and objectives. Pulling together resources and people and making them understand the importance of cooperation to accomplish results are the functions of organizing. While planning helps in deciding what to do, organizing focuses on how to do it by properly forming groups. Behavioural scientists and sociologists view organization as comprising human relationships in group activity. In an operational sense, however, organization can be considered as consisting of division of work among people and coordination of their activities towards some common objectives.

An *organization* is essentially a formal structure of people set up to achieve some defined goals. A business unit or a manufacturing unit may be termed a *business organization* or a *manufacturing organization* because these are essentially formal structures consisting of persons who strive to achieve some defined goals.

An organization is imbued with certain attributes. These attributes have been listed here.

- An organization is a group of people who are organized to achieve a common purpose.
- It is an entity, a unit, or an establishment, which utilizes resources to achieve some common purpose.
- It shows a structure of relationships in an enterprise.
- It is a process that helps to relate tasks and abilities of people working in an enterprise to achieve intended goals.

CONCEPT OF ORGANIZATION

An important approach to organization is defining the terms *organization*, *organizing*, and *organizational structure* separately. The term *organization* is used to refer to a social group that is deliberately created and maintained to achieve some intended goals. More specifically, it is defined as a formal social group. It is also referred to as a process of determining activities that are required to achieve intended goals, creating various roles, and ensuring effective operation of the total system. *Organizing* is defined as a management process, which corroborates with the earlier definition of organization as a process of identifying, classifying, grouping, and assigning various activities with adequately defined authority relationships to achieve intended goals. *Organizational structure*, on the other hand, is the outcome of the organizing process. It is a framework of decision-making authority, that is, a system of relationships that govern the activities of the people working in the organization to achieve the intended goals.

Organizational structure helps to determine authority relationships among the members of an organization, and hence, it influences the behaviour of individuals, groups, and divisions within the organization. Among other things, the structure of an organization affects division of tasks, communication systems, decision-making patterns, and finally, the way people relate to each other. Global competition requires organizations to redefine their structure and even to relocate, taking advantage of state-of-the-art technology and communication support. With reduced trade barriers under the WTO regime, a presence in the global market is now the first priority for many organizations. Proximity to markets, 24 × 7 customer support, and economy of scale in operations are some of the factors that have led many organizations to redefine their structure. As testimony, global majors like IBM, Ford, DuPont, and Siemens are spreading their organizational structures internationally. Global competition has also accentuated organizational turbulence which has, in turn, compelled organizations to revisit their structure and the relationships between people in their organization. Use of e-commerce, knowledge and information, workplace diversity, and ethics are also prompting organizations to revisit their established processes and systems and restructure every time to remain up-to-date.

Theories of Organization

From a historical perspective, one can group the theories of organization into three major categories:

1. Classical theory
2. Neoclassical theory
3. Systems theory

The *classical school of thought* was mostly concerned with the micro aspects of organization, that is, their approaches were mostly divorced from societal issues, which in reality interact with an organization. The *neoclassical approach* is the process of relating psychological variables of people. It gives some thought to the social aspects, if not directly, at least indirectly. The *systems approach*, in particular, studies the concept of organization from a macro perspective. This approach recognizes that organization, in reality, is a dynamic process and exists only by interacting with the environment.

Principles of Organization

Due to the diversity in managerial styles, there are no universal principles of organizing. However, the following principles are widely adhered to while organizing:

- Each person should be immediately responsible to one person only and not to several superiors. Tasks *can* be performed when directions come from several superiors, but in such cases, subordinates get confused and this ultimately defeats the purpose of achieving the common goals. It is always better to organize people in such a way that there is only one superior who can give orders and to whom the subordinates are ultimately responsible.
- Authority should be granted to match responsibility. If this is not done, it often leads to a decline in the subordinate's zeal for taking initiative.
- The span of control should be appropriate to the circumstances, so that it is neither too wide nor too narrow.
- Optimal use should be made of specialization.
- The number of levels of management should be kept as low as possible. Too many levels lead to bureaucracy and to distortion or loss of communication.
- The degree of centralization should be appropriate. Too much of centralization may lead to decisional delay as well as delay in implementation of decisions. This has a crippling effect on the organization as they fail to respond quickly to either internal or external changes.
- There should be equitable distribution of work, both in terms of variety and volume.
- Maximum use should be made of the abilities of the staff in the distribution of duties and responsibilities.
- The duties, authority, and responsibility should be defined; otherwise it may lead to 'empire building'.
- The organization should be flexible enough to accommodate change, cutting across hierarchical barriers. Too much rigidity may weaken the competitive strength of an organization.

Human Factors Behind Organizing

Many modern theorists of management stress the need to look at the human factors in an organization and these are certainly as important as the formal factors. Although there is no empirical evidence to justify such views, many organizations emphasize these points. These include factors like grouping of male and female employees, grouping of employees according to age group, marital status, race, religion, etc. It is suggested that these factors be considered to the extent possible while grouping the functions of an organization. It may be difficult for a relatively small organization to implement this type of grouping. In such cases, better coordination plays a more effective role.

Important Steps in Organizing

One can enumerate the important steps in organizing as:

1. Enumeration and grouping of activities of the enterprise consistent with its objectives
2. Assignment of activities to different executives
3. Delegation of authority and placing of responsibility for carrying out the assigned duties
4. Making provision for effective coordination between employees and establishment of definite lines of supervision

Benefits of Organizing

A sound organization entails certain benefits, as explained here:

- **Facilitating management**: A properly designed organization facilitates both management and operation of the enterprise. Management work takes place with certainty and continuity only if appropriate functional groups are constituted to help managers. The grouping and arrangement of activities directly affect operating results. If the important activities are overlooked or subordinated, the results can be detrimental. Successful managers always try to develop a good structure through organizational analysis.
- **Encouraging growth**: The organizational structure is the framework within which an enterprise grows. This requires a flexible structure where changes may be incorporated. Moreover, a sound structure facilitates growth by improving efficiency levels.
- **Optimum use of technological improvement**: The advantages of new technological improvements can be best realized by having a suitable organizational structure. The use of computers is costly but it helps to process the information quickly. This requires a particular organizational structure.
- **Facilitating a humane work environment**: This point emphasizes the psychological satisfaction of all individuals working in the organization. An individual contributes their best when their satisfaction is at the highest level. The level of one's psychological satisfaction mostly depends upon one's work, one's relationships, and one's working environment. A good organizational structure is essential for creating an environment that facilitates psychological satisfaction. The organizational structure also creates provisions for training and promotional avenues of employees.
- **Stimulating creativity**: A sound organization based on specialization stimulates creative thinking and initiative by providing a well-defined area of work with provision for development of new and improved ways of working.
- **Coordination and control**: A sound organization facilitates coordination and control in the enterprise.

Types of Organizations

Organizations have been classified on the basis of various parameters. According to the different approaches, there is a closed systems and an open systems view of organization.

In the *closed systems view of organization*, the interacting elements operate without any exchange with the environment. This means that such organizations require no inputs (human, knowledge, informational, or technological) from the external environment in which it operates. The primary characteristics of such organizations are that they are perfectly deterministic and there is no exchange between the system and the external environment. However, today no organization can truly be closed and totally closed systems exist only in theory.

The *open systems view of organization* stresses on the need for flexibility and adaptability in the organizational structure and also on interdependence of the organization with its external environment. Louis E. Boone and David L. Kurtz (1992) defined *open systems* as 'a set of elements that interact with each other and the environment and whose structure evolves over time as a result of interaction'.

Organizations can also be classified as formal and informal. A *formal organization* is a group of people working together cooperatively under authority, towards goals that mutually benefit the employees and the organization. In formal organizations, jobs are well defined with a definite measure of authority, responsibility, and accountability. An *informal organization*, on the other hand, is a network of personal and social relations that arise spontaneously as people associate with one another. It lays emphasis on people and their relationships. In contrast, formal organizations emphasize official positions in terms of authority, responsibility, and accountability. Informal organizations, therefore, may or may not support the formal goals and objectives. The manager is then required to understand and recognize the informal relationships and integrate both the forms of organization to achieve the intended goals.

SYSTEMS VIEW OF ORGANIZATIONS

From a systems perspective, the organization can be viewed as an aggregation of parts or subsystems. Such aggregation helps in achieving the overall goals and objectives of the organization. Thus, *systems* indicate various inputs, processes, outputs, and outcomes, along with the feedback that help in integrating the organization as a whole. Any change in any of the constituents of subsystems may lead to total change in the organization. Depending on the nature of activities of the organization, systems may be simple or complex. Each constituent of a system, that is, the subsystems may also vary with respect to the specific nature of activities of the organization. Subsystems can be arranged in order of hierarchies depending on their nature and utilization in the total system. For example, if an organization is engaged in social development, then its extent of service to meet the public utilities as an outcome may be the most important subsystem. In contrast, improving the bottom line or the profitability of the organization may be the most important subsystem that directs the activities of a commercial organization. Therefore, the definition of an important subsystem or the constituent of a system varies with the nature of organizational pursuit. Again, each subsystem has its own boundaries. For achieving overall excellence in organizational activities, each subsystem has to be controlled within its specific boundaries to accomplish the goals of the organization. For example, without the desired quality of inputs (a subsystem), an organization cannot achieve increased sales to get the incremental benefit of an improved bottom line, that is, the outcome (a subsystem).

Thus, from a systems perspective, one can consider the organization as a unitary whole. The systems view implies the arrangement of various subsystems, or the arrangement of the activities of an organization, to achieve the larger objectives. From this perspective, one can define a system as an arrangement of the total activities of an organization to accomplish its goals. The systems view provides a new dimension to scientifically interpret various patterns and activities of an organization, which helps in identification of problems, analysing the problems, and taking the required remedial actions to achieve the desired results.

In the systems view, because of interrelations between different subsystems, managers and executives need to coordinate various activities with due cognizance of each constituent of a system, encompassing various departments and sections. Feedback collected in the process of coordination helps in diagnosing the problems and analysing which department can initiate the corrective actions. Such organizations can also concentrate on outcome achievement, bringing the desired changes in the subsystems, designing the appropriate structures, and provoking the desired behaviours. Through this process, organizations can persuade the event to happen rather than wait for the results to accrue in due course of time.

It is clear that organizations make effective use of interrelated networks of subsystems to achieve their goals and objectives. From the systems perspective, one can conclude that an organization has the following attributes:

- The organizational system pursues organizational goals.
- The organizational system is the whole, that is, the summation of all subsystems.
- The organizational system helps in processing or transforming all the subsystems into the final result in the form of output or outcome.
- The subsystems interact with each other and are interdependent in nature.
- The organizational system is situation-specific and environment-specific.

Organizations are viewed as systems made up of subsystems—environmental inputs, resource inputs (men, machines, materials, knowledge processes, etc.)—that produce the outputs through their interactions. Like any other system, organizations also collect information on the functioning of subsystems through the feedback loop and correct any possible malfunctioning, duly adjusting with changing premises of the environment. The systems approach, therefore, facilitates the functioning of an organization in the following ways:

- The systems approach rightly assumes that an organization is a living organism and, in the process, values the dynamic character of the organization.
- The systems approach appreciates the interrelationship between the organization and the environment.
- The systems approach appreciates that the environment of conducting business changes over time, and hence, an organization must make necessary adjustments with the changing environmental premises.
- The feedback loop in the systems approach provides information inputs for enforcing managerial control and decision making.
- The systems approach helps in framing realistic business goals and objectives as it accounts for environmental considerations.
- The systems approach recognizes that every division, department, and unit of an organization is part of a subsystem, and that they are interrelated and interdependent.
- The systems approach ensures that every organization frames its structure by integrating all the subsystems.

Interrelatedness among all internal or external subsystems of an organization helps in managing the transformation of inputs to outputs. The systems approach to organization has many dimensions. In the principles of management, while the organization structure is more important, a comprehensive understanding of the organization as a system can help in framing the appropriate structure.

Organizational Structure and Systems

Organizational structure represents the various forms of interrelations and linkage among divisions, departments, functions, and employees. It prima facie illustrates the way in which each constituent and subsystem of an organization interacts. Conventionally, organizational structure demonstrates the vertical operational responsibilities of each constituent and the people associated with each such constituent, in the form of a chart. Organizational structure is proportional to the size and geographic spread of the organization. The vertical structure of an organization is in conformity with Weber's (1946) theory of bureaucracy. With the complexity of business and with the global spread of the organization in the changing economic environment of today, one can find various forms of organization structure other than the conventional vertical structure. These are flat, networked, matrix, and even virtual organizations. Every organization needs to change its structure every now and then to be able to respond to the changing environmental factors that necessitate scaling up and scaling down the operations (lean management), job compositional shift of employees and corresponding change in the reporting systems (viz. dual reporting in matrix structure or independent functioning without reporting to anyone, etc.), and workforce rightsizing (making many employees redundant). From the systems perspective, therefore, the structure of an organization represents the pattern of grouping employees and their jobs, and relating the same to the overall organization through various constituents and subsystems. Sometimes, organization structure and organization design are erroneously thought to be synonymous. While organizational structure is the mapping of organizational activities through its different constituents and subsystems, organizational design is the set of managerial decisions that help the organization to bring change in the structure.

Organization Structure

Organization structure is the pattern of relational network between different hierarchies and is characterized by the activity–authority relationship chart. *Organization chart* is a useful model of a formal structure that illustrates relationships among employees and social systems, and their interactions with all the systems of an organization. An organization chart has both mechanistic and humanistic elements. The chart should be designed in such a way that employees of the organization face minimum difficulty in executing their jobs in coordination with various departments, to achieve the goals and objectives of the organization.

As the organization structure is a means to the end of achieving business results, it should be designed in such a way that it helps the organization to accomplish predetermined goals.

Drucker's approach

Drucker (1954) suggested three aspects that can help an organization to attain its objectives:

1. Activity analysis
2. Decision analysis
3. Relation analysis

Drucker's approaches to the structure of an organization deviate from the traditional classification of organizational activities into functional operations like marketing, finance, HR, and production in order to design the appropriate structure. Drucker suggested a more analytic study of each function to understand the elements of its activities and accordingly map their contributions to appreciate how they help in achieving the objectives of an organization. Only with such understanding is the effective structuring of an organization possible.

Yet, from another perspective, one can argue that since an organization is an open system, it constantly interacts with various environmental forces to sustain itself and grow. In the process of such interactions, the organization redefines its business goals and objectives, and to accomplish the same, reframes its structure to make it more adaptable to changes.

Mintzberg's approach

Mintzberg (1981) defines *organization structure* as the way to divide employees for different tasks and achieve coordination between them. Based on his analysis, Mintzberg considers the structure of an organization as the configuration of systems and relationships of six elements. These elements interact with the total system and help to achieve the goals and objectives of the organization.

At the operating core level, employees of an organization get involved with the production and services. The strategic part, according to Mintzberg, facilitates in enforcing control. Line managers help in aligning the strategic core with the operating core. Employees at the techno-structure core extend support for designing, planning, and training of the operating core people. The support staff members, who are outside the operating core, extend support to the organization. Thus, both Mintzberg's and Drucker's approaches to the organization structure are distinctly different from traditional precepts.

Types of Organization Structures

Organization structure explains the authority relationships among employees. Through authority relationships, employees of an organization can relate with each other. In addition, the structure of the organization influences behaviour, determines the division of tasks and the pattern of decision making, and lays down the systems of communication. The structure of an organization may be either open or standardized. The ideal structure will, however, depend on the specific nature of the organization. According to Mintzberg (1981), there are five types of organization structures with different behavioural patterns:

1. **Machine bureaucracy (standardized structure)**: Organizations with the structure of machine bureaucracy standardize their work systems and pursue centralized decision-making norms. Due to their typical nature, such organizations make extensive use of standard operating procedures (SOP). Internationally acclaimed large organizations like McDonald's, General Motors Company, and Ford Motor Company conform to the typicality of machine bureaucracy. For their operational convenience, such organizations polarize (maintain hierarchy) to enforce control over different stakeholders. With a rigid boundary, these organizations balance the relationship between themselves and various stakeholders. By nature, these organizations maintain secrecy, and at times exhibit an attitude that dissuades internal cooperation. A narrow-minded attitude prevents internal cooperation and discourages learning for the people. These organizations are so insular that the employees of one department do not even enter another department. Due to the typical nature of their work systems, internal competition among the employees also increases, against the desired collaborative work systems among employees.
2. **Professional bureaucracy**: Organizations with a professional bureaucracy structure manage their operations with professional employees. Such organizations focus less on formalizations of systems and procedures, believe in allowing a high degree of functional autonomy, empower the employees, and encourage learning and competency development to build the employees' capabilities and encourage them to perform well. For collaborative work systems, these organizations also require less control of employees' activities.
3. **Adhocracy or innovative forms**: Organizations with an innovative or adhocratic structure try to develop a distinctive corporate culture. The typical behavioural syndrome of such organizations,

according to Mintzberg, is 'alliance building'. With a decentralized decision-making process, these organizations encourage open communication, healthy interpersonal relations, mutual discussions, and negotiations.

4. **Simple or entrepreneurial forms**: The entrepreneurial form of organization structure is followed by organizations that are run by the entrepreneur. In such organizations, the entrepreneur directs all the activities and, hence, can win the quick trust of employees with flexible norms and systems. Such organizations, however, experience instability when they fail to build mutual trust.
5. **Divisional forms**: Organizations with a divisional structure manage their activities by making several autonomous divisions. Divisions may be in terms of a product or a process. However, though structurally divisions enjoy autonomy, control and decision-making power may not always be with the divisions. When divisions are managed like independent profit centres, it may generate infighting due to conflicts of interests.

Adhocracy means purposefully cracking down a system with a purpose. It was Alvin Toffler (1970) who for the first time used this term. Later on, Mintzberg and others popularized this concept. Characteristically, it is just the opposite of bureaucracy. Waterman (1990) has defined *adhocracy* as an organization that 'cut across normal bureaucratic lines to capture opportunities, solve problems, and get results'. Obviously, due to its typical nature, such an organization is more innovative and capable of meeting any exigency. The adhocratic organization is marked by certain characteristics:

- It is more organic in nature.
- There is less emphasis on formalization of behaviour.
- Employees' training programmes are specialization-specific.
- There is emphasis on mutual adjustment.
- There is less standardization of procedures.
- Job roles are less defined in order to facilitate job interchangeability.
- Decentralization is applied but not in every case.
- Work is allocated to a specialized team.
- Emphasis is on horizontal job specialization.
- Communication cost is high.
- The work culture is non-bureaucratic.
- Cross-functional and cross-departmental task forces are common.

Thus, in organizations with an adhocratic structure, because of absence of hierarchical barriers, employees are given appropriate decision-making authority and can also work in a concerted manner to achieve the intended business results.

From the above discussion on the different forms of organization structure, it is clear that the choice of a specific form is highly dependent on specific organizational preferences and goals. Although the bureaucratic structure of organization is quite common, the bureaucratic model is not a structure—it is more appropriate to call it a design. A bureaucratic model can provide a blueprint that is descriptive in nature. In contrast, adhocracy determines the structural system, which is flexible and adaptive to any change. Effective performance results are more evident in the adhocratic structure.

Both bureaucratic and adhocratic forms of organizations have their relative merits and demerits. Each form tackles different situations. In bureaucratic organizations, work is done systematically with structured guidelines like SOP. As a result, such organizations cannot respond to changes on a real-time basis. On the other hand, adhocratic organizations with their flexible structure can quickly respond to changes.

Due to frequent overlapping of functions and job roles, adhocratic organizations are, however, more prone to conflict and rivalry. In bureaucratic organizations, such conflict and rivalry are less because systems are more regimented and interpersonal relations are more formal. Therefore, one cannot say that either system is right or wrong. Their success or failure is more organization-specific. Organizations can achieve the intended business performance by using either form, provided it fits in with the typical nature of the organization.

Organizational Effectiveness

To understand organizational effectiveness, there is a need to first understand what effectiveness is. *Effectiveness* indicates successful achievement of long-term goals and sustainable performance of an organization. Effectiveness is measured with respect to a specific activity. It can be either a subjective or an objective measurement. For example, behavioural inputs (attitude, values, etc.) that go into performance results can be measured using subjective or qualitative tools. However, other parameters like output rate and value, profitability trend, and customers' satisfaction can be measured only by using objective or quantitative tools. Therefore, *organizational effectiveness* indicates effective achievement of organizational results with resource optimization. Organizational effectiveness in both qualitative and quantitative terms can be achieved through important performance enablers like good interpersonal skills, positive attitude, technical and managerial competencies, and small group activities. For effective performance results, therefore, organizations need to use a relevant form of organizational structure.

Developing an Organization Structure or Design

Designing a new organization structure or reorganizing an existing one calls for careful consideration of current practices and principles of the organization. While there are no formal or strict rules to determine the best organization structure, the following steps can be more effective in achieving enterprise objectives:

1. **Clearly define the objectives**: The first step is to lay down objectives in very clear terms. This will help in determining the type, stability, and basic characteristics of the organization.
2. **Identify the activities and group them into convenient classes**: The next important step involves enumeration of activities necessary to achieve the objectives, the grouping of these activities in a systematic manner, assignment of such groups of activities to personnel, and providing for their coordination. If possible, similar functions should be combined into one position.
3. **Determine the structure**: The manager has to determine the span of supervision, the types of organization, the basis of departmentation, and the pattern of authority structure.
4. **Revise the system on the basis of assessment of personnel and funds**: The last step is to assess the capacities and abilities of not only the individuals available to manage different positions in the organization, but also other resources at the disposal of the enterprise. The ideal organization should then be adapted to function in sync with the reality of the situation.

These are the general guidelines to be followed. Each enterprise should be viewed as a separate case and developed accordingly. It is unwise to follow a particular structural form simply because that proved more effective in one instance. Local conditions, business objectives and policies, scale of operation, nature of work, and above all, the character and abilities of personnel are important factors to be considered while developing an organizational structure.

DYNAMIC ORGANIZATIONAL STRUCTURE AND DEPARTMENTATION

Organizational structure should not be static. An enterprise operates under a highly dynamic environment where the technological, social, political, and economic setting in which it operates, and the people managing the organization, are all in a continuous flux. This calls for adapting the organizational structure to changing conditions so that it can survive and grow. Accommodating changes in the organization requires that the structure be partly modified so as to adjust to changes in the attitudes, ambitions, and abilities of the people involved. Thus, there are different organizational structures based on the grouping of activities into different units. The process of grouping the activities is known as *departmentation*.

Principles of Departmentation

Different bases for grouping the concerned activities result in different methods of departmentation. While grouping, the manager must consider the advantages and disadvantages of each method of departmentation along with the basic factors involved in grouping the activities of the enterprise. Only after such evaluation should one contemplate the kind of composite departmental structure best suited to the requirements of the organization.

The basic considerations in grouping activities are:

- **Specialization**: The organizational structure should divide and group the activities of the concern in such a way that similar and allied activities are, on all occasions, put under one department. Specialization leads to more and better work with the same effort.
- **Control**: Departmentation should be such as to facilitate control.
- **Coordination**: If objectives are to be accomplished effectively, departmentation should not only facilitate control but also help in coordination.
- **Balance**: Departmentation should allow adequate attention to be paid to each of the functions of the enterprise so that different activities are properly balanced.
- **Duplication of sections**: Departmentation should, as far as possible, avoid duplication of sections.
- **Human factor**: Departmentation should not overlook the human factor of the organization. Any possible impact of the structure upon the human factor should be given due consideration.
- **Reduction of cost**: Activities should be grouped in a manner that will best contribute to achieving enterprise objectives and reducing its cost.
- **Recognition of local conditions**: The pattern of grouping should be evolved in such a way that local conditions are given due recognition.

In addition, the following principles should also be given due consideration according to necessity, in departmentalizing activities or functions:

- Ease of direction
- Flexibility
- Optimum utilization of the workforce
- Opportunities for the application of individual talents
- Uniform and consistent policy of operation
- Functional efficiency in production, distribution, and finance
- Clear and comprehensive channels of communication
- Contribution to the survival and prosperity of the business

Process of Departmentation

The process of departmentation may be divided into the following three stages:

1. Primary departmentation, which is achieved by initial break-up of functions into basic activities
2. Intermediate departmentation, which is done by creating departments in the middle levels of the organization
3. Ultimate departmentation, which is accomplished by dividing activities into separate units at the lower levels

Based on the prevalent practices, organizational structure can be divided into four major types:

1. Functional structure
2. Divisional structure
3. Hybrid structure
4. Matrix structure

Patterns Used in Departmentation

The most common patterns are grouping by functions, products, territories, processes, customers, and time. It may be mentioned here that departmentation by numbers used to be an important method in the organization of tribes and armies.

Departmentation by functions

Departmentation by functions refers to grouping the activities of an enterprise into major functional departments. The basic functions are usually classified into production, selling, and financing. The other commonly recognized functions requiring separate groupings are buying, accounting, personnel, and research. However, these functions vary according to the organization. Departmentation by functions is the most widely used basis for grouping activities into administrative units and is found in almost every enterprise at some level or the other. An illustration of a functional organization structure has been given in Figure 3.1.

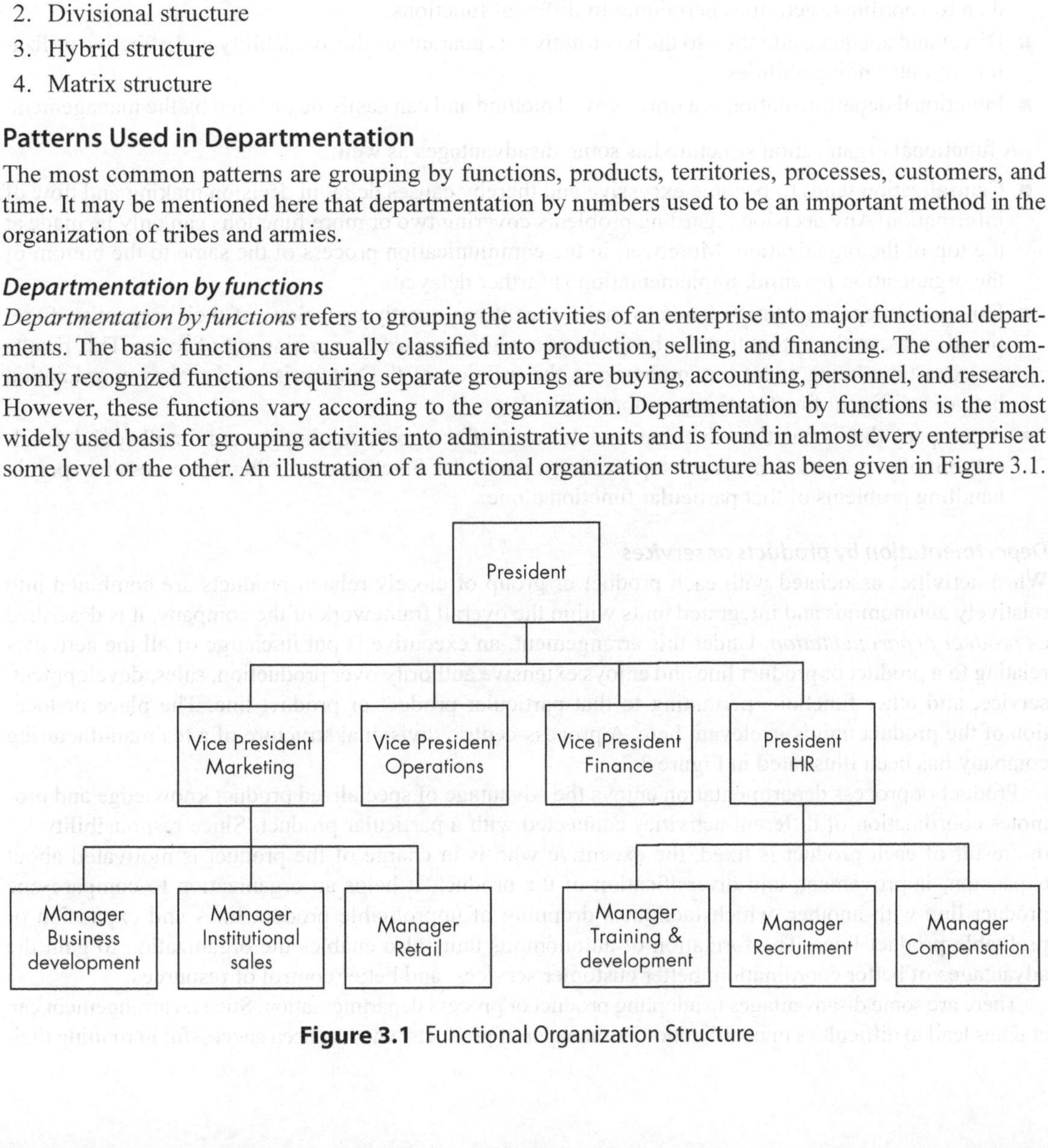

Figure 3.1 Functional Organization Structure

This is a hypothetical organization structure of a multi-product company with both institutional and retail sales.

Some of the advantages of a functional organization structure are:

- Functional departmentation represents a natural and logical way of grouping different activities of the enterprise.
- Such grouping ensures specialization. By concentrating on similar groups of activities, specialized knowledge and skill are acquired which can be utilized for the efficient running of the departments. This leads to economy in operations and efficiency in the use of the workforce and other resources.
- It facilitates coordination within the function. It is easier for a manager in charge of a particular function to synchronize activities and unify efforts of personnel engaged in that particular function, than to coordinate activities pertaining to different functions.
- Direct and adequate attention to the basic activities guarantees the availability and effective utilization of outstanding abilities.
- Functional departmentation is a time-proved method and can easily be justified by the management.

A functional organization structure has some disadvantages as well:

- Centralization tends to become excessive and thereby causes delay in decision making and flow of information. Any decision regarding problems covering two or more functions can only be made at the top of the organization. Moreover, in the communication process of the same to the bottom of the organization pyramid, implementation is further delayed.
- Functional departmentation tends to make executives overtly conscious of their respective functional areas, to the extent that the business as a whole very often remains out of focus. This results in extra time being spent on emphasizing the mission of the enterprise and makes coordination between different functional areas more difficult.
- A company that is functionally organized does not offer a good training ground for all-round development of managers. A manager supervising a particular function more often becomes an expert in handling problems of that particular function alone.

Departmentation by products or services

When activities associated with each product or group of closely related products are combined into relatively autonomous and integrated units within the overall framework of the company, it is described as *product departmentation.* Under this arrangement, an executive is put in charge of all the activities relating to a product or product line and enjoys extensive authority over production, sales, development, service, and other functions pertaining to that particular product or product line. The place or location of the product unit is irrelevant here. A process-centric divisional structure of a tea manufacturing company has been illustrated in Figure 3.2.

Product or process departmentation enjoys the advantage of specialized product knowledge and promotes coordination of different activities connected with a particular product. Since responsibility for the result of each product is fixed, the executive who is in charge of the product is motivated about expansion, improvement, and diversification of the product. It helps an organization to compare one product line with another, which facilitates dropping of unprofitable product lines and expansion of profitable product lines. The formation of autonomous units also enables the organization to gain the advantages of better coordination, better customer services, and better control of resources.

There are some disadvantages to adopting product or process departmentation. Such an arrangement can at times lead to difficulties in coordination. A manager of products who has been successful in running their

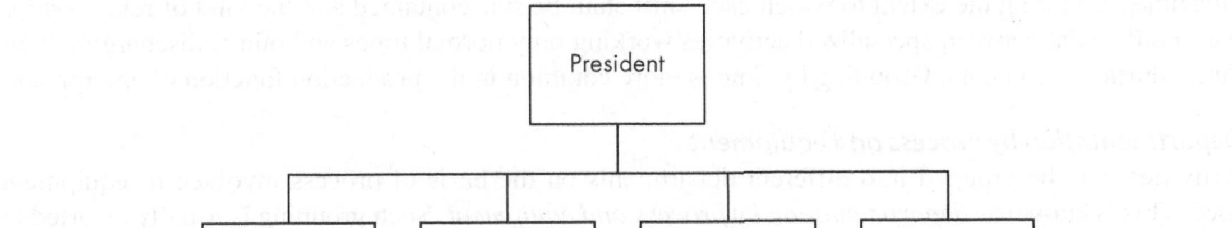

Figure 3.2 Divisional Organization Structure

department may well be prompted to acquire more power for themselves. However, such a situation may be remedied through centralization of certain key activities and shifting major policy decisions to the top of the organization. Also, a product or process departmentation structure requires the organization to hire more persons with general managerial ability, thereby raising the managerial cost. Costs are also increased due to duplication of centralized services and staff activities. At the top management level, it can also create a problem of control due to obvious difficulty in monitoring of activities of various product departments. Apart from that, top management may not like to delegate decision-making powers to departmental heads.

Departmentation by locations or territories

When the activities of an enterprise are physically or geographically dispersed, providing it with local administration is desirable and at times required in the interest of efficiency and economy in operations. This type of organization is viewed as *territorial departmentation.* Koontz (1961) has mentioned two valid reasons favouring territorial departmentation:

1. To avoid absenteeism, that is, to make managers keep local factors in context in decision making
2. To take advantage of certain economies of localized operation

Grouping by locations signifies adaptation to local needs and facilitates prompt actions. Activities within the scope of one's area or authority can be more effectively coordinated and controlled. Such departmentation also offers opportunity to the top management to allow employees to gain experience with minimum risks to the firm. On the other hand, communication gap and delay in decision are some of the major disadvantages that may accrue.

Departmentation by time

When operations extend far beyond the normal work period of an individual, it may well be spread over certain shifts. Such grouping is frequently termed as *departmentation by time.* For enterprises engaged in continuous processes, for example, public utilities and restaurants, departmentation by time is a normal practice. Units so created on time basis perform similar operations. However, there needs to be clear guidelines regarding the extent to which each shift shall be self-contained and the kind of relationships that should exist between specialized activities working only normal times and others discharging their duties during extra hours. Grouping by time is more common in the production function of enterprises.

Departmentation by process and equipment

Activities may be grouped into different departments on the basis of process involved or equipment used. This is known as *departmentation by process and equipment*. Such grouping is usually resorted to in a manufacturing concern. Thus, a cotton textile unit may have separate units for spinning, weaving, dyeing, inspection, and shipping. Such departmentation can help to ensure better supervision, optimal use of equipments, specialization, and avoidance of duplication of investment. In this structure, the same pattern of departmentation as illustrated in the divisional structure is followed.

Departmentation by customers

Customer departmentation is more popular in the sales activities of an enterprise. This pattern is usually followed when a high degree of interest needs to be shown in the welfare and interest of customers. Customers may be classified on the basis of age, sex, income, or taste. This type of departmentation assures full attention to different customer groups. It also helps in enhancing the company's image and goodwill. Since customers are divided into identifiable groups, the pattern permits use of specialized knowledge for each such group.

Hybrid structure

The *hybrid structure* is a form of departmentation that combines both functional and divisional structures. In particular, large organizations adopt this structure to gain the advantages of both functional and divisional structures. The functional structure assures the benefits of economies of scale, in-depth expertise, and resource-utilization efficiencies, while the divisional structure brings the benefits of specialization of products, services, and markets. In India, most of the public sector units and departmental undertakings (like the Railways) follow this structure. A typical hybrid structure of an organization is illustrated in Figure 3.3.

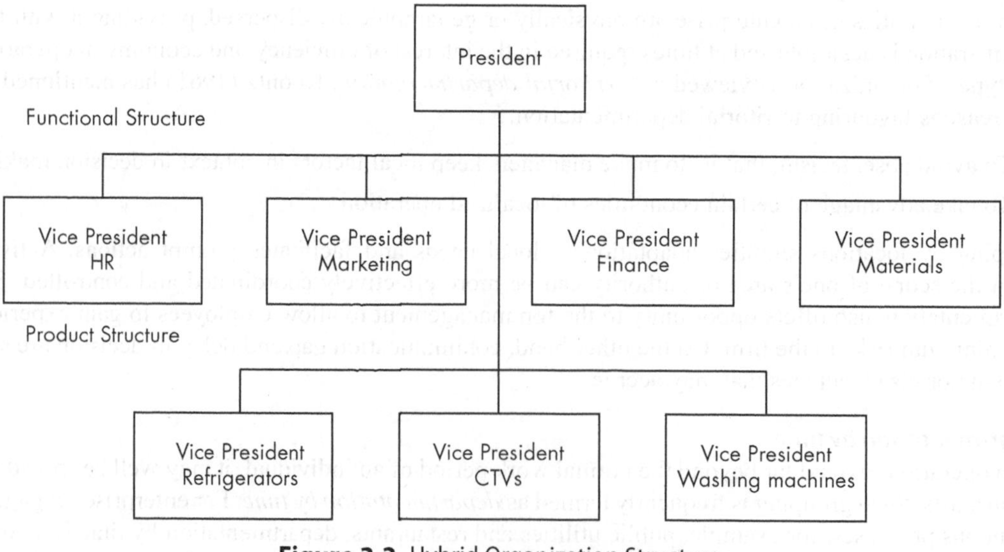

Figure 3.3 Hybrid Organization Structure

A hybrid structure brings the benefits of specialized expertise and economies of scale in prime functional areas. It facilitates adaptability and flexibility in handling diverse product or service lines, territories, and needs of customers, as well as alignment of divisional and corporate goals. However, this structure requires hiring of a large number of staff members both at the corporate level and the functional (operational) level. Control is also difficult to maintain because of a broad organizational structure. Achieving coordination between a division and a corporate functional department is time-consuming, which further creates organizational imbalance.

Matrix structure

In a *matrix structure*, a horizontal set of divisional reporting relationships is superimposed on a hierarchical functional structure. It is also known as grid organization or project or product management organization. It is a combination of functional and divisional forms of organization. Therefore, it is characterized by two chains of command: vertical and horizontal. A typical matrix structure is illustrated in Figure 3.4.

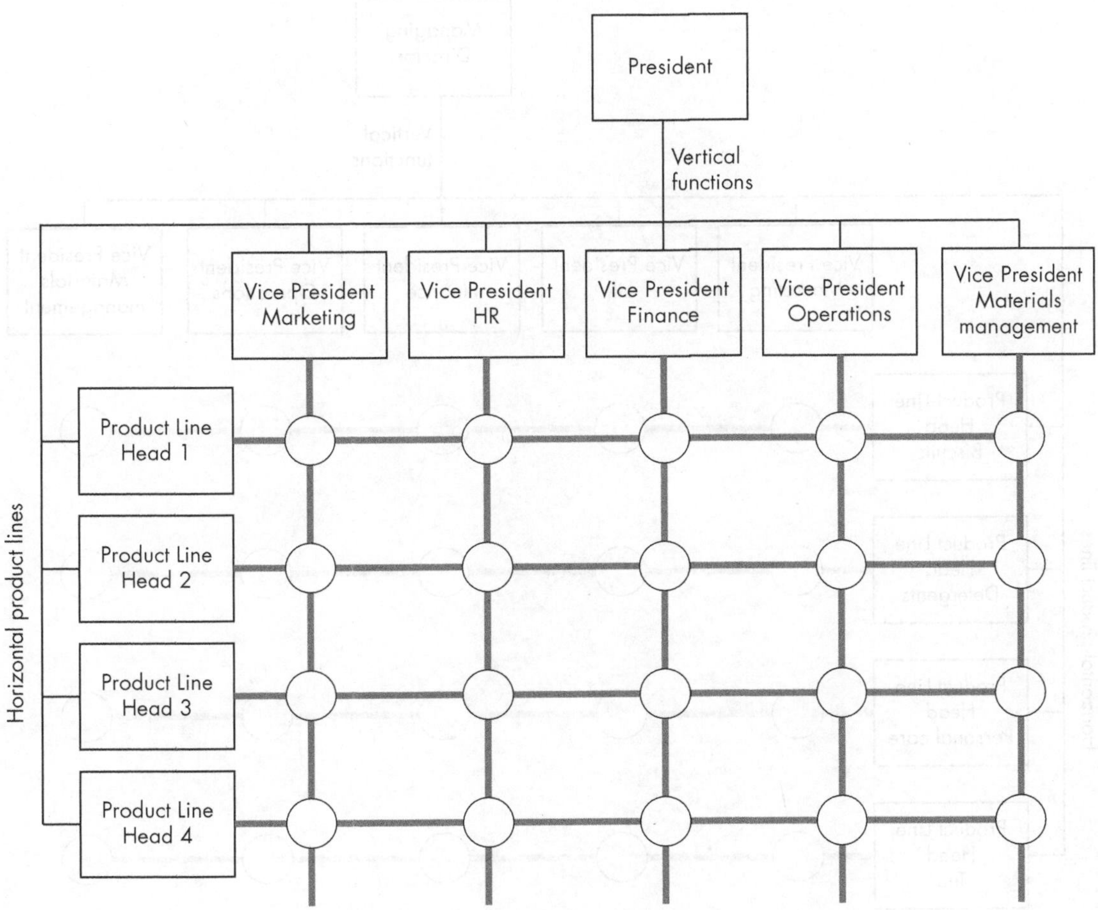

Figure 3.4 Matrix Structure

The advantages of the matrix structure include decentralized decision making, better project or product coordination, improved environment monitoring and resultant response to change, flexible utilization of the workforce and other resources (including support services). On the other hand, this structure requires high administrative costs, creates confusion about authority and responsibility, enhances interpersonal conflicts, and overemphasizes group decision making.

Despite its potential disadvantages, the matrix structure is now widely used to cope with increased environmental pressures and to develop a sound competitive strategy. Unless the whole process is efficiently managed, it is not likely to benefit an organization.

Nowadays, one also observes organizations being structured along the concept of strategic business units (SBU) or independent business units (IBU). SBUs/IBUs are set up as distinct business units to ensure that some products or product lines are promoted as independent businesses. The General Electric Company for the first time used this method of structuring. An illustration of an SBU structure has been given in Figure 3.5.

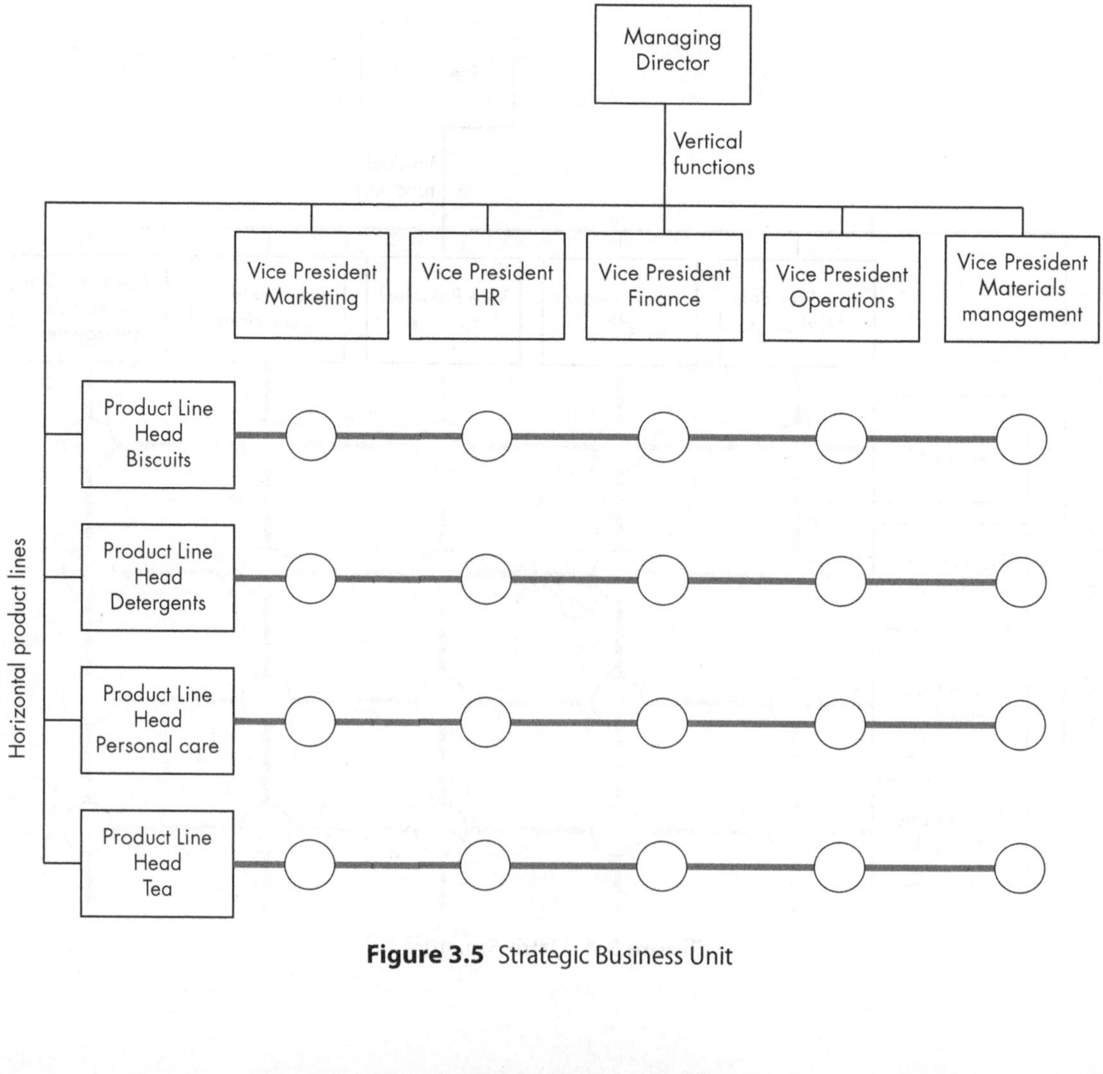

Figure 3.5 Strategic Business Unit

ORGANIZATION STRUCTURE IN A GLOBALIZED WORLD

Business imperatives compel organizations to operate globally. To adapt to global business requirements, organizations may adopt global, international, multi-domestic, transnational, informated, cellular, or networked structures. A *global organization structure* is not locally responsive and it does not believe in optimal sourcing; instead, it concentrates on work activities in one locale, that is, in their country of origin, and follows a centralized approach. They believe in home-base operations even though they do business globally. Strategically, this type of organization offers similar products or services worldwide, irrespective of their acceptance or otherwise in various global markets. An *international organization*, on the other hand, goes beyond home-base operations. They create separate hubs for their various product or service mixes, locating such hubs in those countries where they can get the benefit of optimal sourcing. These hubs in different countries work as 'centres of excellence' and cater to the world market. *Multi-domestic organizations* follow a decentralized, geography-based approach to customize their operations, specific to the requirements of the countries where they do business. They develop specific products and services acceptable to local markets. *Transnational organizations* blend the international and multi-domestic approaches to optimize their location advantages and also to reap the benefits of optimal sourcing. They customize their product and service mix on region basis and at the same time gain the advantages of their worldwide centres of operations. Unilever, Procter & Gamble, and NEC are good examples of this type of organization (Bartlett and Ghoshal 1998). *Informated organizations* manage information up and down the organization, making extensive use of computers and other related supports. They are low in virtualization and high in IT infusion. *Cellular organizations* are characterized by small, autonomous work groups or business units that are self-governed and that can grow, reproduce, and form relations according to their need (Miles and Snow 1984). In fact, they are different from SBUs or IBUs since they can operate more independently, even crossing the boundary of cells. *Networked organizations* develop active linkage between internal and external organizations to meet the knowledge needs. It is a mix of virtualizations and IT infusion and is active in making strategic alliances. Many organizations that survive in a diverse global environment develop a corporate culture that is a learned, shared, relatively enduring, and interdependent system of meanings that classify, code, prioritize, and justify activities both within the organization and towards external environments it has defined as relevant.

VIRTUAL OR NETWORKED ORGANIZATIONS

Information systems have radically changed the world of business and also the way people work. Traditionally, organizational structures were based on location-specific activities and face-to-face communication. With the advancement of information systems, organizations now operate in a distributive environment, with flexibility in the nature and way of work. This is the *e-organization* or *virtual organization*, which does not have a central geographical location. This organization interacts essentially through computer networks. By nature, these types of organizations outsource most of their functions because of their borderless operations and market networks. Several global consulting and high-technology businesses operate through creating a virtual organization, leveraging information systems. In a virtual organization, which may be either temporary or permanent, virtual teams and virtual projects are developed.

Rosabeth Moss Kanter (2001) mentioned the radically transformative nature of the global network—the new e-world which connects everyone with everyone else. This requires a new operating environment as well as new forms of business and organization. To survive in this era of e-revolution, organizations need to be innovative even as they shift from traditional hierarchical bureaucratic systems and structure. Kanter identified certain elements of the e-organization.

According to Kanter, there are four key elements of an effective organizational e-culture:

1. Improved strategy to come out with new products and services
2. Urge to grow through partnerships and collaborations
3. Operate as integrated communities, removing the internal barriers
4. Become talent-dependent or talent-driven

E-organizations have three important features:

1. Managing production processes—encompassing procurement, stock replenishment, payment processing, vendor control, and production control activities—through electronic links
2. Managing customer-centric activities—encompassing marketing, selling, processing of customers' orders, and extending support to customers—through electronic information systems
3. Managing internal processes—encompassing employee services, training, information sharing, and recruiting—through electronic applications

ORGANIZING AS PART OF THE TOTAL MANAGEMENT TASK

Organizing is closely related to other phases of management. This becomes obvious when one considers changes in the organization structure and the effects of such changes on other tasks of management. In fact, changes in organization structure must be matched by changes in the planning, staffing, and controlling phases of management.

Delegation of Authority

Authority delegation is the key to organization. In fact, no organization is possible without delegation because it would then imply the non-existence of subordinates in the organization and one man doing everything. While establishing the organization structure, the manager must group activities, assign them to different individuals in the organization, and delegate authority necessary for their effective and efficient functioning to achieve the mission of the enterprise. Delegation is, thus, an essential process indispensable to organization. The principle of 'span of management' also requires authority to be delegated to subordinates. When the manager delegates authority, he/she creates subordinate positions and thereby makes organization possible. While delegating authority, the manager must know the amount of authority to be delegated and its limit. No manager can delegate authority that they do not have, nor can they delegate all their authority without sacrificing their position as a manager.

Features of authority delegation

Irrespective of the level at which authority is passed on to subordinates, the delegation involves three basic features:

1. Assignment of tasks and duties, that is, indicating what work subordinates must do.
2. Granting of authority, that is, the executive who is delegating authority must transfer sufficient rights or permission to the subordinates to help them accomplish the assigned tasks.
3. Creating an obligation, that is, once duties have been assigned and authority is delegated, responsibility for accomplishment of tasks is spontaneously fixed. According to Fayol, this is exaction of responsibility from the subordinates for accomplishing the assigned tasks.

Thus, duties, authority, and obligation constitute the three important ingredients of delegation. All these three aspects are interrelated and any change in one is bound to call for adjustment in the others.

Principles of delegation

Delegation of authority is made more effective by following certain important principles. These are:

Clarity of delegation Whether specific or general, written or unwritten, delegation of authority must be clear in terms of its contents, functional relations, scope, and assignments. Ambiguity leads to poor results and tends to make the delegation less effective.

Clarity of delegation also implies defining the horizontal and vertical relationships of the position of each subordinate with respect to other positions in the organization. Every subordinate must know what other position exists at their own level in the organization structure and how their position fits in the overall management hierarchy. Every manager must know who are working under them and who are in positions higher to that of their own in the organization. This helps them to seek guidance and also to provide guidance in terms of the scalar chain established in the organization.

Specific and written delegations help both the manager and the recipient of authority. Nevertheless, as one goes up the echelons of organization structure, such specific delegations become more and more difficult to frame.

The principle of clarity should not be taken to mean that authority relations between the subordinates and the seniors once established become immutable. Authority delegation should be adequately modified to conform to any change in the work.

Delegation to be consistent with expected results Before proceeding with actual delegation of authority to the subordinate, the manager should know the precise jobs to be done and the results expected of such delegation. Authority delegation should be restricted to the extent to which it can give results. This principle rests on the assumption that goals are set, plans are made, and jobs are set up to accomplish or implement them. This principle also helps in minimizing the dangers of delegating too much authority or inadequate authority.

No delegation of responsibility The obligation to accomplish the assigned task is absolute and is not partitioned when authority is delegated to the subordinate. The chief executive even after delegation remains accountable to the board of directors for the management and supervision of the whole enterprise. If this principle is violated, three important consequences will follow:

1. If the manager is able to pass on an obligation along with delegation of authority to the subordinate, the rule of single chain of command will be violated.
2. The management at the top shall have great responsibility and yet not be accountable for the results.
3. When a manager is allowed to delegate their obligation, there will be no way of knowing who is accountable for what.

Thus, when authority is delegated, obligations are not passed down the organization; rather, new responsibilities are created at each level.

Parity of authority and responsibility Whenever authority is delegated, responsibility steps in and it coexists with authority. A subordinate can be held accountable for the tasks assigned to them but only to the extent of authority delegated for their accomplishment. By the same rationale, a sales manager cannot be held responsible for production failures for which they were given no authority. Hence, authority and responsibility should relate to the same assignment.

The exception principle Authority is delegated to push down the process of decision making as near the source of information and action as possible. The recipient of authority shall make proper use of it and make all the decisions falling within the scope of their authority. Only in exceptional cases where one cannot make the decision at their level should they refer it upward for consideration by the superior.

By delegating authority, the manager is not absolved of their responsibility. It is, therefore, essential that the manager devises suitable techniques of control to ensure that the authority is properly used and that results are achieved as expected.

Pooling together of the authority of two or more managers before a problem can be solved or a decision made is described as *splintered authority*.

Shared authority Where the superior and the subordinates together come to a decision, it is known as *shared authority*.

Barriers to delegation

There are two main barriers to delegation: the attitude of the executive and the attitude of the subordinate.

Attitude of the executive There are managers who prefer to withhold a larger part of their authority under the pretext that even after delegation they continue to remain responsible for the accomplishment of tasks assigned to them. Such an attitude is self-defeating and results in real limits to delegation.

Certain personal attitudes are important in making delegation real and effective. Every delegation must involve a degree of authority or discretion. The decision taken by a subordinate is not likely to be exactly similar to that of the delegator. Hence, a manager should be receptive to the ideas or initiatives of others. In the same way, for making delegation effective, the manager must not only be willing to push decision-making power down the levels of the organization structure but also be prepared to allow others to make mistakes. It is all the more essential that the manager trusts their subordinates.

Inability to direct well is another barrier to successful delegation by the top executives.

Attitude of the subordinate There are real obstacles to a subordinate accepting delegation. Even when a manager is willing to delegate a part of their authority, the subordinate finds it more convenient and easy to take dictation and guidance from the higher-ups rather than to involve themselves in the creative process of decision making.

Fear of criticism may also deter the subordinate from accepting delegation. Lack of confidence is yet another serious problem.

In addition, lack of necessary information and resources to do the assigned duties may make the subordinate hesitant in accepting delegation.

Decentralization

While *delegation* refers primarily to the entrustment of duties and attendant authority from one individual to another, *decentralization* applies to systematic delegation of authority in an organization-wide context. Delegation can take place from one individual to another and lead to completion of the process. However, decentralization is complete only when the fullest possible delegation is made to all or to most of the people in an organization and they are delegated with a specific kind of authority.

Thus, delegation is the process and decentralization is the result. Delegation is from person to person, whereas decentralization is usually a complete block. Delegation is a must where organization structure is present, whereas decentralization may be optional. In delegation, control lies at the top; in decentralization, control lies in the decentralized unit. An organization can delegate well without enough decentralization. However, this does not mean decentralization can be totally absent in an organization. It always exists in a large or small degree in all organizations.

From the organizational point of view, there is no such thing as absolute centralization or delegation. The existence of the former may be conceptually possible only in a one-man organization.

Delegation involves sharing of either managerial work or operating work between a manager and subordinates, whether they are managers or non-managers. In contrast, decentralization is concerned with the sharing of managerial work only between two managers.

Decentralization versus centralization

Robert Staiger (1995) has suggested that certain things should not be decentralized. These include:

- The responsibility for objective determination
- The responsibility for determination of overall comprehensive business planning and policy
- The final responsibility for business control, that is, control should be reserved at the top
- The responsibility for quality design and quality standards
- Final approval of the budget and other financial plans
- The decision on manner of raising of capital and its application
- The responsibility for deciding various capital projects like large-scale, long-term commitments for a financial project

With the emergence of a participative approach, some of Staiger's observations do not hold much value in today's competitive business environment. To ensure enhanced commitment to deliver results, for example, objectives determination nowadays is made more participative with distributed decision making, rather than being formulated as a centralized decision at the top.

Criteria for decentralization

Earnest Dale (1965) through his research has listed the following criteria for decentralization:

- **The number of decisions**: The greater the number of decisions made down the management hierarchy, the more is the decentralization.
- **Importance and significance of the decision**: The more important and costlier the decision made down the management hierarchy, the more is the degree of decentralization.
- **Effects of decisions**: The more functions are affected by decisions made at the lower levels and, in turn, affect the organization structure, the greater is the degree of decentralization.
- **Checking of decisions**: The lesser the checking required on decisions made lower down the management hierarchy, the more is the decentralization.
- **Decentralization is best where no change has to be made**: In a relatively stable work environment, which need not get influenced by changes in the external environment, the degree of decentralization can be more.

W. Newman (1951) has explained the degree of decentralization in the following terms:

- Where there is complete reservation of authority, that is, absence of decentralization, it is a total case of centralization.
- If plans, policies, and decisions are made at the top, there will be a lesser degree of decentralization.
- Where there is full authority for operating decisions at the lower levels, with practically no reservation or limitation, then it is a high degree of decentralization but not total decentralization.
- If plans, policies, and authorities are pushed down to the lower levels, it becomes a bottom-up organization.

Need for decentralization

Despite the conflicting observations about decentralization, organizations may be required to decentralize or distribute authority in certain circumstances.

According to Louis A. Allen (1958), the need for decentralization arises due to any of the following reasons:

- To reduce or ease the burden of the top executives
- To provide opportunities for greater diversification of product lines
- To pay special attention towards a particular product line or product market
- To promote development of future managerial potential for business
- To boost the morale of all organization members
- To keep pace with technological development, for example, the electronics industry where requirement for decentralization is more because it is growing rapidly

Some of the advantages of decentralization are:

- It reduces the burden of top executives.
- It motivates subordinates to take initiatives and also perform better.
- It boosts the morale of subordinates.
- It helps in development of managerial potential.
- It ensures product-line diversification.
- It ensures division of work.
- It establishes better coordination and operation.
- It ensures effective control, that is, profit-centre decentralization.
- It ensures quicker decisions; decentralization facilitates management by objective (MBO).

Some of the limitations of decentralization are:

- It entails excessive operational cost.
- There is lack of divisibility.
- Non-availability of good executives can be a constraint.
- There is potential wastage of staff service.
- It may result in difficulties in policy control—different decentralized units may have differences in policy approach.
- There may be obstacles in case of an emergency. In emergency situations, the problem could be of getting a quicker decision from the central office.
- There is a potential loss of control.

Problems in achieving decentralization

Achieving decentralization in organizations is not easy. Executives and subordinates are always at loggerheads on decentralization issues. In some organizations, subordinates allege that management adopts the decentralization option to get their part of job done through them. Conversely, some executives believe that decentralization will only add to their woes, as subordinates always need to be guided, which reduces the effective time available for other managerial work.

The main issues in implementing decentralization are:

- Executives may be unwilling to delegate, mainly in the belief that they can do everything better.
- Executives may lack the ability to direct others.

- Executives may not have confidence and faith in subordinates—the superior only gives lip service to decentralization while the subordinate does not even know what their job is. This is often because the executive fears that they might be taken out of their position. Generally, promotee executives belong to this category. One remedy is training the subordinate or bringing in new subordinates.
- The executive may fear a situation where the subordinate develops too much authority.
- Executives may be handicapped by temperamental aversion to taking a chance, notwithstanding the clarity of delegation. The greater the number of subordinates, the higher the chance of decentralization, and greater would be the likelihood of problems faced. To delegate is to take a calculated risk.

The problems in achieving decentralization can be addressed through attitudinal change. One needs to ascertain why the executives are reluctant to delegate. Sometimes, superiors give orders to subordinates and subordinates also show their reluctance to take responsibility. Such reluctance in subordinates to take responsibility can be attributed to the following reasons:

- There may be lack of faith in self and a sense of dependence, with the subordinate preferring to refer back the work to the superior.
- The fear of criticism has a crippling effect. If something goes wrong and the superior publicly criticizes the subordinate, it will have a negative effect.
- Subordinates may refuse to take up responsibility because of lack of information and resources.
- Subordinates avoid taking up responsibility due to work overload.
- Lack of positive incentive and inducement may also deter a subordinate from assuming responsibility.

The application of decentralization requires social and administrative adjustment of attitudes and behaviour patterns of the individuals involved. In a dynamic society, such adjustment is a common occurrence. This adjustment can take place keeping in view that every individual behaves differently. Even the best plan will not be achieved until and unless personal adjustments are made.

LINE AND STAFF RELATIONS

Basically, organizations are tightly knit together by the cord of authority relationships, whatever the way of structuring an organization. Such authority relationships act as a cohesive force and integrate the whole organization. The types and degree of authority vary with the decision-making levels. Different authority relationships basically revolve around line and staff relationships. *Line functions* are those that have a direct influence on accomplishing the objectives of an organization. *Staff functions* help the line to work effectively to accomplish organizational objectives. However, in reality, it is difficult to separate direct and supportive functions. In fact, based on the nature of the organization, such categorization of line and staff functions varies. In a manufacturing organization, production and sales are considered as line functions, and finance, purchase, personnel, maintenance, quality control, etc., are classified as staff functions.

Line and staff functions are defined on the basis of two viewpoints: functional viewpoint and authority relationships viewpoint. Allen defined line functions as 'those which have direct responsibility for accomplishing the objectives of the enterprise' and staff functions as 'those elements of the organization that help the line to work more effectively in accomplishing the primary objectives of the enterprise'. Since organizational objectives determine the line and staff functions, any change in objectives may result in changes in the line and staff functions. Principal distinctions may be made between line and staff as illustrated in Table 3.1.

Table 3.1 Line and Staff Distinction

Line authority	Staff authority
A line manager is a generalist.	A staff manager is a myopic.
A line manager directs others.	A staff manager assists others.
A line manager delegates authority.	A staff manager serves authority.
A line manager trains subordinates.	A staff manager investigates the problem.
A line manager uses sanctions.	A staff manager solves special problems.
A line manager exerts control over subordinates.	A staff manager makes plans.
A line manager has veto power.	A staff manager supports the line.
A line manager takes operating decisions.	A staff manager provides ideas to the line.
A line manager has the final responsibility.	A staff manager has special expertise.

Line and staff managers are expected to work harmoniously to achieve organizational goals. Yet, their relationship is one of the major sources of conflict in most organizations. Since such conflicts lead to loss of time and organizational effectiveness, it is always desirable to identify the sources of such conflict and initiate necessary actions to overcome the same. Theoretically, it is impossible to differentiate line and staff functions, which is also one of the reasons why conflicts cannot be avoided. Line and staff conflicts can be grouped into three categories: conflicts due to the viewpoint of the line, conflicts due to the viewpoint of the staff, and conflicts due to the nature of line and staff relationships.

Conflicts due to the viewpoint of the line can be understood in terms of the following factors:

- **Lack of accountability**: Line managers generally perceive that staff managers are not accountable for their actions. Such lack of accountability on the part of the staff can cause neglect of the overall organizational objectives. Staff managers are quick to take credit for achieving results that have come through because of the efforts of line managers. On the other hand, blame for anything that goes wrong is promptly put on the line. Such perceptions are one of the most important sources of conflict between line and staff.
- **Encroachment on line authority**: Line managers often allege that staff managers encroach upon their authority by giving recommendations on matters that are outside their purview. Such encroachment influences the working of their department and often leads to hostility, resentment, and reluctance to accept staff recommendations.
- **Dilution of authority**: Staff managers often dilute the authority of line managers and also belittle the latter's responsibility.
- **Theoretical basis**: Being specialists, staff managers generally think within the ambit of their specialization. They fail to relate their suggestions with the actual reality and are unable to understand the actual dimensions of a problem. This is because they are cut off from the day-to-day

operations. This may result in impractical suggestions, making it difficult to achieve organizational goals.

Conflicts due to staff viewpoint can arise due to the following factors:

- **Lack of proper use of the staff**: The staff alleges that line managers often take decisions without any input from the staff. The line just informs the staff after taking decisions. Moreover, even in cases where the line takes its own decision without consulting the staff, the staff is made responsible if anything goes wrong.
- **Resistance to new ideas**: Line managers often resist new ideas as they feel that implementing new things would imply that something is wrong with the present way of doing work. Such rigidity of line managers dissuades the staff from implementing new ideas in the organization and this adds to their frustration.
- **Lack of proper authority**: The staff often alleges that despite having the best solutions to the problems in their areas of specialization, they fail to contribute to organizational goals due to lack of authority.

Conflicts that arise due to the very nature of line and staff relationships can be explained in terms of the following factors:

- **Different backgrounds**: Line and staff managers are usually from different backgrounds. Normally, line people are senior to staff in terms of organizational hierarchy and levels. Staff people are relatively young and better educated. Some of them may even look down on the line. Such complex relationships create an atmosphere of mistrust between line and staff.
- **Lack of demarcation between line and staff authority**: In practice, it is difficult to make a distinction between line and staff authority. Overlapping and duplication of work create a gap between authority and responsibility of line and staff. Each tries to shift the blame to the other.
- **Lack of proper understanding of authority**: Failure to understand authority causes misunderstandings between the line and the staff. This leads to encroachment and creates conflict.

To overcome line and staff conflict, it is necessary for an organization to follow certain norms:

- **Clarity in relationships**: Duties and responsibilities of the line and the staff should be clearly laid down. Relationships of the staff with the line and their scope of authority need to be clearly defined. Similarly, for line managers also, they should be made responsible for decision making and they should have corresponding authority for the same. The line should be allowed the freedom to modify, accept, or reject the recommendations or advice of the staff.
- **Proper use of the staff**: Line managers must know how to maximize organizational effectiveness by optimizing the expertise of staff managers. They are required to be trained on the same. Similarly, staff managers should also help the line to understand how the staff can help the line to improve their activities.
- **Completed staff work**: This denotes careful study of the problem, identifying possible alternatives for the problem, and providing recommendations based on the compiled facts. This will result in closely engaged staff work and encourage pragmatic suggestions.
- **Holding the staff accountable for results**: Once, the staff becomes accountable, they will be cautious about their recommendations. The line, in turn, will also have confidence in staff recommendations as they become accountable for the results.

SPAN OF MANAGEMENT

Span of management is the limitation of the number of subordinates who can be effectively supervised by a manager in the discharge of their management duties. The incapacity of human beings restricts the number of persons who can be managed effectively. Actual spans in business organization indicate that there is no particular perfect number that can be universally applied; however, all management experts agree that there is a definite span limiting the number of subordinates who can be managed effectively by one executive. There are various approaches to determining the ideal span of management:

- **Classical approach**: This approach deals with generalizations embodying specific numbers of subordinates for an effective span. Classicists have suggested spans of upper and top levels from three to seven to eight subordinates. However, the recent operational approach has suggested that there are too many variables in management and no exact number can be fixed.
- **A. V. Graicunas' theory on superior–subordinate relationships (1933)**: A. V. Graicunas, a French management consultant, analysed superior–subordinate relations and classified these relationships into three forms. His study did not emanate from empirical observation, but was rather based upon theoretical projection by mathematics. His formula is based on geometric increase in the complexities of managing as the number of subordinates increases. The three types of superior–subordinate relationships identified by him are:
  i. **Direct single relationships**: Such relationships arise from the direct and individual contacts of the superior with the subordinates. Thus, if A as a superior has three subordinates, namely, X, Y, and Z, there would be three direct single relationships.
  ii. **Direct group relationships**: This arises between the superior and the subordinates in all possible combinations. Thus, a superior may consult their subordinate with a second in attendance, or with all their subordinates or with various combinations of them. Depending upon possible combinations, there would be nine relationships like X with Y, Y with Z, X with Y and Z, and so on.
  iii. **Cross-relationships**: These are mutual relationships among subordinates necessary for working under a common superior, such as X and Y, and Y and X. The two relationships are different because in the first case Y consults X and in the second case X consults Y, and in both cases the situations may be different. There are six cross-relationships for the subordinates.

On the basis of the analysis of the three types of superior–subordinate relationships, Graicunas developed the following mathematical formula:

If n = number of subordinates, then

$$\text{Direct single relationships} = n$$

$$\text{Direct group relationships} = n\left(\frac{2^n}{2} - 1\right)$$

$$\text{Cross-relationships} = n\,(n-1)$$

$$\text{Total relationships} = n\left(\frac{2^n}{2} + n - 1\right)$$

On the basis of this formula, the possible relationships with a variable number of subordinates rise very rapidly.

Where there are four subordinates under one superior, the relationship will be:

$$4\left(\frac{2^4}{2}+4-1\right)=44$$

When the subordinates are increased by one, that is, from 4 to 5, the number of relationships will be:

$$5\left(\frac{2^5}{2}+5-1\right)=100$$

Wide Versus Narrow Spans

Span of management directly affects the number of levels in the organization. *Wider spans* of management lead to flat organization structures, whereas *narrow spans* of management result in tall organization structures.

A narrow span, which results in many levels in the organization, creates problems in terms of both cost and efficiency. First, the levels are very expensive because it requires more supervisory staff, which leads to larger expenses in the form of executive remuneration. Expense is further increased on account of additional subordinates for the larger number of managers. Hence, at both executive and operative levels, cost increases. Secondly, communication in a tall organization has several limitations. Communication through scalar chain has to travel various levels, which not only delays it from reaching the appropriate points but also runs the risk of the communication getting distorted or sometimes being missed absolutely. Thirdly, narrow span (tall structure) presents problems in coordination and control, as the top management is much farther away from the operatives where actual work is performed. However, encouraging lower-level managers to develop cross-relationships can eliminate this problem. Fourthly, narrow span also adversely affects employee morale. A subordinate who finds himself/herself submerged at the bottom of the organization pyramid feels sensitive about the fact that they get no recognition from the top organization (leadership). Due to such placement, they get very few opportunities to develop self-reliance and initiative, and hardly enjoy any feeling of belongingness. Hence, employees may be less enthusiastic in their jobs.

Finally, narrow spans also reduce opportunities for management development. Too many levels hardly allow for delegation of any real authority and limit the supervision to very few activities at lower levels. The result is that the subordinate is deprived of the benefit of managing a larger number of related activities.

Notwithstanding their limitations, tall structures have certain advantages such as reinforcing of the authority relationships through emphasis given to status and providing opportunity for promotion because of the many positions involved.

A wide span or flat structure calls for supervision of too many people. Supervision will become less effective because the manager will not have sufficient time and energy to attend to each of their subordinates. The large number of contacts may also distract them to the extent that they neglect important questions of policy.

Advantages in a flat structure are that the communication chain is shorter and that it is free from hierarchical control. Subordinates enjoy a greater degree of autonomy and develop an independent spirit. The flat structure also reduces organizational cost since lesser numbers of executives are required.

The factors responsible for a wide span may be identified in terms of:

- the trend towards decentralization,
- improved communication technology,
- the increasing size of organizations, and
- the new pattern of leadership evolving from a growing acceptance of group processes.

While deciding the span, the attendant advantages and disadvantages of the two options should be carefully examined in terms of tangible as well as intangible factors, and the actual span should be determined keeping in view all the pertinent factors in a particular situation at a given time.

Factors Determining Spans

The determination of the span of management depends upon the number of relationships that can be managed by a superior. As such, the important determinant is the manager's ability to reduce the frequency and time impact of superior–subordinate relationships, though this ability itself is determined by several other factors. Factors that determine the optimum span may be stated as follows:

- **Ability of executives**: The supervisory ability of executives is composed of the capacity to comprehend problems quickly, to get along well with people, and to command respect and loyalty from subordinates. In addition, communication skill, decision-making prowess, leadership ability, and controlling power are important determinants of supervisory ability. Accordingly, executives differ from one another in their ability to supervise others. When the ability is high, a larger number of subordinates can be supervised.
- **Capacity of subordinates**: Efficient and trained subordinates can discharge their duties satisfactorily without much help and direction from the superior. In such a case, the span may be larger because a superior will be required to devote less time in managing them. Thus, changes in subordinates may make the span narrower.
- **Nature of work**: When the work involves routine and repeated efforts or where the executive manages similar functions, they become well versed with their jobs and can handle a larger number of subordinates. On the other hand, activities and functions with a degree of variability and that are probably more complex in nature increase the number of interrelationships and demand more time from the executive. Such a situation will warrant a fewer number of persons to be handled by the supervisor.
- **Time required to be spent on supervision**: Every manager needs to use part of their time in contacting/attending to persons as well as in doing the administrative job of planning and policymaking. These functions are not directly related to guiding the subordinates. Hence, the span to a great extent varies on the availability of time for supervision.
- **Delegation of authority**: Ambiguous or inadequate authority delegation directs a disproportionate amount of time of the manager in counselling and guidance of subordinates. Where subordinates are delegated with authority that is clearly defined as well as sufficient to carry out the assigned duties, and provided they are well trained, they would considerably reduce the time and attention required of the senior. Here, the span of the executive can be large.
- **Degree of decentralization**: An executive operating in a decentralized set-up is relieved of much of the burden of making programmed decisions and can afford to supervise a relatively larger number of subordinates.
- **Use of objective standards**: Reviewing the performance of subordinates can be done either by personal observation or through use of objective standards. In the latter case, the manager is saved of

many time-consuming relationships and can concentrate on points of strategic importance, thereby widening the span of supervision.

- **Territorial continuity of functions supervised**: Where functions are geographically separated, supervision of components and personnel becomes more difficult and time-consuming. The manager must spend considerable time in visiting the separate units and make use of more time-consuming formal means of communication. Geographic continuity of functions supervised by the manager, therefore, reduces his/her span of control.
- **Availability of staff assistance**: When an organization is equipped with staff services, subordinates gain much of their guidance on methods, schedules, and personnel problems from staff experts and, thus, require fewer contacts with line managers. The manager normally gets involved only when the staff fails to run the show. Thus, provision of staff assistance helps executives to supervise a large number of subordinates.

Allen has suggested specific points to be considered while determining spans: (1) diversity, (2) dispersion, (3) complexity, (4) volume, and (5) attitude towards delegation.

Additional factors that determine spans in an organization include:

- Training of the manager
- Capacity and mindset of subordinates
- Dynamic and complex nature of activities
- The degree to which objective standards are established
- The extent of delegation and the clarity of delegation
- Existence of a good communication system
- Degree of decentralization

OPEN SYSTEMS APPROACH IN ORGANIZATIONS

The systems theory has unearthed the process of understanding the complex world of systems. In organizations, systems theory is applied through systems analysis. It is done through systems thinking, which helps one to study the organization, its patterns, structures, and events. Thus, systems thinking provides one with a broader perspective to identify the actual issues and their causes, acting more like a diagnostic tool, and accordingly facilitates the appropriate process of intervention to correct the organizational odds.

One can list the six systems principles in the following manner:

1. Organizational systems follow patterns of events in a cycle.
2. Each pattern of event indicates some specific phases, and at each phase, the behaviour of the organization changes.
3. Systems interpret patterns and events in their organizations.
4. Systems seek balance with the organizational environments.
5. When systems do not interact with their environment, they become limited.
6. A circular relationship exists between the overall system and its parts.

Traditionally, an organization is viewed as a closed system. The closed systems perspective considers everything to be deterministic; hence, the organization structure should be more or less fixed, depending on the preferences of a specific organization. However, in the changing dynamics of today, the open systems approach to organization is considered superior and practical. This approach has been characterized by importation of energy, throughput, output, cycles of events, negative entropy, information input, steady or dynamic homeostasis, differentiation, integration and coordination, and equifinality. Such characteristics actually emerged from the consideration of the organization as a living system. According to Boone and Kurtz (1992), *cycle of events* is a process in an open systems organization through which it receives inputs from the environment and then transforms them and generates output. Negative entropy represents the ability of the organization to autonomously repair itself and then survive and grow by importing resources from its environment and transforming them into outputs. Organizations through steady or dynamic homeostasis maintain equilibrium over a period of time. Through differentiation, organizations develop structures and develop specialized functions. The equifinality principle of the open systems organization helps in achieving objectives through several different courses of action.

The operational research or management science approach has emerged as a separate discipline from the systems perception of organization. It is an extension of the systems analysis and systems engineering approach. *Operational research* conceptualizes the general pattern of conceiving, designing, and implementing with some given specifications, optimizing resource utilization in an efficient and effective manner. In the process it also tries to reduce the negative side effects. The systems engineering approach encompasses technological, organizational, and societal systems. It follows four different stages: systems analysis, systems design, implementation, and operation. At the systems analysis stage, the organization defines the systems, identifies different subsystems, and establishes their interrelationships. At the systems design stage, the organization builds the systems model, optimizing the resources. At the implementation stage, the final design is built, keeping in view various eventualities so that it can cope with uncertainties. Finally, at the operation stage, supports are provided to continue with the designed systems, documenting the activities involved, user manuals, training, etc. Thus, both systems analysis and systems engineering provide a general way of thinking of practical situations requiring the creation of a system that achieves some predefined purpose.

The term *orchestra organization* is used in the open systems perspective because like an open systems organization, an orchestra organization, too, is a complex set of interdependent subsystems. An open systems organization takes inputs from the environment, processes them, and produces outputs. Efficient interactions with the environment and various subsystems determine the success of an organization. When the organization is efficient, it not only considers relationships and reciprocal influences between the organization and its environment, it even considers extending its sphere beyond the formal boundary, through an efficient boundary-spanning subsystem. *Boundary-spanning subsystems* play the buffering role to account for external organizational uncertainty. *Processes* or *throughputs* in a typical orchestra organization are specialized functions that are distinct and interdependent. Even the coordinating function is considered as throughput, as it helps in the goal of achieving the output.

In this chapter, the basic issues surrounding the organizing of activities have been discussed. The success of an organization largely depends on the way it organizes its activities. While organizing, it is necessary to follow certain basic principles and what may be applicable for one organization may not be the right fit for another. While there are many forms of organizational structures, selecting an appropriate structure for an organization largely depends on their style of managing activities and priorities. A manager has to study all facets of the organizational life before finalizing a structure. The structure sets the culture and it often creates an organizational climate. Hence, changing an existing structure requires careful study of the problems. Quite often, the changing strategies of an organization influence structure. Globalization has now intensified competition among organizations. It has also led to the emergence of various new issues like market consolidation through mergers and acquisition, addressing multicultural complexities, and corporate governance aspects. For obvious business reasons, organizations around the world now focus on achieving economies of scale by locating their manufacturing and back-office jobs in countries that offer competitive wage costs. All these now require organizations to experiment with their structure and identify the best fit. It is always desirable that an organization's structure is chosen based on a consideration of multidimensional aspects.

Case CEOs Can Work as a Team: Lessons from Wipro

Wipro, India's third largest software company, after the departure of its former CEO Vivek Paul, was directly controlled by Azim Premji, chairman and owner (by virtue of owning a more than 80 per cent stake in the company), who also had to act as CEO. The roles of chairman and CEO were difficult to manage simultaneously, but Premji demonstrated efficiency in handling all matters including operations. In fact, during Premji's tenure, Wipro grew almost three times in revenue (from USD 1.35 billion in 2005 to USD 4 billion in 2008). In the CEO's role, Premji had to look after day-to-day functioning, which, however, became counterproductive at times. Premji himself realized the conflict brought about by his involvement in the day-to-day functional nitty-gritty since the chairman's role was more strategic, and in a turbulent global market, it was more important for the chairman to reinforce the strategies of the company to sustain itself and grow amidst competition.

In mid-April 2008, Premji appointed two CEOs, perhaps not a very common step in the corporate world. Girish Paranjpe and Suresh Vaswani, two veterans of Wipro, were appointed as CEOs of the company. Wipro's IT business is also divided into two organizations, namely Wipro Infotech and Wipro Technologies. Wipro Infotech's business domains cover India, Asia Pacific, and West Asia, while Wipro Technologies provides business, technology, and process solutions to businesses in various countries. Operationally, Wipro follows a matrix structure encompassing three verticals and two horizontals. The *verticals* are technology, enterprise, and financial services. Technology verticals look after product engineering and telecom services. Enterprise verticals cover the businesses of manufacturing, healthcare, and retail. Financial services verticals focus on the banking and financial services industry (BFSI). The *horizontals* are global business practices specializing in testing, packaging, and technology infrastructure services and business process outsourcing (BPO) operations. Each vertical and horizontal was headed by executives who reported to two CEOs. Premji believes that since both the CEOs had been groomed in-house and had worked together for years, they worked as a team. The 'two-man army' model was also considered by the CEOs as the better option to take the company on the growth path.

Usually, the instance of joint CEOs is seen in cases of mergers, and is mainly meant to dispel any apprehension on the part of minority stakeholders. However, globally, the performance of joint CEOs has a poor track record. An example of an unpleasant experience with two chairmen can be traced to the global fast-moving consumer goods (FMCG) major Unilever. The company functioned with two chairmen for almost 75 years. Ultimately, the joint leadership structure could not be sustained by the company and from 2005 onwards, it had to switch over to the single-leadership model.

In contrast, for Wipro, the joint leadership worked well. With increased business volumes and revenue earnings, Wipro perhaps is an example to emulate and proof that joint leadership can also work well.

CASE QUESTION

Read the case carefully and draw an organizational structure with two CEOs, fitting them in a matrix structure. Develop your structure using Wipro as a model.

SUMMARY

- Organizational structure helps to determine the authority relationships among the members of an organization, and hence, it influences the behaviour of individuals, groups, and divisions within the organization.
- There are various terms related to organization that can be defined separately, such as organization, organizing, and organizational structure. The term *organization* is used to refer to a social group that is deliberately created and maintained to achieve some intended goals. *Organizing* is defined as a management process. *Organizational structure*, on the other hand, is the outcome of the organizing process.
- Organizations are viewed from a systems perspective as systems denote a collection of parts (or subsystems) that are integrated to accomplish the overall goal of an organization.
- There are five types of organizational structure according to Mintzberg. They are: machine bureaucracy, professional bureaucracy, adhocracy or innovative forms, simple or entrepreneurial forms, and divisional forms.
- Organizational structures are divided into four major types: functional structure, divisional structure, hybrid structure, and matrix structure.
- The grouping of activities into different units is known as *departmentation*. There are different patterns of departmentation such as departmentation by functions, departmentation by products, departmentation by territories, departmentation by processes, departmentation by customers, and departmentation by time.
- To adapt to global business requirements, organizations may adopt global, international, multidomestic, transnational, informated, cellular, or networked structures. With the advancement of information systems, organizations now operate in distributive environments with flexibility in the nature and way of work. This results in *e-organizations* or *virtual organizations*, which do not have a central geographical location and interact essentially through computer networks.
- Authority delegation is the key to organization. No organization can survive without delegation because it would then imply the non-existence of subordinates in the organization and one man doing everything.
- *Delegation* primarily refers to the entrustment of authority and responsibility to another person or persons. *Decentralization* applies to systematic delegation of authority in an organization-wide context. Therefore, delegation is the process while decentralization is the result.
- *Line functions* are those that have a direct influence on accomplishing the objectives of an organization. *Staff functions* help the line to work effectively to accomplish organizational objectives. There are also various conflicts that arise between line and staff.
- *Span of management* is the limitation of the number of subordinates who can be effectively supervised by a manager in the discharge of their management duties. Span of management is usually classified as wide and narrow.
- The systems theory has unearthed the process of understanding the complex world of systems. In organizations, this theory is applied through systems analysis. Thus, systems thinking provides a

broader perspective to identify the actual issues and their causes, acting more like a diagnostic tool, and accordingly facilitates the appropriate process of intervention to correct the organizational odds. This is known as the *open systems approach.*

KEY TERMS

Adhocracy: Adhocracy means purposefully cracking down a system with a purpose. In organizations with an adhocratic structure, employees are entrusted with decision-making authority because of the absence of hierarchical barriers and because they can work in a concerted manner to achieve the intended business results for the organization.

Boundary-spanning subsystem: A boundary-spanning subsystem plays a buffering role to account for any external organizational uncertainty. When the organization is efficient, it not only considers relationships and reciprocal influences between the organization and its environment, it even considers extending its sphere beyond the formal boundary, through an efficient boundary-spanning subsystem.

Decentralization: Decentralization applies to systematic delegation of authority in an organization-wide context.

Delegation: Delegation refers primarily to the entrustment of duties and attendant authority from one individual to another. When a manager delegates authority, he/she creates subordinate positions and thereby makes an organization possible.

Departmentation: There are different organizational structures based on the grouping of activities into different units. The process of grouping activities is known as departmentation.

Exception principle: Authority is delegated to push down the process of decision making as near the source of information and action as possible. The recipient of authority makes all the decisions falling within the scope of their authority. Only in exceptional cases when they cannot make the decision at their level, they are forwarded to be taken up by the superior. This is known as the exception principle.

Operational research: It conceptualizes the general pattern of conceiving, designing and implementing with some given specifications, thus, optimizing resource utilization in an efficient and effective manner.

Organization structure: It denotes the pattern of relational network between different hierarchies and is characterized by the activity–authority relationship chart.

Organizing: It is defined as a management process of identifying, classifying, grouping, and assigning various activities with adequately defined authority relationships to achieve intended goals

Professional bureaucracy: Organizations with a professional bureaucratic structure manage their operations with professional employees. Such a structure focuses less on formalizations of systems and procedures, believes in allowing a high degree of functional autonomy, empowers the employees, and encourages learning and competency development to build the employees' capabilities and encourage them to perform well.

Span of management: Span of management refers to the limitation of the number of subordinates who can be effectively supervised by a manager in the discharge of their management duties. The incapacity of human beings restricts the number of persons who can be managed effectively.

Strategic business unit: In a strategic business unit (SBU), departmentation of an organization is based on a product line or a product mix, wherein one business head manages its activities independently. Each SBU's competitor groups are different.

REVIEW QUESTIONS

1. Explain the concept of line and staff organization. Why is conflict between line and staff common? How can such conflict be reduced?
2. Describe the advantages and disadvantages of functional and divisional departmentation.
3. What is the important basis of departmentation?
4. Define *organizing*. Explain whether the terms *organizing* and *organization structure* differ.
5. What are the essential elements of organizing?
6. Define *span of management*. Why is it important for structuring an organization?
7. What is *delegation*? List the major benefits of delegation of authority.
8. Explain the difference between *delegation* and *decentralization*. How can one decide the degree of decentralization?
9. Explain the meaning and scope of *authority*, *responsibility*, and *accountability*.
10. Explain a hypothetical matrix organization structure of a multi-product organization, clearly showing the responsibility assigned to every head.
11. Explain the systems view of organization. How does the systems view influence organizational structure and design?
12. Write short notes on the following:
    - i. Matrix organization
    - ii. Hybrid structure
    - iii. Strategic business units
    - iv. Wide versus narrow span of management
    - v. Decentralization
    - vi. Departmentation by time
    - vii. Barriers to delegation
    - viii. Formal and informal organizations
    - ix. Open systems approach

CRITICAL THINKING QUESTIONS

1. A company has retained you to study their existing structure and reporting relationships. The company believes that since they are operating with state-of-the-art technology and their core business is to extend technical support to telecom majors, there is no point in keeping their brick-and-mortar organization structure in all the countries of their operation. They would, instead, prefer to follow a networked structure, with their controlling office in India. Suggest the right course of action to them.
2. If one wants to switch over from a functional structure to a matrix structure, what are the immediate problems one is likely to face and how should one solve those problems?

REFERENCES

Allen, Louis A. (1958). *Management and Organization*. New York: McGraw-Hill.

Bartlett, C. and S. Ghoshal (1998). *Transnational Management: Text, Cases and Readings in Cross-border Management*. Boston: Irwin/McGraw-Hill.

Boone, Louis E. and David L. Kurtz (1992). *Management*. New York: McGraw-Hill.

Dale, Ernest (1965). *Readings in Management: Landmarks and New Frontiers*. New York: McGraw-Hill.

Drucker, Peter (1954). *The Principles of Management*. New York: HarperCollins Publishers.

Gerth, H. H. and C. W. Mills (eds.) (1946). *From Max Weber: Essays in Sociology*. Oxford: Oxford University Press.

Graicunas, A. V. (1933). 'Relations in Organizations', *Bulletin of the International Management Institute*, 7 March, pp. 39–42.

Kanter, Rosabeth Moss (2001). *Evolve!: Succeeding in the Digital Culture of Tomorrow*. Boston: Harvard Business School Press.

Koontz, H. (1961). 'The Management Theory Jungle', *Academy of Management Journal*, 4 (3): pp. 174–188.

Lewin, A. Y. and C. U. Stephens (1994). 'CEO Attitudes as Determinants of Organizational Design: An Integrated Model', *Organization Studies*, 15 (2): pp. 183–212.

Miles, R. E. and C. C. Snow (1984). 'Designing Strategic Human Resource Systems', *Organizational Dynamics*, 13 (1): pp. 36–52.

Mintzberg, H. (1981). 'Organization Design: Fashion or Fit', *Harvard Business Review*, January–February, pp. 103–166.

Newman, W. H. (1951). *Administrative Action*. Englewood Cliffs, NJ: Prentice Hall.

Staiger, Robert (1995). 'International Rules and Institutions for Trade Policy', in Ronald Jones and Peter Kenen (eds.), *Handbook of International Economics*, vol. 2, Amsterdam: North-Holland.

Toffler, Alvin (1970). *Future Shock*. New York: Bantam Books.

Waterman, R. (1990). *Adhocracy: The Power to Change*. Knoxville, TN: Whittle Direct Books.

FURTHER READING

Beer, M., B. Spector, P. Lawrence, D. Quinn Mills and R. Walton (1984). *Managing Human Assets*. New York: Free Press.

Beer, S. (1972). *The Brain of the Firm*. London: Penguin Press.

——— (1979). *The Heart of Enterprise*. New York: John Wiley & Sons.

Bhattacharyya, D. K. (2006). *Human Resource Management*. 2nd ed. New Delhi: Excel Books.

——— (2007). *Human Resource Research Methods*. New Delhi: Oxford University Press.

——— (2009). *Organizational Behaviour*. New Delhi: Oxford University Press.

Bostrom, R. P. and J. S. Heinen (1977). 'MIS Problems and Failures: A Socio-Technical Perspective', *MIS Quarterly*, 1 (3): pp. 17–32.

Brown, Alvin (1945). *Organization: A Formulation of Principle*. Trenton, NJ: Hibbert Printing Company.

Burns, T. and G. Stalker (1961). *The Management of Innovation*. London: Tavistock.

Burton, Richard M., Gerardine De Sanctis and Borge Obel (2006). *Organizational Design: A Step-by-Step Approach*. Cambridge: Cambridge University Press.

Chandler, A. D. (1962). *Strategy and Structure: Chapters in the History of the Industrial Enterprise*. Cambridge, MA: The MIT Press.

Daft, R. L. and A. Y. Lewin (1990). 'Can Organization Studies Begin to Break Out of the Normal Science Straitjacket? An Editorial Essay', *Organization Science*, 1, pp. 1–9.

Emery, F. E. (1980). 'Designing Socio-Technical Systems for "Greenfield" Sites', *Journal of Occupational Behaviour*, 1 (1): pp. 19–27.

Emery, F. E. and E. L. Trist (1965). 'The Causal Texture of Organizational Environments', *Human Relations*, 18, pp. 21–32.

Fombrum, C. J., N. M. Tichy and M. A. Devanna (1984). *Strategic Human Resource Management*. New York: John Wiley & Sons.

Forrester, K. W. (1958). 'Industrial Dynamics: A Major Breakthrough for Decision Makers', *Harvard Business Review*, 36, pp. 37–66.

Galbraith, J. R. (1995). *Designing Organizations: An Executive Briefing on Strategy, Structure, and Process*. San Francisco: Jossey Bass.

Guest, D. E. (1987). 'Human Resource Management and Industrial Relations', *Journal of Management Studies*, 14 (5): pp. 503–521.

Hammer, Michael and James Champy (1993). *Reengineering the Corporation. A Manifesto for Business Revolution*. London: Nicholas Brealey.

Hendry, C. and A. Pettigrew (1990). 'Human Resource Management: An Agenda for the 1990s', *International Journal of Human Resource Management*, 1 (3): pp. 17–43.

Herbst, P. G. (1974). *Socio-Technical Design: Strategies in Multidisciplinary Research*. London: Tavistock Publications.

Katz, D. and R. L. Kahn (1966). *The Social Psychology of Organizations*. New York: John Wiley & Sons.

Kauffman, D. L. (1980). *Systems One: An Introduction to Systems Thinking*. Minneapolis, MN: Future Systems, Inc., S. A. Carlton.

Khandwalla, P. N. (1977). *The Design of Organizations*. New York: Harcourt, Brace Jovanovich, Inc.

Legge, K. (1995). *Human Resource Management: Rhetorics and Realities*. London: Macmillan.

Likert, R. (1967). *The Human Organization*. New York: McGraw-Hill.

Martinsons, M. G. (1997). 'Human Resource Management Applications of Knowledge-based Systems', *International Journal of Information Management*, 17 (1): pp. 35–53.

Maturana, H. R. and F. J. Varela (1987). *The Tree of Knowledge: The Biological Roots of Human Understanding*. Boston: Shambala.

Mintzberg, H. (1979). *The Structure of Organizations*. Englewood Cliffs, NJ: Prentice Hall.

Perrow, C. (1967). 'A Framework for Comparative Analysis of Organizations', *American Sociological Review*, 32, pp. 194–208.

Pettigrew, A. M., R. Whittington, L. Melin, C. Sanchez-Runde, F. Van den Bosch, W. Ruigrok and T. Numagami (2003). *Innovative Forms of Organizing: International Perspectives*. London: Sage.

Prigogine, I. and I. Stengers (1984). *Order Out of Chaos: Man's New Dialogue with Nature*. London: Bantam Books.

Quinn, J. B. (1980). *Strategies for Change: Logical Incrementalism*. Homewood, IL: Irwin.

Robbins, Stephen and Mary Coulter (2002). *Organizational Behaviour*. New Delhi: Pearson Education.

Rockhart, J. (1982). 'The Changing Role of Information Systems Executive: A Critical Success Factors Perspective', *Sloan Management Review*, 23 (1): pp. 3–13.

Stacey, R. D. (1993). 'Strategy as Order Emerging from Chaos', *Long Range Planning*, 26 (1): pp.10–17.

Thompson, James D. (2001). 'Organizations in Action', in J. M. Shafritz and J. S. Ott (eds.), *Classics of Organization Theory*. Fort Worth: Harcourt College Publishers.

Torrington, D. and L. Hall (1991). *Personnel Management: A New Approach*. Englewood Cliffs, NJ: Prentice Hall.

Tyson, S. (1997). 'Human Resource Strategy: A Process for Managing the Contribution of HRM to Organizational Performance', *International Journal of Human Resource Management*, 8 (3): pp. 277–290.

Waterman, R. (1988). *The Renewal Factor*. New York: Bantam.

Woodward, J. (1965). *Industrial Organization, Theory and Practice*. Oxford: Oxford University Press.

4

Staffing in Organizations

After going through this chapter, you will be able to understand:

- the recruitment function in an organization
- the process of recruitment
- the interview process
- the induction programme
- the process of placement of employees after recruitment

International Sourcing of Workforce at British Petroleum

British Petroleum (BP) is one of the world's largest energy companies, providing its customers with fuel for transportation, energy for heat and light, retail services, and petrochemicals products for everyday items. Recruitment of expatriates is one of the strategies for managing its operations in 55 countries. With more than 3,500 expatriates from over fifty countries, BP today successfully manages its business units that are spread across the globe. Expatriates not only function in critical positions, they also make available the right skill sets whenever critical technology-transfer issues are at stake. One of the most important areas in managing expatriates is to design the global relocation programmes with strategic alignment of business models of BP. It requires developing in-house skill sets, focusing on the work priorities of the organizations, and creating robust processes to manage the business functions. Recruiting expatriates through international sourcing, developing their capabilities in the present and future business, and enabling them to adapt to different cultures are some of the areas of concern in the recruitment and placement of expatriates. By leveraging its in-house capabilities, partnering with global consulting organizations, and the effective management of expatriates, BP was able to make its business goal of becoming a global organization realizable.

INTRODUCTION

Job restructuring may not always be adequate for redeploying the existing workforce in an organization, in which case the organization needs to use external hiring for staffing various positions. The external hiring process succeeds human resource planning (HRP). Through HRP, one can estimate the extent of external hiring required after adjustment of the internal workforce.

Recruitment, selection, induction, and placement are important tools for procuring and effectively using human resources in an organization. All of them are together known as the *staffing* function. While *recruitment* involves employing a suitably trained workforce, *selection* helps in choosing the right candidate for the right job. *Induction* is the process of formally introducing a new employee into the organization, and *placement* is about putting everyone in the right kind of jobs after recruitment. This chapter focuses on these four important organizational activities.

In recent years, recruitment has assumed importance due to its increasing emphasis on human resources. The traditional approach to personnel management was to ensure routine activities for the maintenance of human resources in organizations. Today, human resources are perceived to be as important as any other important resource (physical and financial) of an organization. This change in attitude towards human resources has led to the development of new areas for personnel management. The human resources of an organization are the people who are a part of the organization. Broadly, they may be direct employees, part-time employees, temporary employees, consultants, or any person or persons with a variety of other relationships to the organization. Within the area of human resources, there are two major activities. The first activity is concerned with recruitment, selection, placement, compensation, and appraisal of human resources. This is known as *human resources utilization* or *personnel functions*. The other activity is directed at working with the existing human resources and improving their efficiency and effectiveness. This is known as *human resources development (HRD) functions*, which is designed to enable the existing human resources to learn activities that will help them function effectively in their present jobs as well as in identifiable and undefined jobs in the future.

In view of the increasing importance of human resources, it is now imperative for organizations to retain their workforce and at the same time recruit and select the best possible talent. Most organizations are now facing technological changes, resulting in a radical change in the recruitment process. Such technological changes, among other things, call for hiring a workforce with more skills and knowledge. When one considers the recruitment of the workforce for unskilled jobs, there seems to be no apparent problem for the organization, as unskilled labour is abundantly available in a country like India where the rate of unemployment is high. For highly skilled or technologically skilled employees, that is, those who are in managerial positions with professional skills, the recruitment function is more complex and dynamic.

CONCEPT OF RECRUITMENT

The term *recruitment* can be defined as the process of discovering sources of the workforce to meet the requirements or the staffing schedule of an organization and employing effective measures for attracting that workforce in adequate numbers to facilitate the selection of an efficient workforce.

Functions of Recruitment

The first important task of a recruitment cell is to frame a recruitment policy. Framing a recruitment policy calls for a review of the workforce requirement, that is, an effective forecasting of the workforce that will be required in the near future. Workforce planning and workforce forecasting in an organization depend on many important factors including the present nature of work, the possible changes in the future working of the organization, the workforce records and information available in the organization for the present strength, the diversification plans and programmes of the organization, and the likely environmental changes and the changes necessary in the organization to respond to such environmental changes. In principle, most organizations believe in recruiting the best possible workforce from outside the organization. However, the recruitment policy of some organizations considers recruiting employees based on the recommendations of existing employees or recruiting employees from the wards of existing employees.

An example is the Tata group, where there is a system to recruit employees for unskilled/low-skilled jobs, both technical and non-technical in nature, from the wards of the existing employees. Such a policy of recruitment has been accepted in principle and, therefore, in their manufacturing units, the Tata group maintains a separate employment-exchange record to enlist the names and other details of employees' wards to offer them employment as and when a vacancy arises. However, this kind of a recruitment policy is not followed while hiring for managerial jobs. In such cases, companies are looking for the best available talent. Thus, they either advertise such vacancies in leading newspapers and professional journals, or hire the services of recruitment consultants. They also arrange for campus interviews to recruit fresh talent. Recruitment consultants normally maintain a separate data bank of prospective job seekers and can make available lists of prospective managerial candidates to recruiting companies. In addition to the framing of the recruitment policy, each organization carries out a regular forecasting of workforce requirements to make their recruitment a scientific process of selection.

Internal Recruitment

In certain cases, organizations prefer to have their higher managerial vacancies filled internally. In these cases, organizations need to develop their existing workforce by adopting suitable training and development functions. Training and development may not necessarily ensure the availability of the best talent internally. Organizations are then compelled to recruit from outside sources, as mentioned in the preceding section.

Recruitment Policy

A sound *recruitment policy* calls for adopting scientific processes of recruitment. The recruitment policy needs to be framed in a way that managerial turnover can be substantially reduced, as cost of new recruitment is very high. Without a suitable recruitment policy, it may not be possible for the company to select the right candidate for the right job. A sound recruitment policy, therefore, needs to:

- identify, at the outset, the recruitment needs of the organization,
- identify the preferred sources of recruitment,
- frame suitable criteria for selection, and
- consider the cost of recruitment.

RECRUITMENT PROCESS

As discussed earlier, an organization may recruit either from internal sources, that is, by promoting existing employees to higher positions, or from external sources. Thus, internal and external sources of recruitment are used by an organization according to convenience. Recruitment denotes the process of attracting applicants so that the most suitable ones are selected for a particular job or jobs. Internal recruitment may often avoid unpleasantness, but it is not necessarily effective since it does not provide the organization with many alternatives from whom to select the best possible talent. External sources, on the other hand, provide various opportunities to an organization to select the best and the most suitable candidates from widely dispersed fields.

The requisition for recruitment contains a brief description of the post and the qualification and experience required. The head of the human resource department normally signs such requisitions. Both internal and external sources of recruitment are explored according to the type of personnel required.

The major sources of recruitment for different types of personnel are as follows:

- **Employment exchanges**: These maintain a register of candidates seeking various types of jobs. Under Compulsory Notification of Vacancies Act, 1955, employers are required to notify certain types of vacancies to the nearest employment exchange and recruit candidates from the applicants registered with the exchange. Skilled and unskilled workers as well as clerical staff are recruited through employment exchanges.
- **Consultants and private employment agencies**: Consultants and private agencies assist organizations in locating technical and managerial staff. They charge prescribed fees for their services to an organization.
- **Advertisements in periodicals, newspapers, radio, and television**: Advertising in newspapers, magazines, radio, and television is one of the most effective sources for attracting prospective candidates. It also helps in building the image of an organization because through such advertisements the organization makes certain information like their product, their market share, and their turnover value available to the public in general and the target consumers in particular. Since written press insertions or verbal advertisements through audio and audio-visual methods give first-hand information to prospective jobseekers, each organization is required to give out as much factual information as possible regarding their expectations from the candidates; the required age groups, qualifications, and experience; salary and perks attached to the positions and important conditions of service; and the time limit and mode of applying. There are agencies that help organizations in drafting, publishing, and broadcasting these types of advertisements.
- **Deputation**: This is a well-established practice in public sector undertakings and is meant to develop multiple skills in people. Civil servants are often deputed to many senior and mid-level positions for a specified amount of time.
- **Universities and management institutes**: Recruitment from universities and management institutes is effected through campus interviews. Almost all established private organizations select their management trainees through this method. Some organizations even support the academic ambitions of prospective students by sponsoring their courses. Here, the organization and the prospective student sign a bond stating that the latter would join the organization after the completion of the course.
- **Source of existing employees**: Some organizations recruit from the source of existing employees as a way to ensure commitment and loyalty, and also to motivate the existing employees. This type of recruitment, however, is mostly restricted to clerical and unskilled jobs.
- **Trade unions**: Trade unions may recommend candidates for clerical and unskilled jobs. This practice is not in vogue in many organizations. Only in technical training schemes, trade unions are found to influence the organization to induct their recommended candidates as apprentices.
- **Internet/job sites**: Recruitment through the Internet/job sites has become very popular due to its wide reach among focused jobseekers, immediacy, and cost-effectiveness. Due to the Internet's global reach, organizations are also able to attract the best possible talent. Many placement agents have now started this service to raise their business volume.

The next step in the selection procedure is to develop certain specifications for the desired candidate. It means defining the desired background in terms of education, training, personality, and characteristics of candidates applying for a given vacancy. This, in reality, is an exercise to pre-portray an ideal candidate for a job.

Preliminary Screening of Applicants

The number of applications received against any advertised vacancy is usually large. This creates the problem of selecting the right person from the various candidates. Moreover, conducting tests and interviews for all the candidates may not always be feasible or cost-efficient. To deal with such problems, most organizations first do a preliminary screening to sort out candidates before going ahead with the selection process. There are many different ways of doing a preliminary screening. Some organizations conduct short tests for all the applicants. However, using application blanks is considered to be the best method. An *application blank* is a structured job application either in the company's own format or according to the usual practices. Each organization, before moving towards the selection process, develops its own format of standards or potential attributes to be required of the prospective candidates. This also helps them to define the reasons for rejecting certain candidates. For example, for the post of a stenographer, an organization may define the rejection standards as follows:

- Those who have a shorthand speed of below 100 words per minute and a typing speed of below 40 words per minute
- Those who do not have any work experience
- Those who are above thirty five years of age

By checking the application blank of candidates, an organization may reject a good number of them based on the given rejection parameters. The rejection standards may also be mentioned in the advertisement itself so that the number of applicants is minimized. A sample of an application blank has been appended as Annexure 4.1.

Some organizations also adopt the technique of *successive hurdles* as an effective screening process. This technique requires arranging all the selection factors in their order of importance. For example, if for a particular post an aptitude test is considered to be the most important factor, the first step should be to test the aptitude of the candidates. The other successive tests of qualification, job experience, personality, etc., may be conducted provided that the candidates pass these hurdles one by one.

Review of Application Blanks

The application blank form is designed to have detailed information about the applicants. Some organizations have their own printed forms, whereas others ask the candidates to give their particulars in a standard format to elicit information that includes:

- Personal data and biographical information, that is, name, address, telephone number, age, sex, marital status, children, nationality, and education (school, college, university attended, degree/diploma passed, year of passing, subjects, grade or division obtained, etc.); professional qualification and membership of professional bodies; and languages known (ability to read, write, and speak)
- Chronological employment history (with joining and leaving dates in each case), employer's name and address, nature of business positions and duties held, and reasons for leaving (if any)
- Personal circumstances, specifically to know whether the candidate can relocate elsewhere if required

- Medical history, brief details of any serious illness, number of days not present at work during the last few years on medical grounds, record of hospitalization (if any), declaration of any disability, and any major operation
- Interests, hobbies, sports, and other activities
- Any other aspect that the applicant may like to add in support of his candidature

Several other items may also be included in the application blank with regard to the specific requirements of the organization and the job.

Weighted application blanks are also prepared by some organizations to record personal history items associated with the job success of the candidates. For each item in the application blank, weight factors are predetermined. The importance of weight factors varies for different jobs. For example, in the case of a job for unskilled labourers, education may be given less weight, whereas for executive positions, education receives more weight. Application blanks, therefore, help in comparing the applications of different candidates.

Reference Checking

Some organizations ask for references in the application blank itself to get information on a candidate's character and background. It is preferred that such references are individuals who are not a blood relation or have close acquaintance with the candidates. They can be previous employers and teachers, or other authorities from schools/colleges/universities where the prospective employee studied. Organizations try to verify a candidate's background from the references through the phone, through correspondence, or through personal visits. Most organizations send a brief questionnaire to the references along with a confidential note, requesting them to furnish further details.

Psychological Testing

Generally, psychological testing can be used for various purposes like determining training needs and evaluating training programmes, selection and placement, transfer or promotion, and counselling. In an organization, such testing is primarily used for selection and placement. There can be group or individual tests, instrumental tests, aptitude or achievements tests, and personality and interest tests. Group tests are designed to test a group of candidates simultaneously. Individual tests are for individual candidates at a particular point of time. Instrumental tests can be either group tests or individual tests. When it is an individual test, it makes use of different tools to study the individual candidate's skills and familiarity with the job; in case of a group test, it involves a written test to study the written responses of the candidates. Aptitude tests are intended to assess the potentiality of an applicant to learn the job, whereas achievement tests help to assess how effectively the applicant can perform the job. Conventionally, aptitude tests are administered on freshers, that is, those who do not have any past job experience, while achievement tests are intended for experienced candidates and seek to gauge the previous job performance of the candidate. Such tests have considerable relevance for marketing jobs and for managerial and executive positions.

Psychological tests are mostly designed to measure the aptitude and skills of successful job performers. For selection and placement, most organizations retain the services of consultants and experts rather than just relying on psychological testing. This minimizes the chances of error in selecting candidates for different job positions. Since psychological testing is a complex method and is very diverse, the concept of attitude measurement has been briefly introduced here with simple examples and illustrations, together with some conceptual details about different types of measurement and scales.

ATTITUDE MEASUREMENT

An *attitude* is a mental state of an individual according to which they tend to act or respond to objects, situations, etc. In such cases, their feelings, interests, desires, and so on are vested in the objects and situations. During the course of development, a person acquires tendencies to respond to objects. These learned cognitive mechanisms are called attitudes. Change in knowledge is followed by a change in attitude. Attitudes are not only dependent on knowledge since they are also influenced by emotions. Knowledge reinforces attitudes and reinforced attitudes, in the long run, reinforce individual and group behaviour. Hence, attitudes neither constitute behaviour nor are a cause of behaviour, but relate to an intervening predisposition or a frame of reference that influences the behaviour of an individual. When the interests of an individual are not connected in any way with an object or a situation, their responses towards that particular object or situation will then represent their opinion and not their attitude.

An attitude or a psychic state cannot be observed because psychological variables are either dormant or latent. Due to this reason, attitude measurement is quite difficult. Inference, prediction from behaviour data, interviews with structured questionnaires, and scales are the usual tools for attitudinal measurement.

A basic assumption is that a person's attitude can be measured by asking questions about their thoughts, feelings, and likely actions towards the *attitude object*, which can be people, places, events, etc. Attitudes can also be measured by a quantitative technique, that is, each person's opinion can be represented by a numerical score. A particular test item, or other behaviour indicating an attitude, has the same meaning for all respondents, and, therefore, everyone scores identically for a given response. In a typical *attitude questionnaire*, respondents are asked to indicate whether they agree or disagree with a series of belief statements about an attitude object. Attitudes are arranged along an evaluative continuum ranging from favourable to unfavourable. It is never just one belief statement. This is because in most cases one question will simply not address all the different aspects of a person's attitude. For example, in response to only one question, one might say that they are against cannabis, but tobacco causes as much damage to one's health as cannabis. Thus, using only one question significantly increases the likelihood that irrelevant factors, such as the wording of the question, will create errors. If the responses to a number of questions are summed up together, then it becomes a more valid measure because the error associated with individual items tends to cancel out over a number of items. Each *attitude statement* should represent a different and independent view about the *attitude object* and should cover both favourable and unfavourable attitudes, so that the nature of the response to one item does not affect the response to another item. The assumption is that more extreme scale positions represent more important or more strongly held attitudes.

Techniques of Attitude Measurement

Three popular methods of measuring attitudes are:

1. Thurstone scales
2. Likert scales
3. Semantic differential scales

Thurstone scale

The *Thurstone scale* is the first major technique of attitude measurement. Its basic assumptions are:

- Attitudes lie along an evaluative continuum ranging from favourable to unfavourable.
- Ordering of attitude statements should be such that there appears to be an equal distance between adjacent statements on the continuum, that is, judgements can be made about the degree of discrepancy among different attitudes of individuals.

The steps in a Thurstone scale are as follows:

1. Construct an item pool, that is, a large number of statements giving opinions on an issue.
2. Assemble a group of judges (40 to 60 judges for approximately 100–150 statements).
3. Consider a hypothetical scale running from the most favourable point through a neutral point to the least favourable point.
4. Let the judges consider each item and sort all the items into piles (categories) according to the scale. Usually, 11 intervals between the most favourable category and the least favourable one are regarded as subjectively equal. Therefore, statements selected for use in the final scale are those that have high inter-judge agreement (low spread) and are at relatively equally spaced intervals along the continuum.
5. Finally, a desired number of items, for example, a value of 20 is decided upon for the final scale. Let the 20 scale values be evenly spread across the continuum. Respondents score the scale value of each item agreed upon.

In the case of sweeping statements, such as 'women are less reliable employees because they are likely to leave jobs due to family compulsion', the panel should scrutinize all questions before the interview to ensure that none is discriminating. That companies should provide more crèche facilities is an example of an item pool focusing on the issue of equal opportunities for all.

Likert Scale

Respondents place themselves on an attitude continuum and indicate their level of agreement with a belief statement. The attitude continuum of a Likert scale is illustrated in Figure 4.1.

Strongly agree	Agree	Uncertain	Disagree	Strongly disagree
1	2	3	4	5

Figure 4.1 The Attitude Continuum of a Likert Scale

A person's score is summed up and the resulting total can be used as an index of that person's attitude. This forms the Likert scale.

A *Likert scale* is termed a summated instrument scale. This means that the items making up a Likert scale are summed up to produce a total score. In fact, a Likert scale is a composite of itemized scales. Typically, each scale item will have five categories, with scale values ranging from −2 to +2, with 0 as neutral responses. A typical Likert scale has been provided in Figure 4.2.

Semantic differential scale

Semantic differential scales make extensive use of words rather than numbers. Respondents describe their feelings about the products or brands on scales with semantic labels. When bipolar adjectives are used at the end points of the scales, these are termed semantic differential scales. These scales (Osgood et al. 1957) focus on the meaning people give to a word or a concept. Words have two meanings:

1. Semantic or dictionary meaning
2. Connotative meaning (meanings that a word suggests apart from what it explicitly denotes or names)

The assumption is that a hypothetical semantic space of an unknown number of dimensions is prevalent, in which the meaning of any word or concept can be represented at a particular point. The three major dimensions are:

	Strongly agree	Agree	Neither	Disagree	Strongly disagree
If the price of raw materials fell, firms would reduce the price of their food products.	1	2	3	4	5
Without government regulation, firms would exploit the consumer.	1	2	3	4	5
Most food companies are so concerned about making profits that they do not care about quality.	1	2	3	4	5
The food industry spends a great deal of money making sure that its manufacturing is hygienic.	1	2	3	4	5
Food companies should charge the same price for their products throughout the country.	1	2	3	4	5

Figure 4.2 A Typical Likert Scale

1. Evaluation, that is, how good it is (for example, healthy/unhealthy)
2. Potency, that is, how powerful it is (for example, weak/strong)
3. Activity, that is, how active it is (for example, static/dynamic)

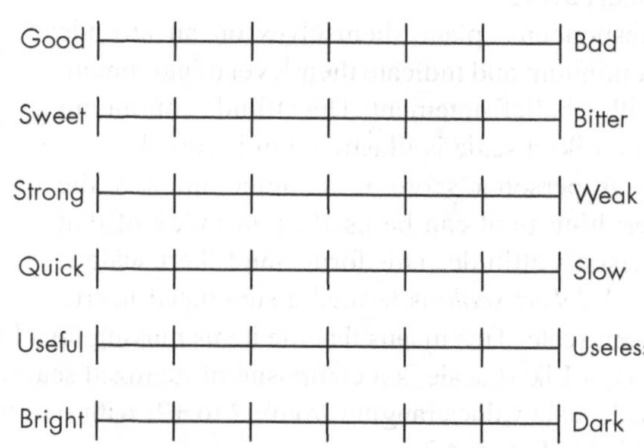

Figure 4.3 Semantic Differential Scale

The midpoint of neutrality is social representations. Ideas and opinions that one holds are moulded by what other people believe and say. 'Our reactions to events, our responses to stimuli, are related to a given definition, common to all the members of the community in which we belong' (Moscovici 1983). Therefore, ideas and opinions are basically social constructions. If social representations are cognitive structures shared on a group basis, agreement between members of that group will increase with age (Augoustinos 1991). Figure 4.3 gives an illustration of a semantic differential scale.

Reliability and validity of attitude measurement scales

Developing a proper scale helps to measure the attitude of newly recruited employees. Each scale has unique properties. Some scales can only establish an association between variables and are limited in their mathematical properties. Other scales have more extensive mathematical properties, while some also hold out the possibility of establishing a cause and effect relationship between variables.

Likert scales are generally more reliable than Thurstone scales. However, validity is still a debatable issue, as results in subsequent attitude measurement exercises, using the same scale, may not always be possible to gather. Nevertheless, using different attitude measurement scales, a near approximation of attitude can be made. When attitude measurement makes use of multiple approaches, results become more appropriate. This is why Glick and Fiske (1996) observed that attitude measurement and behavioural relationship is a complex and subtle business. Some of the problems in attitude measurement can be listed thus:

- Definition of attitude
- Lack of common methods of measurement
- Operationalization of outcome measures
- Self-report

One can use various statistical tools for measurement of attitude. Since attitudes are psychological variables or qualitative variables, the first and foremost task for the rater is to assign numerals to objects, events, or persons. Application of Likert scales, Thurstone scales, etc., can help the interviewer to assign numbers, either discrete or continuous. Analysis of variance, correlation, chi-square test, Kendall's coefficient, and concordance test are some other useful statistical tools for attitude measurement.

The scales that have been described in this chapter are among the most commonly used in attitude mapping for recruitment. There are many more forms of scales. However, familiarity with the scales mentioned here can enable a manager to deal with other scales and successfully conduct research studies.

Levels of Attitude Measurement

There are four levels of attitude measurement: nominal, ordinal, interval, and ratio.

Nominal scale

The *nominal scale* classifies individuals, companies, products, brands, or other entities into categories without any order. This is why this scale is often referred to as a categorical scale. It simply counts the frequency of the cases assigned to various categories. An example of a nominal scale is given in Figure 4.4.

These numbers have no arithmetic properties and the only measure is the mode. This is because by using this scale one simply tries to get a set of frequency counts. Testing of a hypothesis can be done based on the data in the nominal form.

Ordinal scale

Ordinal scales involve ranking along the continuum of the characteristic being scaled. For example, respondents may be asked to rank some brands of shampoo in order of their preferences. An example of an ordinal scale is given in Figure 4.5.

Figure 4.5 gives the researcher the order of preference but does not provide any information about the extent to which one brand is preferred to another. This is known as the *interval* between any two brands.

Which of the following fast-moving consumer goods do you buy at least once a month? (Please tick them)		
Toothpaste	Shampoo	Soap
Deodorant	Hair oil	Detergent

Figure 4.4 Nominal Scale

Order of preference	Brand
1	Sunsilk
2	Rejoice
3	Head & Shoulders
4	Clinic Plus
5	Pantene

Figure 4.5 Ordinal Scale

In addition to the information that is made available through a nominal scale, the ordinal scale can be used to compute the median, quartile, and percentile. One can also compute the rank correlation coefficient (commonly known as Spearman's rank correlation) and Kendall's coefficient of concordance.

Interval scale

The *interval* or *cardinal scale* has equal units of measurement, which makes it possible to interpret not only the order of scale scores but also the distance between them. However, it must be recognized that the zero point on an interval scale is arbitrary and is not a true zero. This, of course, has implications on data manipulation and analysis. Interval scales may be either numeric or semantic. Examples of interval scales in numeric and semantic formats are given in Figure 4.6 and Figure 4.7, respectively.

Ratio scale

The highest level of measurement is a *ratio scale*. This scale has the properties of an interval scale together with a fixed origin or zero point. Examples of variables that are ratio-scaled include weights, lengths, and time. Ratio scales permit the researcher to compare both differences in scores and the relative magnitude of scores. For instance, the difference between 5 and 10 minutes is the same as that between 10 and 15 minutes, and 10 minutes is twice as long as 5 minutes.

The various types of scales used in attitude mapping fall into two broad categories: comparative and non-comparative. In *comparative scaling*, the respondent is asked to compare one brand or product against

Please indicate your views on Sunsilk by scoring them on a scale of 5 down to 1 (5 = excellent; 1 = poor), on each of the criterion listed.

Sunsilk is:	Circle the appropriate score on each line				
Soft	5	4	3	2	1
Nourishing	5	4	3	2	1
Able to make your hair silky	5	4	3	2	1
Possessed of anti-dandruff properties	5	4	3	2	1
Reasonably priced	5	4	3	2	1

Figure 4.6 Interval Scale in Numeric Format

Please indicate your views on Sunsilk by ticking the appropriate responses below:

Sunsilk is:	Excellent	Very good	Good	Fair	Poor
Soft					
Nourishing					
Able to make your hair silky					
Possessed of anti-dandruff properties					
Reasonably priced					

Figure 4.7 Interval Scale in Semantic Format

another. With *non-comparative scaling*, respondents evaluate a single product or brand. Non-comparative scaling is frequently referred to as monadic scaling and this is the more widely used scale in commercial market-research studies.

OTHER MEASURES OF ATTITUDES

Measures of attitude can also be physiological in nature or conducted through attitude surveys.

Physiological Measures

The study of certain syndromes is a way to measure attitude and this is known as physiological measure. Some physiological measures are:

- Skin resistance (Rankin and Campbell 1955)
- Heart rate (Westie and DeFleur 1959)
- Pupil dilation (Hess 1965), that is, attitude inferred by comparing participant's response in the presence of a neutral object and in the presence of the attitude object
- Overt behaviour

Physiological measurement of attitudes faces the following problems:

- Physiological measures indicate intensity and not direction.
- Physiological measures are sensitive to variables other than attitudes (Cacioppo and Petty 1981), for example, vigilance results in lower heart rate, skin response changes in presence of novel or incongruous stimuli, etc.
- The bogus pipeline technique (Jones and Sigall 1971) falsely claims to be capable of determining the truth of the participant's answers through physiological measures. This leads to ethical dilemmas.

Physiological measurement of attitude is a method of overcoming the 'social desirability' bias. Often, it is difficult to eliminate bias in attitude measurement initiatives of an organization. In such cases, the strength and direction of employees' emotional responses are measured by analysing different situations. It is rather difficult for employees to conceal socially undesirable attitudes already ingrained in them (Allen 1975).

Attitude Surveys

To recruit a new incumbent and to evaluate human relations in factories, industries, and different organizations, an attitude survey is indispensable. The study of attitudes is also important in designing a training programme, which is a core human resource management (HRM) function. Attitude surveys focus on feelings and motives behind the employees' opinions about their working environment. There are three basic purposes for conducting attitude surveys:

1. To compare results with other survey results
2. To measure the effect of any change that occurs
3. To determine the nature and extent of employee feelings regarding specific organizational issues and the organization in general

Usually, attitude surveys are carried out by interviewing a person with a structured *close-ended questionnaire*. The skill of the interviewer is very important here for the correct measurement of attitude. While framing the questionnaire, the interviewer should be cautious, as simple questionnaire items will not reveal the attitude of the interviewee. It is important to put *value-laden questionnaire items* and to use behaviourally anchored statements such as asking the respondents to rank *myth statements*.

Attitude measurement can, thus, be done by using myth statements and asking the employees to give their answers against each statement. Some myth statements that can be used in attitude measurement are as follows:

- Hard work ensures better results.
- Never say 'no' to anyone.
- Listen to everybody's problems.
- One who is indispensable is efficient.
- Hierarchical structure should be maintained very rigidly while taking decisions.

Example 4.1 depicts the way in which a value-laden questionnaire works.

Example 4.1 Illustration of a Value-laden Questionnaire

Exhibit 4.1 shows two sample questions from a value-laden questionnaire. The responses of 15 respondents to Question 1 are shown in Table 4.1. Table 4.2 shows how the 15 respondents have ranked Alternative (a) to Question 2. With the help of the given data, answer these two questions:

i. Calculate the weighted average attitude for Question 1.
ii. Quantify all the responses to Question 2.

Exhibit 4.1: Sample Questions

1. Do you think expenditure on training is wasteful? (Respond by selecting any one of the given alternatives.)
   (a) To a large extent
   (b) To some extent
   (c) To a very little extent
   (d) Not at all
2. What, to your knowledge, are the major barriers to effective implementation of flexible working hours in India? Please arrange the factors in order of your perceived preference.
   (a) Lack of awareness
   (b) Difficulty in implementation
   (c) Supervisory problems
   (d) Lack of support from workers
   (e) Lack of support from unions
   (f) Production problems
   (g) Any other (please specify)

Table 4.1 Responses to Question 1

Alternatives	Number of respondents
(a) To a large extent	4
(b) To some extent	4
(c) To a very little extent	5
(d) Not at all	2
Total	15

Table 4.2 Ranks Given to Alternative (a) for Question 2

Respondent	1	2	3	4	5	6	7	8	9	10	11	12	13	14	15
Rank given to (a)	1	3	5	7	1	4	3	2	6	5	1	2	3	4	5

Solution:

i. The first questionnaire item, which reflects the attitude of a person regarding training, can be evaluated by adding the weighted value of individual responses. Table 4.1 shows the responses of the15 respondents to the four alternatives in Question 1.

Now, the weighted average attitude will be as shown in Table 4.3:

Table 4.3 Weighted Average Attitude

Alternatives	Number of respondents	Weighted value	Attitude
(a)	4	4	16
(b)	4	3	12
(c)	5	2	10
(d)	2	1	2

It is evident from Table 4.3 that Alternative (a), that is, 'to a large extent', is the group attitude.

ii. The second questionnaire item allows the respondents to answer by ranking all alternatives in order of their perceived priority. This requires use of the factorial method for quantification of all responses. Let us give an example to illustrate the matter. From Table 4.2, we get the data shown in Table 4.4.

Table 4.4 Number of Respondents to Each Rank for Alternative (a)

Priority/Rank	1	2	3	4	5	6	7
Number of respondents	3	2	3	2	3	1	1

Total number of respondents = 15

Number of priorities/ranks = 7

The weighted score value (*WSV*) will be as shown in Table 4.5:

Table 4.5 Weighted Score Value for Alternative (a) against Ranks 1 to 7

Priority/Rank	1	2	3	4	5	6	7
Total value	3	2	3	2	3	1	1
Weight (factorial)	7	6	5	4	3	2	1
WSV	21	12	15	8	9	2	1

Therefore, the total *WSV* for Alternative (a) = 21 + 12 + 15 + 8 + 9 + 2 + 1 = 68.

In the same way, the total weighted score value for other alternatives can be calculated from the responses obtained against each. Suppose that they are as shown in Table 4.6:

Table 4.6 Total Weighted Score Value for Alternatives (b) to (g)

Alternative	(b)	(c)	(d)	(e)	(f)	(g)
Total *WSV*	65	30	70	55	60	40

The total weighted score value of Alternative (d) is highest. Therefore, Alternative (d), that is, 'lack of support from workers,' represents the attitude/opinion of the group of respondents.

HUMAN RESOURCE MANAGEMENT AND ATTITUDINAL CHANGE

Changing attitudes, values, and motivations are now among the major issues before organizations. Through appropriate HRM interventions, organizations can turn such challenges into advantages, thereby, ensuring optimal working conditions and raising the quality of work life, while keeping pace with the changing human expectations. The following areas of attitudinal changes require HRM intervention:

- Attitudes towards perceived threats to trade union legality and other large-scale efforts to reduce trade union power or cohesion
- Attitudes towards methods of wage negotiations, whether by collective or local bargaining
- Attitudes towards working conditions and any administrative machinery for the discussion or regulation of such conditions
- Attitudes towards worker training or promotion and towards education in general as a means of improving management and industrial skills

As explained earlier, economic restructuring, market globalization, international quality system standards, etc., have, among other things, prompted Indian organizations to go for radical organizational restructuring, which call for adoption of total quality management (TQM) principles in managing human resources. TQM calls for total employee involvement (TEI), employee empowerment, development of small group activities (quality circle forums), value-engineering teams, etc. Translating the TQM requirements into corporate practices, therefore, require attitudinal changes from the top; these may involve developing a more flat organization, de-layering, delegation of authority and responsibility, and an organizational culture where every employee is considered as a member of a well-integrated family.

Most organizations, after selection of employees, also adopt certain approaches that help to develop the potential of the employees and bring positive attitudinal changes in them. Some of these approaches are as follows:

- **Employee empowerment**: Empowerment is to give everyone—instead of a few privileged people with certain positions or certain job titles—the legitimate right to make judgement, form conclusions, reach decisions, and accordingly act. Empowerment, therefore, calls for employee participation in day-to-day problem solving and innovation. Traditional participative forums (works committee, joint consultative machinery, etc.) restrict employee participation in operational areas. Empowerment, on the other hand, demands employee participation in each and every corporate function to the extent that one can accept that the employee is not merely selling his time and labour for a contracted sum of money. The empowered employee acquires necessary skill and authority to make decisions concerning quality and productivity. They initiate changes on their own. Empowerment changes the attitude of the employee as it develops employee ownership and commitment.

- **Promotion of quality circles and developing a culture of total participation**: This strategy is used to infuse attitudinal changes and to facilitate personal involvement of employees. *Quality circles* (QC) have been defined originally by the Japanese Union of Scientists and Engineers (JUSE) as a small group of workers voluntarily performing *quality control* (QC) activities (these activities help organizations to conform to customer requirements while maintaining quality standards) within the workshop to which they belong. These small groups, with voluntary participation from each and every member of the organization, irrespective of their hierarchical levels, continuously engage themselves in promoting quality control activities. Quality circles, in reality, encompass the concepts of self-development and mutual development, and at the same time, reinforce quality control techniques. The concept has gradually gained popularity in many industrialized nations as well as in developing nations.

  Quality control can be related to increased employee motivation and productivity, and hence, it is used as an important HRD tool in organizations. The gamut of knowledge, skill, creative abilities, and aptitude together with values, attitudes, and beliefs of workers and/or other individuals associated with the organization represent the human resources of an organization. Quality circles ensure total involvement of employees through a number of small group forums. Experience shows that many organizations have succeeded in improving their productivity through quality control activities. Thus, increased productivity can be achieved by increased employee motivation, which, in turn, can be better achieved through quality circles than through most other methods, such as complex planning or rigorous execution.
- **Training and development**: Imparting knowledge and value-laden training can help to bring about positive attitudinal changes. In some cases, organizations need to focus on training in areas of human relations like leadership, communication, and motivation. Such knowledge inputs gradually reinforce the attitude of employees.
- **Focus on team spirit**: This helps to create a sense of belongingness and integrate employees with the organization.

INTERVIEW

In the literal sense of the word, an *interview* means a conversation with a purpose. Such purposes are classified under three categories: obtaining information from candidates, giving information to candidates, and motivating candidates. The first purpose is to get information from candidates regarding their background, experience, education, training, and interests in order to evaluate their suitability according to the requirements of the organization. The second purpose is to provide the candidates information regarding the organization, its philosophy, personnel policies, etc. The third purpose is to establish a positive relationship to motivate prospective candidates to join the organization. These purposes form successive stages of an interview and, therefore, the subsequent stages follow only when the interviewers are satisfied with their impression of the candidate in the first stage.

In most organizations, the human resource (HR) department conducts a preliminary interview of the candidates. For a subsequent interview, a committee of executives is formed to select the right candidates. For managerial and executive positions, organizations prefer to retain the service of consultancy organizations with subject experts in the selection committee.

Depending on the job position and the profile of the prospective applicants, the following types of recruitment interviews are conducted:

- **Patterned interview**: This is also known as a structured or standardized interview. It is intended to assess the candidate's emotional strength and stability, industry, ability to get along well with others, extent of self-reliance, willingness to accept responsibility, level of motivation, etc.

- **Indirect or non-directive interview**: This type of interview is meant to help the candidates feel relaxed and free to talk. Interviewers become listeners and allow candidates to reveal their personality and in-depth knowledge in a free and relaxed atmosphere.
- **Direct, planned interview**: It is a simple question–answer session to ascertain the suitability of candidates.
- **Stress interview**: This form of interview assesses candidates' emotional balance under a situation of tension and stress. Such tension is deliberately created through interruptions, provocations, silences, and criticisms, or even by firing questions. Interviewers in such situations deliberately become unfriendly and even, at times, hostile. Such a method is often adopted for the selection of executives who are required to work under stress.
- **Group interview**: This method is intended to assess the leadership ability of candidates. Generally, a topic is given to the candidates to discuss among themselves. The interviewers remain in the background to assess the best leaders, their initiative-taking faculty, poise, adaptability, awareness levels, interpersonal skills, etc.
- **Panel or board interview**: Several interviewers collectively interview a candidate to rate their attributes. Generally, such a panel consists of several experts and each of them interviews a candidate only in those areas on which they have the requisite expertise.

For conducting a successful interview, interviewers should be adequately competent and trained. The interview itself should be conducted in a suitable place. It should be well planned with job descriptions and information about applicants being adequately studied. Interviewers should be free from any conceivable prejudice. Interviewees should be allowed to feel relaxed and the beginning and the end of an interview should be made in a friendly manner.

The limitations of the traditional selection process, such as failure to select the right persons for the right jobs or too much emphasis on written tests and interviews eventually resulted in the development of a psychometric method. This method enables one to quantify the attributes that can be used to select candidates in order of their merit. Many organizations today are making use of this method to ensure proper selection of employees.

INDUCTION AND PLACEMENT

Placement is the next stage after induction (a process that familiarizes employees with the organization) when employees are assigned their jobs according to suitability.

Induction

After the selection of employees, the first step is to orient them to organizational life. The *induction* or orientation programme of an organization is a process to guide and counsel the employees to familiarize them with the job and the organization. This process helps an organization to clarify the terms and conditions of employment as well as specific job requirements, and also helps to inculcate confidence in the minds of the new entrants.

Objectives of an induction programme

The general objectives of an induction programme are:

- To introduce new employees to the organizational environment, exposing them to the mission, history, and traditions of the organization, its achievements and future challenges, and its personnel policy and expectations from the new employees

- To create a positive attitude in the minds of the new employees
- To create proper awareness in the new employees, enabling them to understand the business of the organization
- To provide opportunity to interact with other fellow employees and also with other managerial employees of the organization

Components of an induction programme

A good induction programme should cover a number of areas that can be conveniently distributed under two points of view, namely, the organization's point of view and the employee's point of view.

Organization's point of view The areas to be covered are:

- History, mission, objectives, and philosophy of the organization
- Its product, production process, operations involved, state of technology
- Its past achievements, present status, and future growth plans
- Structure of the organization and the functions of different departments
- Delegation of authority and decision-making process
- Personnel policies, other miscellaneous policies, practices, and regulations
- Job descriptions and responsibilities
- Expectations from new employees

Employee's point of view The areas to be covered are:

- Job responsibilities
- Office procedures
- Grievance-handling procedures
- Salary and perks
- Service rules governing hours of work and overtime
- Rules covering probation, confirmation, promotion opportunities, transfer, etc.
- Retirement and superannuation benefits
- Employee services and welfare activities
- Employee's participation in small group activities and question schemes
- Performance evaluation

Steps in an induction programme

An induction programme essentially involves the following steps:

1. **General orientation**: It includes guided tours in different departments of an organization; introduction to fellow employees, supervisors, and executives; and informing about the organization's mission, philosophy, achievements, and future plans. Some organizations have printed manuals, which they give to their new employees. The purpose of such general orientation programmes is to build a sense of pride in the minds of the new employees and also create interest in them about the organization.
2. **Specific orientation**: This is intended to help new employees get acclimatized to their new work environment. The supervisor or the departmental boss of the employee takes them on a round to their place of work and imparts vocational guidance for their particular nature of work. They are told about the technology, environment, and other facilities available in the organization. The prevailing practices and customs are specified, as are the particular expectations from an employee.

Targets and key result areas (KRAs) are given to executives and managerial employees to make them aware of what the organization expects from them.

3. **Follow-up orientation**: This is conducted after some time has lapsed after the initial induction of an employee, preferably within a period of six months or so. The purpose of such orientation is to give guidance and counsel to employees to ensure that they are reasonably satisfied and gradually settling down.

Employee socialization process

Employee orientation and induction constitute what can be termed as the *employee socialization process*. In today's world, socialization is a continuous process due to the fact that organizations have become dynamic. For new employees, David A. Decenzo and Stephen P. Robbins (1999) identified that the socialization process involves three distinct stages, which are explained here:

1. **Pre-arrival stage**: At this stage, individual employees come to an organization with certain values, attitudes, and expectations. At the selection stage itself, a prospective employee needs to be enabled to understand to what extent his perceived mapping gets along with the organizational culture and systems. It is the duty of the persons involved in the selection process to facilitate this. Today, because of the availability of information about organizations through different media, including the Internet, an enthusiastic individual may also have some preconceived ideas about the organization. Therefore, it is better to first understand from the individual what they understand about the organization and then help them to synchronize this information with the reality. This helps the individual to take the right decision.
2. **Encounter stage**: At this stage, perceptions formed earlier by an individual are reaffirmed through a well-planned induction programme. Any dichotomy between an employee's perceptions and organizational perceptions needs to be properly identified and removed through a higher socialization process.
3. **Metamorphosis stage**: At this final stage of socialization, employees understand the organization and identify themselves with it. Employees develop a sense of belongingness and become contributors to achieving organizational goals and objectives.

As explained earlier, socialization is a continuous process since organizations are now required to go for restructuring and re-engineering every now and then, keeping pace with the changing environment.

Placement

After the initiation programme is over, an employee is put to a specific job, for which they have been selected. Most organizations put new employees on probation for a specified period of time, after which they are confirmed or made permanent, provided they match the requirements of the organization. The personnel department periodically reviews the progress of such employees, taking feedbacks on their performance from their controlling authority. Some organizations also have a system to extend the probationary period if the employees fail to match organizational expectations. Such placement is known as *differential placement*.

Placement is defined as assigning job profiles to employees that have been identified as suitable for them, based on the selection techniques. However, such a definition would be meaningless if a particular employee is recruited against a particular vacancy. Generally, the question of placement arises when a group of trainees are recruited. In such cases, to identify the true potential of an employee, organizations make provision for short-term placements during which phase employees are allowed to work on different jobs through a systematic job-rotation programme. At a later stage, the permanent placement is determined matching the employees' competence, knowledge, skills, and interests.

Importance of Induction and Placement

A combination of factors—common use of high technology, increased level of knowledge and skills of new job entrants, and production restructuring and flexibility coupled with changing perceptions about human resource—have transformed the human resource function in an organization. In the case of India, despite the problem of unemployment, there still exists a dearth of knowledge and skilled workers, and because of that, a dearth of executives and managers. Market globalization has further intensified the competition. The development of total quality management philosophy, among other things, demands a radical change in the product mix and service mix of an organization. All these things together have now increased the scope of job mobility for employees with the appropriate knowledge and skills.

Unfortunately, retaining employees for the long term is an utterly neglected area in the Indian corporate sector. Many organizations spend several millions of rupees in job advertisement, conducting tests and interviews, hiring the services of consultants and psychologists, etc., for selecting a managerial employee. However, weak induction programmes, without adequate emphasis on building confidence and a sense of belongingness in the minds of the new employees, results in quick separation and subsequently the wastage of a colossal sum of money for the organization. Such instances are quite common in public sector units. Very recently, a leading organization from the Tata group lost a few hundreds of their young engineers and professionals, who left en masse to join elsewhere.

Some organizations do not review the progress of their new employees, who, despite being unproductive, automatically become permanent employees after completion of their probationary tenure.

Thus, a good induction and placement programme needs to ensure employees' retention by keeping their motivation high, while simultaneously getting rid of unproductive employees within the organization.

STAFFING COSTS

Staffing or recruitment costs are one of the critical areas that require systematic control by the organization. One needs to understand at the outset the basic areas of staffing costs in an organization.

Areas of Staffing Costs

Some of the basic areas of staffing costs are:

- **Sourcing**: Sourcing costs are incurred to source candidates. Such costs may be incurred on print advertisements, online job posting, managing a resume bank, or managing the recruitment management systems. To contain the cost of sourcing, recruitment managers first need to segment the cost according to category and then adopt suitable strategies to contain the cost. For example, employer brand-building can attract prospective job seekers who apply online of their own accord. Similarly, promoting employee referral scheme can be more cost-effective than print advertisements, etc.
- **Screening**: Screening costs are calculated based on the time spent to process the profiles of candidates, shortlist the candidates, and arrange for the interview. Automatic profile tracker can process online job applications in a cost-effective way. For manual job applications, profile matching or

screening is done based on the standard protocol and, hence, the time spent on such screening by administrative employees can be added back to the cost of screening. At times, organizations may be required to conduct preliminary phone interviews before sending the final call for the interview. Recruitment managers need to manage all these costs to achieve efficiency.

- **Interviewing**: Interviewing cost depends on a number of factors. It is now the convention for organizations to reimburse the travelling costs of outstation interviewees. Similarly, interview panel members, especially when they are inducted from outside the organization, need to be paid. Even the time spent by in-house panel members is included in the cost of recruitment. During the interview process, services of administrative and other support staff members are required and this is also part of the interviewing cost.
- **Hiring**: Cost of negotiation, referral fees, fees of recruitment agencies, costs of employee relocation after selection, costs for reference checking, medical check-ups, signing bonus (if any), etc. are part of the cost of hiring. In addition, there may be induction or orientation programme costs, costs for mentors (if any), costs for enrolment in benefits scheme, and costs for uniforms, mobile phones, and laptops (when provided to the new employees).

Apart from the direct costs of recruitment, organizations can also count in the cost of lead time to recruit (calculated in terms of loss of production due to the time taken for recruitment), cost of wrong recruitment (evident through recruitment validation based on performance appraisal), etc.

Recruitment Ratios

Recruitment cost being a significant cost factor, organizations refer to various recruitment ratios to assess the trend and accordingly, wherever required, intervene to contain costs. Some of the commonly used recruitment ratios are explained here.

Recruiting cost ratio

The *recruiting cost ratio* (*RCR*) measures the cost of recruitment based on the amount spent by the HR department in recruiting new employees. A simple calculation of the same is as follows:

$$RCR = \left(\frac{\text{Total staffing costs}}{\text{Total compensation recruited}}\right) \times 100$$

Total staffing costs include recruiter travel, events, costs for job fairs, paperwork, supplies, recruiter salaries, bonuses offered to new hires, and any other expenses a department needs in order to function properly. Total compensation recruited refers to newly hired employees' salaries or hourly wages for that year.

If adding these numbers results in a low percentage, then that department is on the right track to becoming more efficient. If the percentage is higher than it should be, it calls for reviewing where the department is spending money and the types of positions that were filled to justify costs, in order to find ways to cut costs in the future.

Recruiting efficiency

This is another metric used to determine how efficient HR is about recruiting new hires and balancing expenses. After figuring out the recruiting cost ratio, one should subtract one from the percentage to figure out how efficient the department is. Recruiting efficiency numbers should be high in order to be considered efficient. Becoming more efficient may require hiring more employees during the year to justify costs, cutting costs by travelling less, or not participating in job fairs that cost too much and yield little. Tracking how people find the company is an excellent way to judge companies that are successful and those that are not. These metrics may be good starting points if one has not been using metrics to measure the recruiting process so far. Understanding the amount being spent on recruiting and the success rates will give a good idea on where the improvements should be made.

New hire performance

When gauging new hire performance, it is important to be consistent and maintain a record of all new hires in each department. In order to do this, one needs assistance from the hiring manager.

Before implementing this metric, grading systems must be discussed with hiring managers so that a universal system is determined. This can be a grading system or a point system. All managers should understand the system and be willing to use it.

The best time to evaluate new hires is between 90 and 180 days after they started working for the organization. By compiling new hire performance data, one can see how well the new hires have adjusted and then conclude if additional training is required or if more information needs to be passed on to the new hires during the recruitment or orientation stages.

If, for example, a manager notices that a large number of new hires leave the organization before their evaluation period is up, the reason will need to be investigated, also because this will affect the company's reputation over time. There are many possible reasons behind new employees leaving, such as:

- Incorrect information given during recruitment stage
- Inadequate training
- New hires not given the position they were originally hired for
- Policy changes implemented after being hired
- Shift changes implemented after being hired
- Family/personal issues

These are all possibilities that will have to be investigated.

Tracking new hire performance will also provide insights into the types of personalities that stay with the company and those that do not. This may help while recruiting in the future.

Case Staffing Solutions of Knowledge Hub: Lessons from the KPO Industry

Knowledge process outsourcing (KPO) has witnessed a big boom in India in recent years which is forecasted to continue through 2012. Most information technology-enabled services (ITeS) companies in India have a share in the global KPO market due to the availability of highly skilled professionals at a relatively cheaper rate. Knowledge Hub, one of the new-generation KPO companies in India, operates from Mumbai and serves the information needs of 12 multinationals in Europe and America. As a step towards increasing their global presence, multinationals are now strategically collecting information using a structured protocol. Knowledge Hub deploys IT-empowered domain specialists to serve their clients' information needs, whose inputs are filtered based on the protocol and then mailed to the clients after every 24 hours. Depending on the business volume, one or two clients are assigned to an accounts manager, who ensures information compilation through the domain specialists. Domain specialists are not allowed to interpret the information. Accounts managers arrange the information before the reports are dispatched to their clients, duly listing the facts and possible client-specific implications from the business point of view. Job allocation is, thus, done in such a way as to ensure that information overlapping is avoided and so that no one can single-handedly prepare the report. This is done for the protection of the clients' business interests.

In the business process outsourcing (BPO) industry in India, we find many entrepreneurs who were erstwhile working with BPO companies. The success of these entrepreneurs is mostly due to their competitive cost-effective services, which an organized BPO cannot afford to offer. Many such entrepreneurs also perform the re-outsourced jobs of their parent BPO companies. Knowledge Hub understands this and, accordingly, segments their jobs in such a way that no one can master the entire job process to become an independent service provider in the KPO business.

Knowledge Hub's recruitment system is highly structured and every selection is done after the prospective candidates cross successive hurdles. Every job applicant, apart from having their domain-specific knowledge and expertise, needs to possess business acumen, strong analytical and quantitative skills, a flair for research, an eye for details, understanding of interrelatedness of information and of businesses of various sectors, strong communication skills, and finally, the capability to chase deadlines. Each candidate goes through psychometric and aptitude tests, a series of case-study rounds, and two or three interviews.

Knowledge Hub deliberately recruits from second- or third-rung business schools and technical institutes as a way to ensure retention of employees. Fresh engineering and MBA graduates start with an initial cost to company (CTC) of INR 100,000. After the completion of their training (six months) and probationary period, they are put into managerial scales, depending on their performance record. The boom in the KPO business has, however, significantly increased job mobility for KPO employees. With every job switch, KPO specialists can enhance their compensation stake by at least 20 per cent. Keeping this trend in view, Knowledge Hub has implemented a recruitment management system whereby prospective candidates are encouraged to apply online using a structured format. The attached profile tracker quarantines the misfits and instantly sends them automatic computer-generated replies. The shortlisted candidates are taken through the recruitment process, which is scheduled on an ongoing basis every month. Thus, the IT-enabled recruitment management system helps the company to source human resources on a continuous basis. Knowledge Hub's continuous recruitment endeavours are to put at least 10 per cent of the knowledge pool in bench (recruit but delay job placement) to manage the workforce crisis due to the sudden high rate of attrition. All of Knowledge Hub's earlier endeavours to check attrition had failed over time, resulting in their shift of focus to scientific staffing solutions to have people available at the time of need. The company's recruitment management system ensures quick and accurate processing of applications and in the process reduces the cost and time expended per hire. Sourcing and screening are the two most important cost factors behind the recruitment of a workforce. For Knowledge Hub, both of these are well within their control.

CASE QUESTION

Read the case and identify how similar staffing solutions can benefit another attrition-prone industry in India, namely pharmaceutical research. Develop your answer by mapping it to an organization within the industry.

SUMMARY

- Recruitment, selection, induction, and placement are important tools for procuring and effectively using human resources in an organization. All of them are together known as the *staffing function.*
- *Recruitment* involves employing suitably trained workforce. The functions of recruitment in an organization start with the framing of a recruitment policy. After this, organizations move on to workforce planning to assess the workforce requirement, by using different forecasting tools. Workforce planning depends on factors, such as nature of work, possible change in the future working of the organization, present availability of workforce, diversification plans and programmes of the organization, change in the work processes, and available technology.
- Recruitment can be from both internal and external sources. The recruitment process basically tries to attract the best possible talent. In the case of internal recruitment, documents on the prospective candidates are already available with the organization and, hence, the selection process is easier. Recruitment through external sources involves a more rigorous process that includes steps, such as preliminary screening, review of application blanks, reference checking, psychological testing, and attitude measurement. This process is followed by an interview. Depending on the staffing position, it can be a patterned interview, an indirect or non-directive interview, a direct planned interview, a stress interview, a group interview, or an interview by a panel of board members. In some cases, more than one type of interview is conducted.
- After the process of recruitment, *selection* of employees is made and these employees are taken through the process of induction. *Induction* or orientation programmes guide and familiarize new employees with the jobs and the organization. An interactive process of induction helps in clarifying the terms and conditions of employment and specific job requirements, and also inculcates confidence in the new entrants. This process is also known as *employee socialization.*
- The staffing cycle ends with *placement,* which means putting the newly recruited employees into specific jobs. Initial placement of employees may be on probation basis and on satisfactory performance during probation, such employees may be confirmed. Some organizations take employees through compulsory job rotation before final placement.
- Lastly, to measure the effectiveness of recruitment, organizations use different recruitment metrics, such as recruiting cost ratio, recruiting efficiency, and new hire performance.

KEY TERMS

Follow-up orientation: A follow-up orientation gives guidance and counsel to employees to ensure that they are reasonably satisfied and gradually settling down. It is conducted after some time has lapsed from the point of the initial induction of an employee.

Induction: Induction is the process of formally introducing a new employee into an organization.

Metamorphosis stage: Metamorphosis stage is the final stage in employee socialization. At this stage, employees understand the organization and identify themselves with it. They develop a sense of belongingness and become contributors to achieving organizational goals and objectives.

Placement: Placement involves putting everyone in the right kind of jobs after recruitment.

Recruitment: Recruitment is the process of discovering sources of the workforce to meet the requirements or the staffing schedule of an organization and employing effective measures for attracting that workforce in adequate numbers to facilitate the selection of efficient employees.

Staffing: Staffing is the process of effectively using human resources in an organization through the steps of recruitment, selection, induction, and placement.

REVIEW QUESTIONS

1. Define *recruitment*. What are the important recruitment functions? Why are such functions important for an organization?
2. What is *internal recruitment*? Why is it important for an organization? Do you think it is necessary to have a recruitment policy for an organization?
3. What are the different recruitment processes? Briefly state their merits and demerits.
4. Briefly discuss the importance of the selection process and mention the steps involved in this process.
5. You have been retained by an organization to select a few management trainees. What process do you think you should consider and why?
6. What is the objective of an induction programme? What are the important areas that need to be considered for an effective induction programme?
7. What are the steps involved in an induction programme? In what ways have induction and placement now become important for Indian organizations?
8. Define *attitude*. Why is the study of attitude necessary for the human resource development (HRD) profession?
9. What are the different tools for attitudinal measurement? From an organizational point of view, discuss in detail at least two measurement tools with due emphasis on their relative merits and demerits.
10. A company has retained you to study the attitudes of fifty employees towards a recently introduced pension scheme. Develop at least five structured close-ended questionnaires using Likert's item analysis scale, and interview the employees. Analyse all the responses using the factorial method and measure the attitude of the employees.
11. Write short notes on the following:
    - i. Differential placement
    - ii. Follow-up orientation
    - iii. Stress interview
    - iv. Application blank
    - v. Deputation
    - vi. Successive hurdles
    - vii. Employee empowerment and attitudinal change

CRITICAL THINKING QUESTIONS

1. Your company has asked you to recruit management and engineering trainees by visiting campuses. Draw a campus recruitment programme assuming that you have to give mandate of selection on the spot.
2. You have been asked by your company to prepare a policy document on internal recruitment. Prepare it by drawing the policy statement and the outcome of such a policy document.

REFERENCES

Allen, V. L. (1975). 'Social Support for Nonconformity', in L. Berkowitz (ed.), *Advances in Experimental Social Psychology*, vol. 8, pp. 1–43.

Augoustinos, M. (1991). 'Consensual Representations of Social Structure in Different Age Groups', *British Journal of Social Psychology*, 30, pp. 193–205.

Cacioppo, J. T. and R. E. Petty (1981). 'Electromyograms as Measures of Extent Affectivity of Information Processing', *American Psychologist*, 36, pp. 441–456.

Decenzo, David A. and Stephen P. Robbins (1999). *Human Resource Management*. New York: John Wiley & Sons.

Glick, P. & Fiske, S. T. (1996). 'The Ambivalent Sexism Inventory: Differentiating hostile and benevolent sexism', *Journal of Personality and Social Psychology,* 70, pp. 491–512.

Hess, E. H. (1965). 'Attitude and Pupil Size', *Scientific American*, 212, pp. 46–54.

Jones, E. and H. Sigall (1971). 'The Bogus Pipeline: A New Paradigm for Measuring Affect and Attitude', *Psychological Bulletin*, 76 (5): pp. 349–364.

Moscovici, S. (1984). 'The Phenomenon of Social Representations', in R. M. Farr and S. Moscovici (eds.), *Social Representations*. Cambridge: Cambridge University Press.

Osgood, C. E., G. Suci and P. Tannenbaum (1957). *The Measurement of Meaning*. Urbana, IL: University of Illinois Press.

Rankin, R. E. and D. T. Campbell (1955). 'Galvanic Skin Response to Negro and White Experimenters', *Journal of Abnormal and Social Psychology*, 51, pp. 30–33.

Westie, F. R. and M. L. DeFleur (1959). 'Autonomic Responses and Their Relationship to Race Attitudes', *Journal of Abnormal and Social Psychology*, 58, pp. 340–347.

FURTHER READING

Bhattacharyya, D. K. (2006). *Human Resource Management*, 2nd edition. New Delhi: Excel Books.

——— (2009). *Organizational Behaviour–Concepts and Applications*. New Delhi: Oxford University Press.

Daft, R. L. (1995). *Understanding Management*. Orlando, FL: Harcourt Brace & Company.

Davenport, T. H. (1993). *Process Innovation: Reengineering Work through Information Technology*. Boston, MA: Harvard Business School Press.

Dessler, Gary (1998). *Human Resource Management*, 7th edition. New Delhi: Prentice Hall.

French, W. L. (1990). *Human Resource Management*, 4th edition. Boston, MA: Houghton Mifflin.

Handy, C. (1989). *The Age of Unreason*. London: Century Business.

Herzberg, F. (1966). *Work and the Nature of Man*. Cleveland, OH: World Publishing Co.

Robertson, I. and M. Smith (1985). *Motivation and Job Design: Theory, Research, and Practice*. St. Paul: West Publishing Co.

Rush, H. (1971). 'Job Design for Motivation: Experiments in Job Enlargement and Job Enrichment'. New York: The Conference Board.

Annexure 4.1
Application Blank

APPLICATION BLANK

Name of the Post: ....

Advertisement Number: ....

Applicant's Photograph

PERSONAL DATA

Full Name: Ms/Mr..

Date of Birth: ....

State: ....

Marital Status: ....

Nationality: ....

Category (whether SC/ST): ....

Height: .... cm   Weight: .... kg

Vision: ....

Normal/Corrected: ....

Spectacle Lens Numbers: ....

Address to be written to: ....

Permanent Address: ....

Landline Number: ....

Mobile Number: ....

Father's/Husband's Name and Occupation: ....

If you have any relative employed in/or on the board of our company, please give details: ....

....

Details of previous employment in this company or its sister concerns, with reasons for leaving: ....

....

Continued ...

Details of previous employment elsewhere, with reasons for leaving: ....

....

Languages (Speak/Read/Write): ....

....

EDUCATION

Examinations	School/ College	From:	To:	Major subjects	Class, percentage of marks, and rank

SCHOLASTIC ACHIEVEMENTS

School				
College				

TRAINING

Name of the Firm/Institution	From:	To:	Details of training	Stipend, if any

WORK EXPERIENCE

Employer	From:	To:	Position held and nature of work	Salary per month (basic total)

Continued ...

EXTRA CURRICULAR ACTIVITIES

Types of Activities	At School	At College	Elsewhere
Official positions held			
Sports participation			
Extracurricular participation			

Have you ever been convicted? If so, give full details: **Yes/No** ....

Have you had any major illness, operations, or accidents?: **Yes/No**..........

Any other information that you would like to furnish: ....

Name and addresses of three persons other than relatives to whom we may write for reference: ....

Name: ....

Address: ....

Minimum Salary Expected: ....

We appreciate the time and effort your have spent in completing this application. Please check your application to ensure that you have completely and accurately answered each and every question.

I declare that the particulars given above are, to the best of my knowledge, correct and complete, and undertake to inform the company immediately of changes, if any, in respect of my particulars given above. I confirm that there is no legal bar in my applying or for accepting the above-mentioned employment.

Date: .... *Signature of the applicant*

I have verified the certificates and testimonials where necessary.

Date: .... *Officer-in-charge*

5

Directing Through Motivation

After going through this chapter, you will be able to understand:

- the meaning and characteristics of direction
- the concept of motivation
- the process of motivating employees
- the relation of motivation to employees' morale and productivity
- the different theories of motivation

Employee Motivation at Fortune Furnitech

To correctly identify the tools of motivation, an innovative furniture manufacturer, Fortune Furnitech, which engages qualified designers from NID, Ahmedabad, made use of two scales—a satisfaction scale and a dissatisfaction scale. The purpose of using dual scales was to understand the needs of the employees and take suitable action to ensure greater productivity and loyalty. The *satisfaction scale* starts from zero and goes up. This scale tracks the degree of employees' liking of their job roles. The *dissatisfaction scale,* on the other hand, starts from the highest value and moves to zero, where zero indicates minimum dissatisfaction. It tracks the degree of dissatisfaction related to the workplace environment and the compensation package.

The company made use of the two scales to improve employees' satisfaction and reduce dissatisfaction. The company then decided to focus on gaining better productivity and greater loyalty by increasing the level of employees' motivation. Some of the areas of improvement identified by using the two scales were as follows:

- Appreciation of achievement of goals
- Opportunity to grow with new educational courses
- Opportunity to rise through a career-development map
- Opportunity to participate in the process of decision making in an organization
- Opportunity for employees' involvement and commitment
- Opportunity to be identified with the vision of the company
- Benefits for the family
- Company events and family get-togethers
- Quality of work life

Apart from these areas, employees indicated the need to improve their salary, workplace environment, healthcare plan, and their managers' sensitivity to their needs. The company, therefore, retained a compensation design expert and came out with a compensation plan incorporating all the aspects needing improvement. A review of the compensation plan indicated that the company could substantially increase the motivation level of their employees, their commitment to their jobs and productivity by making the changes suggested in the plan.

INTRODUCTION

Directing as a managerial function initiates organized action with the purpose of fulfilling organizational objectives. A manager accomplishes organizational goals and objectives by directing. Directing involves issuance of directives and guidance to subordinates. Hence, it is an interpersonal aspect of management. Through effective directing, an organization tries to create an appropriate work culture to reap the dormant potentiality and creative talents and abilities of people. Since directing inculcates beliefs, hopes, ambitions, and an interaction pattern, it requires an understanding of human nature and behaviour. The different elements of direction include issuing instructions, supervision, motivation, leadership, and communication.

Some of the characteristics of direction are:

- Direction follows the principle of the scalar chain, that is, managers at the top level direct middle-level managers, who in turn direct operations-level people, who implement the plans.
- Direction does not end by just giving instructions; it also calls for monitoring of performance of subordinates, that is, supervision.
- Direction encompasses all hierarchical levels in the organization. Every manager at their level of function needs to give direction to people to accomplish organizational goals and objectives.
- Direction is a continuous function. Once managers give direction, the process does not end. At every stage, managers need to guide, teach, motivate, and lead their subordinates.
- Direction essentially deals with the human factor.

This chapter discusses the concept of direction through motivation.

MOTIVATION IN ORGANIZATIONS

To motivate means to incite. *Motivation* creates a desire or willingness to work in the manner in which it needs to be done. This is distinct from the capacity to work. Motivation is an urge in the employee to act towards fulfilling their needs and, thereby, the needs of the organization. Various management gurus including Frederick W. Taylor, George Elton Mayo, Mary P. Follet, Henri Fayol, Abraham Maslow, Douglas McGregor, Frederick Herzberg, Chris Argyris, and David C. McClelland have contributed to the theories of motivation. The principal focus in this chapter is the behavioural aspects of motivation.

Process of Motivation

Throughout the world, motivational perceptions of employees are evolving in response to a number of key variables. The conventional motivational reinforcers, either extrinsic or intrinsic, are gradually losing importance. It is no longer possible to identify and indicate one single motivational tool commonly applicable to a cross-section of employees. Yet, one can appreciate the relative importance of one or the other tool for a particular segment of employees belonging to some homogenous organizations.

Motivational factors are perceived needs of employees and the satisfaction of these factors contributes to employees' performance and productivity. Motivation, per se, can be better defined as a process governing choices. This process arouses enthusiasm and persistence about pursuing a certain course of action and may be internal or external to the individual. The process of motivation starts with a physiological or psychological deficiency, or due to a need that activates behaviour or a drive that is aimed at a goal or an incentive. All the definitions, therefore, authenticate that motivation is a behavioural syndrome that develops when there is a perceived incongruence in employees' needs and expectations. With the widening of the perceived gap, employees feel demotivated and their level of performance and productivity may dip. Contrarily, if the gap gets reduced, employees feel motivated and put in their best efforts towards achieving organizational objectives. From the organizational point of view, the process of motivation follows certain defined steps, which as a continuum need to be periodically reviewed and adjusted accordingly. This helps to maintain the motivation of employees, which is evident from their behavioural congruence with organizational objectives.

In the first stage, it is important to identify the need deficiency of employees, if any. Need deficiency revolves around extrinsic and intrinsic needs. *Extrinsic needs* are those needs that are related to material and tangible gains. Increased pay, incentives, bonus, better medical facilities, better retirement benefits, and better canteen facilities are examples of extrinsic needs. *Intrinsic needs*, on the other hand, are related to mental satisfaction and are abstract in nature. Increased status, challenge, a sense of belonging, scope for growth and creativity, recognition, and a sense of achievement are examples of such needs. Identification of need deficiency is possible through direct observation of employees' behaviour and through a survey using a structured questionnaire. However, employees, by and large, feel sensitive about giving responses to a survey questionnaire, fearing that they will be identified and singled out for giving any response that criticizes organizational policy. Confidentiality in survey responses can be ensured through a secret opinion poll, where the questionnaire does not require any employee's identity. For better results, it is desirable to integrate survey findings with a personal interview, which can be in the form of an open discussion with employees by their respective seniors. Some organizations try to document such information from a 360 degree performance appraisal, incorporating certain items in the appraisal form itself. Existence of need deficiency can also be understood from the trend of employees' performance and using that to develop a performance index or productivity index.

In the second phase of the motivational process, organizations try to identify an appropriate strategy to close the perceived need deficiency of employees. This is known as *compensation strategy*. There are many innovative ways to close need gaps of employees without drastically impairing the budget. For example, the need for increase in pay can be ensured by reducing deferred benefits, that is, non-wage labour cost (NWLC), and including the reduced amount in the current pay of employees. This is particularly important for those organizations that employ mostly young people in an exploratory age group (less than 35 years). Similarly, linking pay and performance facilitates development of a proper compensation structure to reward and also to motivate good performers. On the other hand, any gap in fulfilling intrinsic needs can be reduced by adopting an enabling organization structure, which, among other things, fosters creativity and growth.

In the third phase of the motivational process, organizations enforce goal-directed behaviour. *Goal-directed behaviour* enhances performance and productivity of employees, which further influences the compensation strategy and other motivational reinforcers.

Likewise, the cycle continues as an ongoing process in an organization. At the end of the continuum, all needs are again re-evaluated to understand the emerging need deficiency, if any. In Figure 5.1, a model of the motivational process has been provided as a continuum.

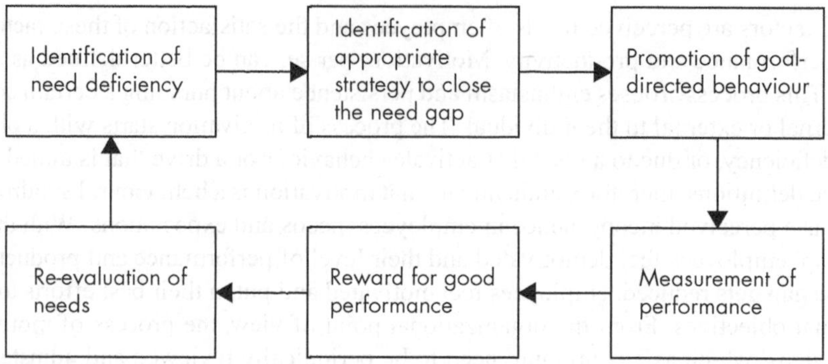

Figure 5.1 A Model of Motivation

Objectives of Motivation

Motivation enhances performance and improves productivity. Therefore, motivation fulfils the following objectives of an organization:

- **Productive use of resources**: Physical, financial, and human resources are the most important resource constructs for an organization. Proper utilization of resources is possible when people in the organization feel motivated. Motivation leads to goal-directed behaviour, which in turn facilitates productive utilization of all resources. Important measures for productive use of resources are total factor productivity indices and labour productivity indices. *Total factor productivity indices* consider the sum-total efficiency of all the factors of production, while *labour productivity indices* consider labour efficiency.
- **Increased efficiency of employees**: Motivation augments employees' willingness to work and boosts their efficiency levels. Increased efficiency also contributes to cost reduction.
- **Quality consciousness**: Thirdly, a motivated employee also becomes quality-conscious, as they behaviourally identify themselves with the organization and try to put in extra effort and care into their jobs. Motivation, therefore, strengthens the quality objectives of an organization.
- **Realization of organizational objectives and strategies**: Fourthly, by promoting goal-directed behaviour, motivated employees help to realize organizational objectives and strategies.
- **Enabling organizational structure**: Motivation promotes a friendly work culture, morale, an increased sense of responsibility, a sense of belonging, integration of individual identity with organizational identity, teamwork, participative decision making, etc. All these aspects together create an environment for creativity and growth and truly transform an organization to become an enabling force.
- **Organizational stability**: Motivation ensures organizational stability by reducing employee turnover and absenteeism.

Mechanism of Motivation

The word *motivation* is used to describe the drive that impels an employee to work. Therefore, the process starts with physiological (extrinsic) or psychological (intrinsic) needs that have to be satisfied, which activate the drive to achieve a goal. Thus, the mechanism of motivation starts with a need that activates a drive towards a goal. This has been explained in Figure 5.2.

At this stage, it is important to understand the basic differences between motive, motivation, and motivating. *Motives* are the reasons behind any action. On the other hand, *motivation* is the inner state that activates and directs the behaviour of individuals towards certain goals. The inner state of an individual is

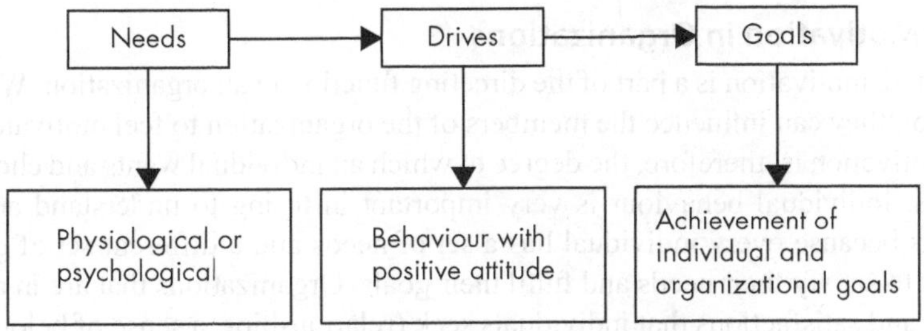

Figure 5.2 Mechanism of Motivation

created out of a perceived need imbalance. The degree of imbalance decides whether it is a strong motive or a weak motive and, accordingly, the person propels themselves into action. Thus, motives create drives that energize people into action. While motive energizes action, the degree of work behaviour indicates the level of motivation. If an employee performs well, putting forth their best efforts, their motivation is considered to be high, while in the reverse scenario, it is be considered to be low. *Motivating* implies inducements to energize work behaviour. This is a managerial role since it satisfies both individual and organizational needs. Managers try to sustain a motivating environment to get work done in an effective and efficient manner. For this purpose, they need to understand the strength of motive in employees. The process of identification of need deficiency has already been explained earlier. Since needs or motives are the reasons for work behaviour, managers need to plot the motives with their respective degree of importance, which can be done as illustrated in Figure 5.3.

In Figure 5.3, A, B, C, D, E, and F denote different motives, which are compensation, promotional opportunities, functional autonomy, creativity, challenge, and flexibility in policies, respectively. Using a Pareto diagram, a manager can optimize the motive strength. This is because the Pareto principle suggests that every problem (the problem being the motive strength in this case) is the result of a few causes and all causes are not equally important, that is, 'a vital few: trivial many'. This means that by taking care of 10 to15 per cent of motive strengths, managers can reduce the need gaps in 70 to 80 per cent areas. This is possible due to the interdependence and interrelationship in motive strengths. A typical Pareto diagram has been provided in Figure 5.4.

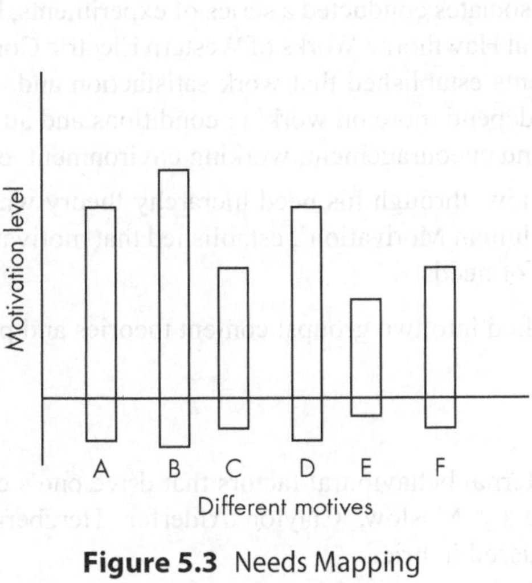

Figure 5.3 Needs Mapping

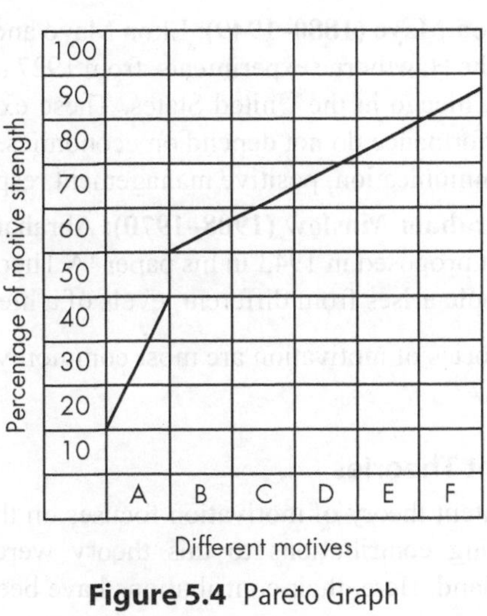

Figure 5.4 Pareto Graph

Significance of Motivation in Organizations

As already explained, motivation is a part of the directing function in an organization. When managers act as a good motivator, they can influence the members of the organization to feel motivated and deliver the desired results. Motivation is, therefore, the degree to which an individual wants and chooses to engage in certain behaviours. Individual behaviour is very important in trying to understand and then influence motivation. This is because every individual has a set of needs and a different set of goals. Individuals behave differently to satisfy their needs and fulfil their goals. Organizations that are in a position to fulfil some of the needs and satisfactions that individuals seek (relationships, a sense of belonging, intellectual stimulation, mental and physical challenges, self-development, etc.) are better able to motivate them.

For organizations, motivation is important because motivated employees contribute to:

- Higher productivity (that is, they produce more for a given level of resources as compared to poorly motivated workers)
- Better quality work with less wastage
- A greater sense of urgency (things happen quicker when they need to)
- Greater engagement by giving feedback and suggestions for improvements (motivated workers take more ownership of their work)
- Greater engagement by demanding more feedback from superiors and management
- Target achievement by working at 80 to 95 per cent of their ability

THEORIES OF MOTIVATION

There are various theories of motivation. The three major proponents of motivational theories are:

1. **Frederick W. Taylor (1856–1917)**: Taylor is known as the father of scientific management. In his work *Principles of Scientific Management* (1911), he observed that the prosperity of the management and the workforce are interdependent. People are inherently capable of hard work but they show such qualities irregularly. To harness such potential, pay and rewards (incentives) must be linked to achievement of 'optimum goals'. While good performers receive rewards and better pay, bad performers lose on this count.
2. **Elton Mayo (1880–1949)**: Elton Mayo and his associates conducted a series of experiments, known as the Hawthorne experiments, from 1927 to 1932 at Hawthorne Works of Western Electric Company in Chicago in the United States. These experiments established that work satisfaction and, hence, performance do not depend on economics. They depend more on working conditions and attitudes, communication, positive management response and encouragement, working environment, etc.
3. **Abraham Maslow (1908–1970)**: Abraham Maslow, through his need hierarchy theory which he first proposed in 1943 in his paper 'A Theory of Human Motivation', established that motivation of people arises from different levels of a hierarchy of needs.

The theories of motivation are most commonly classified into two groups: content theories and process theories.

Content Theories

The content theory of motivation focuses on those internal behavioural factors that drive one's efforts. Pioneering contributions to this theory were made by Maslow, Clayton Alderfer, Herzberg, and McClelland. Here, their contributions have been discussed in brief.

Maslow's theory of hierarchy of needs

The premises of Maslow's hierarchy of needs (1943) theory can be summarized as follows:

- The wants and desires of human beings influence their behaviour. Wants and desires that are already satisfied do not act as motivators. People's motives or behaviours reflect their unsatisfied wants and desires.
- The needs of people are arranged in the order of their perceived priority or hierarchy. Perceived need factors of people vary.
- People can advance from one level of need hierarchy to another only when their preceding need factors are satisfied. For example, without satisfaction of lower-order needs like physiological and safety needs, people cannot advance to a higher order where a sense of belongingness and other social needs matter more.
- The more people advance to higher-order needs, the more they display their satisfaction and motivation to work.

Maslow's need hierarchy theory divides human needs into five distinct categories as depicted in Figure 5.5.

Physiological needs are the basic needs of human beings which are essential for survival. Such needs include food, water, air, clothing, and shelter. From the organizational point of view, such needs are met through one's salary and basic working conditions.

Safety needs ensure protection from the economic and physical environment. People expect some reasonableness in their perceived environment to minimize the degree of uncertainty. Job security, a degree of continuity, order, structure, and predictability comprise the nature of such needs. Organizations fulfil such needs of employees by ensuring a protective work environment.

The *need for belongingness and love* arises after satisfaction of the earlier two lower-order needs. These are also known as social needs. People along this need level develop a strong sense of affiliation and become concerned with love, affection, belongingness, acceptance, and friendship. Organizations meet such needs by providing an appropriate work culture to help employees identify with the organization.

At the *self-esteem need* level, employees look for satisfaction of their esteem or egoistic needs. Esteem needs pertain to self-respect and respect from others. Self-respect is ensured by achieving competence, confidence, personal strength, adequacy, achievement, independence, and freedom. Respect from others comes from prestige, recognition, acceptance, attention, status, reputation, and appreciation. To fulfil such needs of employees, organizations provide challenging work assignments, performance feedback, performance recognition, a participative work culture, tools of empowerment, opportunities for participation in decision making, etc.

At the *self-actualization* stage, employees desire to become what they are capable of becoming. They want to create something of their own using their talent, capacity, and potential. Organizations try to fulfil such needs of employees by nurturing an environment that fosters creativity and growth.

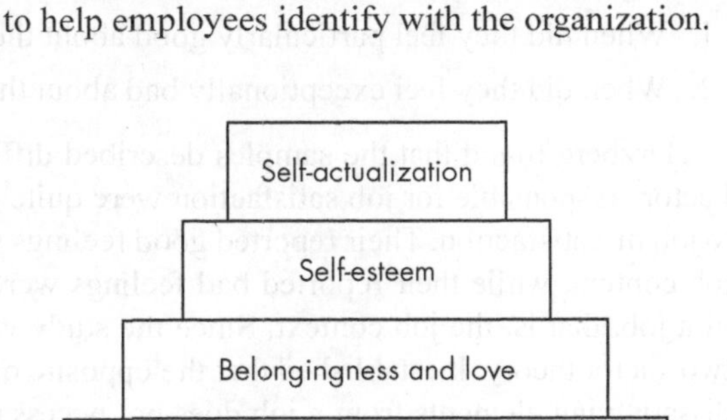

Figure 5.5 Maslow's Theory of Hierarchy of Needs (*Source:* A. H. Maslow, *Motivation and Personality*, 3rd ed., R. D. Frager and J. Fadiman (eds.), © 1997, Pearson Education, Inc., Upper Saddle River, NJ. Adapted with permission.)

The concept of needs helps managers understand human behaviour at work. It also accounts for interpersonal variations in human work. Another important aspect is that motivation is defined as a constantly changing force, which makes it a dynamic model.

Despite the advantages, the theory is criticized on the following counts:

- The theory has no empirical support. It is not even a theory of work motivation since Maslow did not intend to relate his theory to work motivation. Maslow's theory was, in fact, popularized by others (McGregor, etc.) as a work motivation theory.
- Different needs cannot be put into strictly defined levels. In fact, a hierarchy of needs is simply a misnomer. An employee who is motivated by self-actualization may still have lower-order needs like food and shelter.
- The theory is not culturally aligned. It is more aligned to western values while sidelining the East. Work is perceived differently in different cultures. Hence, motivation to work is different across countries and it also varies within a country from one work group to another. Therefore, the theory cannot be applicable to heterogeneous work groups.
- Maslow's existential philosophy is questioned on the basis that people may like to remain content with the satisfaction of their lower-order needs. They may not want to move further up the hierarchy.
- It is time consuming to follow Maslow's theory to diagnose the need deficiency of employees. Even after such a diagnosis, an organization may not be able to develop a tailor-made model for employee motivation.

Herzberg's two-factor theory or motivation–hygiene theory

Herzberg (1959), extending the work of Maslow, developed the two-factor theory of motivation. His study is based on the responses of 200 accountants and engineers drawn from eleven industries in the Pittsburgh area. With the help of critical incident methods (which require facts to be collected for subsequent analysis of causal factors of the human system), he asked the samples to respond on two aspects:

1. When did they feel particularly good about their job?
2. When did they feel exceptionally bad about their job?

Herzberg found that the samples described different types of conditions for good and bad feelings. Factors responsible for job satisfaction were quite different from factors they perceived as contributors to job dissatisfaction. Their reported good feelings were found to be associated with job experiences and job content, while their reported bad feelings were found to be associated with the peripheral aspects of a job, that is, the job context. Since the study was based on a two-factor hypothesis, it is called the two-factor theory. It established that the opposite of satisfaction is not dissatisfaction and that removing dissatisfying elements from a job does not necessarily make the job satisfying. Herzberg classified the factors into two categories: (1) motivation factors and (2) hygiene or maintenance factors.

Herzberg mentioned six motivation factors: (1) recognition, (2) advancement, (3) responsibility, (4) achievement, (5) possibility of growth, and (6) job content or the work itself.

While these factors contribute to creating a motivating environment, their absence does not cause dissatisfaction. Therefore, these factors are the satisfiers.

Similarly, Herzberg mentioned ten hygiene or maintenance factors: (1) company policy and administration, (2) technical supervision, (3) interpersonal relations with subordinates, (4) salary, (5) job security, (6) personal life, (7) working conditions, (8) status, (9) interpersonal relations with supervisors, and (10) interpersonal relations with peers.

These factors are context factors. Their existence creates an environment for doing work. However, these factors by themselves cannot motivate people to work. According to Herzberg, their absence can dissatisfy people but their presence per se cannot satisfy people. Therefore, these factors are the dissatisfiers.

The crux of the two-factor theory of motivation, therefore, is that managers should cater to both satisfiers and dissatisfiers. Mere improvement of hygiene factors cannot guarantee a motivating environment. In Figure 5.6, the essence of Herzberg's theory has been presented with the help of a diagram.

Herzberg's theory is the first of its kind based on field research. While Maslow's work was based on clinical observations (laboratory-based findings), Herzberg did his study to understand motivation in the work environment. Herzberg's study recommends actions that managers can take to improve motivation in the work environment. His emphasis on context factors shifts the focus away from the traditional concept of money as the most potent factor of work motivation. Herzberg contributed an alternative approach to motivation by placing emphasis on job enrichment. Herzberg also gave a double dimension to the aspect of employee needs, instead of sticking to their absolute categorization into five distinct levels, as was done by Maslow.

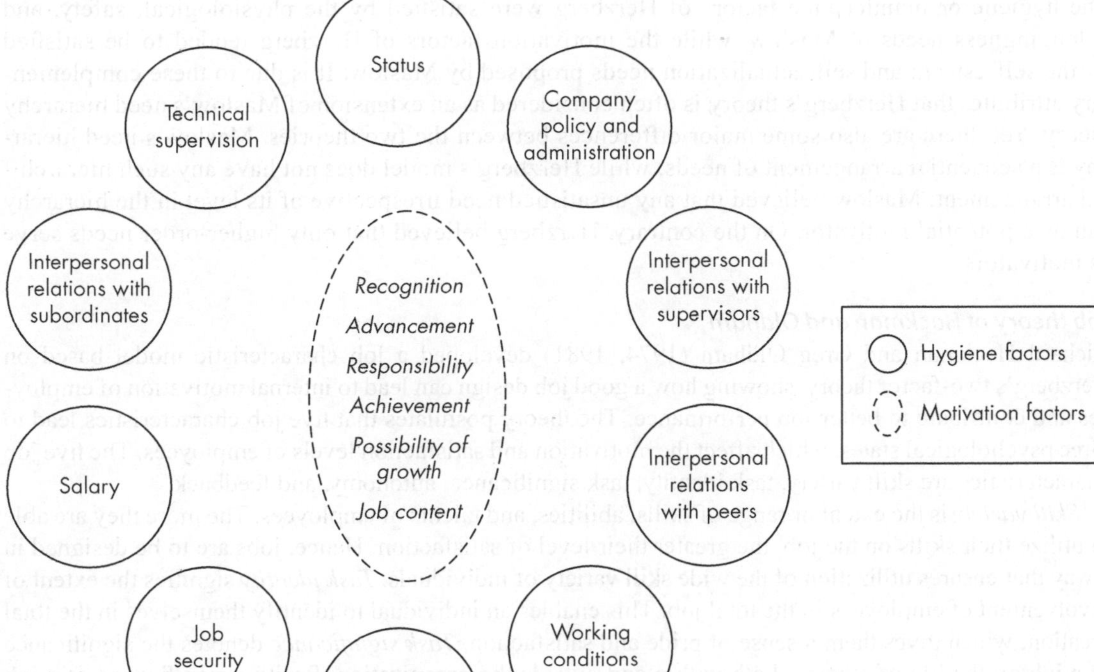

Figure 5.6 Hygiene Factors and Motivators

However, despite all the listed merits, Herzberg's theory has been subjected to the following points of criticism:

- It is limited by its methodology. When things go well, people tend to take credit for themselves. On the other hand, they attribute failure to the external environment.
- Herzberg's theory is method-bound. One cannot get similar results with other methods. The critical incidents method may cause people to recall only recent incidents or experiences. However, experiences can be inconsistent. Moreover, while narrating a critical incident, respondents may take it as an opportunity to give vent to their opinions rather than stick to narrating the reality. Thus, survey findings become more opinion-laden.
- Herzberg's theory talks more about job satisfaction than job motivation.
- The theory ignores situational variables as it is not backed by adequate research in different work environments.
- Even though the theory assumes a relationship between job satisfaction and productivity, the methodology applied by Herzberg limits its focus to job satisfaction.

Comparison of Maslow's and Herzberg's models

Herzberg's framework is largely compatible with Maslow's hierarchy of needs. Maslow referred to needs or motives, while Herzberg dealt with goals and incentives that tend to satisfy those needs. The hygiene or maintenance factors of Herzberg were satisfied by the physiological, safety, and belongingness needs of Maslow, while the motivation factors of Herzberg tended to be satisfied by the self-esteem and self-actualization needs proposed by Maslow. It is due to these complementary attributes that Herzberg's theory is often considered as an extension of Maslow's need hierarchy theory. Yet, there are also some major differences between the two theories. Maslow's need hierarchy is a sequential arrangement of needs, while Herzberg's model does not have any such hierarchical arrangement. Maslow believed that any unsatisfied need irrespective of its level in the hierarchy can be a potential motivator. On the contrary, Herzberg believed that only higher-order needs serve as motivators.

Job theory of Hackman and Oldham

Richard Hackman and Greg Oldham (1974, 1981) developed a job characteristic model based on Herzberg's two-factor theory, showing how a good job design can lead to internal motivation of employees and contribute to better job performance. The theory postulates that five job characteristics lead to three psychological states, which affect the motivation and satisfaction levels of employees. The five job characteristics are skill variety, task identity, task significance, autonomy, and feedback.

Skill variety is the extent or range of skills, abilities, and talents of employees. The more they are able to utilize their skills on the job, the greater their level of satisfaction. Hence, jobs are to be designed in a way that ensures utilization of the wide skill variety of individuals. *Task identity* signifies the extent of involvement of employees in the total job. This enables an individual to identify themselves in the total creation, which gives them a sense of pride and satisfaction. *Task significance* denotes the significance of a job on the life of others—both within and outside the organization. Positive significance of a job gives psychological satisfaction to the person who does it. *Autonomy* is the extent of freedom given for a job. The degree of autonomy depends on the extent of independence given to an employee in deciding about job scheduling, formulating the procedures, decision making without interference of others, etc. The greater the job autonomy, the greater is the job satisfaction and, therefore, the motivation. *Feedback* provides the opportunity to assess the right or wrong ways of doing a job.

The three psychological states that an individual experiences are described as follows:

1. Skill variety, task identity, and task significance provide 'experienced meaningfulness'.
2. Autonomy provides 'experienced responsibility'.
3. Feedback ensures 'experienced knowledge of results'.

Once an employee experiences these three psychological states, they feel intrinsically rewarded, which results in intrinsic motivation.

Based on their study, Hackman and Oldham developed a motivating potential score (MPS) that measures the propensity of a job to become motivating. The formula is presented here:

$$\text{Motivating potential score} = \left(\frac{\text{Skills variety} + \text{Task identity} + \text{Task significance}}{3}\right) \times \text{Autonomy} \times \text{Feedback}$$

ERG theory

Alderfer (1967) of Yale University developed the ERG theory based on empirical research. He modified Maslow's five levels of needs to three levels and labelled them as needs for existence, relatedness, and growth. The ERG theory differs from Maslow's need hierarchy theory in the following ways:

- Instead of a five-level need hierarchy, the ERG theory considers only three need levels.
- The need hierarchy theory postulates rigid progression from one level of needs to another, while the ERG theory assumes that more than one need may be operative simultaneously. This means that employees working on their growth need may remain unsatisfied in relatedness and existence needs.
- The basic postulate of ERG theory works on a frustration–regression model. If for any reason employees are continually frustrated due to inability to satisfy their needs at one level, they intensify their desire to satisfy lower-level needs. For example, a failure to get recognition is compensated by the desire to make more money. On the other hand, Maslow suggests that people will stay at a certain need level till they are able to satisfy it.

The ERG theory is pragmatic in its approach because it considers individual differences among people. Individual differences in terms of education, family background, and culture can alter the motive strength vis-à-vis perceived need factors. The theory is more appealing, intuitive, and logical than Maslow's need hierarchy theory. Despite such advantages, the theory does not offer any clear-cut guidelines. It just indicates that people will be motivated to behave in a particular way to satisfy one of the three sets of needs, that is, need for existence, need for relatedness, and need for growth. Moreover, the theory is yet to be backed by adequate research.

McClelland's three needs theory (achievement motivation theory)

McClelland (1977), through his study of twenty years at Harvard University, documented differences in the needs of people and narrowed them to three important areas:

1. **Achievement need (popularly known as nAch)**: People in this need category have the drive to excel, that is, to achieve in relation to a set of standards. They like a challenge and they like to succeed in a competitive environment. They willingly work hard and volunteer for work that fully stretches their ability. This category of people does not get motivated by money. They feel more motivated with a sense of accomplishment and achievement.

2. **Affiliation need (popularly known as nAff)**: This need emerges from the desire for friendly and close interpersonal relationships. Employees try to fulfil such needs through satisfying relationships with the organization, peer groups, work teams, etc. Since people in this need group try to identify themselves with the organization, they prefer to foster a friendly work culture and try to meet their needs through friendly relations.
3. **Power need (popularly known as nPow)**: People in this need group try to gain satisfaction by controlling others. This need emerges from the desire for superiority and people in this need category look for leadership positions in organizations.

McClelland highlighted the importance of matching the individual and the job. People with a high achievement need prefer challenging job assignments, while those with a low achievement need prefer a job situation that ensures stability, security, and predictability. By manipulating the achievement need, organizations can get complex jobs accomplished by high achievers. However, McClelland's work is criticized on many important counts including the ways in which a sense of achievement or other associated motives can be inculcated in an adult employee. McClelland contends that this can be taught and, thus, motives related to achievement can be developed in an adult. This contention is not tenable in the literature available on psychology. Secondly, McClelland contends that needs can be changed through education and training. However, psychologists contend that needs are permanently acquired. Thirdly, the thematic appreciation test (TAT) used for the study by McClelland is also subject to criticism since interpretation of responses using TAT is subject to the researcher's bias.

Theory X and theory Y

McGregor (1957) of the Massachussetts Institute of Technology (MIT) defined *organizations* as psychological entities and implied that they can be characterized by one's assumptions about the things that motivate people. The basic hypothesis is that managerial decisions and actions are based on certain assumptions about human nature and human behaviour. McGregor proposed two distinct views and assumptions about human behaviour: a negative view labelled theory X and a positive view labelled theory Y. Managers subscribing to the negative view (theory X) believed that employees are lazy, dislike work, dislike responsibility, and need to be coerced to get the work done. Managers subscribing to the positive view (theory Y) believed that employees like work, are creative and responsible, and can exercise self-direction. Motivational implications of McGregor's analysis can, therefore, be best analysed in the context of Maslow's need hierarchy theory. Theory X assumed that people can be motivated by satisfaction of lower-order needs, while theory Y assumed that people can be motivated by satisfaction of higher-order needs.

The assumptions of managers subscribing to theory X and theory Y, as observed by McGregor, are presented in Table 5.1.

Cognitive or Process Theories of Motivation

Content theories of motivation emphasize the importance of inner needs. On the contrary, cognitive models or process theories of motivation propose that people take conscious decisions about their job behaviour. Therefore, to motivate, organizations must understand the ways in which an individual takes decisions and the amount of effort they put into the job. Expectancy theory, equity theory, and performance satisfaction model are some of the important approaches used to understand cognitive or process theories of motivation.

Expectancy theory

This theory essentially emphasizes that people feel increasingly motivated if they perceive that their effort will result in successful performance and that successful performance will ensure desired results.

Table 5.1 Theory X and Theory Y

Theory X assumptions	Theory Y assumptions
The average human being inherently dislikes work and will always try to avoid work.	People can exercise self-direction and self-control in achieving the objectives to which they have committed.
Due to the inherent human tendency to avoid work, people must be coerced, controlled, directed, and threatened with punishment to get work done by them.	Commitment to objective is a function of rewards associated with their achievement. People, therefore, have the capacity of using their imagination, intensity, and creativity for the solution of organizational problems.
The average human being prefers to be directed, avoids responsibility, is less ambitious, and likes security above all things.	The average human being learns (under proper conditions) not only to accept but also to seek responsibility.
For motivating employees, the organization has to enforce strict control with a stick and restrict the motivational reinforcements to those areas that fulfil their lower-order needs.	Organizations are able to only partially utilize people's potential. The potential of people needs to be developed so that they can work according to their full potential towards common objectives. By and large, they can be motivated by the satisfaction of their higher-order needs.

The expectancy theory is variously known as instrumentality theory, path–goal theory, and valence–instrumentality–expectancy (VIE) theory. It has its roots in the cognitive concepts of Kurt Lewin (1951) and Edward Tolman (1951) as well as in the choice behaviour and utility concepts of classical economic theory. It was Victor H. Vroom (1964) who finally formulated an expectancy theory as an alternative to the content models of work motivation. The theory identifies relationships among variables that affect individual behaviour in a dynamic environment. It is an attempt to understand how people determine their extent of effort for a job and how such effort gets influenced by their perceived expectation. The strength of a tendency to act in a certain way depends on the strength of expectation of the outcome that is likely to accrue upon accomplishment of the job. Hence, *motivation*—the strength of drive towards an action—is a product of the strength of one's desire (valence) and the perceived probability of getting something good with a certain action (expectancy). This relationship can be depicted in the following manner:

$$\text{Valence} \times \text{Expectancy} = \text{Motivation}$$

Valence is the degree of desirability of certain outcomes. It is, therefore, the strength of an individual's preference for a particular outcome—which may be a promotion, a pay rise, recognition, etc.—after they successfully accomplish the job. Since people may have positive or negative preference for an outcome, valence may be negative or positive. Hence, valence may vary from −1 to +1.

Expectancy is the perceived possibility of a particular outcome that will follow after an action. It is, therefore, the strength of belief that an act will be followed by particular outcomes. The strength of expectations is based on past experience. People expect that the same things that have occurred in the past will happen in the future. As expectancy is an action-outcome association, it may range from zero to one. If employees perceive no possibility of an outcome from certain acts, their expectancy will be zero, while the value of expectancy will be one when they feel with certainty (from their experience of an action-outcome relationship) that they are likely to achieve something.

Vroom has used one more term between expectancy and valence, which is usefulness or instrumentality. *Instrumentality* is the belief that the first-level outcome will lead to the second-level outcome. For example, one may be motivated to give performance of a superior level due to the desire to get promoted. Here, first-level outcome (superior-level performance) is seen as being instrumental to second-level outcome (promotion). Therefore, the strength of motivating a workforce to perform a certain act will depend on the sum of the products of the valences (including instrumentality) and the expectancies, which can be represented as follows:

$$\text{Motivation strength} = \Sigma V \times I \times E$$

It is widely held that the content theories oversimplified the complex process of work motivation. In contrast, Vroom's model highlights the importance of organization behaviour and clarifying the relationships between employees and the organization. The model also has a cognitive dimension since individuals are viewed as thinking and reasoning beings and they are not seen as simply acting for the satisfaction of their unfulfilled needs.

Despite certain unique features in Vroom's approach, his theory was criticized on account of the following aspects:

- It needs to be adequately tested in different work environments.
- Employees may not always take a conscious decision. It has been observed that they are also prone to take thoughtless decisions. Later, they may try to rationalize the action with their own logic.
- Linkages between efforts and performance and between performance and rewards may not be linear. Organizational policies may further complicate the process. For example, promotion may be awarded on the basis of seniority, educational background, etc.
- The theory is complex. In real-life situations, managers may have time and resource constraints to deal with during implementation.

Equity theory

This theory owes its origin to several contributors including Festinger, Heider, Homans, Jacques, Patchen, and Weick. However, James Stacy Adams's (1963) contribution is most widely acknowledged in this respect. The theory proposes that in a work environment, motivation is influenced by one's perception of how equitably they are treated as compared to others. The theory is also known as 'social comparison theory' or 'inequity theory'. Employees try to perceptively reduce their inequity through such comparison or by establishing a hypothetical relationship of exchange. An individual accounts for the amount of work they put in and the corresponding rewards they receive for the same, and then they compare the efforts and rewards of a similarly placed person in the organization. If equity exists, the individual feels satisfied. However, if it is a case of inequity, it propels them into action to create a condition of equity. Since inequity propels action, it is the motivator. The greater the perceived inequity, the greater is the motivation to reduce it. While doing this, individuals can make any of the following choices:

- Change or alter inputs
- Change or alter outcomes
- Distort inputs and outcomes

- Distort inputs and outcomes of others whom they compare with themselves
- Select a different referent for comparison
- Withdraw from the field

The equity theory is a promising theory of work motivation as well as job satisfaction. Due to this reason, it has generated extensive research. Since the theory works on the basis of perception in a process of social comparison, it is by default dynamic.

The theory is criticized on the following counts:

- It is complex and difficult in application.
- Perceptions are difficult to measure or assess.
- Choosing a 'comparison other' may not be always correct.
- A given factor may be an input as well as an outcome.
- The study is based on laboratory experiments rather than real-life situations in organizations.

Performance satisfaction theory

Layman W. Porter and Edward W. Lawler (1968), based on Vroom's expectancy model, observed that performance leads to satisfaction contrary to the belief that satisfaction leads to performance. Another interesting observation made by them is that motivation (efforts), performance (accomplishment), and satisfaction are separate variables. This observation is again in contrast to the belief that motivation leads to performance, which in turn leads to satisfaction. Efforts (force or motivation) do not directly lead to performance. It is mediated by abilities, traits, and role perceptions. After performance, the rewards that follow and the way they are perceived determine the level of satisfaction. The theory is illustrated in Figure 5.7.

As illustrated in Figure 5.7, whether an individual will make an effort depends on interaction between the value of reward (Box 1) and the perceived effort-reward probability (Box 2). Effort (Box 3) is the motivation to work. Performance (Box 6) is not the direct consequence of effort. It is the product of effort (Box 3), abilities and traits (Box 4), and role perceptions (Box 5). Performance leads to certain outcomes in the form of intrinsic rewards (Box 7A) and extrinsic rewards (Box 7B). Both intrinsic and extrinsic rewards provide satisfaction (Box 9). However, such a reward-satisfaction relationship is moderated by the perceived equitability of rewards (Box 8).

Attribution theory and locus of control

Harold Kelley (1967, 1973) advocated this theory that is mainly concerned with the cognitive process by which an individual interprets behaviour attributed to certain parts of the relevant environment. Such causal relationships or attributes are interpreted by an individual due to his own behaviour or due to others' behaviour. Fritz Heider contended that perceived internal forces (ability, efforts, and fatigue) and external forces (others' supervision, machines, methods, climate, rules, and procedures) together determine the behaviour of an individual. Since the perceived causes are the determinants of work behaviour, and perception differs, people behave differently in a given situation. The concept of locus of control is different from the concept of attribution. While attribution theory is concerned with identifying the causes of one's own behaviour as well as others' behaviour, locus of control theory is applicable only to one's own self. Employees may perceive that their behaviour is either internally or externally controlled. Since external control factors (which influence their own behaviour) are beyond their own control, employees believe that their rewards and punishments are dependent on factors like fate, luck, or chance. On the other hand, in the case of internal control factors, they feel that they can influence their

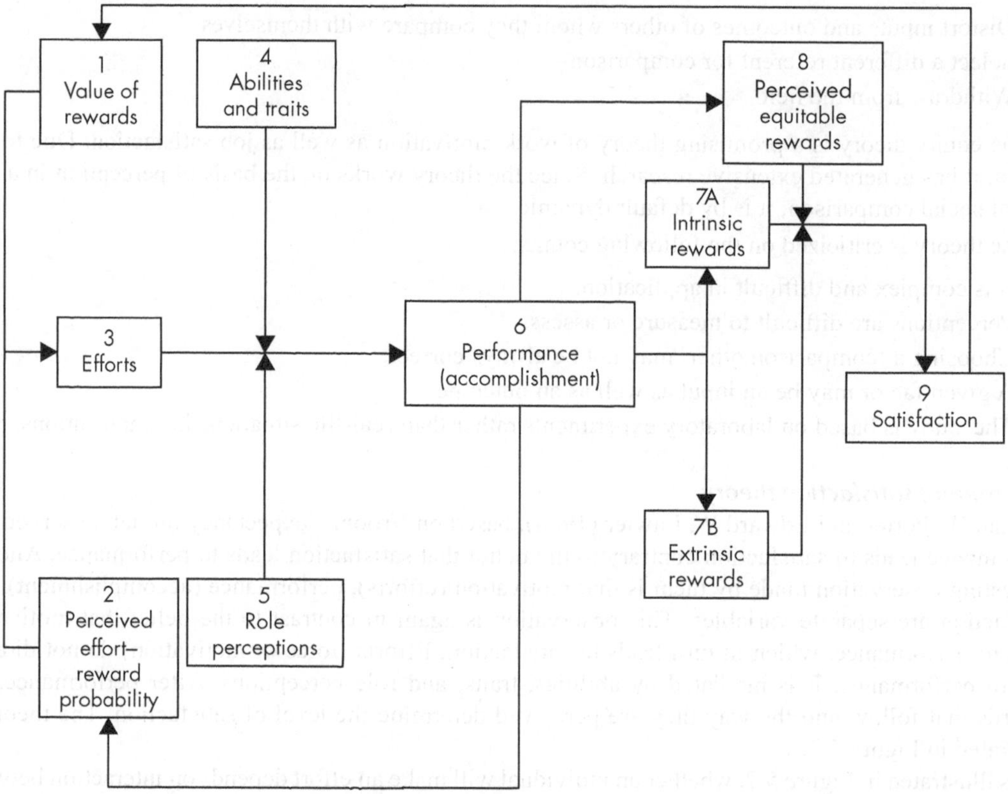

Figure 5.7 Porter and Lawler's Motivation Model (*Source:* L. W. Porter and E. E. Lawler (1968). *Managerial Attitudes and Performance*, Homewood, IL: Richard D. Irwin, Inc. Reprinted with permission.)

outcomes through their own ability, skills, or effort. Julian Rotter (1966) developed a 23-item scale for measurement of locus of control and it is known as the internal–external (I–E) scale.

Goal setting theory

Edwin Locke (1968) considered two cognitive determinants of behaviour: values and intentions (goals). Emotions and desires represent the form of values and value judgements. Intentions are goals to satisfy desires or emotions (values). This results in consequences, feedback, and reinforcement. The study suggests that individuals are willing to work hard when they know what is required of them. Setting specific attainable goals is related to high-level performance.

Miscellaneous Theories on Motivation

There are certain theories that revolve around the core content or process theories. They have been briefly discussed here.

- H. A. Murray (1938) developed the manifest needs theory, which is basically a multivariate approach to the structure of needs. The basic difference between Murray's formulation and Maslow's and Alderfer's formulations is that Murray does not suggest a hierarchical order of the various types of needs. Based on several years of clinical observations at Harvard Psychological Clinic, Murray argues that the intensities of various personality-related needs, taken together, represent a central motivating force.

- R. W. White's competence motive theory (1959) (somewhat similar to the power motive theory) relates motivation to the desire of employees for mastery over their physical and social environs (Cornell study).
- S. Schachter's affiliation motivation theory (1959) relates motivation to the strong need for affiliation.
- C. Argyris's maturity–immaturity theory (1957) relates motivation to an environment that serves both the needs of the organization and the needs of the members of the organization (Yale study).
- W. F. Whyte's money motivation theory (1955) suggests that people are primarily motivated by the desire to make money. However, Whyte also suggests that monetary incentives should not be considered in isolation from other incentives that are not monetary.
- The Michigan studies by R. Likert and D. Katz (1948) emphasized that a productivity-motivated work team is really a function of a particular type of supervisory style. Since productivity has its roots in employee motivation, it can be harnessed by carefully designing an organization in which the individual develops a feeling that they are of some importance to the organization.

L. C. Megginson (1977), for the sake of convenience, has classified the leading theories of motivation into three groups:

1. **Perspective theories**: Taylor's scientific management approach, various human relations theories, McGregor's theory Y, etc., which, in effect, tell the management to motivate people.
2. **Content theories**: Maslow's hierarchy of needs theory, Herzberg's two-factor theory, McClelland's achievement need theory, etc., which try to identify the causes of behaviour.
3. **Process theories**: Various behaviouristic theories that believe in the stimulus-response relationship, viz. motivation (for example, Skinner's behaviour modification theory) and cognitive theories (for example, Vroom's expectancy theory and Porter–Lawler's future-oriented expectancy theory) dealing with the genesis of behaviour.

Indian Studies on Motivation

This discussion will mainly focus on the relevant Indian studies that have tried to understand the underlying motive forces determining the behaviour and performance of employees.

Not many empirical studies on motivation and its related aspects have been carried out in India. There are some studies on industrial workers and a few others on technical personnel, supervisors, and managers. Most studies have attempted to find out the job-satisfaction variables, which have been construed as the motivational variables. The first such study in India is by S. K. Bose (1951) on industrial workers, and this study has paved the way for other researchers to investigate into the perceived importance of job factors to workers. Most of the studies relating to industrial workers, during the period 1951–1971, have rated adequate earnings, job security, the supervisor or manager, and personal life as the main factors that determine the behaviour of employees. Some of the major Indian studies are mentioned here.

- H. C. Ganguli's study (1964) on first-line supervisors (size of sample = 44) has ranked incentives, adequate income, promotional opportunities, job security, and sympathetic treatment from superiors as the important job factors vis-à-vis motivation.

- The study by D. K. Lahiri and S. Srivastava (1967) on middle-management personnel (size of sample = 93) has ranked good organizational policies and administration, better scope for promotion, good salary, good superior–subordinate relationship, and opportunity for growth as the major determinants of satisfaction.
- The study by M. P. Sawalapurkar and others (1968) on middle-level managers (size of sample = 30) has ranked nine job factors in the following order of importance: job content, opportunity for advancement, job security, supervisor, company, working conditions, facilities, working hours, and grievance redressal.
- The study by O. Padaki and A. M. Dolke (1970) on job attitudes of supervisors (size of sample = 15) (based on Herzberg's two-factor theory) has found the major dissatisfiers to be lack of recognition, unfavourable superior–subordinate relationship, lack of technically competent supervision, unfavourable organizational policies and administration, and inadequate salary.
- G. V. S. Rao's study (1970) on bank managers (size of sample = 60), which intended to test Herzberg's two-factor theory, has found promotions, company policies, and one's salary on the dissatisfaction scale.
- L. Narain's study (1971) on public sector managers (size of sample = 1,213) has ranked eight factors in the following order of importance: feeling of worthwhile accomplishments, recognition, decision-making authority, opportunity for personnel growth and development, promotional opportunity, prestige of the organization in the community, pay and fringe benefits, and job security. As far as need deficiencies are concerned, he has found that promotion, recognition, and personal growth and development show very high degrees of dissatisfaction, in that order.
- S. K. Bhattacharyya's study (1972) on managers (size of sample = 210) has shown lack of participation in goal setting, inadequacy of pay, inadequate job authority, and lack of opportunity to help people on the dissatisfaction scale.
- The study by D. M. Pestonjee and G. Basu (1972) on executives (size of sample = 80) has shown promotion and growth, recognition, prestige, organizational policies and administration, and autonomy as the major determinants of satisfaction.
- The study by S. Singhal and H. S. Upadhyay (1972) on supervisors (size of sample = 22) has determined opportunities for promotion, job security, working conditions, work group, opportunities for training, competent and sympathetic supervisors, adequate income, etc., as major motivational factors.
- K. G. Agarwal (1977) has sharply criticized Indian studies on work motivation, alleging that such researches suffer from a number of inconsistencies mainly because they have been carried out practically as a part of the job and were conducted for employees with the aim of helping them reduce production costs. Thus, the measures suggested by such researches have often proved to be short-term remedies and the much-discussed theories on motivation have functioned more like fads or fashions instead of being substantial and lasting points of reference. In tandem with U. Pareek (1974), Agarwal has developed a stratification model of work motivation with variables like social systems, self-status, and roles. Pareek (1974) has assumed the societal system to be a very important variable in the field of motivation as it causes or determines the behaviour of an individual in an organization.
- B. R. Sharma's study (1986) on administrators in Delhi (size of sample = 67) has found the power motive to be the main guiding force for motivation.
- Another study by Sharma (1986) on supervisors (size of sample = 3,378)—drawing samples from 50 manufacturing organizations both in the public sector and the private sector—has obtained score values for different factors that influence motivation, as presented in Table 5.2. The study has been carried out on a three-point scale, namely low, medium, and high frequencies.

Table 5.2 Factors of Motivation (Results of Sharma's Study)

Factors	Score values (%)
Superintendent–management relations	63.21
Monetary benefits	60.30
Objectivity and rationality	56.00
Recognition and appreciation	51.32
Welfare facilities	48.39
Scope for advancement	47.32
Grievance handling	45.83
Training and education	43.46
Participative management	39.68

- The study by S. Neelamegham and D. K. Vaid (1986) on motivation of the sales force (size of sample = 116) has found the highest need deficiencies with respect to prospects of promotion and recognition for good work.

By analysing the causal factors of industrial disputes, one can understand the perceived need gaps in Indian organizations. Table 5.3 has used information from various yearbooks on Indian labour to analyse such factors of industrial disputes. It establishes that Indian workers still have a large need gap in terms of extrinsic factors.

It is important to note that the major Indian studies are on supervisory and managerial personnel. Moreover, most of the studies have been carried out with a small sample, using only conventional methods like ranking and percentage calculation. Some studies have been carried out simply to authenticate Herzberg's two-factor theory, while some others are highly opinionated studies without much adherence to the norms of sampling and survey methods. In most of these cases, suitable and structured close-ended questionnaires were not administered and simple inferences after informal discussions with the samples—mostly drawn without following proper sampling procedure—were used as the premise. Another feature of most Indian studies is that they are based on the experiences of single industrial units. Representative results are difficult to obtain from a survey based on a small sample drawn from a single unit.

MOTIVATION AND MORALE

Morale is a cognitive concept encompassing feelings, attitudes, and sentiments that together contribute to a general feeling of satisfaction in the workplace.

Like morale, motivation is also a cognitive concept but it is different from morale on certain important aspects. Motivation stimulates individuals to action to achieve desired goals. It is, therefore, a function of need and drive. It mobilizes energy, which enhances the potential for morale. Morale, on the other hand, is the individual or group attitude towards a particular subject. It is a function of freedom or restraint towards

Table 5.3 Causal Factors of Industrial Disputes

Cause group	Years							
	1994		1995		1997		1998	
	Number of disputes	Percentage of total	Number of disputes	Percentage of total	Number of disputes	Percentage of total	Number of disputes	Percentage of total
Wages and allowances	354	29.4	320	30	305	23.4	233	21.2
Personnel	194	16.2	195	18.3	261	20.0	175	16.0
Retrenchment	19	1.6	10	0.9	7	0.5	8	0.7
Lay-off	3	0.2	4	0.4	7	0.5	6	0.6
Indiscipline	185	15.2	145	13.6	246	18.9	225	18.9
Violence	20	1.7	14	1.3	13	1.0	7	0.6
Leave and hours of work/shift	17	1.4	21	2.0	31	2.4	14	1.3
Bonus	92	7.8	79	7.4	112	86	123	11.2
Gherao	1	0.1	1	0.1	–	–	–	–
Non-implementation of agreements, awards, etc.	37	3.1	43	4.0	43	3.3	32	2.9

Charter of demands	55	4.6	61	5.7	68	5.2	97	8.8
Workload	10	0.8	10	0.9	9	0.7	6	0.6
Surplus labour	1	0.1	–	–	1	0.1	–	–
Betterment of amenities	16	1.3	18	1.7	34	2.6	12	1.1
Suspension/change of manufacturing process	1	0.1	–	–	–	–	1	0.1
Standing orders/ rules/service/ conditions/safety measures	50	4.2	52	4.9	34	2.6	13	1.2
Others	118	9.8	57	5.4	85	6.5	89	8.1
Not known	21	1.7	29.	2.7	37	2.8	49	4.5
Total	1,164	100	1,059	100	1,293	100	1,092	100

Source: Based on information from the Indian Labour Yearbook.

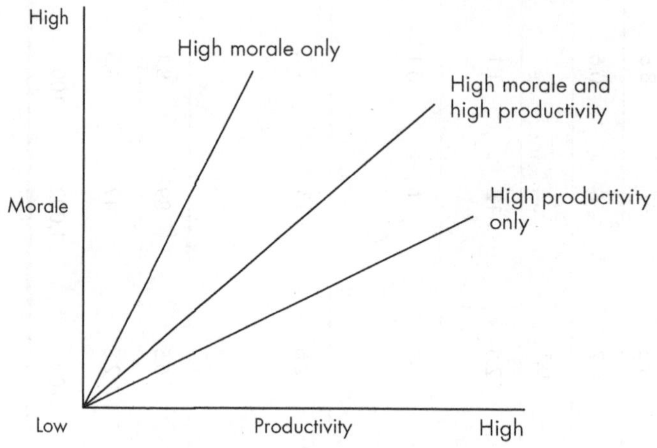

Figure 5.8 Morale and Productivity

some goal. It mobilizes sentiments, which form an important part of the organizational climate. Attitudes and sentiments, that is, morale, per se, affect productivity. High morale is an index of good human relations, which, among other things, reduces labour turnover, absenteeism, indiscipline, grievances, etc.

Factors that affect morale are primarily attitude and the level of job satisfaction of individual employees. From an organizational point of view, such factors can be delineated into organizational goals, leadership style, attitude of co-workers, nature of work, work environment, and the individual employee.

High morale is conventionally considered to be a contributor to high productivity, but such a correlation may not always be true. This is because high productivity may be the outcome of many other organizational initiatives that are independent of employee morale. Hence, even with low employee morale, high productivity is achievable. This can be illustrated using the model of Professor Keith Davis (1982) given in Figure 5.8.

Case Human Resource Development Is Not Enough: The Case of New Life

In spite of rapid technological reformations, New Life, a manufacturer of state-of-the-art lifestyle products, continues to believe that human resources are its backbone. A part of the new generation penetrating the lifestyle products business, New Life always needs to develop new products and generate a demand for them to strengthen its position in the market. In no time, however, New Life found other competing organizations aping its product ideas and introducing matching substitutes at a much lower price. For New Life, establishing a brand identity for new products requires a minimum incubation period of three to five years, while new competitors appear in the market in less than six months' time. This means that New Life cannot retain its share in the market, since its customers settle for price-efficient substitutes. An example is the price band of New Life's chewing gum, which was almost 50 per cent higher than that of other newly established competing organizations. This led to a significant market loss for New Life, after the initial surge in demand. New Life then went for product differentiation through stepped-up R&D activities. New Life repositioned their chewing gum with sweeteners that were harmless for children and diabetic patients, without, however, naming it as sugar-free as this would create a niche market of only diabetic patients. 'Healthy Chew' was the new brand name of their chewing gum, which reduced bad breath, protected teeth and gum, and even had the fragrance of almond and chocolate, making customers feel as if they are taking a bite of crispy candy. The first thing that New Life did before introducing it was to get the name 'Healthy Chew' patented.

New Life could do all these things because of its innovative workforce, which with its killer instincts ('do or die' attitude) always believes in change. New Life believes that its people are the key input for its continuous pursuit of product innovation. Human resource development (HRD) at New Life systematically reviews the competencies of people and meets the gap through various interventions. For New Life, training and development is the last priority. They make use of job rotation, employee empowerment, and career development as major instruments to develop its human resources.

New Life systematically conducts surveys through a human resource development questionnaire (HRDQ) and an organizational effectiveness questionnaire (OEQ) to track the feel of their workforce on its HRD practices. Based on the findings of these two questionnaires, New Life designs the HRD programmes, helping its people to align with the HRD actions of the organization.

Technological change in lifestyle product manufacturing is very high and takes place at very short intervals. Of late, New Life is observing that its people are unable to keep pace with the new requirements and have proved to be ineffective in many areas.

The CEO of the company believes that despite the various HRD interventions, something is missing, as many New Lifers join their competitors before they complete their probation period of one year.

CASE QUESTION

As the general manager of New Life, identify the possible reasons for employees to be lured away by competitors and suggest a detailed course of action.

SUMMARY

- Motivation and leadership are the two dimensions of direction. Theoretically, *direction* is defined as guidance or inspiration. Apart from motivation and leadership, issuance of instructions, supervision, and communication also play an important role in direction. Characteristically, direction follows the principle of the scalar sign and it does not end just by giving instructions. Direction also requires regular performance monitoring. As a continuous function, direction encompasses all hierarchical levels, focusing on human factors.
- To motivate means to incite. It is to create a desire to do a task or a willingness to work in the manner in which one wants it done, which is distinct from the capacity to work. *Motivation* is also defined as a force that gives rise to particular forms of behaviour to accomplish a particular task.
- From the organizational point of view, the process of motivation follows certain defined steps, which as a continuum need to be periodically reviewed and adjusted accordingly. The process starts with the identification of the need deficiency of employees and leads to determining the appropriate strategy to close the perceived need gap. Subsequently, organizations enforce goal-directed behaviour of employees to enable them to meet their need gap. In the process of motivating employees, organizations can ensure productive use of resources, increased efficiency, quality consciousness, and realization of organizational objectives and strategies, and also create an environment for creativity

and growth, which can together culminate in organizational stability and reduce employee turnover and absenteeism.

- There are many motivational theories. Starting from Taylor, who emphasized the linking of incentives for increased level of performance, to Abraham Maslow, who suggested the identification of need deficiency and then developed suitable motivational reinforcers, to the modern theories of McClelland (achievement need theory) and Victor Vroom (expectancy theory), the list goes on. According to Megginson's analysis, they can be classified as perspective theories, content theories, and process theories.
- Motivation and morale are often considered as the same concept, though mistakenly so. *Morale* is the more inherent mental condition or attitude of employees which creates the work atmosphere. *Motivation*, on the other hand, induces goal-directed behaviour in employees.

KEY TERMS

Attribution theory and locus of control: This theory concerns itself with the cognitive process by which an individual interprets behaviour attributing to certain parts of the relevant environment.

Equity theory: The theory proposes that in a work environment, motivation is influenced by one's perception of how equitably they are treated compared to others.

Expectancy theory: This theory emphasizes that people feel increasingly motivated if they perceive that their effort will result in successful performance and that successful performance will ensure desired results.

Goal setting theory: The theory considers two cognitive determinants of behaviour: values and intentions (goals). Emotions and desires represent the form of values and value judgements, while intentions are goals to satisfy desires or emotions (values). Setting specific attainable goals is related to a high level of performance.

Job characteristic model: This model shows how a good job design can lead to internal motivation of employees and contribute to better job performance. Five job characteristics that lead to employee motivation are skill variety, task identity, task significance, autonomy, and feedback.

Morale: Morale is a cognitive concept encompassing feelings, attitudes, and sentiments that together contribute to a general feeling of satisfaction in the workplace.

Motivation: Motivation is the desire to do a task or a willingness to work in the manner in which one wants it done, which is distinct from the capacity to work.

Performance satisfaction theory: This theory, based on Vroom's expectancy model, proposes that performance leads to satisfaction, contrary to the belief that satisfaction leads to performance. It considers motivation (efforts), performance (accomplishment), and satisfaction as separate variables.

REVIEW QUESTIONS

1. Define the term *motivation*. Why it is so important for HR managers?
2. Which motivational tool will you like to use for knowledge workers? Will your approach be different for operators on a shop floor?
3. Critically review the contribution of Maslow and Herzberg to the theories of motivation. Do you think they have any relevance for new-generation workers?

4. How do you distinguish between process theories and content theories of motivation?
5. Distinguish between *motivation* and *morale*. Discuss how morale can influence productivity.
6. Can motivation be defined as perception? What are the circumstances in which perception can influence the motive strength of a worker?
7. Write short notes on the following:
   i. Job satisfaction
   ii. Performance satisfaction theory
   iii. Motivation and morale
   iv. Theory of expectancy
   v. Motivation and productivity

CRITICAL THINKING QUESTIONS

1. A large manufacturing organization with a global presence has a macro policy of recruiting people from diverse disciplines. However, during the process of shortlisting, the organization puts stress on screening the family backgrounds of the prospective employees, apart from the educational and skill requirements. In the process, the organization is able to ensure that prospective candidates are from high-income families. Do you think such a policy is compatible with the process of designing the motivational reinforcers for the company? Give adequate justification for your answer.
2. A knowledge-intensive IT company has booked orders in excess from a number of international clients which require time-bound execution of the projects. The company's analysis revealed that to meet customers' requirements, it would need to recruit new hands and at the same time motivate the existing employees to deliver their best. Thus, the company wants to make employee motivation a strategic tool to meet its deadlines. Explain the ways in which this can be done.

REFERENCES

Adams, J. (1965). 'Inequity in Social Exchange', in L. Berkowitz (ed.), *Advances in Experimental Social Psychology*, pp. 267–299. New York: Academic Press.

——— (1963). 'Toward an Understanding of Inequity', *Journal of Abnormal Psychology*, 67(5): pp. 422–436.

Agarwal, K. G. (1977). 'Self, Role, Status and Motivation: Towards Stratification Theory of Work Motivation', *Indian Journal of Industrial Relations*, 10 (3): pp. 379–386.

Alderfer, Clayton P. (1967). 'An Organizational Syndrome', *Administrative Science Quarterly*, 12 (3): pp. 440–460.

Argyris, C. (1957). *Personality and Organization*. New York: Harper & Row.

Bhattacharyya, S. K. (1972). 'Perception of Organizational Characteristics in Relation to Need Gratification among Indian Managers', *Indian Management*, November, pp. 29–34.

Bose, S. K. (1951). 'Man and His Work', *Indian Journal of Psychology*, 26, pp. 1–20.

Fayol, H. (1949). *General and Industrial Management.* Translated by C. Storrs. London: Pitman.

Ganguli, H. C. (1964). *Structure and Process of Organisation*. Bombay: Asia Publishing House.

Hackman, J. R. and G. R. Oldham (1974). 'Motivation through Design of Work: Test of Theory', *Organizational Behaviour and Human Performance*, 16 (2): pp. 250–279.

——— (1981). 'Relationship between Organizational Structure and Employee Reactions: Comparing Alternative Frameworks', *Administrative Science Quarterly*, 26, pp. 66–83.

Herzberg, F. (1966). *Work and the Nature of Man.* Cleveland, OH: World Publishing.

——— (1959). *The Motivation to Work.* New York: John Wiley & Sons.

Jones, M. R. (ed.) (1955). 'Deficiency Motivation and Growth Motivation', *Nebraska Symposium on Motivation.* Lincoln: University of Nebraska Press.

Keith, Davis (1982). *Human Behaviour at Work: Human Relations and Organizational Behaviour.* New Delhi: Tata McGraw-Hill.

Kelley, H. H. (1967). 'Attribution Theory in Social Psychology', in D. Levine (ed.), *Nebraska Symposium on Motivation*, vol. 15, pp. 192–238. Lincoln: University of Nebraska Press.

——— (1973). 'The Process of Causal Attribution', *American Psychologist*, 28, pp. 107–128.

Lahiri, D. K. and S. Srivastava (1967). 'Determinants of Satisfaction in Middle Management Personnel', *Journal of Applied Psychology*, 3, pp. 251–265.

Lewin, Kurt (1951). *Field Theory in Social Science.* New York: Harper & Row.

Likert, R. and D. Katz (1948). 'Supervisory Practices and Organizational Structure as They Affect Employee Productivity and Morale', *American Management Association*, Personnel Series, 120, pp. 14–24.

Locke, E. A. (1968). 'Towards a Theory of Task Motivation and Incentives', *Organizational Behaviour and Human Performance*, 3 (2): pp. 157–189.

——— (1968). 'Toward a Theory of Task Motivation and Incentives', *Organizational Behavior and Human Performance*, 3 (2): pp. 157–189.

Maslow, A. H. (1943). 'A Theory of Human Motivation', *Psychological Review*, 50 (4): pp. 370–96.

McClelland, D. C. (1977). *Human Behaviour at Work.* New Delhi: Tata McGraw-Hill.

McGregor, Douglas (1957). 'The Human Side of Enterprise', *The Management Review*, 46 (11): pp. 3–20.

Megginson, L. C. (1977). *Personnel and Human Resource Administration*, 3rd ed. Homewood, IL: Richard D. Irwin, Inc.

Murray, H. A. (1938). *Explorations in Personality.* New York: Oxford University Press.

Narain, L. (1971). 'Managerial Motivation in Public Enterprises', *Lok Udyog*, 9, pp. 861–875 and p. 883.

Neelamegham, S. and D. K. Vaid (1986). 'Sales Force Motivation: Challenging Task', *Indian Management*, 25 (12): pp. 21–25.

Padaki, O. and A. M. Dolke (1970). 'A Study of Job Attitudes'. Ahmedabad: ATIRA Research Monograph.

Pareek, U. (1974). 'A Conceptual Model of Work Motivation', *Indian Journal of Industrial Relations*, 10 (1): pp. 15–23.

Pestonjee, D. M. and G. Basu (1972). 'A Study of Job Satisfaction of Indian Executives', *Indian Journal of Industrial Relations*, 8, pp. 3–16.

Porter, L. W. and E. E. Lawler (1968). *Managerial Attitudes and Performance.* Homewood, IL: Richard D. Irwin, Inc.

Rao, G. V. S. (1970). 'Determinants of Job Satisfaction in Managerial Personnel', *Indian Manager*, 1, pp. 55–62.

Rotter, J. (1966). 'Generalized Expectancies for Internal versus External Control of Reinforcements', *Psychological Monographs*, 80: pp. 1–28.

Sawalapurkar, M. P. et al (1968). 'Job Motivation of Middle Managers', *Indian Journal of Applied Psychology*, 5, pp. 7–10.

Schachter, S. (1959). *The Psychology of Affiliation*. Stanford, CA: Stanford University Press.

Sharma, B. R. (1986). *Motivational Crisis in Indian Administration: A Case of Existential Sickness*. New Delhi: Indian Institute of Public Administration.

Singhal, S. and H. S. Upadhyay (1972). 'Psychology of Men at Work: Employees Perception of Job Incentives', *Indian Journal of Industrial Relations*, 8, pp. 17–30.

Skinner, B. F. (1953). *Science and Human Behavior*. New York: Free Press.

Taylor, Frederick W. (1911). *The Principles of Scientific Management*. New York: Harper & Row.

Tolman, Edward (1951). 'A Psychological Model', in Talcott Parsons and Edward A. Shils (eds.), *Toward a General Theory of Action*. New York: Harper Torchbooks.

Vroom, V. H. (1964). *Work and Motivation*. New York: John Wiley & Sons.

White, R. W. (1959). 'Motivation Reconsidered: The Concept of Competence', *Psychological Review*, LXVI (5): pp. 297–330.

Whyte, W. F. (1955). *Money and Motivation*. New York: Harper & Row.

FURTHER READING

Argyris, C. (1964). *Integrating the Individual and the Organization*. New York: John Wiley & Sons.

Atkinson, John W. (1966). *An Introduction to Motivation*. New Delhi: Affiliated East-West Press.

Bhattacharyya, Dipak Kumar (2006). *Human Resource Management*, 2nd edition. New Delhi: Excel Books.

——— (2007). *Human Resource Research Methods*. New Delhi: Oxford University Press.

Flippo, E. B. (1989). *Principles of Personnel Management*. Tokyo: McGraw-Hill.

Haimann, Theo (1989). *Supervisory Management for Healthcare Organizations*. St Louis, MO: The Catholic Health Association.

Haimann, Theo and Raymond L. Hilgert (1977). *Supervision: Concepts and Practices of Management*. Cincinnati, OH: South-Western Publishing Co.

Haimann, Theo and William G. Scott (1974). *Management in the Modern Organization*, 2nd edition. Cambridge, MA: Houghton Mifflin.

Herzberg, F., B. Manser and Snyderman (1967). *The Motivation to Work*. New York: John Wiley & Sons.

Herzberg, Frederick (1966). *Work and the Nature of Man*. Cleveland, OH: World Press.

Koontz, Harold and Cyril O'Donnell (1959). *Principles of Management: An Analysis of Managerial Functions*, 2nd ed. New York: McGraw-Hill.

——— (1968). *Principles of Management: An Analysis of Managerial Functions*, 4th edition. New York: McGraw-Hill.

Maslow, Abraham (1968). *Toward a Psychology of Being*, 2nd ed. New York: Van Nostrand.

Mayo, E. (1933). *The Human Problems of an Industrial Civilization*. New York: Macmillan.

——— (1949). *The Social Problems of an Industrial Civilization*. London: Routledge & Kegan Paul.

——— (1945). *The Social Problems of an Industrial Civilization*. Boston, MA: Harvard University.

Rotter, J. B. (1967). 'A New Scale for the Measurement of Interpersonal Trust', *Journal of Personality*, 35, pp. 651–665.

Urwick, L. and E. F. L. Brech (1945). 'The Making of Scientific Management', 2, *Management in British Industry*. London: Pitman.

Yoder, Dale (1970). *Personnel Management and Industrial Relations*. New York: Prentice Hall.

6

Directing Through Leadership

After going through this chapter, you will be able to understand:

- the theories of leadership
- the difference between a leader and a manager
- the different styles of leadership
- why leadership is essential for managing an organization
- the process of developing leadership in an organization
- the influence of leadership on the work environment of an organization

Human Resources of ONGC

With a dedicated team of about 40,000 professionals, today, ONGC is one of the best-managed public sector companies in India. ONGC reaches performance figures that surpass even its own targets. With progressive policies in scientific planning, acquisition, utilization, training, and motivation of the team, the company has achieved a remarkable place in the oil and gas industry. A large pool of ONGC professionals are scientists encompassing geologists, geophysicists, geochemists, drilling engineers, reservoir engineers, petroleum engineers, production engineers, engineering and technical service providers, financial and human resource (HR) experts, and IT professionals. ONGC has been quite successful in managing such a large knowledge pool, which is no mean achievement.

ONGC's HR vision is to attain organizational excellence by developing and inspiring the true potential of the company's human capital and providing opportunities for growth, well-being, and enrichment. Within the ambit of such a vision, the HR mission of the company has been framed with an aim towards creating a value- and knowledge-based organization by inculcating a culture of learning, innovation, and teamwork, and by aligning business priorities with aspirations of employees, leading to the development of an empowered, responsive, and competent human capital.

Among other HR objectives, ONGC emphasizes on training the business leaders of tomorrow, primarily to achieve its strategic intent of meeting the challenging demands of the business environment. With a focus on world-class systems and participative work culture, ONGC has today reached its global leadership position through people leadership.

INTRODUCTION

The word *leader* first appeared in the English language in the 1300s. It stems from the root word *leden*, which means 'to travel' or 'show the way'. The term *leadership* followed around five centuries later. It is usually accepted that the first scientific study on leadership was done in the United States. Fields as divergent as political science, psychology, education, history, agriculture, public administration, management, anthropology, biology, military sciences, philosophy, and sociology have all contributed to the understanding of leadership and many of them have established sub-fields in the study of leadership. In virtually every culture, the earliest literature deals with accounts of heroes and the results of their leadership. Joseph Campbell (1991), while working on various myths, finds the concept of leadership in every culture. Leadership arises in response to a need. It essentially derives from the uncertainties and dangers built into the human condition (Lee G. Bolman and Terrence Deal 1991). Conditions that develop leadership vary from situation to situation and from one historical time to another. Due to this reason, it is difficult to generalize the term 'leadership'. Leadership in a battlefield is different from leadership in a business organization. Leadership at the corporate level (highest level) of an organization is different from effective leadership at the shop-floor level (operation level). Hence, a universal model of leadership is unthinkable.

Leadership is the only subject on which more than 3,000 studies have so far been carried out and more than 2,000 definitions have been given by management researchers and thinkers. Even then, it is difficult to define leadership in its entirety.

In any work situation, when two or more persons come together to work for a goal, a structure or a group develops and the leadership emerges. The reasons for success and failure with regard to business, sports, or any movement can be attributed to the leadership. Hence, *leadership* can be defined as an activity that influences people to strive willingly for group objectives. It exists only in relationships and only in the imagination and perceptions of 'followers'.

Even though there is a lot of disagreement over the meaning of leadership, it is commonly agreed upon that leadership is very important since it makes a substantial difference to organizations. It is typically a solution for most organizational problems.

LEADERSHIP

Leadership is a process of influencing people to achieve intended goals in a given situation. Based on this definition, the characteristics of leadership can be listed as the following:

- **It is a personal quality**: This quality makes other people follow a leader. The quality of a leader is the aggregation of their intelligence, communications skills, emotional balance, inner drive, energy, and other managerial skills (conceptual, technical, human relations, etc.). To make others follow or to exert others to do the work requires the presence of all these qualities. The degree of requirement of these qualities will, however, depend on the situation.
- **It is a process of influencing others**: It is only through the process of influencing that a leader makes others work towards achieving goals. People may lack initiative or the urge to work, or they may be demotivated. Such behavioural characteristics may seriously impede the achievement of organizational objectives. A good leader, through their influence, can turn the situation around and make people work towards achieving goals.
- **It regulates individual behaviour**: Individual behavioural attributes may stand in the way of achieving group goals. A leader can regulate individual behaviour through the process of influencing and

make an individual submit to group norms. For example, by following the approach of 'discipline without punishment', as advocated by John Huberman (1964), a leader can correct the undisciplined behaviour of an individual and help them to become a good performer.

- **It is based on a relationship between leaders and followers**: A leader succeeds by developing relationships with followers. They cannot flourish in a vacuum. This is the reason why leadership is also known as followership. In order to develop such a relationship, a leader has to have confidence. A two-way relationship can be developed through effective interpersonal relationships and also through participative decision making, which is taking decisions through a group consensus.
- **It is a continuous process**: Leadership is not a one-time exercise of influence of a leader on their subordinates or followers. In order to be a good leader, the manager should sustain the leadership continuously.
- **It is situational**: Leadership is exerted in situations that vary from time to time. Responding to varying situations requires different leadership approaches. One situation may require taking a lenient view, while another may require being tough. Since an organization requires the ability to respond to changes in order to remain competitive, leaders are also required to constantly change their approach. This requires leaders to develop multi-skills and multi-abilities to come out as winners.

Functions of Leadership

Leadership is a means of directing. It represents that part of executive activities by which a leader guides and influences the behaviour of the subordinates and the group towards some specified goals by personally working with them and understanding their feelings and problems. In recent years, management experts, psychologists, sociologists, and behavioural scientists have tried to identify the functions of leadership in varied ways and from different viewpoints. Some of the views are explained here.

Sociological view

Among the sociologists who did in-depth studies on the functions of leaders, the opinion of P. Selzink (1984) may be considered as the most appropriate. According to him, the leadership function entails setting goals, shaping and reshaping organization, and reconciling internal and external forces. In fact, it is the creative function of the leader that calls for viewing and reviewing organizational environment, work accomplishment, and determining near and remote goals.

A review of the work of other sociologists highlights that the leader is supposed to build goals and determine the policies to be fed into the social structure of the enterprise. It is the fundamental duty of a leader to ensure that the enterprise does not merely survive but grows in stature as well. Leaders should be in a position to gauge the desired changes, movements, and functions for the enterprise to steer it towards the larger goals. Another important function is to manage and mitigate internal conflict. It is a hard fact that conflict is almost always imminent in big organizations due to diverse opinions, views, beliefs, and values. The effectiveness of leaders lies in their endeavours to win the consent of several groups and put them to work in accomplishing the objective and the enterprise mission.

Psychological view

According to psychologists, people will best respond in terms of output if the organization provides opportunities for them to appraise and appropriate their basic, social, and ego needs. As a matter of fact, one of the basic functions of managers and executives (leaders) is to devise the necessary motivational system to meet the needs of employees. It should, however, be kept in mind that though the above arrangement is sound from the viewpoint of motivation, it is not adequate to precisely specify the scope of exercise of leadership on the part of the management.

Other views

Management experts have, of late, given a lot of attention to identifying the exact function of leadership. According to their study, the leadership function can be viewed as directing, responding, and representing. Eminent scholar Leonard Sayles (1979) viewed *directing* as the primary function of leadership. In big organizations, where divergent views and a number of groups exist, it is essentially through the means of directing that all of them are unified and coordinated for a central purpose. In this regard, managers and executives have to take the required initiative with an intelligent approach and a rational attitude.

Management experts consider *responding* as the second function of leadership. It signifies responsiveness to the initiatives of subordinates. It may often be noticed that subordinates ask for guidance, assistance, advice, and help from their superiors. Moreover, subordinates want to be appreciated for the services rendered by them. The quality of leadership helps the superior to appraise the needs of their subordinates and meet them intelligently.

The other essential function of leadership is *representing*. It signifies that superiors properly and effectively represent the interests of the total group both among their peers and to the higher level in the managerial hierarchy. This aspect of subordinate thinking may be observed in cases where subordinates initiate action that is required to be accomplished by their superiors or higher-level personnel. The leadership quality enables executives to represent such group effort and get positive responses.

Effective leadership creates a congenial environment for employees not only through influence but also by responding to their problems, feelings, aspirations, and ambitions. At the same time, it enhances the image of the organization in the larger world outside. Thus, the functions of a leader can be listed as the following:

- To develop teamwork in the organization
- To act as an important change agent in the organization
- To balance the use of power
- To act as a representative of subordinates
- To be a counsellor to employees
- To help employees to optimally utilize their time
- To help in achieving organizational effectiveness
- To enhance the level of motivation and morale of employees
- To inculcate human values in the organization
- To increase the level of commitment and loyalty of employees towards the organization

LEADERSHIP AND MANAGEMENT

A good leader may be a poor manager and a good manager need not be a leader. Warren Bennis and Burt Nanus (1997) suggested that 'managers do things right and leaders do the right thing'. Yet, the terms 'manager' and 'leader' are used interchangeably. However, leadership and managership are not the same. One finds the existence of *leadership* even in unorganized groups, while *managership* exists only in organized and structured groups. A manager is more than a leader. Due to their positional role, a manager has to organize and control the activities of people towards the accomplishment of objectives.

As a manager one has to perform all the functions of management, but as a leader, one has to direct, that is, influence people to achieve goals. Therefore, leadership is a part of management and not management in its entirety. It is often said that 'all managers are leaders but all leaders are not managers.'

To stretch the debate further, one can examine the views of major contributors in this field. Their main contention is that leaders and managers vary in their orientation towards goals, conceptions about work, interpersonal styles, and self-perceptions. W. French (1987) while distinguishing between a leader and a manager said this: 'Leaders are often dramatic and unpredictable in style. They tend to create an atmosphere of change, which can even lead to chaos. They are often obsessed by their ideas, which appear as visionary and consequently excite, stimulate and drive other people to work hard to create reality out of fantasy. Managers are typically hardworking, analytical, tolerant and fair-minded. They have a strong sense of belonging to the organization, and take great pride in perpetuating and improving the status quo.'

Another view states that leadership is just one aspect of what a manager must possess. Leaders are only involved in influencing subordinates towards the achievement of organizational goals. Robert P. Vecchio (1988) pointed out that leadership can exist on a formal or an informal basis. John Kotter (1991) even said that leadership and management are distinctive, complementary activities necessary for success in the business environment.

Management functions include planning, organizing, staffing, directing, and controlling. In order to direct their subordinates, the manager must motivate, communicate, supervise, guide, and lead. Thus, it is the directing function that propels a manager to become responsible for effectively and successfully leading their subordinates. Managing is more effective if those who manage are also the leaders. Since a part of a manager's job involves getting things done through the efforts of other people, being a skilful leader will help because leadership can substantially influence the results. Thus, leadership is an essential part of successful management, as explained in terms of the following points:

- The leader guides and directs by eliminating uncertainties as to what should be done, and thereby coordinates individual efforts in order to streamline them into one direction.
- The leader motivates people and integrates individual needs with the needs of the organization.
- The leader represents the group to the outside world and the outside world to the group. The group looks upon the leader as a source of information and satisfaction.

Hence, a leader provides direction, drive, and representation. It is, however, argued that since managers have the authority to provide incentives, reprimand, fine, deprive, or otherwise punish people in the organization, management leadership is more potential than real. Discipline and conformity can be maintained through hierarchy and fear of loss of employment.

Leadership should not be made synonymous with management. A leader need not be a good manager since managing involves more than leading, while a manager can do reasonably well even when they are not a leader. Leadership may be considered as one of the significant prerequisites to managerial effectiveness. A list of the differences between managers and leaders has been provided in Table 6.1.

Formal and Informal Leadership

The organization structure is characterized by a hierarchy of positions that are manned by individuals in a scalar chain. Officially, every manager enjoys the power to lead and secure support of their subordinates. Managers are then leaders because they have the formal authority to direct, motivate, and lead people. This kind of leadership is known as *formal* or *managerial leadership*. Informal leaders are not delegated any

Table 6.1 Managers Versus Leaders

Managers	Leaders
A manager is more than a leader.	A leader need not be a manager.
The term *management* is a wider term.	*Leadership* is a narrow term.
A manager fits in an organized structure.	A leader may also be in an informal group.
A manager exercises different functions of management to achieve group goals.	A leader exercises influence on people to achieve group goals.
The authority of a manager stems from their positional role, that is, it is delegated from the top.	A leader earns their authority by virtue of their skills, knowledge, and abilities.
A successful manager has to be a good leader.	Leaders need not be managers.

authority to lead; rather, they acquire the authority to guide and lead. *Informal leadership* is spontaneous and is a part of informal organization. If properly handled, informal organization offers a good training ground for formal leaders to develop and test their leadership skills.

Significance of Leadership

Leadership is important to an organization. This aspect can be appreciated in terms of the following points:

- **It improves motivation and morale of employees**: A successful leader influences the behaviour of an individual and thereby enhances the involvement of individual employees in their work. By creating confidence in employees and sustaining their enthusiasm and involvement in achieving organizational goals, the leader enhances the motivation and morale of employees. Even in a situation of crisis in an organization (for example, a bad phase in terms of profitability due to market slowdown), a leader can sustain a high level of commitment and motivation from employees, which may ultimately help the organization to turn around. That is why good leaders are considered to be *turnaround agents* in organizations.
- **It leads to higher performance**: Leadership pushes the group to strive for results, that is, achieving organizational goals. With an increased level of commitment and motivation, employees perform better. Higher performance leads to increased productivity, which results in increased profitability even in a competitive market.
- **It is an aid to authority**: Leadership is a process of influencing others. Mere use of authority by managers may not lead to results. When managerial authority is enriched with good leadership, employees start cooperating. Therefore, while formal exercising of authority may not result in success, authority with leadership proves to be more effective.
- **It determines organizational success**: In the process of unifying group efforts to achieve organizational goals, leadership enhances organizational effectiveness. A good manager alone cannot achieve this.
- **It helps to respond to change**: Organizations need to quickly respond to changes. However, any change in technology, process, methods, and plans (including strategic plans) always encounters resistance from

people working in the organization. Leadership can play a crucial role in implementing change in organizations by creating an environment conducive to change. People follow leaders and they like to emulate the examples set by leaders, and this helps to make the process of change smooth and successful.

- **It inculcates values in the organization**: A value-based organization earns increased commitment and loyalty from employees. Since a good leader is inspirational, good leadership also successfully instils human values, which shapes the attitude of employees towards work.

Principles of Leadership

The basic principles of leadership can be grouped as the following:

- **Leaders must know themselves and continuously seek self-improvement**: To know one's self, one has to understand attributes like *being, knowing,* and *doing.* Seeking self-improvement means continually strengthening such attributes, and this can be accomplished through reading, self-study, classes, etc.
- **Leaders must be technically proficient**: As a leader, one must know their job and the job of their followers.
- **Leaders must seek responsibility and take responsibility for their actions**: A leader must guide their organization to new heights. In the process of guiding, things may go wrong at times. They must not blame others but take responsibility themselves. They must analyse the situation, take corrective action, and move on to the next action.
- **Leaders must make sound and timely decisions**: Using problem solving, decision making, planning, and various controlling tools, a leader must make sound and timely decisions.
- **Leaders must set an example**: A leader is a role model for followers. The followers must not only be told what they are expected to do, but also be able to see their leader guiding by example.
- **Leaders must know people and think about their well-being**: Leaders must know the nature of their followers and be nurturing and caring towards them.
- **Leaders must keep followers informed**: Transparency in information enhances commitment from the followers. Hence, a leader must know how to communicate and keep their followers informed.
- **Leaders must develop a sense of responsibility in their followers**: Development orientation requires inculcating good character traits in followers, which will help them to carry out their professional responsibilities.
- **Leaders must ensure that tasks are understood, supervised, and accomplished**: This also requires transparent communication with followers.
- **Leaders must train followers as a team**: Inculcating the team spirit and culture enables a leader to accomplish goals.
- **Leaders must develop full capabilities of an organization**: By developing the team spirit, a leader develops an organization to its fullest capabilities.

Factors of Leadership

The four major factors of leadership are:

1. **Follower**: Different people require different styles of leadership. For example, a newly recruited person requires more supervision than an experienced one. Similarly, a follower with poor motivation requires a different approach than one with a high degree of motivation. Thus, the fundamental

starting point is a good understanding of human nature, that is, needs, emotions, and motivation. Leaders must know and understand their followers.

2. **Leader**: One must have an honest understanding of what one is, what one knows, and what one can do. Also, it is the followers and not the leader who determine whether a leader is successful. If a follower does not trust or lacks confidence in a leader, then they will be uninspired. Hence, to be successful as a leader, one has to convince one's followers and not themselves or their superiors.
3. **Communication**: A leader leads through two-way communication. Communication need not always be verbal; it may also be non-verbal. For instance, through personal selling (their behaviour), a leader sets the example. This also communicates to followers. A leader should not ask their followers to perform anything that they would not be willing to do. What and how a leader communicates either builds or harms the relationship between a leader and their followers.
4. **Situation**: All situations are different. What one does in one situation may not always work in another situation. A leader must use their judgement to decide the best course of action and the leadership style needed for each situation. For example, one may need to confront an employee about inappropriate behaviour, but if the confrontation is too late or too early, too harsh or too weak, the results may be disastrous.

LEADERSHIP AND ENVIRONMENT

Every organization has a particular work environment that dictates to a considerable degree how its leaders respond to problems and opportunities. This environment is largely also a legacy of past leaders and sustained by its present leaders. Leaders exert influence on the environment in three ways:

1. **The goals and performance standards established by them**: Successful organizations have leaders who set *high standards* and *goals* in terms of strategies, market leadership, plans, presentations, productivity, quality, and reliability.
2. **The values established by them for the organization**: *Values* reflect the concern that the organization has for its employees, customers, investors, vendors, and the surrounding community. These values define the manner in which business will be conducted and the type of business that the organization will engage in.
3. **The business and people concepts established by them**: *Concepts* define what products or services the organization will offer and the methods and processes for conducting business.

The goals, values, and concepts make up the organization's 'personality' and determine how outsiders and insiders observe the organization. This personality defines the roles, relationships, rewards, and rites that take place in the organization.

There are two distinct forces that dictate how to act within an organization:

1. **Roles**: *Roles* are the positions that are defined by a set of expectations about the behaviour of any newly recruited person. Each role has a set of tasks and responsibilities that may or may not be spelled out. Roles have a powerful effect on behaviour because one is paid for the performance of the role; there is prestige attached to a role; and there is a sense of accomplishment or challenge.
2. **Relationships**: *Relationships* are determined by tasks. Some tasks are performed alone, but most are carried out in relation to others. The tasks will determine who the role holder is required to interact with, how often, and towards what end. Also, the greater the interaction, the greater is the liking.

This, in turn, leads to more frequent interaction. Human behaviour is such that it is hard to like someone whom one has no contact with and, therefore, one tends to seek out those whom one likes. People tend to do what they are rewarded for, and friendship is a powerful reward. Many tasks and behaviours that are associated with a role are brought about by these relationships. Hence, new tasks and behaviours are expected of the present role holder because a strong relationship was developed in the past, either by the present role holder or by a past role holder.

Each organization also has its own distinctive culture. It is a combination of the founders, past leadership, current leadership, crises, events, history, and size. This results in rites, that is, routines, rituals, and a certain way of doing things. These rites impact individual behaviour with regard to what it takes to be in good standing (the norm) and direct the appropriate behaviour for each circumstance.

The *climate* is the feel of the organization and the individual, and shared perceptions and attitudes of the organization's members. While *culture* is the deeply rooted nature of the organization that is a result of long-held formal and informal systems, rules, traditions, and customs, climate is a short-term phenomenon created by the current leadership. Climate represents the beliefs about the 'feel of the organization' by its members. This individual perception of the 'feel of the organization' comes from what the people believe about the activities that occur in the organization.

Organizational climate is directly related to the leadership and management style of the leader, based on the values, attributes, skills, and actions as well as the priorities of the leader. The *ethical climate*, then, is the 'feel of the organization' about the activities that have ethical content or those aspects of the work environment that constitute ethical behaviour. The ethical climate, therefore, is the awareness about whether everything is being done in the right manner or whether everyone is behaving in the way they ought to behave. The behaviour (character) of the leader is the most important factor that impacts the climate.

On the other hand, culture is a long-term, complex phenomenon. Culture represents the shared expectations and self-image of the organization. It consists of the mature values that create tradition or the way things have always been done. Things are done differently in every organization. The collective vision that defines the institution is a reflection of its culture. Individual leaders cannot easily create or change culture because culture is a part of the organization. Culture influences the characteristics of the climate by its effect on the actions and thought processes of the leader. However, everything a leader does will affect the climate of the organization.

LEADERSHIP AND POWER

Power, in the case of leadership, is divided into six categories. However, each category can be linked with another, as they are interrelated. *Expert* and *informational power* is concerned with skills, knowledge, and information wherein the holders of such abilities are able to utilize and influence others. Technicians and computer personnel can be placed in this category. *Reward* and *coercive power* involve the ability to either reward or punish persons being influenced, in order to gain compliance. *Legitimate power* is power that has been confirmed by the very role structure of the group or the organization itself, and is accepted by all as correct and without dispute. The power vested in the armed forces or the police force is an example of legitimate power. *Referent power*, on the other hand, involves those being influenced identifying with the leader. An example is film personalities using their image to enter the political arena.

Most leaders make use of a combination of the six types of power, depending on the leadership style used. Authoritarian leaders, for example, use a mixture of legitimate, coercive, and reward powers to dictate the policies, plans, and activities of a group. In contrast, a democratic or participative leader would use mainly referent power, involving all members of the group in the decision-making process.

Leadership Styles

The problem of a leadership style is basically concerned with deciding the extent to which a manager should be dictatorial and the extent to which they are supposed to be participative or consultative. Leadership styles can be categorized as follows:

- Authoritarian or leader-centred or autocratic style
- Democratic or participative or consultative or group-centred style
- Laissez-faire style
- Paternalistic leadership

Autocratic style of leadership

The *autocratic style of leadership* is characterized by centralization of authority and decision making and very limited participation by the subordinates of the group. The autocratic leader accomplishes results through use of authority, fear of deprivation, punishment and other coercive measures. Since it is negative in character, an authoritarian approach will succeed only in the short run and will fail to motivate subordinates for better performance in the long run. Resentment, absenteeism, and a higher turnover rate for employees are some of the common consequences of this approach. However, the autocratic style still deserves consideration because of the following reasons:

- There may be very little time for participation, particularly in a situation of crisis.
- Confidential matters may not permit normal consultation.
- A leader may have more knowledge and thereby compensate for no participation by subordinates.

Democratic style of leadership

The *democratic style of leadership* allows substantial participation by members of the group in the management and decision-making processes. Subordinates are frequently consulted by the manager on wide-ranging problems and are allowed sufficient freedom to communicate with the leader and also with their fellow subordinates. The democratic style of leadership is based upon a positive assumption about human beings. It encourages a cooperative spirit and development of the skills of subordinates to make them capable of managing higher responsibilities. This style of leadership contributes substantially to the satisfaction of the subordinates.

Laissez-faire style of leadership

In the *laissez-faire style of leadership*, the leader depends largely upon the group and its members to establish their own goals and make their own decisions. The leader is passive and assumes the role of just another member of the group. Tasks are assigned in general terms. The laissez-faire approach is meant for selective application, though. If the subordinate is intelligent, highly qualified, and experienced, and desires self-fulfilment, a manager may follow this approach without much risk. This style of leadership is, therefore, confined to a small creative or development group.

A manager is not always free in the choice of leadership style in a given situation. Feelings and attitudes long cherished are difficult to change. While a democratic style of leadership may work better, in some work situations, the manager should be able to occasionally switch to the autocratic style so that people are led effectively. Generally, the choice of the style of leadership depends upon the following factors:

- Skill, personality, and values of the manager
- The expectations, aspirations, needs, and values of subordinates
- Factors such as type of structure, clarity or ambiguity in defining work and objectives, nature of the problems, and the pressure of time
- Composition of the people in the group, for example, differences in education, interests, motives, loyalty, etc.

Paternalistic style of leadership

In the *paternalistic style of leadership*, the leader assumes their function like a father. The leader treats the followers as members of a family and guides them as the head of the family. They prefer to help the followers do their work, guide and protect them, and keep them happy while working. This type of leader tries to provide their followers with good working conditions, fringe benefits, and employee services. Followers under this style of leadership work harder to accomplish the job.

Leadership Attitudes

In order to improve a manager's ability to lead, certain attitudes need to be cultivated. These are generally identified as empathy, objectivity, and self-knowledge.

- **Empathy**: It is generally described as the ability of a person to look at things or problems from another person's point of view. It involves projecting one's self into the position of the subordinates who are being directed and led. The manager should not assume that subordinates will understand the things and problems as they themselves perceive them. People differ in their experiences, abilities, and understanding of things. Each person has their own value system and attitudes. Thus, in order to understand their feelings and problems, and lead them successfully, the manager should put themselves in the position of the subordinates.
- **Objectivity**: In the task of leading, the manager should not be guided by any preconceived notion about the attitude and behaviour of subordinates. Problems and their causes should be observed objectively and unemotionally. Thus, a manager should not be annoyed with their subordinates simply because the results are poor or change is resisted. They must observe everything as it is and analyse objectively. Only by being objective and detached in their behaviour towards members of the group can the manager assess the feelings and problems of each member of the group, and guide them properly. However, this behaviour needs to be learnt and acquired.
- **Self-awareness**: A manager may think that they are fair and objective, but subordinates may view them to be otherwise. A manager should, therefore, know how they appear to others and the effect of their attitude and behaviour on the subordinates. Self-knowledge will help the leader to improve and cultivate those habits and attitudes that produce favourable responses from the subordinates. For instance, if self-awareness helps a manager to learn that instructions are not properly understood, the manager can attempt to improve their ability to communicate.

Leadership Skill

As a leader, one has to play many roles in the organization to achieve the intended goals and objectives. What skill sets are important is difficult to define. However, from a general perspective, one can classify the degree of requirement of such skill sets as follows:

- **Human skill**: In order to enlist the cooperation of subordinates, a leader has to successfully resolve people-oriented issues rather than job-related issues. They must understand human behaviour and know people's needs, sentiments, emotions, and motivations, and their contemplated actions and reactions with regard to a particular situation. Therefore, without the human relations skill, which emphasizes understanding people, one cannot be a successful leader. Two essential human skills requirement—empathy and objectivity—have already been discussed while explaining leadership attitudes. Apart from these two skills, a good leader should also have communication, teaching, and social skills, which form a part of human skills. In order to have the ability to persuade, inform, stimulate, direct, and convince the followers, leaders should have good communication skills. Communication is transfer of information in the form of an understandable message. It helps in establishing and disseminating the goals of an enterprise, and enables the leader to create a climate in which people want to perform. Expecting the followers to perform would not be possible unless leaders themselves successfully demonstrate how to accomplish a particular task. The teaching skill, therefore, is also an important component of human skills. Similarly, to win the confidence and loyalty of followers, leaders should also have the requisite social skills. Social skills require a leader to understand the followers and be helpful, empathetic, and friendly with them.

- **Conceptual skill**: This skill requires viewing the organization from an overall perspective. A leader should have the ability to look at the organization as a whole. They should be able to relate various functions of the organization and perceive how changes affect these functions. Understanding of the organization, understanding of the competitors, understanding of financial status, and understanding the most important functional aspects and their interrelationships are the essential requirements of conceptual skills.
- **Technical skill**: Technical skill involves specialized knowledge, analytical skill, and competence (competence is the aggregation of skill, knowledge, and ability) for doing a job. Apart from these, principles, procedures, and operations of a job also add to technical skill. Therefore, expecting followers to do the job without the leaders themselves possessing the requisite technical skill is not practical.
- **Personal skill**: To have the followers give their best, leaders should also have personal skills like intelligence, emotional maturity, personal motivation, integrity, and flexibility of mind.

LEADERSHIP THEORIES AND STUDIES

There are four major categories of leadership theories, as explained here:

1. **Participative leadership theories**: The Hawthorne studies (1927–1932), Kurt Lewin (1947), and Rensis Likert (1967) discuss about participative styles of leadership, which lead to increased job satisfaction and higher performance.
2. **Contingency theories**: These theories basically argue that the right or effective leadership style varies according to the context. For example, Blake and Mouton's (1985) managerial grid has been influential in practices of organizational development.
3. **Instrumental theories**: These leadership theories put stress on task- and person-oriented behaviour—for example, participation, delegation—by the leader to gain effective performance from others.
4. **Inspirational theories**: These theories include charismatic leaders and transformational leadership. The leaders in this category appeal to values and vision, and enthuse others thereby raising their confidence and motivating them. This leadership comes from their compelling vision that draws in commitment and acceptance of change, and offers the potential for anyone to grow and develop with the vision. The words that are commonly used are trust, loyalty, devotion, commitment, inspiration, and admiration. A recent overview comes from R. J. House and B. Shamir (1993)

who see it as the ability of a person to get an intense moral commitment and a strong identification from subordinates. They list a number of behaviours ranging from articulating the vision, passion, and self-sacrifice to risk taking, symbolic behaviours, etc.

F. E. Fiedler (1971), one of the pioneers of the contingency school, offered a continuum ranging from task-focused to people-focused leadership. This is known as *Fiedler's contingency approach.* He argued that the most effective style depends on the quality of relationships, relative power position between the leader and the led, and the nature of the task. He also argued that the style adopted is relatively stable and a feature of a leader's personality, and can, therefore, be predicted. He distinguishes between tasks-oriented and relations-oriented leaders.

The situational leadership dimensions proposed by Paul Hersey and Kenneth H. Blanchard (2001) are linked to task and relational behaviour. *Task behaviour* focuses on defining roles and responsibilities, whereas *relational behaviour* is more about providing support to teams. The extent to which either is used depends on the person's job maturity and psychological security. The situational leadership model looks at elements around delegation, participation, selling, or telling. On the other hand, the path–goal theory looks at what leaders must do to motivate people to perform well and to get satisfaction from work. It draws on the expectancy theory of motivation and it has four leadership styles: supportive, directive, participative, and achievement-oriented.

'Good leaders are made, not born.' On the strength of one's desire and willpower, one can become an effective leader. Good leaders develop through a continuous process of self-study, education, training, and experience. Leadership influences others to accomplish a mission, task, or objective, and directs the organization in a way that makes it more effective. A leader carries this out by applying leadership attributes (belief, values, ethics, character, knowledge, and skills). Mere authority to accomplish certain tasks and objectives in the organization does not make one a leader.

According to Bernard M. Bass (1985, 1990a, 1990b, 1995), there are three basic ways to explain how people become leaders. They are:

1. Some personality traits may lead people naturally into leadership roles. This is the *trait theory*.
2. A crisis or an important event may cause a person to rise to the occasion, which brings out extraordinary leadership qualities in an ordinary person. This is the *great events theory*.
3. People can choose to become leaders. People can learn leadership skills. This is the *transformational leadership theory*. It is the most widely accepted theory today.

The basis of good leadership is an honourable character and selfless service to the organization. Leadership can be demonstrated in everything one does that affects the organization's objectives and the well-being of the people involved. A respected leader concentrates on what they *are* (beliefs and character), what they *know* (job, tasks, human nature), and what they *do* (implement, motivate, provide direction). People want to follow a leader because they want to be guided by those they respect and who have a clear sense of direction. To gain respect, leaders must be ethical. A sense of direction is achieved by conveying a strong vision of the future.

Some of the widely acclaimed studies on leadership are described here.

Iowa Leadership Studies

In the 1930s, Ronald Lippitt and Ralph K. White under the supervision of Lewin conducted studies at University of Iowa by forming hobby clubs for 10-year-old boys. Each club was put under a different style of leadership: authoritarian, democratic, and laissez-faire. The authoritarian leader took on a directive approach and did not allow any participation. The democratic leader encouraged discussion and participation, and the laissez-faire leader gave complete freedom. Under such experimental conditions, the satisfaction, frustration, and aggression levels of the boys were studied while giving them the tasks of making masks, model airplanes, murals, and soap carvings. The results of the study showed that boys under democratic leadership performed better than those who were under authoritarian and laissez-faire leadership. However, the results of the study were not considered compatible with a formal organizational environment for pre-adolescent boys or for adequately controlling the variables. Even then, the study by Lewin et al (1939) is considered a pioneering study since this was the first attempt to experimentally determine the effects of leadership styles on a group.

Ohio State Leadership Studies

In the 1950s, the business research group of Ohio State University with an interdisciplinary team (psychologists, sociologists, and economists) of researchers analysed leadership influence on different groups. For their study, the researchers used a structured leader behaviour description questionnaire (LBDO). They identified two structures of leadership. They were the consideration and initiating structures of leadership that were quite widely accepted by heterogeneous groups ranging from air force commanders to school superintendents. The questionnaire could result in high or low readings for a leader in either structure, or their readings may be a combination of both. With the *consideration structure*, the leader shows thoughtful concern for others. With the *initiating structure*, leaders show concern about adhering to the patterns of organization, channels of communication, and established procedures, during their interaction with their followers. The research studies were published in 1957 by the Bureau of Business Research, Ohio State University.

Michigan Studies on Leadership Styles

In the Michigan studies on leadership styles (conducted at the same time as the Ohio State leadership studies), Likert and his group identified two major styles of leadership—employee participation and production orientation. The study, published by Likert in 1967, found that the employee-centred style resulted in higher productivity, higher job satisfaction, and higher performance in comparison to the production-centred style.

Managerial Grid

Robert R. Blake and Jane S. Mouton (1985) have integrated the authoritarian and democratic concepts in what is known as managerial grid. They recognized that leadership styles are not just authoritarian or democratic but are an admixture of the two philosophies, and these styles vary in nature according to the situation.

In the managerial grid, five types of leadership based on concern for production (task-oriented) and concern for people (relationship-oriented) are located in the four quadrants as shown in Figure 6.1. Theoretically, though, there are eighty one possible positions on the grid and each such position reflects one leadership style.

As depicted in Figure 6.1, concern for production is represented in the horizontal axis. Production becomes more important to the leader as their rating advances on this horizontal scale. A leader with a rating of 9 on the horizontal axis has maximum concern for production. Concern for people is illustrated on the vertical axis. People become more important to this leader as their rating of 9 on this vertical axis shows maximum concern for people.

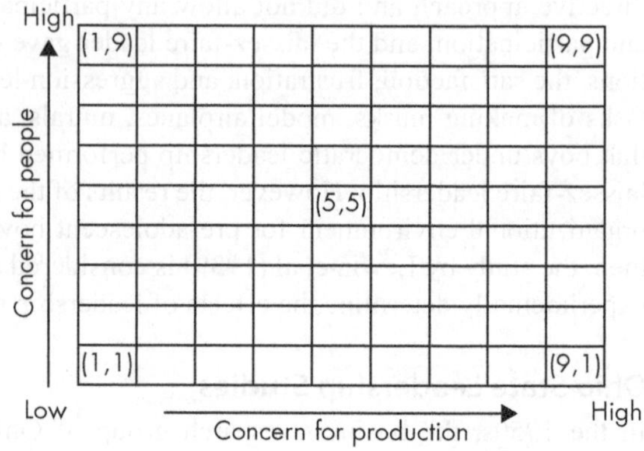

Figure 6.1 Managerial Grid

The five leadership styles are as follows:

1. **Impoverished (low-low; 1, 1)**: Leader exerts minimum effort, avoids controversy and confrontation, and takes the position of an observer.
2. **Country Club (low-high; 1, 9)**: Leader extends the greatest attention to the needs of people with regard to satisfying relationships, which leads to a comfortable and friendly work atmosphere.
3. **Task-oriented (high-low; 9, 1)**: This is the authoritarian, task-oriented, low-human-relation model. Efficiency in operations results from arranging the conditions of work in such a way that human elements interfere to a minimum degree.
4. **Middle of the road (middle; 5, 5)**: This type of leader compromises between high production and employee satisfaction at optimum level for ensuring effective performance by the group.
5. **Team (high-high; 9, 9)**: This is the style of a team leader. This leader is extremely concerned about the tasks as well as the people. They are concerned about work accomplishment by committed people and foster interdependence through a 'common stake' in the organization. They also strive for a relationship of trust and respect.

The grid approach is widely accepted in organizations since it helps managers to identify their individual leadership styles, based on which they develop a framework for the ideal leaders and develop suitable training programmes. However, the approach lacks empirical evidence.

An important extension of the managerial grid approach is W. J. Reddin's (1970) three-dimensional grid, which is also known as 3-D management. The three-dimensional axes represent task orientation, relationship orientation, and effectiveness. By adding an effectiveness dimension to task orientation and relationship orientation, Reddin tried to integrate leadership styles with the situational variables. *Task orientation* (TO) is defined as a leader's direction to followers to achieve goals. It is concerned with planning, organizing, and controlling. *Relationship orientation* (RO) is defined as the extent of personal relationships of leaders with followers. It is achieved through mutual trust and respect of followers' ideas. If the style of a leader is appropriate to a given situation, it can be called effective, and vice versa. *Effectiveness* and *ineffectiveness* are measured in terms of appropriateness of behaviour in a given situation. Four styles of leadership are to be found based on this model: (1) separated, (2) related, (3) dedicated, and (4) integrated.

The four styles of leadership represent four basic types of behaviour. A *separated leader* is concerned with correcting deviations. A *related leader* accepts others, is not bothered about time, looks to the organization as a social system, loves to work with others, and receives cooperation from others (followers) by setting examples. A *dedicated leader* dominates and is interested only in production. They do not identify with subordinates and only work through exercise of power. An *integrated leader* gets themselves and their followers involved with the organization. Such a leader emphasizes teamwork. All of these styles may be effective in one situation but cannot be used interchangeably. Table 6.2 illustrates the four styles by categorizing these into two types—a less effective style and a more effective style.

Table 6.2 Styles of Leadership

Basic style of leadership	Less effective style of leadership	More effective style of leadership
Integrated	Compromiser	Executive
Dedicated	Autocrat	Benevolent autocrat
Related	Missionary	Developer
Separated	Deserter	Bureaucrat

Continuum of Leadership Behaviour

Robert Tannenbaum and Warren H. Schmidt (1973) have explained a range of possible leadership styles on a continuum from authoritarian to free rein.

Figure 6.2 illustrates the continuum of leadership behaviour. On the left side of the continuum, leaders enjoy a high degree of control and believe in less delegation of authority. On the extreme right side, leaders give their followers freedom and allow them to show initiative in work-related matters. A leader moves along the continuum influenced by three forces—the forces operating in the leader, the forces operating in the followers, and the forces operating in the situation.

1. **Forces in the leader**: These forces are influenced by the value system of the leaders, their confidence in their followers, their inclinations, and their level of tolerance of uncertain situations.

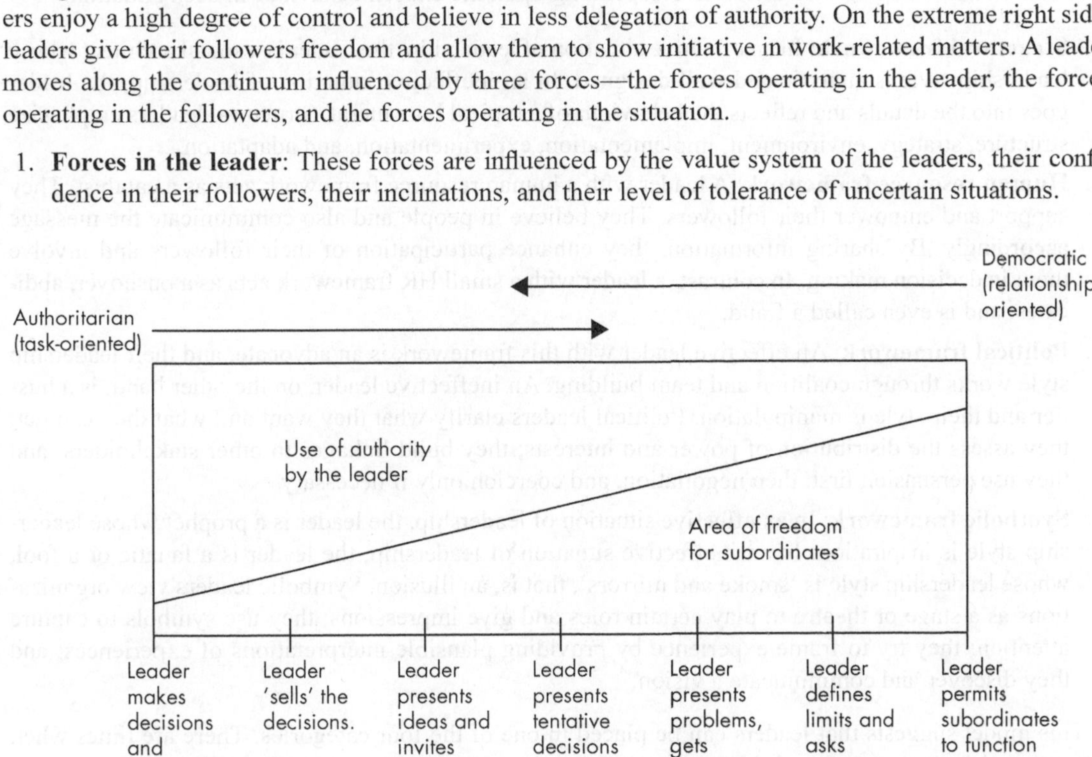

Figure 6.2 Tannenbaum and Schmidt's Continuum (Source: Robert Tannenbaum and Warren H. Schmidt (1973). 'How to Change a Leadership Pattern', *Harvard Business Review*, 3(51): p.180.)

2. **Forces in the followers**: These forces are influenced by the followers' tolerance for ambiguity, readiness to assume responsibility for decision making, interest in understanding problems, level of understanding organizational goals, and their experience with and expectations from leaders.
3. **Forces in the situation**: These forces include the organization and its values, traditions and problems, group effectiveness, and the pressure of time.

The continuum theory provides a wide range of leadership behaviour and its success depends on the behavioural modification of the leader according to the needs of the situation. The basic difficulty in the theory lies in the fact that it supports one-dimensional thinking. It suggests that increase or decrease of any particular type of behaviour may decrease or increase the other types of behaviours. This is a limitation of the theory since a leader does not necessarily become less task-oriented if they become more employee-oriented. The Ohio studies have also corroborated this observation.

Four-framework Model of Leadership

In the *four-framework approach*, Bolman and Deal (1991) suggested that leaders display leadership behaviours in one of four types of frameworks: structural, human resource, political, or symbolic. The style can be either effective or ineffective depending upon the chosen behaviour in each situation.

1. **Structural framework**: In an effective situation of leadership, the leader is a social architect whose leadership style is analytic and well designed. In an ineffective situation of leadership, the leader goes into the details and reflects the behaviour of a typical bureaucrat. Structural leaders emphasize structure, strategy, environment, implementation, experimentation, and adaptation.
2. **Human resource framework**: A leader with a human resource framework acts as a catalyst. They support and empower their followers. They believe in people and also communicate the message accordingly. By sharing information, they enhance participation of their followers and involve them in decision making. In contrast, a leader with a small HR framework acts as a pushover, abdicates, and is even called a fraud.
3. **Political framework**: An effective leader with this framework is an advocate, and their leadership style works through coalition and team building. An ineffective leader, on the other hand, is a hustler and their style is manipulation. Political leaders clarify what they want and what they can get; they assess the distribution of power and interests; they build linkages to other stakeholders; and they use persuasion first, then negotiation, and coercion only if necessary.
4. **Symbolic framework**: In an effective situation of leadership, the leader is a prophet whose leadership style is inspiration. In an ineffective situation of leadership, the leader is a fanatic or a fool, whose leadership style is 'smoke and mirrors', that is, an illusion. Symbolic leaders view organizations as a stage or theatre to play certain roles and give impressions; they use symbols to capture attention; they try to frame experience by providing plausible interpretations of experiences; and they discover and communicate a vision.

This model suggests that leaders can be placed in one of the four categories. There are times when one approach is appropriate and times when it is not. In any case, any one of these approaches alone is inadequate. Therefore, one should be conscious of all four approaches and not rely on just one approach. For example, during a major organizational change, a structural leadership style may be more effective than a visionary leadership style; during a period when strong growth is needed, the visionary approach may be better.

Based on the various studies conducted on leadership, the related theories can be grouped into four types: (1) trait theory of leadership, (2) behavioural theory of leadership, (3) situational theory of leadership, and (4) great man theory of leadership

Trait Theory of Leadership

The trait theory seeks to determine the personal characteristics of effective leaders. It points out that personal traits or personal characteristics make a person an effective or successful leader. Charles Bird (1940) examined twenty lists of traits attributed to leaders in various surveys and found that none of the traits appeared on all the lists. Leaders are attributed with a wide variety of traits ranging all the way from neatness to nobility. They are presumed to display better judgement and engage themselves in social activities. The study of the lives of successful leaders reveals that they possessed many of these traits. According to the trait theory, persons who possess the following traits or personal characteristics can become successful leaders:

- **Good personality**: Physical characteristics and the level of maturity determine the personality of an individual. The success of a leader to a great extent depends on their personality.
- **Intellectual ability**: The level of intelligence of a leader should be higher than that of the followers. Intellectual ability enables a leader to analyse the situation accurately and take a decision accordingly.
- **Initiative**: A leader should have the initiative to undertake activities on time.
- **Imagination**: A leader must be able to visualize trends and adopt the right course of action to achieve the desired result.
- **Maturity**: A leader should have emotional maturity and a balanced temperament. Maturity is reflected through behavioural tolerance.
- **Desire to accept responsibility**: Accepting responsibility for one's actions (irrespective of the results) creates a positive impression in the minds of the followers.
- **Self-confidence**: A leader's self-confidence will motivate the followers and boost their morale.
- **Flexibility and adaptability**: A leader should have an open mind to accept others' viewpoints. This will foster innovation and creativity in the organization.
- **Objectivity and fairness**: In dealing with followers, a leader should be objective and fair. This trait requires a leader to be honest, fair, impartial, and unbiased, and to be a person of integrity.
- **Consideration**: By being considerate to followers, a leader ensures their cooperation in all endeavours.

One of the major limitations of the trait theory is that it assumes leadership to be an inborn quality. This is not always correct. The quality of leadership can be developed through training. One can emerge as a leader also through successful handling of a crisis situation. This happened in the case of Russi Mody when, on 1 May 1947 at the Jamshedpur plant of Tata Iron and Steel Company, he successfully pacified the militant workmen beating up executives and supervisors in what was an outburst of their grievances.

A particular trait or some traits may help a leader to successfully manage a situation but they may fail in other situations. It is also difficult to find a leader with all the listed traits. There is no quantitative tool to measure a trait or traits. Absence or presence of traits can only be understood when a situation occurs and a leader manages the situation.

The list of personal traits is only indicative and not exhaustive. Moreover, personal traits are only a small part of leadership. In order to be a successful leader, one must also have other qualities. Hence, measuring leadership quality only on personal traits may be wrong.

Behavioural Theory of Leadership

According to this theory, a particular behaviour of a leader provides greater satisfaction to the followers. Such behavioural attributes enable followers to recognize a leader. This theory is based on the premise that a leader plays a role using their conceptual, human, and technical skills, which influence the behaviour of followers. Behaviour is not a trait; it sets a particular role pattern. For example, one leader may have a nurturing parent behaviour, which empathizes with the problems of followers and even cajoles them when they fail to deliver. Another leader may have a critical parent behaviour, which depicts a critical nature in dealing with such situations. Such a leader never appreciates, but only reprimands.

The behavioural theory cannot justify why a particular leadership behaviour is effective in one case but fails in another. For example, the nurturing parent behaviour may be effective in stopping recurrence of failure on the part of subordinates in one case, but it may not work in another case where followers take advantage of such behaviour and repeat the same action. The critical parent behaviour could be better in the second situation. This theory also does not recognize the traits of leaders.

Situational Theory of Leadership

This theory views leadership as emerging from situations. It gives importance to the way in which a leader performs in a given situation. A follower tends to follow a leader who is capable of fulfilling their aspirations in a particular situation. The leader duly recognizes the need of the situation and performs accordingly. Hence, such a leader's style may differ from situation to situation. The example of Russi Mody is again appropriate here—he emerged as a leader because of his proactive way of dealing with militant workmen.

A major limitation of this theory is that it emphasizes the leadership of a person in a given situation. It does not state anything on leadership across situations. Since the situation changes, the same style in all situations may not guarantee success. A suitable example here is of trade union leaders. Followers may reject the leadership of a trade union leader who fail to meet their expectations in a different situation.

Great Man Theory of Leadership

This theory emphasizes that leaders are born and not made. Hence, great leaders are natural leaders. It is partly true that some leadership qualities cannot be acquired even through training, notably qualities like a commanding personality, charm, courage, intelligence, persuasiveness, and aggressiveness. In a way, this theory states that leadership qualities are inborn and, hence, all people cannot become leaders.

This theory is not scientific and also has no empirical basis. In many cases, it can be proved that this theory is absurd. It also does not explain who the leaders are, how they emerge as leaders, and how they behave and emerge as achievers.

Case Life Savers: The Saga of a Benevolent Employer

Life Savers—an internationally acclaimed pharmaceutical major with multiple patents in medicines for lifestyle diseases—continuously emphasizes the need to develop human resources. The company spends more than 10 per cent of their annual business turnover on human resource development (HRD) activities. The HRD department is well managed by experts of international repute, who regularly come up with innovative programme designs, at times, even going beyond their business requirements. Life Savers values individual development, making it their priority. Their HRD philosophy asserts that unless people pursue their self-development, they cannot contribute to the development of the organization. Life Savers invites all employees to draw their own lists of training requirements at the beginning of the year. Employees' perceived training requirements are matched with the performance feedback reports, and with a minimum fifty per cent match, the final list of training programmes is drawn.

Life Savers, however, observed that the difference between the employees' perceived training requirements and performance evaluation-mandated training programmes was quite wide. Their age-old practice of participative training had now started facing a great challenge. Moreover, the HR department's employee attrition figures clearly showed that the attrition curve was quite high, surpassing the industry average. Life Savers even lost almost 10 per cent of their highly skilled workforce, including R&D scientists, within three months. Life Savers anyway pays a very competitive salary with unmatched opportunities for career progression. As a result, the high rate of attrition increased their workforce replacement cost, leading to a cascading effect on their product pricing in a fiercely competitive market.

Life Savers found to their surprise that in patented formulations, the price rise significantly reduced their sales volume. When patients started complaining that the price of Life Savers medicines was prohibitive, physicians started prescribing alternative formulations available at a competitive price level.

At this stage, you as the HR manager have been asked to review your present HR systems and suggest some result-oriented changes.

CASE QUESTION

Discuss your line of action.

Case GE and Jack Welch's Style of Leadership

John Francis Welch Jr, better known as Jack Welch, transformed General Electric (GE) into a world-class organization during his tenure as CEO of the company from 1981 to 2001. With a presence in more than 100 countries of the world, about 340,000 employees, and more than 100 billion dollars of annual revenues, GE has become a household name globally. From an incubator to a coffin, whatever one buys, the presence of GE seems ubiquitous. With a diversified business portfolio encompassing aircraft engines, medical diagnostics, lighting, appliances, nuclear power, broadcasting, plastics, and financial services, GE today is an example of corporate excellence. During Jack Welch's time, GE could make more than 1,000 acquisitions to expand their business portfolio. Jack Welch's principle of leadership, which made GE an organization of excellence, is anti-bureaucracy. This principle of GE put stress on managing each unit like a separate business, irrespective of its size and the nature of its activities. Welch harped on this aspect, clearly stating that achieving excellence would be possible only when they manage each unit like a small business unit with entrepreneurial skill and zeal.

CASE QUESTION

Analyse the reasons for GE's success.

SUMMARY

- *Leadership* is a process of influencing people to achieve intended goals in a given situation. Through leadership abilities, leaders and managers exert influence on others, regulate individual behaviour, and establish the relationships between leaders and followers.
- Leadership improves the motivation and morale of employees, leads employees to achieve a higher order of performance, unifies group efforts to achieve organizational goals, helps to respond to change, and inculcates values in the organization.
- Good and competent leadership is determined by certain principles such as continuous pursuit of self-improvement, technical proficiency, urge to seek out and take responsibilities for actions, ability to take sound and timely decisions, concern about the followers' welfare, developing capabilities and the sense of responsibility in followers, and developing followers as team members.
- Just as leadership is influenced by the prevailing work environment in the organization, leaders, too, exert influence on the environment by three types of actions: establishing the performance goals and standards, establishing the values, and integrating people with the organization. Leaders also set the culture and climate of the organization. *Culture* sets the way of doing things, while the *climate* gives the feel of the organization (evident from the individual and shared perceptions and attitudes).
- The functions of leadership can be understood from sociological, psychological, and various other perspectives. The *sociological perspective* considers that leaders set goals and shape or reshape organizations through the process of reconciliation of internal and external perspectives. The *psychological perspective* believes that leadership is more effective when leaders or managers take into account the psychological constructs of employees. Various other views consider leadership to be the process of directing, responding to situations, and representing the organizations.
- Leadership and power are closely connected to each other. Power, in the case of leadership, is divided into six categories; however, each can be linked with another as they are interrelated. They are expert power, informational power, reward power, coercive power, legitimate power, and referent power. Most leaders make use of a combination of these six types of power, depending on the leadership style used.
- Leadership styles depend on the specific traits of the leaders and the nature of followers. It can be autocratic, democratic, participative, consultative, group-centred, laissez-faire (free rein), or paternalistic. *Autocratic leadership* is characterized by centralization of authority and decision making, while *democratic leadership* is characterized by substantial participation by members of the group in the management and decision-making processes.
- There are many theories of leadership. Four major categories are participative, contingency, instrumental, and inspirational theories. *Participative leadership* theories emphasize employees' participation, which lead to increased job satisfaction and higher performance. *Contingency theories* suggest that leadership style varies with respect to the context. *Instrumental theories* emphasize task- and person-oriented behaviour. *Inspirational theories* define the attributes of charismatic and transformational leadership.
- Some of the widely acclaimed studies on leadership are the Iowa leadership studies, the Ohio State leadership studies, and the Michigan studies on leadership styles. The *Iowa studies* tested three different styles of leadership—authoritarian, democratic, and laissez-faire. They established that people perform better under the democratic leadership style. The *Ohio studies*, led by an interdisciplinary

team, used a structured leader behaviour description questionnaire (LBDO) and identified two different structures of leadership—consideration and initiating. The *Michigan studies* identified two major styles of leadership—employee participation and production orientation. An employee-centred style led to higher performance compared to a production-centred style.

KEY TERMS

Autocratic style of leadership: The autocratic style of leadership is characterized by centralization of authority and decision making and limited participation by subordinates of the group. The autocratic leader accomplishes results through use of authority, fear of deprivation, punishment, and other coercive measures.

Democratic style of leadership: This style of leadership is characterized by substantial participation by members of the group in the management and decision-making processes. Subordinates are frequently consulted by the manager on wide-ranging problems and are allowed sufficient freedom to communicate with the leader and also with their fellow subordinates.

Laissez-faire style of leadership: Under this style of leadership, the leader largely depends upon the members of the group to establish their own goals and make their own decisions. The leader is passive and assumes the role of just another member of the group, and tasks are assigned in general terms. This style of leadership is usually confined to a small creative or development group.

Leadership: Leadership is a process of influencing people to achieve intended goals in a given situation. Sociological view of leadership: This view considers that the leadership function includes setting of goals, shaping and reshaping of organizations, and reconciling internal and external forces.

Paternalistic leadership: Paternalistic leaders treat followers as members of a family, guide and protect them, keep them happy, and motivate them to work.

Psychological view of leadership: This view believes that leadership is more effective when leaders or managers take into account the psychological constructs of employees.

Relationship orientation: Relationship orientation (RO) is the extent of personal relationships of leaders with followers. It is achieved through mutual trust and respect.

Task orientation: Task orientation (TO) is a leader's direction to followers to achieve goals. It is concerned with planning, organizing, and controlling.

REVIEW QUESTIONS

1. Briefly describe the history of leadership. Why is leadership so important in modern organizations?
2. Is *leadership* different from *management*? Explain.
3. What are the important characteristics of leadership?
4. Explain the significance and principles of leadership.
5. How does the environment affect leadership styles? Can the culture and climate of an organization affect leadership?
6. Describe the important factors of leadership.
7. List out the functions of a leader. What is the principle objective of a leader in an organization?
8. Is leadership an exercise of power? Explain the relationship between leadership and power.

9. Discuss different leadership styles. How do leadership styles differ from organization to organization and from person to person within the same organization?
10. What are the important attitudinal elements of effective leadership?
11. Explain the important skills of leadership. Do you think the application of such skill sets is uniform in every situation?
12. Briefly explain the theories of leadership.
13. 'Leaders are born and not made.' Do you agree with this statement? Justify your answer.
14. Discuss the theory of managerial grid. How is it different from the 3-D leadership model?
15. What is *continuum leadership behaviour*?
16. Explain the leadership framework. Is it necessary for leaders to follow a particular framework of leadership in every situation?
17. What is the *trait theory of leadership*? How is it different from the *behavioural theory*?
18. Explain the relationship between situational theory and great man theory of leadership.
19. What is *formal* and *informal leadership*? Does an informal leader follow any particular style of leadership?
20. Write short notes on:
    i. Leaders and followers
    ii. Communication and leadership
    iii. Laissez-faire style of leadership
    iv. Transformational leader
    v. Paternalistic leader
    vi. Leadership and empathy

CRITICAL THINKING QUESTIONS

1. In a collective bargaining situation, management and union leaders (as representatives of workers) deliberate on work-related issues and come to a consensus. Both the management and the union representatives indulge in the power game. However, the leadership styles are different for the management and the trade union representatives. Explain the rationale for such differences in leadership style.
2. Narendra Kumar, a production manager in a cement manufacturing unit, achieved the highest production target and even exceeded the level of expectation of the company. In a board meeting, Kumar's performance was discussed at length and the company promoted him to the position of general manager (operations), creating a new position to bring all production shops under him. The post-promotion performance of Kumar was also laudable. However, resentment against Kumar started increasing day by day. This aspect was not given much thought by the top management of the company. Finally, one day, Kumar was physically assaulted by a group of workers who accused him of showing apathy to their problems. The incident persuaded the management to suspend 12 workmen who were found to be directly involved. This enraged the other workers of the company and they resorted to a total shutdown of production with the demand that their colleagues be reinstated and Kumar removed from his charge. Identify Kumar's leadership style and suggest how he can continue to be a good performer while remaining a favourite of the workers. You may cite actual examples from the corporate world to justify your answer.

REFERENCES

Bass, Bernard M. (1985). *Leadership and Performance Beyond Expectation*. New York: Free Press.

——— (1990a). *Bass and Stogdill's Handbook of Leadership*. New York: Free Press.

——— (1990b). 'From Transactional to Transformational Leadership: Learning to Share the Vision', *Organizational Dynamics*, 18 (3): pp. 19–31.

Bass, Bernard M. and B. J. Avolio (1995). *Multifactor Leadership Questionnaire (MLQ) for Research: Permission Set*. Redwood City, CA: Mind Garden.

Bennis, Warren and Burt Nanus (1997). *Leaders: Strategies for Taking Charge*. Harper Business.

Bird, Charles (1940). *Social Psychology*. New York: Appleton-Century.

Blake, Robert R. and Janse S. Mouton (1985). *The Managerial Grid III: The Key to Leadership Excellence*. Houston, TX: Gulf Publishing Co.

Bolman, Lee G. and Terrence Deal (1991). *Reframing Organizations: Artistry, Choice and Leadership*. San Francisco: Jossey-Bass.

Campbell, Joseph (1991). *The Power of Myth: Interviews with Bill Moyers*, Society Series, vol. 6, 2nd edition. Oxford: Basil Blackwell.

Fiedler, F. E. (1971). 'Validation and Extension of the Contingency Model of Leadership Effectiveness: A Review of Empirical Findings', *Psychological Bulletin*, 76 (2): pp. 128–148. University of Washington.

French, W. (1987). *The Personnel Management Process: Human Resources Administration & Development*, 6th edition. Boston, MA: Houghton Mifflin.

Halpin, A. W. and B. J. Winer (1957). 'A Factorial Study of the Leader Behavior Descriptions', in R. M. Stogdill and A. E. Coons (eds.), *Leader Behavior: Its Description and Measurement*. Columbus, OH: Bureau of Business Research, Ohio State University.

Hersey, Paul, Kenneth H. Blanchard and Dewey E. Johnson (2001). *Management of Organizational Behaviour: Leading Human Resources*. New Delhi: Pearson Education.

House, R. J. and B. Shamir (1993). 'Toward the Integration of Charismatic, Visionary, and Transformational Leadership Theories', in M. M. Chemers and R. Ayman (eds.), *Leadership Theory and Research: Perspectives and Directions*. San Diego: Academic Press.

Huberman, John (1964). 'Discipline Without Punishment', *Harvard Business Review*, 42 (4): pp. 62–68.

Kotter, J. P. (1991). 'What Leaders Really Do', *The Best of the Harvard Business Review*, pp. 73–82. Boston, MA: Harvard University.

Lewin, K. (1947). 'Frontiers in Group Dynamics', *Human Relations*, 1 (1): pp. 5–42.

Lewin, K., R. Lippitt and R. K. White (1939). 'Patterns of Aggressive Behaviour in Experimentally Created Social Climates', *Journal of Social Psychology*, 10, pp. 271–301.

Likert, R. (1967). *The Human Organization: Its Management and Value*. New York: McGraw-Hill.

Reddin, W. J. (1970). *Managerial Effectiveness*. New York: McGraw-Hill.

Sayles, Leonard R. (1979). *Leadership*. New York: McGraw-Hill.

Selznick, Philip (1984). *Leadership in Administration: A Sociological Interpretation*. Berkeley, CA: University of California.

Tannenbaum, Robert and Warren H. Schmidt (1973). 'How to Change a Leadership Pattern', *Harvard Business Review*, 3 (51): p. 180.

Vecchio, Robert P. (1988). *Organizational Behaviour*. Chicago, IL: Dryden.

FURTHER READING

Avery, G. and E. Baker (1990). *Psychology at Work*. New York: Prentice Hall.

Bhattacharyya, Dipak Kumar (2009). *Organizational Behaviour*. New Delhi: Oxford University Press.

Davis, Keith (1999). *Human Behaviour at Work*. New Delhi: Tata McGraw-Hill Publishing Company Limited.

Koontz, Harold and Heinz Weihrich (1993). *Essentials of Management*. New Delhi: Tata McGraw-Hill Publishing Company Limited.

Kotter, John P. (1996). *Leading Change*. Boston, MA: Harvard Business School Press.

Kouzes, James M. and Barry Z. Posner (1987). *The Leadership Challenge*. San Francisco, CA: Jossey-Bass.

Lamb, L. F. and K. B. McKee (2004). *Applied Public Relations: Cases in Stakeholder Management*. Mahwah, New Jersey: Lawrence Erlbaum Associates.

Likert, R. (1961). *New Patterns of Management*. New York: Harper & Row.

Likert, R. (1961). *New Patterns of Management*. New York: McGraw Hill.

McFarland, Lynne Joy, Larry E. Senn and John R. Childress (1994). *21st Century Leadership: Dialogues with 100 Top Leaders*. New York: The Leadership Press.

Raven, B. and J. Rubin (1976). *Social Psychology: People in Groups*. New York: John Wiley & Sons.

Robbins, Stephen P. (2005). *Organizational Behaviour*. New Delhi: Pearson Education.

Selznick, P. (1957). *Leadership and Administration*. New York: Harper & Row.

Tannenbaum, Robert, Irving B. Weschler and Fred Massarick (1979). *Leadership and Organization*. New York: McGraw-Hill.

Terry, G. (1960). *The Principles of Management*. Homewood, IL: Richard Irwin, Inc.

7

Introduction to Control

After going through this chapter, you will be able to understand:

- the concept of control
- the interdependence of control and other functions of management
- the various steps involved in the controlling function
- the methods of control
- the importance of control
- the various tools and techniques of control

Human Resource Management in Schilling Robotics

A Schilling press release announced on 10 July 2008 that Schilling Robotics, a global leader in the production of sub-sea control systems and remotely operated vehicles (ROVs), appointed Gil Llacuna as the vice president and corporate controller. Schilling also appointed Sally Larocca as the vice president of the human resource (HR) department, making both of them reportable to John Kehoe, Schilling's senior vice president and chief financial officer. Founded in 1985, Schilling Robotics is a robotics technology company that today produces control systems, ROVs, and other sub-sea equipment primarily for deep-ocean petroleum and gas exploration, and production around the world. The company is now growing at 40 per cent per year. Headquartered in Davis, California, the company also has offices in Houston and Texas in the United States and in Aberdeen, Scotland. In 2008, it became an employee-owned company, and the total staff at the end of 2007 was numbered at 275.

Many believe that Schilling's success is attributable to its emerging technology-intensive processes. However, it is not possible for a relatively young company such as Schilling to sustain a growth rate of 40 per cent with only technological supremacy. Realizing this, Schilling envisaged the need for efficient control of all resources including human resources to ensure optimization and, at the same time, to nurture professionalism.

One does not know yet whether such an approach is a precursor to the institutionalization of a human-resource-control approach in the corporate world, but it is clear that even a technology-intensive company such as Schilling also believes that effective human resource management with a control approach is the way to achieve a high rate of growth.

Source: 'Schilling Robotics, Inc.: New Controller (Gil Lacuna) and Human Resources Head (Sally Larocca) Join ROV Leader Schilling', Available at http://www.schilling.com/about-us/news/Documents/press2008jul10.pdf, 10 July 2008.

INTRODUCTION

The first *feedback control* concepts and control systems emerged from the regulator used in James Watt's steam engine in 1775. Hence, the term *control* primarily originated from industrial applications. With the broader use of automatic control systems in the later 1920s, and their subsequent theoretical treatment in 1932, the extent and ramifications of the term *control* has encompassed the management discipline as well. In the case of industrial applications, the digital computer and microprocessor of the 1960s increased the capabilities of the process of control. Today, many industries allocate at least 10 per cent of their capital investment towards instrumentation and control. In many manufacturing processes, instrumentation and control systems become the major determinants of the ultimate quality of the end products.

IFB Agro is an organization that has been a pioneer in processing liquor. The manufacturing plant is located in Nurpur, close to the southern fringes of Kolkata in West Bengal. The company primarily produces the base raw material, that is, rectified spirit, for the liquor industry by processing the industrial molasses. Industrial molasses being primarily an agro-based material, its yield (rectified spirit) widely varies. The chief chemist of the plant is always busy manipulating the fermenting, which largely depends on the breeding rate of costly, imported yeast. The quantum of yeast to be given in every material load is decided based on the visual inspection of the molasses, which is sourced from all over the world. However, their breeding rate and the quality of fermentation can be ascertained only through instrumentation and control. Reading the data from the attached indicators, the chief chemist decides the quantum of variation in the quantity of yeast. This explains the importance of the control function in industrial applications.

Since the beginning of the industrialization process, efficient planning, organizing, directing, and controlling of organizational activities have received a lot of attention (W. Pindur, S. E. Rogers, and P. S. Kim 1995). Right from the first articulation of classical management thoughts, the imperative for control has been emphasized. Max Weber (1947) is largely credited with institutionalizing the control systems in organizations. In management, the application of control helps in monitoring plans and variances, reviewing results, recommending resources, taking corrective action, and keeping plans within the boundary. Simons (1995) introduced the levers of control framework that gives managers a means to manage the tension between value creation and control. Control denotes managing and measuring value. *Simons' levers of control* is a formal, information-based routine or procedure that can help in maintaining and altering the patterns of behaviour of people in an organization.

In management, the functions of planning, organizing, and directing set the pace, while control ensures that results are achieved in line with the goals and objectives decided by the management. Like planning, controlling is also a never-ending process of management. Through periodic intervention, management ensures that the activities of an organization conform to plans. Therefore, planning and controlling are intimately related. Like planning, controlling also has the same characteristics of unity, continuity, flexibility, and pervasiveness. By comparing actual results with the plans, management enforces control to accomplish the goals. Through the process of control, management can understand the possible difficulties in achieving results as per plan and accordingly conduct periodic reviews to keep pace with changing requirements. Like planning, controlling is also a managerial function and it cannot be delegated. The planning process can be made participative in order to increase the commitment of employees down the hierarchy, but controlling can never be delegated. Based on periodic reviews, the management suggests remedial action, alteration of plans, change in the structure of the organization or in the staffing process, or even change in the process and style of direction. All of these things are a part of the process of control. In fact, control completes the total sequence of the managerial process. Some authors distinguish between the terms *control* and *controlling*. While *control* involves keeping the organizational activities and functions on the right track and duly aligning them with plans, *controlling* is defined as the process of control. The process of control means the ways in which managers enforce control by developing performance standards, comparing ongoing performance, and taking corrective steps. In this book, the terms *control* and *controlling* have been used interchangeably.

A *control system* is a device or a set of devices to manage, command, direct, or regulate the behaviour of other devices or systems. *Management control systems* (MCS) gather and use information to evaluate the performance of organizational resources, including human, physical, and financial. Such control systems influence the behaviour of the organizational resources to implement organizational strategies. R. Anthony and V. Govindarajan (2007) defined management control as the process by which managers influence other members of the organization to implement strategies. Hence, as a tool it steers the organization to achieve its strategic objectives. MCS encompasses organizational structure, human resource management, and the organization's culture. According to J. Maciariello and C. Kirby (1994), a management control system is concerned with coordination, resource allocation, motivation, and performance measurement.

Control is an essential function of management in every organization. The management process is incomplete and sometimes useless without the control function. The control function is concerned with ensuring that the planning, organizing, staffing, and leading functions result in the attainment of organizational objectives. In other words, control is a tool that helps organizations to measure and compare their actual progress with regard to the established plan.

The term *control* has different meanings in different contexts. In the management context, *control* refers to the evaluation of performance and the implementation of corrective actions to accomplish organizational objectives. Some people confuse control with supervision. *Supervision* is a part of control which helps identify deviations from the established standards of performance.

CONTROL

Control, as a basic function in managing an enterprise, is concerned with the task of ensuring that what is performed is kept within prescribed management channels to achieve organizational objectives. In business organizations, such control has an important role as it is a means of telling the employee what they are expected to do.

Moreover, in an organization, maintaining discipline is a process of control. It is widely believed that control has the primary function of keeping an organization working efficiently and effectively. In tandem with this belief, it is suggested that an organization employ a workforce that can be brought under control. Control is the phase of the managerial process concerned with maintaining organizational activity within allowable limits. It is the management action to adjust operation of the organization to its predetermined standards. As a result, control may be instituted to set new goals, formulate new plans, change the organizational structure, improve staffing, and bring in major techniques of directing.

The means of control available to management are many and varied. These include policies, procedures, organizational charts, forecasts, budgets, schedules, reports, audits, and almost any other administrative device that helps to define the work of employees.

Control can be defined as the efforts of the people that are controlled. Efforts can be broken down into three areas:

$$\text{Input} \rightarrow \text{Process} \rightarrow \text{Output}$$

Therefore, *control* can be comprehensively defined as a function of management that involves measuring and correcting the subordinates' performance of activities so as to ensure that the organizational plans and objectives are achieved. Control also means to know the extent to which actions are in accordance with plans and issued instructions, to report and analyse errors and deviations, and to initiate adequate corrective actions.

Control is always dependent on other functions of management. A manager cannot measure whether their subordinates are operating in the desired way unless they have a plan. Further, without organizational structure, one cannot ascertain who should make evaluations and who should take corrective actions. In the absence of effective direction, a manager cannot signify the impact of corrective action on actual performance. Thus, different phases of the management process need to be effectively linked together. All these functions of management greatly facilitate the control process.

Characteristics of Control

The function of control has the following characteristics:

- Control and planning are closely related. In fact, the terms *planning* and *control* are used interchangeably in the nomenclature of departments that carry out production planning, scheduling, and routing. It emphasizes that there is a plan that directs the behaviour and activities in an organization. Control measures these activities and suggests corrective action to remove deviations, if any. Thus, control implies the existence of certain goals and standards. These goals and standards are provided by the planning process. Control is the result of particular plans, goals, and policies. Since one can control future happenings and not the past, it is a forward-looking concept. However, in the process of control, the past performance is used as a reference point because no one can measure the outcome of a happening that has not yet occurred. Based on such analysis, managers suggest corrective actions for the future period.
- Control is both an executive process and a system of an organization. As an executive process, control is a process that modulates the operation of other processes so that a particular goal is achieved. Each manager has to perform a control function in the organization. According to the level of the manager in the organization hierarchy, the nature, scope, and limit of the control function are set. Administrative control constitutes the most comprehensive control. All other types of control are subsumed under it.
- Control is a continuous process. Although this function enables the manager to exercise control at the point of action, it follows a definite pattern and timetable, month after month and year after year on a continuous basis.
- Control is a coordinated, integrated system. This emphasizes that even if data is collected for one purpose, all data should be reconciled with each other. In a sense, a control system is a single system but it is more accurate to think of it as a set of interlocking subsystems.
- Control is neither the beginning of the management process nor is it the end function. It is present through every stage of the management process.
- Control is a dynamic process.
- Control is exercised at all levels of management.
- Control is identified with individuals.
- Control does not necessarily mean curtailment of the rights of subordinate managers and individuals.
- Control is not similar to interference. In fact, control implies *control by facts* rather than *control by means*, and it also implies correlation of many controls in place of superimposed control.

Prerequisites of a Good Control System

Two prerequisites must exist before a manager can devise or maintain a system of control:

1. **Control requires planning**: A control technique must be based upon clear and integrated plans. In a way, control is the reverse side of planning. The plans formulated by management become the standards by which desired actions are measured. Hence, a plan is the foremost requirement of control.
2. **Control requires organizational structure**: The goals, objectives, and strategies of an organization require each and every person to contribute to their accomplishment and to share responsibilities. Accepting one's responsibilities and accounting for them can be imposed at all levels of management and the points of deviation can be easily located. Hence, control vouches for the necessity of a suitable organizational structure.

Essential Features of a Good Control System

A good control system is an important prerequisite for organizational success. This is applicable to HR control systems as well. Some of the essential features of a good control system are listed as follows:

- Control must reflect the nature and needs of the activity.
- Control should be so designed that an activity, its implementation procedures, and its very purpose become apparent. The control system should be adequate enough to enable one to understand the need of the activity, its implementation, and its achievement.
- Control should report deviations promptly.
- Effective control systems detect deviations before they actually occur. Managers should be provided with information as soon as possible to prevent failures.
- Control should be objective. Evaluation of the performance of a subordinate should not be a matter of subjective determination, that is, control should be definite and objective. A subordinate will respond favourably to objective standards and impartial appraisal of their work performance.
- Ideal control is instantaneous, self-correcting, and forward-looking. Managerial control is not exactly similar to mechanical or electronic control. Normally, there exists a time lag between recording and reporting the deviations and the corrective actions to become operative. A manager should, therefore, structure the control system in such a way that deviations are predicted well in time and corrective actions initiated before substantial deviations occur. This type of control is *forward-looking control*.
- If it becomes necessary to revise the plans in order to accomplish objectives, the control system must have the scope to adapt itself to new developments. The basic idea is that control should remain workable under dynamic business conditions including the failure of the control system itself. Flexible plans tend to make the control system adaptable to new situations. This is known as *flexible control*.
- Control is exercised through managerial positions and, as such, they should reflect the organization pattern. Each managerial position should be provided with adequate authority to exercise self-control and take corrective actions. The flow of control information should be consistent with the prevailing organization structure. This type of control is *organizationally suitable control*.
- A control system should be economical in the sense that the cost of its installation and maintenance is justified by its benefits. An elaborate control system may sometimes have to be discarded because

cost and benefit considerations do not warrant its installation. Thus, a small company can hardly afford the extensive system of control practised by large companies.

- *Strategic point control* points out exceptions at critical points. All deviations are not of equal importance and do not require the same amount of attention. It is, thus, one of the essential requirements of an effective control system to highlight the critical or limiting points that deserve close management attention for appraisal and adjustments. Thus, an efficient control system discriminates between important and unimportant factors and thereby makes the system more effective and less costly.
- Control specialists often recommend sophisticated and advanced techniques of control to prove their expertise, and tend to overlook the question of their being understandable to managers in the organization. There are also cases where employees lack sufficient motivation to learn the new system. In either case, control loses its effectiveness. Thus, while launching a system of control, management should ensure that it is properly understood by everyone who has to manage it. Mathematical formulae, complex break-even charts, and detailed statistical summaries, though useful, may fail as effective control devices if their meaning is not properly communicated to the executives who have to use them.
- An effective control system should indicate deviations and suggest corrective actions promptly and in time. Mere recording of deviations and errors and taking responsibility to fix them are not sufficient unless these are followed by suitable actions to prevent the recurrence of such deviations and errors.
- The modern control system is worker-focused rather than work- or job-oriented. If any corrective action is called for, the persons accountable for the results are to be located for initiating remedial actions. *Worker-focused control* is generally associated with higher productivity.
- A manager responsible for control needs a continuous flow of information relating to actual performance so that deviations are promptly corrected and in time. Information that flows back to the manager for this purpose is nothing but feedback. Thus, this is *feedback control*. Feed-forward information flows back from the manager to the performers. Information may be informal or formal feedback. Informal feedback is through personal contact, informal discussion, and personal observation. Financial statements, reports, statistical analysis, and other written communications are examples of formal feedback. In every organization, information is circulated formally as well as informally.
- Control should be motivating; it should not be coercive.
- A control system should motivate both the controller and the controlled. The design of a control system should be such that it aims at motivating people by fulfilling their needs.
- There should be a degree of managerial self-control.

Types of Control

The control function is broken down into three types according to the stages at which they are applied:

1. **Preliminary control**: *Preliminary control* (or *feed-forward control*) is exercised during planning and the assignment of resources. Preliminary control ensures that human resources meet the job requirements, materials meet acceptable levels of quality and are available at the proper time and place, equipments are on hand when needed, and financial resources are available in the right amount and at the right time.

2. **Monitoring**: *Monitoring* (or *concurrent control*) examines actual ongoing operations to ensure that objectives are being met. The principal means by which concurrent control is implemented is through the directing or supervisory activities of managers. Through on-the-spot observation, managers determine whether the work is proceeding in the manner defined by policies and procedures. The

delegation of authority provides managers the power to use financial and non-financial incentives to achieve concurrent control. The standards guiding ongoing activity are derived from job descriptions and from policies established by the planning function.

3. **Evaluation**: *Evaluation* (or *feedback control*) focuses on end results. The corrective action is directed at either improving the process of resource acquisition or modifying future operations. This type of control examines historical results to guide future actions. The methods employed in corrective action include cost–benefit analysis, audit, quality control, performance evaluation, and impact assessment.

In Table 7.1, the three types of control as implemented in the different stages of production have been presented.

The types of control can also be demarcated as strategic control, tactical control, and operational control, which are explained in detail in the succeeding sections.

Strategic control

Strategies are selected and implemented over time. However, since strategies are forward-looking and designed to accomplish the objectives in the future, it is necessary to enforce control. To establish *strategic control*, it is important to allow time between initial implementation and achievement of intended results, steer the organization through different stages of activities, and then correct the actions and directions of the organization based on certain developments in the external environment and in the internal situation of the organization.

Table 7.1 Types of Control

Stage of production	Type of control	Process of enforcing control
Inputs: ■ Capital ■ Labour ■ Raw materials ■ Market information ■ Equipment ■ Knowledge	Feed-forward control	By monitoring inputs in conformity with the standards before they are used in the process of transformation
Transformation process: ■ Planning ■ Organizing ■ Staffing ■ Leading ■ Controlling	Concurrent control	By monitoring and regulating stage-wise activities that form a part of the transformation process to ensure that activities conform to the prescribed organizational standards
Outputs: ■ Goods ■ Services ■ Profits ■ Waste materials/scrap appraisals	Feedback control	By checking the final outputs—goods or services—to understand the degree of conformance to standards and goals

Organizations enforce strategic control through premise control, implementation control, strategic surveillance, and special alert control. *Premise control* systematically and continuously checks whether or not the premises set during the planning and implementation process are still valid. For example, a bank may adopt an aggressive marketing strategy to achieve 15 per cent annual growth, establishing a planning premise that not more than 10 per cent would be their non-performing assets. Therefore, premise control should ensure monitoring of the non-performing assets at branch level on a regular basis. *Implementation control* assesses whether the overall strategy results relate with the incremental steps and actions. For example, an internationally known fast food centre decided to maintain a 3:1 company–franchise ratio of ownership as part of their expansion strategy, to ensure control over quality of foods, rates, etc. However, growth of competition in this business later forced them to reverse the ratio to accelerate their ability to open new locations. *Strategic surveillance* monitors a broad range of internal and external events that are likely to threaten the course of the company's strategy. For example, IBM, in marketing their large and expensive mainframe computer, also targeted libraries worldwide in addition to corporate houses. *Special alert control* is enforced to rapidly reconsider the organizational basic strategy based on sudden changes. For example, the recent global meltdown prompted many organizations worldwide to scale down their activities and to practice lean management.

Tactical control

Tactical control focuses on assessing the implementation of tactical plans at department levels, monitoring results, and taking corrective actions, if necessary. Middle-level managers make use of this control for achieving departmental goals and objectives, and accordingly carry out programmes and meet budgets.

Operational control

Operations managers also need control methods appropriate to their level of strategy implementation. Their primary concern is allocation and use of company resources. *Operational control systems* guide, monitor, and evaluate progress in meeting annual objectives. Usually, the steps taken for operational control include: (1) setting standards of performance, (2) measuring actual performance, (3) identifying deviations from standards, and (4) initiating corrective action or adjustment.

Operations managers enforce operational control making use of budgets, schedules, and key success factors.

SIMONS' LEVERS OF CONTROL

Simons' levers of control is a framework to denote managing and measuring of value. One can understand the process of enforcing control by understanding this framework. The various levers of control according to this framework are as follows:

- **Internal controls**: These are the customary safeguards that a company establishes to protect company assets and ensure reliable record-keeping. Internal controls are structural, staff, and systemic checks and balances that guard against duplication, inaccuracy, mischief, and inadequate documentation.
- **Belief systems**: Belief systems relate to the fundamental values of an organization. These enforce control by obtaining commitment to the organization's vision, core values, mission statements, vision statements, credos, and statements of purpose.

- **Boundary systems**: These are what an organization must have so that it can stake out the territory for each participant encompassing codes of conduct, predefined strategic-planning methods, asset-acquisition regulations, and operational guidelines.
- **Diagnostic control systems**: These must be put in place by a company so that it can optimize outcomes and get the work done, that is, output measurement, valuation standards, incentive systems, and compensation systems.
- **Interactive control systems**: Smart organizations use these for tracking new ideas, for triggering new learning, and for properly positioning the organization for the future by incorporating process data into management interaction and face-to-face meetings with employees, and by challenging data, assumptions, and action plans of subordinates.

PROCESS OF CONTROL

To enforce control, an organization adopts certain steps. These steps help in establishing the control systems and make the process of control structured and meaningful. The steps adopted are:

1. **Establishment of standards**: The first essential element of any control process is to know what hould be the result. This requires projecting the future and determination of goals and standards. *Standards* are the criteria of performance. Since plans are the yardstick against which control must be defined, it follows that the first step in the control process is to establish plans. Standards may be tangible or intangible, vague or specific, but they must be expressed in such a manner that the people concerned understand them and realize that the accomplishment of assigned duties will be measured against them. Standards relating to factors like employee morale and loyalty, results expected of a training programme, and public relations cannot generally be stated in quantifiable terms. Such intangible and somewhat abstract standards need special care. As there is a large number of standards that can be established to judge performance, it is better that standards are set at strategic control points. While determining strategic control standards, management should be economical, comprehensive, and balanced.

   Control standards are most effective when they are related to the performance of a specific individual, because a particular individual can be made responsible for specific results. However, sometimes accountability for a desired result is not so simply assigned; for example, the decision regarding investment in inventory is affected by purchase, rate of production, and sales. In such a situation, where no one person is accountable for the levels of inventories, standards may be set for each step that is being performed by a particular individual.
2. **Measurement of performance**: The second basic step in the control process is the evaluation of performance. This requires measuring the work in terms of control standards and communicating the appraisal to persons responsible for taking corrective actions. Measurement of performance must be in units that correspond to the units of standards. Performance evaluation is not a post-mortem of past events. It is not intended to solely determine the mistakes. Assessment of performance and mistakes enables the manager to predict future problems. Hence, performance evaluation should be conducted on a forward-looking basis so that any deviation may be detected in advance of their actual occurrence and avoided through appropriate actions. Appraisal of actual or expected performance becomes an easy task if standards are properly determined and if the methods of measuring performance are expressed in physical and monetary terms, such as production units, sales volume, and profits. Performance related to subjects that are qualitative and

intangible, such as human relations and employee morale, cannot be measured precisely. For such purposes, techniques like psychological tests and opinion surveys may be applied. Such techniques draw heavily upon intuitive judgement and experience, and these tools are far from exact. However, Peter Drucker opined that it is not necessary that measurements be rigidly quantitative. For measuring tangible and intangible performance, measurements must have the following characteristics:

- They must be clear, simple, and rational.
- They must be relevant.
- They must direct attention and efforts where they should go.
- They must be reliable, self-announcing, and understandable without a complicated interpretation or philosophical discussions.

3. **Comparing actual and standard performance**: Comparison of actual and standard performance involves two steps:
   i. Finding out the extent of deviations
   ii. Identifying the causes of such deviations

   There is no uniform practice for determining variations/deviations. Deviations depend upon the type of activity. For example, a very minute variation in engineering products may be much more significant than a wide variation in other activities. Through an analysis of the causes of deviations, a manager can pinpoint the areas that need corrective measures and take necessary actions.
4. **Correction of deviations**: This is the last step in the controlling process. It requires that actions be taken to maintain the desired degree of control in the system or operation. In fact, correction of deviations is the point where control grows together with other managerial functions like planning, organizing, staffing, and directing. Due to this, many persons hold the view that correcting deviations is not a step in the control process. Correction may be done through re-drafting the plans, changing the organization structure, re-staffing, or better direction of subordinates.

Methods of Control

In order to ensure that the control systems run smoothly, organizations follow certain methods. Conforming to methods makes the control systems practical and result-oriented. These methods include:

- **Policies**: *Policies* are an important means for implementing preliminary control since these are guidelines for future action. There is a distinction between setting policies and implementing them. Setting a policy is included in the planning function, whereas implementing a policy is a part of the control function.
- **Job descriptions**: *Job descriptions* are a part of the control function since they predetermine the activities, responsibilities, and authority of the job holder.
- **Quality control of materials**: The materials to be used in the production process must conform to quality standards. Suppose the management decides that it will accept a maximum level of five per cent of defective items from a supplier. In technical terms, it is stated as ± 5 per cent deviations. Supplied material is then inspected by selecting a random sample and the percentage of defective items in that sample is calculated. A decision is taken based on the sample observations, and supplied items are sentenced as either accepted or rejected.

Thus, preliminary control systems for materials are established as a routine because the decision to accept or reject supplied materials is required to be taken frequently. The standard should be easily measurable and the sample should be easy to draw. The decision to accept or reject (or draw another sample) can be based upon simple instructions. Thus, the decision becomes automatic. An instruction for drawing samples to a quality control inspector may read thus: 'If sample defectives are equal to or more than five per cent, take another sample. If sample defectives in the second lot also exceed five per cent, reject the lot.'

- **Budgets**: The principal means of controlling the availability and interest cost of financial resources is *budgeting*. Budgets should anticipate the flow of activity during the operation cycle and plan for the availability of cash to meet obligations. A standard budget items list can serve as a checklist for the manager. This ensures that all necessary items have been considered. For example, organizations may include recommended ratios or percentages for each item as a guide for managers. Workforce cost of a project may be restricted to a maximum of 30 per cent of the total cost.
- **Audit**: *Audits* are a principal source of information that enables a manager to evaluate a programme. A *management audit* focuses on the efficiency of doing a project. A *financial audit* examines the financial aspects of the project.

  The manager periodically receives a set of financial statements. These statements summarize and classify all transactions in terms of assets, liabilities, income, and expenses, which together constitute the principal components of an organization's financial structure. Analysis of the financial audit information enables the manager to determine the adequacy of the organization's financial planning and budgeting in terms of performance measures and standards. In measuring the financial adequacy, managers in most cases do a cost–benefit analysis, interpreting various ratios.
- **Standard cost analysis**: *Standard costs* are predetermined costs as per the industry standard. For example, labour cost may have a fixed proportion in manufacturing and service sectors. For call centres, such cost is 30 per cent. Information on the standard cost system enables a manager to compare actual costs with standard costs and understand the reasons for variances, if any, and decide what corrective action is appropriate.
- **Employee performance evaluation**: This is one of the most important and difficult feedback control techniques. For any organization, their ultimate source of competitive strength lies with its people. Effective performance of people can make one organization better than the other. Employee performance evaluation is important for this reason. However, employee performance is difficult to measure because objective performance standards are difficult to develop. One of the important methods of evaluation is periodic performance appraisal. Scientific structuring of the performance appraisal form makes the task easier. The most effective way is to develop individual key performance areas (KPAs) and key result areas (KRAs) in qualitative and quantitative terms (which are targets given to employees), in line with the overall organizational objectives (management by objectives). Care should be taken to ensure that KRAs and KPAs are developed through a participative approach, that is, through mutual consensus. Another approach in evaluating employee performance is comparison with labour productivity ratios. Standard productivity ratios can be developed either internally or by benchmarking or comparing with other organizations.
- **Impact assessment**: Many organizations, through analysis of their decisional impact, try to measure the implications of their plans and how far the planned objectives are met. Control is accordingly enforced through alteration of plans. Thus, to provide better customer services, a new-generation

private sector bank may decide to introduce online banking. However, online banking services may create problems due to inadequate technological support at customers' end. The bank may find it better to improve customer services through more ATMs and introducing credit cards or debit cards. Hence, impact assessment helps in effective control of customer services.

- **Graphic charts and diagrams**: Organizational activities can be graphically displayed on charts, graphs, and network diagrams. Such graphical displays help employees to visualize the relationship of activities and the time requirement for each operation. Control is enforced when the time requirement exceeds or is likely to exceed the standards displayed in the charts and diagrams.

Usage of Control

One may summarize the usage of control in terms of the following points:

- Control is used to standardize performance for increasing efficiency and reducing costs with the help of time and motion studies, inspections, written procedures, or work schedules.
- Control is used to conserve company assets through allocation of responsibilities, separation of operational, custodial, and accounting activities, and adoption of proper authorization and record keeping.
- Control is used to standardize quality through inspection, statistical quality control, and product specifications.
- Control is used for providing limits to delegated authority without further approval from the management at the top. Instruments for such control include organization and procedure manuals, policy directives, and internal audits.
- Control is used to measure job performance through special reports, internal audits, budgets, standard costs, and output per hour or per employee.
- Control is used for planning future operations through sales and production forecasts, budgets, cost standards, and other standards of measurement.
- Control is used to help the top management in keeping various plans and programmes in balance through a master budget, a policy manual, an organization manual, and the use of coordinating committees and management consultants.
- Control motivates personnel through promotions, rewards for suggestions, profits sharing, and other methods of recognizing achievements.
- Control facilitates resource optimization.

Importance of Control

The importance of control can be understood in terms of the following benefits:

- **Insurance value of control**: The risk of non-conformity of actual performance with intended goals is largely estimated by controlling. The basic function of control lies in regulating operations in such a way as to ensure the achievement of predetermined objectives. Continuous review of work progress for making necessary adjustments in operations brings the performance back into line or holds it in line with intended goals.
- **Basis of future action**: Evaluation of final results makes available facts and information for future planning and organizing. Such evaluation helps in planning for repetitive operations, in planning

for the next step in non-repetitive operations, in introducing organizational changes, as well as in rewarding, punishing, or disciplining subordinates. As a matter of fact, long-range planning becomes impossible unless control information flows continuously between work projects for keeping plans on the proper track.

- **Indication of managerial weakness**: Control helps to keep a check on other functions for ensuring successful management. The problems of control stem mainly from deficiencies in related management functions. Before accomplishing the work, there may appear to be several unknown and unforeseen situations that cannot be covered by initial planning, organizing, and directing efforts. It is the control function of management that reveals and feeds back necessary information for locating managerial weaknesses and for addressing these through remedial actions.
- **Facility of coordination**: Coordination is facilitated by the control function of management. In the context of predetermined goals, control keeps all activities and efforts within their fixed boundaries and steers them towards common goals through coordinated directives. By determining who needs what information, control becomes instrumental in maintaining horizontal communication between chains of command. Waste of time, money, and efforts can be successfully avoided through the control function of management.
- **Extension of decentralization**: A consistent pattern of executive behaviour and action can be maintained by controlling the use and application of standing plans throughout the organization. By requiring subordinates to exercise self-control for regulating their own performance and to refer only exceptional problems to the superior executive, top management can concentrate on overall planning and control without being buried in minor details.

Shortcomings of Control

The control system has a number of shortcomings and these are briefly described here.

- **Lack of satisfactory standards**: There are many activities involving intangible performance for which no satisfactory standards can be established. Hence, quantification of output and identification of level of achievement is not always possible.
- **Imperfections in measurement**: Intangible performance creates difficulties in measuring results for evaluation. Behavioural activities are evaluated through executive thinking. Moreover, measurement of every aspect of work is not feasible on economic grounds.
- **Limitations of corrective action**: There are several limitations in taking corrective actions and avoiding mistakes. Operating conditions of business may change due to external forces over which management has no control. Managerial mistakes in studying market demand can be known only when products are finally put on the market. Within the organization, minor deviations are bypassed on the grounds of practical expediency; all reasons for deviations are not ascertained because of cost and time involved in investigation; and persons accountable for bad results cannot be singled out in many situations. Moreover, lack of authority and absence of timely information may make the corrective actions irrelevant in character.
- **Human reactions to control**: Control invites greater opposition from subordinates because of its interference with their individual actions and thinking. The pressure on work put through controlling may result in reducing the quality of work and ignoring of long-range goals in favour of short-range targets that look to evading censure through falsifying reports and covering up inefficiencies in other ways. If the control system is of a close and detailed type, it is likely to create more adverse effects among lower-level managers.

TOOLS OF CONTROL

Various tools are used in organizations to enforce control. These include control limits, control charts, Gantt charts, precedence diagrams, PERT, and control ratios. The most commonly used tool of control is a control chart. A control chart covers the following aspect of control functions:

- Concept and use of control limits and control charts
- Control actions that may be taken in response to a reported variance
- Calculation and evaluation of control ratios

Control Limits

Standards are set in advance as a basis for comparison with actual results to reveal any variation from the expected performance. However, standards should not be viewed too rigidly because they may be set at different levels (basic, current, attainable, or ideal) and, thus, variances from the standard (favourable or adverse) may be expected. Standards are only estimates and they also reflect the average performance that is expected over a period of time.

Variance limits may be established to exercise the control function. A *limit* is an allowance for a variance (plus or minus). Once a limit is established, it would not require investigation and control action unless and until the limit is exceeded. While the concept of a variance allowance is relatively straightforward, the setting of the limit in practice is difficult. A combination of experience and judgement and the application of statistics (for example, standard deviation) may be used to decide a control limit.

Control Charts

Control charts are used to present variance data over a period of time in relation to the control limits set. It is a graphical display of a sample quality measure versus a sample number (or time). The centre line represents the average value of the quality characteristic corresponding to the in-control state. The two parallel horizontal lines are the upper control limit and the lower control limit. A sample control chart that is commonly used in organization has been provided in Figure 7.1.

Gantt or Bar Charts

One of the most popular techniques used for production planning, scheduling, reporting, and control is the Gantt or bar chart. This technique graphically represents the progress of a project versus the time frame within which it must be completed. Gantt charts are excellent graphical representations for scheduling the execution of various project activities. They are simple and easily understood models for communicating information to all levels or for project management and supervision. To prepare a Gantt chart, the following steps are taken:

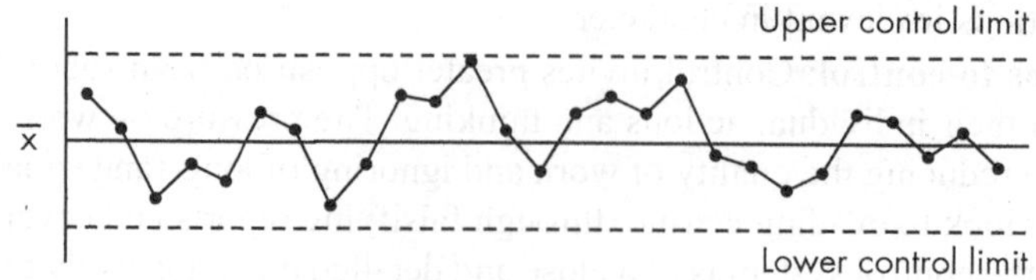

Figure 7.1 Control Chart

- Break down the project into discrete component activities
- Establish the sequence of execution of the activities
- List the activities that can be done simultaneously
- Estimate the duration of these activities

In the *Gantt chart*, the horizontal axis represents the time scale for completing the project. The unit of time scale used can be day, week, or month, depending upon the total length of the project. The listing of the project tasks or activities is shown in the first left-hand column. Horizontal bars drawn on the row representing that activity render the schedule of each activity, graphically showing its starting, duration, and completion times. For this reason, Gantt charts are also called bar charts or bar diagrams. The bars are drawn according to a time scale laid out across the top of the chart; the length of each bar represents the estimated time needed for carrying out the corresponding activity. A Gantt chart has been illustrated in Figure 7.2.

Precedence Diagrams

Precedence diagrams are designed to bridge the gap between manually operated planning systems like the Gantt chart and systems that are designed for computers, such as critical path method (CPM) and programme evaluation and review technique (PERT). However, these diagrams are rarely used as control tools in modern organizations. One of the most commonly used precedence diagrams is digitally accurate response tracking (DART), which is used in disaster management programmes. DART establishes relationships showing the precedence of activities by arrows connected to sets of boxes.

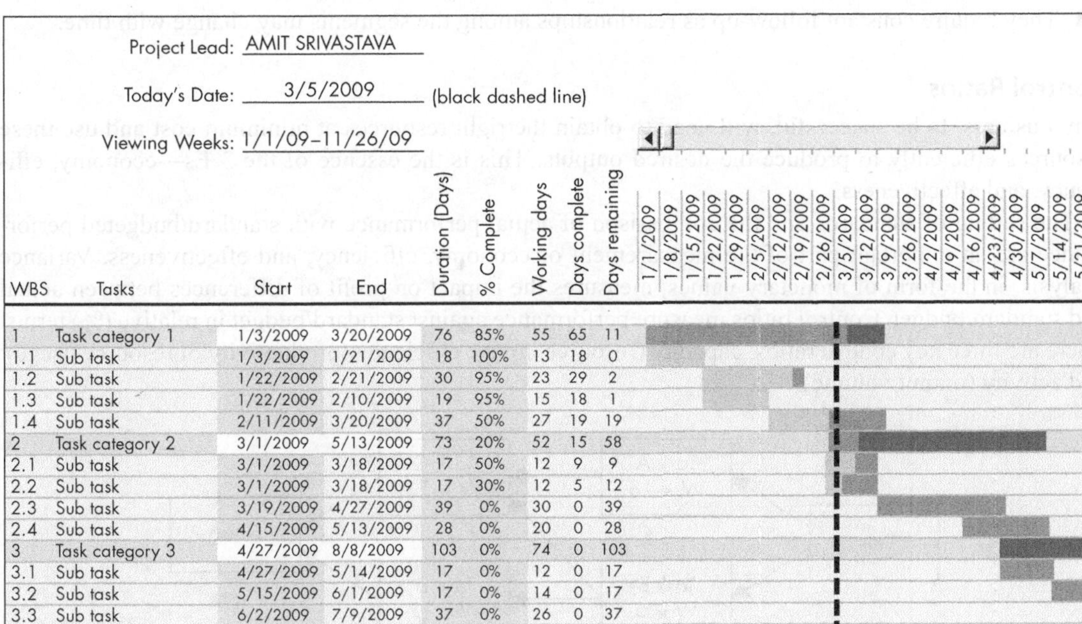

Figure 7.2 Gantt Chart

PERT

The programme evaluation and review technique is one of the most popular network models. Network models are visual aids that may be used to monitor and control activities. They are especially suited for disaster relief programmes because no project is routine or repetitive. The two most commonly used network models are PERT and CPM. While PERT is based on CPM, there is a fundamental difference between the two. PERT is applicable where there is no established system of doing the task and therefore no exact basis for estimating the required time to complete each task. CPM, on the other hand, is applied to jobs that are established or have been done before, and where it is possible to predict performance accurately. The PERT model has been illustrated in Figure 7.3.

Properly constructed, PERT/CPM models can provide the following benefits to managers:

- They help to reappraise the existing system design and identify duplication and overlapping.
- They help management to evaluate the subsystem change on other subsystems and/or the total system. A change in type of output or a change in scheduling in a particular subsystem can affect operations in other areas. This effect can be determined in units of time, money, facilities, or other resources.
- They encourage introspection of an existing system and provide the framework for visualizing the make-up of a proposed system.

PERT/CPM models are limited by the following drawbacks:

- They provide no guarantee for effective system design since there is always the possibility of variations in performance.
- There always exists the danger of assuming relationships among segments which do not exist, ignoring important relationships that should be considered, or weighing existing relationships improperly.
- They require constant follow-up as relationships among the segments may change with time.

Control Ratios

Any business, to be successful, will need to obtain the right resources at minimum cost and use these resources efficiently to produce the desired outputs. This is the essence of the 3 Es—economy, efficiency, and effectiveness.

The setting of standards and the comparison of actual performance with standard/budgeted performance are an important part of the measurement of economy, efficiency, and effectiveness. Variance analysis, in the form of monetary values, measures the impact on profit of differences between actual and standard/budget. Control ratios measure performance against standard/budget in relative (%) terms. There are three key control ratios: capacity (resource input), efficiency (productivity of resource usage), and activity (output volume).

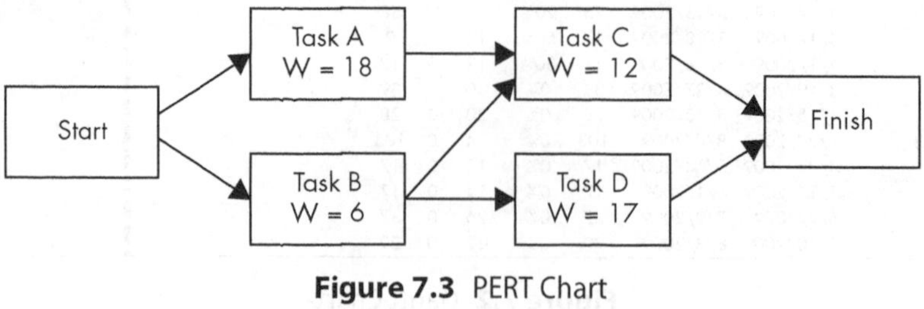

Figure 7.3 PERT Chart

The basis of performance measurement via these control ratios is the concept of the standard hour (the amount of work achievable at standard efficiency levels in an hour). The standard hour provides a common basis for the measurement of work done, typically in a production (factory) environment. Actual hours worked on a variety of tasks can be compared with budgeted hours, with the output achieved measured in standard hours.

The capacity ratio typically measures the utilization of labour resource in terms of total hours worked in comparison with those budgeted. The usual formula for the calculation of the capacity ratio is:

$$\text{Capacity ratio} = \frac{\text{Actual hours worked}}{\text{Budgeted hours}} \times 100\%$$

A capacity ratio of 100 per cent would mean that budgeted hours were worked. A ratio that is lesser than 100 per cent would indicate hours worked are lesser than the budget, and a ratio that is greater than 100 per cent would indicate that the hours worked are greater than the budget.

The efficiency ratio measures how well the labour resource has been used in comparison with the standard set. The formula for the calculation of the efficiency ratio is:

$$\text{Efficiency ratio} = \frac{\text{Standard hours of output}}{\text{Actual hours worked}} \times 100\%$$

An efficiency ratio of 100 per cent would mean that the productivity of labour was exactly on standard. An efficiency ratio lesser than 100 per cent would indicate that the productivity is less than the standard, and an efficiency ratio greater than 100 per cent would indicate that the productivity is greater than the standard.

The activity (also called volume or production volume) ratio typically measures the output achieved compared with budget. The usual formula for the calculation of the activity ratio is:

$$\text{Activity ratio} = \frac{\text{Standard hours of output}}{\text{Budgeted hours}} \times 100\%$$

An activity ratio of 100 per cent would mean that output was on budget. A ratio that is lesser than 100 per cent would indicate that the output is lesser than the budget, and a ratio that is greater than 100 per cent would indicate that the output is greater than the budget.

The activity ratio is a function of the resources utilized (capacity ratio) and how well they are used (efficiency ratio). Thus, the activity ratio can be expressed as:

$$\text{Activity} = \text{Capacity} \times \text{Efficiency}$$

CONTROL TECHNIQUES

There are various techniques of control such as functional task analysis, budgetary control, and manufacturing control systems.

Functional Task Analysis

This technique identifies and describes the functions or activities that must be performed in order to ensure that all operations are performed completely. The result of this process is a list of the various activities and specific tasks needed for business to function on a day-to-day basis. It also includes the functions needed for the business to remain competitive and respond to change creatively and proactively. An example of a functional task analysis form is given in Figure 7.4.

Budgetary Control

As budgets provide standards of performance, they usually become the basis for control. All results and performances are measured and appraised against budget standards, which are developed through a comprehensive budgetary programme. Control exercised for the execution of budget is known as *budgetary control*. Budget making is also concerned with the planning function. Budgetary control coordinates all the activities of business in order to centralize control, though responsibilities are delegated to each manager involved.

Manufacturing Control Systems

The design of the control system in manufacturing directly relates to the mode of production (MOP) and the organizational culture. Modern production systems make use of distributed control systems (DCS). *Distributed control systems* refer to a dynamic system in which control is distributed or decentralized throughout the system. Under distributed control, one controlling agent controls each subsystem. Therefore, distributed control requires an organization to enforce control through networks. For manufacturing, DCS typically uses customized processors as controllers. Input and output modules form component parts of the DCS. The processor receives information from input modules and sends information to output modules. The input modules receive information from input instruments in the process and transmit instructions to the output instruments in the field. Computer buses or electrical buses connect the processor and modules through multiplexer or de-multiplexers. Buses also connect the distributed controllers with the central controller and finally to the human–machine interface (HMI) or control consoles.

Distributed control systems can only be used in a continuous or batch-oriented production system, for example, oil refining, petrochemicals, power generation and distribution, pharmaceuticals, food and beverage manufacturing, cement production, steelmaking, and papermaking. Depending on the scale of production and the size of the plant, DCSs may be large or small. Similarly, the number of input–output points may also vary. Also, a typical DCS may have functionally and geographically distributed digital controllers to execute from 1 to 256 or more regulatory control loops in one control box. In such cases, the

Functional time-use analysis form			
Name:		Day/Date:	
Position:		Dept:	
TASK DESCRIPTION	START TIME	FINISH TIME	TOTAL TIME

Figure 7.4 Functional Task Analysis Form

input/output (I/O) devices integrate with the controller by a remote-controlled field network. In job-shop production systems, however, DCS may not be applicable since the manufacturing process there is highly customized and control in manufacturing requires manual checking of the quality standards and norms. However, the tools and measuring instruments used to support this manufacturing process may be self-regulating and capable of enforcing control autonomously.

Case Ciziko: Testing Time for Market Intelligence Control

Enforcing control through direct supervision was all along considered as the strategic approach to achieve the business goals of Delhi-based family-owned construction chemical organization Ciziko. Ciziko is a known brand in the north Indian market, where real estate business has witnessed an unprecedented pace of growth over the decades. Professional real estate companies always prefer Ciziko due to its quality products and their lifelong guarantee. Ciziko's product ranges include roof-treatment chemicals, anti-termite and anti-insect chemicals, quick-fix chemicals for cement mix, and earthquake-resistant chemicals. Ciziko's nature of business demands strict quality control in production and continuous building of customers' confidence through direct visit to sites and guidance to construction people through a 24 x 7 free helpline. The salespeople are essentially chemical engineers from premier engineering colleges who undergo compulsory on-site induction and training for three months after recruitment. During this phase, Ciziko requests its customers to allow the new recruits to understand the application and usages of their chemicals by learning on the job. Each trainee is also required to perform masonry jobs and act as a helper to the masons. This process helps the salespeople to not only understand the use of the chemicals closely, but also develops their confidence about interacting well with customers in the future. Moreover, Ciziko has become the preferred choice among masons since they feel that allowing the engineers to work with them during induction is tantamount to recognition of their importance and shows respect to their profession.

Ciziko enforces control on its sales force with a two-tier approach. In the first tier, Ciziko makes sure that every individual in its sales force is achieving its sales target, and in the second tier, Ciziko ensures that every salesperson fulfils the satisfaction level of customers. Therefore, buying a Ciziko product should inculcate a sense of pride in every customer. No customer should buy a Ciziko product with suspicion. It is more like buying an insurance policy, that is, a customer should not be pressured into buying a policy (or a Ciziko product) due to the salespeople's manipulation. 'Buy it because you need it' is Ciziko's marketing strategy, though the marketing department views it critically because it often stands against achieving their sales target. Ciziko, however, is very particular about it, as the company's value system endorses this philosophy and believes that customers will eventually feel compelled to buy its products when they realize their utility value. In fact, using Ciziko's products ultimately become one of the unique selling propositions (USPs) for the real estate business. Ciziko's products are proprietary items and the profit margin is considerably higher since customers consider the purchase of Ciziko products as more of an investment than an expense.

After closing every sales deal, Ciziko's Red Force screens the sales process to understand the degree of violation of company norms, if any. The degree of violation is quantified by in-built sales systems, and individual salespeople are immediately tracked and informed.

With more than 0.5 per cent cases of violation, salespeople lose their incentives and sales commissions, and when it exceeds one per cent, they are dropped from the market and sent for retraining. With successive failures, salespeople even risk their jobs. Ciziko helps its sales force to understand on its own where it stands vis-à-vis Ciziko's value systems on marketing. Such a self-tracking control system gradually makes salespeople conscious about the self-control.

Initial market success in northern India prompted Ciziko to consolidate its market position at an all-India level with an ambitious expansion programme. Ciziko's philosophy was at this time put to a real test. With its salespeople scattered in every nook and corner of the country, Ciziko found this task difficult, as Red Force's market intelligence was not sustainable in local market conditions in the southern, western, and eastern parts of the country. The customer-care centre of Ciziko, based at New Delhi, failed to track the market pulse and ultimately, Ciziko lost its market reputation.

CASE QUESTION

You are required to help Ciziko develop foolproof control systems. Suggest your line of action.

Case Managing Without Control

Chevron Corporation, a leader in the petroleum industry, is practising 'direct participation' as an efficient process of designing and implementing change. This has helped the company to develop a response capability for the workforce (using their 'collective wisdom') to outmanoeuvre competitors. The system works like this:

- Organize large-scale conferences (two to three days) involving a variety of stakeholders.
- Discuss issues that require change.
- Bring multiple perspectives while choosing the line of action.
- Select the line of action.
- Communicate the line of action throughout the organization.
- Implement identified changes.

Encouraged by the results, one of the largest automobile manufacturers in India, which employs mostly engineers even in its shop floors, emulated the practices of Chevron. Since the Indian organization was professional and the employees were highly educated, it followed a matrix structure, creating a number of positions for project heads who had been given the task of managing independently after the finalization and implementation of participative plans. The system started with much enthusiasm and brought hope that the results would be better in a sluggish competitive market. However, the annual review indicated that the company could only achieve 70 per cent of its target. There was no system of intermediate review by the top management. The company had to drop its new system and revert to the old hierarchical structure.

CASE QUESTION

What is your lesson from the case?

SUMMARY

- Control ensures that actions conform to plans and this is achieved by comparing the actual performance with the plans. Control is required to be enforced at all levels of management. The term 'control' has different meanings in different contexts. In the management context, control refers to the evaluation of performance and the implementation of corrective actions to accomplish organizational objectives. Some people confuse control with supervision. Supervision is a part of control; it helps identify deviations from the established standards of performance.
- Characteristically, control and planning are closely related, and these two terms are used interchangeably. Control can be both an executive process and a system of an organization. Effective control systems need to be continuous, integrated, in process, dynamic, and all-encompassing.
- Depending on the specific nature of the requirement of an organization, control practices vary. *Forward-looking control* is most widely practised in organizations. This type of control is instantaneous, self-correcting, and forward-looking. It helps in predicting deviations well in time and taking the necessary corrective actions. *Flexible control systems* can adapt themselves to new developments, as may be required from time to time in a dynamic work environment. Effective control must match with the organizational requirements and should be economical. It should be strategically used in order to closely monitor situations that are critical to the organization. It must be simple to understand and capable of suggesting corrective action.
- Essentially, control can be of three types: preliminary control, monitoring, and evaluation. *Preliminary control* is exercised during planning and assignment of resources to be used in an operation. *Monitoring* (or *concurrent control*) examines actual ongoing operations to ensure that objectives are being met. *Evaluation* (or *feedback control*) focuses on end results. The corrective action is directed at either improving the process of resource acquisition or modifying future operations.
- The other way of classification of control is based on the assumption that depending on the hierarchical level, the nature of control differs. From this perspective, control can be strategic, tactical, and operational. *Strategic control* is enforced through premise control, implementation control, strategic surveillance, and special alert control. *Tactical control* focuses on assessing the implementation of tactical plans at departmental levels, monitoring results, and taking corrective actions, if necessary. *Operational control systems* guide, monitor, and evaluate progress in meeting annual objectives.
- To enforce control, organizations adopt certain steps like establishment of standards, measurement of performance, comparing actual and standard performance, and correction of deviations. Organizations enforce control through policies, job descriptions, quality control of materials, budgets, audits, standard cost analysis, employee performance evaluation, impact assessment, graphic charts and diagrams, etc. Control is important for an organization because of its insurance value, its capability to suggest future courses of action, its ability to indicate managerial weakness, and to ensure coordination and extension of decentralization.
- Various tools and techniques are used in organizations to enforce control. The most commonly used control technique is a control chart. A *control chart* helps to decide control limits and can report variations from such limits. A control chart also helps in calculation and evaluation of control ratios. Other control techniques are functional task analysis, budgetary control, and manufacturing control systems. *Functional task analysis* identifies and describes the different

functions or activities that must be performed in order to ensure that all operations are performed completely. *Budgetary control* provides standards of performance, which become the basis of control. *Manufacturing control systems* directly relate to the mode of production (MOP) and the organizational culture.

KEY TERMS

Control: Control can be comprehensively defined as a function of management that involves measuring and correcting the subordinates' performance of activities so as to ensure that the organizational plans and objectives are achieved. Control also means to know the extent to which actions are in accordance with plans and issued instructions, to report and analyse errors and deviations, and to initiate adequate corrective actions.

Control charts: Control charts are used to present variance data over a period of time in relation to the control limits set. It is a graphical display of a sample quality measure versus a sample number (or time).

Evaluation: Evaluation (or feedback control) focuses on end results. The corrective action is directed at either improving the process of resource acquisition or modifying future operations. This type of control examines historical results to guide future actions.

Gantt or bar charts: This technique graphically represents the progress of a project versus the time frame within which it must be completed. Gantt charts are excellent graphical representations for scheduling the execution of various project activities.

Management control system: A control system is a device or a set of devices to manage, command, direct, or regulate the behaviour of other devices or systems. Therefore, a management control system (MCS) gathers and uses information to evaluate the performance of different organizational resources including human, physical, and financial resources.

Monitoring: Monitoring (or concurrent control) examines actual ongoing operations to ensure that objectives are being met. Concurrent control is implemented mainly through the directing or supervisory activities of managers. Through on-the-spot observation, managers determine whether the work of others is proceeding in the manner defined by policies and procedures.

Operational control: This type of control helps in guiding, monitoring, and evaluating progress in meeting annual objectives.

Preliminary control: Preliminary control (or feed-forward control) is exercised during planning and assignment of resources to be used in operations. Preliminary control ensures that human resources meet the job requirements, materials meet acceptable levels of quality and are available at the proper time and place, equipment is on hand when needed, and financial resources are available in the right amounts and at the right times.

Strategic control: To establish strategic control, it is important to allow time between initial implementation and achievement of intended results, steer the organization through different stages of activities, and correct the actions and directions of the organization based on certain developments in the external environment and in the internal situation of the organization.

Tactical control: This type of control focuses on assessing the implementation of tactical plans at department levels, monitoring results, and taking corrective actions, if necessary.

REVIEW QUESTIONS

1. Discuss in what way planning and controlling are related.
2. What is *feedback* and *feed-forward control*?
3. 'Control is an all-pervasive function of management.' Do you agree with this statement? Justify your answer.
4. Define *strategic control*. How is it different from *tactical control* and *operational control*?
5. Can the control function be delegated? Justify your answer.
6. What are the different techniques of control? Which techniques would you recommend as the most suitable for achieving organizational goals?
7. What is a *performance standard*? How are performance standards decided? How do performance standards help in the controlling function?
8. Imagine a situation of planning without control. What would be the implications for an organization? Justify your answer.
9. What are the requirements of a good control system? Discuss with examples.
10. Write short notes on:
    i. Control charts
    ii. Control ratios
    iii. Project evaluation and review technique (PERT)
    iv. Gantt chart
    v. Budgeting and budgetary control

CRITICAL THINKING QUESTIONS

1. Many organizations now enforce control through ERP systems. Visit the Web sites of Oracle, SAP, or major Indian software developers. Identify a module that can help in controlling their functions. Give the details of your selected module and describe the way in which it can enforce control.
2. A knowledge-intensive organization decided to introduce distributed control systems, delegating the control function to supervisors. Supervisors are empowered to initiate corrective actions whenever they observe any deviation. However, resource support and authority still lie with their departmental heads. In a situation like this, do you think the company took the right decision by introducing the distributed control systems?

REFERENCES

Anthony, R. and V. Govindarajan (2007). *Management Control Systems*. Chicago, IL: McGraw-Hill/Irwin.

Drucker, Peter (1954). *The Practice of Management*. New York: Harper.

Maciariello, J. and C. Kirby (1994). *Management Control Systems: Using Adaptive Systems to Attain Control*. Upper Saddle River, NJ: Prentice Hall.

Pindur, W., S. E. Rogers and P. S. Kim (1995). 'The History of Management: A Global Perspective', *Journal of Management History*, 1 (1): pp. 59–77.

Simons, R. (1995). *Levers of Control: How Managers Use Innovative Control Systems to Drive Strategic Renewal.* Boston, MA: Harvard Business School Press.

Weber, Max (1947). *The Theory of Social and Economic Organization* (translated by A. M. Henderson and Talcott Parsons). The Free Press.

FURTHER READING

Argyris, C. (1964). *Integrating the Individual and the Organization*. New York: John Wiley & Sons.

Bhattacharyya, D. K. (2002). *Production and Operations Management*. New Delhi: Excel Books.

——— D. K. (2008). *Organization Behaviour*. New Delhi: Oxford University Press.

——— (2010). *Industrial Management*. New Delhi: Vikas Publishing.

Koontz, H. (1961). 'The Management Theory Jungle', *Academy of Management Journal*, 4 (3): pp. 174–188.

Ouchi, W. G. and A. M. Jaeger (1978). 'Type Z Organization: Stability in the Midst of Mobility', *Academy of Management Review*, April, pp. 305–314.

8

Coordination in Organizations

After going through this chapter, you will be able to understand:

- the nature and characteristics of coordination
- the importance of coordination
- the principles of coordination
- the objectives and purposes of coordination
- the various types of coordination
- the concepts of internal and external coordination

Coordination—a Factor of Performance

Organizations that follow a behavioural model emphasize self-managed work teams. Members of self-managed teams are independent enough to coordinate their own work. On the other hand, in bureaucratic organizations, due to the pervasive culture of competition, coordination and control are imposed. The members of such organizations do not collaborate with each other. Bureaucratic organizations believe that employees need to be told what to do. Their work needs to be controlled and coordinated with a traditional approach of command and control. Although the core objective of coordination is to monitor the activities of people and ensure that results are being accomplished according to the plan, in behavioural organizations, such an objective focuses more on self-coordination on the premise that the very nature of work is interdependent. Thus, the basic premise of coordination lies in the theory of *dependency*, which is the relationship between two or more elements, where change in one element induces change in the other element or elements. Irrespective of its nature, coordination primarily needs to focus on organizational goal achievement. For bureaucratic organizations, coordination is based on *authority*, which is defined in terms of administrative rules, procedures, and practices. Behavioural organizations emphasize on shared values and the individual, and the team members are guided by autonomous self-coordination. Therefore, even if the goal of coordination is in tandem with achieving the business goals of the organization, the approaches may still be different.

INTRODUCTION

To accomplish organizational goals and objectives, one needs to look beyond the planning and organizing functions. Coordination through 'unity of action' ensures harmonization and synchronization of group efforts and thereby helps in achieving the desired results. Managers bring unity of action into the process of managing while performing the basic functions of planning, organizing, staffing, and controlling. It is important primarily because of individual differences in understanding, timing, effort, and approach towards accomplishment of organizational goals. Managerial efforts to ensure unity of action are known as *coordination*. Coordination is all-pervasive and it is the essence of management. It is the management of interdependence in work situations. Even in networked organizations, where employees are globally dispersed, coordination is important. In such organizations, electronic communication is very important since streaming technology and video conferencing with time synchronization help in direct communication and coordination of activities. An example would be a software project manager at Cognizant Solutions operating from India with the project team members operating from three different countries—the United States, France, and Germany. In this case, the team members' jobs are interdependent due to the specific nature of the turnkey project being undertaken. The project manager coordinates with the team members through video conferencing.

CONCEPT OF COORDINATION

Henri Fayol (1949), L. A. Allen (1973), and Ordway Tead (1951) consider coordination to be a separate management function, while others suggest that coordination is not a separate function but is inbuilt with all other management functions. Tead defined *coordination* as 'the effort to assure a smooth interplay of the functions and forces of the different component parts of an organization to the end that its purpose will be realized with a minimum of friction and a maximum of collaborative effectiveness'. Fayol (1930) emphasized internal coordination by suggesting the following three action plans:

1. Each department of an organization should work in proper harmony with the rest.
2. Each department or division should be informed of its share in the group task.
3. The working schedule of different departments should be constantly attuned to circumstances.

Therefore, within the organization, both vertical and horizontal coordination must be achieved so that all employees are aware of how their functions relate to other functions and how they contribute to the achievement of goals. *Vertical coordination* is between the jobs of individuals at different levels of organizational hierarchy. *Horizontal coordination* is between different departments at the same level in a chain of command.

At this stage, it is also important to clarify the meaning of external coordination. Any business organization operates in a dynamic environment. Forces exogenous or external to an organization have great influence on its success and failure. Therefore, coordinating external forces is also important to accomplish organizational goals.

Characteristics of Coordination

The basic characteristics of coordination can be explained as follows:

- **It is a dynamic and continuous process**: Coordination helps in achieving organizational objectives through coordinated group efforts. Organizational objectives are constantly changing in accordance with organizational budgets and priorities. Budgets are made annually and priorities keep getting changed to keep pace with the environmental forces. Coordination is, therefore, a dynamic and continuous process.

- **It applies to group efforts**: Coordination is necessary to integrate group activities with the organizational objectives. Organizations integrate individual as well as group activities through vertical and horizontal coordination.
- **It integrates and harmonizes diversified efforts**: To achieve goals and objectives, an organization segregates its activities into different parts. Each part of an activity is taken care of by individuals working in a group. Each such part forms a specific task and aggregation of tasks leads to achievement of common goals. Hence, individual efforts need to be harmonized and integrated in order to accomplish organizational goals. This is achieved through effective coordination.
- **It emphasizes unity of efforts**: Unity of efforts is ensured by channelizing individual and group efforts towards accomplishment of organizational objectives. As organizing is a complete process, harmonizing the diversified efforts of individuals is essential to achievement of results. This is accomplished through coordination, including vertical and horizontal coordination.
- **It is the basic responsibility of managers**: All managers, irrespective of their functional specializations and hierarchical levels, need to coordinate to achieve the goals and objectives of an organization. Hence, coordination is the responsibility of all managers.
- **It is the essence of management**: All managerial functions require coordination. Several proponents of the concept of coordination regard it as the essence of management to accomplish group goals, instead of viewing it as a separate managerial function. Therefore, coordination is considered as an all-pervasive function of management which permeates planning, organizing, staffing, directing, and controlling.
- **It is the maintenance of systems**: An organization is a system of group efforts. Coordination recognizes the diversity and interdependence of organizational systems and the importance of synthesizing individual and group efforts with the organizational systems. The systems approach considers the organization as a network of mutually dependent parts. It ensures the integration of these parts for accomplishment of goals and objectives.
- **It is a conscious action**: Coordination cannot be achieved spontaneously. It emanates from the conscious and concerted action of management.
- **It avoids interruptions in operations**: Interruptions in operations may arise due to several reasons. Coordination helps in avoiding interruptions and in timely accomplishment of organizational goals.
- **It eliminates overlapping or duplication of work**: Coordination can eliminate the problems of overlapping and duplication, and thereby ensures optimal utilization of the resources of an organization.

Based on the characteristics of coordination, one can locate six valid coordinating mechanisms for organizations, as was also suggested by H. Mintzberg (1981). They are:

1. **Direct supervision**: This is more visible in entrepreneurial organizations.
2. **Standardization of work**: This is adopted in machine organizations.
3. **Standardization of skills**: In professionally managed organizations, standardization of skills is visible.
4. **Standardization of outputs**: This is evident in diversified organizations.

5. **Mutual adjustment**: This is more in practice in innovative organizations.
6. **Standardization of norms**: Missionary organizations adopt standardization of norms to follow the principles of equity.

Importance of Coordination

So far, coordination has been understood as a primary method of synchronization of organizational activities which serves to avoid interruptions in operations and to ensure unity of action among individuals and groups, which together help to accomplish organizational goals. The need for coordination can be understood in terms of three categories:

1. **Division of labour**: Coordination is important because of growing specialization.
2. **Interdependence of units**: Coordination is important because of growth in size of organizations.
3. **Integration of the individual with the organization**: Coordination is important due to diversity of human nature.

The relevance of coordination in organizations has been discussed in detail here.

- **Coordination facilitates specialization**: Division of labour and specialization require segregation of the organization into different parts, though all these parts function towards achieving a common goal or goals. Integration of these segregated parts requires coordination.
- **Coordination leads to unity of action**: Coordination provides unity of action to diversified skills, activities, and perceptions. Diversity is inherent in an organization due to differences in human attributes and characteristics. Moreover, due to globalization, cross-country movements of workers have increased, resulting in employment of culturally diversified people in the same organization. Through coordination, such diversity can be reconciled and unity of action restored to achieve intended organizational goals.
- **Coordination balances inequality and ensures teamwork**: Individual differences may create imbalances, thereby making it difficult to accomplish organizational goals. Coordination helps to balance inequalities and ensures that activities are performed through teamwork.
- **Coordination helps in harmonizing individual and organizational goals**: Individual goals are largely influenced by individual needs. Hence, it may be different from group goals and organizational goals. Conflict between these goals may be a deterrent to accomplish the desired results. Coordination through the process of harmonization integrates individual goals with organizational goals.
- **Coordination is important for differentiation and integration**: Coordination helps in synergizing differentiated work units and authority centres. Differentiated work units and authority centres are inevitable in an organization due to the requirement of specialization.
- **Coordination reduces personality conflicts and eliminates organizational rivalry**: Complexity of individual characteristics creates personality conflicts. Such conflicts automatically develop rival groups. Coordination helps in eliminating conflicts and rivalries by encouraging friendly and cooperative relationships at the workplace. Conflicts and rivalry are counterproductive.
- **Coordination facilitates interdependence**: Even though an organization works by segregating its activities into different functional areas, each and every function is interdependent. Such interdependence cannot be achieved without coordination. Similarly, interdependence also promotes

mutuality in an organization. Mutuality involves positively relating and interrelating with people. It develops cooperation and fosters a culture where everyone strives for both the individual and the team to win. Coordination also helps a growing organization by developing an effective network of a huge number of people working in the organization.

- **Coordination promotes employeeship**: *Employeeship* brings changes in the balance of power in the relationship between employer and employee. Responsibility, initiative, loyalty, and commitment are the values that every organization aspires to achieve and tries to inculcate in their workforce. Employeeship develops such values by reducing the power imbalance, which enables employees to take responsibilities, develops loyalty and initiative, and ultimately aligns company goals with individual goals by developing a shared vision.
- **Coordination develops self-managed teams and leadership**: Coordination helps to link strategy with the individual employees' knowledge by developing a knowledge pool. This helps an organization to enhance the competence of their employees and makes it possible for them to respond to the competitive environment.

The given points amply prove that coordination is an important prerequisite for the success of any organization. That is why Chester Barnard (1938) opined thus: 'The quality of coordination is the crucial factor in the survival of an organization.'

Principles of Coordination

The fundamental principles of coordination have been enunciated by Mary Parker Follet (Parker 1984) focusing on the following aspects:

- **Direct control**: Direct personal contact helps to coordinate activities of individuals. It helps in bringing about agreement on different managerial actions and decisions, duly clarifying possible misunderstandings among employees. Therefore, direct contact is considered as the most important principle of coordination.
- **Early start**: Coordination is more effective in the early stages of planning and policy framing. Through coordination, employees are involved in these two processes and such participation enhances their sense of commitment to the organization. Therefore, direct contact should start right from the beginning so that all employees working in an organization are aware of the plans and programmes beforehand.
- **Reciprocity**: This principle of coordination requires relating the human resource, materials, and the environment reciprocally with the organization. In a total situation, all factors are reciprocally related. For example, when A works with B and B in turn works with C and D, all of them are influenced by each other and, therefore, contribute to the situation in totality.
- **Continuity**: Coordination is a continuous process. It never ends. This is because the ultimate aim of coordination is to achieve organizational goals and every organization operates in a dynamic environment. Environmental forces, which set the competitive arenas for an organization, have to be aligned with the organizational goals, which keep on changing. Every manager, therefore, constantly works to achieve coordination. In this context, the principle of continuity is important for coordination.

Other important principles of coordination are pervasiveness, unity of action, subordination of individual interest to organizational interest, unity of command and direction, teamwork, mutuality, employeeship, synergy, integration, and interdependence.

Objectives and Purposes of Coordination

There are five objectives or purposes that an organization usually seeks to realize through coordination.

1. Coordination plays a crucial role in eliminating conflict through reconciliation of goals, both among individuals and between individuals and the organization.
2. An important purpose of coordination is total accomplishment through synergy. Total accomplishment exceeds the sum of individual efforts. It means that the individual efforts of employees when added would be less than their total achievement through coordination, as coordination eliminates duplication by correlating the activities.
3. Another purpose of coordination is to achieve economy and efficiency. Avoidance of duplication of efforts through coordination helps in eliminating wastage of human resources, materials, and machines.
4. Coordination helps to achieve good personal relations, which enhance employees' morale and productivity.
5. Some organizations also intend to reduce employee turnover through coordination. High employee turnover means less retention, which is not a desirable situation.

Types of Coordination

There are four types of coordination: (1) vertical coordination, (2) horizontal coordination, (3) internal coordination, and (4) external coordination.

Vertical coordination

Vertical coordination is between different levels of an organization to ensure that all levels are in harmony and in line with the organizational policies and programmes. This is achieved through delegation of authority by directing and by controlling.

Horizontal coordination

Horizontal coordination is between departments on the same level of managerial hierarchy. Coordination between production and marketing departments at the same level of organizational hierarchy is an example of horizontal coordination. This is achieved by forming cross-functional teams and self-managed teams.

Internal coordination

When vertical coordination and horizontal coordination are accomplished within an organization, it is called *internal coordination*. Internal coordination is achieved through the following techniques:

- **Coordination through effective supervision**: *Supervision* ensures harmonious and reciprocal performance of subordinates. It synchronizes and coordinates subordinates' efforts both among themselves and in relation to other groups. Such collaborative efforts of individuals and groups to achieve organizational objectives are possible through coordination, which is best achieved through supervision.
- **Coordination through organizational processes**: Suitable organizational processes help to achieve coordination. Proper grouping of activities, assignment of job to the subordinate, proper authority delegation, etc., are some of the organizational processes that support coordination.
- **Coordination through personal contact**: Another important technique of achieving coordination is personal contact. *Personal contact* reciprocally relates one function with another and this is

achieved through development of interpersonal and horizontal relationships of people working in the organization. This promotes cooperation and collaboration due to mutual understanding.

- **Coordination through effective communication**: Transparency through communication is important to achieve coordination. Transparency is maintained by keeping people informed from time to time about internal and external changes, making them understand the changed situation, and coordinating their efforts to achieve intended goals. Communication can be made through letters, documented procedures, reports, bulletins, and the personal behaviour of managers. Communication does the important task of dovetailing information for the benefit of the organization. People react to communication quickly, provided it is properly coordinated. That is why effective communication is considered to be an important technique of coordination.
- **Coordination through group meetings**: Fayol (1930) pointed out that lack of coordination is more visible when a department knows nothing about others or fails to relate them to the organization as a whole. This is primarily due to watertight compartments in a traditional hierarchical structure where people lack initiative and loyalty. Coordination is essential to address such a situation and this can be best achieved by periodic group meetings and conferences of departmental heads. Group meetings help people to better understand the organizational needs and allow them to exchange ideas and know the plans and activities of their own department and also the organization as a whole.
- **Coordination through liaison officers**: Particularly for large organizations, direct personal contact among managers of various units and functions may not be frequent. Such a gap is often filled through liaison officers.

W. H. Newman (1951) suggested the following techniques or measures as tools for achieving better coordination:

- A simplified organization with clear-cut procedures and a network of formal and informal relations among people by grouping various functions into homogenous and non-overlapping units helps to achieve better coordination.
- Harmonized programmes and policies help to coordinate at the planning stage itself. Involving people at this stage facilitates re-examination and checking of programmes and policies of one department against those of another, which helps to integrate the organization as a whole.
- Well-designed methods of communication help to achieve better coordination.
- Voluntary coordination can be achieved by instilling objectives among the members of groups, developing generally accepted customs and terms to make it easy for people to work with one another, encouraging internal contacts to supplement formal communication, providing liaison officers, and forming committees to promote personal contact and informal exchange of ideas and views.
- Coordination can be made strong through personal guidance. The supervisor then plays the role of a mentor to coordinate the tasks of subordinates.

External coordination

The success or failure of an organization depends on a number of external forces. No organization can operate in isolation; it has to continuously interact with dynamic environmental forces and devise strategies to respond to such forces in order to survive. *External coordination* facilitates such processes by integrating the organization with dynamic external forces. At the outset, the organization has to know what the pertinent external forces are. After such identification, the organization has to analyse their potential impact and take suitable remedial measures to cope with the same. Important external forces may be the changing expectations of stakeholders (like suppliers, customers, investors, employees, or even the society), a changing competitive situation, technological advancement, changing government policies and regulations, etc. To facilitate external coordination, a number of techniques are adopted by an organization. Management concepts have been developed for more effective external coordination, for example, customer relationship management (CRM) to align the organization with customers and supply chain management (SCM), which helps to increase market share and multiplies customer satisfaction.

Case Coordination: An Integral Part of Management

No organization can survive without addressing the issues pertaining to functional and operational interdependencies. Only effective coordination of activities can address such issues. The need for coordination can be better understood when organizations face problems due to isolated managerial decisions, taken without thinking about their implications on the overall organization.

Problems of this nature were encountered by a leading steel manufacturer in India. The company makes extensive use of the latest automotive technology in the manufacturing process. The entire production process, right from transporting iron ore from their captive mine on a conveyor belt to rolling for the finished output, follows the assembly-line system. Each work station is equipped with a dedicated workforce and the required equipments and machinery to perform time-bound jobs. Being an automated production system, supervisors coordinate the process primarily through instrumentation control. It requires frequent adjustment to keep pace with the flow of production. For each work station, dedicated maintenance crews have been provided to ensure zero maintenance problems as far as possible, thus optimizing the utilization of machines and equipments.

Manufacturing operations in the company are headed by the general manager of the plant, who by virtue of his position is the senior-most executive in the organization. The general manager is supported by functional heads of different departments such as HR, finance, and marketing. Typically, the problem of maintenance in the company is far below the industry average, that is, very less. Even then, the company needs to provide for dedicated maintenance crew members as any eventual problem in the production process will increase the machine downtime (time during which the machine fails to function), with a lot of unfinished goods left in the pipeline. Minor breakdowns can culminate in prolonged stoppage of production. To motivate the maintenance people, the general manager decided to introduce the following incentive scheme:

'For every maintenance-free month, each member of the maintenance team will receive an incentive at 10 per cent of their base pay.'

The general manager's decision was in direct violation of the prevailing policies of the company which state: 'Maintenance, being a time-independent problem, maintenance people will not receive incentives. However, for their long period of work, whenever required, they will receive the overtime, as per the policy of the company.' Realizing this, the finance and HR heads rushed to the general manager and persuaded him to defer the announcement of the incentive scheme till the issue of amendment of the prevalent policy was discussed in the next plant-level committee meeting, represented by the management and the union. The general manager, however, construed it as a violation of his authority and announced the decision on incentive payment to the maintenance crew. Immediately after his announcement, the operations people declared that since their workmanship was instrumental to proper machine maintenance, they should also receive the same incentive for every maintenance-free month, or else, they would go on strike.

CASE QUESTION

Identify the problem of coordination in this case. Which management approach could have prevented this problem of coordination?

SUMMARY

- *Coordination* through unity of action ensures harmonization and synchronization of group efforts and thereby helps in achieving the organizational goals. Coordination is all-pervasive and is the essence of management. It is management of interdependence in work situations. Some authors consider coordination as a separate management function, while others suggest that coordination is not a separate function but is inbuilt with all other management functions.
- Characteristically, coordination is a dynamic and continuous process of achieving organizational objectives. It applies to group efforts as it facilitates integration of individual efforts vertically and horizontally to achieve the goals and objectives of the organization. Through unity of efforts or actions, coordination channelizes individual and group efforts towards accomplishment of organizational objectives. It is the basic responsibility of managers to maintain the work systems through conscious action.
- According to Mintzberg, coordination is the mechanism of standardization of work, standardization of skills, standardization of outputs, and standardization of norms for mutual adjustments among the people through direct supervision of their work.
- From an organizational perspective, there are different types of coordination, such as vertical coordination, horizontal coordination, internal coordination, and external coordination. *Vertical coordination* is between different organizational levels. *Horizontal coordination* is between departments on the same level of managerial hierarchy. Vertical coordination and horizontal coordination are together known as *internal coordination*. *External coordination* requires the organization to continuously interact with dynamic environmental forces and devise strategies to respond to such forces in order to survive.

KEY TERMS

Coordination: Managerial efforts to ensure unity of action is known as coordination. It is the management of interdependence in work situations.

External coordination: An organization has to continuously interact with dynamic environmental forces and devise its strategies to respond to such forces in order to survive. This process of integrating the organization with dynamic external forces is known as external coordination.

Horizontal coordination: Horizontal coordination is between departments on the same level of managerial hierarchy. This is achieved by forming cross-functional teams and self-managed teams.

Internal coordination: When vertical coordination and horizontal coordination are both accomplished within an organization, it is called internal coordination.

Unity of action: Unity of action is ensured by channelizing individual and group efforts towards accomplishment of organizational objectives.

Vertical coordination: Vertical coordination is between different levels of the organization to ensure that all levels are in line with the organizational policies and programmes. This is achieved through delegation of authority by directing and by controlling.

REVIEW QUESTIONS

1. Explain the term *coordination.* Why is it important for an organization?
2. What are the important characteristics of coordination?
3. What are the important principles of coordination? Are such principles common to all types of organization?
4. What are the important objectives achieved by an organization through coordination?
5. Explain the different types of coordination. What is the difference between *internal* and *external* coordination?
6. Explain the different tools and techniques for achieving coordination. Is there any difference between internal and external coordination tools?
7. 'Coordination is the essence of management.' In the context of this statement, discuss the relationship between coordination and managerial functions.
8. Write short notes on:
   i. Coordination and cooperation
   ii. Horizontal coordination
   iii. Vertical coordination
   iv. Unity of action
   v. Voluntary coordination

CRITICAL THINKING QUESTIONS

1. You are the CEO of a geographically dispersed networked organization. You are required to suggest a coordination system to your cross-country project team leaders, who are executing projects simultaneously in more than one country. The project team leaders often allege that they are unable to coordinate with their team members due to time differences. Suggest your proposed model of coordination.
2. As a manager of a departmental store, you observe that coordination among counter salespersons is extremely important. Salespersons manage each counter with specific and non-duplicating items of sales. Their performance is determined based on the volume and value of items they are able to sell. Salespersons rotate between counters on a daily basis. When a customer enquires about some items and they are not available in a particular counter, the salesperson is supposed to direct the customer to the correct counter. Your company gives performance incentives based on individual results. Of late, you have started observing that salespersons do not coordinate among themselves, resulting in a drop in the sales of the store as a whole. What could be the appropriate steps for enhancing coordination among the salespersons?

REFERENCES

Allen, Louis A. (1973). *Professional Management*. New York: McGraw-Hill.

Barnard, Chester I. (1938). *The Functions of the Executive*. Cambridge, MA: Harvard University Press.

Drucker, Peter (2000). *Management*. New York: Harper & Row.

Fayol, Henri (1930). *Industrial and General Administration.* Translated by J. A. Coubrough. London: Pitman.

——— (1949). *General and Industrial Management.* Translated by Constance Storrs. London: Pitman.

Mintzberg, H. (1981). 'Organization Design: Fashion or Fit', *Harvard Business Review*, January–February, pp. 103–166.

Mooney, James D. and Allen C. Reilly (1939). *The Principles of Organizations*. New York: Harper & Brothers.

Newman, W. H. (1951). *Administrative Action*. Englewood Cliffs, NJ: Prentice Hall.

Parker, L. D. (1984). 'Control in Organizational Life: The Contributions of Mary Parker Follet', *Academy of Management Review,* 9(4): pp. 736–745.

Tead, Ordway (1951). *The Art of Administration*. New York: McGraw-Hill.

FURTHER READING

Bhattacharyya, D. K. (2005). *Business Management*. Kolkata: Santra Publications.

——— (2009). *Organizational Behaviour*. New Delhi: Oxford University Press.

Brech, E. F. L. (1953). *Principles and Practice of Management*. London: Longman, Green & Co.

McFarland, Delton E. (1970). *Management Principles and Practices*. London: The Macmillan Co.

9

Organizational Forms

After going through this chapter, you will be able to understand:

- the differences between the various types of organizational forms
- the concept of a globally integrated enterprise

Suitable Organizational Forms

Global organizations today are facing extremely intense competition, pressures on margins, heightened customer demands for flexibility and speed, and a volatile labour market. In such an environment, organizations that distinguish themselves from their competitors are inevitably those that effectively leverage their human resources. Market leaders, such as AT&T, L.L. Bean, GE, Coca-Cola, Sun Microsystems, IBM, and Microsoft have integrated HR departments that employ strategic human resource management by linking the HR function to the objectives of the organization. In these companies, HR executives are a part of the organization's top strategy and policymaking committees. The HR function proactively drives change to maximize the organization's alignment with its corporate strategy while decision making is decentralized and aligned around a common understanding of the organization's values, vision, and strategy. The HR department is also staffed by specialists that work with line managers to promote the corporate strategy through integrated aspects of HR management (strategy and planning, job analysis, recruitment, hiring, training, etc.). High-performance companies also integrate HR management with other key support functions, such as total quality management, knowledge management, and information technology. By clarifying the common vision, increasing empowerment, and decentralizing decision making, difficult decisions on how to restructure in the best possible way to create a more rational, integrated, international HR function are made more effectively. The result is a lean, decentralized yet integrated HR department that leverages the greatest competitive advantage from the organization's most important asset—its human resources.

INTRODUCTION

There are many forms of business organizations. It may be owned by one person or a group of persons. If it is owned by one person, it is called *sole proprietorship*. All other forms of business organizations are known as *group ownership*, for example, the joint Hindu family firm, the partnership firm, the joint stock company (public or private), and the cooperative undertaking. Government-managed organizations may be a *departmental undertaking*, a *government undertaking*, or a *government enterprise*. Organizational structure and systems largely depend on the type of organizational forms. For example, a sole proprietorship organization operates on a small scale and, therefore, may follow a highly centralized decision-making system and a more flat or horizontal structure, so that the owner or proprietor can be involved in day-to-day business activities. Since the proprietor gets directly involved in routine business activities, they may prefer a wider span of control. In contrast, a professionally managed, large public limited joint stock company may prefer a bureaucratic hybrid structure for operational flexibility. This structure is mostly adopted by departmental undertakings (wholly owned by the government).

SOLE PROPRIETORSHIPS

Sole proprietorship is the single ownership form of business. A sole proprietor runs their business as an entrepreneur and is personally responsible for all business outcomes, which include personal obligation for all liabilities. It means a creditor can raise the claims against a sole proprietor, as their liabilities are unlimited. Even when a sole proprietor chooses to carry out business under a different name for the firm after formal registration, they cannot immune themselves from their personal obligations and liabilities.

Sole proprietorship is the most common form of business organization. The advantages of this form are:

- It is easy and inexpensive to formulate and operate administratively.
- It offers the maximum managerial control.
- Business income is taxed as personal (ordinary) income to the owner.

The disadvantages of the sole proprietorship organization are:

- It is difficult to raise large amounts of capital.
- There is unlimited liability.
- It is difficult to transfer ownership.
- The company has limited life.

As sole proprietorships are owned and operated by a single individual, this form of business organization ensures maximum management control. In small sole proprietorship firms, owners get personally involved in all aspects of purchasing, inventory control, production, sales, accounting, personnel and customer relations, as well as financial and general management issues. Such direct control by owners can be initially beneficial for the organization; however, as the firm grows, owners may find it difficult to be involved in all aspects of the business. In such cases, owners are required to hire helping hands to share control of the business activities. Some owners may feel reluctant to share control, resulting in disruption of business activities. Some owners may also prefer to induct their family members to take control of business. In either scenario, the sole proprietorship organization runs the risk of being reduced to a traditional family-managed business, with not much professionalism in management of the organizational affairs.

Since a sole proprietorship organization is owned by a single individual, the business is restricted by the scarcity of financial resources and this may stand in the way of growth and business diversification. In today's competitive market, even a small sole proprietorship organization requires substantial financial resources to make capital purchases (land, facilities, equipment, cars, and offices) and to meet increasing operating expenses (salaries, wages, and supplies). Paucity of funds may restrict a sole proprietor from scaling up their business activities. Their self-financing ability may not be always strong enough to cater to rising business investment and expenses. Moreover, borrowing money from intermediaries to finance their business activities may not always be cost-effective. All these aspects hinder the business expansion plan of sole proprietors and force them to scale down their activities.

Another major constraint in such type of organization is its limited lifespan. In India, there are many examples of well-known sole proprietorship organizations that have had to wind up with the death of the proprietor, that is, the owner who had started the organization.

PARTNERSHIPS

Partnership is a business that is owned and operated by two or more individuals. Theoretically, a partnership is an agreement between two or more persons who combine their resources in a business to make profit. Persons who are entering into an agreement are known as partners and collectively they constitute a partnership firm or organization. Partners provide capital and share the responsibility for running the firm on a mutual agreement. In a partnership agreement, it may be such that some invest in terms of monetary resources while some others take the responsibility of running the business. Such terms and conditions are spelt out in the partnership deed. Hence, characteristically, in partnership firms, one finds involvement of two or more persons, contractual relations between the persons, lawful business, sharing of profit, agency relationship, unlimited liability, and non-transferability of interest.

The advantages of a partnership include:

- It is easy and inexpensive to form and operate administratively.
- There is potential for large managerial control.
- Business income is taxed as personal (ordinary) income to the owner.
- One may be better able to raise larger amounts of capital in partnership than in a sole proprietorship.

The disadvantages of a general partnership include:

- Raising capital can still be a constraint.
- There is unlimited liability.
- It is difficult to transfer ownership.
- The company has limited life.

Thus, the advantages and disadvantages of general partnership are similar to those of sole proprietorship. Partnerships are generally easy and inexpensive to set up and operate administratively. Managerial control remains concentrated in the partners and is significant when the number of partners is small. Nevertheless, control is diluted with increase in the number of partners. This can become a disadvantage if the partners find themselves unable to work together. The challenge to partnerships and to sole proprietorships extends beyond conflicts with the partners. Divorce and other legal disputes may threaten the survival of the partnership when a claimant to a portion of the business assets demands their equity.

Depending on the nature of the partnership agreement, it could be partnership at will, particular partnership, joint venture, or limited partnership. Similarly, partners can be active, sleeping, or dormant. Further, they can be partner in profits only, sub-partner, partner by estoppels or holding out, etc. *Partner by estoppels* means a person who is construed as partner when they represent themselves to others either by their spoken works or writing, or by conduct, as if they are a partner in the firm. Some of the essential requirements for the success of a partnership firm are good faith, a common approach, a written agreement, registration, adequate capital, skills, talents, and stability.

JOINT STOCK COMPANIES

A *joint stock company* is a voluntarily incorporated association of persons in business. It is called joint stock because the capital contributions are jointly made, dividing it into transferable shares of fixed value. Essentially, a joint stock company has limited liability, a common seal, and perpetual succession. It is a creation of law. It is construed as a person but is artificial, invisible, and intangible, existing only in the eye of the law. A joint stock company is identified by one of these terms—'limited' or 'ltd', 'incorporated' or 'inc.', 'corporation' or 'corp.'. Whatever the term, it must appear with the corporate name on all documents, stationery, and so on, as it appears on the incorporation document.

Since a joint stock company is a legal entity, separate from the owners and managers, it can own assets, incur liabilities, and engage in specified activities. Ownership in the joint stock company is represented by shares on the equity, which may be either a general equity or a preferential equity. *General equity shareholders* can take part only in the distributable profit of the company as dividend. *Preference shareholders* can get a fixed rate of return irrespective of the profit accrued or not. They get the dividends before other equity claims. Ownership can easily be transferred by selling shares in the corporation. Likewise, the corporation has an unlimited life because when the owner dies, the ownership shares are simply passed on to their heirs. The easy transfer of ownership, separation of management and ownership, and limited liability features of a joint stock company together create an organization structure that can combine several activities and functions in a well-coordinated framework. It is designed to raise large sums of equity capital. Shareholders in a joint stock company do not get involved in the management process of the organization. Shareholders' risk is limited to the amount of fund invested by them. Due to easy transferability, they can easily walk out and dissociate themselves from the stakes of the company, simply by disposing of their shares.

The formation of a joint stock company is quite complicated. Since it is a separate legal entity, it requires incorporation complying with all required statutory provisions. In India, such incorporation formalities and other statutory compliance for the formation of a joint stock company are regulated by the Companies Act, 1956. Some companies may prefer to operate in closely held conditions and, therefore, form a private limited entity, restricting the number of members to a minimum two and a maximum fifty. They are known as *private limited companies*. Some prefer to form a *public limited company*, with a minimum of seven members and a maximum of any number. In such cases, they become widely spread organizations whose shareholders may be scattered globally. All such organizations are governed by a duly appointed board of directors.

Apart from private or public limited companies, there are also joint stock companies with government stakes. For example, a wholly government-owned organization is known as a *departmental undertaking*. An erstwhile private or public limited company taken over by the government (a case of nationalization) is known as a *government undertaking*, while a new company formed jointly by the government and private promoters is a *government enterprise*.

Apart from these forms, there is the joint Hindu family organization governed by the Hindu law, and multinational and transnational organizations. Joint Hindu family organizations are inherited and headed by the *karta* (the eldest male member in a joint family, who controls all property and all money matters). Multinational or transnational companies expand their business even beyond their own country where they are incorporated.

COOPERATIVE ORGANIZATIONS

Cooperative organizations are different from the rest because they are formed not for the purpose of making profit but to provide its members goods and services at reasonable rates. This form of organization primarily protects and safeguards the economic interests of its members. Thus, *cooperatives* are voluntary associations formed with a service motive wherein the members' share is the primary source of capital and the members get dividend on trading surplus, if any. They also function as a separate legal entity in a democratic way and are governed by state regulations. There are different types of cooperatives including consumer cooperatives, producers' cooperatives, marketing cooperatives, housing cooperatives, credit cooperatives, and farming cooperatives. A cooperative organization structure ensures:

- All members have an equal say (one vote per member, regardless of the number of shares held)
- Open and voluntary membership
- Limited interest on share capital
- Surplus is returned to members according to amount of patronage

The advantages and disadvantages of a cooperative organization have been enumerated in Table 9.1.

MULTINATIONAL ORGANIZATIONS

Multinational organizations are divided into three broad groups as per the configuration of their production facilities. *Horizontally integrated multinational corporations* manage production establishments located in different countries to produce the same or similar products (for example, McDonald's). *Vertically integrated multinational corporations* manage production establishments in a certain country or countries to produce products that serve as input to its production establishments in another country/other countries (for example, Adidas). *Diversified multinational corporations* manage production

Table 9.1 Advantages and Disadvantages of Cooperative Organizations

Advantages	Disadvantages
Owned and controlled by members	Longer decision-making process
Democratic control: one member, one vote	Requires members to participate for success
Limited liability	Extensive record keeping becomes necessary
Profit distribution (surplus earnings) to members in proportion to use of service; surplus may be allocated in shares or cash	Less incentive and possibility of development of conflict between members

establishments located in different countries which are neither horizontally nor vertically integrated (for example, Microsoft and Siemens AG).

There is no single agreed-upon definition of the multinational (or transnational) enterprise. *Multinational corporations* (MNCs) are companies or enterprises that operate in a number of countries and have production or service facilities outside the country of their origin. A commonly accepted definition of an MNC is an enterprise producing at least 25 per cent of the world output outside its country of origin. An MNC is a body that has an integrated philosophy encompassing domestic and global operations. The term is interchangeably used with *multinational enterprise* (MNE) or *transnational corporation* (TNC). It is an organization that has its facilities and other assets in at least one country other than its home country. Such companies have offices and/or factories in different countries and usually have a centralized head office where they coordinate global management. Very large multinationals have budgets that exceed those of many small countries.

Most of the multinational corporations are based in developed countries. They try to keep their domestic identity by maintaining their central office in a particular country, while their back office functions in countries where they operate. Using such a model, they become a globally integrated enterprise.

MICRO-MULTINATIONALS

Micro-multinationals are the types of organizations that try to become a global organization through Internet-based communication tools. Basically, they are small business entities (mostly software companies) and they coordinate their activities across borders through the Internet. They establish their dispersed virtual business with employees, clients, and resources located in various countries. They enjoy economy of scale since their cost of operation becomes relatively less due to use of cheaper Internet, telephone, and travelling costs. Hence, these types of organizations grow quickly, creating unique business opportunities.

GLOBALLY INTEGRATED ENTERPRISES

The *globally integrated enterprise* is a term coined in 2006 by Sam Palmisano, CEO of IBM Corp., to denote a company that fashions its strategy, its management, and its operations in pursuit of a new goal—the integration of production and value chains around the world. This is also known as the multinational model of the twentieth century. For IBM, this was a successful model to grow internationally, understand customers and local market requirements, and cultivate local talent. Now, such enterprises can locate functions anywhere in the world, based on the right cost, skills, and environment. Palmisano mentioned the *law of global integration* to be driven by three forces—economics, expertise, and openness.

TRANSNATIONAL ORGANIZATIONS

The term *transnationalism* indicates specific strategies of MNCs/TNCs to control production facilities in more than one country through direct foreign investment. Recent examples in this regard are Ford and General Motors. These companies can be called *transnational organizations*. They enjoy specific advantages of global markets, availing low-cost trans-shipment of their finished goods in markets where they can get a bargain price. For example, in China, many multinationals have their own production facilities not for the China market but for other markets where the price offer is competitive.

FEATURES OF INTERNATIONAL ORGANIZATIONS

In a global economy, international competition plays a pivotal role, primarily played out through multinational and transnational organizations. In developed countries like the United States, 70 per cent to 85 per cent of the economy is influenced by multinational organizations. Managing these types of organizations requires philosophies and systems that are different from those of domestic organizations. International business operations can take several different forms. There are four basic types of organizations: namely geocentric, polycentric, regiocentric, and ethnocentric. These differ in the degree of international activities. Geocentric organizations are global hybrids but believe in decision making in their global headquarters and focus more on the ability than the nationality. Ethnocentric organizations follow the home country's systems and even recruit their own managers. Regiocentric organizations are global hybrids and believe in decision making locally. Polycentric organizations also believe in the host country's systems and prefer recruiting managers from the host country.

A multinational corporation has autonomous units that operate in several countries. Shell, Philips, and ITT are three typical examples of MNCs. MNCs allow autonomy to their subsidiaries in different countries to run their business independently. Subsidiaries are empowered to manage local issues like tastes and preferences of customers and design of new products while subscribing to these preferences, and to adopt strategies to tackle political pressures and economic trends. The degree of such independence may even imply non-integration with the headquarters. The global corporation, another form of an MNC, maintains control of operations since they treat the world market as a unified whole. Companies like Matsushita and NEC subscribe to this form and they try to maximize their efficiency on a global scale. Typically, these companies function like a domestic company except for the fact that they view the world as their marketplace. A transnational corporation achieves both the local responsiveness (like an MNC) and the efficiency of a global organization. They make use of networked structures to coordinate their specialized facilities located around the world. In this way, transnational organizations provide autonomy and independence to their units across the world, making all the units function as an integrated whole. Well-known examples of transnational companies are Ford, Unilever, and British Petroleum.

A primary feature of international organizations is that they are strong enough to influence the world economy in the following ways:

- Production and distribution extend beyond national boundaries
- Systematic transfer of technology among the units located in different countries
- Direct investments in several countries
- Capability to influence balance of payments of countries of their operation
- Capability to exert political impact
- Capability to overcome the barriers of nationalism

Advantages of MNCs

Some of the advantages of MNCs are:

- With more investment and increase in economic activity, MNCs generate more employment. In the process, MNCs enhance production facilities and bring positive changes in the local economy.
- MNCs improve the balance of payments of a country. Balance of payments, that is, a positive foreign exchange position, occurs with the direct inflow of capital, which leads to import substitution and export promotion.

- MNCs facilitate transfer of technology and in the process benefit the local economy to enjoy efficiency and effectiveness in the factors of production.
- MNCs help in generating revenues for the government of the beneficiary country through taxation. MNCs' tax payouts enable the country to allocate more to public expenditures on infrastructure development, thereby bringing positive changes in the economy.
- MNCs help in saving precious foreign exchanges.

Disadvantages of MNCs

Some of the disadvantages of MNCs are:

- MNCs often scale down their production facilities and close down operations in a situation of economic uncertainty. Consequently, people employed in MNCs often lose their jobs. Such uncertainty may lead to internal problems in the country.
- MNCs often exert control over the local government, both economically and politically. Such control may even go against the interests of the nation as a whole. This is done by lowering the internal price structure. Through transfer pricing, MNCs can reduce their profits in the countries where they operate and, thus, deprive their host countries of legitimate tax payouts.
- MNCs can create environmental imbalances by extracting natural resources and polluting the environment of the host countries.
- By competing with local firms, MNCs can kill the local organizations.
- MNCs may repatriate their profits to their own country of origin and, thereby, deprive the host countries of the benefits of new investment.

Case The Complex Organizational Web of Cisco

The form of an organization encompasses organizational structure, resources, culture, governance system, and the overall relationships with the external environment. The traditional organizational structure is a vertically designed relationship sketch, indicating hierarchical positions in respective functions or divisions. With the changing business scenario brought about by globalization, many organizations today have switched over to networked structures. Networked structures require an inclusive approach for decision making and, therefore, empower people who are geographically apart. Networked organizational structures can cope with the complexity of cultural and sociopolitical differences by maintaining a skeletal number of persons in work sites, whose proximity to the place help in maintaining or synchronizing organizational relations with the stakeholders. The only difference between the networked structure and the hierarchical centralized structure is in terms of enforcement of control. However, in the changing business systems, control is being replaced by facilitation, which the management can ensure by leveraging advanced communication technologies.

Cisco, a leader in switches, routers, and other Internet-based technologies, was founded by a group of computer scientists. By leveraging the expertise of the founders, the company was able to come out with an Internet operating system (IOS) that helps in sending streams of data from one computer to another. During the initial years, Cisco had a flat organizational structure, which later changed to a structure comprising cross-functional teams. Cisco is so structured that the key decisions are taken by councils, boards, and work groups. Such specially formed committees, which totalled 60 as of 2009, work at different levels and are essentially cross-functional in nature. This approach of Cisco helped it to gain speed, flexibility, and quick decision-making ability. As a result, Cisco is perhaps one of the leading global organizations today capable of responding to environmental changes within the shortest possible time. Also, the company is recognized as one of the most agile and innovative in a rapidly changing industry, operating on a global scale. Breaking away from the traditional command and control model, the company is now able to replicate the model of collaborative decision making with a networked structure. Even in a situation of economic downturn, the company is able to pursue an aggressive growth strategy.

However, many corporate observers believe that Cisco's approach to organizational structure and distributive decision making through committees, in reality, slows down the decision-making process. Management by committee impedes innovation. Going by the track record of Cisco's performance, though, this is not tenable. With its approach, Cisco has grown to be a highly diversified, knowledge-intensive company operating on a global scale.

While addressing the business performance of the company in November 2009, John T. Chambers, Chairman and CEO, Cisco Systems, Inc., observed thus: 'This is business as usual at Cisco, given our collaborative structure of councils, boards, and working groups to be able to effectively execute on multiple fronts. Time will tell if we are right but the tangible results indicate that the business models based on collaboration may be the most effective way to drive a successful global business today.'

The complex organizational web of today's Cisco is a lesson for many, but others are still sceptical, fearing loss of control and delay in responding to changes.

CASE QUESTION

Critically comment on Cisco's organizational form.

SUMMARY

- Organizational structure and systems largely depend on the organizational form. There are many organizational forms such as sole proprietorships, partnerships, joint stock companies, and cooperative organizations.
- *Sole proprietorship* is owned by a single person. *Partnership* is a business that is owned and operated by two or more individuals. A *joint stock company* is a voluntarily incorporated association of persons in business. *Cooperative organizations* are formed not for the purpose of making profit but to provide its members goods and services at reasonable rates.
- Multinational organizations (a particular organizational form) are divided into three broad groups as per the configuration of their production facilities, namely horizontal, vertical, and diversified. *Horizontal multinational corporations* manage production establishments located in different countries to produce the same or similar products. *Vertical multinational corporations* manage production establishments in a certain country or countries to produce products that serve as input to its production establishments in another country/other countries. *Diversified multinational corporations* manage production establishments located in different countries which are neither horizontally nor vertically integrated.
- Another important organizational form is the *micro-multinational* that tries to become a global organization through Internet-based communication tools.

- A *globally integrated enterprise* strategically integrates its production and value chain worldwide. MNCs/TNCs become transnational to control production facilities in more than one country through direct foreign investment.
- Characteristically, multinationals transfer technology among their units, make direct investments in different countries, influence balance of payments of countries of their operation, exert political impact, and, thus, overcome the barriers of nationalism.

KEY TERMS

Cooperatives: Cooperatives are voluntary associations formed with a service motive wherein the members' share is the primary source of capital and the members get dividend on trading surplus, if any.

Globally integrated enterprise: The globally integrated enterprise denotes a company that fashions its strategy, its management, and its operations in pursuit of a new goal—the integration of production and value delivery around the world.

Joint stock company: A joint stock company is a voluntarily incorporated association of persons in business. It is called joint stock because the capital contributions are jointly made, dividing it into transferable shares of fixed value.

Micro-multinationals: Micro-multinationals are small businesses enabled by Internet-based communication tools. These companies start operating in different countries from very early stages.

Multinational corporations: A multinational corporation (MNC) is a company or enterprise that operates in a number of countries and has production or service facilities outside the country of their origin. It is a body that has an integrated philosophy encompassing domestic and global operations.

Partnership: Partnership is a business that is owned and operated by two or more individuals. It is an agreement between two or more persons who combine their resources in a business to make profit.

Sole proprietorship: Sole proprietorship is the single ownership form of business. A sole proprietor runs their business as an entrepreneur and is personally responsible for all business outcomes, which include personal obligation for all liabilities.

Transnational organizations: A transnational organization owns or controls production facilities in more than one country through direct foreign investment.

REVIEW QUESTIONS

1. Discuss the advantages of a joint stock company over sole proprietorship and partnership.
2. Discuss the differences between *cooperatives* and *joint stock companies*.
3. Discuss the concept of multinational and transnational organizations. How are they different from other forms of organization?
4. Write short notes on:
   i. Sole proprietorships
   ii. Partnerships
   iii. Cooperative organizations
   iv. Joint stock companies

CRITICAL THINKING QUESTIONS

1. Your company is an Indian MNC with a presence in eleven countries. Cross-country presence is essential for your company for basing the manufacturing facilities in proximity to the market, as the industrial paints and chemicals that you manufacture deteriorate in quality while being shipped from India. You want centralization of corporate-level decision making in your Indian head office located in Mumbai. However, due to operational reasons, you also allow functional autonomy to your country-specific strategic business units. Often, this leads to decisional errors and substantial loss of business revenue. Identify some possible solutions.
2. Your company is a multinational and engaged in production of industrial chemicals. Your company engages workers from the country of their operation, but all managerial and supervisory employees are recruited from your company's place of origin. Even the compensation packages are different. Identify the forms of your company and then critically comment on your company's functioning.

FURTHER READING

Bhattacharyya, D. K. (2005). *Business Organization*. Kolkata: Santra Publications.

——— (2010). *Industrial Management*. New Delhi: Vikas Publishing.

Dale, Ernest (1965). *Management Theory and Practice*. New York: McGraw-Hill.

Drucker, Peter (1954). *The Principles of Management*. New York: HarperCollins Publishers.

Hofstede, G. (1997). *Culture and Organizations: Software of the Mind*. New York: McGraw-Hill.

Koontz, H. (1961). 'The Management Theory Jungle', *Academy of Management Journal*, 4(3): pp. 174–188.

Massie, Joseph L. (1986). *Essentials of Management*, 4th ed. New Delhi: Prentice Hall.

10

Business Environment and Social Responsibility

After going through this chapter, you will be able to understand:

- the concept of the business environment and the social responsibilities of businesses
- the reasons for an organization's responsibility towards society
- the advantages and disadvantages of social responsibilities of businesses
- the various issues related to the business environment
- the use of various tools and techniques to analyse the business environment of organizations

Make Your Business Responsive to the External Environment

Organizations are open systems. Therefore, the external environment in which they operate is very important. Organizations need support from their environment if they are to survive and perform well. The environment is the key factor in determining the level of availability of resources and the ease with which an organization can carry out its activities. For example, poor macroeconomic policies lead to high interest rates, fluctuating currencies, and a host of conditions that make it difficult for some organizations to perform well.

All organizations are required to respond to the external environment through their boundary-spanning subsystem. Each organization is embedded in a particular environment that provides multiple contexts that affect the organization and its performance. Important points that should be remembered include the impact of these environmental forces on the mission, performance, and capacity of the organization; the level of hostility of the environment; and the major opportunities and risks resulting from the environment. An enabling environment is made up of administrative, technological, political, economic, sociocultural, and stakeholder factors (Lusthaus, Anderson, and Murphy 1995). This premise is consistent with theories of strategic management and serves as a helpful categorization system.

Organizations need to be able to diagnose an enabling environment, and also become competent enough to both influence and adapt to it as that environment evolves (Savedoff 1998). Rules, ethos, and capabilities are three important components through which organizations respond to external environmental cues. The importance of the external environment is very apparent in international financial institutions that are affected by each rise and fall in the world economy.

INTRODUCTION

The *business environment* has two dimensions: namely the task environment and the mega environment. The *task environment* is internal to an organization; the *mega environment* is exogenous to the organization though it influences the task or internal environment. Change of work process for internal restructuring of the organization is a construct of task or internal environment. Increase in global competition is the construct of mega or external environmental issues that affect the organization. Both task and mega environmental issues significantly affect the working of the organization. For example, an increased spate of global competition may require organizations to focus on new product development, which among other things also requires changes in the task environment. Globally, the business environment is continuously changing. Therefore, organizations need to develop the required mechanism to quickly respond to changes in the task and the mega environment.

Corporate social responsibility (CSR) indicates a deliberate socially responsible behaviour of an organization. Even though globally there are many corporate governance mandates, both in terms of business norms and legislation, many organizations fail to integrate their social responsibility with their business practices. It is important to understand that only complying with the legislative requirements of corporate social responsibility is not enough—organizations need to make it their deliberate choice. The carbon discharge to the environment by many organizations during their process of manufacturing may not attract the pollution control norms, but installation of effluent-treatment plants to arrest the carbon deposition for its subsequent economic use may be a deliberate choice and fulfilment of organizational social responsibility. Similarly, organizational social audit may not be the statutory requirement, but voluntary social audit and its disclosure carries a better image and reflects a high degree of social responsiveness for the organization. Similarly, waste recycling, adherence to pollution control norms, correct financial results disclosure, compliance with labour laws, etc., are good examples of organizational responses to the social norms. In India, the Tata group is a notable role model, whose care for social responsibility, even going beyond the statutory requirements, has today created a win-win situation such that Tata Steel enjoys substantial cost benefits, sourcing materials from their community development centres. Similarly, the Murugappa Group, based in the southern part of India, enjoys social prestige because of their obvious care for the society. Organizational investment in the employees' quality of work life also adds value to the society. *Quality of work life* can be defined as the perceived personal needs of employees which they try to satisfy while they work for the organization. Among other things, employees look for social integration with their work organization and seek to relate their society with their working life. From an organization's point of view, important constituents of social responsibility encompass all the stakeholders of the organization. J. R. Schermerhorn (1989) suggests eight important areas of organizational social responsibility. These are:

1. Ecology and environmental quality which covers pollution control, dispersion of industrial waste, and effective land use, including beautification
2. Consumerism, that is, truth in lending, advertising, and business

3. Community needs, that is, meeting the education and health requirements, providing effective solutions to local problems, and enabling voluntary participation in community development works
4. Government relations
5. Taking cognizance of the minorities and disadvantaged persons
6. Labour relations
7. Shareholder relations
8. Philanthropy, that is, financial support to the promotion of art and culture, offering scholarships for education, and financial support for charities

SOCIAL RESPONSIBILITY OF BUSINESS

From socioeconomic perspectives, the social responsibility of organizations extends beyond profit maximization. It argues for the necessity of profit maximization addressing the needs of the society. Although addressing social needs may not pay back in the short run, and it may even have an adverse impact on profitability, it is now proved worldwide that ultimately organizations can gain substantially. By meeting social expectations, it is possible for an organization to sustain itself in the long run and grow. The obligation of any business to protect and serve public interests is known as *social responsibility of business*. Apart from profit-making, organizations perform numerous social functions since they are a part of the society. Social responsibility requires an organization to take care of those who are instrumental to the existence of the organization. Broadly speaking, they are the stakeholders of the organization and they also include the society at large. Social responsibility, therefore, implies that an organization must not harm the society at large while it does its business activities. Organizations' concern about their social responsibility dissuades them from adopting any unfair means in the pursuit of profit. They voluntarily take part in activities related to social responsibility in order to meet the expectations of various stakeholders. Therefore, the importance of social responsibility for business is manifold. Some of the ways in which it is important are:

- It creates goodwill for the business among the public.
- It creates a positive public image.
- It helps in long-term survival and growth of business.
- It provides satisfaction to employees and this factor is directly related to productivity.
- Consumers become more conscious about their rights.

Corporate social responsibility, also known as corporate responsibility, corporate citizenship, responsible business, sustainable responsible business (SRB), or corporate social performance, is a form of corporate self-regulation integrated into a business model. Ideally, a CSR policy would function as a built-in, self-regulating mechanism whereby business would monitor and ensure their adherence to law, ethical standards, and international norms. All business would embrace responsibility for the impact of their activities on the environment, consumers, employees, communities, stockholders, and all other members of the public sphere.

Organizations need to demonstrate their social responsibilities to various stakeholders by complying with the following aspects:

- Ensuring reasonable returns on investment to investors/shareholders
- Prompt repayment of loans to financial institutions

- Paying salaries and ensuring social security to employees
- Providing care and comforts to employees at the workplace and meeting statutory requirements like holidays, maternity leave, sick leave, and overtime payment
- Payment of taxes to the government
- Providing quality goods and services to customers according to their money's worth

Reasons for Social Responsibility

Organizations need to be socially responsible to address the interests of various groups. Some of the reasons can be listed as follows:

- **Favourable public image**: The activities of a business towards the welfare of the society help it to earn goodwill and a positive reputation. Moreover, people prefer to buy products of a company that engages itself in various social welfare programmes. A good public image also attracts honest and competent employees.
- **Compliance with government regulation**: To avoid conflict with government regulations, business firms should discharge their duties voluntarily. For example, if a business firm pollutes the environment, it will come under strict government regulation and this may ultimately force the firm to close down its business. Instead, the business firm should engage itself in maintaining a pollution-free environment.
- **Ensuring survival and growth**: Every business is a part of the society and for its survival and growth, support from the society is very essential. Every business utilizes the available resources like power, water, land, and roads. So, it should be the responsibility of every business to spend a part of its profit on the welfare of the society.
- **Employee satisfaction**: Besides a good salary and a healthy work atmosphere, employees also expect other facilities like proper accommodation, transportation, education, and training. The employers should try to fulfil the expectations of employees because employee satisfaction is directly related to productivity and it is also required for the long-term prosperity of the organization. For example, if a business spends money on training its employees, it will have more efficient people working towards its success and will, thus, earn more profit.
- **Consumer awareness**: Consumers have become more and more conscious about their rights. They may protest against the supply of inferior and harmful products by forming groups. This has made it obligatory for businesses to protect the interests of their consumers by providing quality products at the most competitive price.

Advantages for Socially Responsible Organizations

Socially responsible organizations derive the following benefits:

- **Public expectation**: Public opinion supports a business pursuing a social goal.
- **Long-term profits**: Better community image and relations lead to long-term profits.
- **Ethical obligation**: A business should have a conscience since it is regarded as right to have one.
- **Public image**: A business creates a favourable public image by pursing social goals.
- **Better environment**: A socially responsible organization attracts better staff.
- **Discouragement of further government regulation**: Bad behaviour attracts government intervention.
- **Balance of responsibility and power**: Any imbalance encourages irresponsible behaviour.

- **Stockholder interests**: Society views a socially responsible company as posing less risk and, hence, is willing to pay more for its share.
- **Possession of resources**: A socially responsible company can provide assistance to the public and charitable projects due to the possession of resources.
- **Superiority of prevention over cures**: A socially responsible business can act on some problems before they become too serious.

Disadvantages for Socially Responsible Organizations

Socially responsible organizations may also encounter certain disadvantages such as:

- **Violation of profit maximization**: Businesses should do what they do best, that is, maximize profit.
- **Dilution of purpose**: Waste of time and resources can lead to dilution of the purpose of the organization.
- **Costs**: A socially responsible business may have to absorb the cost of its social programme or pass it on to its customers.
- **Too much power**: A business becomes too powerful if it pursues both economic and social goals.
- **Lack of skill**: Business persons may not be good at dealing with social issues.
- **Lack of accountability**: Social leaders, unlike political leaders, are not held responsible for their social activities.
- **Lack of broad public support**: The public is divided on whether a business should be involved in social activities.

THE BUSINESS ENVIRONMENT

The business environment is of two types. As mentioned in the introduction, one is an internal or task environment and the other is the mega or external environment.

Broadly, anything could be an internal or task environmental issue when it requires change in the internal processes and systems of work. Even global competition (a construct of mega environment) could be instrumental in bringing change in the task environment. The 24 × 7 customer-care service or helpline is a good example of the confluence of task and mega environments.

Some of the internal or task environmental issues are:

- Hours of work and the effect on production
- Music at work
- Noise level at work
- Illumination
- Miscellaneous factors like mundane and repetitive work

In another way, business environmental issues can be classified as micro, macro, and internal. *Micro environmental issues* influence the organization directly, viz. customers, suppliers, etc. Even though the word *micro* is interpreted as small, in this context it is used to signify those driving forces that directly influence the functions of organizations. It requires organizations to effectively manage their relationships with customers and suppliers. *Macro environmental issues* are those forces that influence the organization indirectly, viz. globalization, threat from new entrants in the market, etc. All other factors that are internal to the organization are classified as *internal environmental factors*. A good test to identify internal environmental factors is to use the 'five Ms' model, signifying men, money, machines, materials, and markets. Some organizations believe in classifying the business environment as the external, the specific, and the general.

Analysis of the Business Environment

Using various techniques, organizations perform the analysis of the business environment and accordingly prepare their response strategies to survive in the market. Some of these techniques are explained here.

PEST analysis

Analysis of the business environment is essentially a continuous process and requires consideration of all aspects of organizational activities, more particularly the planning aspects. With any change in planning premises, plans have to be redrawn and changed, which by default becomes a deterrent for the organization. For example, an organization's business environment per se consists of the internal environment (employees, technology, finances, etc.), the micro environment (customers, agents and distributors, suppliers, competitors, etc.), and the macro environment (political, legal, social/cultural, economic, and technological factors).

The macro environment can be put through the PEST analysis. A template of PEST analysis has been provided as Figure 10.1.

The four factors that can affect the business environment according to PEST analysis are:

1. **Political factors**: These factors exert influence on the business in the form of changing regulation, institutional support, and the degree of stability of the government. Some of the important areas of consideration are:
   - ❑ Degree of stability of the political environment
   - ❑ Influence of government policies on regulation and taxation matters
   - ❑ Ethics and values of the political parties that run the government
   - ❑ Influence of government policy on the economy
   - ❑ Perspectives of the government on culture and religion
2. **Economic factors**: Economic factors, that is, the state of the economy both in the short term and the long term, are considered by organizations with reference to their marketing strategies, more particularly for new product launching. Some of the important areas of consideration are:
   - ❑ Rate of interest
   - ❑ Level of inflation or recession
   - ❑ Level of employment per capita
   - ❑ Per capita gross domestic product (GDP)
   - ❑ Long-term economic stability
3. **Sociocultural factors**: Such factors vary across countries. Social and cultural incongruence often stands as the most important barrier to international trade. Some of the important areas of consideration for such analysis are:
   - ❑ Religious fanaticism
   - ❑ General attitudes of people towards international products and services

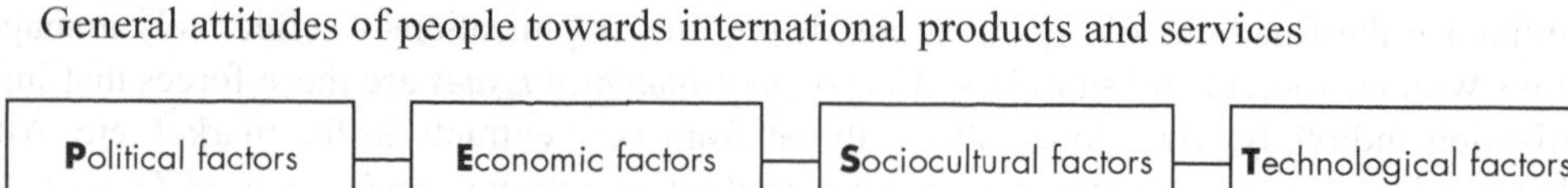

Figure 10.1 PEST Analysis

- ❑ Gender diversity in the society
- ❑ Major nature of economic activity
- ❑ General education and income levels of people
- ❑ Mortality level of people in general

4. **Technological factors**: Technology per se is the dominant factor behind the competitive advantage of an organization and even a nation as a whole. It is an important driver of globalization. While analysing the technological factors, organizations need to consider a number of issues. They need to consider whether the technology:
   - ❑ Helps in achieving economy of scale in production (cost-effectiveness) and ensures high level of quality
   - ❑ Helps the organization to develop innovative products and services
   - ❑ Brings positive changes in distribution logistics and communication systems
   - ❑ Offers value-added customer services

SWOT analysis

SWOT analysis is a simple framework for generating strategic alternatives from a situation analysis. It is applicable to strategy framing at either the corporate level or the business unit level, and therefore, is also applicable in framing marketing plans. SWOT (sometimes also referred to as TOWS) stands for strengths, weaknesses, opportunities, and threats. The SWOT framework was described in the late 1960s by Edmund P. Learned, C. Roland Christiansen, Kenneth Andrews, and William D. Guth. As it concentrates on issues that potentially have the most impact, the SWOT analysis is useful when organizations need to address a complex strategic situation within the shortest possible time. Therefore, SWOT analysis performs a strategic situation analysis. In Figure 10.2, a template of SWOT analysis has been provided.

An internal and external situation analysis can produce a large amount of irrelevant information. The SWOT analysis can serve as an interpretative filter to reduce the information to a manageable quantity of key issues. A SWOT analysis classifies the internal aspects of the company as strengths or weaknesses and the external situational factors as opportunities or threats. Strengths can serve as a foundation for building a competitive advantage, while weaknesses may be a hindrance. By understanding the four aspects of its situation, an organization can better leverage its strengths, correct its weaknesses, capitalize on its opportunities, and successfully withstand potential threats.

Strengths Internal aspects of the company that can be capitalized upon to give it a competitive advantage	**W**eaknesses Internal aspects of the company that might hinder its growth and need to be eliminated
Opportunities External situational factors that can facilitate the company's growth	**T**hreats External situational factors that can be detrimental to the company

Figure 10.2 SWOT Analysis

Although SWOT analysis helps in reducing various situational factors into a manageable number of issues that the organization needs to consider, often it oversimplifies in classifying the environmental factors applicable to a particular organization. It often makes arbitrary classification of factors pertaining to strengths, weaknesses, opportunities, and threats.

TOWS matrix

TOWS and SWOT are basically acronyms. It is just arranging the same words—strengths, weaknesses, opportunities, and threats—in the reverse order. On an operational level, the basic difference between TOWS and SWOT lies in their degree of emphasis. While TOWS emphasizes the external environment, the emphasis of SWOT is more on the internal environment. The externally focused TOWS matrix, which helps to weigh different options for organizations to frame strategies, has been illustrated in Figure 10.3.

Hence, *TOWS matrix* helps to identify strategic alternatives by combining the internal and external environmental factors. While doing this, more emphasis is given on taking stock of external environmental issues.

The BCG growth-share matrix

The *BCG growth-share matrix* is a portfolio planning model developed by Bruce Henderson of the Boston Consulting Group (BCG) in the early 1970s. It is based on the observation that a company's business units can be classified into four categories based on combinations of market growth and market share relative to the largest competitor. Hence, the term *growth-share matrix* is used to indicate the BCG matrix. Market growth serves as a proxy for industry attractiveness and relative market share serves as a proxy for competitive advantage. The growth-share matrix, thus, maps the business unit's positions within these two important determinants of profitability.

This framework assumes that an increase in relative market share will result in an increase in the generation of cash. This assumption is often true because of the experience curve. In the experience curve, increased relative market share implies that the company is moving forward relative to its competitors, thus developing a cost advantage. A second assumption is that a growing market requires

	External opportunities (O)	**External threats (T)**
Internal strengths (S)	*'Maxi-maxi' strategy (SO)* Strategies that leverage strengths to maximize opportunities	*'Maxi-mini' strategy (ST)* Strategies that leverage strengths to minimize threats
Internal weaknesses (W)	*'Mini-maxi' strategy (WO)* Strategies that minimize weaknesses leveraging opportunities	*'Mini-mini' strategy (WT)* Strategies that minimize weaknesses and avoid threats

Figure 10.3 TOWS Strategic Alternatives Matrix

investment in assets to increase capacity and, therefore, results in the consumption of cash. Thus, the position of a business on the growth-share matrix provides an indication of its cash generation and its cash consumption.

Henderson reasoned that the cash required by rapidly growing business units can be obtained from the company's other business units that are at a more mature stage. This option generates significant cash for the organization. Through investment, the company becomes the leader in market share in a rapidly growing market, and in the process can move along the experience curve to develop the cost advantage.

The four categories of BCG matrix are:

1. **Dogs**: *Dogs* have low market share and a low growth rate, and thus, neither generate nor consume a large amount of cash. However, dogs are cash traps because of the money tied up in a business that has little potential. Strategically, organizations need to withdraw from the business.
2. **Question marks**: An organization in a *question mark* state grows rapidly and consumes huge cash. However, due to low market shares, such business does not generate enough cash. This results in huge cash consumption without corresponding increase in cash earnings. This is the reason that a question mark business is often called a problem child. However, a question mark business can grow and eventually become a star and a cash cow when the organization emerges as the market leader. This requires fresh investment in technology to bring changes in the production process. Alternatively, if the organization ceases to be a market leader, with increased cash consumption the question mark will eventually degenerate into a dog and then withdrawal from business becomes the only option. Therefore, before making fresh investments, the company needs to understand the potential to grow in the market.
3. **Stars**: *Stars* generate large amounts of cash because of their strong relative market share, but they also consume large amounts of cash because of their high growth rate. Therefore, the cash in each direction approximately nets out. If a star can maintain its large market share, it will become a cash cow when the market growth rate declines. The portfolio of a diversified company always should have stars that will become the next cash cows and ensure future cash generation.
4. **Cash cows**: As leaders in a mature market, *cash cows* exhibit a return on assets that is greater than the market growth rate and, thus, generate more cash than they consume. Such business units should be 'milked' to extract profits. However, the cash consumption should be limited, mostly through new investments in technology. When an organization has a multiple products portfolio, cash cows can provide the cash to turn around a question mark business into a market leader. The relative positions of the firm's entire business portfolio can be displayed in a single diagram. Such a diagram has been provided in Figure 10.4.

The BCG matrix is losing its importance due to the following weaknesses:

- The model assumes market growth rate and relative market share as the two determinants of profitability. However, there are other factors as well that determine the competitive advantage of an organization.
- As per this model, the definition of the market primarily considers the breadth of the market, but there may be a situation when an organization dominates in a small niche market due to its premium range of products.

Despite such limitations, the BCG matrix is still considered the simplest tool to understand the business portfolio of an organization and the primary basis for allocating resources across strategic business units (SBUs).

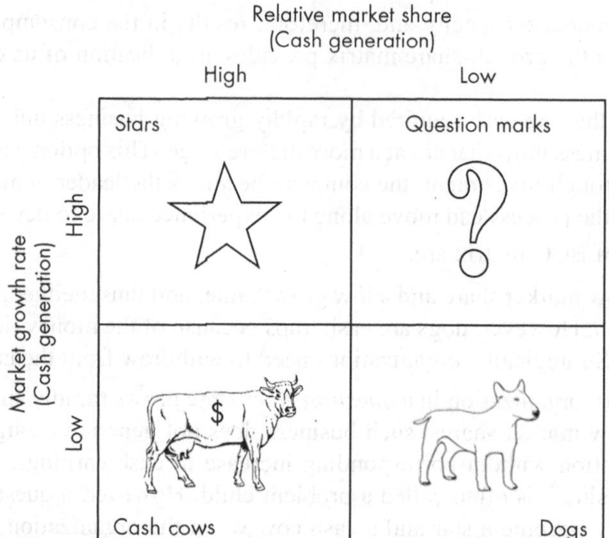

Figure 10.4 BCG Matrix (*Source*: http://www.bcg.com/about_bcg_history_1968.aspx. Reproduced with permission of The Boston Consulting Group, Inc. All rights reserved.)

The McKinsey/General Electric (GE) matrix or industry matrix

The *McKinsey/GE matrix*, developed by McKinsey and General Electric, can be considered an improved version of the BCG matrix. For example, the McKinsey/GE matrix uses the term *market attractiveness* instead of *market growth* (used in the BCG matrix). Market attractiveness is a more inclusive term than market growth. Further, in the McKinsey/GE matrix, the term *competitive strength* is used against *market share* (used in BCG matrix) to measure the dimension of the competitive position of a strategic business unit.

Factors of market attractiveness The analysis of market attractiveness is essentially subjective. The following factors can be used to assess the market attractiveness:

- Market size
- Market growth
- Market profitability
- Pricing trends
- Competitive intensity/rivalry
- Overall risk of returns in the industry
- Opportunity to differentiate products and services
- Segmentation
- Distribution structure (for example, retail, direct, and wholesale)

Factors of competitive strength The factors of competitive strength are:

- Strength of assets and competencies
- Relative brand strength

- Market share
- Customer loyalty
- Relative cost position (cost structure compared with competitors)
- Distribution strength
- Record of technological or other innovation
- Access to financial and other investment resources

Product/market matrix

The *product/market growth matrix* helps in deciding the market and product growth strategy of an organization. The model suggests that organizational attempts to grow depend on factors like whether the markets are new or whether the organization wants to position existing products in new or existing markets (Ansoff 1957). A typical model of the product/market matrix is provided in Figure 10.5.

The output from the product/market matrix is a series of suggested growth strategies that set the direction for the business strategy. These are described here.

- **Market penetration**: *Market penetration* is a growth strategy where the business focuses on selling existing products in existing markets. Market penetration seeks to achieve four main objectives:

  i. **Maintain or increase the market share of current products**: This can be achieved by a combination of competitive pricing strategies, advertising, sales promotion, and perhaps more resources dedicated to personal selling.

  ii. **Secure dominance of growth markets**: This is possible through consistent and aggressive marketing.

  iii. **Restructure a mature market by driving out competitors**: This would require a much more aggressive promotional campaign, supported by a pricing strategy designed to make the market unattractive for competitors.

  iv. **Increase usage by existing customers**: This is done by introducing schemes such as loyalty programmes.

  A market penetration strategy is very much about 'business as usual'. The business focuses on markets and products that it knows well. It is likely to have substantial information on competitors and on customer needs. It is unlikely, therefore, that this strategy will require much investment in new market research.

	Present product	**New product**
Present market	Market penetration	Product development
New market	Market development	Diversification

Figure 10.5 Product/Market Matrix

- **Market development**: *Market development* is a growth strategy where the business seeks to sell its existing products in new markets. There are many possible ways of approaching this strategy, such as:
    - ❑ New geographical markets (for example, exporting the product to a new country)
    - ❑ New product dimensions or packaging
    - ❑ New distribution channels
    - ❑ Different pricing policies to attract different customers or create new market segments
- **Product development**: *Product development* is a growth strategy where a business aims to introduce new products in existing markets. This strategy may require the development of new competencies and modified products that will appeal to existing markets.
- **Diversification**: *Diversification* is the growth strategy where a business markets new products in new markets. This is an inherently riskier strategy because the business is moving into markets in which it has little or no experience. Therefore, to adopt a diversification strategy, a business must have a clear idea about what it expects to gain from the strategy and an honest assessment of the risks involved.

Michel Porter's five competitive forces analysis

Michel Porter referred to five competitive forces and recommended that every organization, before adopting their strategy (related to marketing), consider these forces so that the best strategy can be adopted. These forces have been discussed in Table 10.1.

Porter suggests that the organization should account for the five competitive forces and also make effective use of the three generic medicines—cost leadership, differentiation, and change in business focus.

Table 10.1 Michael Porter's Five Competitive Forces Analysis

Competitive force	How it influences the organization
1. Rivalry	The degree of competition that the company is facing because of the existence of more number of players in the market.
2. Bargaining power of customers	The extent to which customers can bargain. With the increased bargaining power of customers, the firms' competitive position in the market weakens. Hence, any marketing strategy needs to be adopted keeping in view the degree of bargaining power of customers.
3. Bargaining power of suppliers	The extent to which suppliers can bargain. Suppliers' bargaining power also weakens the firms' strategic position.
4. Availability of substitutes	The opportunity for customers to substitute their requirements. With increased opportunity, a firm's competitive position weakens.
5. Entry restriction	Entry restriction is either imposed by the government or the regulatory bodies (in the form of licensing, etc.), or it is a natural restriction due to a long gestation period (the phase during which the firm cannot make any profit), or there are physical barriers created by the company itself, occupying scarce resources like land. Presence of any form of restriction benefits the organization.

If the firm enjoys cost leadership, they will continue to enjoy competitive advantage. Also, to fight against the competitive forces, firms may decide to go for product differentiation to distinguish them from competitors or change their business focus altogether. For example, IBM changed their business focus from desktop manufacturing to IT-enabled services, as the price competition from HP, Dell, etc., was mounting.

The Shell nine-celled directional policy matrix

The *Shell nine-celled directional policy matrix*, which was developed by Shell, is another improved version of the BCG matrix. The horizontal axis of the matrix represents the prospects for profitability, while the vertical axis represents the competitive capability of the organization. Each cell implies different strategic decisions.

The nine zones of this matrix have been explained here:

1. **Leader**: Resources are focused on strategic business units.
2. **Try harder**: It maybe dangerous in the long run, but for the present it is fine.
3. **Double of quit**: Gambling on potential major SBUs for the future is possible.
4. **Growth**: Enough resources are focused on market growth.
5. **Custodial**: One must not commit any resources for long-term gain; rather, one should make quick money.
6. **Cash generation**: Like a cash cow, one should earn as much as one can and put the surplus elsewhere.
7. **Phased withdrawal**: One should move cash to SBUs with greater potential. This zone is repeated as the ninth zone as the firm uses the same strategy when their business is in an average state as well as unattractive state.
8. **Disinvest**: One should liquidate or move assets as quickly as possible.

The Arthur D Little (ADL) strategic condition matrix

The Arthur D Little (ADL) strategic condition matrix guides one to frame strategy keeping in view two perspectives—competitive position and industry maturity. *Competitive position* is understood in the context of the organization's market reach, market share, etc. *Industry maturity* is the reflection of the 'industry life cycle'. A model of this matrix has been provided in Figure 10.6.

According to this matrix, the competitive position of any organization can be listed under five categories:

1. **Dominant**: Extraordinary position (literal monopoly in the market)
2. **Strong**: Comparatively powerful
3. **Favourable**: Competitive strengths in certain market segments
4. **Tenable**: May face erosion by stronger competitors that have a favourable, strong, or competitive position
5. **Weak**: In a vulnerable position

According to the ADL strategic condition matrix, there are six generic categories of strategy that can be employed by individual SBUs. These categories are: (1) market strategies, (2) product strategies, (3) management and systems strategies, (4) technology strategies, (5) retrenchment strategies, and (6) operations strategies.

Company's competitive position	Stages of industry maturity			
	Embryonic	Growth	Maturity	Ageing
Dominant				
Strong				
Favourable				
Tenable				
Weak				

Figure 10.6 Arthur D Little (ADL) Strategic Condition Matrix (Reproduced with permission from ADL)

Scenario Planning for Environment Analysis

Scenarios are the alternative views of the future primarily based on some events or changes that have occurred or are likely to occur. Both the Delphi technique and the nominal group method help in drawing scenario plans, and depending on the issues and the time constraint, organizations choose the appropriate method to minimize the risk of forecasting based on scenario plans. These methods have been explained in detail in Chapter 2 under 'Delphi Technique' and 'Nominal Group Method'.

Case Impact of CSR: Grasim (A Flagship Company of Aditya Birla Group)

Corporate social responsibility is integrated with the Aditya Birla Group's value systems. The founder father of the group, G. D. Birla was an ardent believer of trusteeship in management, which entails that the organization generates wealth and holds a trust for different stakeholders. In another way, it means that since the society is a stakeholder in the organization, principles of trusteeship require the organization to invest a part of the profits in fields other than business, that is, for the cause of the society. Aditya Birla, the grandson of G. D. Birla, further refined the approach to corporate social responsibility by waiving the concept of 'sustainable livelihood', which is also known as chequebook philanthropy. His belief was: 'Give a hungry man fish for a day, he will eat it and the next day, he would be hungry again. Instead, if you taught him how to fish, he would be able to feed himself and his family for a lifetime.'

Taking cues from his predecessors, the present chairman of the group, Kumar Mangalam Birla, institutionalized the triple bottom-line accountability towards corporate social responsibility, representing economic success, environmental responsibility, and social commitment. Corporate social responsibility, therefore, is now an integral part of the group's activities. Today, the group caters to different aspects of social work covering an estimated 3,700 villages and seven million people.

All the companies of the group—Grasim, Hindalco, Aditya Birla Nuvo, Indo Gulf, and UltraTech—have their independent rural development cells, which implement various socially relevant projects. Planning for social development projects is done through participatory need assessment of the communities around the plants. Projects are undertaken with a one year to three years rolling plan, with clear and measurable targets. Each project is audited by external agencies to measure the degree of achievement in qualitative and quantitative terms.

All the social projects of the group are undertaken in partnership with government bodies, district authorities, and village panchayats, as well as with the direct beneficiaries—the villagers. The various agencies, including non-governmental organizations (NGOs), with whom the group collaborates in executing the social projects are United Nations Population Fund (UNFPA), State Innovations in Family Planning Services (SIFPSA), CARE India, Habitat for Humanity International, United Nations Children's Fund (UNICEF), and World Bank. Partnering and collaboration helps the group to ensure that their investment in social causes does not get duplicated, as many other agencies also undertake social projects.

A stocktaking of the group's commitment to social responsibilities for the year 2007–2008 indicates that the group made significant contribution in a number of areas, as given in Table 10.2.

Apart from the areas listed in Table 10.2, the group invested in social welfare activities like mass marriage programmes and drug de-addiction campaigns. The group's investment in infrastructure

Table 10.2 Aditya Birla Group's Contributions to Social Issues in 2007–2008

Area	Nature of activities and the beneficiaries
Healthcare	Medical camps benefited 41,112 villagers. Special health check-ups conducted for 2,359 students of 26 schools. Eye camps performed 2,414 cataract operations and distributed free spectacles to 1,179 people. In addition, the group has invested in treatment of tuberculosis, medical diagnostics, cleft-lip surgery for 260 children, artificial-limb fitment for 170 physically impaired persons, organizing blood-donation camps, AIDS prevention and control, provision for drinking water, mother and child care, etc.
Education	Helped schools to reduce the dropout rates of students, free education facilities extended through *Balwadis* programme benefiting more than 2,000 students, investment in job-oriented industrial training benefiting 102 students, capacity-building training on computers, conducted adult-literacy programmes, made provision for midday meals in schools, etc.
Sustainable livelihood	Investment in agriculture focusing on productivity enhancement and reducing the dependency on monsoon benefited nearly 6,000 farmers, sustainable living and organic farming, animal immunization in veterinary camps, setting up of milk-collection centres, building of water-harvesting structures, vocational training, etc.
Women self-help groups	Capacity-building programme through training in tailoring and providing of sewing machines at subsidized rates benefiting 1,535 women, who are now capable of earning their livelihood. Formation of 211 self-help groups through which 2,550 women were empowered through savings, skills training, and income generation.

development included construction and repair of approach roads, setting up troughs and drinking-water structures, setting up of health centres and facilities, construction of low-cost toilets, construction of dams for water storage and irrigation, and setting up of bus stands.

The group believes that all of these endeavours are the result of translating their philosophy of 'compassionate care'. This is the reason that despite a worldwide economic slowdown, during the financial year 2008–2009, Grasim Industries achieved consolidated net revenue of INR 186,030,000,000 (9 per cent higher than the preceding year). Although the net profit during this period was lower by 16 per cent (INR 21,870,000,000), it was more attributable to high interest rates and also to the higher provision for depreciation. This was borne by the fact that the cash profit for the year was INR 39,390,000,000, which was higher by 6 per cent compared to the previous year. With its presence in cement, powered by captive power plants, logistic infrastructure, and a waste heat recovery system, the company achieved stupendous growth during the year. The other core businesses of the company like viscose staple fibre (VSF), chemicals, and sponge iron have made it possibly the most vibrant diversified company in India.

The company's commitment to social responsibility is evident from their vision statement, which states:

'To actively contribute to the social and economic development of the communities in which we operate. In so doing, build a better, sustainable way of life for the weaker sections of society and raise the country's human development index.'

CASE QUESTION

Take stock of Grasim's commitment to corporate social responsibilities and explain the underlying philosophy behind it. Do you think the same philosophy should prompt other companies and groups to be socially responsive?

SUMMARY

- Business environment has two dimensions: the task environment and the mega environment. *Task environment* is internal to an organization, while *mega environment* is exogenous to it.
- *Corporate social responsibility* indicates a deliberate socially responsible behaviour of an organization. It encompasses areas like ecology and environmental quality, consumerism, community needs, government relations, diversity issues, labour relations, relationships with stakeholders, and philanthropy.
- Organizations emphasize corporate responsibility to address the interests of various groups. It helps an organization to create a favourable public image, ensures compliance with government regulations, stabilizes the growth of the organization, ensures employee satisfaction, increases consumer awareness, etc. Organizational social responsibility is also criticized on the grounds that it dilutes the motive of profit maximization. However, through practising corporate social responsibility, organizations can sustain themselves and grow in the long run.
- Along with corporate social responsibility, it is also important for an organization to account for internal and external environmental issues. *Internal* or *task environmental issues* are working hours, music at work, noise level at work, illumination, factors like mundane and repetitive work, etc. *Micro environmental issues* influence the organization directly, viz. customers, suppliers, etc. *Macro environmental issues* influence the organization indirectly, viz. globalization, threat from new entrants in the market, etc.

- Analysis of business environments can be done using various tools and techniques such as PEST analysis, SWOT analysis, TOWS matrix, BCG matrix, McKinsey/GE matrix, product market/growth matrix, Porter's model, Shell matrix, ADL matrix, and scenario planning. *PEST analysis* helps in understanding political, economic, sociocultural, and technological factors. Likewise, *SWOT analysis* also helps in accounting for the environmental factors. SWOT stands for strengths, weaknesses, opportunities, and threats. *TOWS matrix* is an arrangement of SWOT in the reverse order, differing only in the degree of emphasis. The *BCG growth-share matrix* is a portfolio planning model that classifies a company's business units into four categories based on combinations of market growth and market share relative to the largest competitor.
- The *McKinsey/GE matrix* helps to overcome the disadvantages of the BCG matrix, replacing the term *market growth* with *market attractiveness*. The *product/market growth matrix* helps in deciding the market and product growth strategy of an organization. This model suggests that organizational attempts to grow depend on factors like whether the markets are new or whether the organization wants to position existing products in new or existing markets. Michel Porter referred to five competitive forces and recommended that every organization, before adopting their strategy (related to marketing), consider these forces—rivalry, bargaining power of customers, bargaining power of suppliers, availability of substitutes, and entry barriers.
- The *Shell nine-celled directional policy matrix* is an improved version of the BCG matrix. The horizontal axis of the matrix represents the prospects for profitability, while the vertical axis represents the competitive capability of the organization. The *Arthur D Little (ADL) strategic condition matrix* guides one to frame strategy keeping in view two perspectives—competitive position and industry maturity. Finally, scenario planning helps in environment analysis. This type of planning becomes more effective by using the Delphi technique or the nominal group method.

KEY TERMS

Cash cows: As leaders in a mature market, cash cows are businesses that exhibit a return on assets that is greater than the market growth rate and, thus, generate more cash than they consume.

Corporate social responsibility: Corporate social responsibility indicates a deliberate socially responsible behaviour of an organization in terms of its business practices.

Diversification: Diversification is a growth strategy where a business markets new products in new markets.

Dogs: Dogs are businesses that have low market share and a low growth rate, and they neither generate nor consume a large amount of cash.

Market development: Market development is a growth strategy where the business seeks to sell its existing products in new markets.

Market penetration: Market penetration is a growth strategy where the business focuses on selling existing products in existing markets.

Mega environment: The mega environment is exogenous to the organization though it influences the task or internal environment.

Product development: Product development is a growth strategy where a business aims to introduce new products in existing markets.

Question marks: A question mark business grows rapidly and consumes large amounts of cash, but they do not generate much cash as they have low market shares.

Stars: Stars are businesses that generate large amounts of cash because of their strong relative market share, but they also consume large amounts of cash because of their high growth rate.

Task environment: The task environment is internal to an organization.

REVIEW QUESTIONS

1. Discuss the rationale behind an organization's responsibility towards society.
2. What are the *mega* and *task environment issues* that affect an organization?
3. What are the types of advantages and disadvantages that organizations experience while becoming socially responsive?
4. Explain the difference between *SWOT analysis* and *TOWS matrix*. How can these two tools help an organization to understand the possible environmental impact on their business?
5. Critically evaluate the BCG matrix. How would the McKinsey/General Electric matrix be a better alternative to the BCG matrix?
6. Explain Porter's model of five competitive forces. How can this model help an organization to perform an analysis of the environment?
7. Write short notes on:
   i. Strategic condition matrix
   ii. Shell's nine-celled directional matrix
   iii. Scenario planning
   iv. Delphi technique
   v. Task environment

CRITICAL THINKING QUESTIONS

1. Your company produces life-saving drugs using patented molecules. Your research and development facilities are outsourced to Germany and you can only get information that is specific to your core manufacturing areas. You were apprised that some of the German researchers could observe molecular disorder while the molecules mixed with other chemical agents during the process of production. Using Porter's model, suggest a possible action plan. If required, you can also make use of other models.
2. ONGC has made forays into the retail petroleum, oil and lubricant (POL) business. The details are given in the ONGC Web page http://www.ongc.net/archives1.asp?fold=archives%5CMar03&file1=Ongcnews&file2=ongcnews4.txt. On the basis of the information provided there, create a product/market matrix and analyse whether ONGC's market penetration strategy in the retail (POL) business has been successful.

REFERENCES

Ansoff, H. Igor (1957). 'Strategies for Diversification', *Harvard Business Review*, September–October, pp. 113–24.

Learned, Edmund P., C. Roland Christiansen, Kenneth Andrews and William D. Guth (1969). *Business Policy, Text and Cases*. Homewood, IL: Richard D. Irwin.

Lusthaus, C., G. Anderson and E. Murphy (1995). *Institutional Assessment: A Framework for Strengthening Organizational Capacity for IDRC's Research Partners.* Ottawa: International Development Research Centre (IDRC).

Savedoff, William D. (ed.) (1998). *Organization Matters: Agency Problems in Health and Education in Latin America.* Washington, DC: Inter-American Development Bank.

Schermerhorn, J. R. (1989). *Management Jar Productivity.* New York: John Wiley & Sons.

FURTHER READING

Aghion, P. and J. Tirole (1997). 'Formal and Real Authority in Organizations', *Journal of Political Economy*, 105 (1): pp. 1–29.

Bhattacharya, C. B., Sankar Sen and Daniel Korschun (2008). 'Using Corporate Social Responsibility to Win the War for Talent', *MIT Sloan Management Review*, 49 (2): pp. 37–44.

Bhattacharyya, Dipak Kumar (2009). *Organizational Behaviour: Concepts and Applications.* New Delhi: Oxford University Press.

——— (2010). *Cross-cultural Management: Text and Cases.* New Delhi: PHI Learning.

——— (2010). *Industrial Management.* New Delhi: Vikas Publishing.

Cavanagh, Gerald, Dennis J. Moberg and Manuel Velasquez (1981). 'The Ethics of Organizational Politics', *Academy of Management Review*, 6 (3): pp. 363–374.

Dowell, G., S. Hart and B. Yeung (2000). 'Do Corporate Global Environmental Standards Create or Destroy Market Value?', *Management Science*, 46, pp. 1059–1074.

Huselid, M. (1995). 'The Impact of Human Resource Management Practices on Turnover, Productivity, and Corporate Financial Performance', *Academy of Management Journal*, 38, pp. 635–672.

International Organization for Standardization (ISO) (2009). 'Social Responsibility: ISO 26000'. Available at http://www.iso.or/sr.

Kaliski, B. (ed.) (2001). 'Ethics in Management', *Encyclopedia of Business and Finance*, 2nd ed., vol. 1. New York: Macmillan Reference.

——— (ed.) (2001). 'Social Responsibility and Organizational Ethics', *Encyclopedia of Business and Finance*, 2nd ed., vol. 1. New York: Macmillan Reference.

Klassen, R. and C. McLaughlin (1996). 'The Impact of Environmental Management on Firm Performance', *Management Science*, 42, pp. 1199–1214.

Schumpeter, Joseph A. (1942, 1950). *Capitalism, Socialism, and Democracy.* New York: Harper & Row.

Sen, Sankar, C. B. Bhattacharya and Daniel Korschun (2006). 'The Role of Corporate Social Responsibility in Strengthening Multiple Stakeholder Relationships: A Field Experiment', *Journal of the Academy of Marketing Science*, 34 (2): pp. 158–66.

Smith, Adam (1776, 1937). *The Wealth of Nations.* Toronto: Random House.

Wood, D. (1991). 'Corporate Social Performance Revisited', *Academy of Management Review*, 4, pp. 691–718.

11

Ethics and Values in Organizations

After going through this chapter, you will be able to understand:

- the concepts of ethics and values
- the steps involved in the implementation of a code of ethics
- the benefits of ethical practices in organizations
- the concepts of stakeholders and ethical organizations
- the way to build an ethical culture in organizations
- different views on managerial ethics
- ethical decision making

Do Not Compromise on Ethics

Ethics and values in organizations have become a focus of the media globally. Enron, WorldCom, Tyco International, and Lehman Brothers are some of the international organizations that came under the focus of the media for not following ethical practices. In India, the most recent case is of Satyam Computer Services Limited (now known as Mahindra Satyam). Unethical practices in organizations have now become a social issue. It is due to this reason that corporate governance issues have become more stringent around the world, and non-compliance with these attracts attention from the regulatory bodies. Ethical issues encompass all areas of corporate practices. Therefore, ethics requires giving due attention to all stakeholders. While fulfilment of customers' expectations is one important area of ethics, it also needs to be extended to meeting the needs of internal customers like employees. This is particularly important since organizations expect their employees to comply with their code of ethics and behave accordingly. Most employee-related decisions such as promotion, increment, training, and development are based on employees' performance evaluation reports. Hence, by emphasizing the ethical dimensions in regular performance appraisal systems, organizations can integrate an expectation of ethics into employees' formal role identities to make ethical conduct more relevant at work. This is possible because employees emulate such practices and when they observe any unethical decision being taken by their managers in performance-related issues, they get confused and question their ethical behaviour.

This is why Videocon introduced the COMBED model, that is, communicate, behave, and demand while you manage people. At a critical juncture of transition from the legacy-bound culture of Philips (Videocon acquired some Philips units), Videocon had to implement this model in order to help employees understand that the management practises what it preaches. A similar focus on ethical behaviour is enforced by organizations such as Infosys and Oil and Natural Gas Corporation Limited (ONGC) as well. Hence, making ethics the basis of organizational policies is not enough; it first requires true compliance by employees at the managerial level, and only then are employees down the chain motivated to emulate them.

INTRODUCTION

Values and ethics are an integral part of all organizational activities. They encompass all activities of an organization including leadership and decision making. Values are those abstract principles that are valued by others, individually or collectively. It is essential for any organization to adopt a vision that is consistent with its core values. Core values of an organization may be integrity, professionalism, teamwork, customer satisfaction, employee welfare, etc. Honesty and loyalty are ingredients of integrity. When values are shared by all members of an organization, they become the basis of making judgements, assessing probable outcomes of contemplated actions, and choosing among alternatives. All members of the organization align their activities with respect to the values. Yet, in another way, values can be considered as what one judges to be right. Values are moral, ethical, and professional attitudes of character. Values guide action. They are the basis of the behaviour of people. Thus, values can be defined as the basis for judgements that are important for the organization to achieve success in its core business. Values constitute what is considered to be right in a profession, individually or organizationally. They are the beliefs of a person or social group regarding issues in which they have an emotional investment (either for or against something). Morals have a greater social element in comparison to values and tend to have a broad acceptance. Morals are far more about good and bad than any other value. Thus, one judges others more strongly on their morals than their values. A person can be described as immoral, while there is no word for describing them if they are not following their values. Thus, morals are motivations based on the ideas of right and wrong. Ethics, on the other hand, is to behave in a manner considered to be right or moral. Ethics are a set of rules that are explicitly adopted by a group of people. Values determine what is right or wrong, while doing right is known as ethics. To behave ethically is to behave in a manner consistent with what is right or moral. Ethics are, thus, internally defined and adopted, whilst morals tend to be externally imposed on other people. Therefore, ethics can also be defined as a system of moral values since everyone is shaped to a large extent by their cultural setting.

Many empirical studies and research substantiate that ethical organizations achieve better business results. It is due to this reason that organizations globally are increasing their social responsiveness and ethical practices to fulfil the expectations of all stakeholders. Due to technology-intensive communication systems, organizations' involvement in unethical business practices has now become more transparent. Whether it is a case of child labour exploitation by McDonald's in China, the Indian carpet industry or the Bangladesh garment industry, or suppression of information regarding adverse effects of products or services, organizations get immediately identified and socially reprimanded, resulting in a loss in business and long-term sustainability. Therefore, ethical issues now encompass every citizen of the world. Stakeholders are no longer just limited to shareholders or investors. A stakeholder could be anyone who has any interest in or involvement with, dependence on, or made any contribution to the organization. Therefore, every organization needs to embrace values, morals, and ethics to be socially acceptable and to ensure long-term sustainability.

CONCEPTS OF ETHICS AND VALUES

Values are the principles and priorities that help one to take decisions. J. H. Thorp (2005) defines values as the 'core principles that define for individuals what are ideal personal standards. Values are in hierarchies that are unique to each individual and culture. As a result, values are personal standards that help people determine the relative value, worth, and importance of standards to their lives'. Values are reflected in the way one treats people, the approach to one's work, and one's basic work ethic. They are relatively stable over time. Research claims that most values are formed by age five or six.

There are two types of values: namely terminal and instrumental. *Terminal values* are desired states of existence, while *instrumental values* are desirable modes of behaviour. Similarly, values can also be defined in terms of espoused versus enacted. *Espoused values* are values that one wants others to believe they hold, while *enacted values* are values-in-use, that is, what they actually practice.

Terminal values are developed through the process of upbringing with a cue from people's happiness, freedom, and friendship. Since the process of upbringing by default does not guarantee happiness, one also develops some instrumental values that guide and shape people's lives, motivate them to be cheerful and responsible, and show self-control. Cultural influences also cause major differences in people's values. Generally, Americans want everything immediately, have little patience with waiting, and are pushy. Japanese workers tend to be more patient with regard to job promotions and are willing to stay with the company in the long run. Germans believe more in analytical decision making, with less interest in brainstorming and quick decision making. To ensure value-based business practices, every organization chooses its values from a number of alternatives. Choosing alternatives impulsively or thoughtlessly does not lead to formation of values. Therefore, organizations need to carefully weigh the consequences to make an intelligent choice while deciding what their values are.

Ethics, on the other hand, comprises the standards of conduct that indicate how one should behave based on moral duties and virtues, primarily based on the principles of right and wrong. There are two aspects to ethics. One is to discern right from wrong and the other one is to do what is right, good, and proper. Therefore, ethics encompasses the concept of values. Thorp (2005) defined ethics as 'the implementation of what a group's value system defines as good or bad, and the behaviour necessary to fulfil ideal states. When an individual's conduct is consistent with her group's values, then she has acted ethically. Being ethical is not about acting out of one's own values'. A common philosophical definition of ethics is in terms of the science of conduct or the values of management. It is the framework of values for moral behaviour. Ethics, therefore, is a social glue to serve the interests of the society at large. Ethics are the basic ground rules by which people live their lives since they are accepted by the majority. When it pertains to business, ethics is generally considered as the act of learning what is right and what is wrong in the workplace and then taking the decision to do the right thing. Thus, ethics refers to the standards of conduct that explain how one should behave, based on moral duties and virtues. Ethics, therefore, translates the concept into action. It is in this respect that ethics is different from values, and these two terms are not interchangeable. Ethics is how a person behaves and values are the beliefs and attitudes that shape ethical behaviour.

Code of Ethics

A code of ethics and, therefore, a code of conduct specify the ethical standards that members of the organization, either individually or in a group, should comply with in order to stay as a member of the group. They are generally formally stated and members are required to accept them as part of their membership of the group while accepting employment. A *code of ethics* consists of documented and transparent statements underlying the expected behaviour of the members of the organization that reflect on their day-to-day working, including decision making. After recruitment, during induction or socialization of employees, most organizations orient their new hires to their code of ethics. The code of ethics varies between organizations. This is because it is dependent on the vision and mission of the organization, and is also influenced by culture. Thus, values and ethics vary between individuals and across cultures. G. Hofstede's theory on cultural dimensions (2001) helps to understand clashes on cultural values. Long-term values versus short-term values affect many aspects of organizational life. Four key ethical principles are egalitarianism, utilitarianism, individual rights, and distributive justice. Organizations following a utilitarian approach in ethics make decisions based on their outcomes and consequences. Ethical behaviour is influenced by moral intensity, ethical sensitivity, and the situation.

Although theoretically a code of ethics and a code of conduct are different, operationally they are considered to be the same. The *code of ethics* is more like the statement of values and beliefs that the organization endorses. The *code of conduct*, on the other hand, translates the values (documented in the code of ethics) into specific behavioural standards. Thus, the code of conduct is a certain set of principles outlining dos and don'ts. To be more specific, the code of ethics is a general guideline on the values, while the codes of conduct translate such values into business practices. One can also say that the codes of conduct are rooted in the mission of the organization, as mission translates vision into action.

Components of a code of ethics

It is difficult to embrace a universal approach to frame the code of ethics for every organization. However, keeping in mind certain components, it is possible for an organization to customize their code of ethics. The components are as follows:

- **Preamble**: It is a brief background statement that articulates the organization's basic mission and values.
- **Personal integrity**: It is a pledge based on one's own personal integrity that represents the organization's commitment to dealing with others in a fair and truthful manner.
- **Professional excellence**: It constitutes characteristics and behaviour, such as respect for others, fair evaluation, and positive regard, which become a model for the board, the staff, and the volunteers to follow.
- **Accountability and responsibilities**: This emphasizes good stewardship, the organization's responsibilities to its constituents, and the constituents' responsibilities to the organization.
- **Equal opportunity and diversity**: It establishes the organization's commitments in hiring and other personnel practices.
- **Conflict of interests**: It represents a mandatory value statement that specifically mentions that all decisions are in the best interests of the organization.

When organizations develop their code of ethics using the given framework, they get the best results in terms of value-laden conduct and behaviour, and also in terms of ethical managerial practices. A code of ethics is necessary since members of the organization can then assess their conduct themselves and take decisions in compliance with it. A sample code of ethics is provided at the end of the chapter as Annexure 11.1.

Benefits of a code of ethics

A documented code of ethics sets the standards and can help in resolving any ethical dilemmas. It provides clear guidelines to tackle both internal and external relationships of organizations, and also for decision making that is compliant with one's ethics and values. Members of the organization can also integrate their personal values with that of the organization and restrain themselves from any ethical violation. All stakeholders of the organization feel happy since ethics-compliant decisions benefit them.

Steps to implement a code of ethics in the workplace

After developing the code of ethics, organizations follow certain steps to implement it. Although the implementation mode varies from organization to organization, certain steps can be listed based on the practice of excellence and by emulating the examples of world-class organizations. They are:

1. Identify the chairperson for the ethics committee. Such a person needs to be from the top management and someone who can endorse their own values and also create a culture that compels others to follow them.
2. Make the members of the board agree on the code of ethics.
3. Identify the issues relating to values and ethics. This is done by duly listing the issues that are perceived by employees as well as the management as being sensitive in nature.
4. Emulate the best-practices models of world-class organizations and select the best fit, keeping in mind its degree of compatibility in meeting organizational needs.
5. Develop the code of ethics with due cognizance of specific organizational needs.
6. Understand its degree of compatibility both within and outside the organization.
7. Document the finalized code of ethics and make it transparent for all stakeholders. Many organizations publish their code of ethics on their Web sites.
8. Make the code of ethics compulsory for all employees.

Ben & Jerry's ice cream, founded in 1978, set up a code that begins with a mission statement. The code goes on to state the company's mission related to product quality, economic mission, and social mission. Similarly, Gap Inc.'s (founded in 1969) code contains specific statements for each group with which the company has a relationship, viz. 'commitment to ethical sources', 'code of vendor conduct', 'code for global compliance team', etc. A code of ethics addressing multiple operations or specific functions often becomes necessary, particularly for organizations that conduct global operations.

Training in Ethics

After documentation of the code of ethics, it is necessary to train all employees in the organization. Training in ethics yields better results when it is conducted by the leaders of the organization, through setting an example for everyone to follow. It requires customization of examples on ethical dilemmas specific to a job or a function. Thus, the best approach to ethics training is to customize it keeping pace with the needs of the organization. Much as the purpose of such training is to transform people so that they embrace ethical practices in their behaviour and decision making, organizations also need to reinforce it with incentives and rewards. Violation of the code of ethics can also be made an important disciplinary issue. Such an approach is, however, often criticized since it provides negative cues to employees for complying with ethics. Helping people to voluntarily comply with the ethics requirement of the organization is more important. It can be achieved through systematic audit and monitoring of ethics by a duly constituted ethics committee, and by mentoring and counselling employees. Thus, the process of implementation of ethics in the workplace needs to be structured keeping in mind all the relevant issues, so as to derive all the benefits of ethical practices.

Benefits of ethical practices in the organization

Although ethical practices are often construed as compliance with the requirements of stakeholders, from an organizational perspective, these can also provide many advantages. Some of these advantages are:

- **Competitive advantage**: Customers favour organizations that are known for their ethical practices. Ethical violation reduces the company's market share, reduces their sales and revenues, and adversely affects their bottom-line.

- **Better staff attraction and retention**: Ethics-compliant organizations develop a strong brand image and such employer branding helps to attract and retain competent people, eventually contributing to their sustainable competitive advantage. On the other hand, ethical violation can lead to a high attrition rate, recruitment of average performers, and an overall increase in cost of inefficiency.
- **Investment**: Ethics-compliant organizations also attract investors since people repose their confidence in those who show integrity and a sense of responsibility, and are trustworthy.
- **Morale and culture**: Ethics-compliant organizations create a workplace where employees feel compelled to work. Ethical organizations develop high integrity and become socially responsible and globally considerate, and all these things make such organizations less prone to stress, attrition, and dissatisfaction. Therefore, by complying with ethics, organizations develop a work culture free from stress, which makes employees feel happier and become more productive.
- **Reputation**: Building the reputation of an organization takes years of efforts, while ruining it may require just one act of violation. Ethically responsible organizations are less prone to scandals and disasters. They also become more sensitive to any such practices that may adversely affect the reputation of the organization.
- **Legal and regulatory reasons**: Even though compliance with ethics has so far been voluntary and observed by organizations for their long-term business interests, globally, ethical issues are likely to come under legal and regulatory norms, making it compulsory for organizations to comply with them. Hence, early preparations by organizations will benefit them in the long run when ethical issues become legally enforceable.
- **Legacy**: Ethical consideration changes our perception of a legacy, which is not a pile of money at the cost of others' sufferings, but decisions and business practices that are beneficial to humankind. Hence, for organizations, the test of a real legacy is ethical decision making.

Stakeholders and ethical organizations

Identification of stakeholders on the basis of their relationship with the organization is common. Another approach used to identify stakeholders is by understanding the impact of the activities of the organization on people. Another premise is that when an organization recognizes its responsibilities towards a group, they become stakeholders to the organization. Thus, an organization can develop a stakeholder model on the basis of its relationship (needs and interests), degree of impact (large or small), and acknowledgement of responsibilities towards the group. The degree of stakeholders' relationships with organizations may vary with the nature of activities of organizations. Some examples of stakeholder groups are shareholders, trustees, guarantors, investors, funding bodies, distribution partners, marketing partners, licensors, licensees, approving bodies, regulatory authorities, endorsers and 'recommenders', advisors and consultants (these people have something at stake too), employees (staff, managers, directors, non-executive directors, etc.), customers, suppliers, the local population (community), the regional general public, national general public, international communities, and humankind.

To measure the degree of linkage of organizations with diverse stakeholder groups, one can make use of a weighted analysis. Such an analysis helps to assess, analyse, compile, and prioritize stakeholder needs from the perspective of the organization. A basic template for stakeholder analysis helps one to perform this task. Such a template is provided in Table 11.1.

Table 11.1 Stakeholder Analysis Template

Stakeholder group	Effect/interest/expectation/ needs/rights/quantification	Percentage significance or weighting	Priority or ranking
Shareholders			
Trustees			
Guarantors			
Investors			
Funding bodies			
Distribution partners			
Marketing partners			
Licensors			
Licensees			
Approving bodies			
Regulatory authorities			
Endorsers and 'recommenders'			
Advisors and consultants			
Employees: staff, managers, directors, non-executive directors			
Customers			
Suppliers			
The local population (community)			
The regional general public			
National general public			
International communities			
Humankind			

BUILDING AN ETHICAL CULTURE IN ORGANIZATIONS

Ethical values and culture are critical to organizational performance. To what extent an organization embraces ethical values and culture can be understood from its business practices. Organizations are, therefore, required to measure, understand, and make changes from time to time to improve their ethical values and culture. Although individual perceptions of ethics and values are often construed as the basis of ethical behaviour in organizations, it is the organizations themselves who have to take the responsibility to align such individual perceptions with the organizational ethical culture. Such *ethical culture* consists of the ethical environment of an organization, which influences ethical or unethical behaviour of the members of the organization. Organizations can persuade an unethical person to behave ethically. Research findings by A. Y. S. Chen, R. B. Sawyer, and P. F. Williams (1997) suggest that the 'ability to see and respond ethically may be related more to attributes of corporate culture than to attributes of individual employees'. Therefore, the ethical tone of an organization could be an integral part of an organization's ethical way of functioning. For example, organizational culture and ethical research have shown that the ethical tone of an organization impacts upon:

- Efficiency and effectiveness
- Decision-making processes
- Staff commitment and job satisfaction
- Staff stress
- Staff turnover

While doing business, organizations need to comply with the ethics of intellectual property, knowledge, and skills. Even though these are not physical objects whose possession can be easily determined, ethical violations in such cases can still drag the organization into a difficult phase. Ethical violation in these areas may occur due to patent infringement, copyright infringement, and trademark infringement.

Every organization is required to improve their ethical culture, making ethics a fundamental aspect of good managerial practices. The outcome of ethical practices can be understood when people in the organization behave with honesty and integrity, and understand right from wrong.

Different Views on Managerial Ethics

Organizational ethics can be understood from various perspectives, including the perspectives of various stakeholders. Keeping in view the multidimensionality of managerial ethics, one can list the different views on it in terms of the following:

- **Utilitarian view**: According to this view, decisions are based on their outcomes or consequences (for example, provide the greatest good for the greatest number by laying off 20 per cent of the staff so that the rest of the 80 per cent can keep their jobs).
- **Rights view**: According to this view, decisions are based on protecting the basic rights of individuals (for example, legally protecting privacy even at the cost of productivity and efficiency).
- **Theory of justice view**: According to this view, one seeks to impose and enforce rules fairly and impartially, exceeding the legal requirement (for example, helping those who are underrepresented or lack power, that is, one gives consideration to justice as opposed to entitlement).

From an organizational perspective, one finds an extensive use of utilitarian views on managerial ethics.

Factors Affecting Managerial Ethics

Some of the factors that affect managerial ethics of an organization can be listed as:

- Degree of moral development of employees (it can be measured in terms of degree of independence from outside influence)
- Degree of perceived protection of self-interest
- Degree of perceived fulfilment of expectations of stakeholders
- Degree of perceived protection of personal ethical principles
- Characteristics of individual employees
- Perceived values about right and wrong
- Ego strength and personality of individual employees
- Structured and documented rules, regulations, policies, job descriptions, and code of conduct of the organization
- Culture of the organization

ETHICAL DECISION MAKING

Ethical dilemmas are more evident in organizational decision making. Managers often encounter such dichotomous situations while protecting the organization's prime interest, that is, profit-making. Compromising on quality to meet the deadline for target achievement, artificial pegging of prices to increase the profit margin, less or no payment of taxes, violating pollution-control norms, and depriving workers of their legitimate wages and incentives are some of the peculiar syndromes of ethical dilemmas in decision making. Regulatory norms cannot always do the moral policing; organizational initiative to embrace ethical practices is required, instead. Non-compliance with ethical decision-making requirements can be witnessed in many cases. Often, organizations attribute it to competitive pressure, but non-compliance just for the sake of profit cannot be justified. Managers can justify their decisions by choosing one of the following alternatives, and they may even term these decisions *ethical*.

- **Utilitarian approach**: This approach to ethical decision making focuses on the common good of the people. For example, if a labour-intensive organization substitutes their production process with the latest state-of-the-art technology, unskilled people may lose their jobs, or the number of the total workforce required may fall drastically, but it is in the larger interest of the organization and its other stakeholders. Thus, a temporary setback can lead to long-term sustainability of the organization, which is seen as the common good for the society in general. It is for the managers to articulate what is for the common good and what is not.
- **Moral rights**: Ethical decisions on moral rights are based on moral principles and, therefore, are independent of decisional consequences or outcomes. Such ethical decisions are rigid in nature and are based on the dos and don'ts that are the guidelines of the organization. Therefore, such decisions need not always be for the common good.
- **Universalism**: This type of ethical decision follows the principles of the Golden Rule. The core of the Golden Rule essentially lies in the following two aspects:
  - i. To what extent a particular action applies to all people under all circumstances
  - ii. To what extent the decision makers would like others to impose such decisions on them
- **Cost-benefit approach**: Under this method, ethical decisions are taken balancing the costs and benefits between the decisions taken and the decisions not taken. Weighing the costs of decisions against the competitive advantages and disadvantages, it is possible for managers to justify their decisions.

Ways to Test Ethical Decisions

One can test the ethical quotient of decisions by measuring the degree of the following aspects:

- **Transparency**: To what extent communicating such decisions make the decision makers happy
- **Effect**: To what extent the decision makers considered the ill effects of decisions while finalizing the same
- **Fairness**: To what extent the decisions can be considered fair by all cross-sections of people (that is, all stakeholders) in the organization

When all the questions are answered positively, the decisions can be said to be ethical. Therefore, *ethical decision making* is in compliance with ethical issues while keeping in view the three aspects of transparency, effect, and fairness.

Steps in Ethical Decision Making

The process of ethical decision making requires the following steps:

1. Understand the potentiality of the groups affected by the decision
2. Understand the relevant issues and practices, and their impact on the decision
3. Ensure decisions are not vitiated by personal bias and prejudices
4. Ensure decisions are finalized considering various alternatives
5. Address all the shortcomings of the decision, including the long-term risks involved
6. Choose the decisions in compliance with existing principles, values, and standards
7. Ensure that the decision makers take responsibilities for the decisional outcomes
8. Ensure that the decisions are evaluated and necessary changes are made in the ethical standards of the organization

Case Market Penetration and the Question of Business Ethics

An international soft drink major, in its second spell in India, was very aggressive in its product positioning strategy, literally eliminating the local soft drink bottlers. With the traditional perception that Indians like to get more for less, the international brand initially introduced 300-ml bottles against the conventional local bottlers' 250-ml bottles at the same price band. However, a test mismatch did not give it the opportunity to position its products successfully in the market. After sweetening its product according to the results of the test, it reintroduced its brand but there was no major change in its market position.

The company then tried to understand the major weaknesses of local bottlers. A careful study indicated that local bottlers used bottles that could be refilled again and again. These bottles were not a standard saleable item and required huge lead time to procure. Hence, if empty bottles did not reach the bottling plant, local bottlers could not refill them again and make them available in the market.

Soft drinks are usually bought on an impulse and the highest sales take place in summers. Due to this reason, the company started procuring the bottles of local bottlers during that time and destroying them. By the time the local bottlers could understand the game plan, the company positioned its brand in the market. In no time, the local bottlers' bottling process came to a grinding halt. The company then proposed to the local bottlers that they bottle the company's brands as their franchise. To survive, the local bottlers had to agree and this allowed the company to position its brand successfully, making local varieties unavailable.

CASE QUESTION

Multinational soft drink organizations could not achieve success in China. Analyse the reasons behind their failure and draw up a proactive action plan to counter the market penetration strategy adopted by the soft drink major in India as explained in the case study.

SUMMARY

- Values and ethics are an integral part of all organizational activities. *Values* are defined as those abstract things that are important to or valued by others, individually or collectively. Values are important while an organization frames its vision. Values are the principles and priorities that help one to take decisions.
- *Ethics* are the standards of conduct that indicate how one can behave based on moral duties and virtues, primarily based on the principles of right and wrong. There are two aspects to ethics. One is to discern right from wrong, and the other one is to do what is right, good, and proper. Therefore, ethics encompass the concept of values.
- After documentation of the code of ethics, it is necessary to train all employees of the organization. Training in ethics yields better results when it is conducted by the leaders of the organization, through setting an example for everyone to follow. From organizational perspectives, implementation of a code of ethics can provide many advantages. Some of these advantages are in terms of competitive advantage, attraction and retention of talented employees, attraction of investors, morale and culture, a good reputation for the organization, and compliance with legal and regulatory norms.
- As values and ethics meet the needs of stakeholders, it is important to identify stakeholders on the basis of their relationship to the organization. Another approach to identifying stakeholders is by understanding the impact of the activities of the organization on people. Ethical values and culture are critical to organizational performance. To what extent an organization embraces ethical values and culture can be understood from its business practices. Organizations are, therefore, required to measure, understand, and make changes from time to time to improve their ethical values and culture.
- Ethical dilemmas are more evident in organizational decision making. Managers often encounter dichotomous situations while protecting the organization's prime interest, that is, profit-making. Compromising on the quality to meet the deadline for target achievement, artificial pegging of prices to increase the profit margin, less or no payment of taxes, violating pollution-control norms, and depriving workers of their legitimate wages and incentives are some of the peculiar syndromes of ethical dilemmas in decision making.

KEY TERMS

Code of conduct: The code of conduct translates the values (documented in the code of ethics) into specific behavioural standards.

Code of ethics: A code of ethics consists of documented and transparent statements underlying the expected behaviour of the members of an organization that reflect on their day-to-day working, including decision making.

Ethical culture: It is the ethical environment of an organization which influences ethical or unethical behaviour of the members of the organization.

Ethical decision making: Ethical decision making takes place in compliance with ethical issues while keeping in view the three aspects of transparency, effect, and fairness.

Ethics: Ethics comprises the standards of conduct that indicate how one can behave based on moral duties and virtues, primarily based on the principles of right and wrong. There are two aspects to ethics. One is to discern right from wrong, and the other one is to do what is right, good, and proper.

Values: Values are the principles and priorities that help one to take decisions.

REVIEW QUESTIONS

1. Explain the meaning and importance of *corporate ethics*. Do you think compliance with ethics will deter from achieving the business goals of an organization? Justify your answer.
2. In designing ethical guidelines for managing the behaviour of people in an organization, what are the important areas one should consider? Illustrate your answer by explaining any such area (discipline, promotion, transfer, etc.) with a suitable description of the related ethical issues.
3. Explain how an ethical culture can be built in an organization.
4. Write short notes on:
   i. Code of ethics
   ii. Ethical decision making
   iii. International business ethics
   iv. Ethics in production

CRITICAL THINKING QUESTIONS

1. Visit some recent press reports on ethical violation in organizations. Critically examine those reports and suggest what could be the possible course of action for your chosen organization to avoid such ethical violation.
2. Study the ethical compliance report of any Indian organization. Relate its degree of compliance with its business achievement and give your comments and observations.

REFERENCES

Chen, A. Y. S., R. B. Sawyer and P. F. Williams (1997). 'Reinforcing Ethical Decisions Through Corporate Culture', *Journal of Business Ethics*, 16, pp. 855–865.

Hofstede, G. (2001). *Culture's Consequences: Comparing Values, Behaviors, Institutions, and Organizations Across Nations*, 2nd edition. Thousand Oaks, CA: Sage.

Thorp, J. H. (2005). 'Values and Ethics for CPAs in a Changing World', *The CPA Journal Online*, 75 (8): p. 18.

FURTHER READING

Andrews, K. R. (1989). 'Ethics in Practice', *Harvard Business Review*, September–October, pp. 99–104.

Badenhorst, J. A. (1994). 'Unethical Behaviour in Procurement: A Perspective on Causes and Solutions', *Journal of Business Ethics*, 13, pp. 739–745.

Bailey, J. E., J. R. Schermerhorn, J. G. Hunt and R. N. Osborn (1991). *Managing Organizational Behaviour*. Brisbane: John Wiley & Sons.

Chonko, L. B. and S. D. Hunt (1985). 'Ethics and Marketing Management: An Empirical Examination', *Journal of Business Research*, 13, pp. 339–359.

Coser, L. A. (1977). *Masters of Sociological Thought: Ideas in Historical and Social Context*, 2nd edition. New York: Harcourt Brace Jovanovich.

Ferrell, O. C. and S. J. Skinner (1988). 'Ethical Behavior and Bureaucratic Structure in Marketing Research Organizations', *Journal of Marketing Research*, 25, pp. 103–109.

Hegarty, W. H. and H. P. Sims, Jr, (1978). 'Some Determinants of Unethical Behaviour: An Experiment', *Journal of Applied Psychology*, 63 (4): pp. 451–457.

——— (1979). 'Organizational Philosophy, Policies and Objectives Related to Unethical Decision Behaviour: A Laboratory Experiment', *Journal of Applied Psychology*, 64 (3): pp. 331–338.

Laczniak, G. R. and E. J. Inderrieden (1987). 'The Influence of Stated Organizational Concern Upon Ethical Decision Making', *Journal of Business Ethics*, 6, pp. 297–307.

Neck, C. P. and G. Moorhead (1995). 'Groupthink Remodelled: The Importance of Leadership, Time Pressure, and Methodical Decision-Making Procedures', *Human Relations*, 48 (5): pp. 537–557.

Rich, A. J., C. S. Smith and P. H. Mihalek (1990). 'Are Corporate Codes of Conduct Effective?', *Management Accounting*, 72, pp. 34–35.

Zey-Ferrell, M. (1979). 'Predicting Unethical Behaviour Among Marketing Practitioners', *Human Relations*, 32 (7): pp. 557–569.

ANNEXURE 11.1
The Infosys Code of Ethics

Corporate Governance

Corporate governance is about maximizing shareholder value legally, ethically and on a sustainable basis, while ensuring fairness to every stakeholder—our customers, employees, investors, vendor-partners, the governments of the countries in which we operate, and the community. Thus, corporate governance is a reflection of our culture, policies, our relationship with stakeholders and our commitment to values.

We believe that sound corporate governance is critical to enhance and retain investor trust. Accordingly, we always seek to ensure that we attain our performance rules with integrity.

Our Board exercises its fiduciary responsibilities in the widest sense of the term. Our disclosures always seek to attain the best practices in international corporate governance. We also endeavor to enhance long-term shareholder value and respect minority rights in all our business decisions.

We continue to be a pioneer in benchmarking our corporate governance policies with the best in the world. Our efforts are widely recognized by investors in India and abroad. We have undergone the corporate governance audit by ICRA and CRISIL. ICRA has rated our corporate governance practices at CGR 1. CRISIL has assigned CRISIL GVC Level 1 rating to us.

We have complied with the recommendations of the Narayana Murthy Committee on Corporate Governance constituted by the Securities and Exchange Board of India (SEBI).

Corporate Governance Philosophy

Our corporate governance philosophy is based on the following principles:

- Satisfy the spirit of the law and not just the letter of the law
- Corporate governance standards should go beyond the law
- Be transparent and maintain a high degree of disclosure levels
- When in doubt, disclose
- Make a clear distinction between personal conveniences and corporate resources
- Communicate externally, in a truthful manner, about how the company is run internally
- Comply with the laws in all the countries in which the company operates
- Have a simple and transparent corporate structure driven solely by business needs
- Management is the trustee of the shareholders' capital and not the owner

Board Composition

At the core of our corporate governance practice is the Board, which oversees how the management serves and protects the long-term interests of all our stakeholders. We believe that an active, well-informed and independent Board is necessary to ensure the highest standards of corporate governance. The majority of the Board, eight out of 15, are independent members.

Further, we have audit, compensation, investor grievance, nominations and risk management committees, which comprise independent directors.

As a part of our commitment to follow global best practices, we comply with the Euroshareholders Corporate Governance Guidelines 2000, and the recommendations of the Conference Board Commission on Public Trusts and Private Enterprises in the U.S. We also adhere to the UN Global Compact Program.

Source: http://www.infosys.com/about/what-we-do/pages/corporate-governance.aspx. Reproduced with permission from Infosys.

12

Communication and Negotiation in Organizations

After going through this chapter, you will be able to understand:

- the concepts of communication and negotiation
- the various types of communication
- the features of effective communication techniques
- the psychological and behavioural influences on communication
- the barriers to communication
- the concept of transactional analysis

Communicate According to Cultural Overtones

In a global business environment, organizations integrate their mode of communication with issues of cross-cultural communication. One can appreciate the importance of cross-cultural communication when people from different cultures interact face to face. One of the functions of culture is to provide a highly selective partition between each person and the outside world. Therefore, culture in its many forms designates what one pays attention to and what one ignores (Hall 1976). In cross-cultural negotiations, the most difficult part is to secure an agreement. In international trade, negotiation is an important dimension of every sale or purchase, which could be either good or bad for both parties. Therefore, in a globalized world, international negotiation is now a necessity. International negotiation is conditioned by the respective countries' cultures. For example, in Korea, signing a contract in red ink symbolizes that the result would be bad.

Most countries adopt one of two approaches with respect to a negotiated agreement. The first type of agreement is *explicit* in nature. It covers all the aspects of the contract, including the contingencies and the required level of cooperation from both parties. Here, personal relationships between the parties are redundant. The other type of agreement is an *implicit*, broad, and oral agreement, where the negotiating parties accommodate unforeseen changes and form personal relationships. In an implicit agreement, communication is extensive and it covers all subjects, even beyond the substantive aspects of the negotiation. In the United States, the agreement is explicit in nature with the contract culminating in a series of negotiations, with a clear outlining of rules, regulations, procedures, and standards to bind both the negotiating parties. In China, however, the agreement is an implicit, oral agreement which is the starting point and is essentially based on the human relationship, that is, the bonding of friendship. Therefore, the ultimate terms of reference in Chinese negotiation-based contracts are determined in the future, depending on the circumstances.

INTRODUCTION

Communication is a process of interaction with people and the environment. Through such interaction, two or more individuals influence the ideas, beliefs, and attitudes of each other. Such interaction takes place through the exchange of information by means of words, gestures, signs and symbols, and expressions. In organizations, communication is a continuous process of giving and receiving information, which also helps in building social relationships. The word *communication* is derived from the word *communis*, which means common. Commonness of understanding is an essential component of all kinds of communications, more particularly in organizational communication. Without a common understanding, communication in organizations creates misunderstandings and people are then left without any direction.

In organizations, one talks about a shared vision. Effective communication mechanisms are needed to develop a shared vision. Even in day-to-day operational issues, communication plays a great role in clarifying doubts and in making the efforts of various individuals result-oriented. In all ancient texts, there is enough reference to non-verbal communication between humans, nature, and animals. Communication with nature and animals was considered the best way to reinforce learning in the Indian *gurukul* system. Therefore, communication is as old as civilization. Even before the advent of civilization as we know it, non-verbal communication was in existence among humans, nature, and animals. In organizations, however, verbal communication (use of language) is more important today. Communication between organizations and the outside world has become more effective and global with the use of a common language. With the globalization of markets, the English language as a medium of communication has been accepted even by countries like China, Japan, Russia, France, and Germany, where the emphasis earlier was on communicating in their own languages to trade with the world.

COMMUNICATION

An all-inclusive definition of communication is difficult to develop. However, from an organizational point of view, communication has the features of interaction, interchange, sharing, and commonness.

Elements of Communication

The various elements of communication are as follows:

- Communication is a two-way process. It involves a sender and a receiver. The sender or receiver can be an individual or a group.
- All communication carries a message. A message can be a directive, an enquiry, a feeling, an opinion, an idea, information, etc.
- Communication can occur only when there is commonness of understanding between the sender and the receiver. The commonness includes factors like common culture, common language, and a common environment. Words, phrases, idioms, proverbs, gestures, and expressions are deeply embedded in culture and possess high communicating potential for people from similar backgrounds.

- Communication must be able to evoke a response from the receiver, evident in the form of some behavioural changes.
- The method of communication can be verbal or non-verbal (signs, gestures, expressions, etc.).
- Sender, message, method, receiver, and response of receiver are the five elements that constitute the process of communication.

Nature of Communication

Communication can be broadly divided into two categories. They are verbal communication and non-verbal communication.

Verbal communication is the use of words and languages between two or more individuals for interaction. It can be either oral or written. Hence, speaking, listening, reading, or writing is all classified under verbal communication. Since this type of communication elicits immediate feedback, extensive use of verbal communication is made in organizations.

Non-verbal communication can occur without the use of words. This type of communication sensitizes the senses and evokes responses depending on the way human beings interpret a particular cue. It is often referred to as *body language*, that is, any body movement of the communicator which carries some meaning. Gestures, facial expressions, glances, stares, smiles, and raising of finger are examples of body language, which carry some meaning. In organizations, non-verbal communication is very important for interpersonal relations.

Based on organizational practices, communication can be further divided into internal and external communication, formal and informal communication, downward and upward communication, horizontal and diagonal communication, and the grapevine. Flow of information within the organization is known as *internal communication*; this may be either formal or informal in nature. *External communication* takes place between two organizations, that is, between the organization and others outside the organization. *Formal communication* is official communication, while *informal communication* takes place within the formal organization, between the members. *Downward communication* is between superiors and subordinates, and *upward communication* is between the subordinates and the superiors. In the first case, the superiors communicate with the subordinates, while in the second case, the subordinates communicate with the superiors. *Horizontal communication* takes place between two equals, that is, between persons working at the same level in the organization. *Diagonal communication* takes place cutting across hierarchical barriers. However, this is formal in nature. For example, direct communication from a field salesperson to the vice president (HR) is diagonal in nature. They are functionally apart and also hierarchically different. Apart from this, for globally dispersed organizations, one also uses the *grapevine*, which entails a system of network communication.

ORGANIZATIONAL COMMUNICATION

Communication is a means by which people are linked together in an organization to achieve a common purpose. No group activity is possible without communication. Managers lacking in the ability of communication will not be able to either build a proper chain of authority or improve relationships. One must also appreciate that interpersonal communication and organizational communication are different in nature, though interpersonal communication skills form the base. With interpersonal communication skills, managers are able to communicate well in the organization by adopting some common frame of reference, assessing individuals, and building relationships. In all forms of communication, one not only transfers information but also provides behavioural inputs. Hence, organizational communication is considered to be a unified activity that enables the process to achieve some specific goals. *Organizational communication* provides social inputs into social (organizational) systems by which managers try to modify behaviour to effect change. High integrity of the sender and consistency in verbal and non-verbal messages increase the chance of acceptance of the communication by the receiver. In an organization, managers internally communicate at different hierarchical levels, groups, and departments, and externally to customers, suppliers, and other external stakeholders. Managers must be efficient in all such communications. Oral communication skills are very important for managers. This type of communication is different from other types of communication. While a manager gives oral presentations, it is important to understand the purpose and the audience, and then frame the style of delivery. Thus, organizational communication basically intends to influence action in a positive way to achieve organizational goals. Such purposes of an organization can be listed as the following:

- To establish objectives
- To establish a link between plans and actions
- To organize human resources so that goals can be achieved
- To create a climate that is conducive to lead, direct, and motivate people
- To enforce effective control

A model of organizational communication is presented in Figure 12.1.

Types of Organizational Communication

In an organization, various types of communication are used. Although it is difficult to draw a fine line between the different types of organizational communication, a general understanding will enable managers to adopt the right approach. For example, business communication is different from the type of communication that is intended for team building. Depending on the organizational requirements, managers make use of different types of communication. These are:

- **Business communication**: Business communication includes all communication that managers need to use in a business context. Effective business communication requires the understanding of both the business and the style of communication. Use of common business English and business correspondence are important requisites in this style of communication. While using business communication, organizations also need to focus on psychological and sociological aspects, special effects design, managem ent, marketing, and information technology.
- **Managerial communication**: Managerial communication emphasizes the achievement of specific organizational objectives by adopting suitable communication strategies. For example, in disciplining an erring worker who is otherwise a good performer, the organization may be required to develop a warning letter, taking care not to hurt the sentiments of the worker, and may also need to argue logically to sensitize the conscience of the worker. Similarly, a letter to a payment-defaulting customer, who otherwise had a good track record of meeting their payments, requires one to be more strategic in communication.
- **Organizational communication**: Organizational communications are made with established communication networks and the communication flow within an organization, thereby nurturing an organizational climate. Suitable organizational communication strategy ensures transparency and makes people adaptable to a particular communication culture. It also streamlines communication systems within the organization.
- **Human relations and team building**: Human relations and team building are intended to harmonize interpersonal relations. Interpersonal communications are limited not only to co-workers; they

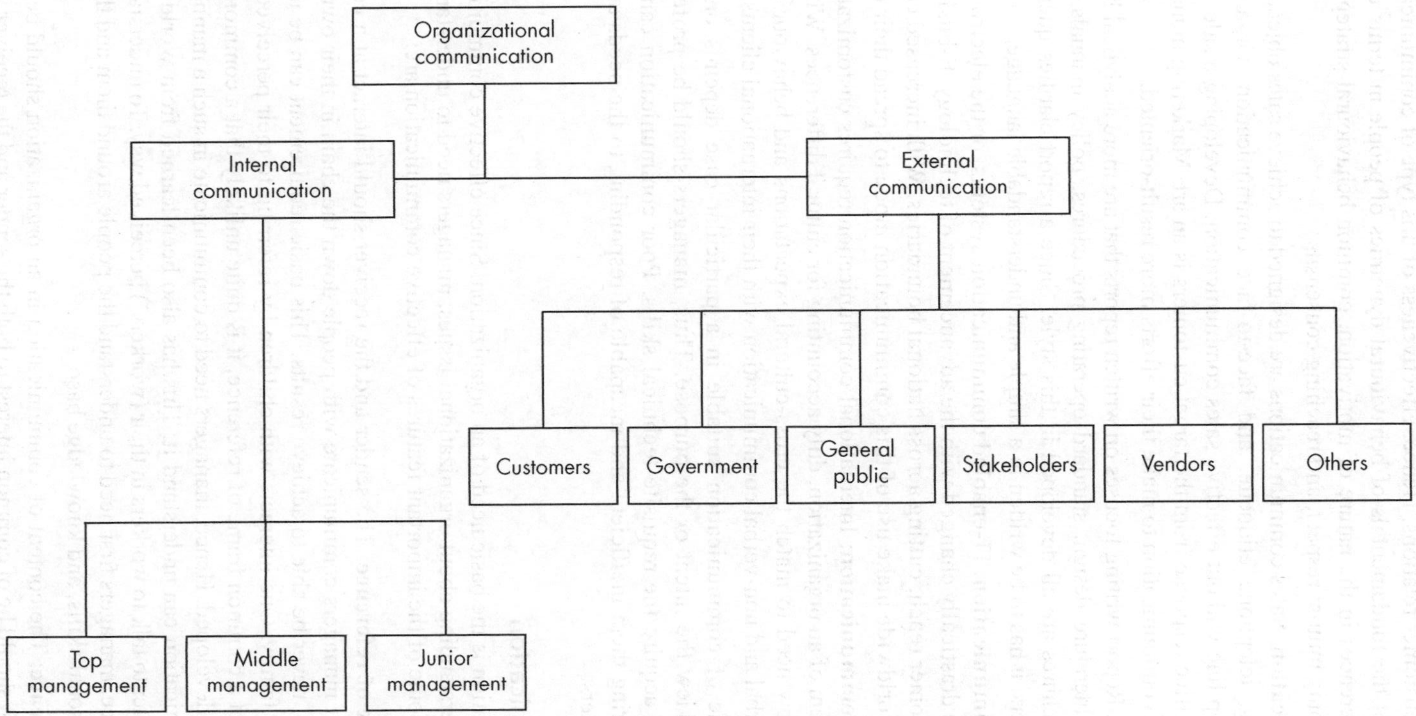

Figure 12.1 Organizational Communication

even extend to customer relations. Hence, effectiveness of this type of communication requires an understanding of the fundamentals of behavioural dynamics of people in terms of differences in perception, differences in the nature of motivation, common behavioural strategies, establishing rapport, developing mutual respect, and reaching consensus.

- **Sales communication**: Sales communications are designed to achieve sales objectives and encompass advertising, telephone etiquette, and face-to-face communication. Organizations cannot improve their top line without effective sales communication. Developing a sales communication that elicits a positive response from the target customers is an art. Marketing managers get special training in sales communication to make their efforts more result-oriented.
- **Report writing**: Report writing focuses on written reports that are more analytical in nature. A company's product literature design, standard operating procedures, policy manuals, and customers' information brochures are all developed in this style. Since a report clarifies queries that may be raised by the users, it has to be written in a simple and understandable language.
- **Electronic communication**: IT-enabled communication systems, or the electronic communication mode, have drastically changed with the advancement of technology. E-business now facilitates better customer reach, cutting across national boundaries. With increased computerization, organizations worldwide make use of this communication mode to spread their customer reach.
- **International communication**: International communication requires customization of the communication system of an organization, duly accounting for cultural differences. With globalization, organizations now need to match the cross-cultural expectations and behaviour of people while entering into verbal and non-verbal communication with their international clients.

The specific style of communication suitable in a particular case depends on organizational choice, keeping in view the intent or the purpose. Thus, managers should be professional in their communication and acquire the requisite technical skills. Poor communication can cost organizations heavily, rendering them inefficient and incapable of responding to the needs and expectations of various stakeholders.

Effective Communication

Effective communication is the basic need of an organization. Since effective communication develops commonness of understanding about organizational issues, managers need to understand the dynamics of communication. Some of the important features of effective communication are:

- **Common frame of reference**: The sender and the receiver should interact at a common level of understanding. If managers communicate with people down the chain in their own perceived languages, they will never be able to achieve results. This basic requirement can be understood from the concept of a family. One interacts with children by referring to their perceived languages and symbols. Without a common frame of reference, it is quite unlikely that a common level of understanding will be developed. Hence, managers need to communicate in such a manner that receivers of their communication can understand it. This has also been learned from world-class corporate leaders, who prefer to talk to workers in their (workers') perceived way. To understand the common frame of reference, managers first need to understand the people around them and their behavioural pattern, interpersonal skills, and knowledge base.
- **Mutual congruence**: The content of communication in an organization should be of mutual congruence, that is, it should be of common interest to both the sender and the receiver. Many organizational problems are now resolved by adopting the model of goal congruence. Erring workers do not

listen to managers unless managers communicate keeping in view their interest areas. In dealing with collective bargaining issues, unions show reluctance to understand financial rationale or to comprehend the company's financial health; they are more interested in receiving the information in simple factual terms.

- **Compatibility in the language of communication**: In a training session, delivering a lecture in English to workers who are not comfortable with the language serves no purpose. To make the training message clear, one has to communicate to them in their own understandable language. For example, Ishikawa (1985) carried the message of quality to Japan and developed the fish-bone diagram adopting the management concepts of the Americans—Deming and Juran. Cascading the message of quality successfully to the workers' level in their perceived style helped Japan to excel in quality.
- **Compatible environment**: Compatibility in environment, which implies communicating with people of a similar background, ensures effectiveness of organizational communication. A common environmental premise for communication develops in an organization when both the sender and the receiver of the communication are alike culturally, economically, professionally, demographically, and interest-wise. To deal with incompatibility in the environment of communication, managers try to synchronize the environmental premise with the goal-congruence model (identifying the individual's and the organization's goals as the same). Convincing workers about the threat of globalization and competition would be more effective when one tries to draw them to common interest areas, for example, telling them that everyone's interest is at stake unless they together try to achieve the best.

Psychological and Behavioural Influence on Communication

The basic intent of communication is to develop a common understanding. Through communication, one tries to develop relationships based on shared mental maps. Shared mental maps follow a structure and understanding that enriches managers' subjective experience, which they relate with the external reality for a trade-off with the perceptual incongruence between the sender and the receiver of communications. *Perception* is use of the senses to construct mental maps, congruent with one's beliefs and the environment. Cross-cultural differences among people make perceptions less than perfect in three different ways—deletion, distortion, and generalization. *Deletion* occurs due to the limitation of the physical senses. Development of the senses ensues as a natural process through the experience of responding to the environment. Thus, one's beliefs and values develop in a gradual process and they are then used in communication. For example, Douglas McGregor's theory X and theory Y, categorizing people as bad or good, represent the reflection of beliefs and values that might have developed through the process of deletion.

Like deletion, *distortion* in communication also takes place due to the inability to observe the external environment correctly. Distortion also alters perception, since one perceives in a way that supports one's existing beliefs and values. Attributing a strange flying object as an unidentified flying object (UFO) from other planets, or attributing business failure to the ill luck of the CEO, are examples of distortion.

In communication, many beliefs are used that are based on one's perceptions and generalizations. That anything made by Tata is good and others are questionable, is an example of a perception based on generalization. The *generalization* of the environment develops through the process of experience. For example, a situational leader generalizes the environment to decide their style of leadership according to what had yielded results in the past. Some generalizations in communication may be good, while some may be bad.

Changing communication strategies may be difficult for an organization because of the dynamics of human behaviour. Thus, an effective communication strategy in an organization should match with one's mental maps, so that it evokes the desired response.

Group Communication

In organizations, people communicate individually (interpersonal communication) and also in a group. To manage the business complexity, organizations form groups to pool knowledge and resources. This is *group communication.* People in a group solve problems jointly and to coordinate their activities they need to communicate. Exchange of information and communication takes place both between and within the groups. The nature and type of group communication depend largely on the intent or purpose of the group. Communication within a self-directed group is different from communication within a focus group. All the factors that indicate the effectiveness of interpersonal communication also apply to group communication. However, non-verbal communication and listening skills are more important for groups.

Unlike most forms of interpersonal communication, communication in a small group is primarily task-oriented, as small groups are formed to achieve a specific task. In such group communication, adopting a blend and motivational approach is very important to make group members feel comfortable. This helps in reaching group consensus quickly. A *blend approach* resolves differences of opinion, while *motivation* makes members follow through. Hence, group communication requires special skills of managers, including an understanding of group characteristics, group dynamics, specific influence of group members, and the role of leadership. Although there are no specific guidelines for size, type, and purpose of small groups, these vary from organization to organization. The size of a small group may vary from 2 to 20 members, where the goal or purpose remains the same. A strategic group may represent members in the top hierarchical level of the organization, while a task group may involve operations people. Hence, communication style varies from one small group to another.

Similarly, groups can be primary, formal, or informal. Members form *primary groups* for self-satisfaction. *Informal groups* are formed to improve interpersonal relations, rather than to achieve a specific task or objective. *Formal groups* are formed to achieve a specific goal or objective, and they are more task-oriented by nature. Depending on the goals or objectives, formal groups can be informational, provide education and training, and solve problems. Informational formal groups are formed in conferences, meetings, and briefings. In this type of formal group communication, information sharing is ensured by adopting consistency in approach. Members in such formal groups can raise questions and participate in discussions. A formal group that provides education and training may be the training and development department that facilitates employees' development. Problem-solving groups can be either formal or informal while aiming to attain a specific objective.

Depending on the degree of group influence, organizational communication style may differ. A strong group influence makes the group members subscribe to certain assumptions and behavioural norms, which may be either explicit or implicit. The degree of group influence can result in conformity, resistance, competition, or conflict. Although in all cases the manager's role is to communicate in a manner that develops group cohesiveness, competition may result in intra-group conflicts in the organization.

With the spread of globalization, organizations today need to enhance their competitive advantage by developing collaborative capability and increasing their spread globally. This requires organizations to revisit their communication strategies, focusing on virtual teams to cope with uncertainty, ambiguity, and many cross-cultural issues. The problem further mounts in cross-border mergers and acquisitions. With geographically dispersed virtual teams, communication now largely depends on electronic mediums. Majority influence on the communication in a group may vitiate the ultimate purpose, as culturally different minority groups may not be able to participate in decision making. To ensure cohesiveness in group communication, organizations need to share information and provide opportunity to everyone to contribute their viewpoints. Managers, thus, need to study cross-cultural dynamics to avoid confrontation, misunderstandings, and conflict in group communication.

COMMUNICATION BARRIERS

Communication is one of the biggest challenges for an organization. In an organization, whenever two people are put together in a relationship they each bring divergent values, beliefs, expectations, goals, personality types, communication styles, and feelings. Better communication in an organizational relationship is possible only when one recognizes these differences and becomes flexible in accepting and understanding the other person's views, opinions, and communication style. Otherwise, communication barriers may come up.

Communication barriers are the results of several inadequacies that tend to distort communication and affect the ability of managers in achieving organizational goals. Important communication barriers can be listed as the following:

- Distortion due to superior–subordinate relationship
- Semantic distortion
- Distortion due to premature evaluation by the recipient of communication
- Distortion due to perfunctory attention
- Distortion due to failure to communicate
- Distortion due to resistance to change

Alternatively, communication barriers can be broadly classified as external barriers, organizational barriers, and personal barriers.

External Barriers

External barriers to communication are grouped as either semantic or psychological.

Semantic barriers

Semantics is the study of meaning in language. *Semantic barriers* are caused in the process of receiving or understanding the message while coding and decoding ideas and words. In communication, one primarily uses words and each word has several meanings. Therefore, any mismatch in the linguistic capacity of the communicators and the recipients may result in misunderstanding. The Oxford English Dictionary mentions about 25 different meanings for the 500 most commonly used English words. Similar problems exist in other languages as well. Therefore, if not used properly, words may fail to convey real meanings. Semantic barriers may result due to:

- Badly expressed message
- Faulty translations
- Unqualified assumptions
- Use of technical language

Psychological or emotional barriers

Psychological or *emotional barriers* are caused in interpersonal communication. Interpretation of the meaning in a message largely depends on the psychological and emotional state of the parties involved. Such barriers may be caused by the following reasons:

- Premature evaluation
- Lack of attention
- Loss of information in transmission
- Poor retention
- Lack of reliance
- Distrust of communicator
- Failure to communicate

Organizational Barriers

Organizational barriers are also known as structural barriers. Organizations are designed on the basis of a formal hierarchical structure. Apart from this, an organization is created to attain certain identified objectives, which requires regulating of day-to-day activities by developing performance standards and framing rules, regulations, procedures, policies, behavioural norms, etc. All these factors affect the free flow of communication in the organization, unless suitably managed. Superior–subordinate relationships in a formal organization structure inhibit the free flow of communication. Even managers may believe in maintaining distance from subordinates. In such a scenario, communication mostly loses the essence of being *two-way communication*. The reasons for organizational barriers can be listed as the following:

- **Hierarchy**: Several hierarchical levels result in transmission loss and communication may even get delayed or distorted. This particularly happens in upward communication, that is, communication from subordinates to superiors.
- **Status relationships**: Superior–subordinate relationships may block the flow of communication due to status incongruence in a formal organizational structure.
- **Functional specialization**: Fragmenting the organization in accordance with specialization may lead to forming of departmental interests and thereby affect the free flow of communication.
- **Organizational policy, rules, and regulations**: These also stand against effective communication within an organization.
- **Organizational facilities**: To communicate with people in the organization, one requires certain facilities like meetings, conferences, complaint box, suggestion box, open door system, and social and cultural gatherings. Unless such facilities are adequate, communication fails.

Personal Barriers

Factors that are internal to the sender and the receiver of the communication and exert influence on the process of communication are known as *personal* or *interpersonal barriers*. Such interpersonal barriers can be broadly categorized into two types—barriers in superiors and barriers in subordinates.

Superiors act as barriers in communication in the following ways:

- **Nurturing of negative attitude**: Favourable attitude of superiors fosters effective communication, while unfavourable attitude inhibits communication.
- **Fear of challenge to authority**: Such fear often compels superiors to withhold information and dissuades them from communicating effectively.

- **Insistence on proper channel**: Superiors often insist on flow of communication through appropriate channels, which can serve to block the communication.
- **Lack of confidence in subordinates**: Superiors often consider subordinates to be less competent. Such a perception stands against free flow of communication.
- **Conscious ignoring of communication**: Ignoring communication consciously frustrates subordinates.
- **Lack of time**: Superiors may think that they have no time to talk to their subordinates, which results in loss of communication.
- **Lack of awareness**: Superiors may not appreciate the importance and effectiveness of communication.

Subordinates act as barriers to communication in the following ways:

- **Mere unwillingness to communicate**: Such unwillingness may be the result of an unpleasant experience in the past.
- **Lack of incentive**: The prevailing reward and punishment system in the organization is largely responsible for this. If suggestions or any other communication from subordinates do not evoke any response from the superiors, they lose interest in communicating upward.

Methods of Overcoming Communication Barriers

Effectiveness in communication greatly contributes to the success of an organization and to the performance of managers. Therefore, it is imperative for an organization to ensure the free flow of communication overcoming all possible barriers. Some communication barriers cannot be eliminated altogether but can be controlled. To overcome communication barriers, the following methods can be followed by an organization:

- **Employee orientation**: If employees are adequately familiarized with organizational objectives, policies, procedures, programmes, authority relations, etc., it minimizes the communication barriers significantly. Apart from this, employees need to receive communication about the vision, mission, goals, objectives, and strategies of the organization, and if required, they may be involved in developing them. Such participation enhances commitment from employees and transparency keeps them informed. Unfortunately, this aspect often gets neglected in organizations and culminates in conflict and creation of organizational barriers. There are many examples of success stories in the corporate world where employee orientation helped the organization to achieve more than the planned rate of growth. Walmart is an example to emulate.
- **Improving interpersonal relations**: Improved interpersonal relations develop mutuality and employees work together to accomplish organizational goals. This requires superiors to respect the dignity and authority of their subordinates, which in turn develops subordinates' trust in superiors and eliminates status differences. Such an environment in an organization makes it possible for the manager to communicate freely and makes communication a truly two-way process.
- **Empathetic listening**: Due to typical managerial attitude, upward communication often tends to get greatly distorted. Managers often use their status and dominate any discussion with subordinates, who do not get much opportunity to express their feelings and emotions. Lack of listening creates barriers to communication, as managers evaluate information without getting a free and frank response from subordinates.
- **Using proper language**: Barriers to communication are often created due to semantic distortions. This can be avoided by using direct, simple, and meaningful language in communication. Avoidance of technical terms, words with more than one meaning, difficult symbols, etc., makes it possible to eliminate communication barriers.

- **Communication through actions**: Action speaks louder than words. When subordinates communicate information or opinions and superiors do not act upon them, it sends a message back, which dissuades future communication. The same thing happens when superiors act in a manner that differs from what they say. This will lead to a situation where subordinates will only listen and not act. Such barriers require to be eliminated through actions and deeds.
- **Judicious use of the grapevine**: The grapevine is important for communication. However, when managers depend too much on the grapevine, ignoring official channels of communication, it develops a culture of informal communication and thereby creates barriers to communication. Hence, the grapevine needs to be used judiciously.
- **Information feedback**: Communication is essentially a two-way process and, hence, feedback is very important. When there is no information feedback, it creates barriers to communication. Even in face-to-face communication, body language may provide successful feedback.

TRANSACTIONAL ANALYSIS

Eric Berne (1961) founded transactional analysis. It is now widely applied in organizational communications. The basic premise of Berne's transactional analysis is Sigmund Freud's (1949) contribution to the human psyche. Berne suggested that while one communicates, one reflects one's state of mind, which translates as child ego, adult ego, or parent ego. It is possible for a person to reflect all the three ego states simultaneously while communicating with others. Every ego state carries some different meaning. For example, a communication from a *child ego* may be either destructive or happy. While communicating from a *destructive child ego*, a person reflects their uncompromising attitude, without listening to the information provided by others. Such a person can even decide to go wrong, knowing that it is going to be wrong. In contrast, a communication from a *happy child ego* is more accommodative, reposing confidence in the other, stating things are going to happen as they are desired. Since an *adult ego communication* is formal and between two matured minds, which understand the environment, it becomes effective and contributes to organizational effectiveness. However, adult ego communication can only be possible between two like mindsets. Communication from a *parent ego* can be either critical or nurturing. *Critical parent ego communication* shows uncompromising attitude and often becomes very unrealistic. Corporate leaders while communicating with their subordinates often become critical, further damaging the spirit and morale of the people. *Nurturing parent ego communication* is, however, understandable, accommodative, and more facilitative. Berne, therefore, said that it is important for every manager to understand communication dynamics in the context of transactional analysis.

Parent ego is the ingrained voice of authority, absorbed conditioning, learning, and attitudes, which one develops right from childhood. It is formed by external events and influences as one grows from a child to an adult. Child ego develops through one's internal reactions to, and feelings about, external events from one's childhood. This mental imprint embodies everyone's seeing, hearing, and feeling experiences. Since the adult ego is the reflection of one's matured mind, it embodies the experience of dealing with situations. Thus, in a nutshell, one can say that 'parent' is a taught concept, while 'adult' is a thought concept.

Berne (1972) defined ego states as 'coherent systems of thought, feeling, manifested by corresponding patterns of behaviour'. Some theorists, however, prefer the term *body language* to *behaviour* because behavioural impulses may not always be evident; it is, instead, an internally felt experience. According to Berne, each ego state is a distinct system of interacting feelings, thoughts, and potential behaviour.

Transactional analysis is extensively used in organizational development to develop the right change premise, eliminating dysfunctional organizational behaviours.

Transactional analysis can also be defined as the 'language within a language' used to reflect the true meaning, feeling, and motive of the communicator. It helps one to understand the environment and then decide one's choice of ego states while communicating with others. Due to its all-encompassing effects, transactional analysis is used in the theory of personality and communication, and in understanding the behavioural pattern of people.

As a subject, transactional analysis has developed beyond Berne's original theories. Subsequent to his death in 1970, many of his followers extended the concepts further. In the 1980s, Wagner, Joines, and Mountain subdivided the three ego states into a seven elements model.

According to the seven ego states model, one can define a *nurturing parent ego* as either *negative (spoiling)* or *positive (nurturing)*, and a *critical parent ego* as either *positive (structuring)* or *negative (critical)*. The *child ego* can be classified as *adapted*, which may be either *cooperative (positive)* or *resistant (negative)*, and *free*, which may be either *spontaneous (positive)* or *immature (negative)*. Finally, the *adult ego* remains a single entity representing the accounting mode, which can draw on the resources of both parent and child.

Franklin Ernst (1971) developed the OK corral matrix, which is also known as the corralogram, to place life positions in quadrants. In the quadrant, except for the 'I am OK–You are OK' situation, the rest are not healthy positions. The unhealthy positions consist of a one-down position (I am not OK, you are OK) resulting in a feeling of helplessness, a hopeless position (I am not OK, you are not OK), and a one-up position (I am OK, you are not OK) resulting in a feeling of anger.

NEGOTIATION

Negotiation is a decision-making process undertaken by two parties with opposing interests. In conflict resolution, one uses negotiation mostly to settle differences between management and the unions through the collective bargaining machinery. Collective bargaining has already been explained in Chapter 9. Here, one is more concerned about the perspectives of communication in negotiation. In any process of negotiation, two goals are considered—substantive goals and relationship goals. *Substantive goals* are those that help to settle some claims, involving either receiving or giving some benefits. A negotiation for wage increase is an example of substantive goal. *Relationship goals* deal with the outcome of decisions that lead the two negotiating parties to work together subsequent to the negotiation reached. Effective negotiation, therefore, requires resolving the substance issues while nurturing the harmonious relationships between two negotiating parties. Whatever may be the process for negotiation, there are two approaches—distributive approach and integrative approach—that are followed. *Distributive approach* is a win-lose or a zero-sum game approach. On the other hand, *integrative approach* is a collaborative approach where both the negotiating parties try to expand the outcomes of their decisions by sharing the benefits.

A distributive negotiation approach is taken in those cases where negotiating parties intend to settle their differences with mutually exclusive goals. Hence, both the parties intend to withhold as much information as possible and try to obtain maximum information from the other. In such negotiation, it often becomes difficult to take an informed decision since the agreement reached between the parties is without adequate information back-up. In contrast, in integrative negotiation, the goals of the negotiating parties are not mutually exclusive. Hence, none of the negotiating parties gains at the expense of the other. Both the negotiating parties work together to optimize the resources in the best possible manner to gain mutual benefit. In *substantive negotiation*, one always tries to gain tangible benefit, while in *integrative negotiation*, one tries to gain both tangible and intrinsic satisfaction. Hence, in integrative negotiation, the negotiating parties adopt a supportive attitude and show empathy, and take informed decisions.

In some forms of negotiation, one also adopts third-party intervention to reach a conclusive settlement. The involvement of arbitrator and mediator is often required in organizational conflict, particularly in wage-related matters.

Thus, negotiation is a process by which two parties seek to reach an agreement through bargaining. A win-win situation in negotiation is possible when each party is prepared to give up something to achieve something that the other party has. During negotiation an organization has to keep in mind the following steps:

1. What does it want?
2. What can it bargain?
3. What are the demands it can agree to?

These steps can be followed by referring to a list of objectives, for example, what the organization intends to get and what it must get. While negotiating, one must listen carefully; ask questions whenever necessary; and get clarification whenever required. One also tries to summarize the discussion. Things that need to be avoided are argument, interruption, and assumption, and even expressing one's concerns may be done with restraint. To make the negotiation effective, one searches for areas of common interests and also makes use of positive body language. The most commonly agreed-upon model of negotiation involves preparing for negotiation (which involves setting objectives, defining strategy, and gathering data), opening, bargaining, and closing.

Every manager needs to negotiate in one area or the other in their day-to-day work life. To succeed in negotiation, managers must possess analytical ability, empathy, planning ability, interactive skills, and communication skills. Such skills can only be developed through experience. Some theoretical understanding may help but putting the learned theories into practice requires a manager to be a part of negotiation, initially as just a member to watch how seniors play their role in negotiation. Negotiation skills of managers help in the following areas:

- Optimizing time, scope, costs, and quality
- Successfully managing change in the organization
- Optimizing resource allocation
- Managing contracts and vendors
- Managing industrial relations
- Settling industrial disputes

Effective negotiation intends to resolve conflicting situations by striking a win-win solution (acceptable to both the conflicting parties). Depending on the situation, styles of negotiation may differ. For successful negotiation, managers have to prepare beforehand and follow certain well-defined steps, which are as follows:

1. Understand the scale of disagreement, that is, whether it is a major disagreement or a minor one. For major disagreements, thorough preparation (preferably using a worksheet) is necessary. For minor disagreements, the negotiation may turn out to be manipulative. While preparing to negotiate for major disagreements, managers (negotiator) may try to understand the goals (what they intend to achieve through negotiation) and the trades (the extent to which they can stretch in terms of accepting the conditions, involving financial benefits or otherwise).

2. Understand the alternatives, that is, the possible ways to reach a decision, when the original line of action fails.
3. Understand the relationships, that is, account for the history of the relationships and how they may impact the negotiation.
4. Understand the expected outcome, that is, understand beforehand the possible expectations of people from the negotiation.
5. Understand the consequences, that is, pre-analysis of the possible consequences (winning or losing) of the negotiation.
6. Understand the power, that is, analyse the power in the relationship, resource control, etc.
7. Assess the possible results of the negotiation.

It is important for both the negotiating parties to feel positive, observing some detachment from emotional feelings. At the outset, managers try to unfreeze, to ensure that the negotiating group members feel at ease to break the deadlock. The entire negotiation should be conducted in such a manner that everyone commits to the issues of difference and agrees to the line of solution.

Case Negotiating for Success: The Experience of a Walmart Vendor

Frey Farms has been one of the premier vendors of Walmart for quite some time. Walmart vendors usually cannot sustain themselves over a long period of time. This is because Walmart, the world's largest retailer, always focuses on 'everyday low prices' (EDLP) which is its core business philosophy. EDLP requires Walmart to always negotiate with vendors and get a price cut. Thus, negotiating with Walmart can either be a fortune or a misfortune. For many vendors, it can be the 'kiss of death'. The experience of Ms Sarah Talley of Frey Farms in her negotiation with Walmart is a good lesson on negotiation. Frey Farms Produce supplies pumpkins and watermelons to Walmart. Ms Talley always confronts price challenges while negotiating with Walmart. Even then, her farm can sustain itself through innovative management of the supply chain. With the responsibility of managing inventory levels and sales on behalf of Walmart, Frey Farms can save customers money while achieving incremental changes in its own margins.

In the case of Walmart, negotiation precedes agreement, which is the other way round for most organizations. As a result, Walmart inculcates a sense of partnership. Hence, the negotiation process focuses on achieving common goals. Walmart's strategy of sourcing at a rock-bottom price is to meet the need of its EDLP philosophy. At the same time, Walmart appreciates the vendor's issues. The negotiation, therefore, is a collaborative effort to drive the costs down through innovative practices. For Walmart, vendors are partners; hence, negotiation cannot jeopardize the relationship, rather, it can resolve the differences without endangering the perpetuating bond.

The experience of Frey Farms suggests that while negotiating with Walmart, one must not make demands or statements; one must instead be a problem solver. Working together to drive costs down to produce goods at a cheaper rate while addressing mutual interests is the only way to ensure the success of Walmart's negotiation.

Some of the important principles followed by Frey Farms while negotiating with Walmart are: always have a clear agenda, avoid small talk, get to the point, bring the issues to the surface and tackle them head-on, and achieve resolution through face-to-face discussions. For Walmart, the relationship with a vendor is a marriage; hence, bluffing while negotiating is not at all desirable. Communication and compromise is the key to success in negotiating with Walmart.

With such a penny-pinching approach to negotiation, Frey Farms still continues to be the vendor of Walmart for pumpkins and watermelons at a price that other vendors cannot dare to match.

CASE QUESTIONS

1. List out the lessons on negotiations with Walmart.
2. Do you think the lessons from Frey Farms can be a role model for others and inspire them to negotiate in a similar manner?

Source: Information from http://www.negotiations.com/case/negotiating-wal-mart/, accessed on 29 April 2011. The negotiation training experts offer negotiation resources on www.negotiations.com. The Web site also offers in-depth negotiation articles, negotiation Q&As, negotiation book reviews, etc.

SUMMARY

- *Communication* is a process of interaction with people and the environment. In organizations, communication is a continuous process of giving and receiving information, and it helps in building social relationships.
- There are broadly two types of communication—verbal communication and non-verbal communication. *Verbal communication* is the use of words and languages to interact between two or more individuals. *Non-verbal communication* can occur without use of words.
- Effective communication is the basic need of an organization, as it provides a common frame of reference and mutual congruence. Communication binds the people with the organization to achieve a common purpose. No group activity is possible without communication. In all communication, one transfers information and also provides behavioural inputs.
- Business communication includes all communication that managers need to do in a business context. Effective business communication requires both an understanding of the business and a suitable style of communication.
- Psychological and behavioural influence on communication helps to develop a common understanding. Through communication, one tries to develop relationships based on shared mental maps. Cross-cultural differences between people make perceptions less than perfect in three different ways—deletion, distortion, and generalization.
- Communication barriers are the results of several inadequacies that tend to distort communication and affect the ability of managers to achieve organizational goals. Important communication barriers are distortion, semantic distortion, premature evaluation, perfunctory attention, and failure to communicate.
- Transactional analysis is now widely applied in organizational communications. While people communicate, they reflect their state of mind, which translates as child ego, adult ego, or parent ego. It is possible for a person to reflect all the three ego states simultaneously while communicating with others.
- *Negotiation* is a decision-making process undertaken by two parties with opposing interests. In conflict resolution, people use negotiation mostly to settle differences between management and the unions through the machinery of collective bargaining. It is important for both the negotiating parties to feel positive, detaching themselves to an extent from emotional feelings and communicating.

KEY TERMS

Communication: Communication is a process of interaction with people and the environment. Through such interaction, two or more individuals influence the ideas, beliefs, and attitudes of each other.

Communication barriers: Communication barriers are the result of several inadequacies that tend to distort communication and affect the ability of managers to achieve organizational goals.

Group communication: To manage the business complexity, organizations form groups to pool the knowledge and resources. This is known as group communication.

Negotiation: Negotiation is a decision-making process undertaken by two parties with opposing interests.

Non-verbal communication: Non-verbal communication occurs without use of words. It sensitizes one's senses and thereby evokes responses, depending on the way one interprets a particular cue. It is often referred to as body language, that is, any body movement of the communicator which carries some meaning.

Organizational communication: Organizational communication provides social inputs into social (organizational) systems by which managers try to modify behaviour to effect change. In an organization, managers communicate internally at different hierarchical levels, groups, and departments, and externally to customers, suppliers, and other external stakeholders.

Transactional analysis: Transactional analysis is the 'language within a language' used to reflect the true meaning, feeling, and motive of the communicator. It helps one to understand the environment and then decide one's choice of ego states while communicating with others.

Verbal communication: Verbal communication is the use of words and languages between two or more individuals for interaction. It can be either oral or written.

REVIEW QUESTIONS

1. Define the term *communication* and describe its important characteristics.
2. Explain the process of communication.
3. What is the *two-way communication channel*? What are its features?
4. List the important objectives of communication.
5. Describe the essential elements of business communication.
6. What are the different types of communication? Explain their relative merits and demerits.
7. Discuss what are the barriers to communication in an organization? How do they affect organizational efficiency?
8. How can we overcome the barriers to communication?
9. Write short notes on the following:
   i. Formal and informal communication
   ii. Verbal and non-verbal communication
   iii. Upward and downward communication
   iv. Horizontal and diagonal communication
   v. Grapevine
   vi. Body language

CRITICAL THINKING QUESTIONS

1. Your company is a multinational steel major. You have been assigned to visit China to negotiate a deal for getting the sponge iron technology, which is now a part of a major expansion plan. Draw a detailed plan of your negotiation strategies.
2. You have visited a shopping mall. To your surprise, you observe that one of the sales girls is quarrelling with a potential customer, who after a long visual inspection discarded the item of his choice. The contention of the sales girl is that this person literally compelled her to make each and every item available, keeping other customers waiting and finally decided not to buy anything. She had literally wasted her time and also lost numerous other customers. As a communication trainer, suggest what type of training can help the girl to improve and tackle similar situations in the future.

REFERENCES

Berne, E. (1961). *Transactional Analysis in Psychotherapy*. New York: Grove Press.

——— (1972). *What Do You Say After You Say Hello?* New York: Grove Press.

Ernst, F. H., Jr, (1971). 'The OK Corral: Grid for Get-On-With', *Transactional Analysis Journal*, 1 (4): pp. 231–240.

Freud, S. (1949). *An Outline of Psychoanalysis.* Translated by James Strachey. New York: W. W. Norton & Co., Inc.

Hall, E. T. (1976). *Beyond Culture*. New York: Doubleday.

Hovland, C. I. (1951). 'Changes in Attitude Through Communication', *Journal of Abnormal and Social Psychology*, 46, pp. 424–437.

Ishikawa, Kaoru (1985). *How to Operate QC Circle Activities.* Tokyo: QC Circle Headquarters, Union of Japanese Scientists and Engineers.

McQuail, Denis (2000). *McQuail's Mass Communication Theory*, 4th edition. London: Sage Publications.

Weaver, W. (1949). 'Recent Contributions to the Mathematical Theory of Communication', in *The Mathematical Theory of Communication*, C. E. Shannon and W. Weaver (eds). Urbana, IL: University of Illinois Press.

FURTHER READING

Berne, E. (1947). *The Mind in Action.* New York: Simon & Schuster.

——— (1963). *The Structure and Dynamics of Organizations and Groups*. New York: Grove Press.

——— (1964). *Games People Play*. New York: Grove Press.

Bhattacharyya, Dipak Kumar (2006). *Human Resource Management*, 2nd edition. New Delhi: Excel Books.

——— (2009). *Organizational Behaviour: Concepts and Applications*. New Delhi: Oxford University Press.

——— (2010). *Cross-Cultural Management: Text and Cases*. New Delhi: PHI Learning.

Fisher, Glen (1982). *International Negotiation: A Cross-Cultural Perspective*. Sydney: Pergamon Press.

Guetzkow, Harold (1966). 'Relations among Organizations', in *Studies of Behaviour in Organizations*, R. W. Bower (ed.). Athens: University of Georgia Press.

Gulliver, P. H. (1979). *Disputes and Negotiations*. New York: Academic Press.

Moran, R. T. and W. G. Stripp (1991). *Successful International Business Negotiations*. Houston, TX: Gulf Publishing Company.

Novey, T. (2002). 'Measuring the Effectiveness of Transactional Analysis: An International Study', *Transactional Analysis Journal*, 32, pp. 8–24.

Usunier, J. C. (1998). *International and Cross-Cultural Management Research.* London: Sage Publications.

White, Leslie (1959). *The Evolution of Culture*. New York: McGraw-Hill.

13

Organizational Systems, Structure, and Design

After going through this chapter, you will be able to understand:

- the systems view of organizations
- the organizational structure and its relationship with the systems
- the various principles of organizational systems
- the viable systems approach in an organization
- socio-technical systems thinking
- the business process approach to an organization
- the relationship of organizational culture to organizational design

Systems Drive Results

Cisco Systems, Inc. is a worldwide leader in Internet infrastructure. Cisco's organizational transformation was achieved primarily by incubating future leaders within the organization and empowering them to drive the organization through change. To achieve this strategic intent, Cisco introduced proactive performance management systems to track 'potential leaders' and take them through the process of grooming to transform them into 'leaders'. This helped Cisco transform from a loss-inducing venture into a profit-making venture. The quality of Cisco's leadership is a critical success factor that enabled the company to tackle present and future business challenges. The leadership and people development manager at Cisco emphasizes that the company incubates all the passion and principles of leadership to develop people's potential. This approach of Cisco has been responsible for the reinvention of the organization. Such a process of developing leaders within the organization and empowering them with the help of performance management systems has enabled Cisco to emerge as one of the most successful organizations today. Since 2001, Cisco has continuously been one of *Fortune* magazine's '100 best places to work'.

INTRODUCTION

An organization is made up of a group of people with some specific goals, objectives, and activities. It is also defined as the relations among the components of a system. Organization structure denotes the components and relations that bind people working in the organization. The three pillars of organization are the people, the organization itself, and the technology. *People issues* encompass education, training, and attitudes. *Organizational issues* cover strategy, policy, culture, and bureaucracy. *Technological issues* are hardware, software, telecommunications, and information systems. The three different levels of organization structure are strategic, tactical, and operational. The *strategic level* represents the decision-making level, that is, the corporate or the top level of an organization. The *tactical* or *business level* is the middle-management level where strategic decisions are transformed into tactics to achieve strategic intents. The *operational level* represents the actual level of implementation, where first-level employees and workers execute the tactics by adopting action plans.

SYSTEMS THEORY, SYSTEMS ANALYSIS, AND SYSTEMS THINKING

Systems theory has unearthed the process of understanding the complex world of systems. In organizations, systems theory is applied through systems analysis. It is done through systems thinking, which helps to study the organization, its patterns, structures, and events. Thus, systems thinking provides a broader perspective to identify the actual issues and their causes, working more like a diagnostic tool, and accordingly facilitates the appropriate process of intervention to correct the organizational odds.

Principles of Systems Theory

Systems theory identifies certain commonalities in systems. Such commonalities have, in fact, developed certain well-accepted principles of systems for organizations. Since numerous principles were identified as common to systems, Draper L. Kauffman, Jr, (1980) believed that the systems' overall behaviour depends on the organizational structure as a whole. Organizational structure determines the various kinds of behaviour, and behaviour determines various events in the organization. Most managers can only see and respond to events, which is a more reactionary approach rather than a proactive approach. Breaking organizational systems only by responding to events becomes more of an effort, similar to addressing organizational problems as and when they arise. Such organizations, characteristically, adopt incremental strategies (short term) to fix some events.

Based on this discussion, the principles of systems can be listed as the following:

- Organizational systems follow a pattern of events in a cycle.
- Each pattern of event indicates some specific phases, and at each phase the behaviour of the organization changes.
- Systems interpret patterns and events in the organization.
- Systems seek balance with the organizational environment.
- When systems do not interact with their environment, the effect of the environment becomes limited.
- A circular relationship exists between the overall system and its parts.

Viable System Model, Organizational Cybernetics, and Organizational Systems

Organizational cybernetics has emerged as a management systems approach by adopting cybernetic notions for the purpose of organizational and social management, especially by focusing on the viable system model (VSM) postulated by S. Beer (1979). VSM is an important instrument in the operationalizing of the organizational cybernetics approach. According to Beer, cybernetics is 'the science of effective organization'. A system is said to be viable when it is able to adapt effectively to environmental changes, even though such changes are unforeseen. *VSM*, thus, consists of operation (O) with embedded management (M) and environment (E). It is used in organizations to diagnose different elements, in designing information systems, in designing management structure, etc. It is even used in designing organizational vision, mission, and structure. Lastly, it also helps in systematic thinking in organizations.

Chaos Theory

Some scholars subscribe to the view that even in chaos there is a system. The *chaos theory* has emerged from this concept and it studies the complexity of the world to identify principles to understand the organization. The theory deals with the structure of turbulence and is, thus, a study of unpredictable complex systems. Edward Lorenz of MIT, a meteorologist, has given a visual presentation simulating the weather pattern to explain the theory of chaos. This has been presented in Figure 13.1.

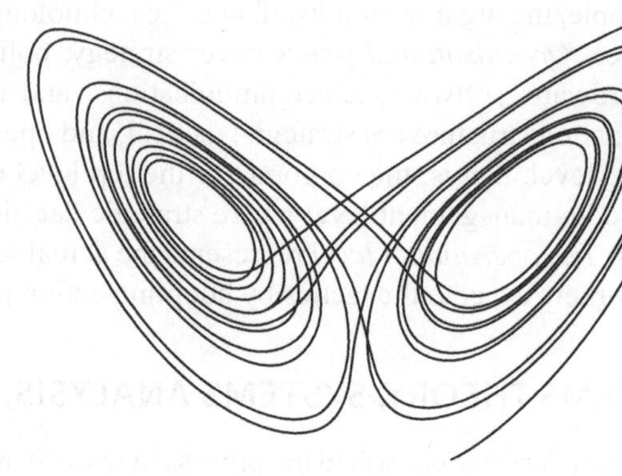

Figure 13.1 The Butterfly Effect

Since Figure 13.1 resembles a butterfly, it is also known as the 'butterfly effect'. The *butterfly effect* refers to the discovery that in a chaotic system it is theoretically possible that a slight change would make no difference whatsoever, but when the system is unpredictable at a certain stage, the future may unfold quite differently, depending upon what little difference occurred.

The chaos theory has emerged from the gestalt theory, which suggests that a whole is greater than the sum of its parts. It is also similar to the systems theory, as it is only concerned with systems. The application of the chaos theory to management depicts organizations as complex and unpredictable because of the relations among the constituents of a system.

The characteristics of a chaotic system are as follows:

- **Sensitivity to initial conditions**: A complex system reacts to different variables at the outset in unpredictable ways. Even starting with the same or slightly different variables in a model will not result in the same outcomes, if the system is complex.
- **Same context may not hold good again and again**: In a complex system, the same context never occurs twice. Hence, in an organization, a team with essentially identical personnel and similar characteristics will never perform in exactly the same way, which means that a system is never exactly the same. In an organization, a strategy or decision will never be made twice even within the same context.
- **Strange attractors (a set of values)**: In chaos theory, the same set of values migrates over time in a given system. This means that attractors (a set of values) in chaos theory act as the influence of gravity. Attractors can be a single fixed point, a collection of points, a complex orbit, or an infinite number of points. In an organization, attractors cause behaviour, which alters over time, depending upon the social, economical, or other forces that drive the system at a given point of time and the way they interact.
- **Fractality**: Literally, *fractal* means a curve or a surface that is independent of a scale. Any segment, if magnified on scale, appears identical to the whole curve. In management analogy, it is assumed that different levels of the organization resemble others and act like a fractal in managerial hierarchy. Therefore, a form of social structure can be examined in relation to the characteristics of the whole system at the macro and micro levels.
- **Bifurcation**: *Bifurcation* is the sudden appearance of qualitatively different solutions to the equations for a non-linear system, as a parameter is varied. In an organization, two different patterns (groups) can emerge to address an issue differently, as complexity increases. This is often recommended as a source of creativity.

Organizations are complex and adaptive systems that have behaviours similar to those found in nature, that is, different stages of stability and chaos. Rather than control an organization, a manager is prompted to take advantage of its complexity. Theorists in management and social organization now believe that organizations are also non-linear dynamic systems, having the same characteristics as natural phenomena (R. D. Stacey 1996). The organization is often seen as a complex adaptive system comprised of the formal and shadow systems, and in this way, the analogy is made between chaos in natural systems and the social organization. Similarly, the long-term behaviour of the organization is unpredictable, akin to the inability to predict hurricanes far into the future. Stacey addresses this issue by stating that managers must learn how to manage the anxiety that accompanies being on the edge of chaos, employing a nearly mystical concept of 'creative destruction'. Stacey ends with optimism, believing that although long-term outcomes are impossible to predict, dealing effectively with change and challenge on a daily basis will ultimately result in success.

Thus, the chaos theory is often used as a way to conceptualize management theory and other social systems. An efficient manager can plan for and expect constant change in the environment. Their goals become not a set of results but a series of contingency scenarios to which they can react in the short run and at some later date in the future. The same principle applies to human society. Tiny changes in one person's state of mind can, on occasions, lead to major changes in society as a whole, or simple acts can lead to unintended consequences.

Socio-technical Systems Thinking

P. G. Herbst (1974) pioneered the concept of *socio-technical systems thinking* based on the studies on coal mining in the 1950s in the United Kingdom. The major landmark in this thought process is that with small self-regulating work teams, organizations get better results. According to this theory, the quality and the quantity of output in any work depend on two distinguishable aspects of the organization. They are the technological system and the social structure of the work system. The social structure of the work system of an organization is partly influenced by the technological system. Therefore, any organization can optimize their performance through suitable modification of their technical and social systems. This concept is also known as the 'social ecology of industry'.

Managers often fail to appreciate that a number of exogenous events are interrelated in such a way that they lead to irreversible generation in the organization (Emery and Trist 1965). Following this line of thinking, Emery and Trist have proposed four ideal types of organizational environment: namely placid randomized, placid clustered, disturbed reactive, and turbulent environments. The survival of an organization would depend upon the compatibility between its strategy and the type of environment it confronts.

System Dynamics

J. Forrester (1958) pioneered the concept of *system dynamics (SD)*. The SD approach involved the use of the concepts and ideas of control theory and control engineering in management and decision making. SD is primarily oriented towards identifying (defining), modelling, and simulating a system (for example, a factory, a city, an economy, or even an entire ecological system) in order to explicate how the system might behave under different policy regimes. The SD approach deals with 'dynamic systems', that is, aggregates of physical and abstract entities, which are distinguishable from their surrounding environment as purposive wholes and exhibit dynamic behaviour. The approach recognizes that certain dynamic systems might behave in a counter-intuitive manner, that is, an unexpected manner, especially due to the way such systems might be constituted. By trying to model dynamic systems and simulating them on a computer, the SD approach seeks to predict their behaviour pattern.

Business Process Approach to Organization

Tracing back history, one finds that the 1980s were the era of automation. In the manufacturing industry, computer numeric control (CNC), direct numeric control (DNC), numeric control (NC), flexible manufacturing system (FMS), robots, etc., were introduced. In contrast to the 1980s, the 1990s were about people. Total quality management (TQM) concepts focused on delegation, total employee involvement, ownership, shared values, cross-functional teamwork, self-managed work teams, employee empowerment, etc. Various models of excellence like the European business excellence model (EFQM), the Shingho prize model, and the people capability maturity model (PCMM) highlighted the role and importance of people and the process-centred approach to manage people in organizations.

There is really no business process model of organizational business processes. Business processes provide critical support to the key value-add (operate) process within manufacturing. In terms of organizational systems and structure, it is better to relate business processes.

Organizational Systems and Human Resource Management

Organizational systems and structure also relate to human resource management (HRM) processes and practices. In organizations, there are broadly two types of HRM models—a prescriptive model and a normative model. A review of four models proposed by different theorists has been conducted here. The four models are as follows:

1. **Michigan model (Fombrun et al. 1984)**: This model has two perspectives—the strategic and environmental perspective, and the human resource perspective. The *strategic* and *environmental perspective* represents the relationship between the people and the organizational strategy as well as the political, economic, and cultural forces that affect them. They have interactive relationships. The *human resource perspective* of the model provides a simple framework to show what the relationship should be between selection, appraisal, rewards, and training, and the effect on performance.
2. **Harvard model (Beer et al. 1984)**: This model consists of two parts, which are the human resource system and a map of the HRM territory. The *human resource system* represents labour relations and personnel administration perspectives under four human resource categories—employee influence, human resource flow, rewards, and work systems. A *map of the HRM territory* shows how HRM is closely connected with both the external environment (stakeholder interests) and the internal organization (situational factors).
3. **Guest's (1987) model**: This model involves seven policies for achieving the four main HR outcomes outlined by the Harvard model. According to Guest, these outcomes will lead to desirable organizational results. In this context it is similar to the Harvard model, but has seven categories instead of Harvard's four. Guest's seven categories are broadly the same as Harvard's categories. For example, where the Harvard model has human resource flow, Guest has manpower flow and recruitment, selection, and socialization; where the Harvard model has work systems, Guest calls these policies organizational and job design. Both models have reward systems. Guest's model has three additional categories—policy formulation and management of change, employee appraisal, training, and development, and communication systems.
4. **Warwick model (Hendry and Pettigrew 1990)**: This model of organization consists of the inner and outer context, and it places more emphasis on strategy. It is based on the Harvard model but concentrates more on strategy. For example, the Harvard model has HRM policy choices that consist of employee influence, human resource flow, reward systems, and work systems, while the Warwick model in the HRM context consists of human resource flow, work systems, reward systems, and

employee relations. Both are the same. The Harvard model uses business strategy in the context of situational factors, while the Warwick model uses business strategy in its inner context.

A major difficulty has been confusion over the types of model being used. Sometimes they are normative or prescriptive, and sometimes they are descriptive or analytical. For example, the Harvard model (Beer et al. 1984) is described by D. Torrington and L. Hall (1998) as an analytical model rather than normative or prescriptive. At the same time, A. Pinnington and T. Edwards (2000) and M. Noon (1994) described the same model as normative. In actuality, the Harvard model is made up of both normative and analytical elements. Another area of confusion is the problem with allocation of various organizational models to a classification. Therefore, two fundamental gaps are to be found in these models, which are:

1. Lack of clarity on type of models (or classifications) and their definitions
2. Absence of a systems engineering-based attempt to model HRM as a business process

EVOLUTION OF THE BUSINESS PROCESS MODEL OF ORGANIZATION

A well-crafted business process extends support to the organization. It exists to support all other processes within the organization. Therefore, all other processes strengthen the business process. Further, in supporting its customers, the business process must ensure that it maximizes its contribution to the overall business objectives and strategy. The business process is continuous, in tandem with W. Edwards Deming's (1989) advocacy of the plan, do, check, and act (PDCA) cycle for continuous planning and improvement. Therefore, the business process should consist of the following sub-processes, which make up the continuous cycle:

1. Planning (replan) the strategy
2. Implementing the strategy
3. Monitoring the impact on business results

Description of Business Process Models

The business process model, as already stated, consists of three sub-processes. Each of these sub-processes consists of a number of activities. The three sub-processes along with their respective activities can be listed as the following:

1. **Make an organizational strategy**: This sub-process uses business strategy and objectives and requirements of key business processes to formulate an integrated strategy by setting objectives, establishing current capabilities, negotiating appropriate budgets for realistic implementation of plans, and setting policies.
   - **Set objectives**: This activity indicates integration of business strategy and objectives and requirements of other key business processes with organizational requirements and objectives.
   - **Establish current capability**: This activity establishes the current resource capability within the business and its key processes to meet the set objectives.
   - **Plan**: This activity develops a plan, including budgets, which defines the course of action that the business is going to adopt to build upon its current capabilities and develop the potential of its people in line with the stated objectives and requirements.

- **Negotiate budget**: This activity requires the plan to negotiate for financial resources, which will lead to successful implementation of the strategy.
- **Set policies**: This activity sets up policies in different areas matching the strategic requirements to achieve the goals and objectives.

2. **Implement a human resource management strategy**: This sub-process implements a human resource management strategy by controlling HR planning and by monitoring, utilizing, recruiting, assessing, and selecting the right people in order to train and educate them and develop their potential. This is performed by managing HR performance through review and appraisal. This results in redeployment of the HR.
   - **Control human resources**: This activity makes sure that the HR planning is correct and that the human resources are correctly recruited and monitored in accordance with the objectives and requirements of the organization.
   - **Recruit**: This activity is concerned with bringing in HR positions in line with HR requirements, from internal or external sources. It is concerned with upgrading existing people's capabilities within the business in line with the HR objectives.
   - **Manage HR performance**: This activity is concerned with setting targets for individuals, monitoring progress against the targets, and identifying necessary training, education, and development needs as well as deciding rewards and disciplinary actions.
   - **Manage redeployment**: This activity, having identified a deficiency in a job position which cannot be rectified through training, education, or development, is concerned with redeployment of the current job holder within or without the organization.
   - **Negotiate working conditions**: This activity concerns the requirements of people and the capacity of the business. It is related to HR policies and plans (people terms and conditions).

3. **Monitor impact on business result**: This sub-process monitors the impact of the HRM process on business performance through monitoring its contribution to the business strategy and objectives, and other key business processes.
   - **Monitor impact on business strategy**: This activity monitors the impact of the HR strategy on business strategy as well as business performance.
   - **Monitor impact on people satisfaction**: This activity is concerned with establishing how well the business satisfies its employees.
   - **Monitor impact on management process**: This activity is concerned with monitoring how well the HRM strategy and its implementation are satisfying the requirements of management processes. Management process formulates strategy and sets the direction for the whole business.
   - **Monitor impact on operational process**: This activity is concerned with monitoring how well the HRM strategy and its implementation are satisfying the requirements of operational processes. Operational processes consist of getting orders, developing products, fulfilling orders, and supporting products.
   - **Monitor impact on support process**: This activity is concerned with monitoring how well the HRM strategy and its implementation are satisfying the requirements of support processes. The support processes include financial and IT processes that enable the operational process functions.

Thus, by analysing the various types of business process models, one can develop a business process approach to organizations, incorporating various aspects of systems engineering principles.

Types of Business Process Models

Normative models of business process reflect or establish standard ways of behaving. These values or norms set expectations for individuals and groups. Normative models are designed to authoritatively impose on others what should be the case and what should be done. *Prescriptive research-based models* make hypothetical claims that if certain conditions are met, then outcomes that are specified within the model will be achieved. The advantage of normative/prescriptive models, according to some researchers, is that they are more open to scientific testing and that when policies and practices are established in a way that is consistent with the model and integrated with the business strategy, they will lead to desirable outcomes for the people and the organization (Pinnington and Edwards 2000).

Descriptive models describe what organizations try to reflect as having happened or is happening while being implemented. K. Legge (1995) further divides descriptive models into two types—descriptive-functional and descriptive-behavioural. *Descriptive-functional models* state 'what is' rather than 'what should be' the function of an organization. *Descriptive-behavioural models* state more precisely what are the actual behaviours of specialists and managers engaged in organizational activities.

Analytical models of organization refer to the use of logical reasoning for a subject or problem. S. Tyson (1995) mentioned that analytical models of organization should be applicable to both cause and effect, in terms of actions taken to influence the relationships of people in the organization and actions that have a global theoretical basis.

Thus, a normative model of the business process describes what should be the function of an organization and what is good for business. The descriptive model describes 'what is' instead of 'what should be'. An analytical model describes the business process and its causes and effects through the use of logical reasoning. Therefore, an analytical model can be normative or descriptive.

Role of Critical Success Factors in Organizational Design

Critical success factors (CSF) analysis is a method developed at MIT Sloan School of Management by John Rockart to guide businesses in creating and measuring success. It is a widely used top-down methodology that is especially suitable for designing systems as opposed to applications. It is a reductionist method for going from an abstract vision to concrete requirements.

CSF analysis is a key area where satisfactory performance is required for the organization to achieve its goals. Therefore, it is a means of identifying the tasks and requirements for success. At the lowest level, CSFs become concrete requirements; a means to prioritize requirements. The CSF method starts with a vision along with a mission statement. Hence, it is imperative to develop five or six high-level goals and then develop a hierarchy of goals and their success factors. It leads to concrete requirements at the lowest level of decomposition (a single idea). Besides, it also identifies the problems being solved and the assumptions being made. Its cross-referential usage helps in identifying scenarios and problems with requirements. CSF analysis produces results that express the needs of the enterprise clearly and (hopefully) completely allows one to measure success and prioritize goals in a sensible manner. When CSF analysis is used along with traditional usage scenarios, it ensures that the needs of both the user and the enterprise are being met.

Finally, critical success factors (CSF) analysis helps in:

- Understanding an objective and definable end results
- Clear definition of entities and relationships

- Access to source data in required formats
- Understanding data and business context
- Creating and analysing competency database

Therefore, for designing an organization, it is a good idea to ensure that inputs from all the key players are considered. Not only does it help to identify requirements that may have been missed, but it also guarantees some degree of consistency in the organizational model.

Business Process Re-engineering

In most organizations, some degree of business process engineering (BPE) or business process re-engineering (BPR) has taken place. If this is the case, then some documentation is already completed that will guide the project team in defining the requirements of a new system.

When BPE projects are completed properly, the end products include recommendations on what information needs to be collected and used, and who will collect it at what point in the business cycle.

Business process re-engineering is often described as a radical redesign of strategic, value-added business processes to achieve breakthrough performance improvements. BPR is a large-scale overhaul of basic business processes. Therefore, it is the heavy artillery used to tear down old structures and practices and replace them with something new and not something for marginal improvements or fine-tuning.

The three terms that constitute BPR can be explained in the following manner:

1. **Business**: It is the process that supports the development, production, and delivery of products and services. Re-engineering business processes like marketing and selling, administration, logistics, and supply chain can significantly optimize the cost for the organization. It can also lead to improvement in the cycle time, that is, the time taken to complete any recurring task essential to business output and enhance customer satisfaction.
2. **Process**: The core of any business is a set of processes, each of which consists of a collection of activities that use input to create an output of value for the customer. Thus, a process actually documents tasks and activities. The objective of the entire process determines which tasks and activities are to be done and how they should be arranged.
3. **Re-engineering**: Re-engineering of business processes must be a radical reform that reaches the very core of the business; it can not be just a superficial rearrangement of what is already there. It is a comprehensive, one-step turnaround that takes more time and effort than incremental change strategies, and often needs considerable support from systems analysis and information technology.

HUMAN RESOURCE INFORMATION SYSTEMS AND ITS USAGE IN ORGANIZATIONAL DESIGN

Human resource information systems (HRIS) comprises a range of computerized technology used to store, record, link, analyse, and present data about the human element within an organization. In HRIS, while the external environment is connected through the Internet, the intranet allows the organization to communicate from within more rapidly and effectively. HRIS thus encompasses both internal and external information processing. The application of HRIS is now possible in all HR functions to reinforce information sharing, as HR information is now considered as strategic input.

Through the process of integrating the HRM function of an organization, HRIS also facilitates the linking of people and organizational systems with the goals and objectives of business. HRIS achieves integration with the HRM processes and initiatives. It creates an environment within which individuals take responsibility for their own learning, gaining support and commitment from managers.

ORGANIZATIONAL CULTURE

Analysis of organizational culture as an approach to organizational design is a difficult task. The culture of an organization is deep-rooted in its history and it is below the surface of awareness. Any process of change in organizational culture follows certain well-defined and structured steps. Although these vary from organization to organization, one can draw a tentative list as follows:

1. Identify core values and beliefs.
2. Uncover core values and beliefs. These may include stated values and goals, but they are also embedded in organizational metaphors, myths, and stories, and in the behaviour of members.
3. Acknowledge, respect, and discuss differences between core values and beliefs of different subcultures within the organization.
4. Look for incongruence between conscious and unconscious beliefs and values, and resolve by choosing those to which the organization wishes to commit. Establish new behavioural norms (and even new metaphor language) that clearly demonstrate the desired values.
5. Repeat these steps over a long period of time. As new members enter the organization, ensure that they are surrounded by clear messages about the culture they are entering.
6. Reinforce desirable behaviour.

Change in organizational culture is an ongoing process, which is why it may be hard to identify organizations that have completed a successful change. However, one can find examples of change-in-progress in organizations.

ORGANIZATIONAL DESIGN

Effective organizational design depends on the interrelationships of the principles of job specialization, departmentalization, coordination, and line and staff positions. It is defined as the total pattern of structural elements and patterns that are used to manage the overall organization. Effective organizational design is also instrumental to implementing strategies for achievement of organizational goals. Organizational design broadly rests on two models. They are the bureaucratic model and the behavioural model.

Bureaucratic Model

The bureaucratic model rests on Max Weber's theory of bureaucracy (1946), which was highlighted in Chapter 3. The basic premise of this theory is designing an organization by creating an absolute and clear division of labour, with a hierarchy of positions in conformity with the principles of the scalar chain. This is to ensure that the commands run from top to bottom, establishing concise and consistent rules and procedures (for decisional conformity), framing policies and practices, and finally managing the organization impersonally.

In the changing business environment, despite the fundamental strength of the bureaucratic model in simplifying the business process or organizational design, and its operational efficiency and effectiveness, it is criticized due to the following drawbacks:

- It cannot cope with the changing external environment.
- Formal rules and procedures often stand in the way of achievement of organizational goals.
- It often neglects the human aspects of the organization, as it considers people only as an economic rational entity (primarily driven by money).
- It traditionally considers the higher management to be more knowledgeable than those reporting to them, which may not always be true.
- It often creates bureaupathology or a feeling of insecurity among people, particularly those who strive for career advancement. The term *bureaupathology* was advocated by Victor A. Thompson (1961), who had argued that managers in authority become more ritualistic in their behavioural pattern. Such 'pathological' behaviour may be counterproductive in achieving organizational effectiveness and growth.

Behavioural Model

The behavioural model of organizational design is the extension of the human relations school of management thought. The behavioural model duly recognized the weaknesses of the relational and mechanistic characteristics of the bureaucratic model, and emphasized the social and psychological implications of organizational life. The socio-technical systems theory and Likert's system 4 organization theory (1967) are the two known behavioural models used in organizational design.

The socio-technical systems theory approach, pioneered by Trist and Bamforth (1951) along with Tavistock Institute, London, emphasized the need for balancing the human side of an organization with its technical and mechanical side, while designing it. This means that every organization has two systems—social systems and technical systems. Balancing these two systems by using a socio-technical model ultimately leads to effective organizational design. *Social systems* represent both formal and informal human interactions in organizations. It helps to sustain the organization. *Technical systems* represent the tasks involved in producing goods and services in the organization.

Likert's system 4 organization theory deals with eight characteristics of organizations; they are the leadership process, the motivation process, the communication process, the interaction process, the decision process, the goal-setting process, the control process, and the performance process. According to Likert, all these characteristics ultimately lead to four design approaches—systems 1, 2, 3, and 4. *System 1* is described as exploitive authoritative, that is, an extreme manifestation of the bureaucratic organization. In such organizations, managers take all the decisions with no participation by subordinates. *System 2* represents the benevolent authoritative style, which means managers repose trust on subordinates and allow information to flow upward. *System 3* represents the consultative style, where managers have complete confidence and trust in subordinates and even solicit advice from them, retaining, however, the right to decision making. *System 4* represents the participative leadership style, which is the extreme manifestation of a behavioural organization.

In Table 13.1, the two extreme forms of organizational design have been discussed, using Likert's framework.

Situational Aspects of Organizational Design

Technology, environment, size, and organizational life cycle are the four important situational factors in organizational design.

Technology is one of the major contingency factors that influence organizational design. Technology, per se, facilitates the conversion process which transforms organizational inputs (materials, equipment, labour, etc.) into outputs (products and services). Rigorous technological changes in Indian organizations during the post-reform days have played a crucial role in redesigning organizations, including public sector enterprises and departmental undertakings.

Table 13.1 Extreme Forms of Organizational Design

Organizational characteristics	System 1 organization	System 4 organization
Leadership process	There is no trust and confidence in subordinates. Subordinates distance themselves from their superiors and can hardly afford to discuss their work-related problems with them.	There is high confidence and trust in subordinates, who feel free to discuss their work-related problems with their superiors.
Motivational process	Subordinates suffer from physical and monetary insecurity and they nurture an unfavourable attitude towards the organization.	Subordinates feel motivated due to a participatory work environment. They nurture a favourable attitude towards the organization and volunteer to achieve goals and objectives.
Communication process	There is distorted downward communication and subordinates view every communication from the superior with suspicion.	There is free flow of upward, downward, and lateral communication within the organization. Communication is accurate and easily understandable by all.
Interaction process	The interaction is closed and restricted. Subordinates can hardly participate in decision making or have any knowledge of departmental goals, methods, and activities.	The interaction is open and extensive. Subordinates and superiors can affect departmental goals, methods, and activities.
Decision process	This process is highly centralized and occurs only at the top.	Decisions occur at all levels. Therefore, this process is decentralized.
Goal-setting process	This process is located at the top of the organization, which discourages participation.	This process encourages group participation in setting realistic objectives.
Control process	This process is centralized and encourages fixing the blame on others for any mistake.	This process is dispersed and emphasizes self-control and problem solving.
Performance goals	These goals are low and passively sought by superiors, who hardly make any effort to develop the potential of subordinates in the organization.	These goals are high and actively sought by superiors, who commit themselves to developing the potential of subordinates through systematic training.

Environmental issues such as globalization and cultural changes influence organizational structure and design in a big way. Even a bureaucratic or mechanistic organization (resembling Likert's system 1 or Max Weber's bureaucratic model of organization) needs to respond to environmental issues to sustain itself and face the competition. The theory of stable and unstable environments, propounded by T. Burns and G. Stalker (1961), suggests that the environment may remain fairly stable over time and organizations can survive even without redesigning their structure. However, such a possibility is rare now, as the environment for every organization constantly changes. An organic organization (resembling the behavioural model or Likert's system 4) is always prepared to face environmental uncertainties and change accordingly.

Organizational size and *form* also play a crucial role in determining the organizational structure and design. Structural features of large and small organizations widely differ. For example, large organizations necessarily require decentralizing, while small organizations may get the right fit in centralizing their activities.

The hypothesis of an *organizational life cycle* believes in different organizational designs for different stages, including the birth stage, the youth stage, the middle stage, and the maturity stage. Based on the study by R. Quinn and K. Cameron (1983), this theory believes that every organization elevates itself to different stages and, accordingly, its structure and design varies. For example, at the *birth stage*, where activities overlap, organizations become more informal. There may not be any rules and regulations, or structured systems of planning, performance, evaluation, and coordination. At the *youth stage*, some amount of decentralization in decision making takes place, where a few trusted employees are taken into confidence, but the final decision making remains centralized. At the *middle stage*, organizations are reasonably successful and become rather large. Organizational design and structure become bureaucratic with formalized functional departments and supporting staff departments. Authority slowly gets decentralized and largely becomes bound by policies, rules, and regulations. At the *maturity stage*, organizations become very large, mechanistic, and specialized with a structured set of rules, policies, and procedures. The hypothesis of organizational life cycle, therefore, mainly focuses on how an organization frames its design according to the different stages of its life cycle.

Case New Organization Structure in Times of Need: The Experience of Bajaj Electricals

Bajaj Electricals Limited (BEL), a 1938 company engaged in the business of manufacturing and marketing consumer electronics and luminaries, and engineering is a household name in India. The company is recognized for quality and also price-effectiveness. However, since 2001, the company has experienced the brunt of an economic downturn in the country. It has had to face tough competition in most of its product lines, primarily due to the entry of multinational organizations in the country. As a consequence, the company had to experience significant downslide in profits and its turnover.

It was at this time that the company undertook a total restructuring exercise to engineer a complete turnaround. To regain its profits and growth, the company adopted various strategic, operational, distributional, and marketing initiatives. At the same time, to get the best results from such initiatives, the company also changed its organizational structure from a traditionally vertical to a strategic business unit, revamping its supply chains to match the competitive market situation. Side by side, the company also went for a financial restructuring exercise, primarily to identify the possible cost-cutting avenues to gain price efficiency. Simultaneously, with the change in the organizational structure, the company came out with innovative pricing and marketing strategies, which ultimately led to a high rate of growth in 2003.

The company named this the 'Mission Excel' exercise, which involved a comprehensive strategy along with organizational and financial restructuring. After getting encouraging results from this exercise, the company subsequently adopted another slogan, 'Operation Triumph 1001' to become an INR 10.1 billion turnover company by 2007, a more than INR 20 billion turnover company by 2009–2010, and then leapfrog to a quadruple turnover by 2014–2015.

The success of Bajaj in emerging as a winner from a total downturn trend in business, through a change in organizational structure, financial restructuring, and adoption of a comprehensive business strategy, provides the following guidelines for others to emulate for business turnarounds.

- In a business downturn, understand, at the outset, the challenges and issues involved in it.
- Identify the need for change.
- Initiate time-bound change in the organizational structure and processes.
- Understand the required strategic and operational initiatives to turn around the organization.
- Understand the effect of such initiatives on the top-line (revenues) and the bottom-line (profits) of the company.
- Review the existing product portfolio and identify the need for change, if any, either by introducing new products or services, or by phasing out the existing products or services.
- Develop pricing and market segmentation strategies focusing on business growth and increase in profitability.

CASE QUESTION

Can the experience of Bajaj be replicated in each and every organization? Justify your answer.

Case Impact of Change in Organizational Culture

A major multinational company engaged itself in a purposeful process of cultural change. The company had a large number of female employees on its payroll. Although female employees were at par with male employees in terms of their performance track records, they were always being discriminated against. Female employees, therefore, wanted a meeting with the CEO of the company to complain about the discrimination. After a meeting with the CEO and subsequent discussions with the male managers, it was ultimately revealed that discrimination against female employees as well as other minorities was true. This problem was identified as conflict with espoused values. The company then developed an 'Aspiration Statement,' which included desired beliefs, attitudes, and behaviour. The statement specified the company's commitment to communication, ethical management practices, employee empowerment, and recognition for those who contribute to the mission of the company. These stated beliefs were further reinforced by training sessions on leadership, diversity, and ethics. The performance evaluation of employees became linked with the 'Aspiration Statement'. However, the experience of the company underscored the fact that change in organizational culture takes a long time.

CASE QUESTION

From this case, we find that the issue of gender neutrality and diversity can only be institutionalized through the purposeful process of cultural change. Indian software major Infosys also values diversity and emphasizes gender neutrality. Explain how Infosys was able to institutionalize a workplace diversity programme?

SUMMARY

- An *organization* is made of a group of people with some specific goals, objectives, and activities. Organization is also defined as the relations among the components of a system. *Organization structure* denotes the components and relations that bind people working within the organization. The three pillars of an organization are the people, the organization itself, and the technology.
- Systems theory has unearthed the process of understanding the complex world of systems. In organizations, systems theory is applied through systems analysis. It can identify certain commonalities in systems. Such commonalities, in fact, develop into certain well-accepted principles of systems for organizations.
- *Organizational cybernetics* emerged as a management systems approach by adopting cybernetic notions for the purpose of organizational and social management, especially by focusing on the viable system model (VSM).
- *Chaos theory* studies the complexity of the world to identify principles to understand organizations. The theory deals with the structure of turbulence, that is, the study of unpredictable complex systems.
- *Socio-technical systems thinking* suggests that the quality and the quantity of output in any work depend on two distinguishable aspects of the organization: the technological system and the social structure of the work system.
- The concept of system dynamics makes effective use of control theory and control engineering in management and decision making.
- Manufacturing systems are now inbuilt with self-regulating systems. Process- and people-integrated systems like total quality management (TQM) focus on delegation, total employee involvement, ownership, shared values, cross-functional teamwork, self-managed work teams, employee empowerment, etc.
- Organizational systems can be understood from prescriptive and normative perspectives. *Normative models* of business process reflect or establish standard ways of behaving. These values or norms set expectations for individuals and groups. *Prescriptive research-based models* make hypothetical claims that if certain conditions are met, then outcomes that are specified within the model will be achieved.
- *Business process re-engineering (BPR)* denotes documentation that guides a project team in defining the requirements of a new system.
- *Human resource information systems (HRIS)* comprises a range of computerized technology used to store, record, link, analyse, and present data about the human element within the organization.
- Effective organizational design depends on the interrelationships of systems principles, technology, environment, size, and organizational life cycle.

KEY TERMS

Business process re-engineering (BPR): BPR is a radical redesign of strategic, value-added business processes to achieve breakthrough performance improvements.

Butterfly effect: The butterfly effect refers to the discovery that in a chaotic system it is theoretically possible that a slight change would make no difference whatsoever, but when the system is unpredictable at a certain stage, the future may unfold quite differently, depending upon what little difference occurred.

Critical success factors (CSF): CSF analysis is a method to guide businesses in creating and measuring success. It is a reductionist method for going from an abstract vision to concrete requirements.

Human resource information systems (HRIS): HRIS comprises a range of computerized technology used to store, record, link, analyse, and present data about the human element within the organization.

Organizational design: Organizational design is the total pattern of structural elements and patterns that are used to manage the overall organization.

Socio-technical systems thinking: This theory suggests that the quality and the quantity of output in any work depend on two distinguishable aspects of the organization: the technological system and the social structure of the work system.

Systems dynamics (SD): This approach involves the use of the concepts and ideas of control theory and control engineering in management and decision making. SD is primarily oriented towards identifying (defining), modelling, and simulating a system in order to explicate how the system might behave under different policy regimes.

Viable system model (VSM): A system is said to be viable when it is able to effectively adapt to environmental changes, even if such changes are unforeseen. VSM consists of operation with embedded management and environment.

REVIEW QUESTIONS

1. Explain briefly the business process models for organizational structure and design.
2. Explain the systems view of organization. How does the systems view influence organizational structure and design?
3. Discuss the difference between *normative models* and *prescriptive models*.
4. How can the viable systems model and the socio-technical approach influence organizational structure and design?
5. What is *HRIS*? What are the key challenges before an organization for implementing HRIS in the HRD function?
6. Write short notes on:
   i. Open systems approach
   ii. Cybernetics
   iii. Bureaupathology
   iv. Situational variables in organizational design

CRITICAL THINKING QUESTIONS

1. You have been retained by a company engaged in the business of private life insurance. The company offers customized life insurance policies, keeping in view the changing needs of customers. 90 per cent of the life insurance policies so far sold by the company are customized in nature, while the residual 10 per cent are standard policies, conforming to their structured table. Lately, the company has started facing trouble in post-sales administration and operation, resulting in a serious setback in customer services. The company wants you to suggest a line of action.

2. Dhar Enterprises Limited manages its activities with standard operation procedures (SOP), which require protocol-bound behaviour. The company's marketing division always struggles through its nose to achieve targets. A strong internal audit team monitors all activities of the company. The marketing department's activities have now figured in a non-compliance with SOP list in spite of the department successfully achieving its targets. As an expert in organization systems and design, suggest the approach you will take to rectify this disorder.

REFERENCES

Beer, M., B. Spector, P. Lawrence, D. Quinn Mills and R. Walton (1984). *Managing Human Assets*. New York: Free Press.

Beer, S. (1979). *The Heart of Enterprise*. New York: John Wiley & Sons.

Burns, T. and G. Stalker (1961). *The Management of Innovation*. London: Tavistock Publications.

Deming, W. Edwards (1989). *Out of the Crisis*. Cambridge, MA: MIT Press.

Emery, F. E. and E. L. Trist (1965). 'The Causal Texture of Organizational Environments', *Human Relations*, 18, pp. 21–32.

Fombrun, C. J., N. Tichy and M. A. Devanna (1984). *Strategic Human Resource Management*. New York: John Wiley & Sons.

Forrester, K. W. (1958). 'Industrial Dynamics: A Major Breakthrough for Decision Makers', *Harvard Business Review*, 36, pp. 37–66.

Guest, D. E. (1987). 'Human Resource Management and Industrial Relations', *Journal of Management Studies*, 14 (5): pp. 503–521.

Hendry, C. and A. Pettigrew (1990). 'Human Resource Management: An Agenda for the 1990s', *International Journal of Human Resource Management*, 1 (3): pp. 17–43.

Herbst, P. G. (1974). *Socio-technical Design: Strategies in Multidisciplinary Research*. London: Tavistock Publications.

Kauffman, D. L. (1980). *Systems 1: An Introduction to Systems Thinking*. Minneapolis, MN: Future Systems, Inc., S. A. Carlton.

Legge, K. (1995). *Human Resource Management: Rhetorics and Realities*. London: Macmillan.

Likert, R. (1967). *The Human Organization*. New York: McGraw-Hill.

Noon, M. (1994). 'HRM: A Map, Model or Theory?', in P. Blyton and P. Turnbull (eds.), *Reassessing Human Resource Management*. London: Sage Publications.

Pinnington, A. and T. Edwards (2000). *Introduction to Human Resource Management*. London: Oxford University Press.

Quinn, R. and K. Cameron (1983). 'Organizational Life Cycles and Shifting Criteria of Effectiveness: Some Preliminary Evidence', *Management Science*, 29, pp. 33–41.

Rockart, John F. (1979). 'Chief Executives Define Their Own Data Needs', *Harvard Business Review*, 57 (2): pp. 81–93.

Stacey, R. (1996). *Complexity and Creativity in Organizations*. San Francisco, CA: Berrett-Koehler Publishers.

Thompson, Victor A. (1961). *Modern Organization*. New York: Alfred A. Knopf.

Torrington, D. and L. Hall (1998). *Human Resource Management*, 4th edition. London: Prentice Hall.

Trist, Eric and K. Bamforth (1951). 'Some Social and Psychological Consequences of the Longwall Method of Coal Getting', *Human Relations*, 4, pp. 3–38.

Tyson, S. (1995). *Human Resource Strategy: Towards a General Theory of HRM*. London: Pitman Publishing.

Weber, M. (1946). *From Max Weber: Essays in Sociology*, in H. H. Gerth and C. W. Mills (eds.). Oxford: Oxford University Press.

FURTHER READING

Allen, Louis A. (1958). *Management and Organization*. New York: McGraw-Hill.

Bhattacharyya, D. K. (2006). *Human Resource Management*, 2nd edition. New Delhi: Excel Books.

——— (2007). *Human Resource Research Methods*. New Delhi: Oxford University Press.

——— (2009). *Organizational Behaviour: Concepts and Applications*. New Delhi: Oxford University Press.

——— (2010). *Cross-cultural Management: Test and Cases*. New Delhi: PHI Learning.

Boone, Louis E. and David L. Kurtz (1992). *Management*. New York: McGraw-Hill.

Brown, Alvin (1945). *Organization: A Formulation of Principle*. Trenton, NJ: Hibbert Printing Company.

Emery, F. E. (1980). 'Designing Socio-technical System for Greenfield Sites', *Journal of Occupational Behaviour*, 1 (1): pp. 19–27.

Fombrum, C. J., N. M. Tichy and M. A. Devanna (1984). *Strategic Human Resource Management*. New York: John Wiley & Sons.

Hammer, Michael and James Champy (1993). *Reengineering the Corporation: A Manifesto for Business Revolution*. London: Nicholas Brealey Publishing.

Hilborn, Robert C. (2004). 'Sea Gulls, Butterflies, and Grasshoppers: A Brief History of the Butterfly Effect in Non-linear Dynamics', *American Journal of Physics*, 72, pp. 425–427.

Kanter, Rosabeth Moss (2001). *Evolve! Succeeding in the Digital Culture of Tomorrow*. Boston: Harvard Business Publishing.

Koontz, H. (1961). 'The Management Theory Jungle', *Academy of Management Journal*, 4 (3): pp. 174–188.

Martinsons, M. G. (1997). 'Human Resource Management Applications of Knowledge-based Systems', *International Journal of Information Management*, 17 (1): pp. 35–53.

Maturana, H. R. and F. J. Varela (1987). *The Tree of Knowledge: The Biological Roots of Human Understanding*. Boston, MA: Shambala.

Mintzberg, H. (1981). 'Organization Design: Fashion or Fit', *Harvard Business Review*, January–February, pp. 103–166.

Prigogine, I. and I. Stengers (1984). *Order out of Chaos: Man's New Dialogue with Nature*. London: Bantam Books.

Robbins, Stephen and Mary Coulter (2002). *Organizational Behaviour*. New Delhi: Pearson Education.

Roberts, Charlotte and Art Kleiner (1999). 'Five Kinds of Systems Thinking', in Peter M. Senge, Art Kleiner, Charlotte Roberts, George Roth, Rick Ross, and Bryan Smith, *The Dance of Change: The Challenges to Sustaining Momentum in Learning Organizations*. New York: Doubleday.

Rockhart, J. (1982). 'The Changing Role of Information Systems Executive: A Critical Success Factors Perspective', *Sloan Management Review*, 23 (1): pp. 3–13.

Stacey, R. D. (1993). 'Strategy As Order Emerging from Chaos', *Long Range Planning*, 26 (1): pp.10–17.

Thompson, James D. (2001). 'Organizations in Action', in J. M. Shafritz and J. S. Ott (eds.), *Classics of Organization Theory*. Fort Worth: Harcourt College Publishers.

Toffler, Alvin (1970). *Future Shock*. New York: Bantam Books.

Torrington, D. and L. Hall (1991). *Personnel Management: A New Approach*. Englewood Cliffs, NJ: Prentice Hall.

Tyson, S. (1997). 'Human Resource Strategy: A Process for Managing the Contribution of HRM to Organizational Performance', *International Journal of Human Resource Management*, 8 (3): pp. 277–290.

Waterman, R. (1988). *The Renewal Factor*. New York: Bantam Books.

——— (1990). *Adhocracy: The Power to Change*. Knoxville, TN: Whittle Direct Books.

14

Technology Management in Organizations

After going through this chapter, you will be able to understand:

- the concept of technology management and its various sociological issues
- the link between technology and innovation
- strategic technology management
- human resource management and technology management
- the process of technology planning and technology transfer
- various models of technology and their influence on organizational structure and design

Get a Competitive Edge Through Technology

Technology transfer and globalization are interconnected and interdependent. Theoretically, the increased level of technology transfer in the wake of globalization is attributed to technological determinism. *Determinism* is the philosophical proposition that views every event, one's behaviour and cognition, one's decisions, etc. as being causally determined by an unbroken chain of prior occurrences. Technological determinism describes the relationship between social and technological aspects. It considers technology to be either the cause of cultural change or the effect of cultural change. Technological determinism revolves around two general ideas:

1. The process of technological development follows a predictable and traceable path, which often cannot be linked to cultural influence.
2. The technology itself has inherent effects on society.

Technological determinism has been defined as an approach that identifies technology, or technological advances, as the central causal element in processes of social change. As technology is stabilized, its design tends to dictate users' behaviours, consequently diminishing human agency. With the advancement of technology, the pace of globalization has increased manifold. Countries across the globe are developing new products using technology in applications, processes, and services. It is also creating the compelling need to develop human resources by imparting new skills, knowledge, methods, and information.

Globalization has drastically improved access of technological latecomers to advanced technologies, and to the extent that technological upgrading is important for development, technology provides a unique opportunity for low-income countries to raise per capita income. Most theories of economic growth explain the persistent poverty in developing countries as being partly due to differences in technology between rich and poor countries.

INTRODUCTION

The term *technology* is often confused by the commercial and the industrial sectors. In the service sector, technology indicates information technology. In a manufacturing unit, technology means high-end machineries and equipments, which substitute the traditional manual work process. From another perspective, technology is considered to be a science and an outcome of firms' research and development initiatives. Chris Floyd in his *Managing Technology for Corporate Success* (1997) defined technology as 'the practical application of scientific or engineering knowledge to the conception, development, or application of products or offerings, processes or operations'. Floyd further argued that technology is important due to two critical reasons:

1. To achieve success in business by sustaining one's competitive position
2. To promote a culture of innovation through technology for long-term sustainability

By achieving the first objective, organizations can achieve product or service differentiation, reduce costs, develop new business opportunities, and facilitate and support strategic change. By differentiating products and services, an organization can sustain its market share in a fiercely competitive market. Similarly, cost reduction is achieved through technology. An organization achieves cost reduction both by acquiring new technology and by integrating it through mergers and acquisitions. For example, by acquiring Thomson's colour picture tube manufacturing technology and facilities, Videocon of India achieved significant cost advantage in its colour television (CTV) production, to remain a cost leader in the market. Likewise, technology also provides new business opportunities. Organizations use technology as a driver of new business. Globally, one knows of the case of Raychem, the leader in radiation chemistry. Using technology, the company successfully manipulated the physical properties of plastics, metals, and ceramics, leading to the introduction of memory metals, heat-resistant plastics, and specialized circuit-protection devices. In India, IFB Agro, a company that processes molasses to extract rectified spirit (used as core input in the liquor industry), by using a specialized effluent treatment plant (ETP), was able to commercially exploit carbon deposition and convert it into dry ice. Today, its dry ice plant generates more revenue than the mother business of rectified spirit.

The second objective recommends the use of technology as a lever for strategic change. Thomson's hiving off its colour picture tube manufacturing facilities to Videocon is basically considered a part of its strategic move to LCD and plasma technology in television sets manufacturing.

Thus, using technology as a driver for organizational change for both long-term and short-term objectives is now more of a strategic than just a technical issue. This, among other things, requires organizations to focus on people-related issues, considering the fact that technology is an ongoing process of change in an organization.

TECHNOLOGY MANAGEMENT

Technology management is the field of study that imparts skills and knowledge designed to improve the entire process of technological change. Technology not only enhances present competitive strength, but also creates opportunity for future growth of the entire organization. Thus, managing technology or technological change per se is an important area of concern for managers today. Managers, therefore, need to have the vision for any type of investment in technology.

Innovation and technology management are intertwined. *Innovation* translates creative ideas into new products and services, which enhance the competitive advantage for an organization. *Technology* is the skill, knowledge, experience, tools, machines, computers, and equipment used in the design, production, and distribution of goods and services. Integrating innovation with technology ensures the application of technological change to products and organizations.

Some definitions of technology attribute innovation to a change in technology. Organizations need to manage technology effectively, integrating the human factors. The outcome of effective technology management is successful technological change, which enables the organization to use technology as their key driver to competitive advantage.

Issues in Technology Management

Organizational technology issues encompass many concepts. These are briefly discussed here.

Sociological issues

The sociological aspect of technology management considers technology to be the outcome of social processes, involving technology adopters (organization) and others (stakeholders) who are affected by the prevailing culture, political beliefs, and strategies. To effectively ensure technological change, the sociological approach suggests agreement on the social context and communication. Thus, the approach recommends emphasis on innovation, communication, considering technology as a social system, and adopting technological change gradually over a period of time.

Innovation The main attributes of innovative technologies are relative advantage, compatibility, complexity, trial, and observation. *Relative advantage* is the quantitative or qualitative measurement of innovation to understand the degree of change between the past innovation and the present innovation. If the present innovation is better, it receives acceptance from stakeholders and the organization also succeeds by ensuring quick adoption. *Compatibility* of innovation studies the degree of consistency with the corporate value systems, past experiences, habits, and the needs of the stakeholders. High compatibility ensures successful adoption, while low compatibility makes the acceptance slower and even disrupts organizational intent to achieve excellence through technology. *Complexity* in innovation arises due to difficulty in understanding and lack of user-friendliness. More the complexity, slower is the acceptance. The innovation is put on *trial* through pilot testing to reduce any possible risk due to technological change. A successful trial can ensure acceptance as people understand the outcome better. *Observation* is the degree of visibility of the outcome of technological change. Higher the degree of observation, better the degree of acceptance.

Communication In any technological change, communication is the most important aspect. Selecting the appropriate communication channels to carry the message to the receiver is a strategic decision of the organization. In any process of change, this is very important. Whatever may be the communication channel, more emphasis should be given to awareness. During processes of technological change, or processes of general change, many organizations emphasize this aspect by increasing the level of face-to-face communication, by putting aside executives' time for the purpose of talking to people, by clarifying their doubts, etc.

Social system The social system in the form of norms, opinion leaders, change agents, culture, political beliefs, laws, policies, etc. sets the boundaries of innovation, within which technological change can be made by the organization. Incompatibility of innovation with the social system leads to poor acceptance.

Time Although technological change should ideally be introduced in an organization in a gradual manner, often this may defeat the purpose, because slowing the process of change will reduce the opportunity of the organization to sustain its competitive advantage. Therefore, the process of change should be appropriately timed, understanding the degree of adaptability of the people.

Organization structure and design

Technology influences organizational structure and design. Technology alters production processes, systems, and even skill sets of employees. It often redefines the roles of workers and employees as supplements to the production process. Such aspects require changes in the organizational structure. For example, in many manufacturing organizations, the production process is such that it empowers workers as independent process owners, so much so that they themselves control their own jobs and require no supervision. The different models of technology discussed later elaborate on structure and design issues.

Economic issues

In economics, technological change is considered from the point of feasibility in production. John R. Hicks (1932) considers a technological change to be Hicks-neutral when the ratio of capital's marginal product to labour's marginal product remains unchanged. Following Hicks, there were two more bifurcations of this concept of economic neutrality—Harrod-neutral (1948) and Solow-neutral (1956). A technological change is Harrod-neutral if technology is labour augmenting, that is, it benefits labour; it is Solow-neutral if technology is capital augmenting, that is, it benefits capital (investor).

Strategic Technology Management

There are three fundamental areas of practices that facilitate technological change in organizations. First, organizations decide to work differently by quantitative assessment of performance, benchmarking against the best practices and duly appreciating the stakeholders' needs. Second, they direct their scarce resources towards high-value uses by re-engineering critical functions and carefully controlling and evaluating expenditure through specific performance and cost measures. Third, they support major cost reduction and service improvement efforts with up-to-date professional skills and organizational roles and responsibilities required to do the job. Managers ensure this by following certain steps known as strategic technology management initiatives. These steps are:

1. Recognize and communicate the urgency to change technology
2. Get line management involved and create ownership
3. Take action and maintain momentum
4. Anchor strategic planning in customer needs and mission goals
5. Measure the performance of key mission delivery processes
6. Focus on process improvement in the context of technology
7. Manage technology as investments

8. Integrate the planning, budgeting, and evaluation processes
9. Establish customer/supplier relationships between line and technology vendors
10. Position a chief technology officer to review and manage the process of technological change
11. Upgrade skills and knowledge of line professionals

Strategic technology management requires the involvement and commitment of the top leadership. The top leadership should not only define business goals but also initiate, mandate, and facilitate major changes in the technology to support the achievement of the goals. They must appreciate the cost–benefit and risk–return trade-offs associated with technology investments. It is also important to understand that new technology, per se, cannot improve the business performance. New technology is a powerful tool to support work processes and business decisions. Hence, if the existing work process itself is inefficient, then technology cannot provide substantive impact. Accomplishing dramatic improvements in performance usually requires streamlining or fundamentally redesigning existing work processes. Information technology projects must then become focused on improving the way work is done rather than simply automating existing outmoded processes.

Human Resource Management and Technology Management

Human resource management (HRM) has been defined as the process of 'attracting, developing, and maintaining a talented and energetic workforce to support organizational mission, objectives and strategies' (Schermerhorn 2001). D. B. Audretsch and A. R. Thurik (2001) argue that effective HRM practices are becoming increasingly important in the new 'knowledge-based' economy, as companies face the double challenge of the need for more highly trained employees and the shortage of qualified labour.

The HR practices considered for technology management especially focus on the areas of:

- Human resource planning
- Systematic recruitment and selection
- Training and development programmes
- Written job description
- Regular performance appraisal
- Growth plans and strategies
- Management techniques (for example, continuous improvement through total quality management, benchmarking, etc.)

Technology and Organizational Operations

The six areas of organizational operations particularly affected by technology are: (1) designs and engineering, (2) processing fabrication and assembly, (3) automated material handling, (4) inspection, (5) integration and control, and (6) network communications.

Designs and engineering

Changes in the designs and engineering function of an organization are enforced through the following technological reinforcements:

- Computer-aided design/engineering (CAD/CAE)
- Computer-aided design/manufacturing (CAD/CAM)
- Modelling or simulation technologies

Processing fabrication and assembly

In processing fabrication and assembly jobs, the following technological inputs are put into use:

- Flexible manufacturing cells or systems (FMC/FMS)
- Programmable logic control (PLC) machine/s or process/es
- Lasers used in materials processing (including surface modification)
- Robot/s with sensing capabilities
- Robot/s without sensing capabilities

High-speed machining

For achieving operational efficiency, high-speed machining is now considered to be the most significant thrust area for an organization. High-speed machining is ensured through the following technologies:

- Automated material handling
- Part identification for manufacturing automation, like barcoding
- Automated storage and retrieval system (AS/RS)

Inspection

Inspection and quality checks are essential for every organization to sustain their competitive strengths. Technologies that facilitate this are:

- Automated vision-based systems used for inspection/testing of inputs and/or final products
- Other automated sensor-based systems used for inspection/testing of inputs and/or final products

Integration and control

Integration and control, on the one hand, facilitate alignment with the organizational business goals and objectives, and on the other hand, ensure timely intervention to correct any deviation from the plan. Integration and control functions are enforced through the following technologies:

- Manufacturing resource planning (MRP II)/enterprise resource planning (ERP)
- Computer/s used for control on the factory floor
- Computer-integrated manufacturing (CIM)
- Supervisory control and data acquisition (SCADA)
- Use of inspection data in manufacturing control
- Digital remote-controlled process plant control

Network communications

Effective network communications facilitate better coordination and enforce efficiency in organizational activities. Technologies that are used in network communications are:

- Local area network (LAN) for engineering/production
- Company-wide computer networks (including intranet and wide area network [WAN])
- Inter-company computer networks (including extranet and electronic data interchange [EDI])

It is clear that technologies are not just limited to the production and operation functions of an organization, but even extend to other areas including the managerial and strategic functions. Therefore, technology should be considered as an important driver for organizational growth and efficiency.

Implementing technological change is only possible with appropriate HR intervention and with a focus on human resource development issues.

While technology may increase productivity and efficiency, it can also have a negative effect on employees, who may feel trapped, alienated, overworked, and vulnerable, according to a study by Chartered Institute of Personnel and Development (CIPD) (Parry et al. 2007) in the United Kingdom. As per the CIPD report, new technologies may alienate workers because the lack of face-to-face interaction can increase work intensity, de-skill manual labour by replacing traditional skills, increase surveillance and control through electronic monitoring, and create health and safety problems such as eye strain, backaches, and repetitive motion injuries. CIPD, therefore, suggests getting HR help in the design and implementation of new technologies. This will also ensure that employees are proactive in bringing about the process of change.

TECHNOLOGY PLANNING

A *technology plan* serves as a bridge between established standards and organizational practice. It articulates, organizes, and integrates the content and processes of operation in appropriate technologies. It facilitates multiple levels of strategy, policy, and decision making, and allows for resource allocations. Technology planning is an ongoing process and it translates organizational policy and technology needs into concrete actions. It allows organizations to take advantage of technology innovations while minimizing the negative impact of unexpected challenges. Technology planning provides a road map for the implementation of technology and can result in more efficient expenditure of limited resources and an improvement in organizational performance.

However, a technology plan by itself is not enough to ensure change. It is the processes of development, implementation, and evaluation of a technology plan which are considered as essential components of the organizational improvement plan. A well-designed technology plan is a dynamic tool providing guidance for innovation. Technology plans also represent opportunities for dialogue and professional development that encourage organizational decision making.

The first step in technology planning is to select a planning model and then move the process forward. It is considered most useful when it is used within a larger planning process and not simply as an add-on or a one-time discussion. According to C. E. Hopey and J. Harvey-Morgan (1995), a good technology planning process can be summed up in six basic principles.

1. It should be organized and considered a continuous process. It should use a simple and straightforward planning model, and result in a document that clarifies how technology is used for operation, management, assessment, and communications. Organizations do this by taking into account their mission and philosophy, and the prevailing systems and processes.
2. It should be broad but realistic in scope, with economical and technically feasible solutions.
3. It should involve all the stakeholders and technology experts.
4. It should identify the strengths and weaknesses of the organization and also assess how each will impact the implementation of technology.
5. It should formalize the procedures and methods for making technology decisions, including the setting of priorities and the purchase, evaluation, upgrading, and use of technology.
6. It should be driven by organizational goals and objectives rather than by technological developments.

TECHNOLOGY INNOVATION

Technological innovation in an organization leads to increased productivity, quality, sustainability, etc. The pace of technological innovation can be influenced by HR interventions. The HR, as an intermediary, influences technological innovation, raising the bar for employees' competencies, commitment, organizational learning, cohesiveness, etc. Successful innovation requires (bundles of) specific personnel and organizational interventions or practices. Definitions of innovation include the process of making improvements by introducing something new, such as a new idea, method, or device, or the successful exploitation of new ideas that create a new dimension of performance. In economics, the change must increase value—customer value or producer value. Innovations are intended to make someone better off and a succession of many innovations help in the growth of the whole economy. The term *innovation* may refer to both radical and incremental changes to products, processes, or services, and also to solving a problem through technology innovation. Innovation is an important topic in the study of economics, business, technology, sociology, and engineering. Since innovation is considered to be a major driver of the economy, the factors that lead to innovation are also considered to be critical to policymakers. In the organizational context, innovation is linked to performance and growth through improvements in efficiency, productivity, quality, competitive positioning, market share, etc. All organizations can innovate. However, while innovation typically adds value, innovation may also have a negative or destructive effect as new developments clear away or change old organizational forms and practices. Those organizations that embrace innovation may destroy themselves if they do not innovate effectively, whether they are large or small.

TECHNOLOGY TRANSFER

Technology transfer is a term used to describe a formal transferring of new discoveries and innovations, resulting from scientific research conducted at universities, to the commercial sector. One way that universities transfer technology is through patenting and licensing new innovations. The major steps in this process include:

1. The disclosure of innovations
2. Patenting the innovation concurrent with publication of the scientific research
3. Licensing the rights to innovations to industries for commercial development

Technology transfer is the process by which basic technologies are developed into practical and commercially relevant applications and products. It evaluates and manages invention portfolios, oversees patent prosecution, and negotiates licensing agreements. Technology transfer activities include processing and evaluating invention disclosures; filing for patents; technology marketing; licensing; protecting intellectual property arising from research activity; and assisting in creating new businesses and promoting the success of existing firms. The result of these activities will be new products, more high-quality jobs, and an expanded economy. The important elements of technology transfer functions can be listed as follows:

- **Coordinate**: Coordinating between technology users and developers and between researchers and manufacturers is an important element of technology transfer. Access to relevant internal and external resources for individual projects and enterprises improves coordination.

- **Nurture**: Proper nurturing moves technology from a research stage to organization, thereby, providing new business opportunities and entrepreneurship avenues. An effective process of nurturing provides guidance, counselling, and resources.
- **Link**: At this stage, technology transfer catalogues resources related to business enterprises and groups them, and connects future entrepreneurs and researchers and other technology developers to help in the process of starting new products, companies, etc. Such linkages provide referrals for individual business counselling as well as sources of financing or the names of individuals who can help with a particular facet of business development.

TECHNOLOGY AND ORGANIZATIONAL DESIGN

Technology as a situational factor of organizational design has already been focused on in earlier chapters. Here, some specific models that suggest the consideration of technology factors as a situational variable for organizational design will be discussed. Technology is the outcome of knowledge, equipments, and work process used by organizations. Hence, it should not be just construed as machines and equipments. Technology is a major factor behind the improvement in quantity and quality of work. The type of technology selected by an organization is an important determinant of organizational design and structure.

Thompson's Model

James Thompson (1967) developed three classifications for technology: (1) intensive technology, (2) mediating technology, and (3) long-linked technology.

Intensive technology is developed keeping in view a high level of uncertainty. It helps to produce the desired outcomes even in uncertain situations. For example, one particular organization makes use of traditional dedicated technology for production of certain items such as long-playing record players. However, one sees that customers suddenly change their tastes and preferences, and switch to the use of CDs or DVDs. This will render long-playing records obsolete. The organization will also suffer, as it will not be possible to salvage their earlier investments in technology. If the organization had made use of intensive technology like flexible technology and computer numeric control (CNC), this situation of technological obsolescence would have been avoided. Intensive technology also makes workers interdependent and creative. They become capable of solving their work-related problems. With intensive technology, organizations become flexible in decision making, rather than being encumbered by decisions that are bound by standard operating procedures (SOP). Members then resolve their work issues through mutual coordination.

Mediating technology brings together individuals and/or groups to seek a mutually beneficial exchange of values. This form of technological environment is more applicable in the service industry like banks and financial institutions.

Long-linked technology is appropriate for mass-production processes like automobile assembly lines. It depends on highly specialized tasks in a closely controlled sequence of activities to produce the final product.

Thompson's model, hence, argues that each type of technology has specific bearings on the design and structure of organizations.

Woodward's Technologies

Joan Woodward (1965) and her team of researchers studied about 100 organizations in England in the 1960s, to establish the linkage between the size and the structure of the organization. However, they could not establish any such relationship. In their follow-up study, they could find some relationship between the structure and three basic forms of technology, which they categorized as small-batch production technology, long-batch or mass production technology, and continuous-process production technology.

Small-batch production technology is suitable for production of a few varieties of products to meet the specific requirements of customers. Such customized production facilities are generally created by organizations to cater to the specialized demands of the defence sector. In some cases, organizations demand initial technology development cost from the customers, as they dedicate such investments towards meeting customer-specific demands.

Long-batch or mass production technology is used for producing a large volume of standardized products to cater to the demands of large markets. Such organizations automate or mechanize their production facilities, rendering workers as complements to the equipment. This type of technology helps in handling large volumes of production of high-quality goods, which may require dangerous or even monotonous operations. A good example is the technology used for automobile assembly lines.

Continuous-process production technology is a complete mechanized form of production process where machines undertake all the jobs, leaving the people involved to focus on quality inspection and adjustment, monitoring, etc. Most of the chemical processing units like petroleum refineries, chemical plants, and nuclear power plants make use of such technology, where production and processing continue uninterruptedly.

Woodward and her associates termed the differences in the three production technologies 'technical complexity'. From the point of view of organizational design, differences in technology have different connotations. For example, more complex technology (like continuous-process production technology) creates tall organization structures that require more supervision and coordination. Similarly, the span of management of lower-level managers increases from small-batch to mass production technology, while it decreases from mass to continuous-process production technology. Similarly, with more technological complexity, support staff functions increase and organizations become top-heavy (more managers).

Case Innovation in Customer Services of Ford Motors

The Ford Motor Company's ethos is *kaizen,* the famous Japanese approach that believes in never-ending improvement. This ethos of the company is evident in every produced item—Ford, Mazda, Jaguar, Land Rover, Volvo, and all its passenger and light commercial vehicles. 'Value-for-money motoring' is what the company believes in, and this is its mantra for customer retention. However, with increased competition from new players in the market, the company has to look at cost-effectiveness as well.

The first thing that the company came out with was a three-year 100,000 km free maintenance plan for all Ford cars. This innovative maintenance plan was introduced by the company by separating the management and administration from the main streams of production. The maintenance agency of Ford provides the service of Ford cars during the three-year warranty period.

This innovative solution for beating the market competition through price efficiency and customer retention became possible due to the arrangement of vehicle repairs and services through the dealer, who obtained the authority to go ahead with the work with a customer's telephone call to the call centre. The dealer who executes the maintenance work is paid within a cycle time (time required to complete a job from start to finish) of 30 to 90 days, after the electronic receipt of the invoice. The uniqueness of this system is that the dealer does not require any authorization except the first call received from the call centre. The dealer is then required to enter minimum information after logging on to the Web site of the company. The system is so designed that automatic validation for service authorization is received by the dealer online. As the transaction is made through the company Web site, the dealer does not need to submit any service invoice. The electronic 'closed' invoices automatically join an invoice payment queue. Payments to dealers are made on a weekly basis to ensure balanced cash flow in a dealer's account. Thus, the automatic authorization of maintenance reduces the cycle time for handling customer services for any maintenance problem within the period of three years, and at the same time avoids unnecessary wastage in phone calls and paper transaction, ultimately leading to substantial cost savings and increased customer retention.

From the customers' point of view, a three-year maintenance warranty is automatic cost control and is also an indication of the inbuilt quality. Further, it erases the perception that Ford is expensive. With improved relationships with customers, their retention also increases and they become brand loyal. Customers also get the best resale value as the full service history is available with the dealer. What is more unique is that the unexpired part of the free warranty period can be sold, to give additional resale value to the vehicle. Such an innovative arrangement strengthened Ford's brand promise with regard to the quality and longevity of vehicles. Thus, the innovative customer services of Ford Motors became one of the most critical strategic moves by the company to survive in an environment of competition and price war.

CASE QUESTION

Study the case of Ford Motors and critically comment on how innovation in customer services enabled Ford to leapfrog the competition.

SUMMARY

- *Technology* is the skill, knowledge, experience, tools, machines, computers, and equipment used in the design, production, and distribution of goods and services. Technology is important to achieve success in business and also to promote innovation. Technology not only enhances present competitive strength but also creates opportunities for the growth of any organization.
- Innovation and technology management are intertwined. *Innovation* translates creative ideas into new products and services, which enhance the competitive advantage for an organization. By integrating innovation with technology, one ensures the application of technological change to products and organizations.
- Sociological issues in technology management consider technology to be the outcome of social processes, involving technology adopters (organization) and others (stakeholders) who are affected by the prevailing culture, political beliefs, and strategies.
- In any technological change, communication is the most important aspect. Selecting the appropriate communication channels to carry the message to the receiver is a strategic decision of the organization.

- Technology also influences organizational structure and design. Technology alters production processes, systems, and even skill sets of employees. It often redefines the role of workers and employees as supplements to the production process. In economics, technological change is considered from the point of feasibility in production.
- There are three fundamental areas of practices that facilitate technological change. First, organizations decide to work differently by quantitative assessment of performance, benchmarking against the best practices and duly appreciating the stakeholders' needs. Second, they direct their scarce resources towards high-value uses by re-engineering critical functions and carefully controlling and evaluating expenditure through specific performance and cost measures. Third, they support major cost reduction and service improvement efforts with up-to-date professional skills and organizational roles and responsibilities required to do the job.
- A *technology plan* serves as a bridge between established standards and organizational practice. It articulates, organizes, and integrates the content and processes of operation in appropriate technologies. It facilitates multiple levels of strategy, policy, and decision making, and allows for resource allocations.
- The process of *technology transfer* describes a formal transferring of new discoveries and innovations, resulting from scientific research conducted at universities, to the commercial sector.
- Both Thompson and Woodward try to establish the linkage between the size and the structure of organizations through their models. However, they could only find some relationships between the structure of an organization and the basic forms of technology.

KEY TERMS

Innovation: Innovation refers to both radical and incremental changes to products, processes, or services, and also to solving a problem through technology innovation.

Technological determinism: It has been defined as an approach that identifies technology, or technological advances, as the central causal element in processes of social change.

Technology management: It is the field of study that imparts skills and knowledge designed to improve the entire process of technological change.

Technology plan: A technology plan serves as a bridge between established standards and organizational practice. It articulates, organizes, and integrates the content and processes of operation in appropriate technologies.

Technology transfer: It describes a formal transferring of new discoveries and innovations, resulting from scientific research conducted at universities, to the commercial sector.

REVIEW QUESTIONS

1. Explain how technology benefits an organization with some live case examples.
2. Explain why we need to understand technology management.
3. What are the *sociological issues* involved in technology management?
4. Explain how HR issues integrate with technology management?
5. What is *technology planning*? How it is done in an organization?

6. Explain the important elements of technology transfer.
7. Write short notes on:
   i. Innovation
   ii. Technology transfer
   iii. Technology planning
   iv. Technology management
   v. Economic issues of technology management

CRITICAL THINKING QUESTIONS

1. Your organization is a well-known technology provider in the country. You look after the technology transfer protocols. Your organization believes that technology transfer should not be absolute and outright. For one of your clients, your company has assigned you the task of drafting a technology transfer agreement. Draft the agreement keeping these guidelines in mind.
2. It is now accepted that technology issues have HR ramifications. Select a particular organization and study how the HR of that organization participates in technology-related decisions. Develop your report accordingly.

REFERENCES

Audretsch, D. B. and A. R. Thurik (2001). 'What Is New about the New Economy: Sources of Growth in the Managed and Entrepreneurial Economies', *Industrial and Corporate Change*, 10, pp. 267–315.

Floyd, Chris (1997). *Managing Technology for Corporate Success*. London: Gower Publishing Ltd.

Harrod, R. F. (1948). *Towards a Dynamic Economics: Some Recent Developments of Economic Theory and their Application to Policy*. London: Macmillan.

Hicks, John R. (1932). *The Theory of Wages*. London: Macmillan.

Hopey, C. E. and J. Harvey-Morgan (1995). *Technology Planning in Adult Literacy* (*Practice Guide no. PG95-02*). Philadelphia, PA: University of Pennsylvania, National Center on Adult Literacy.

Parry, Emma, Shaun Tyson, Doone Selbie and Raymond Kenneth Leighton (2007). *HR and Technology: Impact and Advantages*. London: Chartered Institute of Personnel and Development (CIPD).

Schermerhorn, J. R. (2001). *Management Update 2001*, 6th edition. New York: John Wiley & Sons.

Solow, Robert M. (1956). 'A Contribution to the Theory of Economic Growth', *Quarterly Journal of Economics*, 70, pp. 65–94.

Thompson, James (1967). *Organizations in Action*. New York: McGraw-Hill.

Woodward, Joan (1965). *Industrial Organization: Theory and Practice*. London: Oxford University Press.

FURTHER READING

Bhattacharyya, D. K. (2007). *Human Resource Research Methods*. New Delhi: Oxford University Press.

——— (2009). *Manpower Development for Technological Change*. New Delhi: Excel Books.

Entorf, Horst and Francis Kramarz (1998). 'The Impact of New Technologies on Wages and Skills: Lessons from Matching Data on Employees and on Their Firms', *Economics of Innovation and New Technology*, 5 (2–4): pp. 165–97.

Huselid, Mark A. (1995). 'The Impact of Human Resource Management Practices on Turnover, Productivity, and Corporate Financial Performance', *Academy of Management Journal*, 38 (3): pp. 635–672.

Ichniowski, Casey, Kathryn Shaw and Gabrielle Prennushi (1997). 'The Effects of Human Resource Management Practices on Productivity', *American Economic Review*, 87 (3): pp. 291–313.

Kuhn, Thomas Samuel (1996). *The Structure of Scientific Revolutions*, 3rd edition. Chicago, IL: University of Chicago Press.

Milgrom, Paul and John Roberts (1995). 'Complementarities and Fit: Strategy, Structure and Organizational Change in Manufacturing', *Journal of Accounting and Economics*, 19, pp. 179–208.

Postman, Neil (1998). *Five Things We Need to Know About Technological Change*. Available at http://itrs.scu.edu/tshanks/pages/Comm12/12Postman.htm. Last accessed on 28 June 2009.

Rogers, Everett (2003). *Diffusion of Innovations*, 5th edition. New York: Free Press.

Zuboff, Shoshana (1988). *In the Age of the Smart Machine: The Future of Work and Power*. New York: Basic Books.

15

Globalization and Business Organizations

After going through this chapter, you will be able to understand:

- the debate on globalization
- the process of development of globalization
- the important players in globalization
- the challenges of globalization for managers
- the different types of approaches to globalization
- globalization and international marketing
- interrelations between globalization and culture
- globalization and talent management

Operate Globally but Manage Culturally

It is said that each nation responds to cultural globalization differently. McDonald's may have proliferated around the world but the ingredients vary to fit in with local customs (from shrimp burgers in Japan to kosher burgers for Jewish customers). Its consumers belong to the working class or the middle class depending on the location, and eating customs vary from fast to leisurely in different contexts. From France to parts of the Middle East, not everyone responds positively to the globalization of what is understood as American culture. In fact, a retreat to fundamentalism and greater rather than lesser nationalism are seen to be notable reactions to globalization in some places (Robbins 1997). It is noteworthy, too, that it is the culture of one nation, America, that is often talked about in relation to cultural globalization, as much as culture originating from all around the world (Beck et al. 2003). There have even been well-known predictions of clashes of culture arising from globalization, against hyper-globalist assumptions about the homogenization or hybridization of culture (Barber 1996; Huntington 1996). However such clashes, insofar as they are real, may have more to do with economic interests and foreign policy rather than culture. Ideas of civilization clashes often over-homogenize cultures and have the effect of demonizing cultures and provoking clashes as much as accurately analysing the world. Sceptics like Paul Q. Hirst and Grahame Thompson (1996) would not want to have too much to do with the suggestion of a clash of civilizations. Nevertheless, such perspectives are amongst those that are sceptical about the growth of a globalized culture.

INTRODUCTION

Organizations around the world are now a part of the global economy. They are engaged in business across borders and linking economies together into a more interconnected world. From a business perspective, globalization raises some issues that have economic and managerial significance, for example, whether globalization affects the economic sovereignty of poor nations, whether it is a threat to jobs, whether it is helping to overcome poverty or creating more poverty, and whether the changes arising from globalization can be managed both at the national and the organizational levels. Another important issue is the ways in which globalization affects domestic organizations. Globalization has already brought unprecedented improvements in material welfare for billions of people. It offers unparallel opportunities to raise living standards across the world. Yet, it is also true that the disparity between the rich and the poor is still too wide. Many attribute this to globalization. To understand such issues and the overall impact of globalization on people and national economies, it is necessary to study this subject.

GLOBALIZATION

Globalization is a phenomenon of cross-border social, cultural, and technological exchange. It is the process of cross-sectoral and international interaction particularly in financial and business spheres, where market economics combined with advances in science and technology have subsumed the entire world into one increasingly integrated system with profound cultural, environmental, and societal implications.

The sociologist Anthony Giddens (1971) defines globalization as a decoupling of space and time, emphasizing that with instantaneous communication, knowledge and culture can be shared around the world simultaneously. Ruud Lubbers (2005), a Dutch academic, defines it as a process in which geographic distance becomes a factor of diminishing importance in the establishment and maintenance of cross-border economic, political, and sociocultural relations. Left critics of globalization define the word quite differently, presenting it as a worldwide drive towards a globalized economic system dominated by supranational corporate trade and banking institutions that are not accountable to democratic processes or national governments. Globalization is an undeniably capitalist process. It has taken off as a concept in the wake of the collapse of the Soviet Union and socialism, as a viable alternate form of economic organization.

Debate on Globalization

Globalization has captured public attention and sparked a debate globally. Issues in the debate cluster around the following areas:

- **Increase in the gap between the rich and the poor**: Globalization has changed the dynamics of the international market. Rich countries by virtue of resource acquisition dominate the world market, leaving behind the poor countries. Even the open market mechanism cannot protect the interests of poor countries. As a result, the gap between the rich and the poor countries widens. As its cascading effect, inequality spreads amongst the people in poor countries.
- **Exploitation of labour**: Globalization has increased the spate of movement of goods, services, and capital. However, cross-country movement of people has not increased proportionally. Wherever movement of labour took place, there are enough evidences to show that the migrant labour have been treated unequally. Globalization is viewed critically due to such cross-border exploitation of labour.

- **Lack of transparency and accountability**: With globalization, multinational and transnational organizations are spreading their business internationally. Such global organizations are socially responsive and comply with business ethics in their own countries. However, in other countries, these organizations often engulf themselves in the veil of secrecy, even violating business ethics and failing to be socially responsive. Such differences in business practices are viewed critically.
- **Dilution of values and the local culture**: On the grounds of business imperative, global organizations with their product and service homogenization dilute the values and the culture of the countries where they go. For example, the term 'McDonaldization of culture' has come into being due to McDonald's fast food products (burgers, etc.) transforming the food habits of people in many countries including India.
- **Violation of environmental regulations**: In the process of globalization, many organizations have violated environment-related regulations. Many host countries, including India, now face such problems from global organizations. This is due to the organizations' obvious focus on short-term profit or business gain, without bothering about the adverse effects on the biosphere of the host countries.
- **Increase in civil strife and violence**: Globalization often sparks ethnic conflict, civil strife, militancy, etc., which defeat the purpose of economic advantages.

Benefits of Globalization

The school of thought that advocates the benefits of globalization has different views on globalization. According to the proponents of these views, globalization brings prosperity to the world through shared resources and ideas. Thus, the various benefits of globalization are:

- **Globalization and worldwide economic activity**: Globalization facilitates the creation of open markets, competition, and the free flow of goods, services, capital, and knowledge. Thus, consumers across the world become the principal beneficiary. Due to new technology and cheaper imports, globalization makes the world economy more efficient and creates new job opportunities, particularly in developing countries.
- **Globalization and national sovereignty**: Due to globalization, the sovereignty of a nation is not abandoned but shared. Even the degree of such sharing is minimal; it is far less than one's normal expectations. The sovereignty of the European Economic Community (EEC) member countries is a case in point. Globalization is a process, not a programme driven by one country or a group of countries.
- **Globalization and global rules**: Since globalization requires developing a framework of rules to bring global economic order, it relatively benefits the economically poor countries. Secured market access for foreign goods and services, protection of intellectual property rights and foreign investment, more reliance on free enterprise, open markets, and more competition, etc., have reduced the need for detailed country-specific government regulations. Rather, the international economic order sustained by international organizations like World Trade Organization (WTO), EEC, North Atlantic Treaty Organization (NATO), and International Monetary Fund (IMF), and by various voluntary agreements and business self-regulation is more effective in framing the rules of global trade which benefit all.
- **Globalization and the gap between the rich and the poor**: Pro-globalization believers say globalization raises the standard of living of the poor globally. Subsequent research also establishes that when income data are adjusted to reflect purchasing power, income inequality between rich and

poor countries also diminishes. Globalization cannot be a standalone solution to global poverty, but it is certainly one of the strategies of eradicating poverty, leveraging the strength of the international community rather than depending only on the national potential of the poor countries.

- **Globalization and information technologies**: One of the key drivers of globalization is information technology (IT). IT opens up huge potential for greater efficiency of organizations through e-commerce, the Internet, and real-time information sharing, anywhere in the world and at any time. IT also enhances access to information and knowledge; two valuable inputs that facilitate product and service innovation and reduce cost. Therefore, IT directly benefits consumers across the world, and proliferation of IT is greatly aided by the process of globalization.
- **Globalization, multinationals, smaller firms, and consumers**: Globalization benefits innovative and competitive organizations, whether small or large. While global companies enter local markets, local companies also enter global markets. Such market penetration increases product quality, widens the range of available goods and services, and reduces the prices. All cross-sections of consumers benefit from the process of globalization. Therefore, globalization benefits all, be it multinationals, small organizations, or consumers.
- **Globalization and financial stability**: Globalization increases capital mobility and also ensures optimum allocation of savings and investment resources across countries through the integration of currency, bond, and stock markets. Capital mobility ensures transfer of technology and production to locations where comparative advantages are the highest. Thus, through capital mobility and cross-country allocation of financial resources, globalization increases financial stability across the globe.
- **Globalization and the environment**: Globalization can promote environmental protection at global, regional, national, and local levels. This is possible firstly by relating the terms of reference for global trade with environmental issues and secondly through voluntary environment protection initiatives by organizations. Moreover, increased trade and investment promote opportunities to exchange more environment-friendly technologies, share good practices, and contribute to building the environmental capacity, particularly in developing countries.
- **Globalization and cultural diversity**: By integrating markets and making products and services available universally, globalization actually creates more diversity, increasing the choice for consumers. This results in greater cultural freedom as customers now have a wider range of choices.
- **Globalization and the WTO**: WTO is promoting the cause of globalization by introducing a rules-based international system to promote more open trade and investment worldwide. In fact, WTO is bringing discipline in international trade so that all the member countries can derive the benefits of globalization.
- **Globalization and labour standards**: Pro-globalization advocates believe that globalization creates new job opportunities in poor countries and raises their labour standards. There is no doubt that after becoming a WTO member country, China has put emphasis on enhancing their labour standards by rectifying many International Labour Organization (ILO) resolutions. On their own, they have also streamlined their labour standards. Abolition of child labour and right to organize are some issues to which all WTO member countries need to subscribe.
- **Globalization and human rights**: Globalization also protects human rights, with human rights issues becoming part of trade agreements between partnering countries. WTO, European Union (EU), and NATO are all vocal on human rights issues. Trade concessions are suspended for countries breaching human rights. Democracy and respect for humanity are two necessary preconditions to attract foreign direct investment.

- **Globalization and the poorest nations**: Globalization benefits the poorest nations, as it stimulates entrepreneurship when such nations get the essential implements of business—finance and technical know-how—from economically advanced countries. The poorest countries get preferential access to export markets and also a debt waiver or reduction, which set the pace for their economic growth.
- **Globalization and employment**: Globalization creates jobs in developing countries but this is not at the expense of jobs in advanced countries. If at all any job reduction takes place in the latter, it is primarily attributable to reasons other than globalization. For example, in Europe the nature of unemployment is structural. In some cases, however, a marginal part of unemployment in industrially advanced countries during the post-globalization phase is attributable to lack of competing skill sets.

Factors Promoting Globalization

After examining the arguments both for and against globalization, it is now necessary to understand the factors that promote globalization. While there are many divergent opinions on this issue, only those factors will be considered which are largely subscribed to by scholars on globalization.

- The most important factor that promotes globalization is the decision by industrialized countries to liberalize, open, and deregulate their economies. Towards this purpose, they first transferred some aspects of economic governance from the public to the private sector and then they placed more reliance on market forces and market mechanisms. The justification to reduce government intervention in economic activities was mandated by the collapse of communism in 1989. Communism used to follow a centrally planned economic system. Analysing the reasons, the IMF (2000) stated that central planning failed on economic grounds because it could not (or would not) respond to market signals to guide resource allocation or permit the competition, which would have put pressure on producers to raise efficiency and to innovate.
- An important factor in the spread of globalization is the information and communications revolution, which started during the late 1980s. Development of information and communication systems facilitated the transfer of ideas, technologies, and knowledge without time lag and eliminated distance barriers. This revolution has been prompted by the Internet, e-commerce, the convergence of computing and telecom technologies, the availability of large-capacity broadband networks, and mobile communications.
- Another factor is the free flow of international capital in liberalized financial markets. Due to globalization, savings can now be optimally allocated across countries to derive the best advantage by their productive use. This process has been encouraged by the flexibility to invest in erstwhile protected sectors even by foreign countries, cross-border mergers and acquisitions, and investments by foreign institutional investors (FII) and foreign direct investments (FDI).
- Technology has been instrumental in enhancing the impact of globalization. State-of-the-art technology facilitates large-scale production at a relatively cheaper rate as well as new product design and development, thereby reducing product life cycles. This necessitates bigger markets to sell products in order to maximize the returns on investment and to take care of the high costs of product development, especially in high-tech areas. Thus, technology has significantly enhanced the globalization movement.

- Globalization has eased the process of technology transfer from one country to another. This has enabled organizations to derive the comparative advantages that production flexibility allows. Such comparative advantages can be proximity to markets, availability of inputs, wage costs, etc. Production flexibility enhances competitive advantages as it reduces costs and enhances productivity.
- Finally, division of labour and production specialization have also contributed to the spread of globalization. By outsourcing, relocating the manufacturing facility, or leveraging the advantages of one country over the other, organizations have now become more efficient and consumers also benefit through lowering of prices.

Process of Development of Globalization

While globalization is regarded as a recent phenomenon, the process started much earlier. Tracing history, one finds that European capitalism had its beginnings in the sixteenth century. This is evident from the first circumnavigation of the earth in the years 1519–1521. Such a discovery later paved the way for expansion in world trade and investment, which continued unabatedly until the late nineteenth century. However, the First World War and the subsequent anti–Free Trade movement brought the process of globalization to a halt. Some attribute this to the Great Depression of 1930.

The point that globalization was inevitable was more emphatically established with the adoption of the Gregorian calendar between 1875 and 1925. Along with the International Date Line and world time zones, one also finds that international standards were agreed upon for telegraphy and signalling during this period. Subsequently, after the end of the Second World War, expansion of capitalism took place with the development of multinational organizations. These organizations became interested in producing and selling in markets around the world. Air travel and subsequent development of international communication further accelerated the pace of progress of international business. Since then, there have been many global changes indicating the triumph of capitalism and the resultant globalization.

IMPORTANT PLAYERS IN GLOBALIZATION

A number of international organizations have reinforced the process of globalization, creating institutional support for multilateral and bilateral trade. Some of these organizations have been mentioned here.

World Trade Organization (WTO)

The *World Trade Organization (WTO)* was established in 1995 to administer the rules of international trade as agreed upon by its member countries. In periodic ministerial meetings, terms of references of international trade are discussed and modalities developed to further the promotion of international trade. Before WTO, there was the General Agreement on Tariffs and Trade (GATT). However, the scope of GATT was only limited to trading in goods. To eliminate such limitations, GATT was replaced by WTO, with much wider judicial powers to resolve international trade-related issues. WTO rules do not allow a country to favour their own organizations to protect them from imports from other countries. Similarly, WTO rules do not allow a country to favour the imports of one country over those from another. The basic premise for the arguments is that growth of trade between countries increases the wealth of everyone. International trade allows the production of goods and services by those who are most efficient, thereby maximizing their availability at the best competitive price and quality. The growth of international trade is helped by the lowering of barriers such as tariffs and import quotas. All these things come under the purview of WTO agreements.

WTO introduction

The WTO was established on 1 January 1995 as a successor to the GATT. The implementation problems of WTO agreements are partly linked with the organizational structure and partly to the specific features of the agreements. The main differences between WTO and GATT are as follows:

- The GATT was a set of agreements and not an organization. The role of the GATT was in the area of export and import of goods, in particular the reduction of tariff and elimination of non-tariff barriers. Agriculture was under a very soft discipline in the GATT and textile was under a special regime in derogation from the normal GATT rules. The WTO, on the other hand, is a full-fledged organization with a permanent secretariat and a well-defined structure. Besides trade in goods, its area of operation extends to intellectual property rights and services. It contains enhanced disciplines in the areas of agriculture and textiles.
- The dispute settlement mechanism of the GATT was relatively weak to deal with the effective implementation of decisions. In comparison, the dispute settlement mechanism of the WTO is much more efficient and comprehensive. It has a better mechanism for the enforcement of rights and obligations and also for ensuring acceptance of decisions.

WTO agreements

WTO agreements cover 12 subjects in the area of trade in goods:

1. Agriculture
2. Textiles and clothing
3. Trade-related investment measures (TRIMS)
4. Sanitary and photo-sanitary measures (SPS)
5. Technical barriers to trade (TBT)
6. Anti-dumping
7. Customs valuation
8. Pre-shipment inspection
9. Rules of origin
10. Import licensing
11. Subsidies and countervailing measures
12. Safeguards

It also covers agreements in the following specific areas:

- General Agreement on Trade in Services (GATS)
- Agreement on Trade-Related Aspects of Intellectual Property Rights (TRIPS)
- Trade Policy Review Mechanism (TPRM)
- Agreement on the dispute settlement undertaking

The ministerial conference, the top policymaking body of the WTO, has met eight times so far: in Singapore (1996), Geneva (1998), Seattle (1999), Doha (2001), Cancun (2003), Hong Kong (2005), Germany (2007), and Geneva (2009). The WTO has 153 member countries.

International Monetary Fund (IMF)

The *International Monetary Fund (IMF)* was established in 1946. Its primary purpose is to strengthen the process of globalization, providing a host of services such as:

- Promoting international cooperation on finance
- Encouraging stability in exchange rates and orderly systems for exchanging money between countries
- Providing temporary assistance to countries suffering from problems related to balance of payments

IMF believes that world prosperity is enhanced by greater exchange between nations and that this can be made possible when everyone agrees to abide by the same rules. Like WTO, IMF also has several member countries including India.

World Bank

The *World Bank* provides loans to poor countries for development projects. The bank provides loans for investment projects such as water and sanitation, natural resource management, and education and health. It also lends for what it calls adjustment projects, which are to support governments undertaking policy reforms such as improved public sector management.

United Nations (UN)

The *United Nations (UN)* has become a promoter of globalization. It was established during the concluding phase of the Second World War. It argues that individual states have a dual role with responsibilities to both their own citizens and to the world society as a whole. The United Nations states that broader global responsibility requires international institutions. It supports the case for reform of international institutions, including its own Security Council, to make them more representative. The United Nations has sponsored a global compact to establish and promote a shared set of core values in the areas of labour standards, human rights, and environmental practices.

Organization for Economic Cooperation and Development (OECD)

The *Organization for Economic Cooperation and Development (OECD)* develops economic and social policies for its member countries, which include the countries of North America, Western Europe (including the Czech Republic, Hungary, and Poland), Japan, Korea, Australia, and New Zealand. It provides economic arguments for globalization, such as data demonstrating the positive contribution made by multinational corporations to economic development.

United Nations Conference on Trade and Development (UNCTAD)

The *United Nations Conference on Trade and Development (UNCTAD)* is a permanent intergovernmental body of the UN that aims to maximize the trade investment and development opportunities of developing economies and to assist in their efforts to integrate into the world economy.

Apart from these organizations, there are many private bodies and social organizations that promote globalization. One of the NGOs in India, Liberty Institute in New Delhi, also promotes the cause of globalization.

GLOBALIZATION AND ITS INFLUENCE ON BUSINESS AND MANAGERIAL PRACTICES

Based on the degree of propensities, multinational organizations can be categorized as ethnocentric, polycentric, geocentric, or regiocentric. Such propensities shape the managerial practices, attitude, and overall business pattern of multinationals. The *ethnocentric* or parochial attitude of multinational organizations is influenced by their belief that they follow the best work approach and practices in their home country. In contrast, a *polycentric attitude* embraces the practices of the host country, as those are the best fit for running the business in that country. A *geocentric attitude* emulates the best practices of global organizations, irrespective of their countries of origin. The *regiocentric approach* focuses on variations of human resource management practices, matching the specific norms and practices of specific geographic areas.

Managers of global organizations are, therefore, required to be sensitive to the diversity aspects, keeping pace with the degree of propensities. Such propensities not only affect the managerial practices but also sensitize the cross-cultural issues, making diversity management a complex process. One finds that the term *multinational organization* is used in a more generic sense, as any organization that operates in multiple countries becomes multinational by default. However, depending on the variation in attitude (influenced by the given propensities), multinational companies can be multi-domestic (when they subscribe to the polycentric approach), centralized (ethnocentric), or a borderless transnational (geocentric). Cultural diversity, which emerges from the variation of such propensities, then becomes the most crucial issue and challenge in a globalized business world.

With respect to the degree of propensities, human resource management (HRM) practices in multinationals vary. Ethnocentric and polycentric approaches are two opposing phenomena. Ethnocentric approaches emphasize a global HRM strategy and, therefore, do not localize the management team. Polycentric approaches, on the other hand, adopt an HRM strategy that empowers the local management team.

Based on the scholarly researches of P. J. Dowling and D. E. Welch (2004) and C. W. L. Hill (2005), the variations in HRM practices of multinational organizations have been listed with respect to the four approaches in Table 15.1.

According to A. M. Francesco and B. A. Gold (1998), in the ethnocentric approach, the cultural values and business practices of the home country are predominant. The headquarters develops a managing and staffing approach and consistently applies it throughout its subsidiaries. Companies following the ethnocentric approach assume that the home country approach is the best and that employees from other parts of the world can and should follow it. Managers from the headquarters develop practices and hold key positions in the subsidiaries to ensure consistency. The polycentric approach is in direct opposition. In the company that applies this approach, the assumption is that each country is different and that the subsidiaries in each country should develop locally appropriate practices under the supervision of local managers. With the geocentric or global approach, organizations try to combine the best from the headquarters and the subsidiaries to develop consistent worldwide practices. Manager selection is based on competency rather than nationality and can be from diverse countries. However, most companies use expatriates for key positions like senior managers, high-level professionals, and technical specialists. Since expatriates tend to be costly, it makes little financial sense to hire expatriates for positions that can be competently filled by foreign nationals. In addition, many countries require that a certain percentage of the workforce be local citizens, with exceptions usually made for upper management.

Table 15.1 Different Approaches to HRM Practices in Multinational Organizations

Type of approach	Nature of HRM practices of multinational organizations
Ethnocentric	This approach leverages the experience of the home country to standardize production. It basically trains the employees of the host country on the organization's areas of core competency under the guidance of expatriate managers, and creates a corporate culture independent of the culture of the host country. The HRM practices, therefore, differentiate between the employees of the host country and those of the home country. The host country's employees often get demotivated, while the cultural myopia of expatriate managers may fail to grab the market opportunities.
Polycentric	This approach enables profit maximization through flexibility because local managers can react quickly to market needs in the areas of pricing, production, product life cycle, and political activity. There is an absence of problems associated with expatriate managers. It also provides continuity in the management of foreign subsidiaries. However, there is no synergy because there is little communication between national units. This approach also limits the experience of host nationals to their own country. Moreover, there is a possibility that the corporate headquarters may become isolated from national units, which in turn may lead to corporate inertia.
Geocentric	This approach follows the concepts of economies of scale and experience curve effect. *Economies of scale* indicate an increase in the production efficiency with an increase in the number of goods produced, while the *experience curve effect* is the reduction in cost with the increase in the number of tasks due to labour efficiency and various other shared experiences. The polycentric pressure for local responsiveness is satisfied because of the need to meet the distinctive characteristics that remain in every market. However, it may be contrary to the host country's desire for the multinational to employ local citizens. It is also expensive to implement because of the need for considerable cross-cultural training and development.
Regiocentric	The policy is varied to suit the nature of the firm's business and product strategy. It allows interaction between executives because of inter-regional transfers and shows some sensitivity to local conditions. It also provides a 'stepping stone' for a firm wishing to move from an ethnocentric or a polycentric approach to a geocentric approach. However, it may produce federalism at a regional (rather than a country) level and constrain the firm from taking a global stance. It may improve career prospects on a national level but the promotions are restricted to the respective regional level, that is, the staff may never attain positions at the corporation's headquarters.

GLOBALIZATION AND INTERNATIONAL MARKETING

International marketing is the application of marketing techniques to international business. The American Marketing Association defines *international marketing* as the multinational process of planning and executing the conception, pricing, promotion, and distribution of ideas, goods, and services to create exchanges that satisfy individual and organizational objectives. It is marketing carried on across national boundaries. Further, it can be defined as the performance of business activities that direct the flow of goods and services to consumers or users in more than one nation. The spread of globalization has broadened the scope of international marketing.

Scope of International Marketing

International marketing has a wide scope in many areas such as:

- Opening branch/subsidiary in countries other than the originating country of business for manufacturing, processing, packaging, or assembly through direct investment
- Negotiating, licensing, or franchising patents, processes, or trademarks with other countries with or without investment
- Joint ventures with organizations in other countries for manufacturing and/or marketing
- Turnkey project consultancy with organizations in other countries

Driving Forces of International Business

The driving forces of international business are summarized along four main points:

1. **Comparative costs**: This theory advocates that factor costs of manufacturing and services vary across countries due to resource availability and specialization. These provide specific advantages to one country over the other. Lately, one finds that multinational and transnational companies are increasingly aggressive in leveraging the comparative costs, and relocating their manufacturing and other back-office activities in other countries to remain globally competitive. Many of them prefer China and other Southeast Asian countries to locate their manufacturing. Fast-moving consumer goods (FMCG) giant Procter & Gamble leveraged this advantage to remain globally competitive.
2. **International product life cycle**: This theory establishes that by dissemination of the results of innovations across national borders, organizations can expand customer reach across national boundaries.
3. **Limited growth of domestic markets**: Confining companies to only domestic operations does not provide much opportunity for them to grow. Adopting the option of product diversification may not be the solution for achieving growth, as it involves huge investments and is risky. Expanding the sale of products to another country presents a better alternative to seek growth. For many companies, while the domestic sales of their products are receding, international sales are on the rise.
4. **Technological change**: Technological improvement and change have expanded the market horizon from domestic to international. Significant improvements in transportation and communication revolutionized the conduct of international business.

Interrelations Between Globalization and Culture

Globalization leads to an accelerated pace of growth in international trade and it is interconnected to all aspects of social life, including culture. In the process of globalization, culture is an intrinsic aspect of complex connectivity. This, however, does not mean that culture itself is globalizing to facilitate exchange of goods and services internationally. What is more important is to appreciate that culture has high, average, or low moderating influence on the process of globalization, the degree of which varies from country to country.

Globalization has, among other things, increased the pace of activities of multinational and transnational corporations. It has also led to a rise in labour migration, international trading, etc. Apart from this, globalization has brought about increased institutional support from World Trade Organization, World Bank, and International Monetary Fund. It is certain that with globalization, production, exchange, and consumption of commodities are no longer confined to local activities. Today, multinationals and transnationals are making low-cost countries their manufacturing hub to cater to the demands of the global market. Thus, culture alone cannot dominate the process of globalization. Rather, culture predisposes actions to keep pace with globalization.

The term *cultural globalization* is often used nowadays. *Cultural globalization* refers to the increase in the exchange of cultural practices between different nations and their people. Such exchange of cultural practices has, however, existed right from the beginning of civilization. The present economic globalization has only served to increase the pace, as it is powered by technology. Today, the same products and the same services are consumed by millions of people across the world. The effect of cultural globalization is so deep-rooted that even the language barrier does not matter; it cannot restrain people from listening to foreign songs or even using some common words and phrases. Apart from technology, the Internet has also increased the momentum of cultural globalization, as people across the world can now freely exchange their ideas and thoughts.

Interestingly, the *Human Development Report* (1999) used the term *cultural insecurity*, mainly to highlight that cultural globalization can even dilute the native culture and ethos through changes in lifestyles, but such cases are very rare. Cultural globalization has, instead, promoted the pace of cultural inclusion, that is, the addition of some new cultural practices, without erasing the existing culture.

GLOBALIZATION AND TALENT MANAGEMENT

One is prone to think that the most conspicuous effect of globalization is the outsourcing of manufacturing to lower-wage countries. This is only a partial effect of globalization, though. In the book, *The World Is Flat: A Brief History of the Twenty-First Century*, Thomas Friedman (2007) mentions how globalization was made possible in entirely new ways by technology. The best way to explain globalization has been expressed by Ichack Adizes (1999). He said that globalization causes changes that cause events, which are at the same time problems and opportunities, which require a solution, which will cause, in turn, more changes and result in more problems and opportunities. So, the faster people are at finding solutions, the faster situations will change among them, forcing them to increase the pace.

Thus, for HR professionals and students, the effect of globalization can be best understood in the context of people-related issues. One has to examine how HR practices are changing in organizations, leading to shifting of jobs towards activities that are directly in contact with the client, towards roles that are characterized as consultants, while others, probably in some faraway Indian or Chinese city, perform the background work. Jobs are changing dramatically and employees, more often than not, will end their career with a different kind of job from what they started with. This will happen not just because they will move up the ladder of corporate responsibility, but also because the jobs they held initially will disappear or because the tools used to achieve results will be so different as to change the entire focus of the job, even if the job title remains the same.

In other words, there will be a need for people who are flexible, ready to learn, willing to study new subjects, and open to change and adapt. This process that ensures achievement of performance targets through the coordinated efforts of human resources is *talent management*.

Recruiters also need to stop hiring people solely for what they know, as their knowledge will become obsolete in a short time; rather, the hiring should be for what they are, their attitudes, and their basic values. Recruiters should then nurture the employees' ability to learn with training and the right environment.

Case Cross-cultural Teamwork Through Lateral Hierarchy: The Experience of DEC

Digital Equipment Corporation (DEC), also known as Digital, is a multinational company with headquarters in Geneva, Switzerland. It manufactures small, medium, and large computer systems and peripherals. The company has adopted lateral hierarchy, particularly in the project planning function in European countries. Cross-cultural teamwork is embedded in DEC's system. Apart from supplying standard products to customers, the company also provides customized systems in accordance with customers' needs. The company has several plants in Europe, a technical centre in southern France, manufacturing and distribution systems in Netherlands, Ireland, and Germany, a customer information centre in the United Kingdom, and a manufacturing plant in Scotland. The company follows a system of guaranteed delivery within 10 days from the date of order placement, irrespective of the nature or type of products (within their product range).

To meet the typical business needs, the company extensively practices cross-cultural teamwork through lateral hierarchy. Among other things, the company has to develop global managers who help in the decision-making process through horizontal collaboration, maintaining the lateral hierarchy. *Lateral hierarchy* is a process of decentralizing managerial decision making, recreating the organization into a microcosm. For the sake of operational flexibility MNCs need to dismantle their global headquarters. For MNCs, market and managerial diversities require valuing the lateral hierarchical system.

DEC's experience in lateral hierarchy, that is, the practice of decentralized decision making through horizontal collaborative decision making, helped the company to meet their core business philosophy of on-time delivery to customers, address complex operational issues, and at the same time train their employees into managers who complement the cross-cultural set-up.

The case of Digital, therefore, truly helps us to understand how a company can achieve excellence through lateral hierarchy, despite the diversities of market and culture.

CASE QUESTION

Read this case carefully and study how McDonald's is successful in maintaining its core values of a consistent level of customer service and quality, despite operating in cross-cultural environments.

Source: Information from James McCalman's (1996) 'The Case of Cross-Cultural Management Teams', *European Management Journal*, 14(5): pp. 509–517.

SUMMARY

- *Globalization* is the process of cross-sectoral and international interaction particularly in financial and business spheres, where market economics combined with advances in science and technology have subsumed the entire world into one single increasingly integrated system with cultural, environmental, and societal implications.
- The debate on globalization centres around issues like the increasing gap between the rich and the poor, the exploitation of labour, transparency and accountability, the dilution of culture and values, the violation of environmental regulations, and the increase in civil strife and violence.
- Despite various debates, it is generally agreed that globalization benefits economic activity worldwide, reduces the gap between the rich and poor countries, increases the access to technology

including information technologies, brings financial stability through increased capital mobility, promotes cultural diversity, makes WTO's roles more effective, and institutionalizes labour standards. Globalization also promotes employment opportunities.

- There are many factors that promote globalization. The most important factor is the decision of industrialized countries to liberalize, open, and deregulate their economies. Other factors are advancement of information and communication technologies, flow of international capital, etc.
- The process of development of globalization started long back in history. However, one finds that it started in a more aggressive form after the end of the Second World War, with the expansion of capitalism and the development of multinational organizations.
- The major players in globalization are World Trade Organization (WTO), International Monetary Fund (IMF), World Bank, United Nations (UN), Organization for Economic Cooperation and Development (OECD), United Nations Conference on Trade and Development (UNCTAD), and major trade blocks created in several countries.
- Globalization influences business and managerial practices. However, the nature of such influence depends on the degree of propensities adopted by multinational organizations. Based on the degree of propensities, multinational organizations can be categorized as ethnocentric, polycentric, geocentric, or regiocentric.
- Globalization brings positive changes in the process of international marketing. International marketing is the application of marketing techniques to international business. Multinationals now open branches/subsidiaries in other countries; negotiate, license, or offer franchise opportunities; make joint ventures; and execute turnkey project consultancy. With comparative costs, international product life cycles, limited growth in domestic markets, and technological change, the scope of international business expands.
- In the process of globalization, culture is an intrinsic aspect of complex connectivity. This, however, does not mean that culture itself is globalizing to facilitate exchange of goods and services internationally. What is more important is to appreciate that culture has high, average, or low moderating influence on the process of globalization, the degree of which varies from country to country.
- With the increased spate of job mobility across the globe, globalization also brings major changes in managing the workforce talent.

KEY TERMS

Ethnocentric approach: This approach leverages the experience of the home country to standardize production. It basically trains the employees of the host country on the organization's areas of core competency under the guidance of expatriate managers. It also creates a corporate culture independent of the culture of the host country.

Geocentric approach: This approach follows the concepts of economies of scale and experience curve effect. The polycentric pressure for local responsiveness is satisfied because of the need to meet the distinctive characteristics that remain in every market. However, it may be contrary to the host country's desire for the multinational to employ local citizens. It is also expensive to implement because of the need for considerable cross-cultural training and development.

Globalization: Globalization is a phenomenon of cross-border social, cultural, and technological exchange. It is the process of cross-sectoral and international interaction particularly in financial and business spheres, where market economics combined with advances in science and technology have subsumed the entire world into one increasingly integrated system with profound cultural, environmental, and societal implications.

International marketing: International marketing is the multinational process of planning and executing the conception, pricing, promotion, and distribution of ideas, goods, and services to create exchanges that satisfy individual and organizational objectives.

Polycentric approach: This approach enables profit maximization through flexibility because local managers can react quickly to market needs in the areas of pricing, production, product life cycle, and political activity. However, this approach limits the experience of host nationals to their own country.

Regiocentric approach: This approach allows interaction between executives because of inter-regional transfers and shows some sensitivity to local conditions. It also provides a 'stepping stone' for a firm wishing to move from an ethnocentric or a polycentric approach to a geocentric approach. On the other hand, even if it may improve career prospects on a national level, the promotions are restricted to the respective regional levels.

Talent management: It ensures achievement of performance targets through the coordinated efforts of human resources.

REVIEW QUESTIONS

1. Explain the term *globalization*. What are the views against globalization? Do you agree with these views?
2. What are the positive aspects of globalization?
3. Discuss the factors influencing the globalization process.
4. Briefly explain the history of globalization.
5. Who are the major players in globalization? In what way, do such players reinforce the process of globalization?
6. Explain the role of WTO in globalization.
7. Write short notes on:
   i. OECD
   ii. UNCTAD
   iii. IMF
   iv. Cultural diversity
   v. Polycentric approach

CRITICAL THINKING QUESTIONS

1. Visit the Web site of Dabur India, the Ayurveda and FMCG company that exports its products to several countries. Carefully study its product mix and describe the approach to globalization adopted by the company. Critically comment on its approach, duly interpreting its export market position.

2. A French company recently introduced a range of cosmetic products in the Indian market. Although, its products were selling well in the European market, in India, it could not consolidate its market position. You are recognized as an expert in the international market. You have been given the task to suggest to the company a line of action to consolidate its market position in India. Explain your course of action.

REFERENCES

Adizes, Ichak (1999). *Managing Corporate Lifecycles: How to Get and Stay at the Top*. Paramus, NJ: Prentice Hall.

Barber, R. B. (1996). *Jihad vs. McWorld*. New York: Times Books/Ballantine Books.

Beck, U., N. Sznaider and R. Winter (eds.) (2003). *Global America? The Cultural Consequences of Globalization*. Liverpool: Liverpool University Press.

Dowling, P. J. and D. E. Welch (2004). *International Human Resource Management: Managing People in a Multinational Context*, 4th edition. London: Thomson Learning.

Francesco A. M. and B. A. Gold (1998). *International Organizational Behavior*. Upper Saddle River, NJ: Prentice Hall.

Friedman, Thomas (2007). *The World Is Flat: A Brief History of the Twenty-First Century*. New York: Picador.

Giddens, Anthony (1971). *Capitalism and Modern Social Theory: An Analysis of the Writings of Marx, Durkheim and Max Weber*. Cambridge: Cambridge University Press.

Hill, C. W. L. (2005). *International Business: Competing in the Global Marketplace*, 5th edition. Boston, MA: McGraw-Hill/Irwin.

Hirst, Paul Q. and Grahame Thompson (1996). *Globalization in Question: The International Economy and the Possibilities of Governance*. Cambridge: Polity Press.

Huntington, Samuel P. (1996). *The Clash of Civilizations and the Remaking of World Order*. New York: Simon & Schuster.

International Monetary Fund (IMF). *World Economic Outlook*. May 2009, p. 174.

Lubbers, Ruud (2005). 'The Shift from Economy to Ecology (A Thematic Essay on the Precautionary Approach and Globalization As They Relate to Principle 6)', *Earth Charter in Action*. Amsterdam: KIT Publishers.

Robbins, J. (1997). 'When Do You Think the World Will End? Globalization, Apocalypticism, and the Moral Perils of Fieldwork in "Last New Guinea" ', *Anthropology and Humanism*, 22 (1): pp. 6–30.

United Nations Development Programme (1999). 'Globalization with a Human Face', *Human Development Report*. New York: Oxford University Press.

FURTHER READING

Bhattacharyya, D. K. (2000). 'Competency Mapping and Manpower Redundancy: A Macro-level Study of Indian Organizations', *Management and Accounting Research*, October–December, 4 (2): pp. 97–105.

——— (2006). *Human Resource Management*. New Delhi: Excel Books.

——— (2007). *Human Resource Research Methods*. New Delhi: Oxford University Press.

——— (2009). *Organizational Behaviour: Concepts and Applications*. New Delhi: Oxford University Press.

——— (2010). *Cross-Cultural Management: Text and Cases*. New Delhi: PHI Learning.

Eckes, George (2001). *The Six Sigma Revolution*. New York: John Wiley & Sons.

Ellis, Kristine (2001). 'Mastering Six Sigma', *Training*, December, pp. 30–35.

Feenstra, R. (1998). 'Integration of Trade and Disintegration of Production in the Global Economy', *Journal of Economic Perspectives*, 12 (4): pp. 31–50.

Hodgetts, R. M. and F. Luthans (1994). *International Management*. New York: McGraw-Hill.

Legrain, Philippe (2002). *The Truth about Globalisation*. London: Abacus.

Levitt, Theodore (1983). *The Marketing Imagination*. New York: The Free Press.

OECD (2001). *Measuring Globalisation: The Role of Multinationals in OECD Economies*. Paris: OECD Publishing.

Robertson, Roland (1992). *Globalization: Social Theory and Global Culture*. London: Sage Publications.

Yip, G. (1992). *Total Global Strategy: Managing for Worldwide Competitive Advantage*. New York: Prentice Hall.

16

Organizational Culture

After going through this chapter, you will be able to understand:

- the concept of organizational culture and its influences on the function of an organization
- organizational culture and globalization
- mergers and their implication on corporate culture
- Hofstede's cultural orientation model
- cultural issues and ways to manage corporate cultural change
- organizational diagnostics
- organizational development
- organizational change

My Microsoft

On 18 May 2006, Microsoft Corporation (Microsoft), the US-based multinational computer technology corporation, announced a plan to significantly revamp some of its human resource management (HRM) practices. The plan named 'my Microsoft' was aimed at addressing employees' concerns and at boosting their morale. According to the plan, the company intended to change its performance review system, increase allotment of stock options, introduce new employee benefits, etc. Since its inception, Microsoft had always been considered a 'great place to work for'. Due to its work culture, generous compensation, and benefit programmes, the company was able to attract and retain the best talent. However, according to HR experts, as the company grew rapidly in size, it lost the popular elements of its work culture. In addition, several racial discrimination lawsuits and anti-trust proceedings affected the company's image severely and reportedly demotivated employees.

With the changes in HRM practices, Microsoft was able to boost employee morale. The employee attrition rate went down from 10 per cent in 2005 to 8.3 per cent in 2007. Some analysts attributed this success to Microsoft's senior vice-president of HR Lisa Brummel's attitude towards dealing with problems. No matter what industry one is in, motivated and engaged employees are critical to success. Successful managers spend a significant portion of the day working to develop their team's skills, improve morale, and drive higher levels of performance.

Microsoft's example illustrates that organizational culture and development also depend on requisite practices and institutional support, including change in the work processes.

INTRODUCTION

Culture constitutes the moral, social, and behavioural norms of an organization. It creates an impact on the beliefs, attitudes, and norms of employees in the organization. Building culture through continuous learning is now a global practice. This is primarily more important for globalization and cross-border mergers and acquisition. Movement of people from one country to another renews the attention on building organization-specific corporate culture to bring order in behaviour and attitudes. To build their own corporate culture, many global organizations have started their own universities. These universities not only focus on competency building through renewal of knowledge and skills, they also ensure that their culture is imbibed to the extent that it becomes deep-rooted in the minds of their people. In India, hardly any organization focuses on building a corporate culture of its own. Indian organizations limit their efforts to general induction programmes at the time of recruitment. A few have also extended the period of induction by three to six months, to orient their employees. However, they restrict it to job- or function-specific domain knowledge.

'When in Rome, do as the Romans do', is the motto espoused by Geert Hofstede (1980). Hofstede, after surveying more than 100,000 employees of IBM with operations in 40 countries, came up with five continuums of culture which organizations around the world translate as their own culture. Whether there should be focus on individualism or collectivism or should it be a power distance approach, depends on the organizational value system. Globally, collectivism is a more desired practice as it promotes team culture by developing common and consistent goals, organizational commitment, mutual accountability, team leadership, and shared rewards. Power distance focuses on distribution of power and adherence to formal channels. The uncertainty avoidance culture harps on the relative importance of rules, long-term employment, and steady progression through well-defined career ladders. Dominant values focus on quality of relationships and job satisfaction and flexibility, while a short term versus long term culture gets reflected in the organizational employment relations.

Like organizational culture, organizational development (OD) is also important. The need for organizational development can be understood from the fact that no organization operates in isolation. In fact, every organization continuously interacts with its environment. This, therefore, requires an organization to balance between the internal features and the characteristics of the external environment, which is part of the contingency theory in organization science. The theory suggests that an organization has to understand the dynamics of its environment in order to be able to adapt to the changing demands of the outside and inside (inside the organization) world. There are many different ways of scanning the organizational environment. After scanning the organizational environment, it is imperative to pursue organizational development in order to match with the requirement to stay updated in a competitive environment. However, to understand the parameters of organizational development, it is imperative to understand various other issues.

Understanding the process of organizational change is important for managers. In practice, the terms *organizational change* and *organizational development* are used interchangeably. Although theoretically they are not the same, operationally, however, one encompasses another. To bring about organizational change, it is important to ensure organizational development. Organizational change is unavoidable for organizations if they are to keep pace with the changing business scenario. Globalization has further increased the pace of change. Increased competition, changing customer expectations, economic uncertainty, etc. are gobbling up age-old organizational systems and practices. All these aspects require managers to revisit their internal business processes, taking stock of the external environmental issues to remain competitive in the market.

CONCEPT OF ORGANIZATIONAL CULTURE

The concept of *organizational culture* has become popular since the early 1980s. There is no consensus about its definition but most authors agree that it is holistic in nature, historically determined, socially constructed, and not quantifiable. Therefore, it is also difficult to change. It is something an organization has, or it can also be seen as something an organization is.

Organizational cultures are different from national cultures. Organizational cultures are manifest in symbols, heroes, rituals, and values. National cultures differ mostly at the level of values. Organizational cultures together are labelled as *practices*.

Hofstede studied the differences in national cultures in over fifty countries and identified five independent dimensions of values. They are power distance, individualism versus collectivism, masculinity versus femininity, uncertainty avoidance, and long-term versus short-term orientation. The differences in national cultures are reflected in solutions to organizational problems. Different national cultures have different preferred ways for structuring organizations and different patterns of employee motivation, for example, limitation of options for performance appraisal, management by objectives, strategic management, and humanization of work.

Research into organizational cultures has helped to identify six independent dimensions of practices: process-oriented versus result-oriented; job-oriented versus employee-oriented; professional versus parochial; open systems versus closed systems; tightly controlled versus loosely controlled; and pragmatic versus normative. The position of an organization on these dimensions is determined in part by the business or industry the organization is in. Scores on the dimensions are also related to a number of other 'hard' characteristics of the organization. These lead to conclusions about how organizational cultures can be and cannot be managed.

Managing international business means handling both national and organizational culture differences at the same time. Organizational cultures are somewhat manageable while national cultures are given facts; common organizational cultures across borders keep multinationals together.

The concept of organizational culture is born from early studies of organizational climate, intertwined with human resources and various sociological disciplines. The true definition is more a matter of perspective. Some authors believe that the organization itself is a culture (Bate 1994). This attributes organizational culture to be more of a metaphor for study through which meanings are constructed and expressed. A more modern view, however, considers organizational culture as a variable rather than a metaphor (Wilson 2001). Variables are organizational practices like performance management (Deal and Kennedy 1982), mechanism for effectiveness and control (Peters and Waterman 1982), recruitment and selection (Guest 1994), training and development (Schein 1968, 1992; O'Reilly 1989), knowledge management practices (Brown 1995), reward systems (Kerr and Slocum 1987), and overall human resource management practices.

Organizational Culture and Globalization

The online Merriam-Webster dictionary defines culture as 'the act of developing the intellectual and moral faculties especially by education'. Another definition states that *culture* is 'the moral, social, and behavioural norms of an organization based on the beliefs, attitudes, and priorities of its members'. Even though the first definition harps on building culture through the act of education, one largely finds its relevance in those corporations that have a unique system of emphasizing continuous learning. Many of them have their own universities, like Sears University, Hamburger University (of McDonald's), and Motorola University.

The Hewlett-Packard corporate culture

An example of a unique corporate culture is Hewlett-Packard (HP). They have been successful in creating a conscious corporate culture, which they call 'The HP Way'. HP's corporate culture is based on respect for others, a sense of community, and plain hard work. This conscious culture was developed and is being sustained through extensive training of managers and all employees. Today, HP's growth and success may be traced to their conscious corporate culture.

HP's culture is marked by commitment to diversity, inclusion, and non-discrimination. Since its formation, HP has demonstrated an ongoing commitment to people and to fair employment practices. As HP has grown and expanded throughout the world, its workforce has become more diverse. HP believes that this diverse workforce helps the company to realize its full potential. Recognizing and developing the talents of each individual brings new ideas to HP. The company benefits from the creativity and innovation that result when HP individuals who have different experiences, perspectives, and cultures work together. This is what drives invention and high performance at HP. HP believes that a well-managed, diverse workforce expands HP's base of knowledge, skills, and cross-cultural understanding, which in turn enable the organization to understand and respond to diverse and changing customers throughout the world. HP's overall commitment is reflected in their diversity and inclusive philosophy, which can be summarized as follows:

- A diverse, high-achieving workforce is the sustainable competitive advantage that differentiates HP. It is essential to win in the marketplaces, workplaces, and communities around the world.
- An inclusive, flexible work environment values differences and motivates employees to contribute their best.
- HP attracts, develops, promotes, and retains a diverse workforce to better serve customers.
- Trust, mutual respect, and dignity are the fundamental beliefs that are reflected in HP's behaviour and actions.
- Accountability for diversity and inclusion goals drive HP's success.

The General Electric corporate culture

Jack Welch, erstwhile CEO of General Electric (GE), created a new corporate culture. The key elements of GE's corporate culture are as follows:

- Redesigning the role of the leader in the new economy, creating followers through communicating a vision, and establishing open, caring relations with every employee
- Creating an open, collaborative workplace where everyone's opinion is welcome
- Empowering senior executives to run far-flung businesses in entrepreneurial fashion
- Liberating the workforce and making everybody a participant by improving vertical communication and employee empowerment

The Southwest Airlines corporate culture

Southwest Airlines is one of the most profitable airlines in the United States. CEO Herb Kelleher described Southwest's corporate culture in an interview published by *American Compensation Association (ACA) Journal* (presently known as *WorldatWork Journal*) in 1995 (Whittlesey 1995) as positive from the very first step. Even during the process of hiring, the company looks for people with a positive attitude and who are interested in performing as a team. Their motto is that if one hires people who enjoy working as a team and take pride in the team's accomplishments, one can build an enthusiastic workforce, which in turn creates a good atmosphere at the workplace. An important thing that the top management emphasizes is communication in every possible form. Demeanour is given a lot of importance, as the way one walks, talks, and acts is also a form of communication. Another important strategy adopted by the top management is to constantly demonstrate the company's pride in the employees while displaying an interest in them as individuals. Hence, it is the top management's vigilance in maintaining the organizational culture with clear rules of behaviour and communication, which is the key to Southwest's success.

The Sears and Walmart corporate cultures

An example of a down-to-earth corporate culture is that of Sears, the second largest retail chain in the world. Sears emphasizes the three Cs, namely a compelling place to work, a compelling place to shop, and a compelling place to invest (resulting from customer satisfaction). Sears believes that when these cultures are practiced, they take into account the overall growth and prosperity of the organization. Incidentally, they also align their performance management system with the three Cs. Similarly, Walmart, the largest retail chain in the world, also believes that all their employees are their associates and as a part of their corporate culture and practices, shares all strategic information with employees. Walmart achieves a significant rate of growth every year.

Mergers and Their Impact on Corporate Cultures

Mergers and acquisitions bring major changes in the corporate culture. There are many cultural issues experienced by organizations throughout the world during the post-merger phase. The issues are as follows:

- Disintegration of organizational value systems takes place. An example would be rent-to-own stores.
- Low employee morale results in poor productivity and conflicts, for example, rent-to-own stores.
- Rationalization (that is, ensuring suitable jobs are provided according to aptitude) and relocation of the workforce can create problems, as was the case with Blue Star.
- The generation gap creates conflict. Examples include the Computer Maintenance Corporation (CMC) and Tata Consultancy Services (TCS) merger and the Bank of Madurai and ICICI merger.
- There may be loss of talent.
- The influence of different cultures (including cross-country cultures) is not always positive.
- Rigidity of blue collar employees to learn new things can pose a problem.
- There is anxiety about receiving the pink slip, as a merger is followed by a rationalization of the workforce.
- Differences in HR style can create adjustment problems.
- There is loss of faith in the management due to the veil of secrecy in mergers.
- There is stalemate in managerial positions (one has to leave or compromise for the new group that is taking over).
- There is reduction in employee enthusiasm.
- Cost control takes place to get a synergy of $2 + 2 > 4$, which can affect the executive pay.
- The benefits of synergy require time to materialize. An example is the IndianOil Corporation (IOC) and Indo-Burma Petroleum Company (IBP) merger. IOC's market share is 54 per cent in petroleum, oil and lubricants (POL) products, but in the retail business, its share is 40 per cent. With IBP, IOC gets to add 1,540 outlets to its existing 7,750 outlets (IBP's market share is 8 per cent).

To make effective merger decisions from an organizational perspective, the following steps are necessary:

1. Ascertain the differences in the basic culture and procedures.
2. Pre-assess the cost implication to integrate the workforce of the merging organization.
3. Plan for voluntary retirement scheme (VRS) for people rendered surplus.
4. Make provisions for increased HR cost for training and redeployment, relocation, and VRS benefits.
5. Accommodate employees (including executives) of the merging organization in the new environment. This was the strategy followed in the Tata and Videsh Sanchar Nigam Limited (VSNL) merger.
6. Develop an integrated culture with inputs from both organizations. This was also followed by Tata and VSNL.
7. Focus on the training and learning process. For example, in the case of the TCS–CMC merger, the TCS executives handle mostly international projects, while CMC executives handle mostly domestic projects.
8. Develop a new organization chart and make it transparent.
9. Align the compensation package, if required even by redesigning, as was done by International Business Machines (IBM) and PricewaterhouseCoopers (PwC).

All these examples illustrate how developing and sustaining a conscious culture in the organization can contribute to its growth and prosperity. Corporate culture as a separate branch has received priority due to globalization and the consequent mobility of people and cross-cultural influence, more particularly for multinational and transnational organizations.

Hofstede's Cultural Orientation Model

Hofstede's cultural orientation model is considered to be one of the best models to appreciate cultural diversity. Hofstede is a Dutch researcher and author of the seminal work *Culture's Consequences: Comparing Values, Behaviors, Institutions, and Organizations Across Nations* published in 2001. In his book, Hofstede describes his pioneering study of IBM affiliates in fifty countries. In fact, his work laid the foundation for the field of comparative management. The model proposed by Hofstede has five continuums, which are as follows:

1. **Individual versus collective orientation**: At this level, behaviour is appropriately regulated.
2. **Power distance orientation**: It explains the extent to which less powerful parties accept the existing distribution of power and the degree to which adherence to formal channels is maintained.
3. **Uncertainty avoidance orientation**: It is the degree to which employees are threatened by ambiguity, and explains the relative importance to employees of rules, long-term employment, and steady progression through well-defined career ladders.
4. **Dominant values orientation**: Dominant values like assertiveness, monetary focus, well-defined gender roles, formal structure, focus on quality of relationships, and job satisfaction and flexibility are covered in this continuum.
5. **Short-term versus long-term orientation**: Through this continuum, one can understand the time frame used, that is, short term (involving more inclination towards consumption, saving face by keeping up, etc.) versus long term (involving preserving status-based relationships, thrift, deferred gratifications, etc.).

Quite often, there is a debate on how cross-cultural influence may persuade an organization to redesign HR policies and reward systems. Such trends influence an organization to re-engineer, more particularly in their approach to team orientation. For example, the theory Z management approach combines American and Japanese management philosophies.

The following attributes are necessary for a company to move to a 'team culture':

- Common and consistent goals
- Organizational commitment
- Role clarity among team members
- Team leadership
- Mutual accountability within the team
- Complementary knowledge and skills
- Reinforcement of required behavioural competencies
- Power (real and perceived)
- Shared rewards

Organizational Culture and Organizational Climate

The correct definition of organizational culture is often a matter of perspective. For some, the organization itself is a culture (Bate 1994). Therefore, culture is a metaphor for study through which meanings are constructed and expressed through social interaction. A more modern view of organizational culture is that it is something that an organization has. Hence, it is more of a variable rather than a metaphor (Wilson 2001). For example, various types of culture have been identified and related to other variables such as performance (Deal and Kennedy 1982). In its evolution within the academic and managerial literature, organizational culture has increasingly become a mechanism for effectiveness and control (Peters and Waterman 1982). Hence, organizational culture sets the organizational climate.

Whether it is a metaphor or a variable, organizational culture translates into organizational climate and even decides the organizational practices. Organizational practices on people-related issues are classified under human resource management, which governs organizational behaviour issues. Hence, culture issues encompass recruitment, selection, training, appraisal and reward systems, and so on.

Recruitment and *selection* are the methods by which an organization sorts the applicants for employment. It is very important as it directly controls the types of people that enter the organization (Guest 1994). In managing the cultural environment, the aim of recruitment and selection processes would be to generate a pool of people who have some familiarity with the organization and its culture (Carroll 1991). Although an organization may not be able to pick and choose its applicants, it can advertise a realistic and comprehensive description of what is required from their employees, both in terms of culture and performance (Brown 1995). This would then indicate to potential applicants the desired state of the organization that they are planning to join and give them the opportunity to judge whether they are compatible. The applied psychologist would be able to offer an accurate job analysis, which would highlight the key aspects of the job in terms of what is required from the person performing it. This could include performance goals and cultural aspects of the employment and, therefore, paint a good picture for any potential applicant.

The *training* and *development* within the organization can also have cultural implications, particularly for the newer recruits. For many authors, these processes are thought of as formal socializations. Training programmes demonstrate the ways in which an organization likes its employees to think and, therefore, the aspects that they must be compatible with, and also add direction to the desired cultural state (Schein 1968, 1991; O'Reilly 1989). Training can be used to orient appropriate beliefs, values, and assumptions in employees, setting the cultural framework in their working environment (Wilson 2001). Although this method is seen as valid, a study by Silvester et al. (1999) of a training scheme designed to bring about change in the organizational culture found that senior managers and trainers were less optimistic about the success of the programme than the trainees themselves. This indicates the level of scepticism surrounding such formal cultural management practices.

Appraisal systems implemented by an organization can affect the organizational culture at several levels (Fletcher and Williams 1996). Organizations that choose to implement appraisal systems imply that the areas that are appraised are more important to them. An applied psychologist trying to put together an appraisal system for an organization would want to consider the implications of the system on the culture of the organization. This consideration needs to occur at a number of levels, including not only what to appraise but also who should do the appraising and even how feedback on the appraisal is given. For example, organizations that aim for an open and relaxed culture might want managers to give one-to-one feedback rather than a written report delivered impersonally (Brown 1995). Indeed, 360 degree appraisal systems are often implemented as an attempt at optimizing fairness within organizations, as these systems gather their data from a range of sources (London and Smither 1995), but this may not suit an organization if it desires a culture that only respects management views.

Appraisal systems often (but not always) lead to *reward systems*, which are frequently thought to be a mechanism for controlling the behaviours and, to some extent, the cognitions of employees. This is because it sets the guidelines as to what employees need to achieve in order to receive pay rise, bonuses, and other rewards that organizations believe are valuable to their staff (Kerr and Slocum 1987). This then is thought to be the organization's statement of its beliefs, values, and assumptions inherent in its everyday life. It is important to note that many organizations have different reward settings for different areas of their business, representing different values in different business settings (Brown 1995). For an applied psychologist, readying to help design a reward system, there is a range of theories relating to what is motivating for employees in the workplace. However, the choice that is made and the structures for reward that are put in place must combine motivational qualities with the goals and beliefs of the organization, alongside a consideration as to how the culture will be manipulated by the values the system introduces.

Interestingly, some studies suggest that the success or failure of performance-related pay (PRP) systems should not be solely judged on their motivational qualities. Such schemes can be used to manipulate the prevalent culture to become more individualistic (if that is what the management wants to achieve). Such reward schemes should be introduced sensitively in an attempt to conserve any team spirit that may already exist. This seems contradictory to the overruling idea of performance-related pay, yet the aim is one of balance where individual goals take precedence over collectivist goals without scrapping team communication altogether.

In human resource practices and personnel management in general, the management of organizational culture can play a large part in the type of decisions made and the strategic directions taken by practitioners. From the view of an applied psychologist, assisting with the design and implementation of various human resource programmes, the culture and climate of the organization should play a role in the preparation and design stages. A thought should be given to the current and future culture of the organization and the impact that any intervention may have (whatever shape or form it may take). The possibility of objective assessment is appealing from a psychological perspective and there is no reason why thinking about psychology and its relation to cultural change and management might not become more prominent in the future.

Organizational Culture and Organizational Structure

Organizational structure is one of the central issues in organizational theory in the twentieth century. Three main theories of organization structure have emerged. They are the archetypical bureaucracy theory, the stakeholder model, and newer ways of thinking, especially reflexive theories.

The *archetypical bureaucracy theory* stems from the theories of Max Weber. Its features are rationality, task specialization, hierarchy and regularity, and there is a strong emphasis on structure as a controlling force. In the *stakeholder model*, on the other hand, rationality is abandoned and structure becomes the framework in which the various stakeholders—leaders, internal parties, and external parties—seek to achieve their own goals.

However, new research on organizational structure has focused on variables such as culture, metaphors, learning forms, and dynamic organizational variants and fields (total quality management, six sigma and lean production, and the related paradigm shift). Both organizational theory and organizational practice reflect on the significance and use of the concept of structure.

CULTURAL ISSUES ACROSS NATIONS

Differences in national cultures have been studied for over fifty countries. They show five independent dimensions of values: power distance; individualism versus collectivism; masculinity versus femininity; uncertainty avoidance; and long-term versus short-term orientation. National culture differences are reflected not only in solutions to organization problems in different countries, but also in the validity of management theories in these countries. Different national cultures have different preferred ways of structuring organizations and different patterns of employee motivation. For example, they limit the options for performance appraisal, management by objectives, strategic management, and humanization of work.

A study by A. Laurent (1983) established that internationally experienced executives show major differences by nationality, in their beliefs on how to manage effectively. While such differences are partly attributable to biographical characteristics like age, education, job, professional experience, hierarchical level, and company type, more important reasons for such change as indicated by Laurent are attributable to international ethos. Thus, nationality is a potent factor to explain psychological attributes and behaviour of people across nations. There are four important characteristics of differences in nationality. These are values, cognitive scheme, demeanour, and language. Hofstede (1980) has already established that nationality affects one's values. A cross-national study by England (1975), comparing managers from the United States, Japan, Australia, Korea, and India, found that nationality accounted for 30 per cent to 45 per cent of the variation in managers' values. *Cognitive schemes* are knowledge of facts, events and trends, and knowledge about future events, alternatives, consequences for the alternatives, etc. Hence, perceptions of people across nations largely stem from nationality constructs (Lord and Foti 1986). Differences in cognitive schema of people across nations, in fact, are a primary reason for recruitment of people from different countries by multinational organizations. *Demeanour* is the outward physical behaviour of people. *Values* also affect the demeanour. Differences in eye contact, punctuality, conversational style, interruption patterns, physiological reactions to emotional stimuli, and other types of behaviour are characterized as demeanour and associated with nationality (Frijda 1986). Finally, nationality has implications on the *language* of people. It is not only the language that people know but also the propensity to know other languages which vary from nation to nation.

Therefore, managing organizational behaviour in a cross-cultural set-up assumes importance. Managers need to understand the characteristic differences of people across nations to achieve efficiency.

MANAGEMENT OF CORPORATE CULTURE CHANGE

The need for culture change for an organization does not always necessitate mergers and acquisitions. It may be also for developing the capability of organizational response to meet the needs of the changing environment. Both Toyota and Honda of Japan had to undergo a corporate culture change to suit the US conditions. Another major Japanese company, Mazda, had to withdraw from the United States due to their failure to adapt to U.S. culture, despite the fact that they entered the U.S. market much before Toyota and Honda. India, too, has experienced a cultural mismatch between the Honda and Hero groups, while Suzuki and Maruti present a successful case of adaptive corporate culture. Many Indian organizations had to redefine their culture to keep pace with the process of globalization.

Culture changes in organizations have to be personally led by the top management. This job cannot be delegated to people down the line. This is primarily due to the top management's power to exert influence to bring about necessary changes. It requires dynamic leadership and understanding of people's behaviour and the changing environmental cue. Due to restructuring, organizations may often be required to go for a change in the skills and the attitudes of their people. These changes succeed culture change. It encounters resistance and non-cooperation from people, but with sustained intervention from the top management, it can be achieved. Culture change also succeeds change in internal practices. Making people innovative, empowered to take decisions, and capable of troubleshooting problems is not so easy. The top management along with their team is required to lead the show, identifying change agents to further the process of cultural transformation.

An example of successful cultural change in an organization is British Petroleum (BP), which is one of the world's largest energy companies. BP provides its customers product bundles ranging from fuel for transportation and energy for heat and light, to retail services and petrochemicals. It manages its business with about 3,500 expatriates from 55 countries. For BP, these expatriates are strategic as they facilitate the process of technology transfer and have specialized skills to do the job. Career development for expatriates ensures stress-free relocation. The entire process is done by BP in such a manner that any cultural incongruity gets suitably addressed.

Organizational culture change is a constant organization-building challenge to broaden, deepen, or modify organizational capabilities and resource strengths in response to ongoing market changes. A focus on customer relationship management (CRM) and developing people's capabilities require organizations to undergo a perceptive cultural change. Managers play the role of a teacher in cultural transformation; they send signals through their practices, which the subordinates emulate.

Building a strategy-fit corporate culture is important for successful strategy execution, which produces a performing work environment and develops *esprit de corps* (enthusiasm) as propounded by Henry Fayol (2002).

Since culture sets the work climate, any change in corporate culture always encounters resistance. Organizations in a changing business environment are always required to take on an adaptive culture, which among other things necessitates receptivity to new ideas, experimentation, innovation, new strategies, and new operating practices. Changing prevailing organizational culture, therefore, requires competent leadership at the top. Apart from symbolic actions from the top leadership, it also requires substantive actions, which demonstrate the degree of commitment of the top leadership. With symbolic and substantive actions from the top management, changing the behaviour of the people in the chain of hierarchy can be achieved automatically.

Similarly, cultural change in organizations requires strong corporate ethics and values. *Ethical norms* develop business principles and moral values of people, which develop their capability to take socially responsive decisions. *Ethical standards* denote integrity, doing the right thing, and genuine concern for stakeholders. To ensure the practice of ethical standards, organizations conduct ethics and values programmes through training, and they form ethics committees, develop a code of ethics, and periodically conduct ethics audit. It is essential for the top management to comply with ethical norms since all employees further down the hierarchical chain are expected to comply with them.

Another important enabler for cultural change is the top leadership. *Leadership* requires understanding of organizational pulses through active listening and talking to people, coaching and mentoring, transparency in information sharing, and encouraging people to be creative and innovative in their work. Since it exerts influence to elicit voluntary participation from organizational members, it requires leaders (top management) to be more proactive in their practices, so that people down the chain can emulate them. Adopting a participative approach in planning and decision making, developing problem-solving capability, and helping the people in the organization to mature are also important prerequisites for successful leadership in bringing about cultural change in the organization. Thus, implementing cultural change in organizations require a series of actions, without, however, any universally accepted sacrosanct practices. What actually leads to this, therefore, depends on specific organizational constructs. In India, there are many such cases of successful cultural transformation. When Videocon, a traditional Indian organization, acquired a legacy-bound multinational like Philips, it took Philips through successive difficult stages of cultural transformation. With sustained efforts from the top management, mostly in tandem with the stated courses of action, it successfully achieved the desired results. In the initial phases of cultural transformation, the top management of Videocon even spent 80 per cent of their time in listening to the people, playing a supportive role to infuse confidence in their apprehensive minds. Organizational cultural change, therefore, is situation-specific.

ORGANIZATIONAL DIAGNOSTICS

Organizational diagnostics are measures that can apply to anyone in the organization and can be aggregated to represent different levels of the organization, such as departments, branches, or the organization as a whole. These are useful diagnostics for gauging the morale of a company's workforce, testing the impact of new policies or procedures, monitoring long-term trends in the workforce, and determining where interventions are needed. Some of the measures that are essential for an organization's growth and development are given here.

Attitudes Towards Work

The different attitudes towards work considered to be essential for organizational growth are:

- **Job satisfaction**: This denotes the degree to which employees are satisfied and happy with their jobs. This becomes clear from a statement like 'I am generally satisfied with the kind of work I do in this job'.
- **Autonomy**: The extent to which employees have a say in the scheduling of their tasks, as well as decisions regarding the procedures to be followed and equipment to be used in their work. This becomes clear from a statement like 'I am able to act independently of my supervisor in performing my job function'.
- **Participation in decision making**: This denotes the extent to which employees participate in setting the goals and policies of the organization. This becomes clear from a statement like 'I can help in making decisions that affect my work'.

- **Role clarity**: This denotes knowledge of exactly what behaviour is expected in one's job. This becomes clear from a statement like 'I know what my job responsibilities are'.
- **Role conflict**: This denotes the extent to which two or more pressures occur together such that complying with one would make doing the other more difficult. This becomes clear from a statement like 'I often have to bend a rule or policy in order to carry out an assignment'.
- **Job involvement**: This denotes the degree to which employees are committed to and involved in their job. This becomes clear from a statement like 'I don't mind spending a half hour past quitting time if I can finish a task'.

Organizational Commitment

The different factors that show the degree of organizational commitment are:

- **Loyalty**: This denotes the feelings of affection for and attachment to one's organization. This becomes clear from a statement like 'If another organization offered me more money for the same kind of work, I would almost certainly accept'.
- **Job security**: This denotes the ability to keep a job for as long as one wants, providing one's job performance is satisfactory. This becomes clear from a statement like 'I can be sure of my job as long as I do good work'.
- **Trust in management**: This denotes the extent to which employees ascribe good intentions to, and have trust in, the works and actions of the management and their organization. This becomes clear from a statement like 'The management at my location acts with sincerity'.
- **Identification**: This denotes the extent to which employees adopt as their own the goals and values of their organization. This becomes clear from a statement like 'I really feel as if this organization's problems are my problems'.
- **Alienation**: This denotes the extent to which employees feel disappointed with their career and professional development. This becomes clear from a statement like 'I don't feel a sense of pride or accomplishment as a result of the type of work that I do'.
- **Helplessness**: This denotes the extent to which employees feel they have few opportunities and alternatives available to them outside their organization. This becomes clear from a statement like 'I feel I have too few options to consider leaving this organization'.

Organizational Climate

The various aspects that constitute an ideal organizational climate are:

- **Support**: This denotes the degree of emotional support employees feel they receive from their organization. This becomes clear from a statement like 'Management here is interested in the welfare of its people'.
- **Communication**: This denotes the accuracy and openness of information exchange. This becomes clear from a statement like 'I am kept informed about changes that affect my work'.
- **Fairness**: This denotes the extent to which employees perceive their workplace to be equitable and free of bias. This becomes clear from a statement like 'Employees in my workplace are treated fairly, regardless of race'.
- **Safety**: This denotes the extent to which employees perceive their workplace to be safe and free of physical danger. This becomes clear from a statement like 'I am often in situations at work where I can easily get physically hurt'.

- **Tolerance for risk**: This denotes the degree to which the organization encourages bold action, risk taking, and independence of thought. This becomes clear from a statement like 'Risk taking is a value supported by our corporate culture'.
- **Flexibility**: This denotes the degree of adaptability and tolerance for ambiguity in an organization. This becomes clear from a statement like 'This organization adapts quickly to changes'.
- **Continuous learning**: This denotes the perceptions on training and development opportunities in one's organization. This becomes clear from a statement like 'There are adequate opportunities to pursue professional development activities beyond the scope of my immediate job'.

ORGANIZATIONAL DEVELOPMENT

Organizational development (OD) is a planned change based on the paradigm of understanding the environment, benchmarking, and action research. OD can, thus, be described as a learning process. The active development of an organization towards its desired corporate identity succeeds only if this change process is undertaken holistically. From a behavioural perspective, this means that the behavioural conditions that lie within the person (qualifications and motivation) as well as those lying outside the person (organizational structure and technology) must be modified. The process of change is also described as a political process. Lastly, the process of change is often examined in terms of whether, and how, basic assumptions within an organization can be decoded through analysis of symbols.

Types of intervention include the person-centred approach, the structural approach, and the relationship approach. The *person-centred approach* requires the development of both social competence that fosters cooperation and general intellectual competence that promotes innovation. The *structural approach* requires moves to reintegrate segregated work sequences and attempts to decentralize decision making. The *relationship approach* requires team development, role negotiations, and survey-feedback methods.

A new approach to organizational development is *organizational transformation (OT)*. OT is associated with re-engineering and many feel that it could be a replacement for organizational development. However, OT is a much harder concept and encounters many problems as re-engineering is succeeded by the problems of downsizing, lean production strategy, and many other humane issues that may ultimately create a strong resistance to change.

Organizational development is a strategy or an effort that is planned and managed from the top, to bring about planned organizational changes for increasing organizational effectiveness through planned interventions based on social philosophy.

Elizabeth Ann Broyles (2007) amply clarifies the need for OD through the following statement: 'Circumstances of an ever-changing market and an ever-changing product are capable of breaking any business organization if that organization is unprepared for change; indeed, in my opinion, if it has not provided procedures for anticipating change.'

Characteristics of Organizational Development

The various characteristics of OD are:

- **Planned organization change**: It identifies the problem and diagnoses the strategies that the organization should develop for improvement. The variables considered in OD programmes are values, attitudes, organizational culture, and team development.

- **Planned intervention**: It is a planned intervention in the existing organization that helps it to become more viable. It, therefore, examines present working norms, values, and possible areas of conflict in the organization and develops better alternatives. The interventionist needs to diagnose different subsystems of the organization and develop alternatives for their better health. The important areas of intervention are planning and decision-making processes, goal setting, team development, organization structure, values and culture, and upgrade of employee skills and abilities.
- **Top management's commitment to OD**: Top management should feel interested in the programme and its outcome, and effectively support efforts in this direction. Unless mutual trust and collaborative relationships are developed between the change agents (which in most of the cases are consultants or professionals) and the management of the enterprise, organizational development efforts may not succeed.
- **Social philosophy as a norm of change**: The bureaucratic model of organization ignores the basic human factors and thereby reduces organizational effectiveness. The interventionist is, therefore, required to use the behavioural science knowledge and develop a system that is more humane and democratic.

Organizational development should not be confused with management development. *Management development* is concerned with the upgrading of managers' skills and abilities, whereas *organizational development*, while it includes management development, is primarily concerned with improving the total system constituting the organization.

Goals of Organizational Development

The important goals of OD are as follows:

- Emphasize the need for changing from a closed system to an open system by inculcating various changes in the organization. Such changes, among other things, also include introduction of the concepts of social philosophy in the organization, making the organization socially responsible and transparent.
- Supplement authority and hierarchical roles with knowledge and skills, replacing traditional authority-assigned roles and creating a more congenial work environment.
- Build mutual trust and confidence in the organization for managing the workforce and reducing conflict.
- Change the structure and roles consistent with the accomplishment of goals.
- Encourage a sense of ownership and pride in the organization.
- Decentralize decision making and take it close to the source of activity.
- Emphasize feedback, self-control, and self-direction.
- Develop the spirit of cooperation, mutual trust, and confidence.
- Develop reward systems based on achievement of goals and development of people's potential.
- Lead in this competitive world.

It is apparent that the goal of OD is basically to change the attitudes of people in the organization to enable them to identify the change areas and implement the desired changes on their own.

Steps in Organizational Development

Robert Black and Jane S. Mouton (1964) suggested a six-phase approach to organizational development:

1. Investigation by each member of the organization of their own managerial styles
2. Examination of boss-subordinate relationship

3. Analysis of work team action
4. Exploration of coordination issues of interrelated teams
5. Identifying and defining major organizational problem areas
6. Planning for executing agreed-upon solutions that result in changes in the organization

Different Stages of Organizational Development

Organizational development progresses through a series of well-defined stages, which can be enumerated as follows:

1. **Identification and diagnosis of the problem**: The required changes in relation to various units in the organization should be identified and diagnosed, duly examining the feedback from employees. Effective identification and diagnosis of the problem should be preceded by an employee survey.
2. **Developing a strategy**: While developing an appropriate strategy, it is necessary to study the people, the subsystem, and the organization as a total system. Strategy is the direction and scope for an organization in the long run, matching resources and the changing environment.
3. **Implementing the programme**: The OD programme should be implemented in a phased manner. Thus, it should be tried at the outset only in a small part of the organization, and only after getting positive results should it be gradually implemented in the total organization. Since total organizational change precedes attitudinal change, that is, change in the values and beliefs of people, the initial thrust should be given to training of employees, improvement of their skills, developing self-awareness, improving interpersonal relationships, reducing conflict, etc.
4. **Reviewing the progress of the programme**: A review of the OD programme should be preferably done by a qualified person who was not involved in designing and developing the programme. This is essential to get an unbiased opinion.

ORGANIZATIONAL CHANGE

Organizational change, per se, is the process of bringing changes in the internal structure, processes, and systems of the organization to make it capable of responding to the external environment and to sustain itself and grow. The process of organizational change follows certain sequential steps. However, before that, one needs to understand the theoretical approaches to organizational change.

Contextual theory of organizational change emphasizes identification of forces and conditions in the internal and external environments of the organization. *External conditions* or *forces* are governmental regulations, technological advances, and various competitive forces that augment market competition. *Internal conditions* or *forces* are the degree of specialization (technology-specific), the level of organizational slack, and lessons from previous change issues. Contextual issues or elements of organizational change, therefore, relate to the success or failure of organizational responses to internal and external environments.

Process theories of organizational change deal with various process issues, addressing the actions taken by organizations in their change initiative. Such organizational actions may be taken to tackle the external environment or the internal environment, and even at the individual level. *External environmental issues* like rules and regulations of various central and state governments as well as local bodies influence organizational employment practices, consumption of energy, production processes encompassing health and safety of workers, environmental pollution, outputs encompassing product safety regulations, etc. In the process of responding to changes in the external environment, organizations are required to bring changes in the operating environment and change the behaviour of employees to achieve the desired goals and objectives. The process theory of organizational change, therefore, focuses on actions or organizational responses to implement changes within the organization and the employees' responses to such organizational mechanisms. Hence, organizations adopting the process theory approach basically become concerned with developing suitable response mechanisms to external environment components that affect the internal activities of the organization, so as to optimize the employees' responses.

Content theory of organizational change deals with causes (conditions of organizations) and the resultant effect based on the change in individual and organizational performance data. Hence, it identifies inbuilt transformational and transactional dynamics of successful organizational change. *Transformational change factors* identify areas that require new employee behaviours as a consequence of external and internal environmental pressures. These factors are leadership, culture, and mission and strategy. *Transactional factors* deal with psychological and organizational variables that predict and control the motivational and performance consequences of a work group's climate. These variables include management practices, structure, systems (policies and procedures), task requirements, and individual skills/abilities.

Need for Organizational Change

Organizational change is basically organic adjustment, and it is needed for different reasons. Some of the important motives behind organizational change can be listed as follows:

- **To set the situation right**: Organizations often need to correct the situation that they feel requires some adjustments or changes. For example, an existing HR policy on variable pay, in a recessionary market, may seem to be incorrect when such pay is based on the value of total sales. An organization may amend this with fixed performance incentive till the market situation rectifies.
- **To fix things that are needed**: Organizations often orchestrate change through external interventions to set right the poor performance areas. This may require alignment of some activities to derive strategic advantages. For example, strategic location disadvantages may require an organization to set up their marketing office in that location and relocate some of their marketing officials there to correct the situation. Similarly, Asian Paints and Dabur, two Indian multinationals, had to set up their manufacturing units across the nation and in foreign countries to derive the advantage of market proximity and to optimize the costs of distribution and supply chain.
- **To grab opportunities to grow**: New market opportunities may motivate an organization to build new capabilities through expansion of their activities or through strategic alliances, identifying business partners, etc. This requires increasing the workforce strength and investing in new resource building. For example, when political pressure mounted in the United States to stop outsourcing of jobs to India, Infosys had to set up their units at Canada to get the outsourced jobs and then route those to their Indian units.
- **To emerge as a different entity**: Often, an organization changes to enjoy flexibility. While adaptability to new situations is essential, flexibility in operations or functions may be the necessity in special circumstances, like developing strategic business units based on product mix or type to make each product type an independent profit centre. To give a competitive edge to each of its products, Kodak formed 34 strategic business units, restructuring its organization to get an edge over Fujifilm.

Philosophy of Organizational Change

Philosophies are the value systems and the guiding force for organizational change. In most cases, one observes that change in organization is motivated by the following core philosophies:

- Adaptability
- Flexibility
- Strategic change
- Behavioural issues
- Participative change process
- Being ethical
- Balancing stakeholders' interests

Steps to Successful Organizational Change

To understand and manage the process of organizational change, John Kotter (1995) suggested an eight-step model. Each step relates the responses of people to the process of change, where people see, feel, and then change. The eight steps are as follows:

1. Increase the urgency, duly activating people through inspiration, so that people move and appreciate the relevance of change objectives.
2. Develop a team to manage organizational change. Such team members will ensure that the right people are put in the right place, addressing the issues of emotional commitment, right skill mix, and hierarchical levels. This process will ensure the success of any organizational change initiative.
3. Develop the right vision—one that is simple, understandable, and shared by all the members of the change team. The real test of a right vision is how far it becomes a shared vision and to what extent people can relate themselves to it. With a shared vision, people can draw the right strategy, matching their emotional and creative needs to successfully drive the organizational change process.
4. Communicate the vision more from the selling perspective, to increase the involvement of all cross-sections of people in the organization, including those who are being affected by the change process, so that they can positively respond to the change process. This would be possible only when change initiatives of the organization respond to people's needs.
5. Empower people so that they can become active in the change action. This would be possible only when obstacles in participation of people in the change process are removed, people are given constant feedback and support, and they are recognized and rewarded for their progress and achievements.
6. Go for change with an incremental approach, that is, short term and step by step. The idea is to celebrate every win in the change process, to pass on the message to the people that results are being achieved. This requires the organization to set aims that are easy to achieve and manageable, and results that are traceable. Strategically, organizations drive the change process with a mantra to do the first thing first, before starting the next stage of change.
7. Do not give up the change initiatives, as it is ongoing. Organizational change requirements never cease to exist. A dynamic organization always encourages change and highlights what they could achieve and what they intend to achieve in the future.
8. Reinforce the change with new values and culture and with more proactive policies in recruitment, promotion, motivation, etc. This will ensure that the change process in the organization is self-sustaining.

Organizational Transition

The term *organizational transition* has been used by many scholars on organizational change, indicating that by implementing change, an organization in fact reaches a transition state, as it moves through the desired conditions and activities to reach the future. Therefore, organizational transition succeeds organizational change. R. Beckhard and R. T. Harris (1987), however, stated that transition is a distinct phase of organizational change which falls between the other two distinct conditions—the present state and the desired future state. The process of organizational transition starts when the organization feels the need or desire for a new future. Such a need emerges from three important sources:

1. Change in external environment, which compels the organization to find faster, cheaper, and better ways to meet the changing needs of customers and other stakeholders
2. Technological change, which requires introduction of a new process and which in turn requires skill renewal and competency development of the existing workforce
3. Top-down change initiatives of managers and executives who prefer to emulate the best practices

The first two needs unfreeze the organization and bring in new work methods. It is a reactive approach, as organizations go for transition or change only after the happenings. The last approach is proactive, as organizations on their own volunteer to change to remain competitive in the market.

Another model of organizational transformation, pioneered by the US-based Healthcare Transformation Institute (HTI) in the 1990s, suggests the following steps:

1. Understanding the opportunities to change
2. Designing a guiding vision for change
3. Measuring the organizational energy (strength) for change
4. Developing a comprehensive plan and commitment to change
5. Developing partnerships (specific working relationships) to implement the change plan
6. Developing leadership to initiate, manage, and sustain the desired change

To understand the degree of preparedness for change, HTI further suggests that organizations should measure their degree of preparedness on a five-point scale. If an organization secures the highest value, say four out of five in all these areas, it may be concluded that transformation is possible.

Irrespective of the nature of the need for organizational change, a clear perspective on the present state and the desired future state of the organization facilitates better management of organizational transition.

Differences Between Organizational Change and Transformation

Organizational change alters the way the organization functions. Change may vary in degree from organization to organization. Whatever may be the degree of change, it is necessary for the organization to survive. Change introduces new ways of doing work and assigns new goals to employees. If the change process continues, the organization can derive the strategic advantage of this process.

Organizational transformation is referred to as a metamorphosis, since the structure, function, activities, and attitudes of people radically change with the process of transformation. The word *transformation* in the context of organization is more appropriate in cases of mergers, acquisitions, corporate gobbling, etc., when culture change in organizations becomes imminent. In such cases, due to change in the management and the way of work, employees of the merged entity undergo a cultural shock. To set them in the right direction, organizations need to transform. Among other things, such organizational transformation succeeds employee rightsizing, hiving off of businesses and redundancies, process changes, etc.

Triggers of Change

Organizational change is necessary to enable organizations to remain competitive, productive, and profitable. The change process is initiated from the top and then is cascaded down through the workforce. It continues till it is integrated with the organization. In the process of integration or implementation, many organizations unsuccessfully adopt a negative approach, which comprises persuading people to change without sharing information with them. Such a negative approach puts organizations into difficulties; resistance to change permeates all areas of activities in the organization, resulting in loss of productivity and fall in the bottom-line (profitability). On the other hand, positive initiatives lead to successful integration and implementation of the change, as people accept the change voluntarily.

Although there are many reasons for organizational change, some of the common reasons are:

- Mergers and acquisitions
- Management restructure
- Introduction of new technology
- Relocation of business premises

At this stage, it is imperative to understand that the impact of change can be striking and can affect all cross-sections of employees of an organization. In some cases, like partial technological change or process changes, organizations may only influence activities of certain departments—more particularly, people who are involved with those departments. Whether it is partial change or all-encompassing change, it is important to reinforce them through required cultural change, new strategies, business plans, process design, training and development, and effective performance management systems. Due to all these reasons, change management first takes stock of the current situation, including the quality of people, and then designs a tailor-made change management programme to ensure success.

Case Strategic Globalization of Business: The Lessons of Barclays

Barclays is one of the leading banks in the United Kingdom. To extend its business beyond the national boundaries, the bank introduced the Barclaycard (credit card) as far back as 1966. To smooth its entry into the global market, apart from introducing new products with wide international acceptance, the bank adopted four medium-term strategies, specifically, defending and extending UK markets, setting up new international markets, developing a world-class global business, and achieving operational excellence. The bank was successful in achieving its strategic intents with its credit card business becoming one of the largest in the world. Today in the European market, Barclaycard is a popular and widely accepted credit card.

The bank has gradually expanded its business in the United States, several European countries, and even Scandinavian, African, and South East Asian countries.

Addressing the cultural and market diversities is a business imperative for the bank, and is also strategically important. Along with its business expansion through the introduction of a new product mix, the bank is also on a cross-border acquisition spree.

The rapid business growth of the company is now a challenge for the HR function of the bank. To achieve consistent people management practices, the bank has put up a platform of people management processes to ensure stability, governance, and control, and also to ensure flexibility in global and local decisions for achieving rapid expansion. HR practices with a global mindset helped the company to synchronize its growth, aligning culturally diverse people to achieve business excellence and growth. The company could establish processes, structures, and frameworks for generic guidance and could also make room for flexibility to accommodate cultural, legal, and social factors that vary with respect to the countries. To make this possible, the company adopted international resourcing, international mobility, talent acquisition and development practices, and global policies and frameworks.

Realizing that policies and frameworks alone cannot serve the purpose, the company also emphasized cultural awareness programmes for the senior leaders to enable them to successfully lead in a global culture. Also, the company adopted cross-cultural training interventions, including a global induction programme to guide employees through the global value systems and the differences in languages.

CASE QUESTION

Read the case of Barclays and document its model of organization culture. Also, suggest how it can be further improved.

Source: Adapted from Sparrow, P. R. (2007). *Barclaycard International: Recruitment in the Context of an Internationalisation Strategy*. Lancaster University Management School, Centre for Performance-led HR Case Study, Number 2007–02, available: http://www.lums.lancs.ac.uk

SUMMARY

- *Culture* is the moral, social, and behavioural norms of an organization. It creates an impact on the beliefs, attitudes, and norms of employees in the organizations.
- Hofstede has identified five independent dimensions of culture: power distance; individualism versus collectivism; masculinity versus femininity; uncertainty avoidance; and long-term versus short-term orientation.
- Every organization aspires to develop a team culture that provides common and consistent goals, enhances organizational commitment, clarifies roles among the team members, develops team leadership, promotes mutual accountability within the team, complements knowledge and skills, reinforces the behavioural competencies, empowers employees, and introduces the system of shared rewards.
- Different national cultures have different preferred ways of structuring organizations and different patterns of employee motivation. For example, limiting the options for performance appraisal, management by objectives, strategic management, and humanization of work. To manage organizational behaviour in a cross-cultural set-up, it is important to understand the characteristic differences between the cultures of people.
- Organizational culture change is a constant organization-building challenge to broaden, deepen, or modify organizational capabilities and resource strengths in response to ongoing customer-market changes. Focus on customer relationship management (CRM) and developing people capabilities require organizations to undergo a perceptive cultural change.

- Managers play the role of a teacher in cultural transformation; they send signals through practices that people down the line emulate. Building a strategy-fit corporate culture is important for successful strategy execution, which produces a performing work environment.
- *Organizational diagnostics* are measures that can apply to anyone in the organization, and can be aggregated to represent different levels of the organization, such as departments, branches, or the organization as a whole.
- *Organizational development (OD)* is a planned change based on the paradigm of understanding the environment, benchmarking, and action research. OD can, thus, be described as a learning process. Types of OD intervention include the person-centred approach, the structural approach, and the relationship approach.
- *Organizational change* is the process of bringing changes in the internal structure, process, and systems of the organization to make it capable of responding to the external environment and to sustain itself and grow. Organizational transition succeeds organizational change. The organizational transition process starts when the organization feels the need or desire for a new future.
- *Organizational transformation* is referred to as a metamorphosis, since the structure, function, activities, and attitudes of the people radically change with the process of transformation. The word *transformation* in the context of organization is more appropriate in the case of mergers, acquisitions, corporate gobbling, etc., when culture change in organizations becomes imminent.

KEY TERMS

Organizational change: It is the process of bringing changes in the internal structure, process, and systems of the organization, to make it capable of responding to the external environment and to sustain itself and grow.

Organizational culture: It is something an organization has, or it can also be seen as something an organization is.

Organizational development: Organizational development (OD) is a planned change based on the paradigm of understanding the environment, benchmarking, and action research. OD can, thus, be described as a learning process.

Organizational diagnostics: Organizational diagnostics are measures that can apply to anyone in the organization, and can be aggregated to represent different levels of the organization, such as departments, branches, or the organization as a whole.

Organizational transformation: It is referred to as a metamorphosis, since the structure, function, activities, and attitudes of the people radically change with the process of transformation.

REVIEW QUESTIONS

1. Define *corporate culture*. Why do organizations across the globe try to create their own culture?
2. Explain Hofstede's cultural orientation model.
3. Discuss how an organization can create a team culture. What are the areas that an organization should change while endeavouring to build a team culture?
4. Give a detailed account of the HP and Sears cultures.

5. What is *organizational development*? What are its important characteristics? How does it differ from *management development*?
6. Write a short note on culture-specific management.
7. Why does an organization require change? What are the important theories of organizational changes?
8. What are the different types of change? How does *planned change* differ from *emergent change?*
9. Write short notes on:
   i. Individual versus collective orientation
   ii. Dominant values orientation
   iii. Uncertainty avoidance
   iv. Power distance
   v. Masculinity and femininity
   vi. OD intervention

CRITICAL THINKING QUESTIONS

1. It is normal practice for organizations to go through cultural transformation after mergers and acquisitions. In India, there are many examples of cross-border mergers and acquisitions. Identify one such unit and critically comment on their cultural transformation process.
2. You have been retained by an organization to help them in OD intervention. The organization feels that this is necessary to bring about an attitudinal change in their employees, as they are now operating in a globally competitive market. Draw up your action plan.

REFERENCES

Bate, P. (1994). *Strategies for Cultural Change*. Oxford: Butterworth-Heinemann.

Beckhard, R. and R. T. Harris (1987). *Organizational Transitions*. Reading, MA: Addison–Wesley.

Blake, Robert R. and Jane S. Mouton (1964). *The Managerial Grid*. Houston, TX: Gulf Publishing.

Brown, A. (1995). *Organizational Culture*. London: Pitman Publishing.

Broyles, Elizabeth Ann (2007). *Resistance to Change in Conservative, Hierarchical Religious Organizations: A Study of Roman Catholic Parishes Shifting from a Top-Down to a Shared Leadership Governance Model*. La Verne, CA: University of La Verne.

Carroll, A. B. (1991). 'The Pyramid of Corporate Social Responsibility: Toward the Moral Management of Organizational Stakeholders', *Business Horizons*, 34, pp. 39–48.

Deal, T. and A. Kennedy (1982). *Corporate Cultures*. Reading, MA: Addison–Wesley.

England, G. W. (1975). *The Manager and His Values*. Cambridge, MA: Ballinger Publishing Co.

Fayol, Henri (2002). *Critical Evaluations in Business and Management*, edited by John C. Wood and Michael C. Wood. London: Routledge.

Fletcher, C. and R. Williams (1996). 'Performance Management, Job Satisfaction and Organizational Commitment', *British Journal of Management*, 7, pp. 169–179.

Frijda, N. H. (1986). *The Emotions*. Cambridge: Cambridge University Press.

Guest, D. E. (1994). 'Organizational Psychology and Human Resource Management: Towards a European Approach', *European Work and Organizational Psychologist*, 4 (3): pp. 251–70.

Hofstede, Geert (1980). *Cultural Consequence: International Differences in Work-related Values*. Beverly Hills, CA: Sage Publications.

——— (2001). *Culture's Consequences: Comparing Values, Behaviors, Institutions, and Organizations Across Nations*, 2nd edition. Thousand Oaks, CA: Sage Publications.

Kerr, J. and J. W. Slocum (1987). 'Managing Corporate Culture through Reward Systems', *Academy of Management Executive*, 1 (2): pp. 99–108.

Kotter, J. P. (1995). *The New Rules: How to Succeed in Today's Post-Corporate World*. New York: Free Press.

Laurent, A. (1983). 'The Cultural Diversity of Western Management Conceptions', *International Studies of Management and Organisation*, 8 (1–2): pp. 75–96. Beverly Hills, CA: Sage Publications.

London, M. and J. W. di Smither (1995). 'Can Multisource Feedback Change Perceptions of Goal Accomplishment, Self-Evaluations, and Performance-related Outcomes? Theory-based Applications and Direction for Research', *Personnel Psychology*, 48, pp. 803–839.

Lord, R. G. and R. J. Foti (1986). 'Schema Theories, Information Processing, and Organizational Behavior', in H. P. Sims, D. A. Gioa and Associates (eds.), *The Thinking Organization*, pp. 20–48. San Francisco, CA: Jossey-Bass.

O'Reilly, C. (1989). 'Corporations, Culture, and Commitment: Motivation and Social Control in Organizations', *California Management Review*, 31 (4): pp. 9–25.

Peters, T. and R. Waterman (1982). *In Search of Excellence*. New York: Harper & Row.

Schein, E. (1968). 'Organizational Socialization and Profession of Management', *Industrial Management Review*, 9, pp. 1–15.

——— (1992). *Organizational Culture and Leadership*, 2nd edition. San Francisco, CA: Jossey-Bass.

Silvester, J., N. R. Anderson and F. Patterson (1999). 'Organizational Culture Change: An Inter-Group Attributional Analysis', *Journal of Occupational and Organizational Psychology*, 92, pp. 1–22.

Whittlesey, Fred E. (1995). 'CEO Herb Kelleher Discusses Southwest Airlines' People Culture: How the Company Achieves Competitive Advantage from the Ground Up', *ACA Journal* (*WorldatWork Journal*), Winter 1995, 4 (4): pp. 8–25.

Wilson, K. G. (2001). 'Some Notes on Theoretical Constructs: Types and Validation from a Contextual-Behavioral Perspective', *International Journal of Psychology and Psychological Therapy,* 1, pp. 205–215.

FURTHER READING

Ackerman, L. S. (1986). 'Development, Transition or Transformation: The Question of Change in Organizations', *Organizational Development Practitioner*, December, pp. 1–8.

Albert, M. and M. Silverman (1984). 'Making Management Philosophy a Cultural Reality, Part 1: Getting Started', *Personnel*, 61, pp. 12–21.

Bhattacharyya, Dipak Kumar (2007). *Human Resource Research Methods*. New Delhi: Oxford University Press.

——— (2010). *Cross-Cultural Management—Text and Cases*. New Delhi: PHI Learning.

——— (2010). *Organizational Change and Development*. New Delhi: Oxford University Press.

Carr, C. (1996). *Choice, Chance and Organizational Change*. New York: Amacom.

Guest, D. E. (1992). 'Right Enough to be Dangerously Wrong: An Analysis of the "In Search of Excellence Phenomenon" ', in G. Salaman (ed.), *Human Resources Strategies*. London: Sage Publications.

Hampden-Turner, C. and F. Trompenaars (2000). *Building Cross-Cultural Competence: How to Create Wealth from Conflicting Values*. New Haven: Yale University Press.

Schein, E. H. (1969). *Process Consultation: Its Role in Organizational Development*. Reading, MA: Addison–Wesley.

——— (1990). 'Organizational Culture', *American Psychologist*, 45, pp. 109–119.

Weick, K. E. and R. E. Quinn (1999). 'Organizational Change and Development', *Annual Review of Psychology*, 50, pp. 361–386.

Woodman, R. (1989). 'Organization Change and Development: New Arenas for Inquiry and Action', *Journal of Management*, 15, pp. 205–228.

17

Managing Conflict and Stress in Organizations

After going through this chapter, you will be able to understand:

- the concepts of conflict and stress in organizations
- the different causes of conflict and stress in organizations
- the process of conflict management
- the process of managing stress

Working Together at Shell Australia

Shell Australia is a major global energy organization operational since 1901. With over 3,000 people from culturally diverse backgrounds, it meets about one-third of Australia's petroleum requirements, catering to more than 50,000 customers. One of its biggest challenges is to manage a multicultural technical team wherein the members need to demonstrate strong affiliation and commitment to the organization and achieve high performance. The usual problems experienced are misunderstandings arising from differences in communication styles, decision-making preferences, and cultural backgrounds. To overcome these, the team required an engaging learning framework which would enable them to develop an agreed set of goals to improve team interactions and performance. To make the team members work in coordination, the company engaged them in an experiential workshop designed to address team interactions and approaches to communicating, managing conflict, and utilizing diversity within the team to achieve business objectives. As a result, the team gained insight into its strengths and addressed the challenges it identified through the process. The trust increased between team members, enabling them to make constructive use of differences in personality types within the team and improve the performance and efficiency of the team, which resulted in tangible business gains.

INTRODUCTION

Employee performance gets affected by conflict and stress in the workplace. *Conflict* implies a clash which occurs due to differences in needs, expectations, and interests of people. Stress is a frequent cause of conflict, and in a reinforcing manner, conflict can further increase the stress. Conflict in organizations could be disastrous unless checked through timely interventions. With conflict and stress, productivity rate goes down and the entire organization suffers. Even then, conflict per se may not always be bad—at times it sparks innovation and creativity, which helps to build long-term organizational capability to grow and survive. For managers, therefore, the responsibility is to manage the conflict in a constructive way, so that people can be motivated to contribute more for the benefit of the organization. Conflict mostly occurs between individuals or groups. Working in a group is now an organizational imperative. Hence, to get the best from a group, successful management of conflict is very important. However, managing individual conflicts also deserves simultaneous attention. Through the management of conflict, organizations can reduce stress and successfully drive the efforts of employees to reach their peak level of performance.

CONCEPT OF CONFLICT

To understand the concept of conflict better, one first needs to understand what leads to behavioural incongruity and competition in individuals. All competition need not involve conflict but all conflict, per se, is embedded in competition, which leads to perceived behavioural incongruity. Similarly, conflict arises due to contesting relational propensities among individuals. With these two preludes, one can say that conflict is a naturally occurring phenomenon with both positive and negative effects depending on its management (Sheppard 1984). It is a phenomenon inherent in all organizations and arises from the differences in goals, needs, interests, attitudes, values, and perceptions during the interaction of groups such as management and labour (Bendix 1989). Essentially, organizations function as a 'means for internalizing conflicts, bringing them within a bounded structure so that they can be confronted and acted upon' (Pondy 1992). Pondy further advocates that conflict is the essence of an organization. This is why organizations cannot be viewed as purposive and cooperative systems—rather, they are the outcome of inbuilt conflicts, which make organizations adapt to changes by effectively managing the conflict. By managing organizational behaviour, developing an appropriate organizational structure, and adopting the systems and processes of a cooperative culture, conflict can be effectively managed. Since conflict is inevitable, its elimination is not possible. Organizational efforts should focus on reducing harmful conflicts, while nurturing the positive ones to promote creativity and innovation. Sheppard (1992) also recommended the elimination of destructive conflict.

Types of Conflict

Fred Luthans (1995) has classified conflicts into four types: intra-individual, interpersonal, inter-group, and organizational.

1. *Intra-individual conflict* arises due to frustration, and frustration arises due to incompatibility between the perceived goals and the actual achievements. When individual employees encounter goal incongruity, they become aggressive and frustrated. Ultimately, they decide to either withdraw from the pursuit of their goals, realizing that nothing is going to be achieved. However, in the final stage of conflict resolution, individual employees may compromise. Goal conflicts can be categorized as approach–approach (cognitive dissonance), approach–avoidance (conflict between organizational goals and individual goals), and avoidance–avoidance (perceptive goal congruence). Further, role conflict and ambiguity are classified under intra-individual conflict. Role conflict and ambiguity mostly arise due to cultural differences.
2. *Interpersonal conflict* arises due to personal differences, information deficiency, role incompatibility, and environmental stress. This type of conflict is resolved through negotiation. The Johari Window (Luft and Ingham 1955) can also be used to analyse interpersonal conflict.

3. *Inter-group conflict* arises due to competition for resources, task interdependence, jurisdictional ambiguity, and status struggle. In organizations, the strategies of avoidance, diffusion, containment, and confrontation are adopted to avoid inter-group conflict.
4. *Organizational conflict* occurs mostly due to structural conflict, hierarchical conflict, functional conflict, line and staff conflict, and formal and informal conflict.

Causes of Conflict

Be it competition or contesting behavioural incongruence, causes of conflict can be best understood through an analysis of the sources of conflict. The causal factors of conflict are as follows:

- **Need-based conflicts**: Employees differ in their perceived needs. Hence, depending on the varied nature of needs, conflict may be due to multiplicity of needs, incongruence of needs, dissatisfaction of needs, and dilemma of choice.
- **Work environment-related conflicts**: Job roles of individual employees, job interactions, line and staff conflict, and finally the job itself are potential sources of conflict.
- **Organizational factors**: Often, organizational factors such as authority and responsibility, excessive or low standardization, transfers, communication, and scarcity of resources become potential sources of conflict.
- **Goal conflicts**: Often, conflict arises due to the differences in goals and objectives, both between individuals and between individuals and the organization. It could be a win–win conflict, a lose–lose conflict, or a win–lose conflict.
- **Individual factors**: People differ from each other in terms of culture, education, status, ideology, attitude, experience, competition, and conflict. Such individual differences could be potential sources of conflict.

Conflict Management

The very first step in *conflict management* is to avoid conflict. However, conflict avoidance may not be possible in all cases. The process of conflict management, in such circumstances, resolves conflict on real-time basis. Although it is true that conflict arises in organizations due to individuals' perceived competition, there is a need to understand that organizations in their own may nurture competition to extract the best from individuals. When such a culture of competition is deliberately created, organizations take extra precautions to make it as friendly as possible. A friendly culture of competition indicates nurturing of the reward schemes in such a way that individual target achievements do not get the maximum weight—it is, instead, balanced and focused on group target achievement. Most of the private sector banks design their employees' compensation structure in such a way that increased pay and incentives become payable to individual employees on 100 per cent achievement. This is a typical example of unhealthy competition and it is bound to spark conflict. However, when organizations distribute such weights to individual, group, and organizational target achievement, the nature of competition becomes friendlier.

In organizations, two types of conflicts are more visible—conflict over right and conflict over interest. *Conflict over right* is more related to employer–employee relationships, which are settled through the processes of collective bargaining and grievance handling, and partially also through enforcement of workplace discipline. *Conflict over interest* relates to perceptions, attitudes, and opinions that differ from person to person. Building a proactive organizational culture through shared vision and mission can alleviate this type of conflict. Conflicts are avoided by organizations through promoting teamwork and cooperation.

Teamwork can only be possible with shared vision, empowerment with stakes in decision making, transparency in information, etc. Collective bargaining, conciliation (inducing friendly feeling), negotiation, mediation (when negotiation fails), and arbitration are the most useful methods of conflict resolution in organizations. However, use of the appropriate conflict management tool must be situation-specific and need-based. Conflict management requires different levels of interaction between people, which may be basic communication, use of positive body language, or simple evasion tactics. This requires training and opportunity to interact and learn through experiences. For example, collective bargaining or negotiation skills are possible to attain through theoretical training but they also require hands-on exposure to the situation, letting learners understand the real-life situation by allowing them to witness the process with their seniors. Slowly, they gain confidence and start contributing to the solution. In the process of interaction, they learn how to escalate and de-escalate the existing situation, realizing the implication of the other person's action. In the process, they master the following skill sets:

- Appropriate selection of policies and strategies to handle a conflict
- Proper understanding of the individual's rights and duties, as also their own rights and duties, to ensure that there exists a proper synergy in actions and interactions
- Understanding of the mechanism of positive response
- Understanding of the process of averting negative behavioural responses
- Recognizing the emotions and feelings of other people
- Understanding of the effects of fear and admiration and the process of controlling these effects
- Nurturing positive attitude and appearance
- Understanding of the behaviour of people
- Mastery over both verbal and non-verbal communication skills
- Understanding of the de-escalation strategy, that is, helping people to control their emotion
- Understanding of the process of tackling the effects of an incident, to render effective post-incident support
- Mastery over counselling skills

Conflict Models and Strategies

Organizational conflict is sensitized by a series of events and extends to all interactions between organizational members, departments, and groups. This makes organizational conflict unavoidable and inseparable from organizational functioning (Lewicki and Spencer 1992). Organizational conflict represents disagreement, differences, or incompatibility within or between individuals and groups (Rahim 1985). With the effective management of organizational conflict, organizations can reach new heights of creativity, innovation, and competitiveness.

The models of conflict provide a conceptual framework for conflict resolution by elaborating the process and actions through which conflict is managed in an organization (M. Patchen 1970). A possible conceptual model of conflict resolution is discussed here.

Stimulating conflict

Managers in organizations stimulate conflict by encouraging friendly competition. This is, however, an example of positive conflict that is used to bring changes in the organizations by harnessing the innovation and creativity of individuals. At times, organizations stimulate conflict by bringing in new people in very senior-level positions (even at the CEO level). These new recruits shake up everything in organizations, including prevailing systems, procedures, standards, and managerial approaches.

Incidentally, it is important to mention that recruiting people at very senior levels is often not liked by organizations, as they always prefer to groom people from within through effective succession planning. However, induction of outsiders is often viewed as a deliberate strategy by organizations to bring changes by inducing positive conflict.

Controlling conflict

In the process of stimulation of conflict, organizations may encounter dysfunctional conflicts that pose a threat to smooth functioning. At this stage, controlling conflict becomes important. The most dominant strategy of conflict control is to expand the resource base to enhance coordination among interdependent groups. To remove employees' attention from dysfunctional conflicts, organizations also set higher goals and try to form work groups of individuals with matching personalities and habits.

Resolving and eliminating conflict

Strategies for resolving and eliminating conflict are adopted in cases when conflict-related tensions disrupt the activities in the workplace, making it impossible to achieve goals and objectives. The ways and means to resolve conflict in such cases include avoidance, smoothing (through stating that things will improve), and compromising (by bringing together the conflicting parties). Irrespective of the approach taken to resolve conflict, the core focus of organizations is avoidance of destructive conflict.

Resolving conflicts in a positive manner

As explained earlier, conflict cannot be eliminated. Rather, it should be effectively managed. At times, organizations need to resolve dysfunctional conflicts by adopting various means. Some of the positive ways to resolve conflict are as follows:

- **Use of 'I' instead of 'you'**: In organizations one often uses the word 'you', but the word 'you' puts the listener on defence, as 'you' sounds more like an order, emphasizing the point that as subordinate, one has to carry out the order of the superior. The use of 'I' is more personal and non-accusatory.
- **Power of anticipation**: Anticipation is pre-study of the reaction of the listeners to the statements made. This ensures respecting others and thus reduces conflicts.
- **Selling of self-interest**: Positive conflict resolution succeeds when managers know the interests of the conflicting persons and then sell their desires and needs. The interests of the conflicting persons or the issues of the conflict per se may be related to money, power, popularity, status, promotion, or security. Hence, managers can effectively sell their interests, appealing to the appropriate needs and desires of the conflicting persons to resolve the conflict positively.
- **Attitude**: While resolving conflict positively, it is important for managers to understand the attitude of the conflicting person. Understanding attitude is difficult, but incongruity between verbal responses and the body language often gives clues to managers to understand the attitude of the conflicting person. Accordingly, managers can decide the strategies suitable for conflict resolution.
- **Clarity**: Lack of clarity often sparks conflict. People without clarity fail to rationally allocate their priorities and efforts to achieve goals and objectives. Hence, eliminating confusion is a step towards positive relationships.
- **Explaining the adverse consequences**: This should not be misconstrued as the use of the stick. It should, instead, be seen as an attempt at helping people understand the possible adverse consequences of continuing to nurture dysfunctional conflicts. Through transparent information sharing and using glass-wall management styles, conflicting employees are often transformed into positive contributors to organizational goals and objectives.

In addition, to resolve conflicts in a positive way, one needs to first resolve internal conflicts and put oneself in the other person's shoes. Thereafter, one must listen to what they need, set one's own priorities, discuss the situation calmly, come to a mutually agreeable solution, and honestly follow up on the decisions taken. These techniques can be used together or separately, depending on the conflict. Conflict should always be dealt with in camera (that is, privately or individually), or else it can create tensions and aggravate the situation. Through effective negotiation, managers should focus on win-win solutions.

STRESS IN ORGANIZATIONS

In workplaces, psychological and physiological functioning of the individuals gets influenced due to a number of incompatibilities, of which conflict is the major one. Conflict and stress are closely related behavioural phenomena. Conflict may increase stress, and stress may lead to work-based conflict. The online Merriam-Webster dictionary defines *stress* as a 'constraining physical, chemical or emotional factor that causes bodily or mental tension'. Managing stress means identifying the symptoms of stress and then making effective use of different stress busters, like humour in the workplace, to help employees feel relaxed and perform efficiently. Effective stress management makes the workplace more enjoyable and increases the productivity level. Global organizations like Hewlett-Packard and Viking Components emphasize stress management, offering their employees a running track, fresh bowls of fruit, weekly neck massage, etc.

Nature of Stress

Stress is an individual's adaptive response to a stimulus that carries excessive psychological or physical demands. The stressor is the stimulus that induces stress. Stress generally follows a cycle known as the general adaptation syndrome (GAS). According to this, individuals have a normal level of resistance to stressful events; some individuals can tolerate a great deal, while others can handle much less. When a stressor is present, in the first stage the individual becomes concerned about the stress. During the second stage, the person attempts to resist the effects of the stressor. In many situations, the resistance phase may end the GAS. However, prolonged exposure to a stressor without resolution may lead to exhaustion and its attendant consequences. Some stress is necessary for optimal performance, but too much stress can have very negative consequences. It is also important to understand that stress can be caused by good as well as bad things.

Stress and the Individual

People handle stress differently. Some thrive on pressure. Others panic at the slightest pressure and would do anything to avoid stress. Cultural backgrounds can affect a person's response to stressors. Stress can have behavioural, psychological, and medical consequences for individuals. Stress can lead people to engaging in harmful behaviour. Stress can adversely affect an individual. Individual stress has direct consequences for organizations. The performance level declines and withdrawal behaviours such as absenteeism and turnover may occur if there is too much stress. People may exhibit poor attitudes when they are under too much stress, which affect their mental health and well-being as well as their physiological well-being

Type A personality profile

Type A individuals are extremely competitive and devoted to work. They have a strong sense of timing and urgency. They are likely to be aggressive, impatient, and very work-oriented. Due to these personality traits, a type A person is much more likely to experience stress than a type B person.

Type B personality profile

Type B individuals tend to be less competitive and less devoted to work. They have a weaker sense of timing and urgency. The type B person is much less likely to experience stress than the type A person. Few people are either purely type A or purely type B.

Causes of Stress in Organizations

Stress can be caused by a variety of factors. Positive stress may result in increased energy, enthusiasm, and motivation. Negative stress has more serious consequences. Common causes are organizational stressors and life stressors.

Organizational stressors

Organizational stressors may relate to task demands, physical demands, role demands, or interpersonal demands.

- *Task demands* are stressors associated with the specific task or job the person is performing. Some occupations are naturally more stressful than others.
- *Physical demands* are stressors associated with the job setting. Environmental temperatures, poorly designed offices, and threats to health can lead to stress.
- *Role demands* are stressors associated with a particular position in a group or an organization. Examples are role ambiguity and the various role conflicts that people experience in groups.
- *Interpersonal demands* are stressors associated with the characteristics of the relationships that confront people in organizations. Examples are group pressure, personality style, and leadership style.

Life stressors

Causes of stress may reside in events that are not directly connected to people's daily work lives. Any significant change in a person's personal or work situation can lead to stress. The top eight life stressors are:

1. Death of spouse
2. Divorce and marital separation
3. Jail term
4. Death of a close family member
5. Personal injury or illness
6. Marriage
7. Loss of job and retirement
8. Marital reconciliation

Approaches to Managing Stress

Burnout is a general feeling of exhaustion that may develop when an individual simultaneously experiences too much pressure and too few sources of satisfaction. Effects of burnout are likely to be constant fatigue and feelings of frustration and helplessness. There are different ways to manage stress to avoid burnout.

Individual approaches to managing stress

People have different ways of managing stress. One way is exercise. Another method is relaxation. Individuals can use time-management techniques to help them manage their schedules. Role management can be used to avoid role overload, ambiguity, and conflict. Finally, people can manage stress by developing and maintaining support groups.

Organizational approaches to managing stress

Organizations have a vested interest in helping their employees manage stress. Organizations can use institutional programmes and wellness programmes. Institutional efforts to manage stress are based on established organizational mechanisms. Organizations can redesign especially stressful jobs, rearrange work schedules, and eliminate rotating shifts. Also, the organizational culture can help manage stress. Wellness programmes are specifically created to help individuals deal with stress. Stress management programmes, health promotion programmes, and other kinds of programmes can be made a part of an organization's wellness focus. Career development programmes can also help minimize stress by showing managers clearly where they are in their career relative to where they would like to be. In developing any type of stress management programme, managers need to balance the costs and benefits.

PROCESS OF CONFLICT MANAGEMENT

Conflict management requires a systematic and structured approach. As highlighted before, conflict cannot be eliminated—it needs to be managed. Some conflict-management strategies that are commonly used by organizations have been discussed here.

Collective bargaining is of central concern to the process of conflict management. It is the mechanism through which labour and management negotiators try and resolve their disagreements by interacting under formal rules, accepted practices, laws, and conventions (Allen and Keaveny 1983). Collective bargaining has the purpose and result of regulating relations between unions and management, and has the effect of redistributing power, reallocating resources, rationalizing authority, and changing the psychological climate.

The *grievance procedure* as a conflict-management strategy is an integral part of the total collective-bargaining process. It serves the general purpose of adjusting disagreements, individual dissatisfactions, and conflict, without recourse to threats of strike and use of force. However, the grievance process can also be used to sustain and feed conflict, especially under circumstances where contract-bargaining relationships between the union and the management have not been established (Kennedy 1954).

Within the area of labour-management disputes, grievance negotiation and bargaining are key strategies used in the management of conflict. Essentially, *negotiation* involves the settlement of differences by means of verbal agreements, while *bargaining* also involves many non-verbal actions that are utilized to resolve a controversy (Pruitt and Rubin 1972). Bargaining may, therefore, involve a number of tactics to elicit concessions from the adversary to resolve the dispute (Pruitt 1972). The tactics used in the bargaining process are, however, dependent on the conceptualization of the issues of conflict. Generally, four types of tactics have been identified, including coordinating mutually satisfactory outcomes, conceding, breaking off negotiations, and persuading the other party to concede using positional commitments, persuasive arguments, or threats (Hartley and Kelly 1986).

Employee Discipline and Grievance Handling as a Workplace Conflict-resolution Strategy

Workplace conflict-resolution strategy depends on enforcement of discipline and grievance-handling systems in the organization. In a broad sense, discipline means orderly and systematic behaviour. Every organization, to ensure operative efficiency, frames certain codes of behaviour for employees to observe under normal practice, contract, statutes, or mutual understanding. Breaking of such behavioural norms creates disciplinary problems. The steps to be followed to handle such problems are: (1) early intervention, (2) identification of problem, (3) clear expectations, (4) feedback, (5) positive reinforcement, and (6) follow-up.

To enforce discipline, organizations adopt various approaches, which may be corrective, positive, or negative. *Corrective discipline* is ideally suited to solve continual performance problems, rather than isolated ones. Discipline itself may be classified as positive discipline and negative discipline. When a person spontaneously abides by the required norms, it is called *positive* or *constructive discipline*. However, when he is compelled to behave in a desired way under threat or fear of punishment, it is termed as *negative*, *punitive*, or *autocratic discipline*. The type of approach followed depends on the organization's policies and strategies and the nature of the workforce.

Positive discipline is achieved through education and training, while negative discipline is enforced by punishment. Indiscipline may be of two types—individual and collective. *Individual indiscipline* is basically a problem of attitude, while problems relating to industrial relations are responsible for *collective indiscipline*.

Walter Kiechel (1990) developed the 'hot stove' rule to administer discipline in an organization. By touching a hot stove, one gets burned. There is an immediate response and it leaves no question of cause and effect. This analogy keeps the discipline impersonal, that is, penalties for a given violation are independent of the personality of the violator.

Whatever approaches are followed by an organization to tackle disciplinary problems, the focus is on individual or collective conflicts.

Collective Bargaining as a Conflict-resolution Strategy

In addition to the enforcement of discipline and maintaining scientific grievance-handling systems, in cases of collective conflict, organizations make use of collective bargaining, which is more of an institutionalized and structured approach. Collective bargaining is a method to determine working conditions and terms of employment through negotiations. Negotiations take place between an employer's organization and workers' organization. The negotiation process helps the two sides to reach an agreement. Collective bargaining is considered to be an economic institution, as trade unionism restricts entry into trade by forming a labour cartel. Discarding this concept, Allan Flanders (1975) advocates that collective bargaining is basically political as it aims to protect dignity rather than economic interests. The Marxist school considers collective bargaining to be a means of social control. The marketing concept considers the process of collective bargaining to be a constitutional system to determine relations between management and trade unions. Finally, the industrial relations concept views collective bargaining as a system of 'industrial governance'. In practice, however, none of these theoretical distinctions are considered. All these theories converge on three basic issues, which define collective bargaining. These are:

1. A means to contract for sale of labour
2. A form of industrial government
3. A system of industrial relations

International Labour Organization (ILO 1986) defines the term *collective bargaining* as negotiations about working conditions, terms of employment, and regulation of relations between an employer, a group of employers, or one or more employers' organizations, on the one hand, and representatives of workers' organizations, on the other hand, with a view to reach an agreement.

In collective bargaining, the object is to arrive at an agreement on wages and other conditions of employment about which the parties start with divergent viewpoints, but ultimately attempt to reach a compromise. As soon as the bargain is made, the terms of agreement are put into operation. On the other hand, the major task of the latter relates to sharing the information and suggestions with regard to issues of common interests including health, safety, welfare, and productive efficiency.

Mary Sur (1965) observes that collective bargaining starts with claims advanced by both sides—demands from the union and statements by the management on how far they can concede to these demands and what they want in return, just as the bazaar vendor and buyer start by quoting prices that are at variance, each knowing that they will have to be somewhat accommodating in the end in order to reach a final agreed price.

The most comprehensive definition of collective bargaining has been provided by the Trade Union and Labour Relations (Consolidation) Act (TULRCA), 1992, Section 178, points (1) and (2) of U.K. Employment Law. Collective bargaining, according to the U.K. Employment Law, is the negotiation connected with one or more of the following:

- Terms and conditions of employment, or the physical conditions in which any worker is required to work
- Engagement or non-engagement, or termination or suspension of employment and the duties of employment of one or more workers
- Allocation of work or the duties of employment between workers or groups of workers
- Matters of discipline
- A worker's membership or non-membership of a trade union
- Facilities for officials of trade unions
- Machinery for negotiation or consultation, and other procedures relating to any of the above matters, including the recognition by employers or employers' associations of the right of a trade union to represent workers in such negotiation or consultation or in the carrying out of such procedures

While employers and employees have different interests, these differences are not irreconcilable. Instead, they are somewhat same like the differences between buyers and sellers in general. Therefore, through bargaining, a deal can be cut which sets the price and regulates the conditions under which employees sell their labour. Some important assumptions to achieve a stable process of collective bargaining are:

- Each side accepts the legitimacy of the other and its right to survive.
- The sides are roughly equal in strength; otherwise, one side will dominate rather than bargain with the other.
- The union legitimately represents the interests of all of those it claims to represent (a claim sometimes questioned by women and members of minority groups).
- Both parties are willing to negotiate seriously with the aim of reaching an agreement.
- If an agreement cannot be reached, it is legitimate for either side to exert economic pressure (strikes or lockouts) in order to induce the other to make concessions. This type of pressure, which is usually regulated by law or generally accepted as rules of fair play, may differ among countries.
- The government plays only a limited direct role in the bargaining.

Case Resolve Conflict Through Discussions: The Case of Robin and His People

Robin Mehata, a US-based technocrat, recently shifted to India, his birthplace, and joined an engineering major at Bangalore as the chief operating officer (COO). Robin heads the entire operation of the Bangalore unit and in addition, because of his background, he is also looking after the design and development unit of the company based in Pune. The Indian company is in the business of customized machine tool design and manufacturing. Machine tools are critical supplementary manufacturing aids for any manufacturing process, including those which still make use of conventional machines in their manufacturing process. With standard machine tools, it is particularly difficult to run the latest technology-intensive manufacturing process. It requires customized solutions for the customer. Robin is a typical workaholic and expects his people to work like him to achieve time-bound targets for the company. In a short-term (quarterly) performance review of his design team members, Robin promoted half a dozen young engineers who were found to be excellent in terms of performance and innovation, and who could even beat deadlines. This decision of Robin made other members of the design team furious, and many of them even stopped talking to Robin. Robin's telephonic instructions to them are now mostly left unattended, and they even ignore the need to inform Robin about the work progress. Their behaviour gradually cascaded to the employees in other departments, and eventually Robin became the talk of the plant. Being an ardent believer of transparent and professional management practices, Robin took it as a challenge.

Robin first took a detailed account of the whole situation, meticulously studied the history of the organization and its age-old systems and procedures, and then started meeting each employee individually. Within a week's time, Robin was able to meet all the employees of the plant. As irritant employees can immediately get sensitized by psychometric assessments, Robin took the approach of convincing them by 'word of mouth'. The first round of individual meetings and discussion was followed by 'ice-breaking sessions' in a team of 15–20 people, where every participant was asked to indicate their expectations from the organization, with a clear mandate that their expectations in general will be ranked after consolidating the information, based on their perceived choices. Robin could identify 10 different expectations from all the employees of the organization. His analysis indicated that 'recognition and rewards' is most sought after. With such 'ice-breaking sessions,' one thing was clear to Robin. It is that everyone aspires to rise through the ladder and get recognized. The expectation to rise naturally leads to the zeal to perform. However, since the typical nature of the work of the company required high-end skill, many old-timers failed to deliver results despite their urge to perform. Robin introduced systematic in-house training and even hired the services of external experts. This was followed by specific trade tests for assessing their application-based knowledge and skill.

The approach of Robin was well taken and within no time, employees started cooperating, delivering their best and showing their eagerness to learn more and more.

CASE QUESTION

Study the case and indicate whether Robin's approach to conflict resolution can be universal (applicable across all organizations). Give reasons to support your argument.

Case Managing Stress in Organizations: The Case of an Industrial Chemical Company

To manage stress at work, a leading collaborative unit of Japan and India engaged in producing industrial chemicals adopted a policy delineating the responsibilities of managers, individual employees, and the organization. The main thrust of the policy was to adopt a proactive approach in matters of stress management, rather than waiting for the problem to arise. The policy document spelled out that the management of stress in the workplace is inseparable from the duties and the job roles of managers and supervisors. Since the company was in the business of hazardous chemicals, stress in the workplace also occured due to occupational health hazards, in addition to work-related stress. To guide the managers and supervisors, the policy document categorized the possible reasons for stress as the following: culture, demands, control, relationships, change, role, and support.

After categorization of possible stress issues that have occurred or likely to occur, managers and supervisors would decide the possible course of action through brainstorming and recommend the same to the top management. After a review, the top management would recommend its implementation within a day or two. To help the workers self-manage the workplace stress, and also the stress that may be exogenous to organizations, a detailed frequently asked questions (FAQ) was also hosted by the company and prominently displayed in canteens, shop floors, etc.

This approach to stress management helped the company to reduce workplace stress significantly. The backup support of counselling also helped the company to reduce the stress exogenous to the organization, like family matters and relationship problems.

CASE QUESTION

Draw lessons from this case study and suggest a solution to a coal mining company, facing high attendance irregularities primarily due to workplace stress.

SUMMARY

- For organizations, conflict may be a challenge or an opportunity; at the same time, it could be counterproductive and affect the health of an organization. The most effective way to manage and resolve conflicts in organizations is to negotiate around the issues that cause conflicts and maintain a cooperative process.
- Resolving conflict is best possible through enforcement of discipline. *Discipline* means orderly and systematic behaviour, which is an important prerequisite for organizational harmony. Absence of discipline or indisciplined behaviour may stand against achievement of organizational objectives.
- To enforce discipline, every organization lays down certain procedures and norms that employees are required to comply with. Approaches to discipline differ from organization to organization, though most of them prefer to adopt a legalistic approach. Disciplinary proceedings follow certain well-defined steps. The problem of discipline can be avoided by adopting a well-defined grievance redressal mechanism within the organization. The principles of natural justice should receive attention while handling grievances or cases of indiscipline in an organization. Handling disciplinary problems in an organization requires specialized knowledge and skills.

- Collective bargaining is another important approach to conflict resolution. *Collective bargaining* is a voluntary process of negotiation between employers and employees to determine various terms of employment. The process ensures organizational democracy. However, it often proves to be an ineffective mechanism for reaching an agreement. In fact, the importance of collective bargaining is receding globally. Most organizations prefer to have enterprise-wide bargaining rather than industry-wide bargaining. Industry-wide bargaining agreements are not implemented by many organizations within the same industry group. The example of the banking industry is relevant in this context. In a collective bargaining situation, HR managers need to play a crucial role in striking a win–win deal. To achieve this, they have to enrich their negotiation skills, practising collective bargaining simulation games on a regular basis.
- Like conflict, stress also leads to a dysfunctional syndrome in organizations. Stress is the result of interactions of the individual with the environment. Often, conflict leads to stress. Therefore, stress can be controlled through the process of managing conflict. Stress could be due to psychological or physiological reasons.

KEY TERMS

Burnout: Burnout is a general feeling of exhaustion that may develop when an individual simultaneously experiences too much pressure and too few sources of satisfaction.

Collective bargaining: This is a method to determine working conditions and terms of employment through negotiations. Negotiations take place between an employer's organization and workers' organization.

Conflict: Conflict implies a clash which occurs due to differences in needs, expectations, and interests of people.

'Hot stove' rule: The 'hot stove' rule suggests administering of discipline in organizations. By touching a hot stove, one gets burned. There is an immediate response and it leaves no question of cause and effect. This analogy keeps the discipline impersonal, that is, penalties for a given violation are independent of the personality of the violator.

Inter-group conflict: This type of conflict arises due to competition for resources, task interdependence, jurisdictional ambiguity, and status struggle.

Interpersonal conflict: This type of conflict arises due to personal differences, information deficiency, role incompatibility, and environmental stress.

Interpersonal demands: These are stressors associated with the characteristics of the relationships that confront people in organizations.

Intra-individual conflict: This type of conflict arises due to frustration, and frustration arises due to incompatibility between the perceived goals and the actual achievements.

Organizational conflict: This type of conflict occurs mostly due to structural conflict, hierarchical conflict, functional conflict, line and staff conflict, and formal and informal conflict.

Physical demands: These are stressors associated with the job setting.

Role demands: These are stressors associated with a particular position in a group or an organization.

Stress: Stress is a 'constraining physical, chemical, or emotional factor that causes bodily or mental tension'.

Task demands: These are stressors associated with the specific task or job the person is performing.

REVIEW QUESTIONS

1. Explain the causes of conflict and how workplace stress adds to conflict.
2. It is said that conflict cannot be eliminated but needs to be managed. Do you agree with this statement? What types of conflict need to be resolved and need not be resolved? Elaborate your answer with examples.
3. A careful study of workplace-related conflict indicates that many conflicts are the result of the organizational environment. If it is so, how can an organization ensure that its environment does not contribute to any conflict?
4. What are the steps necessary for corrective discipline? How is the *positive discipline* approach different from the *negative discipline* approach? Which approach do you consider to be the best approach?
5. What are the causes of undisciplined behaviour in organizations?
6. Briefly describe the common disciplinary problems. Prepare a checklist for resolving such problems.
7. Define *collective bargaining*. What are its important characteristics and what are the prerequisites for its success?
8. To make the collective bargaining process a success, what are the roles of workers and management representatives?
9. Explain the reasons for organizational stress. How can organizations reduce such stress?
10. 'Stress due to individual reasons can also be addressed by the organization.' Do you agree with this statement? Justify your answer.
11. Write short notes on:
    i. Step ladder system of grievance handling
    ii. Power of anticipation
    iii. Life stressors
    iv. Conflict-resolution models
    v. Organizational stressors

CRITICAL THINKING QUESTIONS

1. You have been engaged by an organization to help in resolving perennial conflict situations which hinder the growth of the organization. The organization is engaged in research and development work in the biomedical and biotechnology fields and all research work requires cross-sectional inputs. Draw up an action plan to probe into the problem of conflict. Find out how your line of action can help the organization to reduce conflict.
2. To resolve conflict in your cement-manufacturing unit, your company proposed to develop a conflict-resolution policy. However, you find that since the conflicts are so varied in nature, you cannot take any policy-bound decision to resolve the conflicts. Suggest an approach that would be a better solution.

REFERENCES

Allen, R. E. and T. J. Keaveny (1983). *Contemporary Labour Relations*. New York: Addison-Wesley.

Bendix, Reinhard (1989). *Nation Building and Citizenship*. New Delhi: Eastern Wiley.

Flanders, Allan (1975). 'Collective Bargaining: Prescription for Change', *Management and Unions*. London: Faber & Faber.

Hartley, J. and J. Kelly (1986). 'Psychology and Industrial Relations: From Conflict to Cooperation?', *Journal of Occupational Psychology*, 59, pp. 161–176.

International Labour Organization (1986). *Collective Bargaining: A Workers' Education Manual*, 2nd revised edition. Geneva: International Labour Office.

Kennedy (1954). A collection from the holdings of The John F. Kennedy Library, Boston, Massachusetts. Edited by Paul L. Kesaris. A microfilm project of University Publications of America, Inc.

Kiechel, Walter (1990). 'Hot Stove Rule', available at www.law.cornell.edu/usca, last accessed on 24 July 2007.

Lewicki, R. J. and G. Spencer (1992). 'Conflict and Negotiation in Organizations: Introduction and Overview', *Journal of Organizational Behaviour*, 1, pp. 205–07.

Luft, J. and H. Ingham (1955). 'The Johari Window: A Graphic Model of Interpersonal Awareness', proceedings of the western training laboratory in group development. Los Angeles: UCLA.

Luthans, Fred (1995). *Organizational Behaviour*, 7th edition. New York: McGraw-Hill.

Patchen, M. (1970). 'Models of Cooperation and Conflict: A Critical Review', *Conflict Resolution*, 14 (3): pp. 389–407.

Pondy, L. R. (1992a). 'Overview of Organizational Conflict: Concepts and Models', *Journal of Organizational Behaviour*, 13, pp. 225.

——— (1992b). 'Reflections on Organizational Conflict', *Journal of Organizational Behaviour*, 13, pp. 257–61.

Pruitt, Dean G. and Jeffrey Z. Rubin (1972). *Social Conflict, Escalation, and Settlement*. New York: Random House.

Rahim, M. A. (1985). 'A Strategy for Managing Conflict in Complex Organizations', *Human Relations*, 38 (1): pp. 81–89.

Schelling, T. C. (1963). *The Strategy of Conflict*. New York: Oxford University Press.

Sheppard, B. H. (1984). 'Third Party Conflict Intervention: A Procedural Framework', in B. M. Staw and L. L. Cummings (eds.), *Research in Organizational Behaviour*, 6, pp. 141–190.

Sheppard, B. H. (1992). 'Conflict Research As Schizophrenia: The Many Faces of Organizational Conflict', *Journal of Organizational Behaviour*, 13, pp. 325–334.

Sur, Mary (1965). *Collective Bargaining*. Bombay: Asia Publishing House.

FURTHER READING

Bhattacharyya, Dipak Kumar (2009). *Organizational Behaviour—Concepts and Applications*. New Delhi: Oxford University Press.

——— (2010). *Cross-Cultural Management—Texts and Cases*. New Delhi: PHI Learning.

Brown, L. D. (1992). 'Normative Conflict Management Theories: Past, Present and Future', *Journal of Organizational Behaviour*, 13, pp. 303–09.

De La Rey, C. (1991). 'Inter-Group Relations: Theories and Positions', in D. Foster and J. Louw-Potgieter (eds.), *Social Psychology in South Africa*. Johannesburg: Lexicon Publishers.

Deutsch, M. (1987), 'Theoretical Perspective on Conflict and Conflict Resolution', in D. J. D. Sandole and I. Sandole-Staroste (eds.) (1987). *Conflict Management and Problem Solving: Interpersonal to International Applications*. New York: New York University Press.

Kolb, D. M. and L. L. Putnam (1992). 'The Multiple Faces of Conflict in Organizations', *Journal of Organizational Behaviour*, 13, pp. 311–24.

Laue, J. (1987). 'The Emergence and Institutionalization of Third Party Roles in Conflict', in D. J. D. Sandole &and I. Sandole-Staroste (eds.). *Conflict Management and Problem Solving: Interpersonal to International Applications*. New York: New York University Press.

Pondy, L. R. (1967). 'Organizational Conflict: Concepts and Models', *Administrative Science Quarterly*, 12 (2): pp. 296–320.

Thomas, K. (1992). 'Conflict and Conflict Management: Reflections and Updates', *Journal of Organizational Behaviour*, 13, pp. 265–74.

18

Individual Behaviour and Its Characteristics

After going through this chapter, you will be able to understand:

- the meaning and significance of organizational behaviour
- the concepts of perception
- perception and individual decision-making styles
- personality and its influence on individual behaviour
- attitude and its influence on individual behaviour
- emotional intelligence and its influence on individual behaviour

Tata–Corus: The Post-merger Behavioural Syndrome

Tata's acquisition of Corus Steel, a British company worth USD 13.7 billion, on 31 January 2007 is one of the biggest acquisitions by any Indian company. Tata, a household name in India and recognized as 'the quality people,' is extremely employee-friendly. With an estimated 84,000 people across 45 countries in the world, Tata–Corus today produces 27 million tonnes of steel per annum, and is one of the fifth largest steel manufacturers in the world. Ratan Tata, the chairman, considers this acquisition of Corus to be strategically significant as the company has gained substantial competitive edge in the global steel industry.

Corus, with its long track record of disruptive performance, faced a loss in its strategic direction because of its performance. With the centralization of its functions and increased focus on profitability, emphasis on selling more of high-margin products, sifting of product mix to processing and fabrication, and improvement in customer service, Corus was able to tap the potential of value-added growth opportunities. Since Tata and Corus are culturally different, the management experienced resistance from the newly acquired employees, as many of Tata's ways of management were not considered suitable for managing Corus employees. Further, the cultural incongruence of Tata and Corus employees resulted in several instances of individual behavioural incompatibilities. Although Tata adopted the wait-and-watch strategy in the months following the acquisition, the integration strategy that Tata will eventually adopt to make Corus compatible with Tata will attract attention and analysis.

INTRODUCTION

The study of *organizational behaviour* requires analysis of an organization's structure and functions, and of the behaviour of its people. Behavioural study encompasses both groups as well as individuals. It is an interdisciplinary field and has its roots in sociology and psychology. Organizational behaviour is based on sociology, as the word *organization* itself represents social collectivity. It is linked to psychology because the subject encompasses the study of people, individually and in groups at the workplace (essentially, an organization). Individual and group behaviour is, again, influenced by many factors, which extend to other interdisciplinary fields such as economics, political science, social anthropology, engineering, and human resource management. The scope of organizational behaviour is, therefore, extensive. An organization needs to manage all these aspects so that it can sustain itself in a competitive market.

Theoretically, it is difficult to draw a line between management and organizational behaviour. It can be said that one supplements the other. Some organizational behaviour issues have their roots in the management processes. In fact, the study of management began much before the study of organizational behaviour. Studies in organizational behaviour started in the middle of the twentieth century. Organizational behaviour studies, therefore, draw from management theories to understand aspects such as organizational structure, behaviour of its people, and the issues concerning external and internal fit.

Successful management of organizational behaviour largely depends on the management practices that prevail in an organization. Understanding organizational behaviour, therefore, requires a clear understanding of the basics of management.

Going back in history, one finds that before the Industrial Revolution (which took place in Europe in the middle of the eighteenth century), people used to manage their own economic activity through home-centred production systems. They were themselves the owners of labour, services, and capital. Since participation was spontaneous (as it was their own work), and the size of activities was small (confined to the family members), management as a significant human activity did not get much recognition in those days. With the advancement of technology, communication, and transportation, the domain of the market expanded beyond the neighbourhood areas. It was at this point of time that the organized activity of production in the form of factory-centred production systems began to emerge. People started working in groups to accomplish common goals. It was not possible for individuals or individual households to achieve these goals. An understanding of management and organizational behaviour then became crucial for coordinating the efforts of individuals working in groups.

To understand organizational behaviour, it is essential, at the outset, to understand individual behaviour. The nature and personality of human beings is the root cause of behaviour. Work-related behaviour of people in an organization stems from both environmental and individual factors. *Human behaviour* is broadly classifiable into two characteristics—inherited characteristics and learned characteristics. *Inherited characteristics* usually do not get influenced by external forces. *Learned characteristics*, on the other hand, are the result of interactions with the environment. They also result in permanent change in behaviour. It involves an individual's attitudes, values and perceptions, emotions, and the environment around him. *Perception* is a process of receiving, selecting, organizing, interpreting, checking, and reacting to sensory stimuli. To be more simplistic, through perception everyone processes information and then interprets to deduce a sensible meaning. *Attitude*, on the other hand, is a perception with a frame of reference. It is a stable way of thinking, perceiving, and acting towards a situation or an object. *Personality* is the set of traits and characteristics that form the habit strength and a static response pattern to a certain stimuli. *Values* are basic convictions that depict an individual's moral structure. It helps to determine what is right and what is wrong.

CONCEPT OF PERCEPTION

Perception is mostly considered to be sensory stimuli. Through perception, people deduce some sensible meaning of a situation or information. Thus, perception receives, selects, organizes, interprets, checks, and reacts to stimuli or reinforcers. At the individual level, everyone develops their response to the outside environment through a dynamic inner process. This response is largely influenced by their perception. In managing organizational behaviour, one needs to study the difference between the perceptual and the real world. Moreover, work-related behaviour of an individual is the product of perception. Managers, therefore, need to understand their own perceptions as well as the perceptions of their subordinates.

Perception is a process by which one's sensory impressions are organized and interpreted in order to give meaning to their environment. However, what one perceives can be different from the objective. For an organization to drive people to achieve a common goal, it is important that all cross-sections of employees perceive the same things with reference to organizational goals and objectives; else, it would be difficult to achieve the desired results. A shared vision is possible only when all employees exert their efforts in the same direction to achieve goals. Any perceptual difference may hinder such achievement. As perception influences the behaviour of people, and also their style of decision making, it is very important to organizational behaviour. Some of the characteristics of perception are:

- Perception may be different from the objective reality, that is, what one perceives may be different from what the object or target, or the situation, is.
- There may be disagreement among individuals due to different ways of perceiving the same object or target, or the situation. Company policies on wages and salaries, incentives, promotion, and transfer may be perceived by various employees differently, as employees perceive the situation with their own frame of reference.
- Similarly, perceptions of employees toward the same manager may be different.
- Shaping perceptions of employees of the organization to develop their shared vision is the greatest challenge for any organization, as this helps in achieving the desired results.

Perception as a Process

Perception is a three-phase process of selecting, organizing, and interpreting information. As a process, perception is used to interpret and organize sensation to draw a meaningful experience of the world around everyone. Here, one can draw a borderline between sensation and perception. While *sensation* is the unprocessed result of stimulation of sensory receptors in the eyes, ears, nose, tongue, or skin, *perception* describes the ultimate experience of the world by processing sensory inputs. Thus, perception and sensation can hardly be separated, as they are intertwined. As a process, perception translates sensory impression, guides behaviour, and encompasses all processes that are associated with the recognition, transformation, and organization of sensory information. From this perspective, one can also relate perception to cognitive functions like reasoning, concept formation, problem solving, and memory, and also consider it as sensory motor behaviour. Perception is also known as a *perceptual process*, which is viewed as a complicated interaction of selection, organization, and integration through the process of addition and subtraction from the real sensory world.

There are two distinctly different approaches to perception. J. J. Gibson (1979) argued that perception is the outcome of stimulus. He was strongly in favour of the concept of immediate perception. According to him, the nature of stimulus is primarily responsible for what and how one perceives. Constructivist theories, on the other hand, argue that perception is influenced by people's experience

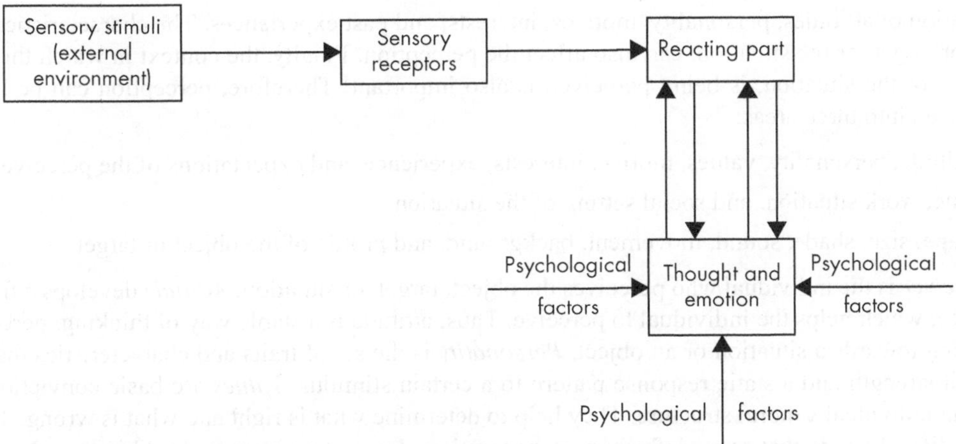

Figure 18.1 The Process of Immediate Perception

and expectations. Theories of attitudinal change and social learning also support the second argument. Figure 18.1 is a conceptual schematic representation of the process of immediate perception.

Sub-processes of perception

There are many sub-processes of perception and they vary from individual to individual. They can be broadly categorized as:

- Internal causation
- External causation
- Sensual stimulation
- Physical environment
- Sociocultural environment

Internal causation occurs due to the internal locus of control, as the perception of people can be attributed to internal factors. On the other hand, *external causation* occurs due to the external locus of control, as perception in such cases can be attributed to external forces or factors. Internal causation is within one's control, whereas external causation is outside one's control. *Sensual stimulation* can be generated by supervisors, new procedures of the organization, new machineries, etc. All these cues first register stimulus through sensory and neural mechanisms. The stimulus is interpreted through one's motivation, learning, and personality; one then behaves overtly or covertly, gets the feedback on one's own behaviour, and faces the consequences. *Physical environment* could be the office, the shop floor, the research labs, the store, and the climate. *Sociocultural environment* is made up of management styles, values, and discrimination.

Factors influencing perception

What influences the perception of people is difficult to categorize. An individual perceiver attaches meaning to an object or a target, or a situation, with their frame of reference. Hence, perception depends on the personal characteristics of the individual perceiver. Such personal characteristics can be the aggregation of attitudes, personality, motives, interests, and past experiences. The characteristics of the object or target, or the situation, can also affect the perception. Finally, the context in which the object or target, or the situation, is being perceived is also important. Therefore, perception can be broadly categorized into three areas:

1. Attitude, personality, values, motive, interests, experience, and expectations of the perceiver
2. Time, work situation, and social setting of the situation
3. Shape, size, shade, sound, movement, background, and profile of the object or target

Perceiver is the individual who perceives the object, target, or situation. *Attitude* develops a frame of reference, which helps the individual to perceive. Thus, attitude is a stable way of thinking, perceiving, and acting towards a situation or an object. *Personality* is the set of traits and characteristics that form the habit strength and a static response pattern to a certain stimulus. *Values* are basic convictions that depict an individual's moral structure. They help to determine what is right and what is wrong. *Motives* are unsatisfied needs that exert influence on perception. *Interest* represents the likings and curiosity level of people. *Past experience* narrows down the perception, that is, it nullifies the interest in objects or targets, or situations. In contrast, objects, targets, and situations that have not been experienced earlier evoke more interest. Finally, from the perceiver's point of view, *expectations* also distort perception, when the gap between what one sees and what one expects widens.

Individual perception is often situation-specific. Time, work, and social settings are the three constructs of a situation. A boss in the office is perceived differently by their subordinates. When the same boss becomes informal with their subordinates in a party, they are perceived differently.

Similarly, objects or targets in relation to their shape, size, shade, sound, silhouette, movement, and background influence one's perception. A police officer in uniform may be perceived as ruthless and tough, while in reality, they may be soft and delicate.

Theories of Perception

Some of the important theories of perception are attribution theory, selective perception, halo effect, contrast effect, projection, and stereotyping.

Attribution theory

Attribution theory explains why people develop explanations attributing a meaning to a given behaviour. It is a general propensity to develop some explanations on one's own about the behaviour of others. In the process of developing one's own explanations, one also tries to determine whether such behaviour is the outcome of internal or external causes, based on a perceived mapping of the degree of distinctiveness, consensus, and consistency.

Internally caused behaviour is considered to be under the personal control of the person responsible. *Externally caused behaviour*, on the other hand, is considered to be the result of outside causes, beyond the control of the individual. A habitual latecomer's late attendance is considered as an internal issue, while an occasional latecomer's late attendance is considered to be an external issue, which may be due to certain reasons like traffic disruption. Therefore, a habitual latecomer has already been distinctly identified. It is considered usual and a result of the internal factor. Consensus is more related to external factors. It is also more relevant in group behaviour. Consistency in behaviour is more related to internal factors or causation. This was illustrated in Elton Mayo's bank wiring experiment (1933), where workers kept the production level constant despite availability of incentives, that is, the opportunity to work to earn more, by producing more.

Fundamental attribution error is caused when one overemphasizes internal causation. This is more evident in performance behaviour. The prevalent downtrend in the market is often overlooked when the marketing team of an organization fails to achieve the target. On the other hand, *self-servicing bias error* is caused when one attributes success to one's own abilities and hard work, and failure to external factors.

Selective perception

Selective perception occurs when people selectively interpret what they see based on their attitude, interest, background, and experience. Such an approach leads to bias in perception, as subsequently it may transpire that what one perceives is wrong. To avoid such selective perception bias, it is important to develop one's perception about an object after adequate study, observation, etc.

Halo effect

Halo effect influences people's perception about an individual based on single characteristics, viz. one's intellectual ability, charisma, or sociability. For example, improvement in sales performance subsequent to the visit of the marketing head is often attributed to the quality of the marketing head. However, this could be the result of hard work and focused attention of the salespeople, who worked under the direction of the local sales head.

Projection error

Projection error occurs when people perceive a person to be their type due to obvious similarity of traits and qualities. Often, their expectations are to find similarity of traits with others. The moment they find such similarity, they perceive that person to be like themselves, and in the process, perception error occurs.

Contrast effects

Contrast effects also distort perception. It is the propensity to evaluate a person in relation to another. Due to this reason, most average candidates for a job interview become successful when other candidates are of below average standards.

Stereotyping error

Stereotyping error occurs when one categorizes people and events into already known categories. Perceiving a woman as a boss often becomes difficult because one stereotypes the woman as the secretary. Similarly, one often stereotypes police officers as corrupt, while they may be honest.

Hence, selective perception, halo effect, contrast effect, projection error, and stereotyping error are all classified under common perception errors, unlike attribution theory.

In an organization, correct perception is important for successful employment interview, performance expectations, ethics profiling, performance evaluation, and employee effort. Moreover, the study of perception is also important to understand individual decision-making styles.

Types of Perception

Perception has three levels of complexity:

1. **Detection**: It refers to whether people can sense that they are being stimulated by some form of energy. For example, a light may be so dim that they can barely detect its presence.

2. **Recognition**: It means being able to identify as well as detect a particular pattern of stimulation.
3. **Discrimination**: It means being able to perceive one pattern of stimulation as different from another. For example, a person may hear slight differences between two similar musical tones. This is an example from psychophysics, which investigates into the relationships between the physical properties of stimulus patterns and the perceived effects of stimuli.

Principles of Perception

The process of perception is based on a number of principles. The first principle is the *principle of closure*, which means a general propensity of people to perceive things as complete and unified. When engineers visualize the entire shape from a prototype, they make use of this principle.

The *principle of constancy* makes people perceive objects as constant in size, shape, colour, and other qualities. For example, an orange is perceived with its characteristic colour under different kinds of light.

The *opposite of the principle of constancy* is also valid. At times, when one views a constant object, it may be perceived as not constant. A good example is a black cube.

Another important principle relates to *perceptual context*, which refers to the influence of surrounding conditions on perception. It is often perceived that reprimands by a teacher are for one's own development.

PERCEPTION AND INDIVIDUAL DECISION MAKING

Decision making has already been discussed in Chapter 2. Decision making is the process to select a course of action from a number of alternatives. Thus, while taking decisions, individual managers get influenced by their perception. In an organization, most employees' individual decisions are based on policy documents; individual preferences can hardly influence these decisions. This is because policy-bound decisions are structured and cannot be discriminated, or else it may create resentment among employees. However, apart from policy-bound, routine, and operational decisions, individual employees need to take decisions in contingent situations. Such decisions are highly influenced by the perception of employees. Although organizations often make use of various mathematical tools to minimize the risk of wrong decisions, perception plays a major role. In order to be a successful manager, one has to necessarily develop decision-making skills.

To avoid errors in individual decisions, organizations often insist on group decision making. In such cases, individual perception can hardly influence the decision. The two most widely used techniques for group decision making are Delphi method and nominal group method. They have been explained in Chapter 2.

Rational Decision Making by Individuals

As a rational decision maker, individual employees or managers in an organization take decisions based on complete availability of information and resource support. Hence, such a decision maker takes time to ensure a flawless and informed decision. Rational decision making follows certain steps and the decision maker, at every step, needs to apply their own perceived ideas to ensure that the plan is flawless. The steps are as follows:

1. **Analysis of opportunities**: Planning requires analysis of opportunities both within and outside the organization. Opportunities need to be weighed in terms of internal strengths and weaknesses of an organization. Opportunities decide the business focus and establish the objectives. For example, the Imperial Tobacco Company (ITC) now considers diversification into retail business as an opportunity

with the changing market scenario, particularly when their tobacco business is increasingly becoming uncertain with the changing regulatory norms globally.

2. **Establishing objectives**: The second step in the planning process is the establishment of objectives. Objectives specify what is to be achieved. It gives direction to all planning in an organization. While establishing objectives, it is essential to specify them in measurable terms to subsequently measure the extent of its achievement.
3. **Determining planning premises**: *Planning premises* are assumptions about the environment which decide the field on which planning is made. These lay down the boundaries. Adequate environment scanning has to be made with emphasis on economic, social, political, and technological factors as well as competitors' plans and government policies. Similarly, internal premises, which are the premises within an organization, have to be studied with focus on organizational policies, resources, strengths, and weaknesses. After such an exercise, plans are to be made. Premises, however, are subject to change. This has recently happened in the case of Reliance. Reliance had to revise its price tag for mobile services several times within a year. From INR 10,000, they have now reduced it to INR 500. Hence, premise control is very important. Most organizations make provisions for a contingent plan due to this reason.
4. **Identification of alternatives**: In the next stage of planning, the organization has to identify different alternatives.
5. **Evaluation**: At this stage, evaluation of different alternatives is done and the best course of action in terms of cost–benefit is selected.
6. **Selection**: At this point, a plan is adopted after evaluating different alternatives. This is the stage of decision making. It is necessary to also decide about a contingent plan at this stage.
7. **Implementation**: At this stage, the plan is put into action. To implement the plan, a manager has to make a series of decisions using their authority, persuasion, and policy. The plan has to be communicated to all cross-sections of people in an organization in order to ensure their participation and support.
8. **Review**: After implementation, the plan has to be reviewed systematically, comparing the outcome with planned actions. This facilitates adoption of future plans and even corrects the deviations in the current plan. Review may even require one to alter the current plan in the light of changing circumstances.

Non-rational Models of Individual Decision Making

One of the problems in rational decision making is the undue loss in time. In reality, all information backup or support may not be available. Secondly, it may not be cost-effective for the organization to lay hands on every possible piece of information to minimize the risk. It is due to this reason that individual decision makers prefer to take decisions based on non-rational models. There are three types of non-rational decision-making models, which are perception-based.

1. **Bounded rationality**: This is, in fact, a non-rational model. In such a case, the individual decision maker tries to justify their decision within the ambit of availability of information and the given resource constraint.
2. **Incremental model**: Decisions taken using this model are essentially short-term and, therefore, lack the long-term perspective. Such decision makers believe in immediate gains, rather than gains in the long run. Hence, they cannot take decisions for projects that can give them long-term sustainability.
3. **Garbage can model**: Such decisions are intuition-based and largely depend on the gut feelings of the individual decision makers. This type of decision maker is more of a gambler than being

averse to risk. Even with 40 per cent probability of success, they do not mind taking decisions. The late Dhirubhai Ambani, founder of Reliance Group, and Jack Welch, the former CEO of General Electric, often used to take decisions based on their intuition and gut feeling. The obvious danger in such type of decision making is that it may or may not succeed.

Perception influences individual decision making in terms of choosing the specific style of decision and also in terms of having a gambling or risk-averse attitude on a specific decisional issue. Again, the preference of the individual decision maker plays a major role.

PERSONALITY AND INDIVIDUAL BEHAVIOUR

Like perception, personality constructs of individual employees also influence their pattern of behaviour. The word *personality* is derived from the Latin word *persona*. It denotes the masks that used to be worn by theatrical players in ancient Greek dramas. Hence, personality is the superficial social image that one adopts. Personality can also be viewed as the reflection of the most dominant characteristics in the behaviour of an individual which are observable (viz. aggressiveness or shyness). It is through personality that an individual makes an overall impression on others in various social settings. A quick comparison of behaviour, character, and personality can be made by attributing behaviour as the external appearance and not the exposition of true feelings of the mind. The *character* is the index of the mind and feelings, that is, behaviour that is endorsed and directed by the mind, while *personality* is self-directed behaviour. Components of personality, therefore, are mind (clarity and understanding), will (steadiness and equality), heart (warmth, expansiveness, and magnetism), vitality (energy), and physique (perseverance and endurance for work).

Individual personality is important because the individual employee's personality refers to their dynamic mental structures and coordinated processes of the mind which determine their emotional and behavioural adjustments to the organization. Personality is dynamic because mental structures of individual employees continuously develop over their lifetime. In organizational behaviour studies, personality and individual behavioural pattern of employees become an important construct to adjust and succeed in work situations. Particularly in a changing business environment, to get the right fit, employers make use of personality tests in selection and recruitment decisions. Apart from this, interest in personality assessment is also important for cultural transformation in an organization. With the understanding of cognitive and emotional bases of human behaviour, personality assessment has gained further importance.

In the given backdrop, personality studies are actually focusing on personality differences—types and traits, that is, some of the characteristics that can differ from each other. Even though traditionally they are considered from a psychological point of view, to understand them holistically requires consideration of biology (with more focus on neurology), evolution and genetics, sensation and perception, motivation and emotion, learning and memory, developmental psychology, psychopathology, psychotherapy, etc. There are various personality theories, but there is no unified approach.

Based on these discussions, the definitional elements of personality can be identified as follows:

- Personality is self-organized, permanent, and a subjectively perceived entity, which is at the very heart of all experiences.
- Personality is something that guides and directs all human activities.
- Personality is the outcome of a series of psychological crisis (Erickson 1948).
- Personality is an individual's unique way of making sense out of life experiences.

Table 18.1 Personality Constructs with Matching Physical Type

Physical type	Physical characteristics	Psychology type	Psychological characteristics
Ectomorphs	Slender, often tall people, with long arms and legs and fine features	Cerebrotonics	Nervous types, relatively shy, often intellectual
Mesomorphs	Stockier people with broad shoulders and good musculature	Somatotonics	Active types, physically fit and energetic
Endomorphs	Chubby people tending to be pear-shaped	Viscerotonics	Sociable types, lovers of food and physical comforts

Numerous studies on personality also relate personality constructs with the physical type of people. In Table 18.1, these physical constructs have been listed.

Different Perspectives of Personality

The study of personality can be made from different perspectives, such as those listed here:

- Trait perspective
- Biological perspective
- Psychoanalytic perspective
- Learning perspective
- Phenomenological perspective
- Cognitive perspective

P. Hersey, K. Blanchard, and D. Johnson (2002) say: 'As individuals mature, they develop habit patterns or conditioned responses to various stimuli. The sum of these habit patterns, as perceived by others, determines their personality.' It can be shown as:

Habit a + Habit b + Habit c + ……. + Habit n = Personality

Fred Luthans (1995) defines personality as 'how people affect others and how they understand and view themselves, as well as their pattern of inner and outer measurable traits, and the person–situation interaction'. He further stressed the importance of personality traits in organizational behaviour. According to him, there are five personality traits that especially relate to job performance. These traits are:

1. Extraversion—sociable, talkative, and assertive
2. Agreeableness—good natured, cooperative, and trusting
3. Conscientiousness—responsible, dependable, persistent, and achievement-oriented
4. Emotional stability—tense, insecure, and nervous
5. Openness to experience—imaginative, artistically sensitive, and intellectual

C. S. and Carver and M. F. Scheier (2000) provide a more contemporary definition of personality, stating that 'personality is a dynamic organization, inside the person, of psychophysical systems that create a person's characteristic patterns of behaviour, thoughts, and feelings'. *Dynamic organization* suggests ongoing readjustments, adaptation to experience, continual upgrading, and maintenance. Personality does not just lie there—it follows a process and is organized.

Characteristics of Personality

The characteristics of personality are as follows:

- Stable personality characteristics develop consistent patterns of behaviour. Characteristics like warm, friendly, cold, hostile, aggressive, and emotional are often found to be stable in some individuals and influence their personalities.
- Personality characteristics may be either common or different. Hence, to understand what an individual has in common and what is different, one must try to assess certain aspects:
  - Like all other people
  - Like some other people
  - Like no other people
- Personality induces people to behave in a manner that may be required by an individual to respond to social and biological pressure.
- Personality is an abstraction based on inferences that are derived from behavioural observation.
- Personality is often some uniqueness in characteristics that differentiates one individual from another.
- Personality is an evolving process and it develops through internal and external influences, which include genetic and biological influences, social experiences, and changing environmental stimulus.

Determinants of Personality

There are several factors that influence the shaping of a personality. One can understand which behaviour has what influence on the personality characteristics of an individual by observing the behaviour of a person. A brief review of such personality characteristics has been provided here.

- **Heredity**: Some characteristics of behaviour are genetic. Some traits like physical height, slimness, dexterity, intellectual capacity, ability to learn, and logical power are also inherited. All such inherited traits have a significant influence on behavioural patterns.
- **Family background**: The socioeconomic status of the family, education of the parents, and other family members shape the personality of an individual to a considerable extent. In fact, family members themselves try to influence the behaviour of children in their attempts to personify their own values, roles, etc.
- **Nature of people with whom one interacts**: People influence each other and such influences shape personality. Due to this reason, personality is constantly evolving and is shaped throughout one's life.
- **Culture**: It shapes one's personal values and predispositions. Culture is the unique characteristic of a social group. The values and norms shared by its members set it apart from other social groups. The essence of culture is the collective programming of the mind. According to anthropological concepts, culture relates to a shared system of beliefs, attitudes, possessions, attributes, customs, and values that define group behaviour. Values are assumptions about 'how things ought to be' in the group. Thus, culture plays a significant role in influencing the behaviour of an individual.

Personality and Individual Differences

Individual difference variables explain how people are similar or different in their behaviour and how this influences their thinking and feeling. People can be classified on the basis of their intelligence and personality attributes. In organizations, it is essential to study the psychological differences among employees because of wide variability in their personality characteristics. One tries to understand how employees are similar or dissimilar, through the study of individual differences. Such study, using psychological and personality attributes, helps to explain and predict individual behaviour and performance.

Based on intelligence and personality characteristics, people differ from each other psychologically. Such differences among individuals can be attributed to gender differences, intelligence differences, personality differences, etc.

Personality Types

The theory of personality types categorizes people into distinct and discontinuous (one or the other) types. It is synonymous with personality styles but is different from the personality trait theory. For example, the difference is that introversion is a *personality type*, while a continuum of introversion to extroversion, which clusters people in the categories of middle or extremes, is a *personality trait*. The trait approach tries to synthesize and formalize these traits in order to explain and predict behaviour. Traits are distinguishing qualities or characteristics of a person. Traits are a readiness to think or act in a similar fashion in response to a variety of different stimuli or situations.

Type A personality

People with type A personality have an entrepreneurial band and they do not mind taking risks to receive the rewards that go along with their work. The type A personality is usually independent, direct, and to the point. A manager with type A personality will always try to influence the subordinates to get to the bottom line. They dislike routine nature of work and get their subordinates involved (through delegation) in performing routine jobs. The type A personality enjoys change but fears routine, repetitive, protocol-bound jobs. They are focused on what they do, sometimes even remaining insensitive to others. This personality construct is evident in entrepreneurs, business owners, managers, and salespeople, or in those involved in other challenging jobs that require direct handling. The type A personality is, therefore, known for its leadership qualities.

Type B personality

People with type B personality love to be part of groups, and in an organization they become the centre of attention. They love excitement and are often impatient and demanding, being of a high-energy type. As they want to be in the limelight, they do very well in sales, advertising, marketing, public speaking, party planning, travel, and other similar positions. They are supportive of subordinates and enjoy being around while the subordinates perform. Since they prefer being liked by others, if others neglect them, they take it rather personally. The type B personality is usually known for its charisma.

Type C personality

People with type C personality thrive on details and accuracy, and show seriousness about everything. Accountants, engineers, computer programmers, and analysts belong to this type. They are usually very neat, dress fashionably, and are calculated and precise in just about everything they do. They do not like hype and prefer to depend on verifiable facts for decision making. Since they are consistent in their actions, they follow a charted procedure. Their actions are reliable. They also become good customer-relation executives as they are sensitive.

Type D personality

People with type D personality do not like change and prefer doing the same thing repeatedly within a set of guidelines. They easily get motivated by security and benefits. They are punctual, consistent, and supportive of others, and usually feel happy and content with themselves. They usually take on clerical assignments.

Personality Opposites

Personality clash takes place in an organization having personality opposites. At the personal level, however, personality opposites may attract each other.

Type A (Leadership)	Type B (Charismatic)
Type C (Detail-oriented)	Type D (Clerical)

Figure 18.2 Personality Opposites

In Figure 18.2, personality opposites have been shown in opposite corners, that is, types A and D are opposites. Similarly, types C and B are opposites. Opposite personalities can complement one another when they try to understand each other's perspectives, but in an organization the opposites need to be properly identified and managed in order to avoid conflicts.

ATTITUDE AND INDIVIDUAL BEHAVIOUR

Attitude is an enduring evaluation (positive or negative) of people, objects, and ideas. Thus, attitudes are evaluative statements or judgements concerning objects, people, or events. Attitude has three components—cognition, affection, and behaviour of people. A particular attitude of a person can be based on one component or the other. *Cognitive-based attitude* is primarily based on beliefs and properties of an attitudinal object. Therefore, the cognitive component of an attitude is the opinion or belief segment of an attitude. Cognitive dissonance theory helps to trace any incompatibility between two or more attitudes or between behaviour and attitudes. *Affection-based attitude* stems from people's feelings (for example, attitudes towards political candidates). Affective component is the emotion or feeling segment of an attitude. *Behaviour-based attitude* is based on self-perception of one's own behaviour when the initial attitude is weak or ambiguous. Behavioural component of an attitude is an intention to behave in a certain way towards someone or something. The affection–behaviour (A–B) relationship comprises moderating variables (that is, importance, specificity, accessibility, social pressures, and direct experience). Self-perception theory uses attitudes behind the action to make sense of the action taken.

For organizational behaviour, people's attitude is especially significant, as job satisfaction, job involvement, and organizational commitment largely stem from the individual employee's attitude. *Job satisfaction* refers to the general attitude of employees towards their job. *Job involvement* helps in psychological identification of people with their job, while *organizational commitment* is the degree to which an employee identifies with a particular organization and its goals, and wishes to maintain membership in the organization. In an organization, people seek consistency among their attitudes and seek to reconcile divergent attitudes to appear rational and consistent.

Attitudinal change in a person takes place with change in behaviour. Cognitive dissonance theory facilitates change of attitude through behavioural reinforcement. Persuasive communication and focus on a particular issue also facilitate such change of attitude. The Yale attitude change model (Havilland et al.) suggests the study of conditions under which people are most likely to change their attitudes. These conditions are source of communication (that is, credibility of speaker), nature of communication, and nature of audience. Communication from a doctor to a patient on a medical issue (communication source), communication that does not intend to influence people (nature of communication), and persuasive communication to distract an audience within the age group of 18–25, are likely to yield better results in attitudinal changes. The elaboration-likelihood model (Petty and Cacioppo 1986), on the other hand, shows that people change their attitudes in two ways—concept (central route to persuasion) and conditions for central route to persuasion (motivation). The *central route to persuasion* motivates people to pay attention to the facts in a communicated message. When facts are logical and compelling, attitudinal changes take place promptly. Therefore, the contents of the message are especially important. In contrast, when facts are not compelling, people get swayed only by peripheral cues such as mood, emotion, and attractiveness of the speaker. Such peripheral cues may serve to enhance motivation but will not induce the attitudinal changes. The *condition for central route to persuasion* is reinforcing motivation by focusing on personal relevance, so that people pay attention to the arguments.

Emotion's influence on attitude changes depends on the routes to persuasion. Emotion or mood manipulation is only effective in the peripheral route to persuasion.

People pay more attention to a speech when the argument is strong and effective in changing their attitudes. People in a sad mood take the central route to persuasion, while in a happy mood they take the peripheral route to persuasion. Therefore, attitudinal changes take place when people take the central route to persuasion, such as fear and greatness of harm, which produce better results in inducing attitudinal changes. Therefore, managers should use the central route to persuasion, duly attempting the arousal of fear, and combining it with a persuasive and appealing message.

A. H. Eagly and S. Chaiken (1993) define attitude as 'a psychological tendency that is expressed by evaluating a particular entity with some degree of favour or disfavour'. From another perspective, attitude is defined as the way one reflects one's values. For example, innate value systems of employees may make them optimists; they always look at the brighter side and work smartly to get a positive outcome. They not only nurture such attitudes in their own behaviour but also view others with the same perspective.

Values are reflected through the way one treats people, in the approach one takes to one's work, and in one's basic work ethic. They are relatively stable over time. Research suggests that most values are formed by age five or six. Value systems develop largely through one's education. The *cognitive part* is developed through one's knowledge, that is, through knowing what is right and what is wrong. The *affective part* develops through experience as it is the emotional side. The *behavioural part* is a blend of knowledge and emotions.

The concept of attitude has a rich history (Fleming 1996). Once used to describe the spatial orientation of physical objects such as statues, the concept has evolved to refer to a person's mental and neural state of readiness (Allport 1935). The function of attitude is to guide the formation of behavioural intentions. Attitude formation and change are viewed as a process of deliberative evaluation and update of belief. Attitudes are thought to impact behaviour indirectly via behavioural intentions.

Attitude theory and research deal with the structure, function, formation, and change of attitudes, and are also concerned with the relationship between attitudes and behaviour. The model of reasoned action (Fishbein and Ajzen 1975), for example, provides a comprehensive approach to all of these aspects. In this model, the internal structure of an attitude is described in terms of beliefs (expectations), which relate the attitude object (a behavioural alternative) to evaluated attributes. More recent approaches, however, assume that a deliberative calculation of expectancy and values is not a necessary condition for either intention formation or attitude formation and change. There is ample evidence to suggest that liking of an attitude object can be enhanced simply by increasing its presentation frequency (Zajonc 1980). Furthermore, if attitudes are frequently activated from memory, they tend to become activated automatically in the presence of the attitude object and then directly impact behavioural decisions (Fazio 1990).

EMOTIONAL INTELLIGENCE

Emotional dimensions of behaviour of people are usually neglected in organizations, as conventionally the emphasis is still on verbal and cognitive intelligence. Human thought process, however, evolves through interaction. Emotional intelligence has attracted attention because it suggests that emotions convey sensible meanings, which require understanding. Emotional intelligence is potentially a useful factor in understanding and predicting individual performances at work. The term *emotional intelligence* was first discussed by J. D. Mayer and P. Salovey (1995). However, their discussions did not evoke much interest among organizations. It was only in 1995 that Daniel Goleman's book *Emotional Intelligence: Why It Can Matter More Than IQ* and his subsequent articles in *USA Weekend* (13–15 March 1998) and *Time Magazine* (2 October 1995) evoked noticeable response from organizational behaviour and human resource management professionals. Goleman's subsequent book, *Working With Emotional Intelligence* (1998), evinced further interest in this subject. Thus, emotional intelligence is the latest development in understanding the relation between reason and emotion. Human thoughts and emotions are adaptively and intelligently intertwined. Today, one integrates emotional intelligence, personality, and intelligence quotient in organizations to achieve excellence in employees' performance. To recruit the right people, one needs to make use of such an integrated approach. Conceptually, emotional intelligence is an umbrella term that captures a broad collection of individual skills and dispositions, usually referred to as soft skills or inter- and intrapersonal skills that are outside the traditional areas of specific knowledge, general intelligence, and technical or professional skills.

Emotional intelligence involves being aware of emotions and how they can affect and interact with traditional intelligence (for example, impair or enhance judgement, etc.). This view fits well with the commonly held notion that it takes more than just brains to succeed in life—one must also be able to develop and maintain healthy interpersonal relationships. Viewed from this perspective, emotional intelligence is nothing new.

Goleman (1995) defined emotional intelligence as the 'capacity for reorganizing our own feelings and those of others, for motivating ourselves, for managing emotions well in ourselves and in our relationships'. The underlying belief in Goleman's hypothesis is that rational thinking alone cannot ensure success. In other words, high intelligence quotient (IQ) alone cannot ensure success. It is due to this reason that organizations endeavour to develop leadership skills and competencies among employees to enhance their emotional intelligence.

Another perspective of emotional intelligence, provided by V. Dulewicz and M. J. Higgs (1998), suggests that emotional intelligence is distinctly associated with competency models of people. They have identified a set of competencies associated with the various aspects of emotional intelligence which are self-awareness, emotional management, empathy, relationships, communication, and personal style. All these aspects of emotional intelligence correspond to competencies such as sensitivity, flexibility, adaptability, resilience, impact, listening, leadership, persuasiveness, motivating others, energy, decisiveness, and achievement orientation.

Aspects of Emotional Intelligence

The essential premise of emotional quotient (EQ) is that one requires effective awareness, control, and management of one's own emotions, and those of other people, to be successful. EQ embraces two aspects of intelligence:

1. Understanding self, goals, intentions, responses, and behaviour
2. Understanding others and their feelings

Domains of Emotional Intelligence

Goleman identified the five domains of EQ as:

1. Knowing one's emotions
2. Managing one's own emotions
3. Motivating oneself
4. Recognizing and understanding other people's emotions
5. Managing relationships, that is, managing the emotions of others

Emotional intelligence embraces and draws from numerous other branches of behavioural, emotional, and communications theories, such as neuro-linguistic programming (NLP), transactional analysis, and empathy. By developing emotional intelligence in these areas and the five EQ domains, it is possible to become more productive and successful at what one does, and also help others to become more productive and successful. The process and outcomes of emotional intelligence development also contain many elements known to reduce stress for individuals and organizations, by decreasing conflict, improving relationships and understanding, and increasing stability, continuity, and harmony.

Using Emotional Intelligence at the Workplace

While experimenting with emotional intelligence, Goleman applied the concept in the workplace to study how emotionally intelligent workers can make a difference in their performance and relationships. Using the emotional competence framework, Goleman could identify the differences between an emotionally intelligent worker and an ordinary worker on two counts—personal competence and social competence.

Goleman has explained the details of the emotional competence framework, with different sub-components, in his book *Emotional Intelligence: Why It Can Matter More Than IQ*. The emotional competence framework helps to appreciate the ways in which people with emotional competence can benefit an organization. They are as follows:

- **Personal competence**: It is the ability to regulate behaviour by redirecting disruptive impulses and moods. It is also the ability to pursue goals. Competencies associated with it are self-control, trustworthiness and integrity, initiative and adaptability, comfort with ambiguity, openness to change, and strong desire to achieve.
- **Social competence**: It is the ability to understand others' emotions and develop the requisite skill to tackle people accordingly. It is linked with six competencies—empathy, expertise in building and retaining talent, organizational awareness, cross-cultural sensitivity, valuing diversity, and service to clients and customers.
- **Self-awareness**: It is the ability to understand one's own moods, emotions, and drives, and their effect on others. The associated competencies are self-confidence, realistic self-assessment, and emotional self-awareness.
- **Social skills**: It is the ability of managing relationships and building networks to get the desired result from others. Associated competencies are leadership, effectiveness in leading change, conflict management, influence/communication, and expertise in building and leading teams. Internal states, preferences, resources, and intuitions are some of the sub-factors that influence social skills.

For developing emotional intelligence at the workplace, Goleman suggests the following steps:

1. Make an assessment of job-related emotional skills.
2. Make an assessment of the available emotional intelligence of individuals at the workplace. Some organizations make use of 360 degree feedback for this purpose.
3. Make an assessment of the extent of readiness of people in the organization to improve their level of emotional intelligence.
4. Make an assessment of the level of motivation of people to learn through experience in order to improve emotional intelligence.
5. Make the process of change in emotional intelligence self-directed, allowing people to develop their own learning plans, matching their own interests, resources, and goals.
6. Help people to focus on their manageable goals, planting the thought in their mind that emotional intelligence development is a gradual process and in pursuing the same, they may often be confronted with their old ways of doing the work.
7. Help people to understand how they can learn through lapses and also how they can prevent relapses.
8. Make performance feedback available to people.
9. Avoid the propensity to believe that emotional intelligence can be developed overnight.
10. Make models of desired behaviour available.
11. Introduce rewards for self-improvement to encourage and reinforce the climate of participation for development of emotional intelligence.
12. Develop objective measurement criteria to evaluate employees' performance.

Hence, promotion of EQ in the workplace may be summarized in terms of:

- Paving the way
- Assessing the organization's needs
- Assessing the individual
- Delivering assessments with care
- Maximizing learning choice
- Encouraging participation
- Linking goals and personal values
- Adjusting individual expectations
- Assessing readiness and motivation for EQ development

To bring changes in the workplace through EQ, organizations focus on the following aspects:

- Foster relationships between EQ trainers and learners
- Encourage self-directed change and learning
- Set goals
- Break goals down into achievable steps
- Provide opportunities for practice
- Give feedback
- Use experiential methods
- Build support

- Use models and examples
- Encourage insight and self-awareness
- Encourage transfer and maintenance of change (sustainable change)
- Encourage application of new learning in jobs
- Develop organizational culture that supports learning

To evaluate the change in the workplace through development of EQ, organizations need to evaluate individual and organizational effect. As a rule, the higher a person's EQ, the less insecurity there is likely to be present, and more the degree of openness that will be tolerated.

High Emotional Quotient = Low Insecurity = More Openness

A person's preparedness to expose their feelings, vulnerabilities, thoughts, etc., is a feature of EQ. Again, the converse also applies. The Johari window (Luft and Ingham 1955) is a concept that illustrates this quite well. Maslow's hierarchy of needs theory is also relevant as self-actualizers naturally have stronger EQ. People struggling to meet lower-order needs, and arguably even middle-order needs such as esteem needs, tend to have lower EQ than self-actualizers. The five stages of the hierarchy of needs explain that all needs other than self-actualization are deficiency drivers, which suggests some EQ development potential or weakness.

There is a strong thread of EQ in S. R. Covey's habits (1989). While explaining the seven habits of highly effective people, Covey first dealt with the habits by defining the reasons as knowledge, skill, and desire, and then emphasized a perceptive view of the world through an emotional bank account, that is, kindness, honesty, keeping promises, managing role expectations, loyalty, and attitude to say 'I am sorry'. The seven habits are the culmination of people's emotions into a maturity continuum and can be listed as the following:

1. **Habit 1**: Being proactive, that is, the habit of personal vision, recognizing the self-freedom and ability to choose how to respond, irrespective of situational cues and consequences.
2. **Habit 2**: Beginning with the end in mind, that is, the habit of personal leadership, knowing where one is going.
3. **Habit 3**: Putting first things first, that is, the habit of personal management, organizing, and executing according to priorities.
4. **Habit 4**: Thinking win–win, that is, the habit of mutual benefit, seeking solutions that allow everyone to win. This ensures successful relationships. A win–win character requires three important traits—namely integrity, maturity, and abundance mentality. With abundance mentality, one can empower people in organizations.
5. **Habit 5**: First seeking to understand, then being understood, that is, the habit of communication. Empathetic listening ensures this habit.
6. **Habit 6**: Synergizing, that is, the habit of creative cooperation, which can only be developed when one values differences and believes in alternatives. Synergy makes one plus one greater than two.
7. **Habit 7**: Sharpening the saw, that is, the habit of self-renewal, emphasizing physical, mental, social/emotional, and spiritual strength.

Covey's seven habits for highly effective people are embedded in emotional intelligence. Hence, managers with high emotional intelligence can develop such habits in order to be effective in their respective areas of work.

Nature of Emotional Intelligence

The concept and meaning of emotional intelligence are still developing. With every new definition, its nature and contexts are becoming much wider. This often leads to the difficulty of listing the nature of emotional intelligence in a few points. A refined definition of emotional intelligence by Mayer and Salovey (1997) extends its meaning as 'the ability to process emotional information, more specifically an ability to recognize the meanings of emotions and their relationships, as well as being able to reason and problem-solve on the basis of them. In particular, it involves one's capacity to perceive and assimilate emotional feelings, to understand the information of these emotions and lastly, the management of them.' Therefore, in tandem with this definition, some of the important components of emotional intelligence are:

- Intelligence
- Information processing
- Potential for learning
- Understanding
- Developing
- Growth

With several such extended definitions, the nature of emotional intelligence now encompasses the following:

- Identification of emotion
- Perception of emotion
- Expression of emotion
- Facilitation of emotional thought
- Understanding of emotion
- Management of emotion

EMOTIONAL INTELLIGENCE, INDIVIDUAL BEHAVIOUR, AND PERFORMANCE

It is often asked whether emotional intelligence influences individual behaviour. Since emotional intelligence in its present form is a relatively new concept, not many studies are available showing direct linkage between emotional intelligence and individual behaviour. However, their relationships can be examined through linkages between components of emotional intelligence and performance. Here, the focus will be on abilities such as being able to motivate oneself, persistence in the face of frustration or failure, controlling one's impulses, monitoring one's own moods, soothing oneself even after facing distressing experiences, empathizing, and hoping for new challenges and opportunities. The various factors contributing to emotional intelligence have been illustrated in Figure 18.3.

The relative advantage of emotional intelligence is that it can be a factor in stress resistance. It is likely to contribute to managing individual performances and help managers in building up effective leadership. Goleman (1995) treated emotional intelligence as a personal-level independent variable in organizational behaviour. Accordingly, the emotional intelligence base of each style of leadership as explained by Goleman is illustrated in Table 18.2.

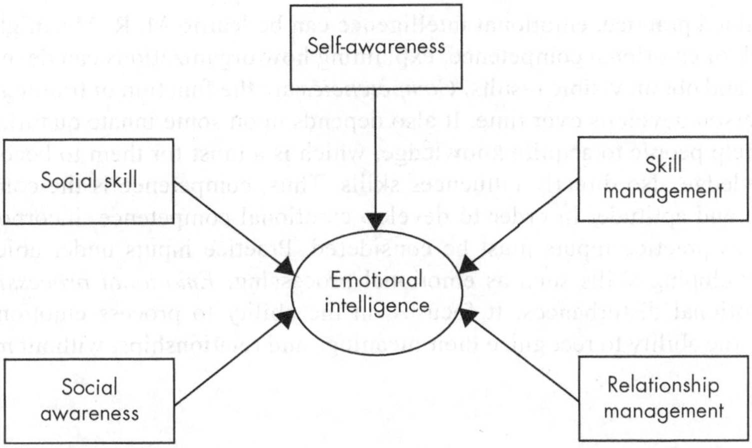

Figure 18.3 Factors Contributing to Emotional Intelligence

Table 18.2 Leadership Style and Emotional Intelligence Base

Leadership style	Emotional intelligence base
Coercive	Desire to achieve, intuition, and self-control
Authoritative	Self-confidence, empathy, and catalyst of change
Affiliative	Empathy, building relationships, and communication
Democratic	Collaboration, team leadership, and communication
Pace-setting	Conscientiousness, drive to achieve, and initiative
Coaching	Developing others' potential, empathy, and self-awareness

Barring the pace-setting and coercive dimensions of leadership style, all other dimensions have a positive correlation with the overall climate of an organization. People with high emotional intelligence could have the following characteristics:

- They are more satisfied with work and life.
- They persist longer and work harder than others.
- They are able to adapt to change more quickly.
- They demonstrate better organizational citizenship and behaviour.
- They are better suited to jobs primarily requiring interpersonal competence.
- They are better team players.
- They are less vulnerable in the face of frustration and stress experience.
- They contribute to organizational climate more positively.
- They are able to work with the diverse nature of the workforce and are successful at ambiguity management.

Through sustained practice, emotional intelligence can be learnt. M. R. McKnight (1991) developed a framework of emotional competence, explaining how organizations can develop this through directed learning and obtain visible results. *Competencies* are the function of training, education, and skills, which a person develops over time. It also depends upon some innate qualities of the person. Innate qualities help people to acquire knowledge, which is a must for them to become emotionally intelligent. Knowledge also directly influences skills. Thus, competence is the combined result of knowledge, skill, and aptitude. In order to develop emotional competence, incorporation of learning programmes as practice inputs must be considered. Practice inputs under able guidance help individuals in developing skills such as emotional processing. *Emotional processing* is a process of absorbing emotional disturbances. It focuses on the ability to process emotional information, more particularly the ability to recognize their meanings and relationships, without manipulating the emotions.

Case Surviving Competition Through Attitudinal Change

With the entry of Korean companies in the Indian electronics industry, many domestic players in India, including legacy-bound Philips, had to revisit their business strategies. With the Korean entry, Philips began to face the real heat of competition. The price competition and the multiple models brought out by the Korean companies rendered their products uneconomical. Consequently, even employees started to believe that the Korean companies would be able to meet their rising salary demands and accede to other negotiable issues involving high expenditure.

Some Philips units were then acquired by a traditional Indian electronics major, Videocon, whose price advantage made it successful in the market, next to the Korean manufacturers. The acquisition was legally challenged and even violently opposed by the trade unions. Many employees resigned quite early on, while those in a higher age bracket even opted for voluntary retirement, for which their parent company, before selling their stake to the Indian electronics major, had made available separate provisions.

To deal with the employee turnover, Videocon adopted a policy of rigorous communication and transparency of information with all cross-sections of employees. The chief operating officer (COO) was advised to spend more than 80 per cent of his time in meeting and talking to all cross-sections of employees, to clarify their doubts and answer their queries, if any. The COO also made it a point to meet employees both in groups and individually in his office at a designated time to discuss any issue that employees could not bring up in the shop floors. In the midst of this, the COO also set an example before managers and executives about being punctual and disciplined at the workplace. Over time, this practice spurred managers to emulate the COO and set an example before the workers. Whenever workers pointed out that things were not moving at the right pace, they were given the freedom to manage those activities, and allowed to take decisions on their own on every aspect of their jobs. The management extended all support and facilitated their activities, and even made it a point for any important visitor to the plant to appreciate how workers could take charge of the shop floor and manage their activities.

Hence, the company identified commonalities between the goals of the management and the employees, and helped the employees understand the value of such shared goals.

This helped the company to reinforce the attitude of workers, who volunteered to cooperate to bring about change. The changed mindset of the workers was then further reinforced by intensive training workshops, which helped the workers to believe that they could scale up their activities and achieve excellence to beat competition.

CASE QUESTION

Like the competition in the electronics industry, we also know about the competition between Unilever (erstwhile Hindustan Lever) and Procter & Gamble, especially with regard to two main product lines, namely, detergent and soap. Unilever was able to successfully counter the attempts of Procter & Gamble to consolidate its market share in India. Visit the Web sites of these companies and elaborate on how Unilever was able to be successful.

SUMMARY

- *Organizational behaviour* is the analysis of an organization's structure and functions, and the behaviour of its people. Behavioural study encompasses both groups as well as individuals. It is an interdisciplinary field and has its roots in sociology and psychology. Organizational behaviour is based on sociology, as the word *organization* itself represents social collectivism. The scope of organizational behaviour is, therefore, extensive.
- To understand organizational behaviour, it is essential, at the outset, to understand the individual behaviour. The nature and personality of an individual human being is the root cause of behaviour. Work-related behaviour of people in an organization stems from both environmental and individual factors. Human behaviour is broadly classifiable into two characteristics—inherited characteristics and learned characteristics.
- *Learning* is the result of interactions with the environment. It involves an individual's attitudes, values and perceptions, emotions, and the environment around them.
- *Perception* is a process of receiving, selecting, organizing, interpreting, checking, and reacting to sensory stimuli. To be more simplistic, through perception one processes information and then interprets to deduce a sensible meaning.
- *Attitude* is a perception with a frame of reference. It is a stable way of thinking, perceiving, and acting towards a situation or an object. *Personality* is the set of traits and characteristics that form the habit strength and a static response pattern to a certain stimulus. *Values* are basic convictions that depict an individual's moral structure. They help to determine what is right and what is wrong.
- For an organization to drive people to achieve a common goal, it is important that all cross-sections of employees perceive the same things with reference to organizational goals and objectives; else, it becomes difficult to achieve results.
- Personality constructs of individual employees also influence their pattern of behaviour. One can view personality as the reflection of the most dominant characteristics in the behaviour of an individual which are observable (viz. aggressiveness or shyness). It is through personality that an individual makes an overall impression on others in various social settings.
- Emotional intelligence is a useful factor for understanding and predicting individual performances at work. It involves being aware of emotions and how they can affect traditional intelligence.

KEY TERMS

Attitude: It is a perception with a frame of reference. It is a stable way of thinking, perceiving, and acting towards a situation or an object.

Attribution theory: This theory explains why people develop explanations attributing a meaning to a given behaviour. The reason is a general propensity to develop some explanations on one's own about the behaviour of others.

Bounded rationality: It is a non-rational model where the individual decision maker tries to justify their decision within the ambit of availability of information and the given resource constraint. One can say that it is thinking on constraint.

Emotional intelligence: Emotional intelligence suggests that emotions convey sensible meanings, which require understanding. It involves being aware of emotions and how they can affect and interact with traditional intelligence.

Emotional processing: It is a process of absorbing emotional disturbances. It focuses on the ability to process emotional information, more particularly the ability to recognize their meanings and relationships, without manipulating the emotions.

Organizational behaviour: It is the analysis of an organization's structure and functions, and the behaviour of its people.

Perception: It is a process of receiving, selecting, organizing, interpreting, checking, and reacting to sensory stimuli.

Personality: It is the set of traits and characteristics that form the habit strength and a static response pattern to a certain stimulus.

Principle of closure: It means a general propensity of people to perceive things as complete and unified—for example, visualization of the entire shape from the prototype.

Principle of constancy: According to this principle, people perceive objects as being constant in size, shape, colour, and other qualities.

Values: They are basic convictions that depict an individual's moral structure. They help to determine what is right and what is wrong.

REVIEW QUESTIONS

1. What is *perception*? What are its characteristics?
2. What are the factors that influence perception? As an engineer, which factor(s) do you think can influence your perception?
3. What is the relationship of perception with individual decision making?
4. Discuss the differences between *emotional intelligence* and *cognitive intelligence*.
5. Discuss how emotional intelligence correlates with the behaviour and performance of an individual.
6. Define the term *personality* and explain its various characteristics.
7. Explain the various theories of personality and distinguish between the descriptive and predictive theories.
8. Explain the influence of behaviour and personality on decision making.

9. Write short notes on:
   i. Incremental model
   ii. Emotional quotient
   iii. Individual behaviour versus organizational behaviour
   iv. Perceptual set

CRITICAL THINKING QUESTIONS

1. For recruitment of customer care executives for an automobile manufacturing organization riddled with customer complaints, you have been asked to suggest some personality assessment tools. Accordingly, select some personality assessment tools and also recommend how the use of such tools will benefit the recruitment and selection process, keeping in mind the unique nature of this job.
2. In a shopping mall with huge footprints, every single salesperson needs to manage more than 100 queries from visiting customers. However, the conversion rate is 10 per cent only. Suggest how a salesperson can visualize the prospects by using their emotional intelligence.

REFERENCES

Allport, G. W. (1935). 'Attitudes', in C. Murchison (ed.), *Handbook of Social Psychology*. Worcester, MA: Clark University Press.

Carver, C. S. and M. F. Scheier (2000). *Perspectives on Personality*, 4th edition. Needham Heights, MA: Simon & Schuster.

Covey, S. R. (1989). *The Seven Habits of Highly Effective People*. Rockefeller Center, NY: Fireside, Simon & Schuster.

Dulewicz, V. and M. J. Higgs (1998). 'Emotional Intelligence: Can It be Measured Reliably and Validly Using Competency Data?', *Journal of Competency*, Autumn, 6 (1): pp. 28–37.

Eagly, A. H. and S. Chaiken (1993). *The Psychology of Attitudes*. Fort Worth: Harcourt Brace Jovanovich.

Erickson, M. (1948). 'Hypnotic Psychotherapy', in E. L. Rossi (ed.) (1980), *Innovative Hypnotherapy, The Collected Papers of Milton H. Erickson on Hypnosis*, vol. 4, pp. 35–51. New York: Irvington.

Fazio, R. (1990). 'Multiple Processes by Which Attitudes Guide Behavior: The MODE Model As an Integrative Framework', in M. Zanna (ed.), *Advances in Experimental Social Psychology*, vol. 23, pp. 75–109. San Diego, CA: Academic Press.

Fishbein, M. and I. Ajzen (1975). *Belief, Attitude, Intention, and Behavior: An Introduction to Theory and Research*. Reading, MA: Addison-Wesley.

Fleming, S. (1996). Leadership for Teacher Empowerment: The Relationship between the Communication Skills of Principals, Transformational Leadership, and the Empowerment of Teachers [doctoral dissertation]. New Orleans, LA: University of New Orleans.

Gibson, J. J. (1979). *The Ecological Approach to Visual Perception*. Boston, MA: Houghton Mifflin Co.

Goleman, Daniel (1995). *Emotional Intelligence: Why It Can Matter More Than IQ*. New York: Bantam Books.

——— (1998). *Working With Emotional Intelligence*. New York: Bantam Books.

Havilland, William A., Harald E. Prins, Dana Walrath and Bunny McBride (2008). *Cultural Anthropology: The Human Challenge*, 12th edition. Belmont, CA: Thomson Wadsworth.

Hersey, P., K. Blanchard and D. Johnson (2002). *Management of Organizational Behavior: Leading Human Resources*, 8th edition. Englewood Cliffs, NJ: Prentice-Hall.

Luft, J. and H. Ingham (1955). 'The Johari Window: A Graphic Model of Interpersonal Awareness', *Proceedings of the Western Training Laboratory in Group Development*. Los Angeles, CA: UCLA.

Luthans, Fred (1995). *Organizational Behaviour*, 7th edition. New Delhi: McGraw-Hill.

Mayer, J. D. and P. Salovey (1995). 'Emotional Intelligence and the Construction and Regulation of Feelings,' *Applied and Preventive Psychology*, 4 (3): pp.197–208.

——— (1997). 'What is Emotional Intelligence?', in P. Salovey and D. Sluyter (eds.), *Emotional Development and Emotional Intelligence: Implications for Educators*, pp. 3–31. New York: Basic Books.

Mayo, Elton (1933). *The Human Problems of an Industrial Civilization*. New York: Macmillan.

McKnight, M. R. (1991). 'Management Skill Development', in J. D. Bigelow (ed.), *Management Skills*. Newbury Park, CA: Sage.

Petty, R. E. and J. T. Cacioppo (1986). 'The Elaboration Likelihood Model of Persuasion', in L. Berkowitz (ed.), *Advances in Experimental Social Psychology,* vol. 19, pp. 123–205. San Diego, CA: Academic Press.

Zajonc, R. B. (1980). 'Feeling and Thinking: Preferences Need No Inferences', *American Psychologist*, 35, pp. 151–175.

FURTHER READING

Ackers, P. and A. Wilkinson (2003). *Understanding Work and Employment: Industrial Relations in Transition*. Oxford: Oxford University Press.

Bhattacharyya, D. K. (2007). *Human Resource Research Methods*. New Delhi: Oxford University Press.

——— (2009). *Organizational Behaviour—Concepts and Applications*. New Delhi: Oxford University Press.

——— (2010). *Cross-Cultural Management—Text and Cases*. New Delhi: PHI Learning.

Budd, J. (2004). *Employment with a Human Face: Balancing Efficiency, Equity and Voice*. Ithaca, NY: Cornell University Press.

Carteret, E. and M. Friedman (1978). *Handbook of Perception*, volumes 1–10. New York: Academic Press.

Feist, J. (1985). *Theories of Personality*, 3rd edition. New York: Harper San Francisco.

Funder, D. C. (1997). *The Personality Puzzle*. New York: W. W. Norton and Company.

Gibson, J. J. (1966). *The Senses Considered As Perceptual Systems*. Boston, MA: Houghton Mifflin Company.

Guest, D. and N. Conway (2004). *Employee Well Being and the Psychological Contract: A Report for the CIPD*. London: Chartered Institute of Personnel and Development.

Hemphill, J. K. (1959). 'Job Description for Executives', *Harvard Business Review*, 37 (5): pp. 55–67.

Johnson, M. (2004). *The New Rules of Engagement: Life–Work Balance and Employee Commitment*. London: Chartered Institute of Personnel and Development.

Jung, C. (1923). *Psychological Types*. London: Routledge and Kepan Paul.

Luft, J. (1961). 'The Johari Window', *Human Relations Training News*, 5 (1): pp. 6–7.

McClelland, D. C. (1973). 'Testing for Competence rather than for Intelligence', *American Psychologist*, 28 (1): pp. 1–14.

Murray, H. A. (1938). *Explorations in Personality*. New York: Oxford University Press.

Myers, I. B. and M. H. McCaulley (1985). *A Guide to the Development and Use of Myers–Briggs Type Indicator*. Palo Alto, CA: Consulting Psychologist Press.

Purcell, J., N. Kinnie and S. Hutchinson (2003). *Understanding the People and Performance Link: Unlocking the Black Box*. London: Chartered Institute of Personnel and Development.

Reed, S. (1973). *Psychological Processes in Pattern Recognition*. New York: Academic Press.

Singh, Shailendra (2002). *Emotional Intelligence for High Performance: High Performance Organizations*. New Delhi: New Age Publication.

Ulrich, D. and W. Brockbank (2005). *The HR Value Proposition*. Boston, MA: Harvard Business School Press.

Warr, P. B. and S. Hoare (2002). 'Personality, Gender, Age and Logical Overlap in Multi-Source Ratings', *International Journal of Selection and Assessment*, 10, pp. 279–91.

Warr, P. B., D. Bartram and A. Brown (2006). 'Big Five Validity: Aggregation Method Matters', *Journal of Occupational and Organizational Psychology*, 78, pp. 377–86.

Warr, P. B., D. Bartram and T. Martin (2005). 'Personality and Sales Performance: Situational Variation and Interactions between Traits', *International Journal of Selection and Assessment*, 13, pp. 87–91.

19

Managing People in Groups

After going through this chapter, you will be able to understand:

- the concept of groups
- the theories of group formation
- the group decision-making process
- the influence of groups on organizational culture
- the process of team development through group formation
- the management of group dynamics and group conflict

Teamwork Pays: Lessons from DSP

Organizational effectiveness depends not only on the talent available in the organization but also on the quality of leadership available. An organization's success depends on the ability of its leaders to align individual goals to business goals and objectives, and bring out the best in all the members of the team through resolution of conflicts and proper team building. The essence of team building is promoting the culture of group dynamics. *Group dynamics* promotes interactions between people, where at least one person takes the lead in conversation to offer their thoughts and opinions freely. In a culture of teamwork, it is essential for the organization to promote group dynamics so that people are largely involved in managing their discussions, which pertain to achieving the organizational goals. A successful transformation of attitude of employees is the prerequisite for the success of organizational change initiatives. The positive attitude of employees results in effective group dynamics and ultimately enhances the decision-making capability of people and their competency.

An example is the Durgapur Steel Plant (DSP), a public sector steel manufacturing unit of Steel Authority of India Limited (SAIL), which promoted the culture of teamwork and quickly bounced back from a state of poor performance. DSP had accumulated huge losses due to a tremendous setback in its performance in successive years. The problem mounted during the first phase of economic globalization and deregulation with price decontrol mechanism announced by the government of India. From a position of captive-market privilege, SAIL units, including DSP, suddenly witnessed a sea change in the market dynamics, which needed the company to quickly respond to the change, transforming the entire organization including the attitude of employees. To promote group dynamics, SAIL emphasized developing a shared vision, urging all its plants to quickly endorse their employees to nurture this vision and reflect it in their day-to-day work.

The integrated steel plant, one of the largest industrial complexes in the state of West Bengal, is today spread over an area of 6.5 square km and employs a workforce of about 16,000. The plant has the rated capacity to produce 2.1 metric tons (MT) of hot metal, 1.9 MT of crude steel, and 1.6 MT of saleable steel.

INTRODUCTION

A *group* symbolizes a cluster of two or more persons with some common characteristics. According to this perspective, the organization as a whole can be called a group. For reasons of survival, human beings always tend to be collective. This phenomenon is evident right from the early days of civilization. Through this process of collectivism and mutual interaction, language and behavioural norms were developed, and they ultimately transcended to the formation of social groups, and also work groups in organizations. The study of groups in organizations, among other things, requires understanding of behavioural dynamics. In organizations, group formation is now a necessity, as it helps to accomplish tasks, to establish a sense of identity, and to facilitate exchange ideas. In organizations, groups are studied in two forms—primary groups and secondary groups. *Primary groups* develop emotional attachment and a culture of their own, and make themselves distinctly different from others by developing their own normative systems. *Secondary groups*, on the other hand, are developed by detaching personal feelings and attachment, to get some specific work done or to achieve a desired level of performance. Work groups in organizations are an example of a secondary group. Primary group is a social group, which can also be an informal group in an organization. The study of work groups in organizations is important to understand the collective psychology of people when they are in groups. Since work process in an organization is now managed through work-group formation, before fitting an individual into a particular work group, one now tries to first assess the degree of compatibility, without which the purpose of the organization may be defeated. The failure of Mazda of Japan in the United States is attributable to such incompatibility, which forced Mazda to withdraw despite being the first (much before Toyota and Honda) to enter the American market. Toyota's current recruitment practices focus more on assessment of such compatibility, which makes it possible to get the right fit and reduce the attrition rate.

Despite such logic behind group formation, a group is often misconstrued as a collection of people. A mere collection of persons cannot be a group because they do not have any interaction, cohesion, and goal commonality. Therefore, a collection of persons (two or more) can only be a group when they have a common purpose or goal, there exists within the group a stable structure (usually hierarchical with a leader), there exist an established set of roles and a standard pattern of interaction, and members in the group identify themselves with the group. Many organizations use the terms *team* and *group* interchangeably. Although differences between teams and groups in organizations hardly exist, the *concept of a group* is more traditional, as it is the outcome of the principles of division of labour, based on job specialization and putting people under one supervisor. The *concept of a team* is more modern, as the test of a team does not essentially require functional commonality, while members of groups strive to achieve a common goal. In a team, members interact interdependently and adaptively to achieve specified, shared, and valued objectives. Members in a team believe in shared commitment.

GROUP DYNAMICS

Group dynamics is an extended thought of Kurt Lewin's concept of *action research* (1948). Lewin's action research argues against the traditional distinction between basic and applied science by suggesting that scientific understanding will occur most rapidly if researchers' and practitioners' efforts are unified.

In an organization, group process is followed. *Group process* understands how an organization's members work together and get things done. An effective way to understand a group process is through studying the group's morale, membership participation, and decision-making style, and how the members get along with each other. By developing a group process, organizations ensure that members develop self-confidence, refine skills, and make friends. Not everyone in a group has the same expectations, does the same thing, or has the same commitment level. Knowledge about how group members interact, share common goals, and work with one another can help managers integrate newcomers and prepare them for the roles, norms, and cohesiveness of the group.

Although Lewin (1935) advocated the term *group dynamics* in the 1930s itself, there is still no consensus on its definition. However, as a first impression, group dynamics can be defined as the structures and processes of group formation and its functioning. The normative view is that group dynamics describes how a group should be organized and conducted. Democratic leadership, member participation, and overall cooperation are stressed. Another view of group dynamics is that it consists of a set of techniques. Here, role playing, brainstorming, the Johari window, transactional analysis, and team building are equated with group dynamics. A third view, which is closest to Lewin's original concept, is that group dynamics relate to the internal nature of groups, how they form, their structure, and the organization. Therefore, *group dynamics* is the behaviour of a group of people under certain conditions and the way they change with the situation. It can also be defined as the branch of social psychology that studies the dynamics of interaction in a small group.

Importance of Studying Groups

People in a group behave differently in comparison to their individual behaviour. In organizations, the primary focus is on issues pertaining to managing people in a group, as the organization per se represents a group. Understanding the group process in organizations helps to assess how people in organizations work together and accomplish results. Managers must know and appreciate how people behave in an organization, interact among themselves, and share common goals. Understanding this aspect helps managers to integrate the new recruits, prepare them for their job roles, make them aware of the norms, and thus achieve the desired group cohesiveness. Managers need to appreciate that people not only play their formal roles in organizations but also play different informal roles. Apart from this, certain normative aspects of groups are also important. Norms need not always be explicit; they can also be implicit. The significance of such group norms can be seen in the bank wiring experiment conducted at Western Electric Company by Elton Mayo (1949), where group norms persuaded workers to contain their productivity despite availability of incentives and opportunities to earn more. Thus, *group norms* can be both positive and negative. While *positive norms* bring a sense of order in an organization, *negative norms* can be against the mutual interests of people and organizations.

Similarly, the study of group cohesiveness is also important in an organization. *Group cohesiveness* binds all members of the organization to remain together for the purpose of achieving the desired results. It is achieved when group members align their individual needs and goals. This is what Henri Fayol referred to as *esprit de corps* while summarizing the principles of management in 1916. A cohesive work group is a precursor to an organization's success. The manager, as a leader of the group, must focus on achieving group cohesiveness.

Apart from these aspects, the study of group development process, group conflict, group decision making, group thinking process, group dynamics, etc., are all important areas of studying groups in an organization. Organizational success largely depends on effective management of work groups.

Important Characteristics of a Group

It is clear that in organizations, groups represent a collection of two or more individuals who work towards a common goal and are interdependent. They interact with each other to achieve group objectives or goals. A collection of people can be called a group when two or more persons share any or all of the following aspects:

- **Interpersonal interaction**: Individuals do not form a group merely by being in the same place; there needs to be interaction between them.
- **Perceptions of membership**: Individuals should be perceptibly aware that they are members of the group.
- **Interdependency and mutual influence**: Any event that affects a group member affects them all; each member influences, and is influenced by, the other member.
- **Mutual goals**: Individuals come together in pursuit of a mutual goal, which is set by using a goal congruence model. When individuals feel that their goals match the goals of other individuals, they pursue goal achievement voluntarily.
- **Motivation**: Group members seek to satisfy some personal need through their joint association.
- **Structured relationships**: Interactions are structured by a set of role definitions and norms.

Types of Groups

Groups have already been categorized into two types—primary and secondary. However, ideally, one can classify groups along two dimensions—size and membership cohesiveness. In terms of *size*, classifications can be made as small/large groups and primary/secondary groups. In terms of *cohesiveness*, groups can be classified as coalitions, expert groups, and in- and outgroups. The generally accepted theory is that the group to which a person pledges complete membership and loyalty is a primary group; in the event of a conflict of interests, this group's well-being would be paramount. Although there is no attempt to assign precise numbers to the primary group size, the criterion is that the group must be small enough for face-to-face interaction between the members.

Individuals may assume membership of groups other than the primary groups. However, such membership may be limited by time, task, or location. As an individual's affinity to such a group becomes higher, it is quite possible that this group may move up to become a primary group. In general, however, it is accepted that primary groups are socializing groups and have a very high degree of membership feeling and interdependency among members.

Based upon an individual's membership status, groups could be classified as *membership/reference groups* or as *in-group/out-group*. The criterion here is that the image of the group is very powerful and it attracts individuals to become a part of the group. Until they get full membership of the group, an individual looks to it as a reference group, the values and activities of which have to be imitated.

Looking at organizational practices, one finds the existence of the following types of groups:

- **Formal group**: This group is defined by the organizational structure. After planning, organizations group the activities and put them under a formal structure, deciding their goals, objectives, and strategies to achieve the same. Formal group members report to their superiors and interact with each other to achieve common goals. Usually, a formal group consists of people whose jobs are more or less homogeneous in nature. On a shop floor, a gang engaged in doing the same job represents a formal group. Similarly, in a call centre, all outbound callers handling the same customer account represent a formal group. Thus, the formation of a formal group is based on job specialization and similarity of skill sets.

- **Command group**: This group is also known as a *task group*. A *task* is defined as the cross-functional activities carried out by group members to accomplish a common goal. A *team* represents the nature of a command group. A command group can be formed by drawing members from various formal groups. For example, organizations may form a command group to achieve success in new product launches. Once the task is achieved, group members may be sent back to their specific formal groups.
- **Power group**: Power is a universal feature of social interaction and plays the most important role in building relationships among group members. In every group, there may be one or more member(s) who is/are more powerful than others. Such a member can, in general, influence the behaviour of other persons. A power group, therefore, indicates the group that enjoys the capability to influence the work and systems of an organization.
- **Committees**: To achieve results, organizations often form permanent or temporary committees, drawing members from various formal groups. Committees also represent cross-functional members. While goals may be specific for a command group, for committees they are varied. For example, to ensure better transparency and accuracy in purchase decisions, various members drawn from the user sections such as finance, marketing, and HR may represent a tender purchase committee (TPC) in an organization. Such a committee may be permanent in nature. Temporary committees in organizations may be entrusted with achieving temporary goals, such as probing a case of fund embezzlement against a particular member.
- **Informal groups**: Informal groups are formed within a formal organizational structure. Informal group members primarily meet their social or affiliation needs by sharing common interests. Thus, informal groups are not organizationally determined; the members themselves form such groups to fulfil their needs for social interaction. In a particular organization, functional proximity primarily determines the formation of informal groups. Apart from this, like-minded people—those who have the same personality and attitude constructs or those who belong to a similar status (in terms of hierarchy or economic status)—also form informal groups. The constructive use of informal groups may benefit an organization. However, inefficient management may render informal groups counterproductive. An informal group may be a friendship group, an interest group, a reference group, or a membership group. *Friendship groups* are formed by like-minded people; those who have common interests form *interest groups*; formation of *reference groups* are based on compatibility of decisions and opinions; and *membership groups* are formed for affiliation-related needs.

GROUP FORMATION

The most basic assumption is that individuals form groups out of propinquity, meaning spatial or geographical proximity. While this may explain why people travelling in the same railway car each day form a weakly bonded group, it cannot explain other complexities involved in group formation.

The *balance theory of group formation* states that persons are attracted to one another on the basis of similar attitudes towards commonly relevant objects and goals. Individuals X and Y will interact and form a relationship because of common attitudes and values (Z).

Once this relationship is formed, the participants strive to maintain a symmetrical balance between the attraction and the common attitudes. When an imbalance occurs between the two, organizations make an attempt to restore the balance. If it cannot be restored, the relationship dissolves. Both propinquity and interaction play a role in the balance theory.

The *exchange theory of groups* is based on reward–cost outcomes of interaction. A minimum positive level (rewards greater than costs) of an outcome must exist for attraction or affiliation to take place. Rewards from interactions gratify needs, while costs incur anxiety, frustration, embarrassment, or fatigue. Propinquity, interaction, and common attitudes are important in the exchange theory.

Stages of Group Development

Being live entities, groups go through a process of evolution, beginning with their birth and moving through maturity, decline, and death. These stages are by no means watertight or even sequential. A brief explanation of the stages (Tuckman 1965) has been given here along with an illustration in Figure 19.1. The stages are as follows:

1. **Forming**: The group defines the expectations of members, the environment in which it operates, and the reasons for its existence. The members get introduced to each other and share their ideas about what the group is seeking to achieve.
2. **Storming**: Members jostle for influence and positions. They try to be collective but encounter differences on issues such as group structure, agenda, and work allocation. There may be arguments and counter-arguments for finalizing a group structure.
3. **Norming**: Group members recognize the need for mutuality and interdependence. They negotiate their differences and arrive at workable approaches, upholding the interests of the group. Ultimately, they come out with the established norms for the group.
4. **Performing**: After reaching a consensus on group norms, members start working together to achieve the intended goals.

It is interesting to note here that the first three stages take a while, during which apparently not much progress is made. However, it must be recognized that these stages lay the foundation for performance. Without these stages, the group will be trapped in trying to come to terms with itself. Also, effective groups are constantly on the lookout for renewal. As the operating environment or the goals change, the group again goes through the first three stages, thereby rediscovering itself.

Ultimately, the group terminates. This happens when the group is unable to satisfy the needs of members within the boundaries that it had set for itself. Members look to other groups to satisfy their needs. The group's existence becomes redundant and it fades away.

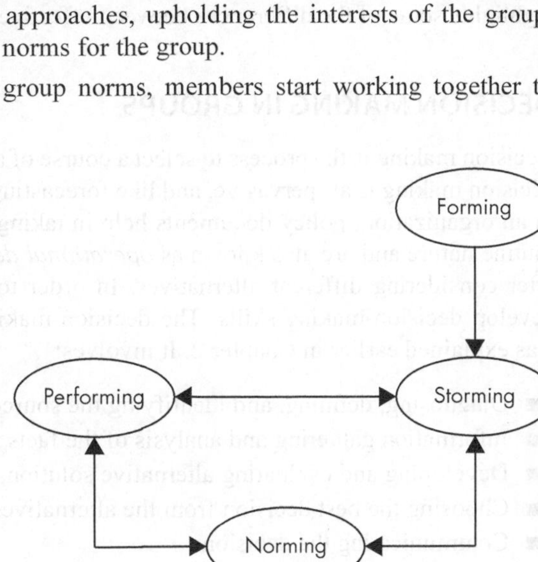

Figure 19.1 Stages of Group Development (*Source:* B. Tuckman (1965). 'Developmental Sequence in Small Groups', *Psychological Bulletin*, 63, pp. 384–399.)

Models of Group Development

There are many models of group development. Some of the well-known models of group development are:

- Recurring phase model
- Equilibrium model
- Sequential stage model

The *recurring phase model* assumes that each group experiences certain dominating issues. Such recurrent issues eventually improve the group participation. In other words, one can say that recurrent issues create a compelling pressure on people to participate in a group. The *equilibrium model*, on the other hand, assumes that the participation in a group improves due to the general propensity of individuals to balance their task relationships (job-related) and their behavioural relationships (interpersonal). Finally, the *sequential stage model* assumes that the improvement process of group participation follows the cycle of forming, storming, norming, performing, adjourning orientation, conflict, emergence, reinforcement, and adjourning.

GROUP EFFECTIVENESS

Group effectiveness is influenced by the degree of task orientation and people or process orientation. By balancing these two aspects, a group achieves its goals and improves the group effectiveness. Hence, the effectiveness of a group depends on its ability to achieve its goals, its ability to maintain itself internally as a cohesive unit, and its ability to change and develop in ways that improve its effectiveness. Table 19.1 highlights some of the differences between effective and ineffective groups.

DECISION MAKING IN GROUPS

Decision making is the process to select a course of action from a number of alternatives. Like planning, decision making is all-pervasive, and like forecasting, decision making is an important part of planning. In an organization, policy documents help in taking managerial decisions, but these are decisions of a routine nature and are also known as *operational decisions*. *Strategic* or *important decisions* are taken after considering different alternatives. In order to be a successful manager, one has to necessarily develop decision-making skills. The decision-making process is similar to strategic planning, which was explained earlier in Chapter 2. It involves:

- Diagnosing, defining, and identifying the source of the problem
- Information gathering and analysis of the facts required to solve the problem
- Developing and evaluating alternative solutions to the problem
- Choosing the best decision from the alternatives available
- Communicating the decision
- Implementing the decision

The advantages and disadvantages of groups are presented in Table 19.2. Even in group decision making, various forecasting tools can be used. Most of these tools have already been presented in Chapter 2.

Table 19.1 Effective versus Ineffective Groups

Effective groups	Ineffective groups
With clarity of goals, congruence between individual goals and group goals is achieved. Hence, goals can be changed depending on the situation.	Goals are imposed. Hence, they receive lesser acceptance from group members.
Such groups facilitate two-way communication and improve mutual understanding in order to avoid confusion.	There is only one-way communication and, therefore, the individual member's ideas and feelings get subdued, leading to frustration among group members.
Such groups encourage participative and distributed leadership among group members and, thereby, facilitate goal achievement and strengthen internal balance.	Leadership is based on authority. Hence, group members' participation is unequal as authoritative leaders emphasize goal achievements.
Equal sharing of power is possible. This provides opportunity for individual goal achievement and needs fulfilment.	Power is mainly derived from role position. Therefore, group members' participation is more formal and rule-bound. Members' disobedience is considered as violation of discipline.
There is flexibility in decision making as well as a participative approach, which encourages group involvement, making the decision-making process more effective.	Such groups have a system of centralized decision making. This minimizes group members' participation and involvement.
Such groups promote positive conflict through group discussions and, thus, improve the quality of decisions.	Even genuine conflicts are suppressed, leading to increased violence and indiscipline.
They emphasize group cohesion. Thus, group members can improve their interpersonal relations, enhancing their level of inclusion and mutual trust.	Rigidity suppresses group cohesion.

Table 19.2 Advantages and Disadvantages of Groups

Advantages	Disadvantages
Groups can exploit a wide range of knowledge, expertise, and innovative ideas.	Groups may block communication, restricting it to only one person.
Groups can ensure consensus in decision making.	Groups may have dominant people who restrict other group members from expressing their views.
Groups can communicate even complex information effectively.	In a group, members may be more status-sensitive and impose self-restriction on participation.
Members in a group are motivated to work harder when they see that everyone is trying their best.	Groups can also have the bad effect of social loafing, which may make members perform less.

Case Infosys: A Culture that Promotes Achieving Excellence Through Group Efforts

N. R. Narayana Murthy started his journey in 1981 with only INR 10,000, with six other co-founders with the objective to provide cost-effective IT services to companies in the developed world, engaging talented Indian engineers. The only aspiration of the company was 'to become the most respected company in the world'. Extending IT services to global clients from India was initially not possible. However, after deregulation and with massive investment in telecommunications, communication links between India and the rest of the world became possible, which enabled the company to connect the mainframes in the United States to form the terminals in India. Such possibilities completely changed the landscape of the company's business. With its own global delivery model (GDM), the company could send software every now and then to any destination on real-time basis. With GDM, the company could also provide services to remote areas, including ongoing maintenance and user support.

While trying to meet the expectations of international clients, the biggest challenge that the company faced was recruiting, enabling, empowering, and retaining the best employees. Murthy realized the need for the company value proposition (marketing statement that sells the company) to shift focus from customers to employees, to make them the best performers. The emphasis on new recruits now is with regard to not only strong technology skills but also the zeal to continue learning. The zeal for ongoing learning is possible only when people are humble, that is, open to learning. It is necessary for Infosys employees to continually acquire new skills and to keep pace with the rapidly changing technology. Also, from the employees' point of view, it is important to quickly rise through the positions, as the growth rate of the company is quite high. 'Powered by intellect' and 'driven by values' are the slogans of the company, and these are reflected in the company's commitment to employees' development through continuous learning. Some of the values that the company advocates are:

- Openness to new ideas
- Subordination of individual egos
- Meritocracy
- Emphasis on logical discussions, powered by data and facts
- Speed
- Imagination
- Excellence in execution

Therefore, managers at Infosys need to know the employees' needs. Understanding such needs and endeavouring to achieve the desired results are the only things that can help them to gain optimal productivity and loyalty of employees. Infosys believes that employees' motivation can make a difference in achieving its business goals. The company believes in 'C-LIFE', that is, 'customer delight, leadership by example, integrity & transparency, fairness and pursuit of excellence'. Customer delight is achieved in terms of commitment to customers, even surpassing their expectations. Practice of leadership by example requires a commitment to set standards in business and transactions, which others in the company will emulate. Integrity and transparency values require employees to be ethical, diligent, and open in dealings. Fairness values are formed from employees' commitment to objectivity that elicits trust and respect from others. Lastly, pursuit of excellence takes place due to employees' relentless commitment to the development of self and team members, which transcends to products and services that are the best in quality.

Murthy, chairman of the board and former chief executive of Infosys, says, 'The first responsibility of a leader is to create mental energy among people so that they enthusiastically embrace the transformation'. He invites his high-performing team members to present themselves before large audiences drawn across the country to showcase how the company values high performers. An ardent believer in self-renewal, Murthy himself chose his job title as the chief mentor of the company. This was a positive attempt to reinvent himself, setting aside his formal managerial authority. Such a decision by Murthy not only set an example before his employees, but also encouraged his successor to become more and more successful at his job.

CASE QUESTION

List the lessons learnt from Infosys and give your comments about whether the practices at Infosys can be effectively implemented at other organizations.

SUMMARY

- A *group* symbolizes a cluster of two or more persons with some common characteristics. From such a perspective, the organization as a whole can be called a group.
- A mere collection of persons cannot be a group because they do not have any interaction, cohesion, and goal commonality. Therefore, a collection of persons (two or more) can only be a group when they have a common purpose or goal, there exists within the group a stable structure (usually hierarchical with a leader), there is an established set of roles and a standard pattern of interaction, and members in the group identify themselves with the group.
- The concept of a group is more traditional, as it is the outcome of the principles of division of labour, based on job specialization and putting them under one supervisor. The team concept is more modern as the test of a team does not essentially require functional commonality, while members of groups strive to achieve a common goal. In a team, members interact interdependently and adaptively to achieve specified, shared, and valued objectives. Members in a team believe in shared commitment.
- Groups can be classified along two dimensions—size and membership cohesiveness. In terms of *size*, classifications can be made as small/large groups and primary/secondary groups. In terms of *cohesiveness*, groups can be classified as coalitions, expert groups, and in and out groups.
- There are many theories of group formation. The *balance theory of group formation* states that persons are attracted to one another on the basis of similar attitudes towards commonly relevant objects and goals. The *exchange theory of groups* is based on reward–cost outcomes of interaction.
- There are different stages of group development, like forming, storming, norming, and performing. *Forming* defines the expectations of group members, for fulfilling which they get together. *Storming* helps the members to be collective. *Norming* recognizes the need for mutuality and interdependence of group members. *Performing* is working together to achieve the group goals.
- Although there are many models of group development, three well-known models are recurring phase model, equilibrium model, and sequential stage model. The *recurring phase model* believes that recurrent issues eventually improve the group participation. The *equilibrium model* assumes that participation in a group improves due to the general propensity of individuals to balance between their typical task behaviours and relationship behaviours. Finally, the *sequential stage model* assumes that the improvement process of group participation follows the cycle of forming, storming, norming, performing, adjourning orientation, conflict, emergence, reinforcement, and adjourning.

- *Group effectiveness* is influenced by the degree of task orientation and people orientation. By balancing these two aspects, a group achieves its goals and improves the group effectiveness.
- *Group dynamics* is the behaviour of a group of people under certain conditions and the way they change with the situation. It can also be defined as the branch of social psychology that studies the dynamics of interaction in a small group.
- *Group process* understands how an organization's members work together and get things done. An effective way to understand a group process is through studying the group's morale, membership participation, and decision-making style, and how the members get along with each other.

KEY TERMS

Group: It symbolizes a cluster of two or more persons with some common characteristics. From such a perspective, the organization as a whole can be called a group.

Group cohesiveness: Group cohesiveness binds all members of the organization to remain together for the purpose of achieving the desired results. It is achieved when group members align their individual needs and goals.

Group dynamics: Group dynamics is the behaviour of a group of people under certain conditions and the way they change with the situation. It can also be defined as the branch of social psychology that studies the dynamics of interaction in a small group.

Group effectiveness: Group effectiveness is influenced by the degree of task orientation and people orientation. By balancing these two aspects, a group achieves its goals and improves the group effectiveness.

Group process: Group process understands how an organization's members work together and get things done. An effective way to understand a group process is through studying the group's morale, membership participation, and decision-making style, and how the members get along with each other.

Primary groups: These groups develop emotional attachment and a culture of their own, and make themselves distinctly different from others by developing their own normative systems.

Secondary groups: These groups are developed by detaching personal feelings and attachment, to get some specific work done or to achieve a desired level of performance.

REVIEW QUESTIONS

1. Explain why people tend to form groups. Is it not possible to survive without forming groups?
2. What are the characteristic features of a group? How do such features contribute to the effectiveness of groups?
3. Explain the process of group decision making. What are the problems encountered by an organization in group decision making?
4. Elaborate on the concept of group norms. How are group norms decided?
5. Write short notes on:

   i. Tuckman's model
   ii. Group dynamics
   iii. Mutual goals

iv. Primary and secondary groups
v. Command group
vi. Power group

CRITICAL THINKING QUESTIONS

1. It is now corporate practice to achieve success through group formation. However, group formation depends on organizational culture. In this context, study any organization's autonomous work-group system, where people work in a group but remain accountable for their individual tasks. Prepare your report with a critical assessment of the culture of your sample organization.
2. Study the group dynamics of a knowledge-intensive software-development company and report its strengths and weaknesses.

REFERENCES

Fayol, Henri (1949). *General and Industrial Management*. Translated from the French edition by Constance Storrs. London: Pitman.

Lewin, Kurt (1935). *A Dynamic Theory of Personality*. New York & London: McGraw-Hill.

——— (1948). *Resolving Social Conflicts: Selected Papers on Group Dynamics*. New York: Harper.

Mayo, Elton (1949). *Hawthorne and the Western Electric Company, The Social Problems of an Industrial Civilization*. London: Routledge.

Tuckman, B. (1965). 'Developmental Sequence in Small Groups', *Psychological Bulletin*, 63, pp. 384–399.

FURTHER READING

Bednar, R. L. and T. Kaul (1978). 'Experiential Group Research: Current Perspectives', in S. Garfield and A. Bergin (eds.), *Handbook of Psychotherapy and Behavior Change*. New York: John Wiley & Sons.

Bhattacharyya, Dipak Kumar (2009). *Organizational Behaviour: Concepts and Applications*. New Delhi: Oxford University Press.

Forsyth, D. R. (1993). 'Building a Bridge between Basic Social Psychology and the Study of Mental Health', *Contemporary Psychology*, 38, pp. 931–932.

Forsyth, D. R. and M. R. Leary (1991). 'Metatheoretical and Epistemological Issues', in C. R. Snyder and D. R. Forsyth (eds.), *Handbook of Social and Clinical Psychology: The Health Perspective*, pp. 757–773. New York: Pergamon.

Freud, S. (1922). *Group Psychology and the Analysis of the Ego*. London: Hogarth.

Hawthorne Studies (1924). Western Electric Company Hawthorne Studies Collection, available at http://oasis.lib.harvard.edu/oasis/deliver/~book00047, last accessed on 15 July 2007.

Janis, Irving L. (1982). *Groupthink: Psychological Studies of Policy Decisions and Fiascoes*, 2nd edition. New York: Houghton Mifflin.

Klein, R. H. (1983). 'Group Treatment Approaches', in M. Hersen, A. E. Kazdin and A. S. Bellack (eds.), *The Clinical Psychology Handbook*, pp. 593–610. New York: Pergamon.

Le Bon, G. (1960). *The Crowd* (translation of *La psychologie des foules*). New York: The Viking Press.

Moreno, J. L. (1932). *Who Shall Survive?* Washington, DC: Nervous and Mental Disease Publishing Co.

20

Capability Development, Innovation, and Creativity

After going through this chapter, you will be able to understand:

- the concept of capability development
- the concept of organizational capability development through the people capability maturity model (P-CMM)
- the structure of P-CMM
- organizational life cycle analysis
- the concept of talent management for capability development
- the process of developing innovation and creativity in organizations
- critical success factors in building organizational capability

P-CMM and Global Organizations

UST Global, Inc. is a leading end-to-end provider of IT services and solutions to more than 1,000 companies globally. UST Global follows a client-centric global engagement model, which combines UST Global's human resources with cost, scale, and quality advantages of offshore operations. Its six sigma practices have already imbibed the client-centric approach in the organizational DNA. With P-CMM's level 5 certification in 2004, UST Global has consolidated its foundation, that is, it has dedicated and qualified people to serve customers with the help of the best HR practices. UST Global admits that P-CMM's level 5 certification and its adoption in practices immensely benefited them internally. With the help of P-CMM, it could successfully address critical people issues and achieve overall organizational improvements. P-CMM enhanced the maturity of UST Global's employees with systematic workforce development programmes, setting priorities for improvement actions, and integrating people with its process improvement, thereby establishing a culture of excellence.

Wipro, on the other hand, first took the initiative to understand the practices in global companies before going for P-CMM's level 5 certification. Accordingly, Wipro extensively studied the HR policies of various companies such as AT&T, General Electric, Tandem, and British Telecom. In 1999, Wipro developed a 'competency dictionary', identifying 24 competency areas spread across the five levels of P-CMM. Wipro also zeroed in on the behavioural issues for each level and listed out the procedures to address them.

Since Wipro competes in critical areas of business globally, P-CMM's level 5 certification helped it to build the capabilities of employees to reach global performance standards and, accordingly, facilitate their growth.

INTRODUCTION

Capability maturity model®* *(CMM)* primarily focuses on the improvement of the process or technology of an organization and not on people. However, while many organizations achieve maturity in terms of process and technology, they often fail to achieve the desired progression in terms of their human resource management (HRM) issues. By integrating the maturity of people with the process and technology, organizations can get better results. It helps in holistic capability development for the organization as a whole. It is due to this reason that professionally managed organizations aspire for the certification of both CMM and people capability maturity model (P-CMM). P-CMM, therefore, is an adaptation of CMM concepts to develop human capabilities for organizations. Although it is targeted especially in software organizations, it can be equally adapted by other organizations. Human capabilities, particularly in software organizations, are more important. With the adaptation of P-CMM, software organizations can attract, develop, motivate, organize, and retain the talent needed to steadily improve software development capability.

Like capability enhancement, *innovation* is also a new technique or idea encompassing products/services, processes, managerial styles, and even organizational structure. It may be technology push or demand pull, or even a combination of both. Research and development (R&D) activities of an organization are examples of such innovation. In an organization, the need for innovation is primarily felt to keep pace with the competition. It has to be essentially customer-focused as this backward linkage facilitates process-centred innovative changes. Just-in-time (JIT) inventory, supply chain management (SCM), business process outsourcing (BPO), flexible manufacturing systems (FMS), product/service customization, strategic backward or forward integration, synergy through merger, acquisition, alliances, or collaboration, organizational re-engineering, total quality management (TQM) or six sigma practices, new work culture as facilitator of organizational change, any R&D initiative for value addition, etc., are all practices that broadly encompass innovation. Also, all these practices stem from customers' explicit or implicit needs.

Mapping customers' needs and taking the initiative to align them to innovation is what is required in this competitive world. Innovation is enabled by proactive HRM practices. Subscribing to innovation without proactive HR practices can hinder rather than foster innovation in an organization. Proactive HR practices, among other things, call for creating a work environment that recognizes creativity, inter-organizational cooperation rather than competition, working with cross-functional teams, productive meetings for innovative results, introducing formal innovation programmes, and being receptive to new ideas and perspectives. Fostering innovation requires a structured approach. It has to be broadly aligned with leadership, values, and culture. Contextual analysis helps in building required innovation teams. Leaders facilitate the teams. Values enable adoption of principles that foster innovation, and culture provides the playing field.

This chapter has discussions on employee capability, talent management, and innovation issues that are meant to enhance organizational capability development.

* Capability Maturity Model, CMM and CMMI are registered trademark of Carnegie Mellon University.

PEOPLE CAPABILITY MATURITY MODEL

P-CMM is a maturity framework that suggests certain key elements to manage and develop the potential of people in an organization. Employees at P-CMM-compliant organizations become more mature, disciplined, and capable or competent, and enhance the organizational performance. Characterizing the human resource practices of organizations, P-CMM helps to identify the level of maturity and accordingly suggests areas of required improvement to make people more result-oriented. Its basic aim is to facilitate the development of a culture of people excellence, integrating the competency development of people with the improvement of the process. The model actually complements the capability maturity model (CMM), which focuses on the process and technology. Organizational excellence can be achieved when one integrates the improvement in the process and technology with the improvement of the human resource. Depending on the level of maturity of the people in an organization, the development practices and techniques change. With a higher level of maturity, such practices and techniques become more sophisticated. Organizations can increase the individual, team, and overall performance by embracing the P-CMM-mandated practices. A typical P-CMM has been reproduced in Figure 20.1.

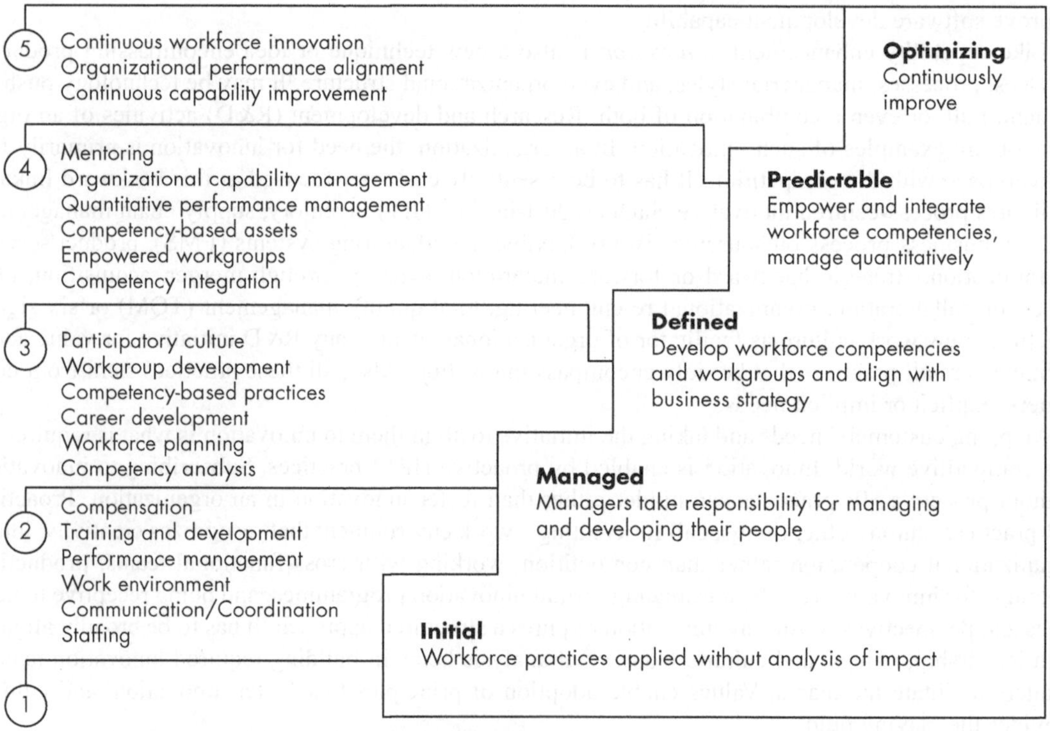

*CMM and Capability Maturity Model are registered in the U.S. Patent and Tradmark Office.

Figure 20.1 People Capability Maturity Model (*Source:* Bill Curtis, William E. Hefley, and Sally Miller. 'People Capability Maturity Model® [P-CMM], Version 2.0'. Software Engineering Institute. Technical Report CMU/SEI-2001-MM-01, July 2001, reproduced with permission from the Software Engineering Institute of Carnegie Mellon University.)

In Figure 20.1, each level of maturity and its key factors are delineated. P-CMM, thus, adapts the maturity framework of the capability maturity model for software, to manage and develop the organizational workforce. It is so designed that organizations can integrate workforce improvement with software process improvement programmes. P-CMM provides the organization with the required guidance to adopt the best practices in human resource management and development, and gain control over the workforce management processes. P-CMM can also be used by all kinds of organizations as a guide for achieving excellence in HRM issues.

Levels of P-CMM

P-CMM describes the key practices at each level of maturity. Following the information and the guidelines, organizations gradually reach the highest level of maturity, that is, level 5. At every level of maturity, processes are transformed to achieve certain distinct capabilities. Each maturity level is characterized by a set of interrelated practices in critical areas of workforce management. For continuous improvement, organizations achieve successive levels of maturity. Level 5 of P-CMM represents the highest level of maturity and capability of the workforce.

Each P-CMM level illustrates some key factors and provides guidance to achieve excellence. By institutionalizing P-CMM, organizations can achieve the desired evolutionary plateau at each level of maturity. Other than level 1, that is, the initial level, at each level of maturity, several key process areas are indicated with the key practices that can enhance workforce capability.

The five maturity levels of P-CMM are:

1. **Initial**: At this level, there are low-maturity organizations that are unable to respond to talent shortages. These types of organizations are characterized by:
   - ❑ Inconsistency in performing practices
   - ❑ Displacement of responsibility
   - ❑ Ritualistic practices
   - ❑ An emotionally detached workforce
2. **Managed**: The key process areas at this level focus on disciplining the workforce activities, emphasizing the following areas:
   - ❑ Work environment
   - ❑ Communications
   - ❑ Staffing
   - ❑ Performance management
   - ❑ Training
   - ❑ Compensation
3. **Defined**: At this level, an organization's core competencies are identified and aligned with the people management activities. Key process areas are:
   - ❑ Knowledge and skills analysis
   - ❑ Workforce planning
   - ❑ Competency development
   - ❑ Career development
   - ❑ Competency-based practices
   - ❑ Participatory culture

4. **Predictable**: At this level, the focus is more on quantitative growth, duly establishing competency-based teams. Therefore, the key process areas are:
   - ❑ Mentoring
   - ❑ Team building
   - ❑ Team-based practices
   - ❑ Organizational competency management
   - ❑ Organizational performance alignment
5. **Optimizing**: The key process areas at level 5 cover the issues that address continuous improvement of methods for developing competency, at both organizational and individual levels. They are:
   - ❑ Personal competency development
   - ❑ Coaching
   - ❑ Continuous workforce innovation

P-CMM helps an organization to select the actions of immediate improvement based on the current maturity level of workers. Apart from the HRM areas, it also encompasses areas like work environment, communication, and developing of culture.

Objectives of P-CMM

The core concepts of P-CMM aim to improve the capability of the organization in building up the capability of people. Some of the core objectives of P-CMM are as follows:

- Improve the capability of software organizations by increasing the capability of their staff
- Ensure that software development capability is an attribute of the organization rather than of a few individuals
- Align the motivation of the staff with that of the organization
- Retain assets (that is, people with extensive skills and capabilities) within the organization

Keeping in view the stated objectives, P-CMM encompasses the following areas of activities related to human resource management:

- Staffing (includes recruiting, selection, and planning)
- Managing performance
- Training
- Compensation
- Work environment
- Career development
- Organizational and individual competence
- Mentoring and coaching
- Team and culture development

Significance of P-CMM

For holistic performance improvement, every organization needs to manage three core components, that is, its people, process, and technology. These components are interrelated. Through CMM, software companies can make lasting cost-effective improvements in software process and technology. However, to sustain such improvements, companies need to bring about desired changes in the management and development of their human resource. P-CMM is the maturity framework that helps in effectively managing and developing the human resources. The importance of P-CMM can be appreciated in terms of the following points:

- It ensures that software development capability is an attribute of the organization rather than of a few individuals.
- It aligns the motivation of individuals with that of the organization.
- It retains human assets (that is, people with critical knowledge and skills) within the organization.
- It describes an evolutionary improvement path from ad hoc, inconsistently performed practices to a matured, disciplined, and continuously improving development of the knowledge, skills, and motivation of the workforce.
- It characterizes the maturity of workforce practices.
- It guides a programme of continuous workforce development.
- It sets priorities for immediate actions.
- It integrates workforce development with process improvement.
- It establishes a culture of software engineering excellence.

Thus, P-CMM guides organizations on strategy and practices. One can construe P-CMM as the road map for organizational growth through the development of human resources.

ORGANIZATIONAL LIFE CYCLE

Organizations, just like human beings, go through different phases in their life cycle. For example, one goes through different phases like infancy, childhood, and teenage. In each phase, one experiences certain developments through which one matures. When one compares the individual life cycle with organizational life cycle, one finds that organizations also go through different phases of development and in the process, mature. Organizational experience in each phase of their life cycle gradually builds organizational capability in managing, which in the process ensures long-term sustainability. Experiences through different phases of the life cycle gradually help organizations to develop the right perspectives to problem solving and responding to the environmental cues. The typical features of an organizational life cycle have been documented in Table 20.1.

Managers need to understand the sequential process of change in different phases of the life cycle, and manage accordingly to avoid deterioration. The typical organizational syndromes in the different phases of a life cycle have been explained here.

Infant Stage

For organizations, this stage starts with a dream. Organizations translate this dream into a vision, and by exploring opportunities, transform the vision into a realizable mission. Since setting up the organization is the result of the promoters' dream, at this stage, action is more important than opinions. This is the reason why an infant organization is characterized as action-oriented, opportunity-driven, and vision-focused.

Growing Stage

This is the stage of formalization of beliefs, values, goals, structure, and actions in the form of culture, norms, rules, and procedures. All organizational members need to reach a consensus for action with a

Table 20.1 Features of Organizational Life Cycle

Features of organizations	Different phases of organizational life cycle			
	Birth	Youth	Midlife	Maturity
Size	Small	Medium	Large	Very large
Bureaucratic nature	Non-bureaucratic	Pre-bureaucratic	Bureaucratic	Very bureaucratic
Division of labour	Overlapping tasks	Some departments	Many departments	Extensive, with small jobs and many descriptions
Centralization	One-person rule	Two leaders' rule	Two department heads	Heavy top management
Formalization	No written rules	Few rules	Policy and procedures manuals	Extensive
Administrative intensity	Secretary, no professional staff	Increasing clerical and maintenance staff	Increasing professional and staff support	Large multiple departments
Internal systems	Non-existent	Crude budget and information system	Control systems in place, budget, performance reports, etc.	Extensive planning, financial resources and personnel added
Lateral teams and task forces for coordination	None	Top leaders only	Some use of integrators and task forces	Frequent at lower levels to break down bureaucracy

shared dream. Organizing the action is facilitated by the structure of the organization. With a strong sense of purpose, all employees of the organization feel committed and deliver the results.

Prime Stage

At this stage, organizations make their vision a reality. This stage usually stretches to a longer duration in the life cycle. Organizations achieve efficiency and effectiveness, become more result-driven, and expand and focus on long-term sustainability.

Ageing Stage

This stage is characterized by decline in the commitment of the employees. Members of the organization question the leadership. The process of ageing becomes more acute if the organization fails to redefine their purpose. It requires revisiting the vision and mission, and providing a new sense of direction to the members of the organization.

Dying Stage

This is the stage of total loss of purpose and hope for rejuvenation. With the increase in questioning, internal problems mount and conflict increases. Recovering from this stage is near impossible.

CAPABILITY DEVELOPMENT

For organizations to succeed in a competitive setting, employees at all levels need to develop and demonstrate behaviour showcasing their capabilities, characteristics, knowledge, talent, and personal qualities for effective performance at work. All businesses are based on some key competencies. The main reason for an organization to create a capability- or competency-based system that focuses on having the right people with the right skills at the right time is that it helps in accomplishing business targets. Capabilities are the need of the hour and they help in designing appropriate capability development models. Therefore, a capability framework is an instrument to identify the critical factors or capabilities required now and in the future for high performance.

Capability development is central to organizational performance, and it requires a systematic management approach to learning and development as an integral part of the workforce planning. Learning and development encompass a wide range of activities designed to improve the capabilities of people. Capabilities comprise not only the technical skills and knowledge people have, but also their attributes, attitudes, and behaviour. Learning and development activities can be designed to deliver specific skills in a short period of time to meet an immediate need, or designed to achieve broader requirements over a longer period. *Capability requirements* is ascertaining or identifying short-term and long-term organizational capability requirements and establishing learning and development strategies and plans that are aligned with desired outcomes as identified by the organization in their planning documents such as corporate plans, business unit plans, and workforce/people management strategies. The capability requirements should cover subject matter, skills and knowledge relevant to the organizational role and challenges, as well as broader capabilities in management and leadership.

A software organization's core is their talent or knowledge pool. In the competitive race of attracting and retaining the best talent, software companies often over-recruit, but due to a lack in their post-recruitment capability development initiatives, most of these recruits become redundant. Capability development in the software industry is particularly crucial due to the shorter knowledge cycle. Therefore, for software organizations, employees' skill or capability development is the most important role. Again, the scope of capability development of software professionals need not be confined to technical areas. Software managers also need to develop their capability in customer relationship management (CRM), negotiation, project management, etc.

For organizations, the terms *capability* and *competency* are used interchangeably. These involve identification of specific job functions of employees, documenting the job specifications, mapping the availability of capabilities, listing the gaps, and putting the right initiatives to meet such gaps. This process serves the purpose of recruitment, keeping pace with the present and future needs of the organization.

Benefits of Capability Development Models

Capability development models benefit organizations in a number of ways, such as:

- Reduction in staff turnover, recruitment costs, training costs, etc.
- Improvement in productivity, performance, training and development
- Reliable and consistence performance data across cultures and geographic borders

- Delivery of comprehensive training and development plans
- Setting up of training and development processes that identify and deliver the most effective sessions
- Identification of employees' capabilities for an organization's future needs
- Analysis of capability gaps

Capability development models provide a capability framework against which staff and supervisors can identify learning and development needs and map their careers. Managers and staff agree on the learning and development needs and a strategy is formulated for meeting those needs as part of the performance management process. Architecting people capability is also a key requirement for managers. Some managers appear to be born with the skill to get along with people, while many may be lacking in such skills. Competence development is, therefore, a lifelong process.

Key Areas of Capability Development

To build a winning team, managers must be capable of developing the human resource. Key focus areas of capability development include the following:

- **Communication**: Lack of information and communication are the major constraints on people's capability. The most important thing is mastering the art of empathetic listening and empathetic communication.
- **Performance management**: Effective performance management requires developing performance standards, cascading business goals to individual goals, group or team performance, developing appropriate performance assessment tools, and ensuring systematic feedback to employees, including periodic performance counselling. Most employees' capability development decisions are taken based on performance results.
- **Resource management**: Employees need to develop their skills in resource optimization. This requires developing the power to think on constraints. Organizations need to make people capable by focusing on empowering, and allowing them to take decisions on their own. Through this process, employees can gradually master the art of resource optimizing.
- **Training**: Capability development is part of a long-term strategy, while plugging skill gaps is a short-term training need. Performance appraisal data can help in assessing the training needs and organizations can accordingly introduce training modules to make people capable of performing.
- **Teamwork**: Introducing a culture of teamwork in the organization helps in many ways. Due to the benefits associated with synergy, a team can deliver more than the aggregate of individual work. It is important for organizations to make people understand that they all work towards achieving a common goal. With a common goal, people can be bound together in a team to achieve the best results.

Talent Management for Capability Development

The capability of individual employees and organizational capability can be improved through talent management. Through the process of talent management, organizations can achieve both short-term and long-term success. It improves the way the organization works and can differentiate it from its competitors, enhancing its competitive advantage (Duttagupta 2005). Through the process of managing talent, an organization can gradually build its culture. It helps in harnessing unutilized or underutilized capability of people to achieve performance results both at the individual and the organizational levels. Hence, *talent management* helps in optimizing the available human resources in an organization. The present generation of workers do not believe in just job security. They value their long-term employability much more. Hence, organizational emphasis on talent management is valued by them (Mintzberg 2004). Henry Mintzberg suggests that to attract and retain the best talent, organizations should focus on talent management catering to the following areas:

- **Developing the culture of learning**: This can be done by investing in visible learning initiatives to benefit all cross-sections of employees, which in the process also develops the culture of learning in the organization.
- **Ensuring employees' mobility**: This is possible when organizations believe in cross-functional mobility, irrespective of the location. This facilitates exposure of employees to different functions.
- **Redesigning jobs**: This requires organizations to focus on job families, rather than rigid job descriptions. Job families are identified by grouping jobs in terms of skill or knowledge proximity. It helps in identifying the possibility of skill interchangeability and accordingly utilizes the talent of employees.
- **Emphasizing on coaching and mentoring**: This develops the potential of the employees helping to hone their talent.
- **Focusing on leadership development**: This helps to develop the potential of future leaders, who can contribute to the organization.
- **Developing a compelling work environment**: This inspires employees to believe in accomplishing the job rather than in time-bound working.
- **Creating a culture of 'inclusion and collaboration'**: Inculcating this mindset is important in order to move away from the traditional culture of 'command and control'.

Along with capability development for the new generation of workers, organizations need to also emphasize special capability development programmes for their ageing workforce, which among other things require focus on periodic skill renewal and skill transition (changing from one skill area to another, wherever possible). Craig Donaldson (2006) emphasized an innovative talent management strategy for organizations to gain competitive advantage. The strategy is to 'buy, build, or move', that is, look at skill strengths and acquire them in either of these ways to make organizations more stable. According to William J. Rothwell (2005), this can be done through environmental scanning and organizational analysis, and by preparing realistic scenarios. *Environmental scanning* is done through the examination of external trends; *organizational analysis* is done by mapping the extent of organizational strengths to withstand future challenges; and *realistic scenarios* pre-decide strategies for any eventuality.

The comprehensive Conference Board (2005) research report on talent management suggests an integrated approach towards talent management. The integrated approach, according to the report, requires embracing of recruitment, retention, professional development, leadership/high potential, performance management, feedback/measurement of talent, workforce planning, and culture.

INNOVATION AND CREATIVITY

Innovation and *creativity* are terms that are often used interchangeably in the workplace. The online Merriam-Webster dictionary defines creativity as 'the ability or power to create, to bring into existence, to invest with a new form, to produce through imaginative skill, to make or bring into existence something new'. Creativity is, therefore, the core competency. It is the talent of employees of an organization. Competitors can replicate the strategies of an organization but not the creative talents of its employees. To encourage creativity, an organization first creates the right environment where employees feel safe to come up with even 'dumb' or 'crazy' ideas. Creativity is often punished in organizations, as creative people spend more time to get ready for action. They are also more difficult to manage. Organizations, therefore, often see them as major wasters of time and money, and even inhibit their creative thoughts. A review of creative literature found the following creative patterns:

- A creative process is a balance of imagination and analysis. It involves idea generation, analysis, and evaluation.
- Creativity does not stem from subconscious processes, as traditionally believed by the classical school of thought. It is a purposeful or directed attempt to generate new ideas under a controlled situation to help organizations leapfrog the competition. Paul E. Plsek (1997) more appropriately used the term *directed creativity*. It is a purposeful generation of creative ideas with a seriousness imbued to its implementation, whenever it matches organizational requirements. Non-implementation of even some ideas (that fit the purpose) will inhibit creativity.

Creativity is the ability or power to create or generate new ideas, while *innovation* is the implementation of creative ideas. Therefore, creativity is the subset of innovation. Since innovation is a holistic concept, it is used interchangeably with creativity.

Competencies, on the other hand, are sets of behaviours that encompass skills, knowledge, abilities, and attributes. Competencies are measurable and these change over time. G. Hamel and C. K. Prahalad (1990) attributed business success only to innovative creativity, knowledge resources, and the expertise, which together create the critical potential of an organization, that is, the core competencies. Other proponents such as Quinn (1992), Drucker (1988, 1992), Porter (1995), Peters and Waterman (1982), Nonaka and Takeuchi (1995), and Senge (1990) also show that developing core competencies helps an organization to build strategic power. Core competencies are difficult to duplicate by competitors because of their distinctiveness. *Core competencies*, therefore, are the critical success factors for an organization. Although there is widespread difference in opinion regarding constituents of core competencies and their relation with knowledge, skill, abilities, and attributes of employees, it is generally agreed that they are created by linking the organization's goals, structure, and culture. Innovation and creativity help to develop core competencies by supplementing the knowledge and skill base of employees. In this respect, directed creativity, that is, purposeful generation of new ideas matching with organizational requirements is more relevant.

Innovation, creativity, and competencies are important facilitators of organizational change. Imperatives for organizational change basically stem from redefining business focus, restructuring, and customer orientation, and they are all aimed at garnering competitive advantage.

Aligning Innovation to Competitive Strengths and Organizational Capability Development

Innovation and creativity can enhance the capability of organizations. In the Indian social system, innovation and creativity are embedded in the age-old theory of social stratification. *Social stratification* refers to the principal mechanism of social order in society from which the concept of class categorization has come up. While caste, class, and elite and professional occupational categories have been used for the analysis of social stratification in India, one finds more use of occupational categories. Among the occupational categories, professional and bureaucratic elites were those who had sustained training to acquire skills for performing professional roles in a formal organizational set-up, and their nature of work was more complex than others.

The Indian *gurukul* system of learning also intended to reinforce innovation and creativity, recognizing the existence of a core essence in each individual. Learning under the *gurukul* system was intended to help students to think independently and understand their interdependent relationship with nature by exploring nature. Over the years, however, this has changed, reducing learning to a formal mechanism, where creativity and independent thought are often punished, as teachers find that creative students in the classroom make it harder for them to do their job.

The competitive compulsion in organizations has put the focus back on the age-old process of nurturing innovation and creativity, in view of their importance in gaining competitive strengths.

To cultivate innovation and creativity, it is important to understand the factors that encourage innovation in an organization. They are as follows:

- Creating a congenial work environment is the most important prerequisite. This requires major attitudinal and cultural changes to provide the right playing field to foster innovation. The desired work environment to nurture innovation and creativity should be full of listening, speaking, evaluating, and questioning. A destructive way of questioning or questioning with a cynical tone may dampen the spirit of innovators. Even giving a negative non-verbal cue, that is, diverting attention, falling asleep, etc., may vitiate the environment. Attitudinal and cultural changes should be reinforced by proper employee compensation; it also requires special rewards for implemented ideas. If ideas are not implemented at all, it sends a wrong signal to creative people, who then start perceiving that their organization inhibits creativity.
- Another important aspect of cultivating innovation in an organization is fostering mutual cooperation. Creating strategic business units (SBU) or independent business units (IBU) does not mean that each SBU or IBU should compete with each other. By leveraging their strengths, an organization should function as an integrated whole and work with cross-functional teams. For example, one finds that in most cases the customer database is common for SBUs in an organization, but SBU heads prefer to have proprietary control over these databases, fearing a clash of interests. Even within SBUs, one finds that executives compete with each other by not sharing information. Such a competitive environment within the organization, unless transformed into a cooperative environment, will not allow creativity to flourish. The competitive trend is prevalent in business schools as well. When students of these schools enter the corporate world, they work with a competitive mindset, which fosters organizational rivalry and competition. One can correct this situation by forming cross-functional teams.
- Having productive meetings and brainstorming also inspire innovation and creativity. Such brainstorming does not mean that only the topmost superior will speak and the others will listen. It implies actual involvement of all members on issues that may or may not pertain to their area of activities. A true productive meeting may not be time-bound; it may even run for several days. This helps in process re-engineering and, at times, leads to re-aligning the business to customers' expectations. Productive meetings help in capturing the 'collective wisdom' of the entire cross-section of employees. This, therefore, develops the innovative and creative response capability, which adds to the competitive strengths. Chevron Corporation, a leader in the petroleum industry, used direct participation (DP), involving employees in innovative thinking for designing and implementing change. In the DP process, a variety of stakeholders meet (for two to three days) to address a problem or an issue that calls for change and produce detailed outputs that can be quickly implemented. It brings multiple perspectives relating to the problem and facilitates identification of changes required to resolve it.
- Formal innovation programmes and techniques are vital to uphold an innovative and creative culture in the organization. Formal innovation programmes in an organization should focus on generating ideas in relation to current and future customer needs, speeding up idea generation with frequent meetings, quickly funding the idea that fits the purpose, and reducing the response time for implementation. Many organizations have adopted the 'incubator' concept for nurturing innovation and creativity. Incubators in leading Indian organizations are like small meditation halls that allow employees to think in isolation, even taking a break from work, and explore issues for creative

solution. Once the thoughts are matured, they are put up for discussion by cross-functional teams for implementation.

- Finally, organizations should also be receptive to new ideas. The mere presence of formal innovation programmes will not help unless an organization shows concern for their implementation. Quite often, innovative ideas are thought to be a criticism of existing systems. In fact, some employees, in the process of presenting new ideas, often unknowingly indulge in criticizing the existing system. This may be dangerous and it requires proper training on how to structure ideas and present them either in writing or in the form of a discussion.

Aligning Innovation and Creativity to Organizational Practices

For aligning innovation and creativity to competitive strategy, it is important to consider the following aspects:

- Innovation should be focused and need-specific.
- There should be a clear documented policy on innovation and creativity explaining how they are captured, if there is a reward system for the best innovative ideas, and the process of implementation.
- Innovation and creativity cannot be outsourced. Hence, emphasis should be on in-house talent. If it is outsourced, it loses its competitive strength as others can replicate it.
- All innovative ideas should be subjected to brainstorming and, if acceptable, should first be tried out in pilot projects.
- For risk hedging, innovative ideas can be benchmarked with other organizations. Hindustan Lever Limited (HLL; now Unilever) succeeded in repositioning Lifebuoy by changing its attributes (from carbolic soap to soap with an inbuilt health essence), but Colgate is struggling behind and trying desperately to retain its market share by increasing product variety.
- Implementation should be closely monitored, preferably by calculating the return on investment (ROI), and it should only be institutionalized after success in the pilot project.
- Finally, innovation and creativity need to be aligned to organizational values, which provide broad guidelines for adoption of principles, vision, mission, and strategies.

CRITICAL SUCCESS FACTORS

Aligning organizations to identified critical success factors (CSF) is yet another creative tool to introduce technological change and promote innovation. CSF analysis was first developed at the MIT Sloan School of Management by John Rockart (1979). It helps an organization to create and measure success. The approach is a top-down reductionist method to deduce simple and concrete requirements from a complex and abstract vision. To be more specific, *critical success factors* are the identified key areas for achieving organizational goals. It starts with a vision and a mission statement. This requires developing some goals in order of hierarchy and making a list of points that would enable the organization to achieve these goals, that is, the success factors. This method enables an organization to measure success by duly prioritizing their listed goals. Thus, CSF results in objective and definable end results. It defines entities and relationships in a business context.

The author has experienced how CSF can help in transforming an organization. IFB Agro Industries Limited, Kolkata, does not have any documented vision and mission statement. However, the employees of the company direct all their efforts to achieve common goals, as set by the top management. As an outsider, the author started asking various executives about their beliefs regarding their personal and organizational practices. Within 15 minutes they all came out with a host of points on issues ranging from customers' satisfaction, quality, cost-competitiveness, and brand building, to social identity, valuing human resources, becoming number one in their area of activity, etc. After this, they were asked to indicate what they should also practice. Continuous process improvement, quality improvement, staying ahead of competitors by periodic benchmarking, product diversification, technological upgrade, and many more points came out in this phase. One coordinator for the batch was then requested to identify the specific points that fit their philosophy, first by simple identification of common points and second by brainstorming. After coming up with 80/20 rules, they then reduced the points to a minimum of four. With just four statements, they could then spell out their vision, that is, the philosophy of the organization. Subsequently, they were asked to translate their vision into a more action-oriented statement—a mission that defines the purpose of existence now.

Unlike a vision, a mission is more specific, keeping in mind the present that an organization has and the future it intends to have, with an eye to aspects of competitiveness. Since a mission statement is action-oriented, it must be dynamic enough to give a message, while putting everything it aims for under a common umbrella, preferably with a single statement. After this, the leaders have to go and sell to people, take inputs from them, and if required revisit. The most important factor is reaching a consensus with everyone.

Thus, by using CSF analysis, an organization can successfully align people with the process of technological change in an innovative way.

BLOCKBUSTING AND PRODUCT IMPROVEMENT

Blockbusting is used to break the functionally fixed mindset. To help employees to practise this technique, the trainer asks the participants to think of an item or an object and list its possible uses, not just limited to its immediate utility. For example, in the case of a ball pen, everyone knows that the pen is for writing. However, one also uses a pen to prick one's ears, bite, scratch one's back, comb one's hair, hold papers together, and so on. All these alternative uses may apparently seem awkward, but they are visibly practised. Moreover, the more one thinks about such alternative uses, the more creative one can become. It is then possible to design a pen that multiplies the utility value to a user, without, however, raising the cost value. The blockbusting technique is very useful in new product design. It is also useful in new technology selection and implementation.

One can also encourage employees to be creative by urging them to think about improvement of any product/service or an object. While doing so, it is important to have employees follow this structured list:

- Product simplification
- Application in new areas
- Automation
- Cost reduction
- Making the product user-friendly
- Better usability, durability, and reliability
- Additional features and functions
- More flexibility
- Better sensory, emotional, and psychological appeal

The list is not exhaustive. Trainers can identify many more improvement means relating to organizational requirements.

Case Lessons from Mitsubishi Chemicals

Mitsubishi Chemicals has a vibrant presence in the industrial chemicals sector in India. In Haldia (West Bengal), they process purified terephthalic acid (PTA), one of the most harzadous chemicals used by industries. Mitsubishi's entry into the Indian market by stepping into areas that were already saturated—the largest market share belonging to Reliance—was never thought to be a prudent business decision. However, the company proved everyone wrong by raising its market share in PTA and becoming number one, beating all competitors.

Like a standard Japanese organization, Mitsubishi believes in teamwork. Even at the shop-floor level, Mitsubishi engages qualified people to achieve results. Processing of PTA requires a series of operations and involvement of multi-skilled people with specialized knowledge. Since it is a continuous-process industry, chemical processing activities take place round the clock. The company needs to shut down the plant only during preventive maintenance. As PTA is a highly explosive and hazardous chemical, the company follows preventive maintenance at predetermined intervals to ensure smooth running of the operations. To ensure effective maintenance work, employees from each cross-section are invited to suggest their perceived areas of processing deficiency, if any, and state how they feel the process can be made more result-oriented. The employees' shared experiences are valued by the company.

One of the essential ingredients of PTA is its absolute transparency. In fact, PTA with high transparency is considered to be the most effective version of PTA. After one preventive maintenance exercise, the quality control team was able to identify a problem with the transparency. Successive brainstorming and innovative exercises helped the company to pinpoint the cause of the problem, which lay with the water sourced from the river used in cleaning the pipelines. Subsequent plant maintenance with duly treated water helped the company to eliminate this problem.

CASE QUESTION

After reading the case, explain how innovation can be made a part of the culture of an organization. Draw lessons for Indian organizations.

SUMMARY

- *Capability maturity model (CMM)* primarily focuses on the improvement of the process or technology of an organization and not on people. Many organizations often fail to achieve the desired progression in terms of their human resource management issues even if they achieve maturity in terms of process and technology. However, by integrating the maturity of people with the process and technology, organizations can get better results. This helps in the capability development of the organization as a whole.
- The *people capability maturity model (P-CMM)* is a maturity framework that suggests certain key elements to manage and develop the potential of people in an organization. Employees of P-CMM-compliant organizations become more mature, disciplined, and capable or competent, and they help to enhance the organizational performance.
- The people capability maturity model describes the key practices at each level of maturity. Following the information and the guidelines, organizations gradually reach the highest level of maturity, which is designated as level 5. At every level of maturity, an organization's processes are transformed to achieve a distinct capability. Each maturity level is characterized by a set of inter-related practices in critical areas of workforce management.

- Organizations go through different stages in their life cycle. Organizational experience in each stage gradually builds up organizational capability in managing, which in the process ensures organizational long-term sustainability. Experiences through the different stages of a life cycle help organizations to develop the right perspectives to problem solving, responding to the environmental cues.
- For organizations to succeed in a competitive setting, employees at all levels need to develop and demonstrate a set of behaviour showcasing their capabilities, characteristics, knowledge, talent, and personal qualities for effective performance at work.
- All businesses are based on some key competencies. The main reason for an organization to create a capability- or competency-based system that focuses on having the right people with the right skills at the right time is that it helps in accomplishing business targets.
- Through the process of managing talent, an organization can gradually build its culture and develop its capability at the individual and the organizational levels. This helps in harnessing the unutilized or underutilized capability of individuals to achieve performance results at both levels.
- *Innovation* implies a new technique or idea encompassing products/services, processes, managerial styles, and even organizational structure. It may be technology push or demand pull, or even a combination of both. Research and development (R&D) activities of an organization are examples of such innovation. In an organization, the need for innovation is felt primarily to keep pace with the competition.
- *Creativity* is the ability or power to create, to bring into existence, to invest with a new form, to produce through imaginative skill, or to make or bring into existence something new. Creativity is therefore, the core competency. Innovation and creativity can enhance the capability of an organization.
- *Competencies* are a set of behaviours that encompass skills, knowledge, abilities, and attributes. Competencies are measurable and they change over time.
- Critical success factors (CSF), and blockbusting and product improvement are some important tools and techniques of innovation.

KEY TERMS

Competencies: Competencies are a set of behaviours that encompass skills, knowledge, abilities, and attributes. Competencies are measurable and they change over time.

Creativity: Creativity is the ability or power to create, to bring into existence, to invest with a new form, to produce through imaginative skill, or to make or bring into existence something new.

Innovation: Innovation implies a new technique or idea encompassing products/services, processes, managerial styles, and even organizational structure.

People capability maturity model: People capability maturity model (P-CMM) is a maturity framework that suggests certain key elements to manage and develop the potential of people in an organization. Employees of P-CMM-compliant organizations become more mature, disciplined, and capable or competent, and they help to enhance the organizational performance.

Talent management: Talent management helps in optimizing the available human resources in an organization.

REVIEW QUESTIONS

1. Define the concept of *capability development*. How does the people capability maturity model (P-CMM) help an organization to build its capability?
2. Explain the structure of P-CMM.
3. What are the important objectives of P-CMM? Why is it important for organizations?
4. Explain the concept of organizational life cycle. Why is it significant for organizations?
5. Discuss the ways in which the process of talent management can help an organization to build its capability.
6. Define *innovation* and *creativity* and illustrate how they are used in new technology selection and implementation in an organization.
7. Examine how an organization nurtures the culture of innovation and creativity. In what ways can HR support the process?
8. What are the *critical success factors* for an organization? How can these be determined? In what way can these facilitate new technology introduction?
9. Write short notes on:
   i. Blockbusting techniques
   ii. Critical success factors
   iii. Competencies
   iv. Social stratification theory
   v. Reward and recognition

CRITICAL THINKING QUESTIONS

1. Your organization is experiencing the typical problem of unity of action. To infuse a sense of direction and bring about unity of action, you are planning to undertake a critical success factors analysis. Explain the process that you are going to adopt and the way in which you are going to do it.
2. Apply a product improvement approach to design a new product for an organization. Illustrate your answer by elaborating on the various stages and explain why you chose this approach.

REFERENCES

Donaldson, Craig (2006). 'Annual Reports Quiet on HR Spend', *Human Resources*, 7 February. Australia: LexisNexis.

Drucker, Peter F. (1988). 'The Coming of the New Organization', *Harvard Business Review on Knowledge Management*, pp. 1–19.

——— (1992). *Managing for the Future*. Oxford: Butterworth-Heinemann.

Duttagupta, R. (2005). 'Identifying and Managing Your Assets: Talent Management', *Intellectual Asset Magazine*, 4 (2): p. 32.

Gibbons, John and Christopher Woock (2005). *Evidence-based Human Resources: A Primer and Summary of Current Literature*. New York: The Conference Board.

Hamel, G. and C. K. Prahalad (1990). 'The Core Competence of the Corporation', *Harvard Business Review*, May–June, 68 (3): pp. 79–91.

Mintzberg, Henry (2004). *Managers, Not MBAs: A Hard Look at the Soft Practice of Managing and Management Development*. San Francisco, CA: Berrett-Koehler.

Nonaka, Ikujiro and Hirotaka Takeuchi (1995). *The Knowledge-Creating Company*. New York: Oxford University Press.

Peters, T. J. and R. H. Waterman (1982). *In Search of Excellence: Lessons from America's Best-Run Companies*. New York: Harper-Collins Publishers.

Plsek, Paul E. (1997). *Creativity, Innovation and Quality*. Milwaukee, WI: ASQ Quality Press.

Porter, Michael E. (1995). 'The Competitive Advantage of the Inner City', *Harvard Business Review*, May–June, pp. 55–71.

Rockart, John F. (1979). 'Chief Executives Define Their Own Data Needs', *Harvard Business Review*, 2, pp. 81–93.

Rothwell, William J. (2005). *Effective Succession Planning: Ensuring Leadership Continuity and Building Talent from Within*, 3rd edition. New York: American Management Association.

Senge, P. M. (1990). *The Fifth Discipline: The Art and Practice of the Learning Organization*. New York: Doubleday Currency.

FURTHER READING

Adizes, Ichak (1988). *Corporate Lifecycles*. Englewood Cliffs, NJ: Prentice Hall.

Bhattacharyya, D. K. (1995). 'Corporate Bodybuilder: The Emerging Role of HRD Professional, A Prescriptive Model for Success', *Indian Journal of Training and Development*, April–June.

——— (2000). Competency Mapping and Manpower Redundancy: A Macro-level Study of Indian Organisations', *Management and Accounting Research*, October–December, 4 (2): pp. 97–105.

——— (2007). *Human Resource Research Methods*. New Delhi: Oxford University Press.

Ceserani, Jonne and Peter Greatwood (2001). *Innovation and Creativity*. New Delhi: Crest Publishing House.

Christiansen, James A. (2000). *Competitive Innovation Management*. London: Macmillan Business.

Fredric, Frank and Taylor Craig (2004). 'Talent Management: Trends that Will Shape the Future', *Human Resource Planning*, 27, pp. 33–41.

Gordon, Edward E. (2000). *Skill Wars: Winning the Battle for Productivity and Profit*. Boston, MA: Butterworth-Heinemann.

Rappaport, Anna, Ed Bancroft and Lauren Okum (2003). 'The Aging Workforce Raises New Talent Management Issues for Employers', *Journal of Organizational Excellence*, 23 (1): pp. 55–66.

Stolovitch, H. D and J. G. Maurice (1998). 'Calculating the Return on Investment in Training: A Critical Analysis and Case Study', *Performance Improvement*, 37 (8): pp. 9–20.

21

Quality Management Practices in Organizations

After going through this chapter, you will be able to understand:

- quality management practices
- the six sigma approach and its role in developing human resources
- lean management practices
- the concepts of employee empowerment and quality of work life (QWL)
- the concept of quality circles and their relevance to total quality management (TQM)
- the Toyota production system
- quick response manufacturing

Lean Management Lessons of Nestlé

Nestlé Purina Petcare (Friskies), Merseyside, United Kingdom, is a part of the Nestlé group. Nestlé Purina Petcare, formerly Friskies Petcare, manufactures dog biscuits for all the major supermarkets including Bonio, Sharpes, and Specials. Committed to developing the workforce, Nestlé Purina embraced the concept of lean management practices. Using the services of a consulting team, CQM Training & Consultancy Ltd, the company carried out a detailed study on the production line; measured the wastage, labour utilization rate, and rework costs; evaluated the scope of multi-shift working; and made extensive use of communication for their commitment to continuous improvement. In the process, the company was able to develop the following tools:

- Team development
- Systematic problem solving
- Process analysis
- Modern manufacturing techniques
- Productivity measures
- *Kaizen*/total productive maintenance (TPM)/lean manufacturing
- Workplace organization—5S methodology

All the listed tools strengthen lean management practices. Using these tools, the company could identify the wastage and, accordingly, save costs. Wastage was identified in the production lines and also in the processes, and its elimination led to savings of GBP 118,000. In addition, lean management practices reduced the company's labour costs, improved teamwork, and facilitated the development of cross-functional learning. The company's experience, therefore, teaches that lean management can not only save costs, eliminating the wastage, it can also develop the potential of the workforce, bring about process improvement, and develop teamwork. Once it is operational, the teams can further the process of its implementation autonomously.

Note: Hiroyuki Hirano from Japan advocated the 5S concept, which helps to bring stability and standardization in workplace organization, and to achieve improved safety, quality, delivery performance, and cost control. 5S is the basis of lean manufacturing, that is, the principles of Toyota Production System (TPS). 5S is construed as the systematic approach to workplace organization, indicating (1) sort *(seiri)*—what is needed and what is not, (2) set *(seiton)*—arranging everything in its place, (3) shine *(seiso)*—cleanliness, (4) standardize *(seiketsu)*—standardize and instill discipline, and (5) sustain *(shitsuke)*—audit and improve the system.

Source: http://www.cqmltd.co.uk/files/NestlePurina, last accessed on 2 December 2011.pdf. Adapted with permission from CQM Training and Consultancy Ltd.

INTRODUCTION

Quality is the totality of features and characteristics of products or services which satisfy stated or implied needs of customers. It is now a must for the survival of an organization. Customers who buy an organization's products or services have certain expectations. If the product or service meets or exceeds those expectations time and again, then in the mind of that customer, it is a *quality product* or *service*. Quality provides a focus for all management concerns—cost reduction, productivity, teamwork, communication, and training objectives like problem solving, decision making, organizational dynamics, and interpersonal skills. These concerns acquire synergy and meaning only when aligned to organizational goals of quality and customer service. Through quality, organizations can also make the human resource development function effective. Through quality improvement programmes, organizations can develop the capability to troubleshoot problems of quality and develop quality as an essential inbuilt attribute of products and services. *Total quality management (TQM)* focuses on adopting an organizational improvement strategy through development of the human resource. Therefore, quality is intertwined with the development of the human resource of an organization.

QUALITY IN ORGANIZATIONS

Organizations worldwide put stress on achieving quality to sustain themselves in a competitive environment, as it lowers cost and at the same time offers value for money to customers. The mission statement of almost every organization declares that achieving quality is their most important priority to grow in a globally competitive market. Traditional focus on product quality has gradually metamorphosed to become quality of the organization. Both for achieving internal efficiency and international acceptance, corporate houses are now getting certification from the International Organization for Standardization (ISO) to establish their quality identity.

Cost of Quality

To appreciate the importance of quality, firstly, it is necessary for the organization to understand the term *cost of quality*. Identification of the cost of quality and appropriate steps to reduce it can help an organization to attain both cost minimization and increased profitability. To analyse the cost of quality, it is necessary to first classify the nature of cost under three groups:

1. **Cost of failure**: Quality may fail either internally, that is, within the organization, or externally, that is, within the customers' premises. Therefore, *cost of failure* can be grouped as either *internal failure cost* or *external failure cost*. Cost of rework, cost of additional raw materials, additional payments required to be made to the workforce, etc. can be included in internal failure cost. In the case of external failure, one considers the costs incurred on re-transportation, repackaging, and servicing and handling of customers' complaints, as well as the cost of loss of goodwill, in addition to the cost to be incurred for internal failure. Experience shows that the cost of failure absorbs 70 per cent of the total cost of quality.
2. **Cost of appraisal**: For verification of quality, the organization has to incur expenses towards inspection. Apart from maintaining an inspection team, certain inspection gadgets and tools are also required. All the expenses incurred on this account are considered the *cost of appraisal*. On this account, usually an organization spends about 28 per cent to 29 per cent of the total quality cost.
3. **Cost of prevention**: *Cost of prevention* is the type of quality cost that is incurred to reduce the other two quality costs. Such expenses are amounts spent on research and development and human resource development. Expenses on this account normally vary between 1 per cent and 2 per cent.

From an international perspective, even though the cost of quality is not accounted for under any separate heading, it is as high as 40 per cent of the cost of production. In Indian organizations, it is typically assumed that in the normal manufacturing process there will be some amount of rejection, known as unavoidable rejection rate (URR), and this may be as high as 22 per cent. In sharp contrast, in some developed countries, more particularly in Japan, they are subscribing to the philosophy of zero defects.

Experience shows that a mere one per cent to two per cent more expenditure on cost of prevention can substantially reduce the expenditure on the other two quality costs. In fact, the rate of such incremental cost benefit is as high as 70 per cent to 80 per cent for an additional one per cent to two per cent expense on cost of prevention.

Thus, it is evident that even though cost of quality is not apparent from the account books, it is a significant factor of wasteful cost, which can be reduced substantially to increase the profitability of an organization. In fact, the process of ISO documentation helps to prune the cost of quality and augment the internal efficiency of an organization. It also helps to achieve total quality management in a phased manner.

Quality Management

With growing global competition, quality management is becoming increasingly important to the leadership and management of all organizations. Quality management principles provide guidance on the application of quality management. By applying the eight principles of quality management, organizations produce benefits for customers, owners, suppliers, and the society at large.

1. **Customer-focused organization**: Organizations depend on their customers and, therefore, should understand current and future customer needs, meet customer requirements, and strive to exceed customer expectations.
2. **Leadership**: Leaders establish a unity of purpose and direction for the organization. They should create and maintain the internal environment in which people can become fully involved in achieving the organization's objectives.
3. **Involvement of people**: People at all levels are the essence of an organization and their full involvement enables the utilization of their abilities for the organization's benefit.

4. **Process approach**: A desired result is achieved more efficiently when related resources and activities are managed as a process.
5. **System approach to management**: Identifying, understanding, and managing a system of interrelated processes for a given objective improve the organization's effectiveness and efficiency.
6. **Continual improvement**: Continual improvement should be a permanent objective of the organization.
7. **Factual approach to decision making**: Effective decisions and actions are based on an analysis of data and information.
8. **Mutually beneficial supplier relationships**: An organization and its suppliers are interdependent, and a mutually beneficial relationship enhances the ability to create value.

Quality management is a comprehensive and fundamental rule or belief for leading and operating an organization, aimed at continually improving performance over the long run by focusing on customers while addressing the needs of all stakeholders. There are many quality management practices that are used by organizations, such as quality circles, Moller's competency model, the Malcolm Baldridge model, the European foundation for quality management (EFQM) business excellence model, quality response manufacturing, and six sigma practices.

Using the ISO/TC176, that is, the International Organization for Standardization's Technical Committee 176 on quality management and quality assurance, a process of consensus developed the ISO 9000 series of standards. These standards provide a clear statement of the eight quality management principles (QMPs) and place them in a business environment/framework.

Successful total quality management requires behavioural and cultural changes in the organization. Three management systems that are aligned with the TQM initiative in an organization are:

1. Organizational management system (OM)
2. Human resource management system (HRM)
3. Total quality management (TQM)

For successful implementation of TQM in an organization, it is necessary to embrace the models of human resource development (HRD) and organizational development (OD). From the earlier definition of TQM, one can, therefore, say HRD + OD = TQM.

TQM practices in organizations are culture-specific. Quality management practices may differ for organizations with presence in different countries, even though it is important that the perceptions of quality be uniform.

Standards

Standards can be defined as documented agreements containing technical specifications and other precise criteria to be used consistently as rules, guidelines, or definitions of characteristics, so as to ensure that materials, products, processes, and services are fit for their purpose. The *International Organization for Standardization* is a worldwide federation of national standards bodies from more than 140 countries, one from each country.

ISO is a non-governmental organization established in 1947. The mission of ISO is to promote the development of standardization and related activities with a view to facilitate the international exchange of goods and services, and to develop cooperation in the spheres of intellectual, scientific, technological, and economic activity. ISO's work results in international agreements that are published as *international standards*.

The term *ISO* is derived from the Greek *isos*, meaning 'equal', which is the root of the prefix *iso* that occurs in a host of terms such as *isometric* (of equal measure or dimensions) and *isonomy* (equality of laws or of people before the law). The term *ISO* is used around the world to denote the organization, thus avoiding a plethora of acronyms resulting from the translation of *International Organization for Standardization* into the different national languages of its members, for example, IOS in English, OIN in French, etc.

ISO 9001:2000 Family of Standards

The new ISO 9001:2000 is an integration of the three familiar standards ISO 9001, ISO 9002, and ISO 9003. ISO 9001:2000 specifies requirements for a quality management system for any organization that needs to demonstrate its ability to consistently provide products that meet customer specifications and applicable regulatory requirements. It aims to enhance customer satisfaction. ISO 9001:2000 has been organized in a user-friendly format with terms that are easily recognized by all business sectors. The standard is used for certification/registration and for contractual purposes by organizations seeking recognition of their quality management system.

Guidelines for ISO 9000 family standards

The guidelines are as follows:

- **Fundamentals and vocabulary:** ISO 9000:2000 establishes a starting point for understanding the standards and defines the fundamental terms and definitions used in the ISO 9000 family. This is needed to avoid misunderstandings in application.
- **Quality management systems requirements:** ISO 9001:2000 is the requirement standard used to assess the ability to meet customer satisfaction and applicable regulatory requirements, and thereby address customer satisfaction. It is now the only standard in the ISO 9000 family against which third-party certification can be carried out.
- **Guidelines for performance improvements:** ISO 9004:2000 is the guideline standard that provides guidance for continual improvement of the quality management system to benefit all parties through sustained customer satisfaction.

ISO 9000 standards in use

If an organization is seeking to establish a management system that provides confidence in the conformance of its product to established or specified requirements, ISO 9001:2000 is used. It is now the only standard in the ISO 9000 family against whose requirements quality systems can be certified by an external agency. The standard recognizes that the word *product* applies to services, processed material, hardware, and software intended for or required by the customer.

There are five sections specifying activities that need to be considered when implementing the ISO system. The first section describes the activities used to supply products. The other four sections relate to quality management system, management responsibility, resource management and measurement, and analysis and improvement. These are relevant to all organizations, which need to demonstrate how they can apply them in their quality manuals or other documentation.

Together, the five sections of ISO 9001:2000 define what everyone should do consistently to provide a product that meets customer requirements and applicable statutory or regulatory requirements. In addition, it seeks to enhance customer satisfaction by improving an organization's quality management system.

QUALITY GURUS AND THEIR CONTRIBUTION TO TQM PRACTICES

According to Philip Crosby (1988), quality is conformance to standards, which an organization expects to meet. The concept of quality comes from defect prevention and not defect correction. This can be achieved only through proper leadership, training, and discipline in work processes. Thus, adherence to quality ensures that an organization achieves defect-free performance standards. Any organization that achieves quality can save money, duly correcting poor performance, and at the same time can emerge as a market leader gaining customers' confidence.

Crosby, recognized globally as a quality guru, based his quality improvement process on 14 steps. By following them, an organization can endeavour to achieve quality improvement. These steps are:

1. Make management committed to quality
2. Form cross-functional quality improvement teams
3. Measure current processes and develop improved processes by duly identifying potential quality problems
4. Evaluate the cost of quality and explain its use as a management tool
5. Raise the quality awareness and personal concern of all employees
6. Take actions to correct problems identified through previous steps
7. Establish progress monitoring for the improvement process
8. Train supervisors to actively carry out their part of the quality improvement programme
9. Hold a 'zero defects day' to let everyone realize that there has been a change and to reaffirm management commitment
10. Encourage individuals to establish improvement goals for themselves and their groups
11. Encourage employees to communicate to management the obstacles they face in attaining their improvement goals
12. Recognize and appreciate those who participate
13. Establish quality councils to communicate on a regular basis
14. Do it all over again to emphasize that the quality improvement programme never ends

According to Crosby, to emerge as an 'eternally successful organization', it is essential for the organization to understand and appreciate the following:

- People routinely do things right the first time.
- Change is anticipated and used to advantage.
- Growth is consistent and profitable.
- New products and services appear when needed.
- Everyone is happy to work there.

From an organizational point of view, quality management requires

- Participative management, which ensures employee involvement in the decision-making process
- Attitudinal change, which reflects through improved responsiveness to customers' (both internal and external) needs
- Effective communication (both internal and external)
- Flexibility, that is, willingness to accept changes, etc.

Most organizations can meet these requirements through continuous education, teamwork, focus groups, and partnership. *Continuous education* can be ensured through quality seminars and training and development. *Quality teamwork* is possible through nurturing of mutual collaboration and cooperation, so that employees endeavour to achieve a common goal. *Focus groups* provide assistance and involvement for problem solving, while *partnership* enhances relationships between individuals, service centres, and customers.

The importance of human resources in the process of quality improvement can be best understood with the following example. Indian leather manufacturing organizations were facing a major crisis in the export market due to improper soaking operations. Improper soaking affects the quality of shoe uppers, which develop multiple wrinkles within a short period of their use and quickly get torn. To improve the quality, the following steps had to be taken.

1. Define the problem
2. Fix the problem
3. Identify the root cause
4. Take corrective action
5. Evaluate and follow up

Crosby's four absolutes of quality management are illustrated through Table 21.1.

In his explanation in *Quality Without Tears*, Crosby (1984) has very correctly exemplified the need for HRD by emphasizing executive education, management education, and education of supervisors, professionals, knowledge workers, and other employees.

W. Edwards Deming (1986), another quality guru, developed six-fold productivity improvement programmes through quality improvement. Such productivity enhancement initiatives help an organization to reduce scrap and rework. Extending Walter Andrew Shewhart's manufacturing approach (1939) to non-manufacturing and human variation, Deming suggested that managers should focus on variability and understand the difference between special and common causes. *Special causes* for quality variation prevent satisfactory performance. Special causes are easily assignable, and after their identification through Deming's statistical quality control methods, an organization can correct the situation through changes of operator, shift, or procedure. *Common causes* are those that occur due to the design or the operation of the processes or systems. Common causes can be easily identified by the operators, but

Table 21.1 Four Absolutes of Quality

Conventional wisdom	The four absolutes	Reality
Goodness	Definition	Conformance to agreed-upon requirements
Appraisal/inspection	System	Prevention of low standards
That's close enough	Performance standard	Zero defects—do it right the first time (DIRTFT)
Cost of indices	Measure	Price of non-conformance

their elimination would be possible only by making use of management authority. Deming suggested a systematic approach to problem solving, using the plan, do, study, and act (PDSA) cycle. This can lead to better results and efficiency for the organization, and for this, it is essential for the organization to ensure the capability development of its people.

Joseph Juran (1951) is another important figure in the context of quality management practices. Along with Deming, he was invited to Japan by the Union of Japanese Scientists and Engineers (JUSE) in 1954. Juran focused on planning, organizational issues, and management's responsibility for quality improvement. Training and HRD activities also play a very crucial role in this respect. Juran's quality planning road map consists of the following steps:

1. Identify who the customers are
2. Determine the needs of those customers
3. Translate those needs into one's language
4. Develop a product that can respond to those needs
5. Optimize the product features to meet one's own needs as well as customers' needs
6. Develop a process that is able to produce the product
7. Optimize the process
8. Prove that the process can produce the product under operating conditions
9. Transfer the process to operations

Kaoru Ishikawa (1990), a quality guru from Japan, suggested the need for company-wide quality improvement initiatives through quality circle movement. Both Ishikawa and Genichi Taguchi (1995) (another quality guru from Japan) emphasized the need for making effective use of technical statistical techniques for quality improvement, simplifying it by use of Pareto diagrams and cause and effect (Ishikawa or fishbone) diagrams. Ishikawa's diagrams can find, sort, and document the causes of quality variation with the participation of employees in quality circles or small-group activities. Similarly, Pareto graphs can plot the quality variation by making use of frequency distribution and can then track how elimination of problems can lead to changes in the quality level. The Pareto principle suggests that organizations should not look for 100 per cent solution of problems, due to the interdependence of one problem with another. It is instead better to get 100 per cent results with the solution of 80 per cent problems. Other techniques like control charts, scatter diagrams, binomial probability distribution, and sampling inspection can also be used for measurement of variability in the quality of products and services.

Company-wide quality control, as proposed by Ishikawa, emphasizes not only the quality of the product but also the quality of after-sales service and the quality of management and the people as a whole. Some of the important points suggested by Ishikawa as the outcome of quality control initiatives are:

- Improvement of product quality and uniformity through reduction in defects
- Improvement in product reliability
- Reduction in costs
- Increase in production volume through rationalization in the production schedules
- Reduction in wasteful work and rework
- Improvement in production techniques
- Reduction in the cost of inspection and testing

- Rationalization of contracts between vendor and vendee
- Enlargement of market
- Improved relationships between departments
- Reduction in false data and reports presentation
- More democratic discussions among the organizational members
- Smooth conduct of meetings
- Rational repairs and installation of equipments and facilities
- Improved human relations

Quality circles were first started in Nippon Telegraph and Telephone Corporation in 1962, and subsequently adopted by organizations throughout the world. The basic aims of quality circle activities are:

- Contributing to the improvement and the development of the organization
- Respecting human relations and nurturing healthy interpersonal relations that create a compelling workplace
- Full deployment of human capabilities and potentialities

Using the cause and effect diagram, members of the quality circle team can identify quality-related workplace problems, issues pertaining to cost reduction, productivity improvement, and workplace safety, and accordingly suggest ways to improve them through mutual participation and cooperation. A model cause and effect diagram is presented in Figure 21.1.

For the overall development of the human resource, organizations need to master seven tools through continuous training and development functions. The seven tools are as follows:

1. Pareto charts
2. Cause and effect diagrams
3. Stratification
4. Check sheets

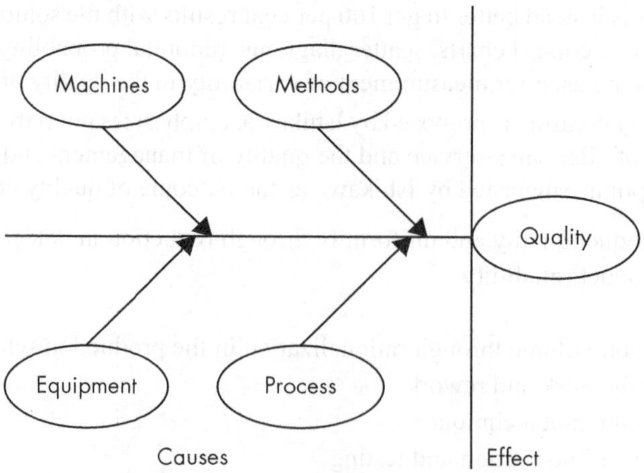

Figure 21.1 Cause and Effect Diagram

5. Histograms
6. Scatter diagrams
7. Shewhart's control charts and graphs

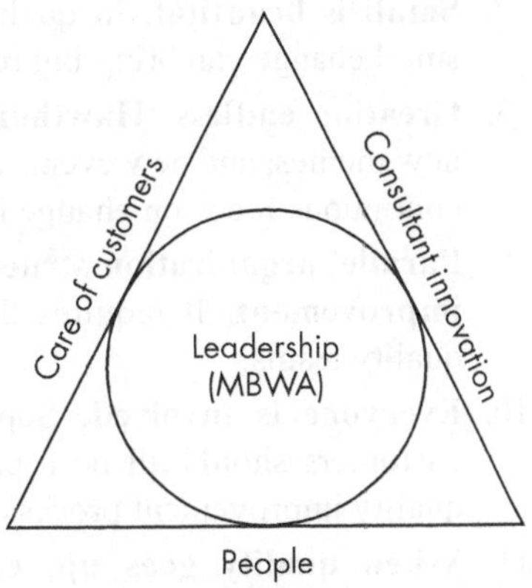

Figure 21.2 MBWA Model (*Source*: McKinsey & Company)

Taguchi's methodology optimizes products and processes before manufacturing, rather than achieving quality through inspection. Taguchi pushed back the concepts of quality and reliability to the design stage to develop an efficient and error-free manufacturing process. Taguchi's methods can also be used to troubleshoot critical manufacturing problems.

Japanese quality guru Shigeo Shingo (1985) helped revolutionize the manufacturing of goods through his improvement principles that result in achieving quality through drastic cost minimization. He has basically provided the strategy for continuous improvement through the creative involvement of all cross-sections of employees.

Tom Peters, an American management guru, evolved a quality improvement strategy with a sales-oriented viewpoint based on his extensive research on successful American companies. He identified leadership as the central factor to the quality improvement process. It is due to this reason that he advocated the idea of replacing the term *management* with the term *leadership*. According to him, 'managing by wandering about' (MBWA) is the basis of leadership and excellence. MBWA enables the leader to keep in touch with customers, innovation, and people, and these three major areas help in achieving excellence in the organization. Peters' MBWA model (1982) is illustrated in Figure 21.2.

By practising MBWA, a leader can perform three major activities, which are:

1. **Listening:** It suggests caring.
2. **Teaching:** The values must be transmitted face to face.
3. **Facilitating:** One should be able to give on-the-spot help.

According to Peters, there are 12 traits of successful quality improvement programmes. These traits are:

1. **Management obsession with quality**: This emphasizes the emotional commitment to quality, practising certain value systems like abolition of rework mechanics in the organization in a phased manner, and an absolute 'no' to shoddy goods.
2. **Passionate systems**: A system without passion is no good for achieving quality. Hence, the quality ideology should bind an organization.
3. **Measurement of quality**: Such criteria should be adequately displayed and transparent to all members of the organization.
4. **Quality is rewarded**: Quality achievement should be aligned with the organizational compensation and reward systems.
5. **Everyone is trained for quality**: All members of the organization should be sufficiently trained to understand the quality imperatives. Training on quality is best possible through creating awareness about cause and effect analysis, statistical process control, and the seven tools mentioned earlier.
6. **Multi-function teams**: Quality achievement is best possible through the formation of cross-functional teams, small-group activities like quality circles, value engineering teams, total quality management teams, etc.

7. **Small is beautiful**: In quality improvement, even a small change can bring big results.
8. **Creating endless 'Hawthorne' effects**: New goals, new themes, and new events are the antidote. Hence, a continuous focus on change is necessary.
9. **Parallel organization structure devoted to quality improvement**: It requires the formation of shadow quality teams.
10. **Everyone is involved**: Suppliers, distributors, and customers should all be a part of the organizational quality improvement process.
11. **When quality goes up, costs go down**: Quality improvement is the primary source of cost reduction.
12. **Quality improvement is a never-ending journey**: All quality is relative; hence, the everyday quality of a product or a service becomes either better or worse—it never stands still. Therefore, organizations should pursue continuous quality improvement programmes.

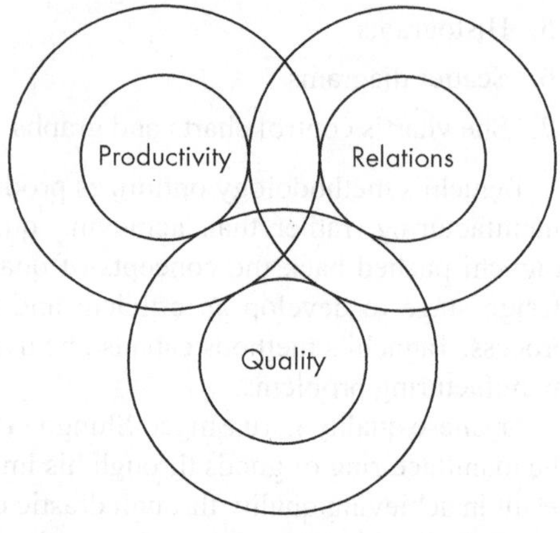

Figure 21.3 Moller's Competency Model (*Source*: Claus Moller (1988). *Personal Quality: The Basis of All Other Quality*. Denmark: Time Manager International. Reproduced with permission from Claus Moller, Founder of Time Manager International.)

Claus Moller (1988), the founder of Time Manager International (TMI) and widely regarded as the European quality management guru, emphasized the need for improving the personal quality of employees to achieve organizational quality. He developed the model of 'putting people first'. Moller believed that the administrative process, rather than the production process, offers more opportunity for overall productivity gains. Hence, to achieve quality, organizations must inspire people to do their best, and this would be possible through the personal development of employees, who can build their requisite competence in the three vital areas of productivity, relations, and quality. Time Manager International documented this model as presented in Figure 21.3.

MODES OF TQM

The different modes used to ensure participation in TQM have been discussed here.

Teams and Teamwork

When TQM is successful, employees at every level participate in decisions affecting their work. The most common vehicle for ensuring employee participation is a team. Teams range in scope and responsibility from problem-solving groups to self-managed work teams that schedule work, assign jobs, hire members, and set the standards and volume of output. A participative work culture is built when quality becomes everybody's responsibility.

Employee involvement practices in organizations may differ according to organizational policies and strategies. Common employment practices are:

- Suggestion system
- Survey feedback
- Quality circles
- Formation of 'quality of work life' team

- Job redesign
- Formation of self-managed teams
- Formation of TQM team

Participative management is an important approach for introducing TQM culture in an organization. It involves all cross-sections of employees in organizational functions. People tend to live together in love and amity. This is to be learnt even from the *Yajurveda* (dates back to 4000 BC–100 BC). In the Indian context, a more organized or institutionalized approach to workers' participation in management dates back to 1920, when Mahatma Gandhi advocated the principles of trusteeship in industry. This idea has further been concretized with the five-year plans (started in 1951 and continuing till today) through enactment of various legislations and policy decisions. Statutory support has now made it mandatory for Indian industries to adopt participative management practices.

Employee Empowerment

Employee empowerment is to confer legitimate rights on employees, irrespective of the nature of their job and hierarchical level, for them to make judgements and take decisions on their own. Hence, employee empowerment can facilitate development of problem-solving abilities of employees. Operationally, in organizations, one empowers employees first by developing their capabilities and second by allowing them the freedom to commit mistakes. Unlike other quality management approaches, empowerment not only calls for employee participation in the operational area, but also allows them to participate in corporate-level decision making, so that employees emerge as a totality. An empowered employee, in other words, is not a mere seller of their time and labour for a contracted sum of money. The empowered employee acquires necessary skill and authority to own. Employee empowerment and involvement and participative management (as important corporate practices) have been used as experiments in several multinational and national organizations. In all these cases, it was identified that employee ownership and commitment (which is possible through employee empowerment) are the two ingredients that achieved efficiency and productivity. Some organizations are even empowering their employees at the strategic level rather than confining their involvement to limited operational activity.

Quality of Work Life (QWL)

Quality of work life is most conventionally defined as those perceived important personal needs that an individual tries to satisfy by working in an organization. Its conceptual foundations, though laid by a host of behavioural scientists, were in reality advocated by Chris Argyris (1975) in his famous work *Personality and Organization.* The socio-technical systems theory, pioneered by Tavistock Institute of Human Relations, London, during the 1960s is considered to be an important QWL construct. The principles of this theory (Cherns 1976) were first published in the journal *Human Relations* brought out by Tavistock Institute. The basic conceptual criteria for QWL incorporate growth and security as important personal needs for an individual. The possibility of furthering one's career within the organization has, therefore, been identified as one of the important criteria for QWL. Although common QWL strategists put more emphasis on job redesign, formation of autonomous work groups, and worker participation in management, there is no unanimous opinion as to what should be construed as QWL factors. The process of QWL can be explained with the help of the following criteria:

- Adequate and fair compensation
- Safe and healthy working conditions
- Immediate opportunity to use and develop human capacities

- Future opportunity for continued growth and security
- Social integration in the work organization
- Work and total life space
- Social relevance of working life

From studies carried out, both in India and abroad, it is evident that the essence of QWL is the opportunity for employees at all levels to have substantial influence over their work environment. This is a result of their participating in the decision-making process relating to their work, thereby enhancing their self-esteem and the overall satisfaction they derive from their work. Hence, QWL calls for an open style of management, which implies sharing of information and genuinely encouraging efforts relating to the improvement of the organization. This makes it amply clear that QWL, in fact, is an important managerial activity to develop the human resource of an organization. The success of TQM programmes largely depend on appropriate HRD interventions like emphasis on continuous training and development activity, encouraging participation in management through small group forums, increasing employees' motivation, looking after the career development of employees, employee empowerment, and infusing attitudinal changes at the top (accepting a more flat organization structure, adopting a democratic approach, becoming receptive to changes on a continuous basis, supporting group performance, etc.).

SIX SIGMA PRACTICES

To add economic value and practical utility for customers and organizations, companies are now looking beyond total quality management practices. It is acknowledged by the corporate world that customers have a rightful expectation to buy quality products at competitive cost. Therefore, organizations should strive for improving the bottom-line (profit). Synergy between these two can be achieved through *six sigma practices*. Six sigma as a business process is allowing organizations to improve their bottom-line by designing and monitoring business activities in a way that minimizes wastes and resources without, however, compromising on customer satisfaction. Six sigma processes are broader than total quality management (TQM) programmes. While TQM focuses on detecting and correcting defects, six sigma recreates the processes to ensure defects never arise right from the beginning. From organizations' point of view, it provides maximum value in the form of increased profits, and from customers' point of view, it provides maximum value in terms of high quality products and services at competitive costs.

Higher sigma values indicate better quality products and lower sigma values represent lesser quality products. At the six sigma level, products are virtually defect-free, that is, there are only 3.4 defects per million opportunities (DPMO).

Like TQM, six sigma also requires thorough changes in the culture and practices of the organization. Essentially, all the tools mentioned in the case of TQM are applicable to six sigma. However, it additionally requires the organization to make people more creative and innovative, as six sigma recreates processes to ensure that defects never arise.

MALCOLM BALDRIGE MODEL

The Malcolm Baldrige model is an important framework to measure the quality level of an organization. Each organization, as per this framework, is evaluated against 1,000 marks on seven broad parameters, which are (1) leadership; (2) strategic planning; (3) customer and market focus; (4) measurement, analysis and knowledge management; (5) human resource focus; (6) process management; and (7) business results. The model's key focus is on strategy formulation and development.

QUALITY CIRCLES AND TOTAL EMPLOYEE INVOLVEMENT

In the new economy, total participation of workers, as opposed to statutory participation, is a must. Participation may be through work committees, departmental councils, and other representative forums. One way to enforce total participation is by forming quality circles (QC) or small group forums.

Quality circles (QC) are an important managerial tool in the organization and can be related to increased employee motivation and productivity. Total knowledge, skill, creative abilities, talents, and aptitudes together with values, attitudes, and beliefs of the workers and/or individuals can represent an organization's effective human resource inventory. The total involvement of employees is ensured by QCs through a number of small group forums. Organizations have succeeded in improving their productivity through QC activities that increase employee motivation. As a result, QCs can guarantee more results than any other method including complex planning and rigorous execution.

Organizations in India have started training their workers and employees on QC concepts for their successful implementation. They are systematic about follow-up activity in connection with setting up QC forums involving all workers, forming homogeneous groups of 8–12 employees, who regularly meet once a week for at least an hour to deliberate on work-related problems and to identify possible solutions to those problems. Many organizations have benefited from the consequent cost minimization, changing methods of production, work simplification, etc. Figure 21.4 gives an illustration of a quality circle.

PEOPLE AND ORGANIZATIONAL COMPETENCIES

This methodology of continuous improvement has been discussed in detail in Chapter 20 in the section 'Innovation and Creativity'.

LEAN MANAGEMENT

Lean management practices consider three primary processes of manufacturing, keeping in mind the value creation for customers. These are product development, order to delivery, and service through the product life cycle. It requires value creation from the standpoint of the customers, examining the current process and experimenting to see how it could perform better, understanding the requirement of the people and processes to support the value creation, and aligning the purpose, processes, and people in search of the perfect process. To achieve the stated intent, organizations focus on eight basic areas, which are as follows:

1. **Strategic vision and core values:** They are designed leveraging the collective expression of all the stakeholders of the organization. They can, therefore, be called shared vision and shared values. They need to be designed in such a way that all members of the organization get the same direction and accordingly contribute. They also create a compelling work culture.
2. **Inspiring leadership:** This is also critical for lean management practices. Leaders persuade members of the organization to deliver a compelling value to their customers. Inspirational leaders can get members to show the required commitment to the strategic vision and defined core values. They motivate, coach, and guide people, and transform them into true performers.
3. **Customer orientation:** This means designing or developing customer-centric products and services. In lean management, it is essential to adopt a customer-centric approach in product design, keeping in consideration the cost, delivery, quality, and overall customer satisfaction. Customers'

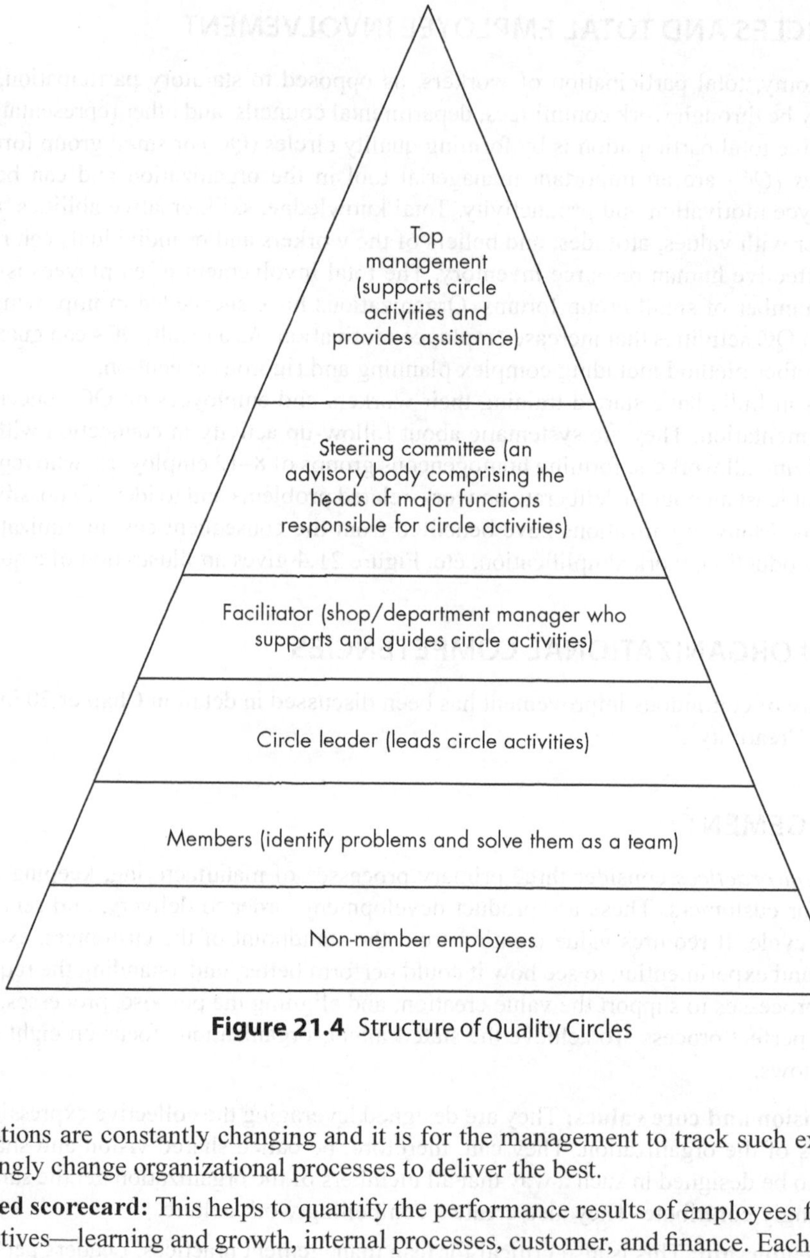

Figure 21.4 Structure of Quality Circles

expectations are constantly changing and it is for the management to track such expectations and accordingly change organizational processes to deliver the best.

4. **Balanced scorecard:** This helps to quantify the performance results of employees from four major perspectives—learning and growth, internal processes, customer, and finance. Each employee contributes to these four areas irrespective of the hierarchical level and functional areas. For effective lean management practices, balanced scorecard is the most effective instrument, as it can scientifically track the development of employees through incremental changes in their performance.
5. **People involvement and engagement:** They require participation of all cross-sections of employees of the organization in the transformation process through lean management. However, ensuring the participation of people is not so simple. It requires explaining the need for transformation

to the people and allowing them the freedom to ask questions and clarify their doubts. Once people participate, they feel increasingly committed to deliver results. An important prerequisite for people to participate is to create a compelling culture for competitive advantage.

6. **Process innovation:** This requires new thinking. It requires challenging the existing process and managing the operations from altogether different perspectives. For example, the Toyota Production System renders one's traditional perceptions (for example, producing in bulk to achieve economies of scale, as per unit cost of production) wrong, making them obsolete. Instead, it recommends the formation of productive cells, and proves that even small assets can create low cost through flow and not the volume. Hence, in the TPS, processes become cells, people become teams, and products and services develop into value streams.
7. **Problem investigation and resolution:** They require clear identification and understanding of the problems, and devising of solutions using various problem-solving tools. A structured model of problem investigation and resolution is DMAIC, which is used as an organizational improvement strategy through six sigma. DMAIC stands for define, measure, analyse, improve, and control.
8. **Organizational processes:** They put all the other seven elements of lean management practices together to achieve the intended results. Organizational processes may be with regard to human resource management, quality management, or any other key business process.

TOYOTA PRODUCTION SYSTEM

Toyota production system was developed in Japan by Toyota Corporation, led by Taiichi Ohno. It was based on two primary concepts—the manufacturing production system of Henry Ford and the Ford Motor, and the supermarket operations in the United States observed during a visit in 1956. The supermarket concept provided the basis of a continuous supply of materials, as the supermarket ensured a continuous supply of merchandise on the store shelves. TPS incorporated just-in-time (JIT) production and *jidoka* techniques to optimize time and human assets in the manufacturing environment, and became the basis for the lean production and lean enterprise movements beginning in the early 1990s.

JIT is a system of production that makes and delivers just what is needed, just when it is needed, and just in the amount needed. *Jidoka* is the practice of providing machines and operators the ability to detect when an abnormal condition occurs, and accordingly ensures immediate stoppage of work. This enables operations to build in quality at each process and to separate people and machines for more efficient work.

Kaizen is the method of continuous improvement of an entire value stream or it is the individual process to create more value with less waste. There are two levels of *kaizen*. *System* or *flow kaizen* focuses on the overall value stream and *process kaizen* focuses on individual processes.

QUICK RESPONSE MANUFACTURING (QRM)

Quick response manufacturing (QRM) is a companywide strategy to cut lead times in all phases of manufacturing and office operations. Focusing on eliminating 'white space' within and between processes, QRM shortens time-to-market on products. QRM is highly effective in companies providing engineer-to-order product solutions.

While these continuous improvement methodologies differ in approach, they all focus on creating customer-defined value in products and services, eliminating the wastage. Wastages occur not only in the manufacturing processes but in other operating and administrative processes as well.

Case Quality Measurement: The Experience of Zed Plus

The European Foundation for Quality Management (EFQM) business excellence model comprises nine criteria broadly categorized as enablers and results. Each criterion has point allocation similar to the Baldrige framework. Enablers are leadership, people, policy and strategy, partnerships and resources, and processes. Results are customer results, people results, society results, and key results.

Using the EFQM business excellence model and the Baldridge framework, one can measure the organizational quality achievement and the corresponding changes in the business scenario.

Without going into the controversy of accurate measurement of quality results, Zed Plus, a professional high-tech security agency, developed its own EFQM-based balanced scorecard, spreading its entire activities into four broad perspectives—customers, people, society, and key results. Zed Plus's adaptive approach in developing a hybrid model using both the EFQM model and the Baldridge framework to measure its quality management practices yielded better results, as the company could understand its sub-parameters and the corresponding measurement criteria for more effective assessment of its quality level.

CASE QUESTION

Critically evaluate Zed Plus's approach. Do you think the company is right in its approach?

SUMMARY

- *Quality* is defined as the totality of features and characteristics of products or services which satisfy stated or implied needs of customers. Quality provides a focus for all management concerns—cost reduction, productivity, teamwork, communication, and training objectives like problem solving, decision making, organizational dynamics, and interpersonal skills.
- *Total quality management (TQM)* focuses on adopting an organizational improvement strategy through development of the human resource. Therefore, quality is intertwined with the HRD activities of an organization.
- Identification of cost of quality and taking appropriate steps to reduce the same can help an organization to attain both cost minimization and increased profitability. Cost of quality may be the cost of failure, the cost of appraisal, and the cost of prevention.
- With growing global competition, quality management is becoming increasingly important to the leadership and management of organizations. Quality management principles provide understanding of and guidance on the application of quality management.
- *Standards* are documented agreements containing technical specifications and other precise criteria to be used consistently as rules, guidelines, or definitions of characteristics, so as to ensure that materials, products, processes, and services are fit for their purpose.
- The *International Organization for Standardization (ISO)* is a worldwide federation of national standards bodies from more than 140 countries, one from each country. The new ISO 9001:2000 is an integration of the familiar three standards ISO 9001, ISO 9002, and ISO 9003. ISO 9001:2000 specifies requirements for a quality management system for any organization that wants to demonstrate its ability to consistently provide products that meet customer specifications and applicable regulatory requirements. It aims to enhance customer satisfaction.

- Quality circles contribute to the improvement and development of the organization, respecting human relations and nurturing healthy interpersonal relations, which create a compelling workplace and ensure full realization of human capabilities and potentialities.
- Globally, companies are now looking beyond total quality management practices. A better synergy between customers' expectations and the bottom-line can be achieved through six sigma practices. *Six sigma* as a business process is allowing organizations to improve their bottom-line by designing and monitoring business activities in a way that minimizes wastes and resources without, however, compromising on customer satisfaction.
- *Lean management practices* consider three primary processes of manufacturing, keeping in mind the value creation for customers. These are product development, order to delivery, and service through the product life cycle. It requires value creation from the standpoint of the customers, examining the current process and experimenting to see how it could perform better, understanding the requirement of the people and processes to support the value creation, and aligning the purpose, processes, and people in search of the perfect process.
- *Toyota Production System (TPS)* is the adoption of the supermarket model of continuous supply of materials on the store shelves to reduce the waiting time and, at the same time, to optimize the inventory holding.
- *Quick response manufacturing (QRM)* is a companywide strategy to cut lead times in all phases of manufacturing and office operations.

KEY TERMS

Employee empowerment: It requires conferring of legitimate rights on employees, irrespective of the nature of their job and hierarchical level, for them to make judgements and take decisions on their own.

ISO: The full form of ISO is International Organization for Standardization. ISO standards ensure common quality systems.

Lean management practices: These practices require value creation from the standpoint of customers, examining the current process and experimenting to see how it could perform better, understanding the requirement of the people and processes to support the value creation, and aligning the purpose, processes and people in search of the perfect process.

Participative management: It involves all cross-sections of employees in organizational functions.

Quality: It is the totality of features and characteristics of products or services which satisfy stated or implied needs of customers.

Quality management: It is a comprehensive and fundamental rule or belief for leading and operating an organization, aimed at continually improving performance over the long run by focusing on customers while addressing the needs of all stakeholders.

Quality of work life: Quality of work life (QWL) is the perceived important personal needs of workers which they try to satisfy by working in an organization. Basic conceptual criteria for QWL incorporate growth and security as important personal needs for an individual. The possibility of furthering one's career within the organization has, therefore, been identified as one of the important criteria for QWL

REVIEW QUESTIONS

1. Discuss the role of quality management practices in achieving organizational improvement.
2. Explain how quality management practices influence the human resource development functions.
3. Explain the concepts of *employee empowerment* and *quality of work life (QWL)*. How do these two approaches supplement quality management practices?
4. Explain the concept of *six sigma*. How can the six sigma approach improve quality in an organization?
5. Discuss whether it is essential for an organization to get ISO certified for formalizing its quality management practices.
6. Discuss how quality circles can strengthen the quality management practices in an organization.
7. Write short notes on:
   i. Quality circles
   ii. QWL
   iii. Employee empowerment
   iv. Quick response manufacturing
   v. Toyota Production System

CRITICAL THINKING QUESTIONS

1. Visit the Web site http://www.tataquality.com/UI/Home.aspx and examine the quality management practices implemented by the Tata Group. Identify the key practices responsible for Tata's success giving your reasons for choosing them.
2. Quality management practices, apart from achieving operational excellence, bring order in the organization, make the organization more quality- and price-competitive, and internally keep employees motivated. Visit any ISO-certified organization and examine the extent of its achievement. Also, point out areas of deficiency, if any.

REFERENCES

Argyris, Chris (1975). *Personality and Organization*. New York: Harper & Row.

Cherns, A. (1976). 'The Principles of Sociotechnical Design', *Human Relations*, 2 (9): pp. 783–792.

Crosby, Philip B. (1984). *Quality Without Tears*. New York: McGraw-Hill.

——— (1988). *The Eternally Successful Organization: The Art of Corporate Wellness*. New York: McGraw-Hill.

Deming, W. E. (1986). *Out of the Crisis*. Cambridge, MA: MIT, Centre for Advanced Engineering Study.

Hamel, G. and C. K. Prahalad (1990). 'The Core Competence of the Corporation', *Harvard Business Review*, May–June, 68 (3): pp. 79–91.

Ishikawa, Kaoru (1990). *Introduction to Quality Control*. Translated by J. H. Loftus. Tokyo: 3A Corporation.

Juran, Joseph (1951). *Quality Control Handbook*. New York: McGraw-Hill.

Moller, Claus (1988). *Personal Quality: The Basis of All Other Quality*. Denmark: Time Manager International.

Nonaka, Ikujoro and Hirotaka Takeuchi (1995). *The Knowledge-Creating Company*. New York: Oxford University Press.

Peters, T. J. and R. H. Waterman (1982). *In Search of Excellence: Lessons from America's Best Run Companies*. New York: Harper & Row.

Shewhart, Walter Andrew (1939). *Statistical Method from the Viewpoint of Quality Control*, edited by W. Edwards Deming. Washington, DC: The Graduate School, Department of Agriculture.

Shingo, Shigeo (1985). *Revolution in Manufacturing: The SMED (Single-Minute Exchange of Die) System*. Cambridge, MA: Productivity Press, Inc.

Taguchi, Genichi (June 1995). 'Quality Engineering (Taguchi Methods) for the Development of Electronic Circuit Technology', *IEEE Transactions on Reliability* (IEEE Reliability Society), 44 (2): pp. 225–229.

FURTHER READING

Bhattacharyya, D. K. (1995). 'Corporate Bodybuilder: The Emerging Role of HRD Professional, A Prescriptive Model for Success', *Indian Journal of Training and Development*, April–June.

——— (2000). 'Competency Mapping and Manpower Redundancy—Macro-level Study of Indian Organisations', *Management and Accounting Research*, October–December, 4 (2): pp. 97–105.

——— (2007). *Human Resource Research Methods*. New Delhi: Oxford University Press.

Ceserani, Jonne and Peter Greatwood (2001). *Innovation and Creativity*. New Delhi: Crest Publishing House.

Christiansen, James A. (2000). *Competitive Innovation Management*. London: Macmillan Business.

Gordon, Edward E. (2000). *Skill Wars: Winning the Battle for Productivity and Profit*. Boston, MA: Butterworth-Heinemann.

Plsek, Paul E. (1997). *Creativity, Innovation and Quality*. Welshpool, Western Australia: Quality Press.

Stolovitch, H. D. and J. G. Maurice (1998). 'Calculating the Return on Investment in Training: A Critical Analysis and Case Study', *Performance Improvement*, 37 (8): pp. 9–20.

Index